Knowledge Information Extraction Research

Knowledge Information Extraction Research

Guest Editors

Lanting Fang
Yubo Song

MDPI

Basel • Beijing • Wuhan • Barcelona • Belgrade • Novi Sad • Cluj • Manchester

Guest Editors

Lanting Fang
School of Computer Science and Technology
Beijng Institute of Technology
Beijing
China

Yubo Song
School of Cyber Science and Engineering
Southeast University
Nanjing
China

Editorial Office
MDPI AG
Grosspeteranlage 5
4052 Basel, Switzerland

This is a reprint of the Special Issue, published open access by the journal *Electronics* (ISSN 2079-9292), freely accessible at: https://www.mdpi.com/journal/electronics/special_issues/50EK4W3G1P.

For citation purposes, cite each article independently as indicated on the article page online and as indicated below:

Lastname, A.A.; Lastname, B.B. Article Title. *Journal Name* **Year**, *Volume Number*, Page Range.

ISBN 978-3-7258-5213-0 (Hbk)
ISBN 978-3-7258-5214-7 (PDF)
https://doi.org/10.3390/books978-3-7258-5214-7

Contents

About the Editors

Lanting Fang

Lanting Fang is an Associate Professor at the School of Computer Science and Technology, Beijing Institute of Technology, China. She received her PhD degree in Signal and Information Processing from Southeast University, where she also worked as a faculty member before joining Beijing Institute of Technology. Her research interests cover a broad spectrum of topics in data mining, natural language processing, and graph neural networks. In particular, she has conducted influential research on dynamic graph representation learning and anomaly detection, where her work has proposed effective models for capturing structural changes in evolving networks. She has published a number of research papers in well-regarded international journals and conferences, and her studies have contributed to both theoretical advances and the design of practical intelligent systems. Beyond publications, she has participated in national and provincial research projects, playing important roles in advancing research on large-scale data analysis and intelligent information systems. Her ongoing work emphasizes the integration of machine learning with real-world data problems, bridging the gap between algorithmic development and domain applications. With her growing academic profile, she remains committed to fostering interdisciplinary collaboration and to training students in the areas of intelligent data processing and cyber-physical systems, helping to build a vibrant and innovative research community.

Yubo Song

Yubo Song is an Associate Professor at the School of Cyber Science and Engineering, Southeast University, China. He received his bachelor's degree in power systems automation, his master's degree in communications and information systems, and his PhD degree in signal and information processing, all from Southeast University. His research interests include network and communication security, physical-layer security, authentication for Internet of Things devices, anomaly detection, privacy-preserving computation, and federated learning. He has participated in numerous national and provincial research projects, including grants supported by the National Natural Science Foundation of China, the National 863 Program, and the National Key R&D Program. His work has addressed topics such as wireless security, blockchain-based authentication, secure data transmission in smart grids, and privacy-aware computation for next-generation networks. In addition, he has contributed to several projects focusing on vulnerability discovery and secure system design. Beyond research, Dr. Song has served as a member of professional organizations such as the IEEE PES Technical Committee on Power System Communications and Cybersecurity, and he frequently reviews for international journals and conferences. He has published more than one hundred papers and holds multiple patents. His achievements have been recognized by awards including provincial and ministerial prizes for scientific and technological progress, university-level teaching honors, and inclusion in Elsevier's list of the World's Top 2% Scientists in 2024.

Preface

The Preface of this Reprint reflects our intention to assemble high-quality research that advances the rapidly developing domains of information extraction and knowledge graphs. These fields not only provide the theoretical foundations and practical tools that allow raw, unstructured, and heterogeneous data to be converted into structured, meaningful knowledge, but also stand at the intersection of computer science, data science, and artificial intelligence. They are essential for enabling new forms of intelligent decision-making, knowledge discovery, and adaptive systems that respond to the growing complexity of today's digital ecosystems.

As the volume of digital information grows at an unprecedented pace, the ability to organize, interpret, and exploit this information has become a central challenge across science, engineering, business, and society. The transformation of data into actionable knowledge requires techniques that capture semantics, contextual meaning, and hidden relationships beyond what traditional approaches can deliver. Knowledge graphs and related extraction methodologies are particularly promising because they facilitate reasoning, interoperability, and integration across domains, allowing information to be reused and extended in ways that enhance both efficiency and innovation.

This Reprint presents a collection of innovative contributions that address methodological advances, system development, and real-world applications. The included articles cover a wide range of topics, from natural language processing and data mining to machine learning algorithms, semantic technologies, and knowledge-driven system architectures. Collectively, they demonstrate the interdisciplinary nature of the field, where theoretical insights are closely tied to practical deployment. Case studies in domains such as healthcare, finance, and e-commerce further underscore how knowledge extraction and graph-based representations can improve reliability, scalability, and trust in decision-making processes.

By bringing together diverse perspectives, the Reprint aims to provide readers with both a comprehensive overview of current progress and an inspiration for future directions. It is designed to be a valuable resource for researchers seeking to explore new algorithms, practitioners striving to implement intelligent knowledge systems, and students aspiring to enter this exciting area of study. In doing so, the Reprint also highlights emerging challenges, including scalability to massive data streams, ensuring interpretability and fairness in automated systems, and integrating domain expertise into machine learning pipelines.

We would like to extend our sincere gratitude to all contributing authors for their dedication, creativity, and commitment to advancing the state of the art. We are equally thankful to the reviewers for their constructive feedback, which strengthened the quality of the contributions, and to the editorial team of *Electronics* for their professional support throughout the process. Without their collective efforts, the successful completion of this Reprint would not have been possible.

Lanting Fang and Yubo Song
Guest Editors

electronics

MDPI

Article

A Study on Toponymic Entity Recognition Based on Pre-Trained Models Fused with Local Features for Genglubu in the South China Sea

Yinwei Wei, Yihong Li * and Xiaoyi Zhou

School of Cyberspace Security, Hainan University, Haikou 570228, China;
21220854000097@hainanu.edu.cn (Y.W.); xy.zhou@hainanu.edu.cn (X.Z.)
* Correspondence: 990638@hainanu.edu.cn

Abstract: Toponymic entity recognition is currently a critical research hotspot in knowledge graphs. Under the guidance of the national ancient book protection policy and the promotion of the wave of digital humanities research, this paper proposes a toponymic entity recognition model (ALBERT-Conv1D-BiLSTM-CRF) based on the fusion of a pre-trained language model and local features to address the problems of toponymic ambiguity and the differences in ancient and modern grammatical structures in the field of the Genglubu. This model extracts global features with the ALBERT module, fuses global and local features with the Conv1D module, performs sequence modeling with the BiLSTM module to capture deep semantics and long-distance dependency information, and finally, completes sequence annotation with the CRF module. The experiments show that while taking into account the computational resources and cost, this improved model is significantly improved compared with the benchmark model (ALBERT-BiLSTM-CRF), and the precision, recall, and F1 are increased by 0.74%, 1.28%, and 1.01% to 98.08%, 96.67%, and 97.37%, respectively. The model achieved good results in the field of Genglubu.

Keywords: toponymic entity recognition; Genglubu corpus; pre-trained language model; local feature; digital humanities

1. Introduction

Genglubu is a kind of ancient navigation guidebook formed through fishermen's long-term practical activities and accumulated experience in fishery production on the islands of the South China Sea and its waters [1]. As a national intangible cultural heritage, Genglubu has constructed a perfect navigation system for the South China Sea, recording numerous geographical entities, including features such as shape and orientation, as well as a large amount of information such as the distance between islands and reefs, the direction of sea currents, and navigational relationships, among which the toponymic entities are the most valuable type of geographic information resources [2]. A toponym is an exclusive name that refers to a specific spatial location [3]. Its naming is usually influenced by a variety of factors, such as history, culture, geology, climate, and folklore, and reflects the comprehensive characteristics of a region in terms of natural conditions, human history, and social culture, and plays an essential role in various fields such as territorial management, mapping, navigation, tourism, and cultural heritage [4]. Toponymic entity recognition (TER), which refers to determining the location boundaries of toponymic entities from natural language texts and making type judgments about them [5], is a subset of the Named Entity Recognition (NER) task, which is of great significance as an upstream task for constructing a knowledge graph in the geography field. Most of the existing research in Genglubu has been conducted from a traditional humanities and social sciences perspective and technology. It has several problems, including a lack of clear knowledge organization and weak correlation between geographic entities. The Opinions on Promoting the Work of Ancient

Books in a New Era states that new technologies should be used to realize the digitization and intelligence of ancient books [6]. Knowledge graphs can not only help the implicit relationships and enhance the correlation between data but can also reduce the difficulty of knowledge dissemination in related fields.

For low-resource domains such as Genglubu, under the guidance of national policy and the promotion of artificial intelligence technology, this paper designs and constructs a toponymic entity recognition dataset (Genglubu Toponym Data, GTData) for the TER task in Genglubu. Meanwhile, we propose a toponymic entity recognition model (ALBERT-Conv1D-BiLSTM-CRF) and analyze and compare it with other models to obtain superior results. It aims to provide a database for the construction of geographic knowledge graphs of the South China Sea and to promote cross-disciplinary development.

The remainder of this paper is organized as follows. In Section 2, we introduce the literature review. Section 3 describes the model structure in detail. Section 4 describes the experimental setup and the analysis of the results. Section 5 summarizes the results.

2. Literature Review

In recent years, deep learning models have been effective in areas such as CV and NLP [7,8], especially in TER [9,10]. Compared with traditional entity recognition methods, deep learning can automatically learn critical features and higher-order abstract features from the original dataset, avoiding the need for domain experts to define rules or carry out complex feature engineering manually. Because it can use many parameters, it has apparent advantages in applying deep semantic knowledge and alleviating data sparsity [11]. It maps raw textual data into a vector or matrix space. It maps words to their corresponding entity classes using different neural networks [12]. The toponymic entity recognition model based on deep learning mainly comprises an embedding layer, a feature encoding layer, and a label decoding layer. Among them, the feature encoding layer mainly includes Convolutional Neural Networks (CNNs), Recurrent Neural Networks (RNNs), Long Short-Term Memory (LSTM), Gated Recurrent Units (GRUs), as well as Hybrid Neural Networks and Attention Mechanisms. CNNs can increase computation speed by parallelizing data processing and, therefore, have a faster computational efficiency. Gritta M et al. proposed a new approach to systematically encoding geographic metadata in conjunction with CNNs [13]. This approach involves converting place names in natural language text into corresponding latitude and longitude coordinates and combining them with map information to improve the robustness of the model with a joint training approach. Kumar A et al. faced the problems of unreliable fields, grammatical errors, and non-standard abbreviations of place name information on Twitter. They proposed a CNN-based model that extracts geolocation information from Twitter and achieves an F1 of 96.0% [14]. CNNs have the problem of missing contextual information when processing long text or sequence data. RNNs are superior to CNNs in terms of performance in processing sequence data and can better capture the dependencies between sequence data. By analytically comparing ARIMA, LSTM, and BiLSTM models, Siami-Namini et al. verified that training data in the opposite direction helps sequence modeling and can significantly improve the accuracy of time series [15]. Chen T et al. proposed a divide-and-conquer approach by first classifying sentences into three different types using Bilstm-CRF and then utilizing 1d-CNNs to perform sentiment analysis on each type of sentence, which effectively improves the performance of sentence-level sentiment analysis [16]. Shen Si et al. proposed an RNN-based Chinese character-level annotation model by combining RNNs and Chinese word features, which significantly improved the F1 value of toponymic entities [17]. Rhanoui M et al. addressed the problems of large data size and conflicting viewpoints in the task of document-level sentiment analysis by constructing a CNN-BiLSTM model for extended text viewpoint analysis using word embedding in Doc2vec. They obtained excellent results on a French newspaper article [18]. Peng N et al. attempted to train NER and disambiguation as a joint task using an LSTM-CRF model, which improved the F1 value by almost 5% on the results of previous studies [19]. Lu W et al. constructed a model for prediction by combining CNNs, BiLSTM, and Attention Mechanisms for nonlinear time series such as stock price and obtained better results [20]. Dong C et al. constructed a BiLSTM-CRF model based on character-level and part-level feature representations for Chinese-named entity recognition. They achieved the best F1 value of 90.95% on the MSRA dataset [21]. With the development of pre-trained language models (PTLM) such as BERT, PTLM can capture most of the semantic information of Chinese characters in a better way compared with previous studies. Ning X et al. introduced bi-directional attention routing and sausage measure to project data onto complex surfaces with nonlinear mapping, which enables the approximation of any nonlinear function with arbitrary accuracy and maintains the local responsiveness of the capsule entities. The experimental results are excellent [22]. Ma K et al. proposed a neural network model based on BERT-BiLSTM-CRF for Chinese place name entity recognition, which performs well on MSRA, GeoTR-20, and other datasets [23]. Ziniu W et al. proposed a hybrid neural network model based on BERT to address the problems of not fully considering the context and ignoring the local features in the NER task by combining the BiLSTM and IDCNN models to extract the features, which resulted in a 4.79% improvement in the F1 value compared with the baseline model on the CLUENER dataset [24].

Deep learning has made superior progress in TER tasks. However, problems that need to be addressed, such as data scarcity, difficulty in contextualizing contextual understanding, and place name ambiguity. These problems mentioned above are also reflected in the field of Genglubu. First, Genglubu has high scarcity as it is a kind of literature containing unique geographical features. Its data samples are small, and the data available for training are limited. These problems cause difficulties for the model in discovering hidden features in the data. Second, the way of documentation in Genglubu differs from modern times, especially the rich contextualized information in Chinese. Finally, the phenomenon that the same name can be used as both a place name and an orientation exists in Genglubu, increasing the ambiguity in the corpus. Based on the above research results, this paper utilizes deep learning models to research toponymic entity recognition in Genglubu.

3. Methods

3.1. Architecture of the Model

The ALBERT-Conv1D-BiLSTM-CRF toponymic entity recognition model proposed in this paper consists of four main components. From top to bottom are the global feature extraction module, local feature extraction module, sequence modeling module, and decoding module, as shown in Figure 1. First, the global feature extraction module consists of the ALBERT layer. It is mainly responsible for mapping text sequences into vectors in a high-dimensional vector space and learning high-quality features and global semantic information of the input text. Second, the local feature extraction module consists of the Conv1D layer. It performs a convolution operation on the output of the ALBERT layer to extract local features that may involve individual characters or phrases by sliding a learnable convolution kernel over the sequence. Again, the sequence modeling module consists of BiLSTM layers. It mainly performs bi-directional modeling of the outputs of the upper layer to better capture the deep semantics and long-distance dependency information of the sequences and further improve the model's ability to characterize the sequences. Finally, the decoding module consists of the CRF layer. It accepts the output sequences from the BiLSTM layer. It improves the accuracy and robustness of the sequence labeling task by calculating the label scores and transfer probabilities to obtain the optimal labeled sequences. Each layer takes on a different function and has a clear order to work together to accomplish the sequence labeling task.

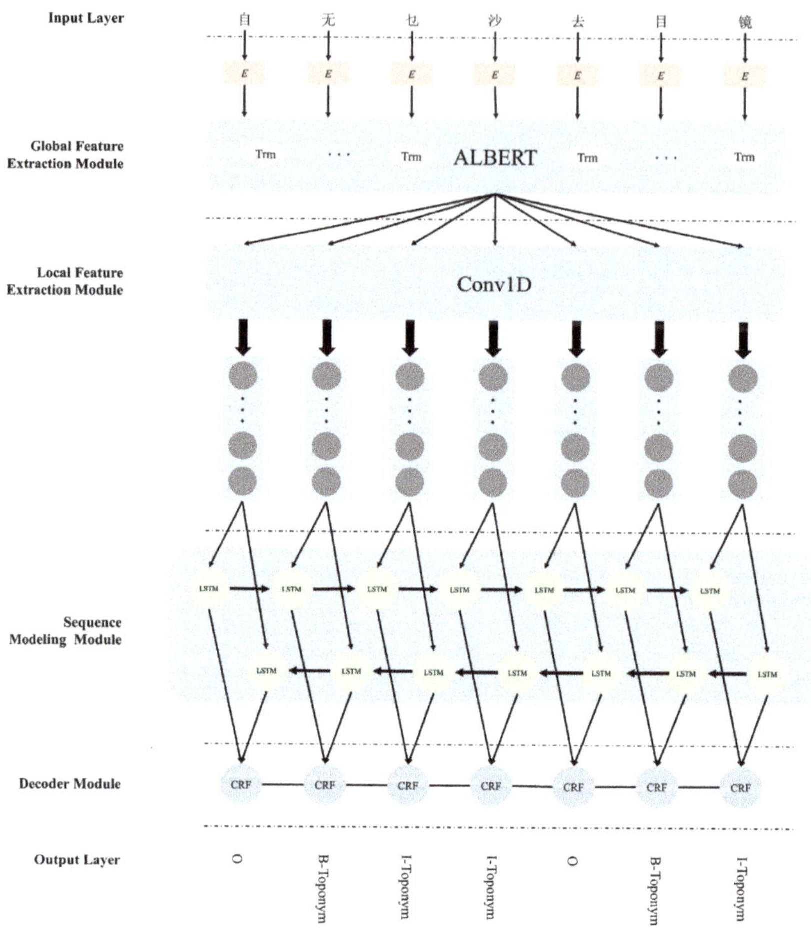

Figure 1. The overall framework of the model.

3.2. ALBERT

A Lite BERT (ALBERT) model is a pre-trained language model that was improved and optimized based on the BERT model, which allows ALBERT to perform better in some natural language processing tasks [25,26]. The ALBERT model uses techniques such as parametric factorization of embedding vectors and cross-layer parameter interactions to reduce the number of parameters significantly, thus improving the model's training speed and generalization performance. It also introduces the Sentence Order Prediction (SOP) task instead of the Nest Sentence Prediction (NSP) task to improve the performance of the downstream tasks [27]. It has the same basic structure as the BERT model: a deep bi-directional coded representation model based on the Transformer encoder. The multi-head attention mechanism in Transformer can make the same word in different sentences form different vector representations, which is effective for solving the multiple meanings of a word.

This paper uses the ALBERT layer to preprocess the input text. It is responsible for extracting the contextual semantic information of the sequence data as a global feature extraction module. Take data "自无乜线至深圈使壬丙三更" as an example, as shown in Figure 2. Suppose the input sequence is $X = (X_o, X_1, \ldots, X_n)$, where X_i denotes the ith token. For each X_i, token embedding, segment embedding, and position embedding are used to obtain E^i_{token}, $E^i_{segment}$, $E^i_{position}$, respectively. The three embedding vectors are weighted and summed according to a specific ratio, and the computation process is as follows:

$$E = \alpha_1 E^i_{token} + \alpha_2 E^i_{segment} + \alpha_3 E^i_{position} \tag{1}$$

where α_1, α_2, and α_3 denote the scaling factor of the three embedding vectors, generally being a real number between [0, 1] and satisfying $\sum_{j=1}^{3} \alpha_j = 1$.

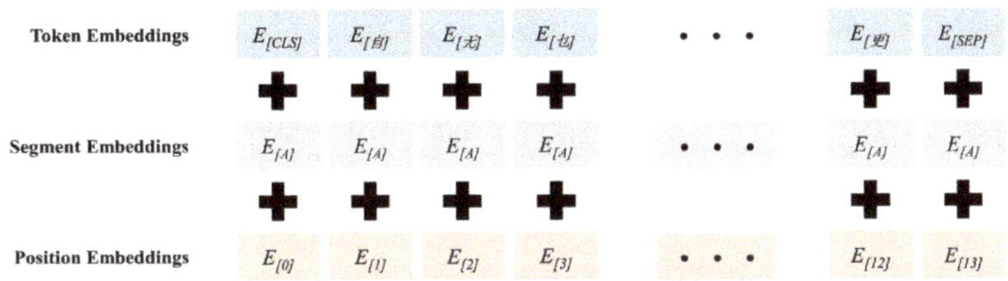

Figure 2. Input vector representation of the ALBERT model.

Then, the ALBERT layer learns the semantic information of each token in the context and is able to capture the long-range dependencies in the sequence. After the encoding process of the multi-layer Transformer, a high-dimensional vector representation $T = (T_0, T_1, \ldots, T_n)$ is obtained, and the specific learning process is shown in Figure 3.

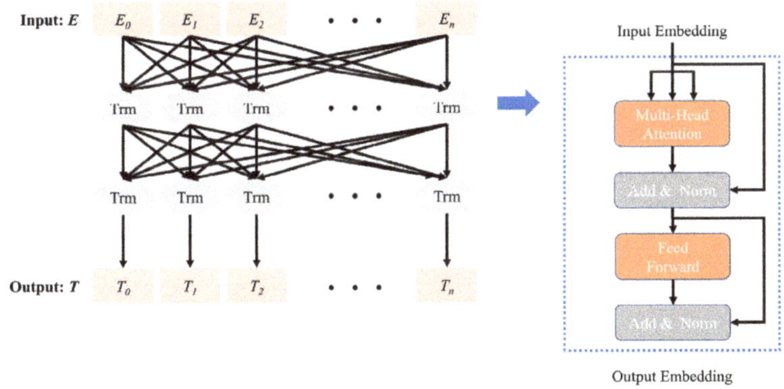

Figure 3. Structure of the ALBERT model.

Among them, the i-layer Transformer encoder calculation process is shown in Equations (2) to (6):

$$t'_i = Layer\ Norm(t_{i-1}) \tag{2}$$

$$t''_i = Multi\ Head\ Attention(t'_i, t'_i, t'_i) \tag{3}$$

$$t'''_i = Layer\ Norm(t'_i + t''_i) \tag{4}$$

$$t''''_i = Feed\ Forward(t'''_i) \tag{5}$$

$$t_i = Layer\ Norm\left(t'''_i + t''''_i\right) \tag{6}$$

where *Layer Norm* is the normalization operation that reduces the effect of internal variable displacements, thus making the model more stable. *Multi Head Attention* is used to capture deep information in the input sequence better. *Feed Forward* is the feed-forward fully connected network that improves the Transformer's nonlinear modeling capabilities and increases the model's degrees of freedom and its representational capabilities [28].

Since Genglubu belongs to the low-resource domain and small-scale dataset, to reduce the risk of overfitting and improve the generalization performance and the training efficiency, the parameters of the ALBERT layer are frozen during the training process. Freezing the ALBERT module makes the training focus on the task-specific layer you added, helping the model better adapt to name entity recognition.

3.3. Conv1D

Conv1D (1D Convolution) is a one-dimensional convolutional layer used in this paper as a local feature extraction module to extract local features from the input sequence with convolution operation [29]. The ALBERT model has excellent results in extracting global features of the input sequence but falls short in extracting local features. When analyzing the corpus features, the local features are crucial in the field of Genglubu, and an enhancement in the local features helps to classify the toponymic entities more accurately. In addition, the spatial structure of the input sequences can be learned, thus helping to improve the model's generalization and reduce the overfitting problem.

After accepting the output vector $T = (T_0, T_1, \ldots, T_n)$ as the input of this module, a series of convolution operations were performed to extract the local features of the sequence and obtain a new feature sequence with more expressive capability $C = (C_0, C_1, \ldots, C_n)$. The computation process is shown in Equations (7) and (8). Assuming that the convolution kernel size is k and the number of output channels is c, the convolution output can be expressed as Equation (7):

$$h = Conv1D(T, W) + b \tag{7}$$

where $W \in R^{k \times d \times C}$ is the convolution kernel tensor and $b \in R^c$ is the bias vector. For the ith output channel, the convolution operation can be expressed as Equation (8):

$$h_{i,j} = relu\left(\sum_{s=1}^{k}\sum_{t=1}^{d} W_{s,t,i} \times T_{j+s-1,t}\right) \tag{8}$$

where $j = 1, 2, \ldots, n-k+1$ denotes the starting position of the convolution operation, and each position j will be given a feature vector $h_j \in R^c$ of c dimension. Based on the above calculation, the new feature sequence is $C = (C_0, C_1, \ldots, C_n)$.

3.4. BiLSTM

Long Short-Term Memory (LSTM) is a recurrent neural network model that processes sequential data. It consists of a recurrent unit, an input gate, a forgetting gate, and an output gate. It effectively solves the problem of gradient vanishing and gradient explosion that occurs when training on long sequences by introducing a gating mechanism that can memorize the information of the input sequence for a long time [30]. BiLSTM consists of a forward LSTM and a backward LSTM, where the forward LSTM processes the input sequence in chronological order, and the backward LSTM processes the input sequence in reverse chronological order. Combining the outputs of the two directions gives the bidirectional hidden state at each moment [31]. It can capture long-term dependencies in sequences better than unidirectional LSTM and improves the expressive power. Here, the transformer is not used instead of BiLSTM. This is because the transformer is based on attention, which weakens the position information in the computation process (relying only on position embedding). Yan H et al. experimentally verified that BiLSTM outperforms Transformer in the NER task, where relative positional information and orientation information are essential, so the BiLSTM model was chosen [32,33]. The structure of the BiLSTM model is shown in Figure 4. The output $C = (C_0, C_1, \ldots, C_n)$ of the Conv1D layer is used as the input to this module. The long-term dependencies of the input sequences are captured with the BiLSTM layer, and the output $B = (B_0, B_i, \ldots, B_n)$ is input to the next module.

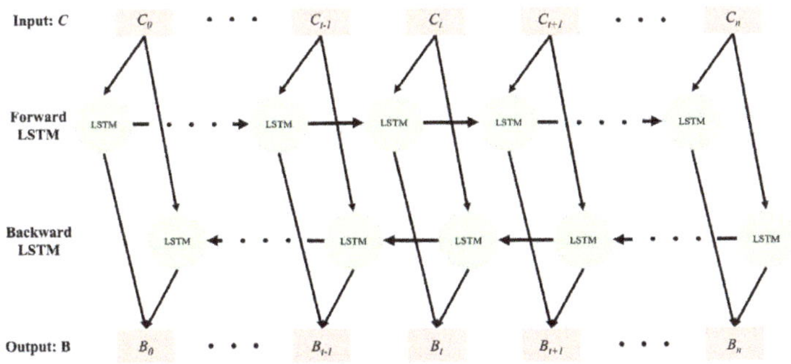

Figure 4. Structure of the BiLSTM model.

For the input sequence $C = (C_0, C_1, \ldots, C_n)$, the BiLSTM module deals with the forward and backward parts of the sequence data, using an LSTM model in different directions with independent parameters. The LSTM module uses C_i to denote the cell state. To avoid confusion and make the formulae clear, the input sequence $C = (C_0, C_1, \ldots, C_n)$ is temporarily expressed as $x = (x_0, x_1, \ldots, x_n)$. In the forward part, for the input x_t, the LSTM unit computes its hidden state and outputs it. Combining with Figure 5, the internal computation process can be expressed as Equations (9) to (14):

$$f_t = \sigma\left(W_f x_t + U_f h_{t-1} + b_f\right) \tag{9}$$

$$i_t = \sigma(W_i x_t + U_i h_{t-1} + b_i) \tag{10}$$

$$o_t = \sigma(W_o x_t + U_o h_{t-1} + b_o) \tag{11}$$

$$\widetilde{c_t} = tanh(W_c x_t + U_c h_{t-1} + b_c) \tag{12}$$

$$C_t = f_t \odot C_{t-1} + i_t \odot \widetilde{c_t} \tag{13}$$

$$h_t = o_t \odot tanh(C_t) \tag{14}$$

where σ is the sigmoid function and $tanh$ is the hyperbolic tangent function, both are nonlinear activation functions; f_t, i_t, o_t are the activation values of the forget gate, input gate, and output gate, respectively; C_t is the cell state, and $\widetilde{c_t}$ is an important parameter used to update C_t, which can be understood as the candidate hidden state; $W_f, W_i, W_o,$ and W_c are the weight matrices of the oblivion gate, the input gate, the output gate, and the cell state, respectively; $U_f, U_i, U_o,$ and U_c are the weight matrices of the previous moment, respectively; and $b_f, b_i, b_o,$ and b_c are the corresponding bias terms, respectively.

The above output is the output result of the forward part, so h_t can be understood as $h_t^{forward}$. The calculation process of the reverse part is similar to that of the forward part, and finally, the outputs of the forward and reverse parts are spliced together. The output result of the reverse part h_t is understood as $h_t^{backward}$, and the final representation is formed, as shown in Equation (15), which serves as the input of the downstream task:

$$B_t = \left[h_t^{forward}; h_t^{backward}\right] \tag{15}$$

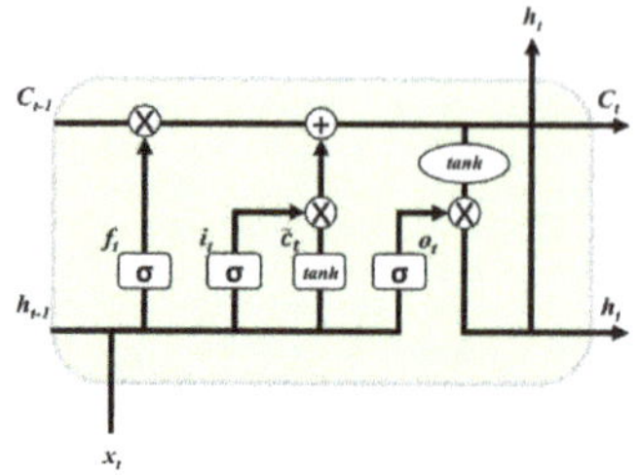

Figure 5. The cell structure of LSTM.

3.5. CRF

Conditional Random Field (CRF) is a discriminative model for predicting the output sequence from the input sequence in a sequence labeling task. It uses conditional probability distributions to model the dependencies between neighboring tags, normalizes the upstream output by learning the transfer probabilities between tags, makes a global optimization of the predicted sequence, and finally, solves for the optimal labeled sequence. In this paper, the CRF layer, as the last part of the model, receives $B = (B_0, B_i, \ldots, B_n)$ as input and gives the optimal labeling sequence by internal computation.

Suppose $B = (B_0, B_i, \ldots, B_n)$ is represented by $x = (x_0, x_1, \ldots, x_n)$ and the label sequence is denoted as $y = (y_0, y_1, \ldots, y_n)$, where y_i is the label corresponding to x_i. This conditional probability calculation process is as follows:

$$P(y|x) = \frac{exp(S(y,x))}{Z(X)} \tag{16}$$

where $Z(X)$ is the normalization factor, which is the sum of the scores computed for all possible labeled sequences and is used to convert the numerator part into a probability distribution. $S = (y, x)$ denotes the scores at a given labeled sequence y and input sequence x, which can be computed from the firing matrix E and the transfer matrix T, as in Equation (17):

$$S(y,x) = \sum_{i=0}^{n} \left(E_{i,y_i} + \sum_{j=0}^{n} T_{y_i,y_j} \right) \tag{17}$$

where the transfer matrix T represents the transfer probability from the previous label to the next label, and the firing matrix E is obtained by mapping the hidden state of each position of the input sequence into the label space. After obtaining the conditional probabilities, optimization algorithms such as stochastic gradient descent are used to maximize the log-likelihood function and update the model parameters. During the prediction process, the predictions are decoded using the Viterbi algorithm to find the labeled sequence predicted with maximum probability.

3.6. Loss Function

The loss function used in this paper is divided into two parts: the cross-entropy loss function and the CRF loss function. The cross-entropy loss function focuses on the model's accurate prediction of entity boundaries and categories. The parameters of the sequence annotation layer are updated by calculating the difference between the predicted sequence labels and the actual sequence labels:

$$Loss_1 = -\sum_{j=1}^{N} \sum_{i=1}^{C} y_{j,i} \ln(S_{j,i}) \tag{18}$$

where N is the number of samples, C is the number of categories, $y_{j,i}$ is the true value of the *i-th* category in the *j-th* sample, and $S_{j,i}$ is the predicted value of the *i-th* category in the *j-th* sample.

The CRF loss considers the dependencies between label sequences to ensure the overall soundness of the generated label sequences. It is modeled using a negative log-likelihood function. For a given input sequence x and actual label sequence y, the $Loss_2$ can be expressed as:

$$Loss_2 = -\ln(P(y|x)) \tag{19}$$

The overall loss function consists of a weighted sum of the two components.

$$Loss = \alpha_1 Loss_1 + \alpha_2 Loss_2 \tag{20}$$

where α_1 and α_2 are generally between [0, 1] and satisfy $\sum_{i=1}^{2} a_i = 1$.

4. Experiment

4.1. Datasets and Data Labeling

The initial data of the GTData dataset comes from more than twenty books of Genglubu, including *Su Deliu, Su Chengfen, Wang Shitao, Zheng Qingneng*, et al. We invited domain experts to annotate and check this dataset to ensure the quality of the dataset, and finally, check it manually as well as by code to ensure the uniqueness of the statements in the dataset. The GTData dataset is shown in Table 1.

Table 1. Genglubu Toponym Data dataset.

Classifications	Training Data	Test Data	Total Data
Number of sentences	2489	620	3109
Number of characters	42,797	10,776	53,573
Number of toponymic entities	5059	1262	6321

The GTData dataset has distinctive features compared with the publicly available datasets MSRA and People's Daily. In terms of average expected length (characters/sentence), GTData (17.23) is much lower than MSRA (48.39) and People's Daily (51.69). In terms of toponymic entity density (toponymic entities/sentence), GTData (2.03) is much higher than MSRA (0.82) and People's Daily (0.87). In addition, there are apparent prefix and suffix phenomena around place-name entities in GTData. Combined with the analysis of the characteristics of the era, these are because the ancient language is shorter and is more conducive to preservation and circulation, so the local characteristics in GTData are critical. The labeling method is the BIO labeling method, which is widely used in NER tasks. For example, for "自乌仔峙去乙辛，用乙辛，二更收。", the specific annotation format is (O, B-Toponym, I-Toponym, I-Toponym, O, B-Toponym, I-Toponym, O, O, O, O, O, O, O, O, O, O, O, O, O, O, O), in which O denotes a non-toponym, B-Toponym denotes the beginning of the toponym, and I-Toponym denotes the interior of the toponym.

4.2. Experimental Setting and Assessment Indicators

The experimental environment of this paper is shown in Table 2.

Table 2. Experiment environment.

Experimental Environment	Configure
Operating system	Ubuntu Server 18.04 LTS 64 bit
CPU	Intel(R)Xeon(R)Platinum 8255C CPU @ 2.50 GHZ
GPU	NVIDIA T4
RAM	32 GB
Python	3.8.0
Pytorch	1.7.1

Precision (P), recall (R), and the F1-score (F1) were used as the evaluation indexes of the experimental results. Their calculation processes are as follows:

$$P = \frac{TP}{(TP + FP)} \tag{21}$$

$$R = \frac{TP}{(TP + FN)} \tag{22}$$

$$F1 = \frac{2 \times P \times R}{(P + R)} \tag{23}$$

where True Positive (TP) is the number of positive samples correctly predicted; True Negative (TN) is the number of negative samples correctly predicted; False Positive (FP) is the number of negative samples incorrectly predicted as positive samples; and False Negative (FN) is the number of positive samples incorrectly predicted as negative samples.

4.3. Parameter Setting

In order to compare the performance of each model, the parameter configurations were uniformly set as in Table 3, and the overfitting problem was avoided using the dropout mechanism [34].

Table 3. Important parameter configurations.

Parameter Name	Value
Hidden dim	768
Max_sequence_length	128
Transformer_layer_num	12
BiLSTM_layer_num	1
Learning rate	10^{-4}
Dropout	0.5
Batch size	32

4.4. Analysis of Experimental Results

According to the above experimental setup, the trend in each evaluation index with Epoch was obtained, as shown in Figure 6. It is clear from Figure 6a that BERT-BiLSTM-CRF, RoBERTa-BiLSTM-CRF, ALBERT-AM-LSTM-CRF, and the model in this paper have a faster decrease in the loss and can achieve lower loss values. In contrast, the benchmark model (ALBERT-BiLSTM-CRF) performs relatively poorly, worse than the previous four, regarding both the rate of loss decline and the value of loss. A faster loss decline indicates that the model can converge faster during the learning process, indicating that the model can learn the patterns and features in the data faster. A low loss value indicates that the model performs better on the test set, which can measure the generalization ability of a model.

Figure 6b represents the trend in precision with epoch, and it can be seen that the ALBERT-BiLSTM-CRF, RoBERTa-BiLSTM--CRF, and ALBERT-AM-LSTM-CRF models have lower accuracy and almost the same effect. In contrast, BERT-BiLSTM-CRF and this paper's model are more effective, especially at epoch = 18; the effect of these two models tends to stabilize, of which the effect of this paper's model reaches 98%, which is slightly better than the BERT-BiLSTM-CRF model. Compared with the benchmark model, the improvement is nearly 0.74%.

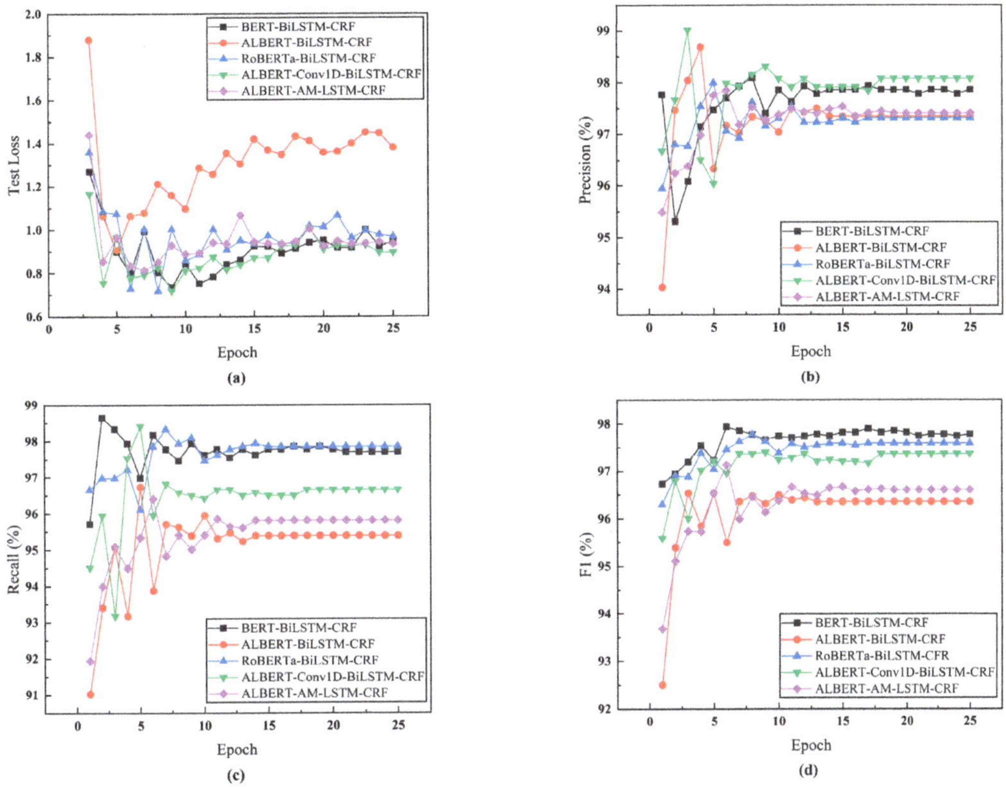

Figure 6. The change trend in each evaluation index with epoch. (**a**) represents the trend in Test Loss with epoch. (**b**) represents the trend in precision with epoch. (**c**) represents the trend in recall with epoch. (**d**) represents the trend in F1 with epoch.

Figure 6c represents the trend in recall with epoch, and it can be seen that the recall of ALBERT-BiLSTM-CRF and ALBERT-AM-LSTM-CRF is significantly lower than the other three models. The BERT-BiLSTM-CRF and RoBERTa-BiLSTM-CRF models have almost the same effect. The model in this paper shows a significant increase in recall compared with the benchmark model due to the introduction of the Conv1D model into the model structure, which can better capture the local features and thus enhance the recognition ability of the model and thus increases the recall from 1.28% to 96.67%. Although it is slightly insufficient compared with BERT-BiLSTM-CRF, it should be considered that in terms of parameters, the model in this paper is much smaller than the previous two models, which significantly saves computational consumption and has higher computational efficiency and lower cost. Therefore, the model in this paper is a superior choice under resource constraints.

Figure 6d represents the trend in F1 with epoch, and the F1-score is an essential indicator for evaluating the model to measure the overall comprehensive performance of the model. It can be seen that the F1 of ALBERT-BiLSTM-CRF and ALBERT-AM-LSTM-CRF have a large gap compared with the other three models. The BERT-BiLSTM-CRF and RoBERTa-BiLSTM-CRF models, as well as the model in this paper, have a more negligible difference in F1, and all perform better. By summarizing the data in the above figure, the performance can be obtained, as shown in Table 4.

Table 4. Effects of different models on toponym entity recognition.

Model	P (%)	R (%)	F1 (%)	Duration of Training (s/Epoch)
BERT-BiLSTM-CRF	97.86	97.70	97.78	66.26
ALBERT-BiLSTM-CRF	97.34	95.39	96.36	60.56
RoBERTa-BiLSTM-CRF	97.31	97.86	97.58	/
ALBERT-AM-LSTM-CRF	97.40	95.82	96.60	59.20
The model in this paper	98.08	96.67	97.37	61.59

We analyzed the four models regarding the loss function, precision, recall, and F1. In summary, in the task of toponymic entity recognition, this paper's model improves by 0.74%, 1.28%, and 1.01% in P, R, and F1 compared with the baseline model ALBERT-BiLSTM-CRF, respectively. As the model in this paper adds a local feature extraction layer based on the baseline model, which enhances the local features of the text data, there is an increase in computational resources, and the training time changes from 60.56 s/epoch to 61.59 s/epoch, which reduces the computational efficiency by 1.7%. Compared with the BERT-BiLSTM-CRF model, F1 is only 0.4% lower. Considering the computational resources and other aspects, the model in this paper is much smaller than the BERT-BiLSTM-CRF model in terms of the number of parameters, so the training efficiency is improved by nearly 7.05%. Therefore, the model in this paper has high performance while significantly saving computational resources and is more suitable for running on equipment with limited computational resources, thus improving the training speed and reducing the training cost.

4.5. Ablation Experiment

In order to further evaluate the impact of each module on model performance, ablation was designed to validate the results by removing the ALBERT, Conv1D, and BiLSTM modules, respectively. The experimental results are shown in Table 5.

Table 5. Results of the ablation experiments.

Model	P (%)	R (%)	F1 (%)
The model in this paper	**98.08**	**96.67**	**97.37**
* ALBERT	93.21	94.47	93.84
* Conv1D	97.34	95.39	96.36
* BiLSTM	95.22	95.31	95.26
* ALBERT-Conv1D	93.37	93.14	93.25
* Conv1D-BiLSTM	94.52	93.86	94.19

Note: * represents the removal of the module.

By ablating the ALBERT, Conv1D, and BiLSTM modules separately, it can be seen that each component contributes to model performance. Among them, the ALBERT module has the most significant impact on model performance, and its extracted contextual semantic information plays a vital role in recognizing place-name entities. Comparing the model with the removal of the BiLSTM module and the full model, we observe a decrease in the performance, which shows that the BiLSTM module plays a vital role in the long-distance dependencies in the whole sequence. In comparison, the Conv1D module had relatively little impact. With Conv1D as the control variable, the performance of the ALBERT-CRF, BiLSTM-CRF, and ALBERT-BiLSTM-CRF models all improved after adding the Conv1D module, which shows that the Conv1D module has a certain positive impact on dealing with the task of toponymic entity recognition in Genglubu.

4.6. Analysis of the Feature Vector

In the TER task, if the labels corresponding to two characters are of the same class, the final higher-order feature vectors of these two characters obtained after deep learning model training will usually have some similarity. The model will make the samples of the same class closer in the vector representation space during the training process. T-SNE (t-distributed stochastic neighbor embedding) is a nonlinear dimensionality reduction technique that maps high-dimensional data into a low-dimensional space while preserving the relative distance between data points. It tends to map similar samples to neighboring locations in the reduced dimensional space, thus preserving the similarity relationship of the data [35].

Therefore, we take one batch of data for the case study of the feature vector (32 data points, a total of 616 characters, 65 characters of the B-toponym category, 97 characters of the I-toponym category, and 454 characters of the O-category). The corresponding feature vectors of the already-trained data are dimensionality-reduced with the t-SNE algorithm to see if meaningful features can be extracted. As shown in Figure 7, the samples corresponding to the same labels form three types of clusters. It can be seen that the model has extracted meaningful features to some extent.

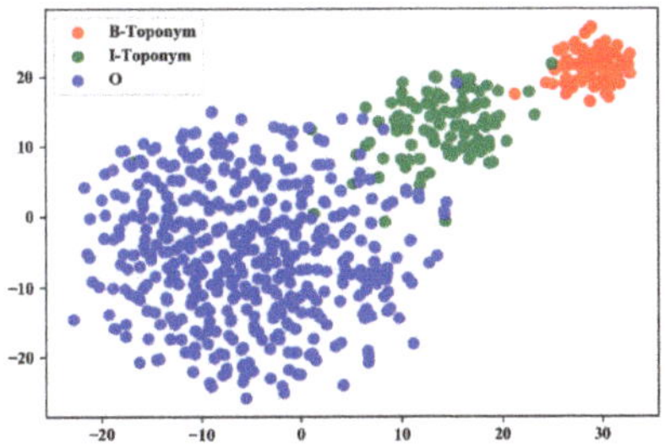

Figure 7. t-SNE visualization of feature vectors.

4.7. Sensitivity Analysis of Hyperparameters

We aimed to provide the performance of these models under different hyperparameter settings by varying the hyperparameters, including the learning rate, batch size, etc., to show the robustness of the proposed method. Due to the excessive permutations of different hyperparameters, we selected several parameter settings with common usage to demonstrate the method.

Based on the hyperparameter tuning experiments, it can be seen from the results in Table 6 that this paper's method exhibits a superior F1 performance than the ALBERT-BiLSTM-CRF model under different parameter settings (the enhancement ranges from 1.40% to 0.66%), which indicates that the model has a certain degree of robustness.

Table 6. Model performance with different hyperparameter settings (F1).

Model	Parameters [1]	Parameters [2]	Parameters [3]	Parameters [4]
BERT-BiLSTM-CRF	97.85	97.78	97.53	97.49
ALBERT-BiLSTM-CRF	96.33	96.36	95.62	96.52
RoBERTa-BiLSTM-CRF	97.35	97.58	97.62	97.42
ALBERT-AM-LSTM-CRF	96.44	96.60	96.27	96.35
The model in this paper	97.40	97.37	97.02	97.18

Note: The parameters are set as follows: [1] The parameters are set to learning rate = 10^{-4}, batch size = 16, epoch = 25, dropout = 0.5. [2] The parameters are set to learning rate = 10^{-4}, batch size = 32, epoch = 25, dropout = 0.5. [3] The parameters are set to learning rate = 10^{-4}, batch size = 64, epoch = 30, dropout = 0.5. [4] The parameters are set to learning rate = 10^{-3}, batch size = 32, epoch = 25, dropout = 0.3.

4.8. Model Generalization Validation

In order to validate the applicability and generalization ability of the model in this paper in the general domain, validation was carried out on the public datasets: the MSRA dataset and the People's Daily dataset, respectively. Since this paper focuses on the task of toponymic entity recognition, a label reset operation was performed on the public dataset, where all non-toponymic entity labels were corrected to the label 'O' in order to facilitate high-quality evaluation of the model performance.

Figure 8a, Figure 8b, and Figure 8c shows the validation results for the GTData, MSRA, and People's Daily datasets, respectively. According to Figure 8b, the model in this paper reduces the precision by 1.01% compared with the ALBERT-BiLSTM-CRF model. However, the recall is improved by 2.17%, the F1 value is improved by 0.77%, and the overall performance is better than the latter. According to Figure 8c, including the pre-trained language model in the BiLSTM-CRF model has degraded the task in terms of performance. This may be because the ALBERT model does not match the features of the toponymic entity recognition task in some respects. It is better at handling sentence-level tasks, while the toponymic entity recognition task focuses more on entity-level tasks. In this paper, the Conv1D model is introduced after the ALBERT module, which makes the model focus on local features better, leading to an improvement in recognition. The experiments show that after introducing the Conv1D model, the precision is improved by 6.77%, the recall is improved by 8.21%, and the F1 is improved by 7.53% compared with the ALBERT-BiLSTM-CRF model. The model in this paper performs better on different datasets, indicating its good generalization and generalization ability.

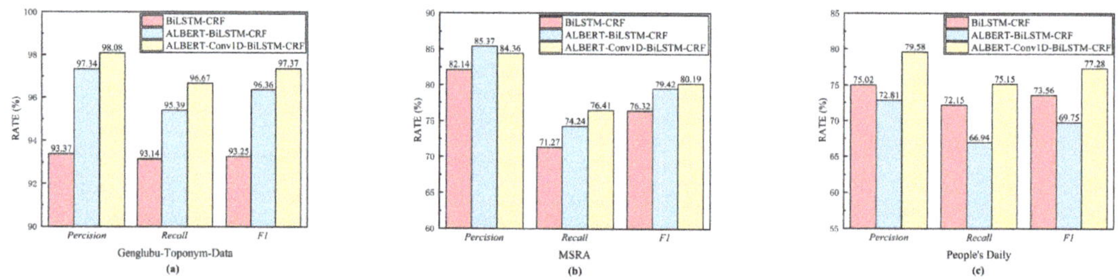

Figure 8. Model validation of common datasets. (**a**) is validation on the GTData dataset. (**b**) is validation on the MSRA dataset. (**c**) is validation on the People's Daily dataset.

5. Conclusions

Most of the existing research in the field of Genglubu in the South China Sea utilizes traditional social science and humanities tools and methods. It lacks effectiveness in the protection and dissemination of Genglubu data. Therefore, facing the problems of a lack of corpus, irregular geographical entity representation, and ambiguity of place names in Genglubu, this paper constructs the GTData dataset and proposes a toponymic entity recognition model based on the fusion of a pre-trained language model and local features (ALBERT-Conv1D-BiLSTM-CRF). Experiments show that compared with other deep learning models, the model in this paper achieves excellent performance on the GTData dataset and the public dataset while considering the computational resources and computational cost. This paper provides a new perspective for the research of Genglubu, helps to reduce the difficulty of its dissemination, and provides a new paradigm for the research of digital humanities. The next step focuses on expanding the featured literature corpus, granularizing the toponymic entities, and improving the model, aiming to improve the performance and robustness of the model and conduct relationship recognition studies to construct a geographic knowledge graph for the South China Sea.

Author Contributions: Conceptualization, Y.W.; methodology, Y.W.; software, Y.W.; validation, Y.W. and Y.L.; formal analysis, Y.W.; investigation, Y.W.; resources, Y.W.; data curation, Y.W.; writing—original draft preparation, Y.W.; writing—review and editing, Y.L. and X.Z.; visualization, Y.W.; supervision, Y.L. and X.Z.; project administration, Y.L. All authors have read and agreed to the published version of the manuscript.

Funding: This work was supported by the National Natural Science Foundation of China (No. 62362025, No. 62163010, No. 62162021) and the Hainan Province Key R&D plan project (No. ZDYF2022GXJS224).

Data Availability Statement: The data that support the findings of this study are available on request from the corresponding author, Yihong Li, upon reasonable request.

Conflicts of Interest: The authors declare no conflict of interest.

References

1. Wang, X. A preliminary study on the South China Sea voyages GENG LU BU Peng Zhengkai transcript. *Qilu J.* **2015**, *6*, 42–50.
2. Li, W.; Zhiguo, G.; Huang, L. Research on the place names of Siam Bay in Guihai Nian Gengliubu in the perspective of digital humanities. *Geogr. Res.* **2021**, *40*, 1529–1542.
3. Berragan, C.; Singleton, A.; Calafiore, A.; Morley, J. Transformer based named entity recognition for place name extraction from unstructured text. *Int. J. Geogr. Inf. Sci.* **2023**, *37*, 747–766. [CrossRef]
4. Lenc, L.; Martínek, J.; Baloun, J.; Prantl, M.; Král, P. Historical map toponym extraction for efficient information retrieval. In Proceedings of the Document Analysis Systems: 15th IAPR International Workshop, DAS 2022, La Rochelle, France, 22–25 May 2022; pp. 171–183.
5. Aldana-Bobadilla, E.; Molina-Villegas, A.; Lopez-Arevalo, I.; Reyes-Palacios, S.; Muñiz-Sanchez, V.; Arreola-Trapala, J. Adaptive geoparsing method for toponym recognition and resolution in unstructured text. *Remote Sens.* **2020**, *12*, 3041. [CrossRef]
6. Meimei, X. Policy driven ancient books protection and digital humanities. *Libr. Inf.* **2022**, *2*, 122–126.
7. Aslan, M.F.; Unlersen, M.F.; Sabanci, K.; Durdu, A. CNN-based transfer learning–BiLSTM network: A novel approach for COVID-19 infection detection. *Appl. Soft Comput.* **2021**, *98*, 106912. [CrossRef] [PubMed]
8. Hwang, S.; Hong, J.E.; Nam, Y.K. Towards effective entity extraction of scientific documents using discriminative linguistic features. *KSII Trans. Internet Inf. Syst. (TIIS)* **2019**, *13*, 1639–1658.
9. Wang, J.; Hu, Y.; Joseph, K. NeuroTPR: A neuro-net toponym recognition model for extracting locations from social media messages. *Trans. GIS* **2020**, *24*, 719–735. [CrossRef]
10. Wang, X.; Ma, C.; Zheng, H.; Liu, C.; Xie, P.; Li, L.; Si, L. DM_NLP at semeval-2018 task 12: A pipeline system for toponym resolution. In Proceedings of the 13th International Workshop on Semantic Evaluation, Minneapolis, MN, USA, 6–7 June 2019; pp. 917–923.
11. Schmidhuber, J. Deep learning in neural networks: An overview. *Neural Netw.* **2019**, *61*, 85–117. [CrossRef]
12. Lample, G.; Ballesteros, M.; Subramanian, S.; Kawakami, K.; Dyer, C. Neural architectures for named entity recognition. *arXiv* **2016**, arXiv:1603.01360.
13. Gritta, M.; Pilehvar, M.T.; Collier, N. Which Melbourne? augmenting geocoding with maps. In Proceedings of the Association for Computational Linguistics, Melbourne, Australia, 15–20 July 2018.
14. Kumar, A.; Singh, J.P. Location reference identification from tweets during emergencies: A deep learning approach. *Int. J. Disaster Risk Reduct.* **2019**, *33*, 365–375. [CrossRef]
15. Siami-Namini, S.; Tavakoli, N.; Namin, A.S. The performance of LSTM and BiLSTM in forecasting time series. In Proceedings of the 2019 IEEE International Conference on Big Data (Big Data), Los Angeles, CA, USA, 9–12 December 2019; pp. 3285–3292.
16. Chen, T.; Xu, R.; He, Y.; Wang, X. Improving sentiment analysis via sentence type classification using BiLSTM-CRF and CNN. *Expert Syst. Appl.* **2017**, *72*, 221–230. [CrossRef]
17. Si, S.; Danhao, Z. Chinese Place Name Recognition Based on Deep Learning. *Trans. Beijing Inst. Technol.* **2017**, *37*, 1150–1155.
18. Rhanoui, M.; Mikram, M.; Yousfi, S.; Barzali, S. A CNN-BiLSTM model for document-level sentiment analysis. *Mach. Learn. Knowl. Extr.* **2019**, *1*, 832–847. [CrossRef]
19. Peng, N.; Dredze, M. Improving named entity recognition for chinese social media with word segmentation representation learning. *arXiv* **2016**, arXiv:1603.00786.
20. Lu, W.; Li, J.; Wang, J.; Qin, L. A CNN-BiLSTM-AM method for stock price prediction. *Neural Comput. Appl.* **2021**, *33*, 4741–4753. [CrossRef]
21. Dong, C.; Zhang, J.; Zong, C.; Hattori, M.; Di, H. Character-based LSTM-CRF with radical-level features for Chinese named entity recognition. In *Natural Language Understanding and Intelligent Applications: 5th CCF Conference on Natural Language Processing and Chinese Computing, NLPCC 2016, and 24th International Conference on Computer Processing of Oriental Languages, ICCPOL 2016, Kunming, China, 2–6 December 2016*; Proceedings 24; Springer International Publishing: Berlin/Heidelberg, Germany, 2016; pp. 239–250.
22. Ning, X.; Tian, W.; Li, W.; Lu, Y.; Nie, S.; Sun, L.; Chen, Z. BDARS_CapsNet: Bi-directional attention routing sausage capsule network. *IEEE Access* **2020**, *8*, 59059–59068. [CrossRef]
23. Ma, K.; Tan, Y.J.; Xie, Z.; Qiu, Q.; Chen, S. Chinese toponym recognition with variant neural structures from social media messages based on BERT methods. *J. Geogr. Syst.* **2022**, *24*, 143–169. [CrossRef]
24. Ziniu, W.; Meng, J.; Jianling, G.; Meng, Q. Chinese named entity recognition method based on BERT. *Comput. Sci.* **2019**, *46*, 138–142.
25. Devlin, J.; Chang, M.W.; Lee, K.; Lee, K.; Toutanova, K. Bert: Pre-training of deep bidirectional transformers for language understanding. *arXiv* **2018**, arXiv:1810.04805.

26. Cui, Y.; Che, W.; Liu, T.; Qin, B.; Wang, S.; Hu, G. Revisiting pre-trained models for Chinese natural language processing. *arXiv* **2020**, arXiv:2004.13922.
27. Lan, Z.; Chen, M.; Goodman, S.; Gimpel, K.; Sharma, P.; Soricut, R. Albert: A lite bert for self-supervised learning of language representations. *arXiv* **2019**, arXiv:1909.11-942.
28. Vaswani, A.; Shazeer, N.; Parmar, N.; Uszkoreit, J.; Jones, L.; Gomez, A.N.; Kaiser, L.; Polosukhin, I. Attention is all you need. *Adv. Neural Inf. Process. Syst.* **2017**, *30*, 1–11.
29. Zhong, L.; Hu, L.; Zhou, H. Deep learning based multi-temporal crop classification. *Remote Sens. Environ.* **2019**, *221*, 430–443. [CrossRef]
30. Greff, K.; Srivastava, R.K.; Koutník, J.; Steunebrink, B.R.; Schmidhuber, J. LSTM: A search space odyssey. *IEEE Trans. Neural Netw. Learn. Syst.* **2016**, *28*, 2222–2232. [CrossRef] [PubMed]
31. Huang, Z.; Xu, W.; Yu, K. Bidirectional LSTM-CRF models for sequence tagging. *arXiv* **2015**, arXiv:1508.01991.
32. Yan, H.; Deng, B.; Li, X.; Qiu, X. TENER: Adapting transformer encoder for named entity recognition. *arXiv* **2019**, arXiv:1911.04474.
33. Guo, Q.; Qiu, X.; Liu, P.; Shao, Y.; Xue, X.; Zhang, Z. Star-transformer. *arXiv* **2019**, arXiv:1902.09113.
34. Srivastava, N.; Hinton, G.; Krizhevsky, A.; Sutskever, I.; Salakhutdinov, R. Dropout: A simple way to prevent neural networks from overfitting. *J. Mach. Learn. Res.* **2014**, *15*, 1929–1958.
35. Van der Maaten, L.; Hinton, G. Visualizing data using t-SNE. *J. Mach. Learn. Res.* **2008**, *9*, 2579–2605.

electronics

MDPI

Article

Demonstration-Based and Attention-Enhanced Grid-Tagging Network for Mention Recognition

Haitao Jia [1,†], Jing Huang [2,*,†], Kang Zhao [1], Yousi Mao [1], Huanlai Zhou [3], Li Ren [4], Yuming Jia [2] and Wenbo Xu [1]

1 School of Resource and Environment, University of Electronic Science and Technology of China, Chengdu 611731, China
2 School of Information and Communication Engineering, University of Electronic Science and Technology of China, Chengdu 611731, China
3 UESTC—Chengdu Quantum Matrix Technology Co., Ltd., Joint Institute of Data Technology, Chengdu 610066, China
4 University of Electronic Science and Technology Library, University of Electronic Science and Technology of China, Chengdu 611731, China
* Correspondence: 202152011709@std.uestc.edu.cn
† These authors contributed equally to this work.

Abstract: Concepts empower cognitive intelligence. Extracting flat, nested, and discontinuous name entities and concept mentions from natural language texts is significant for downstream tasks such as concept knowledge graphs. Among the algorithms that uniformly detect these types of name entities and concepts, Li et al. proposed a novel architecture by modeling the unified mention recognition as the classification of word–word relations, named W^2NER, achieved state-of-the-art (SOTA) results in 2022. However, there is still room for improvement. This paper presents three improvements based on W^2NER. We enhanced the grid-tagging network by demonstration learning and tag attention feature extraction, so our modified model is named DTaE. Firstly, addressing the issue of insufficient semantic information in short texts and the lack of annotated data, and inspired by the demonstration learning from GPT-3, a demonstration is searched during the training phase according to a certain strategy to enhance the input features and improve the model's ability for few-shot learning. Secondly, to tackle the problem of W^2NER's subpar recognition accuracy problem for discontinuous entities and concepts, a multi-head attention mechanism is employed to capture attention scores for different positions based on grid tagging. Then, the tagging attention features are embedded into the model. Finally, to retain information about the sequence position, rotary position embedding is introduced to ensure robustness. We selected an authoritative Chinese dictionary and adopted a five-person annotation method to annotate multiple types of entities and concepts in the definitions. To validate the effectiveness of our enhanced model, experiments were conducted on the public dataset CADEC and our annotated Chinese dictionary dataset: on the CADEC dataset, with a slight decrease in recall rate, precision is improved by 2.78%, and the comprehensive metric F1 is increased by 0.89%; on the Chinese dictionary dataset, the precision is improved by 2.97%, the recall rate is increased by 2.35%, and the comprehensive metric F1 is improved by 2.66%.

Keywords: discontinuous mention recognition; grid tagging; demonstration learning; tag attention; rotary position embedding

1. Introduction

In the realm of human cognition, the concept stands as a paramount bridge between concrete elements and abstract understanding. It epitomizes the embodiment of human understanding of the myriad elements in our world, linking past experiences with present interactions and thereby enabling the crucial cognitive functions of recognizing and comprehending novel phenomena [1]. In essence, the human ability to comprehend and understand relies on associating their knowledge with the concrete world through concepts.

For instance, when the word "冻" (freeze) is mentioned, people can associate it with different concepts or entities such as "寒冷" (cold) and "皮冻" (frostbite), allowing them to perceive, understand, and infer in specific contexts. Furthermore, in the era when intelligent upgrading and transformation have become common demands across various fields, understanding, and interpretation have become some of the core missions of artificial intelligence in the post-deep-learning era. Prior knowledge, such as knowledge of concepts, is also essential to endow machines with cognitive intelligence. Both structured and unstructured texts contain rich concepts or entities. Entities refer to distinguishable and independently existing entities, while concepts represent collections of entities with similar characteristics. For a natural, language sequence like "深海中的鲨鱼令大多人恐惧，其缘由是它们是食肉的动物。" ("Sharks in the deep sea frighten most people; the reason is that they are carnivorous animals".), people need to focus not only on the entity "鲨鱼" (shark) but also on broad concepts like "食肉动物" (carnivorous animal) and "动物" (animal). The comprehensive extraction of both named entities and overarching concepts from textual data is of paramount importance. It serves as a foundational step in the construction of concept knowledge graphs and facilitates a myriad of other downstream tasks.

Entities and concepts in natural language sequences, referred to as mentions in the following text, can be classified into three types: flat, nested, and discontinuous. Flat mentions imply that the words (or characters in Chinese text) in the mention are continuous and that none of its subsequences represent other entities or concepts. Nested mentions mean that the words in the mention are continuous, but they contain subsequences representing other entities or concepts. Discontinuous mentions indicate that the words in the mention are not contiguous. Accurately identifying the boundary of the entity and concept is extremely challenging. Additionally, using a unified model to address these three types of problems and refining the granularity of entity and concept representations has become a research hotspot in recent years.

Moreover, in the past two years, methods based on grid tagging have shown outstanding performance in the unified recognition of entities and concepts [2–6]. Among them, the W^2NER [3] model predicts the boundaries of entities and concepts as well as the adjacency word relationships using two grids. It then decodes the entire entity and concept, unifying the recognition problems of flat, nested, and discontinuous cases. Although this method has achieved SOTA results, there is still room for improvement. The SOTA model only focuses on the relationships between words within the grid, overlooking the impact of labels on the classification of word-pair relationships. Especially for discontinuous cases, it is crucial for the model to learn the word positions that it should pay more attention to, which is essential for improving the recognition of discontinuous entities and concepts.

In grid-tagging algorithms, inspired by Liu et al. [7], capturing the attention of grid tagging on words at different positions is valuable. In this way, this paper utilizes a multi-head attention mechanism to embed grid-tagging representations into the model, modeling the relationships between labels and the relationships between tags and words. However, pure attention mechanisms may lose sequence order information, and preserving the positional information of the sequence is essential for the effectiveness of grid-tagging algorithms.

So far, very few publicly available datasets include discontinuous entities and concepts, and there are no Chinese datasets of this kind. Among the limited publicly available datasets, discontinuous cases account for less than 10%. This paper aims to extract flat, nested, and discontinuous entities/concepts from authoritative Chinese dictionary definitions. However, manually annotated data are always limited. Therefore, in situations where the number of samples is small, the model's learning ability and generalization capability still need improvement.

Additionally, authoritative Chinese dictionaries contain rich conceptual knowledge in the form of vocabulary and phrases. However, most natural language sentences in these dictionaries are short texts due to this nature. Short texts have characteristics such as sparse semantic context, flexible expression, and a lack of annotated data. Traditional algorithms find extracting accurate, complete, and fine-grained conceptual knowledge from these texts challenging. Moreover, as a complex language with limited resources, Chinese has highly flexible expression styles and grammar rules.

In summary, the mining of fine-grained entities and concepts from structured and semi-structured texts face challenges such as significant text noise, abundant missing data, insufficient semantic information, subpar recognition in discontinuous scenarios, and limited annotated data.

The contributions of this paper are as follows:

1. Based on the analysis of practical results obtained from mining mentions of paraphrases in the Chinese dictionary using W^2NER, we address the issue of insufficient semantic information in short texts. Furthermore, with the rise of Large Language Models (LLMs), in-context learning theory performs excellently in its performance by feeding a few task-related samples, which is widely applied in the field of Natural Language Processing (NLP) [8]. Concatenating task-related demonstration in the input text as a prompt is also an advantage for normal-scale models. To enhance the learning ability, inspired by task-specific demonstration proposed in GPT-3 [9], we introduce the concept of in-context learning. Following specific selection strategies, it samples inputs and labels from the training data, designs task-specific demonstration templates, constructs corresponding demonstration sequences, concatenates them with input sentences, and provides information enhancement. Simultaneously, it improves the model's ability to learn from limited samples.
2. To address the issue of lower accuracy in recognizing entities or concepts in discontinuous scenarios with the base model, we introduce a multi-head attention mechanism to capture attention scores for words at different positions based on different labels. The attention features of labels are embedded into the model. Additionally, an iterative mechanism is employed to update the representations of label attention, aiming to extract deep fusion features.
3. To tackle the problem of attention mechanisms losing sequence information, this paper introduces rotary position embedding [10], achieving relative encoding effects in an absolute embedding form. Additionally, we then propose an improved algorithm W^2NER [3], named the Demonstration and Tag attention Enhanced Grid-Tagging Network (DTaE). The overall architecture of DTaE is illustrated in Figure 1.
4. This study selected an authoritative Chinese dictionary and employed a five-person annotation method to annotate flat, nested, and discontinuous entities and concepts in the definitions. Experiments were conducted on the public dataset CADEC [11] and the Chinese dictionary dataset to validate the effectiveness of the proposed model.

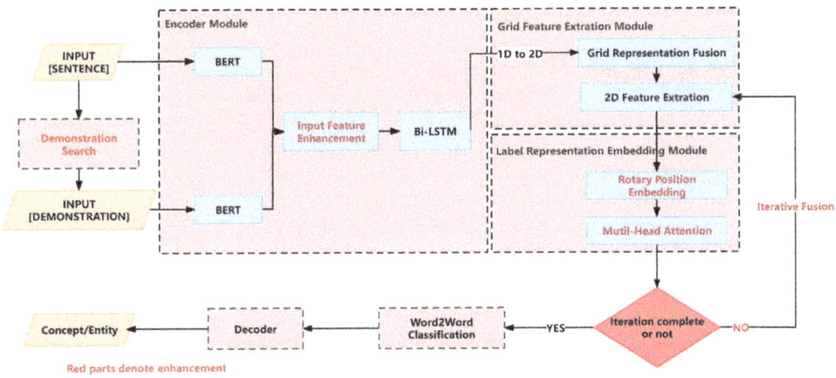

Figure 1. Detailed structure of modules within the enhanced DTaE model.

The subsequent arrangement of this paper is as follows: In Section 2, the current research progress in the relevant field will be introduced. In Section 3, we enhanced the grid-tagging algorithm W^2NER [3] by demonstrating learning and multi-head attention mechanism with rotary position embedding. In Section 4, the evaluation of the model's performance will be conducted.

2. Related Work

Entity and concept recognition aims to detect the boundary and semantic label of an entity or a concept mentioned from an input sentence, which, as a fundamental task in NLP, can be divided into three subtasks: flat, nested, and discontinuous named entity and concept recognition [6]. The earliest conventional research focuses on the recognition of flat mentions. In recent years, it has evolved from the conventional flat mention recognition to overlapped [12] and discontinuous mention recognition [13]. Previous methods can be divided into approximately four types: sequence labeling-based methods, span-based methods, generative methods, demonstration-based learning methods, and grid-tagging methods.

Sequence labeling-based methods treat nested mention-recognition tasks as sequence-labeling tasks, decoding them sequentially based on the order of the sequence. Since a character or word in nested entities can be annotated with multiple distinct labels, conventional sequence labeling models cannot directly recognize nested entities. Most learning models use Bidirectional Encoder Representation from Transformers (BERT) and Bidirectional Long Shot-TERM Memory (Bi-LSTM) to extract word- and character-level features, obtaining the context semantic information of the target word or character [3,7,14–18]. In Tang et al. [15], a multi-task BERT-Bi-LSTM-AM-CRF intelligent processing model was constructed to classify the observation annotation sequence to obtain the named entities in a Chinese text. Methods employing sequence labeling for nested NER attempt to transform multi-label tasks into single-label tasks or modify decoders to accommodate multiple labels. Ju et al. [19] used dynamic stacking of flat entity layers to identify nested entities. The layered-Bi-LSTM-CRF model uses LSTM layers to capture sequential context representations and feeds them back to cascaded CRF layers. The output of the LSTM layers is merged into the current flat NER layer to construct new representations for detected entities, which are then input into the next flat NER layer. This approach fully utilizes the internal information of nested entities, extracting external entities from the inside out. The dynamic stacking of flat NER layers continues until no nested entities are left. Takashi et al. [20] proposed a novel method for learning and decoding nested entities iteratively from the outside in, addressing structural ambiguity problems. They used the Viterbi algorithm to recursively search the scope of each entity to find internal nested entities. This algorithm does not require predefining the maximum length and quantity of entities. Each entity type has its CRF layer to judge whether the decoding meets the constraint conditions. In order to label irregular entities and concepts, Tang et al. [21] proposed an improved schema system named BIOHD containing seven labels to uniformly recognize flat, nested, and discontinuous mentions through the Bi-LSTM-CRF network. However, methods based on sequence labeling have several limitations: they cannot train models in parallel, complex label types lead to sparse label distributions, and there are exposed error issues between layers.

Span-based methods treat nested named entity recognition (NER) as a subsequence-classification problem within a sentence, effectively addressing error-propagation issues [22–27]. The basic idea of these methods is to enumerate all possible subsequences given an input sequence and predict the labels for each subsequence using a classifier. To capture underlying semantic information in the text, approaches like Sohrab et al. [27] classify all possible text fragments as potential entity mentions using deep neural networks. Shared Bi-LSTM networks output representations of text fragments to reduce computational costs and capture contextual semantic information around the fragments. Fisher et al. [26] propose a method where terms or named entities combine into nested structures of named entities. This method recognizes such nested entities in two stages: first, it determines the boundaries of nested entities at different levels, and second, it generates embeddings for each named entity by combining embeddings of smaller terms, predicting the linkage probability between two terms. The representations of each term in the named entity are iteratively updated to recognize nested entities. Span-based methods suffer from high computational costs and lack clear boundary supervision, leading to numerous negative samples, which impact overall algorithm performance. To address these issues, Li F et al. [28] propose a segment-enhanced span-based model for nested NER (SES-NER). This model treats the nested NER task as a segment coverage problem. It models entities as line segments, detects segment endpoints, and identifies positional relationships between adjacent endpoints. It detects outermost segments, generating candidate entity fragments for nested entities to classify text fragments. This model enhances boundary supervision in span representations by detecting segment endpoints, preserving long entities while reducing the number of negative samples and improving operational performance. Despite these advancements, span-based methods still face challenges, including excessive consideration of non-named entity regions, leading to numerous negative samples, high computational costs associated with classifying all subsequences in a sentence, and poor performance in boundary detection.

Generative methods aim to generate a named entity or a concept span sequence to fulfill the recognition task [2,29–31]. J. Straková et al. [30] identified flat and nested entities by generating label sequences and then decoding multi-labels. Tan et al. [31] generated span boundary and corresponding labels to detect flat and nested entities. Yan et al. [2] proposed a unified generative framework for various NER subtasks and utilized the unified pre-trained Seq2Seq model Bidirectional and Auto-Regressive Transformers [32] (BARTs) to address three entity recognition tasks. Yan et al. introduced three-pointer mechanisms to precisely locate entities within input sentences—span, byte pair encoding (BPE), and word—to use the BART model effectively. This framework is easy to implement, offering both performance and versatility. However, it still faces challenges related to decoding ambiguities and the inherent exposure bias problem in the Seq2Seq framework.

Demonstration-based learning methods have been researched widely in auto-regressive language models, with the recent introduction of a few training examples in a natural language prompt [33,34]. This kind of prompt is a task-specific demonstration that aims to make the model understand the training task [35]. Related efforts focused on data augmentation by generating synthetic labeled instances, which generate artificial samples but mostly ignore real training data. Thus, Chen et al. [36] proposed a novel description and demonstration-guided data-augmentation (D3A) approach for sequence annotation. Lee et al. [34] designed a demonstration-based approach for NER few-shot learning, which conducted a systematic study of the demonstration strategy, inspiring us to a great extent.

Grid-tagging methods convert a recognition task into a classification task that tags the relationship of each word pair in a grid transformed from a sentence [3,7,37]. In 2022, Li et al. a unified named entity recognition (NER) model called W^2NER [3]. They predefined three types of word-pair relationships: THW (Tail-Head-Word), NNW (Next Neighboring Word), and Unknown. First, they utilized pre-trained models for embedding to enhance the semantic representation capability of the model. Secondly, they employed advanced span annotation to convert the input into a two-dimensional grid, effectively alleviating decoding ambiguity issues. Next, they used a two-dimensional convolutional network to extract deep two-dimensional features. Finally, they employed joint biaffine and linear classifiers for word-pair relationship classification, obtaining named entities through decoding. This method addressed the challenges of entity boundary recognition difficulties and exposure bias. This approach is highly advanced by unifying the modeling of three types of entities and breaking through the core bottleneck through word-pair relationship classification. Furthermore, Liu et al. [7] improved recognition accuracy by expanding tag definition and the multi-head attention mechanism.

3. Methods

When addressing the challenges of flat, nested, and discontinuous entity types, it is essential to analyze their commonalities and transform them into a unified training task to construct an effective unified model. For entity-recognition problems, it is crucial to accurately identify the boundary words, internal words, and categories of entities. In this context, the state-of-the-art model in the field as of 2022, W^2NER [3], transformed entity recognition problems into word-pair relationship classification problems. In English, this corresponds to words, and in Chinese, it corresponds to characters (hereinafter referred to as "words" without specific mention of "characters"). The algorithmic process is as follows: First, words' semantic features are extracted via BERT-Bi-LSTM from input text. BERT and its variants are heavily used to extract semantic word features in Nature Language Processing and the proposed approach. Some studies [38] recently showed that these tools can often extract semantic meaning and sentiment in a way that matches human-generated text. Then, matrix-form position embedding and upper-triangular region embedding are introduced, combined with word features to construct features. Next, two-dimensional grid features are constructed through Conditional Layer Normalization (CLN), which is easier to extract using convolutional networks. Hybrid Dilated Convolution (HDC) generates a deeply interactive feature of two-dimensional object as well as W^2NER, which is extremely appropriate for handling gird feature extraction [3,39,40]. Subsequently, a joint classifier using Multilayer Perceptron (MLP) and Biaffine is employed to classify word-pair relationships within the grid. Finally, a decoding algorithm is designed to decode entities and concepts in the input text based on word-pair relationships.

Although W^2NER [3] has achieved significant state-of-the-art (SOTA) results in the unified recognition domain, its recognition capability in discontinuous scenarios still needs improvement. The network only focuses on the relationships between words and words, neglecting the influence of tagging on the classification of word-pair relationships. This paper proposes three improvements to address these issues: enhancing input features through demonstrations, strengthening the representation ability of tagging features using multi-head attention mechanisms, and preserving sequence position information through rotary position embedding.

In summary, this paper proposes an improved algorithm based on the state-of-the-art model W^2NER [3], named Demonstration and Tag-aware Enhanced Grid-Tagging Network (DTaE). The specific steps of the algorithm are as follows:

1. Searching for demonstration sentences: During the training phase, a certain search strategy is employed to sample input sequences and corresponding annotated data from the training set. Task-specific demonstration templates are designed, and the obtained input sequences and annotated data are filled into these templates to construct demonstrations. Relevant demonstration sequences are concatenated with input sequences, playing a role in task demonstration and information enhancement.
2. Word feature extraction and sentence feature enhancement: pre-trained models are used to embed input sequences, obtaining word features and sentence features. The demonstration information is also embedded using the same pre-trained model, resulting in a sentence vector indicated by the "[CLS]" token. This vector is weighted using learnable weights and fused with the input sequence's sentence vector to enhance the features. Furthermore, Bi-LSTM networks are utilized to embed the representation vectors of input sequences, introducing more semantic context information.
3. Construction of two-dimensional grid features: The vector representations of the input text are concatenated with position embedding and upper-triangular matrices to create BERT-style input. Conditional Layer Normalization is applied to merge grid representations.
4. Hybrid Dilation Convolution (HDC) for extracting two-dimensional features: Convolutional networks are naturally suited for extracting two-dimensional features. Although single fine-grained dilated convolutions can enlarge the receptive field, they face the grid effect: as the dilation rate increases, the input sampling becomes sparse,

potentially leading to the loss of local information. Multiple fine-grained mixed dilated convolutions are used to extract grid features, enlarging the receptive field while avoiding the grid effect and effectively extracting two-dimensional features.

5. Obtaining tag attention features: Tagging features are constructed, and multi-head attention mechanisms capture the attention weights of different labels at different positions in the input sequence. These attention features are iteratively updated to enhance the model's recognition ability. To address the issue of attention mechanisms losing sequence position information, rotary position embedding is introduced in a relative embedding form, achieving results similar to absolute embedding. This embedding advantage is fully utilized by incorporating rotary position embedding before the aforementioned multi-head attention mechanism.
6. Deepening features: Word-pair grid features and tag attention features are iteratively fused through multiple rounds of the steps mentioned in (4) and (5).
7. Joint classifier: A joint classifier consisting of a multilayer perceptron and biaffine predictors predicts the word-pair relationships for various grid indicators.
8. Decoding: Based on the predicted word-pair relationships within the grid, the decoding algorithm is applied to obtain flat, nested, and discontinuous entities and concepts in the input sequence.

According to the aforementioned process, the algorithm design diagram for our improved grid-tagging model is illustrated in Figure 2.

3.1. Demonstration Search

Demonstration-based learning is a simple and effective auxiliary supervised learning method originating from GPT-3. The core idea is to provide the model with task demonstrations, allowing the input to undergo context learning through these demonstrations in advance. This enables the model to understand better and predict the tasks.

In the context of unified recognition of flat, nested, and discontinuous entities and concepts in short texts, especially in enhancing recognition in discontinuous scenarios to obtain more accurate and granular concepts, this study introduces task-related demonstrations into entity- and concept-recognition algorithms as a means of information enhancement. The goal is to compensate for the lack of rich contextual information and the scarcity of data samples in short texts. The challenge lies in determining reliable search strategies and designing effective demonstration templates.

Search strategies aim to find instances in the training set as demonstrations for the task. This study adopts two demonstration strategies: random search and semantic search. A random seed is set in the random search strategy, and instances of different target types in the training set are counted. Instances of different types are randomly selected, and multiple demonstrations are concatenated to form demonstration sentences. The remaining sentences are used as training data. In the semantic search strategy, highly relevant sentences are searched for each instance of training data to serve as its demonstration sentence. High relevance means semantic relevance at the sentence level, with semantic differences at the word level. Semantic search requires a universal sentence vector representation. Searching for many highly related sentence pairs using BERT incurs significant time costs, and the obtained sentence representations are unsuitable for unsupervised semantic search. SentenceBERT networks can address these issues. This pre-trained model is based on a twin network derived from BERT, which can obtain semantically meaningful chapter vectors. The basic principle is to obtain sentence vectors for two sentences through the twin network, and the pre-training task involves calculating the similarity between the two sentences. We use SentenceBERT(SBERT) [41] to search semantically relevant sentences for input as a demonstration. Constructing highly relevant sentence pairs in the training set, with sentence 1 as the demonstration and sentence 2 as the training data point.

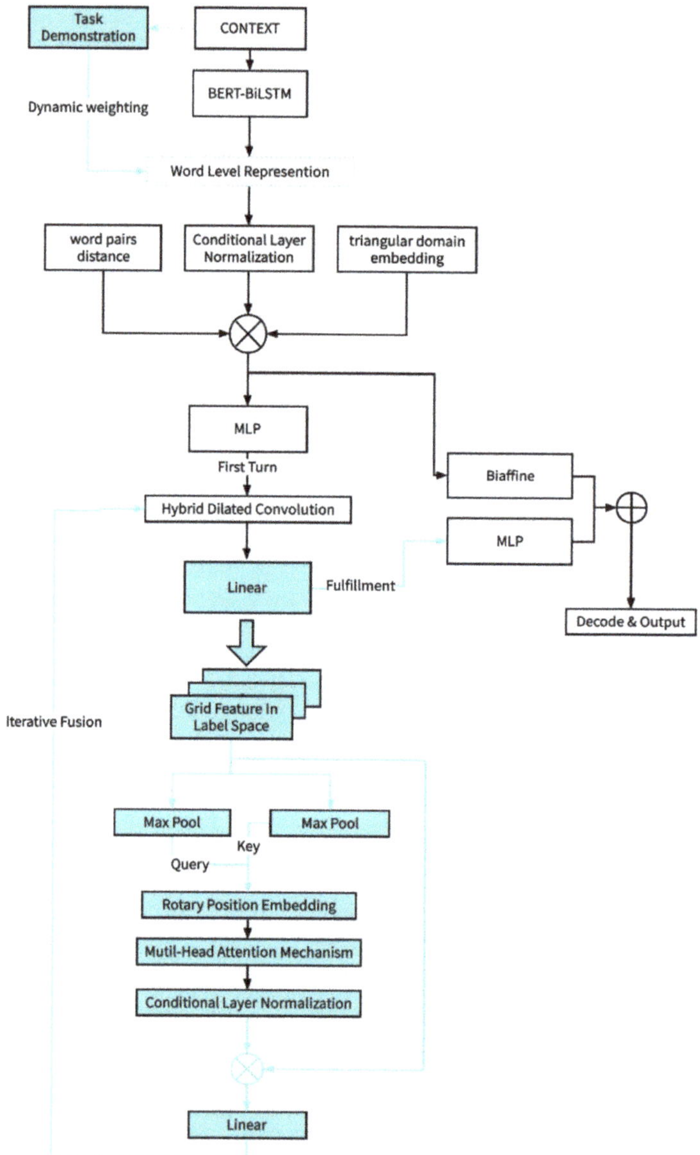

Figure 2. The overall architecture of our model.

Based on the search strategy, instances are searched in the training set to construct demonstrations. Specifically, a task demonstration can be represented as an input sequence $\widetilde{x} = [[SEP], \hat{x}_1, \cdots, \hat{x}_l]$, where l is the length of the sequence. Using instance-oriented demonstration templates, each instance includes an input sentence s and a set of annotated data S_e. If S_e is an empty set, there are no entities or concepts of the target type in the input sentence. Let the target type be $Type$. In this case, the demonstration sentence $\widetilde{x}$ is constructed as s + "There is no entity or concept named Type"., For Chinese demonstration sentences, it would be s + "上句中不存在Type实体或概念。". If S_e contains k entities or concepts, for each entity or concept e_i in S_e, an answer sentence ans_i is constructured: "e_i is entity or concept named *Type*". "or" "e_i 是一个*Type*实体或概念。" "The demonstration sentence $\widetilde{x}$ is then constructed as $s + ans_1 + \cdots + ans_k$".

Based on the above discussion, the two demonstration search algorithms used in this paper are illustrated in Figures 3 and 4.

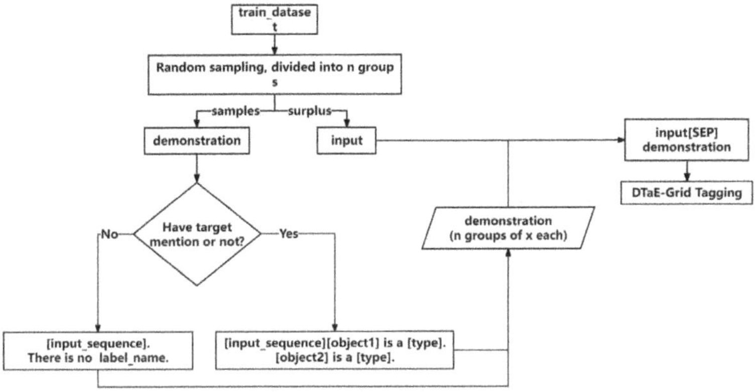

Figure 3. Random search strategy of our model for a demonstration of the search task.

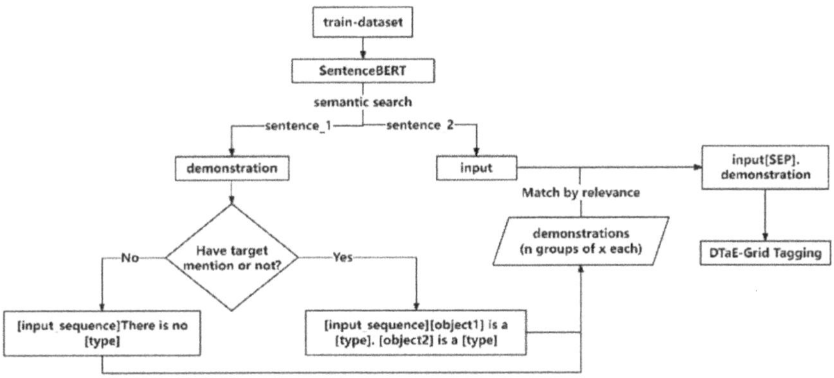

Figure 4. Semantic search strategy for our model for the demonstration of a search task.

3.2. Sequence Embedding

Once the natural language sequence $X = \left[x; \widetilde{x}\right]$ is obtained, it needs to be embedded in three stages: pre-trained model embedding, demonstration enhancement, and context embedding. These stages are essential for obtaining enhanced input representations incorporating information from the pre-trained model and the demonstration data. Specifically, leveraging pre-trained models like BERT, the input sequence X is embedded to obtain semantic representations H', as shown in Equation (1) below, where n represents the length of training data x, l represents the length of the demonstration $\widetilde{x}$, h_x represents the semantic representation vector of x, and $h_{\widetilde{x}}$ represents the representation vector of $\widetilde{x}$.

$$H' = BERT([x_1, \cdots, x_n; [SEP], \hat{x}_1, \cdots, \hat{x}_l]) = [h_x, h_{\tilde{x}}] \tag{1}$$

Next, the representation vector of the demonstration sentence is utilized to enhance the training data, introducing more task-related semantic information into the training dataset, thereby enhancing the semantic representation ability of short texts. Through a dynamic weighting network, $h_{\tilde{x}}$ is integrated into the semantic representation vector of x, obtaining the word-level representation vector H_x, as shown in Equation (2).

$$H_x = WH' + b \tag{2}$$

Here, $W \in \mathbb{R}^{(n+l)\times n}$ represents the learnable weight matrix, and $b \in \mathbb{R}^{n\times 1}$ is the learnable bias. Additionally, Xavier initialization is employed for the weight network to prevent gradient vanishing during backpropagation, ensuring consistency in the variances of inputs and outputs.

Finally, to capture the contextual information of the sequence and enhance the semantic feature representation H_x of sequence x, bidirectional Long Short-Term Memory networks (Bi-LSTMs) are employed. This step further constructs the input features $H \in \mathbb{R}^{n\times d_h}$, where d^h represents the dimensionality of a word representation, as shown in Equation (3).

$$H = BiLSTM(H_x) = [h_1, \cdots, h_n] \tag{3}$$

3.3. Grid Feature Extraction

The algorithm based on grid tagging requires the construction of grids and the extraction of grid features. This part includes grid representation fusion and two-dimensional feature extraction. Inspired by BERT's input structure, which includes position embedding, sentence tokenization, and the sentence sequence, three inputs are constructed to extract grid features: relative distance embedding for word pairs $E^d \in \mathbb{R}^{n\times n\times d_{E^d}}$, upper-lower triangular area embedding $E^t \in \mathbb{R}^{n\times n\times d_{E^t}}$, and grid representation for word pairs $V \in \mathbb{R}^{n\times n\times d_h}$.

Specifically, for a grid $grid \notin \mathbb{R}^{n\times n}$, where each cell represents a word pair (w_i, w_j), their relative distance embedding is proportional to the distance. The embedding values increase with distance, with a distance of 1 embedded as 0, and for distances in the range [4, 7], the embedding is 2, and so on. Following this rule, the relative distance embedding E^d corresponding to the grid can be obtained, with a dimensionality of d_{E^d} for the distance embedding of a single grid.

As mentioned earlier, this algorithm's designed word-pair relationships include the Next Neighboring Word (NNW) and Tail-Head Word (THW) tags. Within a concept or entity, based on tagging characteristics, NNW tags only appear in the upper triangular area or on the diagonal of the grid, while THW tags only appear in the lower triangular area or on the diagonal. Therefore, distinguishing between the grid's upper and lower triangular areas is necessary. To achieve this, the upper-lower triangular area embedding feature E^t is designed, with a dimensionality of d_{E^t} for the embedding of a single grid's upper–lower triangular area.

After the aforementioned embedding process, a one-dimensional sequence of deeply fused semantic features $H \in \mathbb{R}^{n\times d_h}$ is obtained. It is necessary to transform this feature into word-pair representations $V \in \mathbb{R}^{n\times n\times d_h}$. That is, for an n-length sequence, the features of any word pair (w_i, w_j) need to be computed. The relationships between word pairs in the grid have directionality. In other words, one of the necessary conditions for the relationship (w_i, w_j) to be NNW is $1 \le i \le j \le n$. To obtain high-quality grid features while considering the directionality between word pairs, Conditional Layer Normalization (CLN) networks are employed to model the representation $V_{ij} \in \mathbb{R}^{d_v}$ of the word pair (w_i, w_j), as shown in Equation (4).

$$V_{ij} = \gamma_{ij} \odot (\frac{h_j - \mu}{\sigma}) + \lambda_{ij} = CLN(h_i, h_j) \tag{4}$$

where $\gamma_{ij} = W_\alpha h_i + b_\alpha$ represents the gain parameters, and $\lambda_{ij} = W_\beta h_i + b_\beta$ represents the parameters for layer normalization. μ and σ are the mean and standard deviation of vector h_j, calculated as shown in Equations (5) and (6).

$$\mu = \frac{1}{d_h}\sum_{k=1}^{d_h} h_{jk} \tag{5}$$

$$\sigma = \sqrt{\frac{1}{d_h}\sum_{k=1}^{d_k} (h_{jk} - \mu)^2} \tag{6}$$

Concatenating the aforementioned three types of representational features, the fusion of grid representation features is achieved through a multilayer perceptron, resulting in the preliminary fused grid representation feature $C \in \mathbb{R}^{n \times n \times d_c}$, where d_c represents the feature dimension of a single grid, as shown in Equation (7).

$$C = MLP_1([V; E^d; E^t]) \tag{7}$$

To capture the interaction between word pairs at different distances and expand the receptive field, dilated convolution is employed to extract two-dimensional grid features. However, using a single dilated convolution faces the issue of the grid effect. To avoid losing local information and extracting irrelevant long-distance information, a hybrid dilated convolution $DConv_L$ with different dilation rates is employed, where L represents the dilation rate. The fused grid representation feature C is input into the $DConv_L$ network to extract two-dimensional features $Q^L \in \mathbb{R}^{n \times n \times d_q}$, as shown in Equation (8).

$$Q^L = GELU(DConv_L(C)) \tag{8}$$

By cascading different dilated convolutional layers with various dilation rates, we obtain preliminary two-dimensional grid features Q_0, where m represents the number of dilated convolutional networks. The subscript "0" indicates that these features have not yet been iteratively fused with the tag attention features. This process is represented in Equation (9), where d_{wp} represents the embedding dimension of word-pair grid representations.

$$Q_0 = [Q^{L_1}, \cdots, Q^{L_m}] \in \mathbb{R}^{n \times n \times d_{wp}} \tag{9}$$

3.4. *Label Representation Embedding*

Currently, the correct identification of the three types of mentions only occurs when all grid tagging within the mention are predicted. Therefore, embedding tag representations into the model, modeling relationships between tags, and modeling relationships between tags and words can enhance the model's recognition ability in discontinuous scenarios.

In other words, tag representation embedding requires the model to learn the attention of different tags on different word positions, perceiving the roles of different tags and organizing these roles as implicit knowledge. Introducing attention mechanisms to perceive the attention of each tag independently allows the model to learn relevant information in different representation subspaces, enriching the perceptual dimensions.

However, although the multi-head attention mechanism can perceive the roles of various labels from multiple perspectives, it cannot learn the sequence of the sequence. As mentioned above, the sequence order is inevitable for grid tags. Therefore, introducing Rotary Position Embedding [10] (RoPE) into the multi-head attention mechanism allows the sequence information to be retained. RoPE is an advanced form of position embedding that achieves excellent results by implementing relative position embedding in the form of absolute position embedding.

Specifically, the process of tag representation embedding modules is as follows: extracting tag features, introducing rotary position embedding to retain sequence information, obtaining tag attention features through a multi-head attention mechanism, iteratively integrating word-pair features and tag attention features, thus embedding tag representations into the model.

By using a linear network, the word-pair grid features Q_0 obtained from the above steps are mapped to the label space, extracting features for different labels T_p, where $1 \leq p \leq P$, and P represents the number of labels. The extracted features $T_p \in \mathbb{R}^{n \times n \times d_{tag}}$ are represented as follows in Equation (10).

$$T_p = W_p Q_0 + b_p \tag{10}$$

Here, $W_p \in \mathbb{R}^{d_{tag} \times d_q}$ and $b_p \in \mathbb{R}^{d_{tag}}$ are learnable parameters where d_{tag} represents the dimensionality of individual tag features. Concatenating these individual tag features results in the word-pair grid $T = [T_1, \cdots, T_P] \in \mathbb{R}^{n \times n \times (P \cdot d_{tag})}$ mapped to the tag space.

Through the MaxPooling layers $MaxPool_1 \in \mathbb{R}^{n \times (P \cdot d_{tag})}$ and $MaxPool_2 \in \mathbb{R}^{n \times (P \cdot d_{tag})}$, word-pair grid features in both horizontal and vertical directions are obtained: $T_{sub} \in \mathbb{R}^{n \times (P \cdot d_{tag})}$, $T_{obj} \in \mathbb{R}^{n \times (P \cdot d_{tag})}$. These serve as query, key, and value vectors for the multi-head attention mechanism.

Rotary Position Embedding (RoPE) is introduced into the query vector q and key-value vector v. The core idea is to perform the $f(\cdot)$ operation on them separately, ensuring that the equation $< f(q,a), f(k,b) >= g(q,k,a-b)$ holds in the form of absolute positions implementing relative position embedding. The two-dimensional form of $f(\ )$ is as follows in Equation (11), where $\theta = 10{,}000^{-\frac{2i}{d}}$, and this can be extended to multiple dimensions accordingly, where i corresponds to the index.

$$f(q,a) = \begin{pmatrix} \cos a\theta & -\sin a\theta \\ \sin a\theta & \cos a\theta \end{pmatrix} \begin{pmatrix} q_0 \\ q_1 \end{pmatrix} \tag{11}$$

Rotary Position Embedding (RoPE) is introduced separately in T_{sub} and T_{obj} to obtain T_{sub}' and T_{obj}' There are three optional methods, as shown in Equations (11)–(13).

$$f(q,a)_{add} = \left(\begin{pmatrix} \cos a\theta & -\sin a\theta \\ \sin a\theta & \cos a\theta \end{pmatrix} + q \right) \begin{pmatrix} q_0 \\ q_1 \end{pmatrix} \tag{12}$$

$$f(q,a)_{mul} = \left(\begin{pmatrix} \cos a\theta & -\sin a\theta \\ \sin a\theta & \cos a\theta \end{pmatrix} \times q \right) \begin{pmatrix} q_0 \\ q_1 \end{pmatrix} \tag{13}$$

$$f(q,a)_{zero} = \begin{pmatrix} \cos a\theta & -\sin a\theta \\ \sin a\theta & \cos a\theta \end{pmatrix} \begin{pmatrix} q_0 \\ q_1 \end{pmatrix} \tag{14}$$

Subsequently, the tag attention features are obtained using the multi-head attention mechanism, where T_{sub}' serves as the query vector and T_{obj}' serves as the key and value vectors. Let the embedding dimension of each attention head be d_{head}, and there are hn heads in total. The specific calculation process is as follows:

First, for each attention head $head_{hi}, hi \in [1, hn]$, calculate the corresponding attention weights. Map the query vector and the key-value vector to their respective linear spaces using the corresponding linear networks, as shown in Equation (15), where $W_Q \in \mathbb{R}^{(Pd_{tag}) \times d_Q}$, $W_K \in \mathbb{R}^{(Pd_{tag}) \times d_K}$, and $W_V \in \mathbb{R}^{(Pd_{tag}) \times d_V}$ are learnable parameter matrices.

$$\begin{aligned} Q_{head_{hi}} &= T_{sub}' W_Q \\ K_{head_{hi}} &= T_{obj}' W_K \\ V_{head_{hi}} &= T_{obj}' W_V \end{aligned} \tag{15}$$

Then, calculate attention cores using function $s(\cdot)$, and finally, and obtain the attention $Att_{head_{hi}} \in \mathbb{R}^{n\times(Pd_{tag})\times d_{head}}$ for $head_{hi}$ through weighted summation, as shown in Equation (16).

$$Att_{head_{hi}} = \sum_{j=1}^{n} \alpha_{ij} v_{head_{hi},j} = \sum_{j=1}^{n} softmax(s(k_{head_{hi},j}, q_{head_{hi},i}))v_{head_{hi},j} \tag{16}$$

The attention score function $s(\ )$, as shown in Equation (17), employs a scaled dot-product model.

$$s(k_{head_{hi}}, q_{head_{hi}}) = k_{head_{hi}}{}^{T} q_{head_{hi}} / \sqrt{(P \bullet d_{tag})} \tag{17}$$

Next, the attention weights from hn heads are concatenated and undergo another linear transformation, resulting in the tag-aware representation vector $T_{awared} \in \mathbb{R}^{n\times(Pd_{tag})\times d_{att}}$, as shown in Equation (18), where $W_o \in \mathbb{R}^{(hnd_{head})\times d_{att}}$ is a learnable parameter matrix.

$$T_{awared} \in \mathbb{R}^{n\times(P\bullet d_{tag})\times d_{att}} = concat(Att_{head_{h1}}, \cdots, Att_{head_{hn}})W_o \tag{18}$$

Finally, to embed the tag attention vectors into the model and integrate them deeply with the word-pair grid features, the two-dimensional tag attention features $T^{2D}_{awared} \in \mathbb{R}^{n\times n\times(Pd_{tag})}$ are reconstructed through the Conditional Layer Normalization network CLN_1, as shown in Equation (19), where the calculation method of the Conditional Layer Normalization network has been described earlier.

$$T^{2D}_{awared} = CLN_1(T_{awared}, T_{awared}) \tag{19}$$

The final tag-embedded word-pair grid features $Q_1 \in \mathbb{R}^{n\times n\times d_{wp}}$ are obtained using element-wise summation of the word-pair grid features $T \in \mathbb{R}^{n\times n\times(P\cdot d_{tag})}$ and the tag attention features, followed by a linear network, as shown in Equation (20), where $W_{TT} \in \mathbb{R}^{(Pd_{tag})\times d_{wp}}$ represents the learnable parameters.

$$Q_1 = (T^{2D}_{awared} \oplus T)W_{TT} \tag{20}$$

Furthermore, to deeply extract features between words, between words and tags, and between tags, the deep features are iteratively updated as shown in Equation (21).

$$Q_0 = Q_1 \tag{21}$$

Repeating multiple rounds of iterative calculations from Equations (9)–(21) enables the extraction of deeply embedded tag grid word-pair features Q_1.

3.5. Joint Prediction and Decoding

On top of predicting word-pair relationships using a multilayer perceptron, we incorporate a double affine predictor to enhance the classification capability. The calculation process of the double affine predictor is shown in Equation (22), where W, U, and b are learnable hyperparameters.

$$Biaffine(h_i, h_j) = (MLP_2(h_i))U(MLP_3(h_j)) + W[MLP_2(h_i); MLP_3(h_j)] + b \tag{22}$$

Combining the multilayer perceptron and the biaffine predictor, we obtain the relationship probability y_{ij} between word pairs (w_i, w_j) as shown in Equation (23).

$$y_{ij} = softmax(Biaffine(x_i, x_j) + MLP(Q_{1,ij})) \tag{23}$$

After obtaining the relationships between word pairs (w_i, w_j) in the input sequence x, the flat, nested, and discontinuous concepts or entities are decoded in the grid. The decoding algorithm is illustrated in Figure 5.

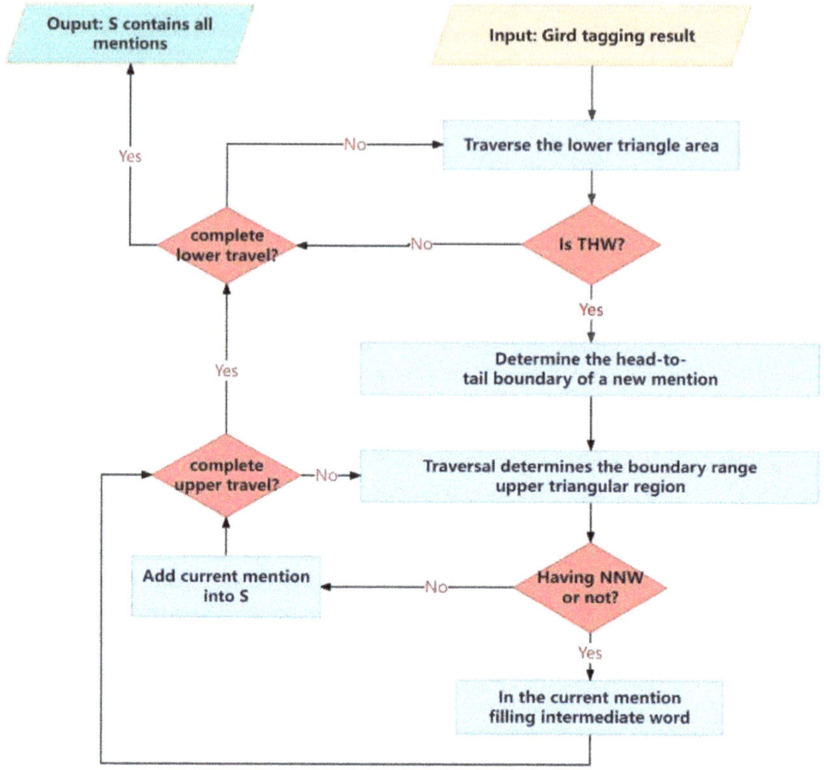

Figure 5. The process of decoding the mentions in the tagging grid.

4. Experiment

4.1. Dataset

Datasets containing discontinuous entities and concepts were selected to evaluate the effectiveness of the model proposed in this paper. Currently, the only free and publicly available dataset meeting the requirements is CADEC. This English dataset comes from the biomedical field and includes only one entity type, Adverse Drug Reactions (ADRs). Discontinuous entities and concepts in this dataset constitute only 10% of the data. Additionally, to test the improved model's performance in discontinuous scenarios and its learning ability in situations with limited samples, all discontinuous data were extracted from the CADEC dataset to create the CADEC-Discontinuous dataset.

Furthermore, for the Chinese lexical resources mentioned in this paper, the Modern Chinese Dictionary compiled by the Institute of Linguistics, the Chinese Academy of Social Sciences, and the Chinese Dictionary jointly compiled by experts from multiple provinces were chosen. Five individuals annotated entities and concepts mentioned in the definitions of these Chinese dictionaries, and the corresponding annotations were determined through voting. To ensure the quality and reliability of annotation, we specifically invited five annotators with backgrounds in linguistics and related fields to participate in this task. These five annotators are all from the linguistics departments of well-known universities, and among them are scholars who have performed in-depth research in Chinese lexicology and semantics. They possess rich experience in areas such as compiling Chinese dictionaries and vocabulary teaching and providing strong assurance for the professionalism and accuracy of this annotation task. In detail, we collected all entities and concepts annotated by these five annotators and had them rate entities and concepts based on five options:

"Completely Agree", "Agree", "Don't Know", "Disagree", and "Completely Disagree". If any annotator was unfamiliar with any term in the target vocabulary, they could choose "Don't Know". Only entities and concepts that received at least three "Agree" (or "Completely Agree") votes were considered in the dataset.

The statistical data for the datasets used in this paper are shown in Table 1 below.

Table 1. The statistical data of the datasets.

Dataset	CADEC				CADEC-Discontinuous				Chinese Dictionary			
	All	Train	Dev	Test	All	Train	Dev	Test	All	Train	Dev	Test
#Sentences	7597	5340	1097	1160	439	306	59	74	1496	1036	230	230
#Entities	6318	4430	898	990	679	491	94	94	4268	2916	639	713
#Discontinuous	679	491	94	94	679	491	94	94	253	172	46	35
%Discontinuous	10.7	11.1	10.5	9.5	100	100	100	100	16.9	16.6	20.0	15.2

The "#" represents the number of statistical data. The "%" represents the percentage of the total statistics.

4.2. Evaluation Metrics

The typical evaluation metrics for assessing model performance include precision (P), which evaluates the ratio of correctly predicted positive observations to the total predicted positive observations; recall (R), which assesses the proportion of actual positive cases that were correctly predicted; and the composite metric F1 score (F1). Precision and recall are conflicting metrics. The confusion matrix divides the different outcomes of classification, as shown in Table 2.

Table 2. The confusion matrix of classification results.

True \ Predict	Positive Samples	Negative Samples
Positive samples	*TP*	*FN*
Negative samples	*FP*	*TN*

The formulas for the above-mentioned metrics are as follows:

$$\begin{aligned} P &= \frac{TP}{TP+FN} \\ R &= \frac{TP}{TP+FP} \\ F1 &= \frac{2 \bullet P \bullet R}{P+R} \end{aligned} \tag{24}$$

4.3. Experimental Results and Analysis

In recent years, significant methods for the unified recognition of three types of entities and concepts include methods based on sequence labeling, methods based on hypergraphs, methods based on sequence-to-sequence, and methods based on grid tagging. The sequence labeling methods assign a tag to each token, such as the LSTM-CRF model based on the BIOHD tagging method proposed by Tang et al. [21] in 2018. The hypergraph-based methods use hypergraphs to represent and infer mentions of different types in the text, as exemplified by the model proposed by Wang et al. [42] in 2019. Sequence-to-sequence methods directly generate word sequences of mentions at the decoder side, with typical examples being the model proposed by Fei et al. [43] in 2021. Grid-tagging methods, the core approach adopted in this study, construct the input sequence into a grid, assign tags to each pair of words in the grid, and then decode mentions (entities or concepts) in the input text based on these tags. Representative models include those proposed by Wang et al. [37] in 2021 and W^{2}NER proposed by Li et al. [3] in 2022.

Here, a total of four sets of experiments were conducted. The results of the first and second sets of experiments are shown in Table 3, the results of the third set of experiments are shown in Table 4, and the results of the fourth set of experiments are shown in Table 5:

1. On the public dataset CADEC, this study compares various typical models in recent years and validates the improvement effect of the proposed DTaE grid-tagging algorithm for unified entity and concept mining tasks.
2. On the Chinese Dictionary dataset, a comparison is made with the baseline model W^{2}NER.
3. The study validates the significant improvement of the proposed DTaE model in unified entity and concept recognition tasks.
4. On the public dataset CADEC, ablation experiments are conducted to verify the effectiveness of the introduced demonstration search module, multi-head attention mechanism, and rotary position embedding in the improved DTaE model.
5. On the non-sequential data from the public dataset CADEC, a comparison is made with the base model W^{2}NER to validate the effectiveness of the proposed DTaE grid-tagging algorithm in non-sequential scenarios and its capability to learn from fewer samples.

Table 3. Comparative experiments on CADEC and Chinese dictionary datasets.

Model		CADEC			Chinese Dictionary		
		P (%)	R (%)	F1 (%)	P (%)	R (%)	F1 (%)
Methods based on sequence labeling	Tang et al. 2018 [21]	67.80	64.99	66.36	/	/	/
Methods based on hypergraph	Wang and Lu 2019 [42]	72.10	48.40	58.00	/	/	/
Methods based on sequence-to-sequence	Fei et al. 2021 [43]	75.50	71.80	72.40	/	/	/
Methods based on grid tagging	Wang et al. 2021 [37]	70.50	**72.50**	71.50	67.59	75.97	71.53
	Li et al. 2022 [3]	74.09 (81.84)	72.35 (**83.80**)	73.21 (82.77)	86.75	86.38	86.56
	Ours Model	**76.87 (83.24)**	71.52 (82.94)	**74.10 (83.55)**	**89.72**	**88.73**	**89.22**

The bold number represents the highest result in each column. The bracket represents the token level. A script for calculating mention-level evaluation metrics on the CADEC dataset can be found in Supplementary Materials.

Table 4. Ablation experiments on public datasets.

Model	Number of Iterations	Attention	RoPE	Demonstration	CADEC		
					P (%)	R (%)	F1 (%)
W^{2}NER	1	/	1	/	74.09	**72.35**	73.21
Ours	6	Y	/	/	74.76	69.38	71.96
Ours	6	Y	Zero	/	76.39	70.91	73.55
Ours	6	Y	Add	/	75.70	68.24	71.14
Ours	6	Y	Mul	/	73.33	68.60	70.89
Ours	6	Y	Zero	Random	76.69	71.00	73.60
Ours	6	Y	Zero	SentenceBERT	**76.87**	71.52	**74.10**

The bold number represents the highest result in each column.

Table 5. Comparative experiments on discontinuous scenarios of public datasets.

Model		CADEC-Discontinuous		
		P (%)	**R (%)**	**F1 (%)**
Methods based on grid tagging.	W^2NER	48.68	63.79	39.36
	Ours Model	51.66	68.42	41.49

To validate the effectiveness of the proposed improved model for unified recognition tasks, comparisons were made with various types of typical algorithms on the public dataset CADEC. As shown in Table 3, the proposed improved model achieved the highest precision and F1 score among all typical models at the cost of a slightly lower recall rate. Compared to all typical models, the improved model in this study showed the highest precision and F1 score. In comparison to the base model W^2NER, the precision improved by 2.78%, and the overall F1 score increased by 0.89%. Furthermore, the performance of the improved model in recognizing the required data for the application scenario in this study was verified using the Chinese Dictionary dataset. Compared to W^2NER, this study's proposed DTaE grid-tagging model demonstrated improvements in three metrics: a 2.97% increase in precision, a 2.35% increase in recall, and a 2.66% increase in the overall F1 score. To further demonstrate the effectiveness of our improvement, Table 3 presents the token-level evaluation metrics on the CADEC dataset, as shown in the brackets. The core of the grid-tagging algorithm is to recognize the word-pair relationships on the grid and then obtain the textual mentions from input sentences through decoding. Our work has achieved significant improvements in recognizing word-pair relationships, which helps to enhance the effect of obtaining mentions through decoding in the entire sentence. However, local errors in recognizing word-pair relationships will affect the overall decoding effect to a certain extent. Therefore, the final performance shows a slighter improvement in mention-level metrics, which does not mean that our improvement is affected by data noise.

To comprehensively assess the trade-off between precision, recall, and F1 score, we conducted tests on the classification using the Receiver Operating Characteristic (ROC) curve. The Area Under the Receiver Operating Curve (AUC-ROC) is used to measure the performance of the classification. The ROC curve has a valuable characteristic: it remains unchanged when there is a change in the distribution of positive and negative samples in the test set. Lable imbalance, where there is a significant difference in the number of negative samples compared to positive samples (or vice versa), is common in real-world datasets. Additionally, the distribution of positive and negative samples in test data may vary over time.

The ROC-AUC curve for token-level classification of word-pair relationships is presented in Figure 6, a script for Figure 6 can be found in Supplementary Materials, where NNW represents the Next Neighboring Word, and THW-ADR stands for the tail head-word of the ADR (Adverse Drug Reaction) entity. More explanations of labels can be found in the aforementioned text. We could find out that both NNW and THW-ADR reach a higher enough area (0.94 and 0.96). And the black dashed line on the diagonal represents the fiducial. It is suggested that our work does improve the token-level performance instead of noise in the evaluation data. This aligns with the characteristics of the grid-tagging method, where both public datasets and our private dictionary exhibit high accuracy at the token level. In summary, our work also maintains this excellent feature.

To validate the effectiveness of the three innovations introduced in this study, ablation experiments were conducted on the public dataset CADEC. As shown in Table 4, embedding label attention features into the model and iteratively merging word-pair grid features led to a 0.67% increase in precision (P), but it resulted in a significant impact on recall due to the loss of sequential information. Furthermore, the introduction of rotary position embedding improved precision (P) by 2.3% and increased F1 score by 0.34%. Additionally, utilizing SBERT semantic search demonstration sentences as input for information enhancement further improved the precision (P) and F1 score. The proposed model achieved the best metrics, as indicated in the last row of the table.

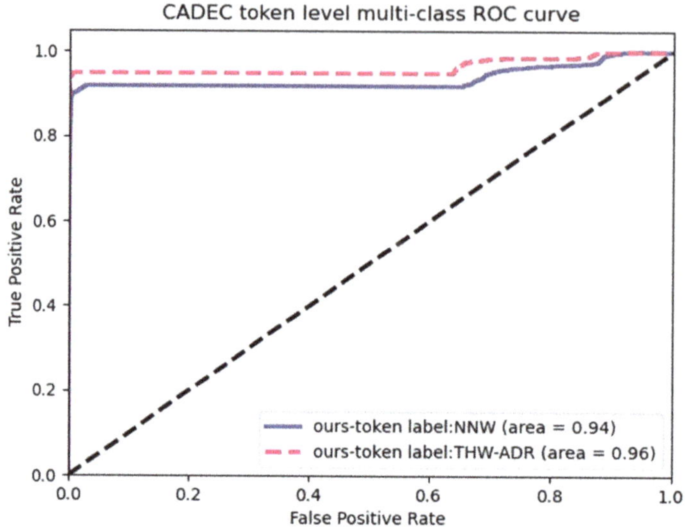

Figure 6. ROC-AUC curve for predicting grid labels on the CADEC dataset.

To rigorously evaluate the proposed model's ability to learn from few-shot and its improvement in recognizing discontinuous scenarios, the flat and nested parts of the data in the public dataset CADEC were removed, retaining only the discontinuous data. The statistics for the CADEC-Discontinuous dataset are shown in Table 1. Based on the experimental results in Table 5, it is evident that the proposed model has achieved the improvement objectives. Compared to the base model, the proposed model demonstrated a 2.98% increase in precision (P), a 4.63% increase in recall (R), and a 2.13% increase in F1 score. The differences in F1 scores among different models on the CADEC-Discontinuous dataset are illustrated in Figure 7.

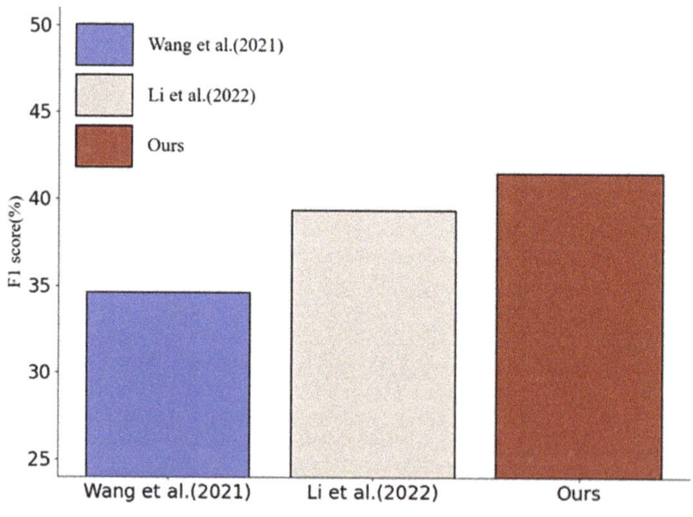

Figure 7. The differences in F1 scores among different models on the CADEC-Discontinuous [3,37].

Additionally, concerning the attention mechanism introduced in this study, attention heatmaps were generated on the CADEC dataset to analyze their effectiveness. For instance, in the sentence "I developed a pain that seems to originate at the base of my neck, travel down to my shoulder blades and then run to my shoulders, elbow, and wrist", there are discontinuous mentions of ADR types such as "pain neck", "pain shoulders", "pain elbow", and "pain wrist". The average attention scores of the three heads for these mentions are shown in Figure 8. Average attention scores between each word pair in the two-dimensional grid formed by the example sentence are shown in Figure 9. It is clear that the colors of grids around each mention are warm, and the attention scores are also high, with an average of around 0.75, shown in the yellow highlighted part of Figure 9.

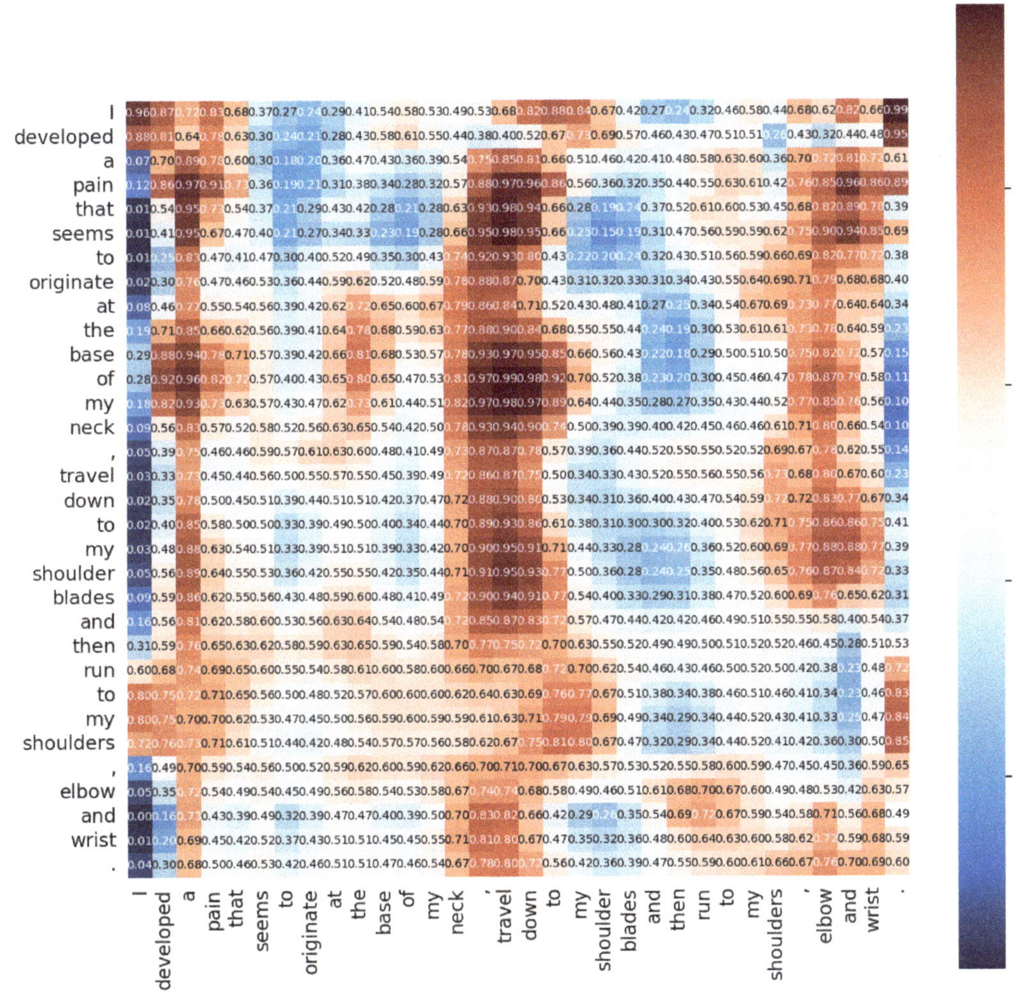

Figure 8. The heatmap of attention weight from an instance in CADEC, where warmer color means higher weight and vice versa for the cool color.

token	I	developed	a	pain	that	seems	to	originate	at	the	base	of	my	neck	.	travel	down	to	my	shoulder	blades	and	then	run	to	my	shoulders	.	elbow	and	wrist	.
I	0.96	0.87	0.72	0.83	0.68	0.37	0.27	0.24	0.29	0.41	0.54	0.58	0.53	0.49	0.53	0.68	0.82	0.88	0.84	0.67	0.42	0.27	0.24	0.32	0.46	0.58	0.44	0.68	0.62	0.82	0.66	0.99
developed	0.88	0.81	0.94	0.78	0.65	0.30	0.24	0.21	0.28	0.43	0.58	0.61	0.55	0.44	0.38	0.40	0.52	0.67	0.73	0.69	0.57	0.48	0.43	0.47	0.51	0.51	0.26	0.45	0.32	0.44	0.48	0.95
a	0.07	0.70	0.89	0.78	0.60	0.30	0.18	0.20	0.36	0.47	0.43	0.36	0.39	0.54	0.75	0.85	0.81	0.66	0.51	0.46	0.42	0.41	0.48	0.58	0.63	0.60	0.36	0.70	0.72	0.81	0.72	0.61
pain	0.12	0.86	0.97	0.91	0.73	0.36	0.19	0.21	0.31	0.38	0.34	0.28	0.32	0.57	0.88	0.97	0.96	0.86	0.56	0.38	0.32	0.35	0.44	0.55	0.63	0.61	0.42	0.76	0.85	0.96	0.86	0.89
that	0.01	0.54	0.95	0.73	0.54	0.37	0.21	0.29	0.43	0.42	0.28	0.21	0.28	0.63	0.93	0.98	0.94	0.66	0.28	0.19	0.24	0.37	0.52	0.61	0.80	0.53	0.45	0.68	0.82	0.89	0.78	0.39
seems	0.01	0.41	0.95	0.67	0.47	0.40	0.21	0.27	0.34	0.33	0.23	0.19	0.28	0.66	0.95	0.98	0.95	0.66	0.25	0.15	0.19	0.31	0.47	0.56	0.59	0.59	0.62	0.75	0.90	0.94	0.85	0.69
to	0.01	0.25	0.83	0.47	0.41	0.47	0.30	0.40	0.52	0.49	0.35	0.30	0.43	0.74	0.92	0.93	0.80	0.43	0.22	0.20	0.24	0.32	0.43	0.51	0.56	0.59	0.66	0.69	0.82	0.77	0.72	0.38
originate	0.02	0.30	0.76	0.47	0.46	0.53	0.38	0.44	0.59	0.62	0.52	0.48	0.59	0.78	0.88	0.87	0.70	0.43	0.31	0.32	0.33	0.31	0.34	0.43	0.55	0.64	0.69	0.71	0.79	0.68	0.68	0.40
at	0.08	0.46	0.77	0.55	0.54	0.56	0.39	0.42	0.62	0.72	0.65	0.60	0.67	0.79	0.86	0.84	0.71	0.52	0.43	0.48	0.41	0.27	0.25	0.34	0.54	0.67	0.69	0.73	0.77	0.64	0.64	0.34
the	0.19	0.71	0.85	0.66	0.62	0.56	0.39	0.41	0.64	0.78	0.68	0.59	0.63	0.77	0.88	0.90	0.84	0.68	0.55	0.55	0.44	0.24	0.19	0.30	0.53	0.61	0.61	0.73	0.78	0.64	0.59	0.23
base	0.29	0.88	0.94	0.78	0.71	0.57	0.39	0.42	0.66	0.81	0.68	0.53	0.57	0.78	0.93	0.97	0.95	0.85	0.66	0.56	0.43	0.22	0.18	0.29	0.50	0.51	0.50	0.75	0.82	0.72	0.57	0.15
of	0.28	0.92	0.96	0.82	0.72	0.57	0.40	0.43	0.65	0.80	0.65	0.47	0.53	0.81	0.97	0.99	0.98	0.92	0.70	0.52	0.38	0.23	0.20	0.30	0.45	0.46	0.47	0.78	0.87	0.79	0.58	0.11
my	0.18	0.82	0.93	0.73	0.65	0.57	0.43	0.47	0.62	0.73	0.61	0.44	0.51	0.82	0.97	0.98	0.97	0.89	0.64	0.44	0.35	0.28	0.27	0.35	0.43	0.44	0.52	0.77	0.85	0.76	0.56	0.10
neck	0.09	0.56	0.83	0.57	0.52	0.58	0.52	0.56	0.63	0.65	0.54	0.42	0.50	0.78	0.93	0.94	0.90	0.74	0.50	0.39	0.39	0.40	0.42	0.45	0.46	0.46	0.61	0.71	0.80	0.66	0.54	0.10
.	0.05	0.39	0.75	0.46	0.46	0.59	0.57	0.61	0.63	0.60	0.48	0.41	0.49	0.73	0.87	0.87	0.78	0.57	0.39	0.36	0.44	0.52	0.55	0.55	0.52	0.52	0.69	0.67	0.78	0.62	0.55	0.14
travel	0.03	0.33	0.73	0.45	0.44	0.56	0.50	0.55	0.57	0.55	0.45	0.35	0.49	0.72	0.86	0.87	0.75	0.50	0.34	0.33	0.43	0.52	0.55	0.56	0.55	0.56	0.73	0.68	0.80	0.67	0.60	0.23
down	0.02	0.35	0.78	0.50	0.45	0.51	0.39	0.44	0.51	0.51	0.42	0.37	0.47	0.72	0.88	0.90	0.80	0.53	0.34	0.31	0.36	0.40	0.43	0.47	0.54	0.59	0.72	0.72	0.83	0.77	0.67	0.34
to	0.02	0.40	0.85	0.58	0.50	0.50	0.33	0.39	0.49	0.50	0.40	0.34	0.44	0.70	0.89	0.93	0.86	0.61	0.38	0.31	0.30	0.30	0.32	0.40	0.53	0.62	0.71	0.75	0.86	0.86	0.75	0.41
my	0.03	0.48	0.88	0.65	0.54	0.51	0.33	0.39	0.51	0.51	0.39	0.33	0.42	0.70	0.90	0.95	0.91	0.71	0.44	0.33	0.28	0.24	0.26	0.36	0.52	0.60	0.69	0.77	0.88	0.88	0.77	0.39
shoulder	0.05	0.56	0.89	0.64	0.55	0.53	0.36	0.42	0.55	0.55	0.42	0.35	0.44	0.71	0.91	0.95	0.93	0.77	0.50	0.36	0.28	0.24	0.25	0.35	0.48	0.56	0.65	0.76	0.87	0.84	0.72	0.33
blades	0.09	0.59	0.86	0.62	0.55	0.56	0.43	0.48	0.59	0.60	0.48	0.41	0.49	0.72	0.90	0.94	0.91	0.77	0.54	0.40	0.33	0.29	0.31	0.38	0.47	0.52	0.60	0.69	0.76	0.65	0.62	0.31
and	0.16	0.56	0.81	0.62	0.58	0.60	0.53	0.56	0.63	0.64	0.54	0.48	0.54	0.72	0.85	0.87	0.83	0.72	0.57	0.47	0.44	0.42	0.42	0.46	0.49	0.51	0.55	0.55	0.58	0.40	0.54	0.37
then	0.31	0.59	0.76	0.65	0.63	0.62	0.58	0.59	0.63	0.65	0.59	0.54	0.58	0.70	0.77	0.75	0.72	0.70	0.63	0.55	0.52	0.49	0.49	0.50	0.51	0.52	0.52	0.46	0.45	0.28	0.51	0.53
run	0.60	0.68	0.74	0.69	0.65	0.60	0.55	0.54	0.58	0.61	0.60	0.58	0.60	0.66	0.70	0.67	0.68	0.72	0.70	0.62	0.54	0.46	0.45	0.46	0.50	0.52	0.50	0.42	0.38	0.23	0.48	0.72
to	0.80	0.75	0.72	0.71	0.65	0.56	0.50	0.48	0.52	0.57	0.60	0.60	0.60	0.62	0.64	0.63	0.69	0.76	0.77	0.67	0.51	0.38	0.34	0.38	0.46	0.51	0.46	0.41	0.34	0.23	0.46	0.83
my	0.80	0.75	0.70	0.70	0.62	0.53	0.47	0.45	0.50	0.56	0.59	0.60	0.59	0.59	0.61	0.63	0.71	0.79	0.79	0.69	0.49	0.34	0.29	0.34	0.44	0.52	0.45	0.41	0.33	0.25	0.47	0.84
shoulders	0.72	0.76	0.73	0.71	0.61	0.51	0.44	0.42	0.48	0.54	0.57	0.57	0.56	0.58	0.62	0.67	0.75	0.81	0.80	0.67	0.47	0.32	0.29	0.34	0.44	0.52	0.41	0.42	0.36	0.30	0.50	0.85
.	0.16	0.49	0.70	0.59	0.54	0.56	0.50	0.52	0.59	0.62	0.60	0.59	0.62	0.66	0.70	0.71	0.70	0.67	0.63	0.57	0.53	0.52	0.55	0.58	0.60	0.59	0.47	0.45	0.45	0.36	0.59	0.65
elbow	0.05	0.35	0.72	0.54	0.49	0.54	0.45	0.49	0.56	0.58	0.54	0.53	0.58	0.67	0.74	0.74	0.68	0.58	0.40	0.46	0.51	0.61	0.68	0.70	0.67	0.60	0.49	0.48	0.53	0.42	0.63	0.57
and	0.00	0.16	0.73	0.43	0.39	0.49	0.32	0.39	0.47	0.47	0.40	0.39	0.50	0.70	0.83	0.82	0.66	0.42	0.29	0.26	0.35	0.54	0.69	0.72	0.67	0.59	0.54	0.58	0.71	0.56	0.68	0.49
wrist	0.01	0.20	0.69	0.45	0.42	0.52	0.37	0.40	0.51	0.51	0.43	0.45	0.55	0.71	0.81	0.80	0.67	0.47	0.35	0.32	0.36	0.48	0.60	0.64	0.63	0.60	0.58	0.62	0.72	0.59	0.68	0.59
.	0.04	0.30	0.68	0.50	0.46	0.53	0.42	0.46	0.51	0.51	0.47	0.46	0.54	0.67	0.78	0.80	0.72	0.56	0.42	0.36	0.39	0.47	0.55	0.59	0.60	0.61	0.66	0.67	0.76	0.70	0.69	0.60

Figure 9. The table of attention weight from an instance in CADEC.

In summary, the proposed improved model DTaE grid-tagging algorithm, without compromising the unified entity/concept recognition effectiveness, introduced the multi-head attention mechanism and rotary position embedding, further enhancing the recognition performance in discontinuous scenarios. Simultaneously, inspired by the in-context learning concept in large language models, the introduction of task demonstrations enhanced the model's ability to learn from a few shots. In the Chinese Dictionary dataset, out of 230 test instances, the model accurately predicted fine-grained entities/concepts in 196 glosses, as depicted in Figure 10, demonstrating the practical predictive effectiveness of the improved model on the Chinese Dictionary data.

```
"sentence": "冻 ： 汤 汁 凝 结 成 的 固 体 或 半 流 体 。",
"true": [
  "冻      [0]",
  "半 流 体      [11, 12, 13]",
  "固 体      [8, 9]",
  "汤 汁 凝 结 半 流 体      [2, 3, 4, 5, 11, 12, 13]",
  "汤 汁 凝 结 固 体      [2, 3, 4, 5, 8, 9]"
],
"predict": [
  "冻      [0]",
  "半 流 体      [11, 12, 13]",
  "固 体      [8, 9]",
  "汤 汁 凝 结 半 流 体      [2, 3, 4, 5, 11, 12, 13]",
  "汤 汁 凝 结 固 体      [2, 3, 4, 5, 8, 9]"
]
```

Figure 10. Example of our model recognizing mentions on Chinese Dictionary data.

5. Conclusions

This paper aims to enhance the model's ability to learn from few shots and improve its recognition capabilities in non-sequential scenarios based on the state-of-the-art (SOTA) model W^{2}NER for the unified recognition of flat, nested, and discontinuous mentions. Three improvements were made to the grid-tagging algorithm W^{2}NER, leading to the proposed Demonstration and Tag-aware Enhanced Grid-Tagging Network (DTaE) model. Specifically, this study introduced task demonstrations as a form of information enhancement during the training phase. The model incorporated tag attention features obtained through the multi-head attention mechanism and preserved sequence position information using rotary position embedding. The model iteratively merged word-pair grid features and tag attention features, embedding tag attention into the model. Through multiple rounds of experiments, the effectiveness of the proposed model was validated on the public dataset CADEC and the Chinese Dictionary dataset annotated in this study.

6. Limitation and Future Work

Our current research is constrained by hardware computational capabilities, confined to relatively smaller pre-training models such as BERT and its variants. However, the emergence of large language models with hundreds of billions of parameters has showcased powerful capabilities not present in traditional pre-training models. More and more efforts are being made to incorporate these large language models. Future work may consider employing language models with a greater number of parameters as our word-embedding tools to better capture semantic information. Additionally, with the development of large language models, prompt methods akin to In-Context Learning have seen significant progress. In the future, exploring In-Context Learning methods and Chain-of-Thought approaches more tailored to large language models as replacements for demonstrations, aiming to achieve enhanced performance, may be worthwhile. Additionally, there is typically a precision gap between the token level and the mention level for grid-tagging methods and similar approaches. Some experiments have shown that the precision of the token level tends to be higher than that of the mention level. Currently, this method lacks a systematic explanation of its characteristics and effective improvement methods. In future work, we will explore ways to enhance mention-level precision on the decoding side to reduce the gap with token-level precision.

Supplementary Materials: The following supporting information can be downloaded at: https://www.mdpi.com/article/10.3390/electronics13020261/s1, We provide two main scripts: a script for calculating mention-level evaluation metrics on the CADEC dataset, and a script for constructing ROC-AUC curves at the token level for multi-class scenarios on the CADEC dataset.

Author Contributions: Conceptualization, H.J., J.H. and H.Z.; Methodology, J.H.; Software, J.H.; Validation, J.H.; Formal analysis, K.Z. and Y.M.; Investigation, H.J.; Resources, H.J.; Data curation, K.Z. and Y.M.; Writing—original draft, H.J. and J.H.; Writing—review & editing, K.Z. and Y.M.; Visualization, K.Z. and Y.M.; Supervision, H.Z., L.R., Y.J. and W.X.; Project administration, H.Z., L.R., Y.J. and W.X.; Funding acquisition, H.J., H.Z. and W.X. All authors have read and agreed to the published version of the manuscript.

Funding: This research was funded by the Sichuan Science and Technology Program (under Grants No. 2022YFQ0052) and the Technology Development Project of China Railway Eryuan Engineering Group Co., Ltd. (under Grant No. KYY2019003(19-22)).

Data Availability Statement: Publicly available datasets were analyzed in this study. The CADEC dataset can be found here: https://pubmed.ncbi.nlm.nih.gov/25817970/. Our research is supported by the aforementioned funding. Due to the confidentiality requirements of the institution, we are unable to provide Chinese dictionary data.

Conflicts of Interest: Author Huanlai Zhou was employed by the company UESTC—Chengdu Quantum Matrix Technology Co., Ltd. The remaining authors declare that the research was conducted in the absence of any commercial or financial relationships that could be construed as a potential conflict of interest.

References

1. Murphy, G. *The Big Book of Concepts*; MIT Press: Cambridge, MA, USA, 2004.
2. Yan, H.; Gui, T.; Dai, J.; Guo, Q.; Zhang, Z.; Qiu, X. A unified generative framework for various NER subtasks. *arXiv* **2021**, arXiv:2106.01223.
3. Li, J.; Fei, H.; Liu, J.; Wu, S.; Zhang, M.; Teng, C.; Ji, D.; Li, F. Unified named entity recognition as word-word relation classification. In Proceedings of the AAAI Conference on Artificial Intelligence, Virtual, 22 February–1 March 2022.
4. Hu, Y.; He, H.; Chen, Z.; Zhu, Q.; Zheng, C. A unified model using distantly supervised data and cross-domain data in NER. *Comput. Intell. Neurosci.* **2022**, *2022*, 1987829. [CrossRef] [PubMed]
5. Lu, J.; Zhao, R.; Mac Namee, B.; Tan, F. Punifiedner: A prompting-based unified ner system for diverse datasets. In Proceedings of the AAAI Conference on Artificial Intelligence, Washington, DC, USA, 7–14 February 2023.
6. Zhang, S.; Shen, Y.; Tan, Z.; Wu, Y.; Lu, W. De-bias for generative extraction in unified NER task. In Proceedings of the 60th Annual Meeting of the Association for Computational Linguistics, Dublin, Ireland, 22–27 May 2022; Long Papers. Volume 1, pp. 808–818.
7. Liu, J.; Ji, D.; Li, J.; Xie, D.; Teng, C.; Zhao, L.; Li, F. TOE: A grid-tagging discontinuous NER model enhanced by embedding tag/word relations and more fine-grained tags. *IEEE/ACM Trans. Audio Speech Lang. Process.* **2022**, *31*, 177–187. [CrossRef]
8. Min, S.; Lyu, X.; Holtzman, A.; Artetxe, M.; Lewis, M.; Hajishirzi, H.; Zettlemoyer, L. Rethinking the role of demonstrations: What makes in-context learning work? *arXiv* **2022**, arXiv:2202.12837.
9. Brown, T.; Mann, B.; Ryder, N.; Subbiah, M.; Kaplan, J.D.; Dhariwal, P.; Neelakantan, A.; Shyam, P.; Sastry, G.; Askell, A. Language models are few-shot learners. *Adv. Neural Inf. Process. Syst.* **2020**, *33*, 1877–1901.
10. Su, J.; Lu, Y.; Pan, S.; Murtadha, A.; Wen, B.; Liu, Y. Roformer: Enhanced transformer with rotary position embedding. *arXiv* **2021**, arXiv:2104.09864. [CrossRef]
11. Karimi, S.; Metke-Jimenez, A.; Kemp, M.; Wang, C. CADEC: A corpus of adverse drug event annotations. *J. Biomed. Inform.* **2015**, *55*, 73–81. [CrossRef] [PubMed]
12. Wang, Z.; Xu, X.; Li, X.; Li, H.; Wei, X.; Huang, D. An Improved Nested Named-Entity Recognition Model for Subject Recognition Task under Knowledge Base Question Answering. *Appl. Sci.* **2023**, *13*, 11249. [CrossRef]
13. Huang, P.; Zhao, X.; Hu, M.; Tan, Z.; Xiao, W. T 2-NER: AT wo-Stage Span-Based Framework for Unified Named Entity Recognition with T emplates. *Trans. Assoc. Comput. Linguist.* **2023**, *11*, 1265–1282. [CrossRef]
14. Jiang, X.; Song, C.; Xu, Y.; Li, Y.; Peng, Y. Research on sentiment classification for netizens based on the BERT-BiLSTM-TextCNN model. *PeerJ Comput. Sci.* **2022**, *8*, e1005. [CrossRef]
15. Tang, X.; Huang, Y.; Xia, M.; Long, C. A Multi-Task BERT-BiLSTM-AM-CRF Strategy for Chinese Named Entity Recognition. *Neural Process. Lett.* **2023**, *55*, 1209–1229. [CrossRef]
16. Li, D.; Yan, L.; Yang, J.; Ma, Z. Dependency syntax guided bert-bilstm-gam-crf for chinese ner. *Expert Syst. Appl.* **2022**, *196*, 116682. [CrossRef]
17. Li, W.; Du, Y.; Li, X.; Chen, X.; Xie, C.; Li, H.; Li, X. UD_BBC: Named entity recognition in social network combined BERT-BiLSTM-CRF with active learning. *Eng. Appl. Artif. Intell.* **2022**, *116*, 105460. [CrossRef]
18. Zhang, W.; Meng, J.; Wan, J.; Zhang, C.; Zhang, J.; Wang, Y.; Xu, L.; Li, F. ChineseCTRE: A Model for Geographical Named Entity Recognition and Correction Based on Deep Neural Networks and the BERT Model. *ISPRS Int. J. Geo. Inf.* **2023**, *12*, 394. [CrossRef]
19. Ju, M.; Miwa, M.; Ananiadou, S. A neural layered model for nested named entity recognition. In Proceedings of the 2018 Conference of the North American Chapter of the Association for Computational Linguistics: Human Language Technologies, Orleans, LA, USA, 1–6 June 2018; Long Papers. Volume 1.
20. Shibuya, T.; Hovy, E. Nested named entity recognition via second-best sequence learning and decoding. *Trans. Assoc. Comput. Linguist.* **2020**, *8*, 605–620. [CrossRef]
21. Tang, B.; Hu, J.; Wang, X.; Chen, Q. Recognizing continuous and discontinuous adverse drug reaction mentions from social media using LSTM-CRF. *Wirel. Commun. Mob. Comput.* **2018**, *2018*, 2379208. [CrossRef]
22. Su, J.; Murtadha, A.; Pan, S.; Hou, J.; Sun, J.; Huang, W.; Wen, B.; Liu, Y. Global pointer: Novel efficient span-based approach for named entity recognition. *arXiv* **2022**, arXiv:2208.03054.
23. Zaratiana, U.; Tomeh, N.; Holat, P.; Charnois, T. GNNer: Reducing overlapping in span-based NER using graph neural networks. In Proceedings of the 60th Annual Meeting of the Association for Computational Linguistics: Student Research Workshop, Dublin, Ireland, 22–27 May 2022.
24. Zaratiana, U.; Tomeh, N.; Holat, P.; Charnois, T. Named Entity Recognition as Structured Span Prediction. In Proceedings of the Workshop on Unimodal and Multimodal Induction of Linguistic Structures (UM-IoS), Abu Dhabi, United Arab Emirates, 7–8 December 2022.
25. Wan, J.; Ru, D.; Zhang, W.; Yu, Y. Nested named entity recognition with span-level graphs. In Proceedings of the 60th Annual Meeting of the Association for Computational Linguistics, Dublin, Ireland, 22–27 May 2022; Long Papers. Volume 1.
26. Fisher, J.; Vlachos, A. Merge and label: A novel neural network architecture for nested NER. *arXiv* **2019**, arXiv:1907.00464.
27. Sohrab, M.G.; Miwa, M. Deep exhaustive model for nested named entity recognition. In Proceedings of the 2018 Conference on Empirical Methods in Natural Language Processing, Brussels, Belgium, 31 October–4 November 2018.

28. Li, F.; Wang, Z.; Hui, S.C.; Liao, L.; Zhu, X.; Huang, H. A segment enhanced span-based model for nested named entity recognition. *Neurocomputing* **2021**, *465*, 26–37. [CrossRef]
29. Su, J.; Yu, H. Unified Named Entity Recognition as Multi-Label Sequence Generation. In Proceedings of the 2023 International Joint Conference on Neural Networks (IJCNN), Gold Coast, Australia, 18–23 June 2023.
30. Straková, J.; Straka, M.; Hajič, J. Neural architectures for nested NER through linearization. *arXiv* **2019**, arXiv:1908.06926.
31. Tan, Z.; Shen, Y.; Zhang, S.; Lu, W.; Zhuang, Y. A sequence-to-set network for nested named entity recognition. *arXiv* **2021**, arXiv:2105.08901.
32. Lewis, M.; Liu, Y.; Goyal, N.; Ghazvininejad, M.; Mohamed, A.; Levy, O.; Stoyanov, V.; Zettlemoyer, L. Bart: Denoising sequence-to-sequence pre-training for natural language generation, translation, and comprehension. *arXiv* **2019**, arXiv:1910.13461.
33. Hu, N.; Zhou, X.; Xu, B.; Liu, H.; Xie, X.; Zheng, H.-T. VPN: Variation on Prompt Tuning for Named-Entity Recognition. *Appl. Sci.* **2023**, *13*, 8359. [CrossRef]
34. Lee, D.-H.; Kadakia, A.; Tan, K.; Agarwal, M.; Feng, X.; Shibuya, T.; Mitani, R.; Sekiya, T.; Pujara, J.; Ren, X. Good examples make a faster learner: Simple demonstration-based learning for low-resource NER. *arXiv* **2021**, arXiv:2110.08454.
35. Gao, T.; Fisch, A.; Chen, D. Making pre-trained language models better few-shot learners. *arXiv* **2020**, arXiv:2012.15723.
36. Chen, Z.; Qian, T. Description and demonstration guided data augmentation for sequence tagging. *World Wide Web* **2022**, *25*, 175–194. [CrossRef]
37. Wang, Y.; Yu, B.; Zhu, H.; Liu, T.; Yu, N.; Sun, L. Discontinuous named entity recognition as maximal clique discovery. *arXiv* **2021**, arXiv:2106.00218.
38. Lynch, C.J.; Jensen, E.J.; Zamponi, V.; O'Brien, K.; Frydenlund, E.; Gore, R. A Structured Narrative Prompt for Prompting Narratives from Large Language Models: Sentiment Assessment of ChatGPT-Generated Narratives and Real Tweets. *Future Internet* **2023**, *15*, 375. [CrossRef]
39. Zeng, D.; Liu, K.; Lai, S.; Zhou, G.; Zhao, J. Relation classification via convolutional deep neural network. In Proceedings of the COLING 2014, the 25th International Conference on Computational Linguistics: Technical Papers, Dublin, Ireland, 23–29 August 2014.
40. Wang, L.; Cao, Z.; De Melo, G.; Liu, Z. Relation classification via multi-level attention cnns. In Proceedings of the 54th Annual Meeting of the Association for Computational Linguistics, Berlin, Germany, 7–12 August 2016; Long Paper. Volume 1.
41. Reimers, N.; Gurevych, I. Sentence-bert: Sentence embeddings using siamese bert-networks. *arXiv* **2019**, arXiv:1908.10084.
42. Wang, B.; Lu, W. Combining spans into entities: A neural two-stage approach for recognizing discontiguous entities. *arXiv* **2019**, arXiv:1909.00930.
43. Fei, H.; Ji, D.; Li, B.; Liu, Y.; Ren, Y.; Li, F. Rethinking boundaries: End-to-end recognition of discontinuous mentions with pointer networks. In Proceedings of the AAAI Conference on Artificial Intelligence, Vancouver, BC, Canada, 2–9 February 2021.

electronics

MDPI

Article

Robust Soliton Distribution-Based Zero-Watermarking for Semi-Structured Power Data

Lei Zhao [1], Yunfeng Zou [1], Chao Xu [1], Yulong Ma [1], Wen Shen [2,*], Qiuhong Shan [3], Shuai Jiang [3], Yue Yu [3], Yihan Cai [3], Yubo Song [3,4] and Yu Jiang [3,4]

1 State Grid Jiangsu Marketing Service Center, Nanjing 210003, China; zhaolei@sgcc115.wecom.work (L.Z.); 13814099766@163.com (Y.Z.); mmxcan@163.com (C.X.); mayulong0107@126.com (Y.M.)
2 State Grid Smart Grid Research Institute Co., Ltd., Nanjing 210003, China
3 School of Cyber Science and Engineering, Southeast University, Nanjing 210003, China; qiuh_shan@163.com (Q.S.); 220224992@seu.edu.cn (S.J.); 220224906@seu.edu.cn (Y.Y.); 220224837@seu.edu.cn (Y.C.); songyubo@seu.edu.cn (Y.S.); jiangyu@seu.edu.cn (Y.J.)
4 Purple Mountain Laboratories, Nanjing 211189, China
* Correspondence: shenwen@geiri.sgcc.com.cn

Abstract: To ensure the security of online-shared power data, this paper adopts a robust soliton distribution-based zero-watermarking approach for tracing semi-structured power data. The method involves extracting partial key-value pairs to generate a feature sequence, processing the watermark into an equivalent number of blocks. Robust soliton distribution from erasure codes and redundant error correction codes is utilized to generate an intermediate sequence. Subsequently, the error-corrected watermark information is embedded into the feature sequence, creating a zero-watermark for semi-structured power data. In the tracking process, the extraction and analysis of the robust zero-watermark associated with the tracked data facilitate the effective identification and localization of data anomalies. Experimental and simulation validation demonstrates that this method, while ensuring data security, achieves a zero-watermark extraction success rate exceeding 98%. The proposed approach holds significant application value for data monitoring and anomaly tracking in power systems.

Keywords: robust zero-watermarking; data security; semi-structured data; text watermark; error correction coding; power data protection; robust soliton distribution

1. Introduction

In the field of electric power, the integrity and security of data are crucial for the stable operation of power systems. However, online collaboration channels in power marketing often support a vast number of user transactions. With the comprehensive promotion of Marketing 2.0 in the future, the integration of all online collaboration channel operations into an omnichannel business introduces increased complexity and variability in the business processes. Consequently, data security issues and threats become more prominent and severe [1]. One major concern is the need for power business systems to provide interface data for interaction with third-party terminals, posing a risk of data leakage. If sensitive data is compromised in certain critical business interfaces, the structure and functionality of the entire business activity chain can be severely impacted. Therefore, it is crucial to identify key nodes in the business chain, define protection priorities, and swiftly and accurately trace the source of data leakage in the event of anomalies such as data breaches.

To address the challenge of tracking data anomalies, researchers have actively explored various methods and technologies. These include machine learning-based data anomaly detection methods [2], such as Support Vector Machines (SVM), decision trees, random forests, or deep neural networks, which involve learning and modeling power data.

Statistical methods for anomaly detection [3,4], relying on statistical principles and models like outlier detection and probability distribution, compare the actual observed values of power data with expected values to detect anomalies. Time series analysis methods [5,6] can identify periodic and trending changes in power data. Additionally, data visualization techniques map power data into a graphical space, and anomaly detection methods [7–9] assess anomalies based on the position and distribution of data points in the graphical space. However, these methods require extensive data learning, and since power data has confidentiality requirements, they are not suitable for tracking anomalies in power data.

Furthermore, in recent years, digital watermarking technology has found widespread applications in areas such as data protection and data source authentication, and is extensively used for data tracing. Data watermarking involves embedding watermark information into data, akin to digital signatures or markers, with the aim of providing data integrity, source authentication, copyright protection, and preventing unauthorized data replication or tampering.

In the realm of digital watermarking technology, text watermarking is a topic that has received comparatively less attention in discussions about information hiding. Yet, power data often contains a substantial amount of textual data. Research on text watermarking dates back to 1997, when several text watermarking methods were proposed. Early text watermarking methods included structure-based watermarking, grammar-based watermarking, semantics-based watermarking, and image-based watermarking. It is crucial to control the intellectual property of textual content by analyzing the implementational nature and underlying logical principles of text content. The differences in text watermarking methods also impact the effectiveness of protecting digital text [10]. In structure-based watermarking, lines, letters, and spaces in the watermark carrier text are shifted to embed watermark bits [11]. In grammar-based watermarking, the grammatical structure of the text is utilized for watermark embedding. Mikhail J. Atallah and others first proposed a natural language watermarking scheme using syntax trees and transformations applied to syntax trees of structured text in 2000, preserving all properties of the text [12,13]. Semantic-based watermarking primarily uses the semantic content of the text for embedding watermarks. Atallah et al. first introduced a semantic watermarking scheme in 2000 [12,14,15]. However, the functionality of semantic-based text watermarking relies on language features, and techniques based on synonyms lack resilience against random synonym substitution attacks. In image-based text watermarking methods, text images serve as the source for watermark embedding. However, text watermarking algorithms using binary text images lack robustness against re-typing attacks and have limited applicability [16]. While text image authentication is straightforward, considering text as an image is often impractical.

Nevertheless, there has been limited work on watermark injection for semi-structured textual data, despite the fact that textual content in power data is often transmitted in a semi-structured form. Semi-structured data offers flexibility and scalability, effectively handling various data types and formats, providing convenience for data analysis and processing [17,18]. Some typical applications of semi-structured data include Extensible Markup Language (XML), JavaScript Object Notation (JSON), and others.

The aforementioned text watermarking schemes are generally not applicable or effective for semi-structured textual data. Moreover, these schemes are often not robust enough against typical attacks, such as deletion. Additionally, when protecting power data, the specific meaning of the data is crucial, and any modification or tampering would render the data invalid. Traditional text watermarking methods mentioned above typically involve modifying the data itself to embed watermark information. Therefore, there is a need to propose a robust watermarking scheme for protecting semi-structured data without modifying the data content.

In summary, this paper addresses the challenge of ineffective traceability caused by localized changes in power data. Through an analysis of power data and its circulation scenarios, we propose a semi-structured power data tracking scheme based on robust zero-watermarking. The main contributions are as follows:

(1) For the format of power data, we propose a novel scheme for robust zero-watermark embedding and extraction in semi-structured data. This scheme embeds watermark information into the feature sequence of semi-structured data without modifying the data, ensuring data integrity and privacy.
(2) The scheme integrates erasure codes and redundant error correction codes theory. The watermark to be embedded is divided into blocks, and a transfer matrix is used to obtain an intermediate sequence. Subsequently, error correction coding is applied to the intermediate sequence. Finally, the encoded watermark information is embedded into the feature sequence. The encoded watermark can detect block damage, and even after losing damaged blocks, it can still recover the original watermark information, significantly enhancing robustness.
(3) Experimental results demonstrate that our scheme ensures data integrity and exhibits high robustness, security, and accuracy.

The rest of this paper is organized as follows: Section 2 introduces the basic concepts of zero-watermarking technology. Section 3 establishes the system model of the semi-structured power data tracking scheme based on robust zero-watermarking, providing detailed explanations of power data preprocessing, and the embedding and extraction methods of robust zero-watermarking. Section 4 conducts experimental and analytical demonstrations of our proposed scheme. Finally, Section 5 provides a brief summary.

2. The Concept of Zero-Watermarking

Zero-watermarking technology, as a means of data labeling and authentication, has found widespread applications in the field of information security and is well-suited for protecting power data. Traditional watermarking algorithms struggle to balance the invisibility and robustness of watermarks simultaneously. Wang et al. [19] introduced the concept of "zero-watermarking". Unlike traditional watermarking algorithms, zero-watermarking algorithms construct watermarks using rich and robust feature information of the protected target data, without embedding any watermark information in the original data. Zero-watermarking technology requires the involvement of a trusted third-party entity or an entity with equivalent functionality for watermark ownership authentication and verification. When applying robust zero-watermarking technology to data anomaly tracking, in cases of data tampering or leakage, the trusted third party or an equivalent entity can leverage its credibility, invoke the authenticated and stored zero-watermark, and compare it with the anomalous data to determine the watermark information at the time of the data anomaly, swiftly and accurately tracing the source of the data anomaly [20].

In zero-watermarking schemes, the watermark information is not actually embedded in the original data itself; instead, the watermark carrier uses certain features of the original data for generation. These features remain stable before and after the transmission of the original data to ensure the effectiveness of the zero-watermark extraction process.

Zero-watermarking schemes comprise two main phases: zero-watermark embedding and zero-watermark extraction and verification. Watermark embedding is performed by the watermark owner and is then released on a trusted third-party certification entity. During watermark extraction, the verifier requests the stored zero-watermark from the trusted third-party certification entity and combines the features of the data in their possession to complete the watermark extraction process, verifying the watermark owner and the data source. In this algorithm, a trusted certification entity is a fundamental requirement for the original data owner to register their legitimate identity. When there are issues with data ownership or watermark source, this trusted third party serves as a decision authorization entity.

The general process of zero-watermark embedding is illustrated in Figure 1. Firstly, the data owner extracts the robust feature information of the data to be protected and obtains feature values based on these features. These feature values are then encoded into a feature sequence capable of embedding watermark information. Next, the data owner selects specific watermark information as proof of identity and encodes this information. The encoded feature sequence is used as the watermark carrier, and the encoded watermark is embedded, resulting in the zero-watermark sequence for the data. Finally, the zero-watermark sequence and the data to be protected are stored on a trusted third-party certification entity or an entity with equivalent functionality for subsequent identity verification of the watermark owner.

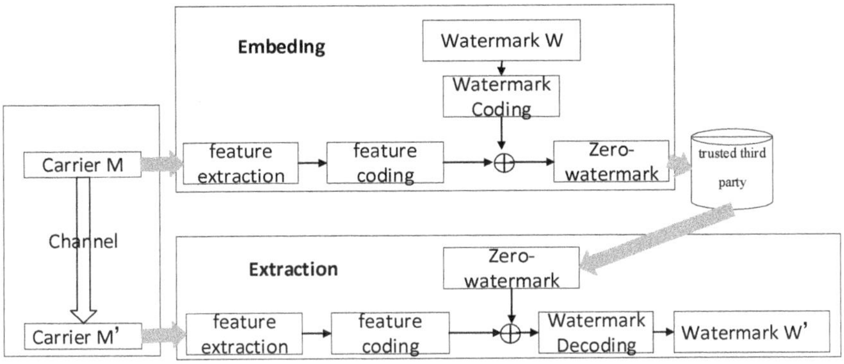

Figure 1. The schematic diagram of the zero-watermark embedding and extraction process.

The main idea behind zero-watermark extraction is to combine the zero-watermark sequence stored in the trusted third-party certification entity or an equivalent entity with the feature sequence extracted from existing data through a series of operations to recover the watermark information. This process verifies the identity of the data owner. The general process of zero-watermark extraction and verification is depicted in Figure 1. Firstly, the robust feature information of the data to be verified is extracted, and feature sequences are obtained based on these features. The feature sequence is then combined with the zero-watermark sequence stored in the trusted third-party certification entity or an entity with equivalent functionality through the inverse operation of embedding. This process recovers the watermark information. Finally, the original watermark information stored in the trusted third-party certification entity or an entity with equivalent functionality is compared with the recovered watermark information for similarity. This determines the identity of the data owner, completing the extraction and verification of the watermark.

3. Robust Soliton Distribution-Based Zero-Watermark Scheme for Semi-Structured Power Data

The proposed semi-structured power data tracking scheme based on robust zero-watermarking extracts the watermark sequence from the corresponding zero-watermark stored in a trusted third-party entity when data leakage occurs. This process enables the identification of nodes through which the data has passed, ultimately locating the source of data leakage.

Before embedding the watermark information into the watermark carrier, preprocessing is performed on both. Feature extraction is applied to the original semi-structured power data to construct a feature sequence, serving as the watermark carrier and identifying effective embedding positions. The watermark information is then segmented, and a transmission matrix is constructed to transform these segmented fragments into an intermediate sequence. These intermediate sequences undergo further encoding through error correction coding to resist a variety of attacks, enhancing robustness. The encoded sequences are then embedded into the watermark carrier, generating the zero-watermark sequence. The zero-watermark sequence is stored in a trusted third-party entity. During the zero-watermark extraction and verification at the receiver end, successful extraction is possible even if the received zero-watermark sequence has been intentionally or unintentionally modified.

In the context of power business data, the majority of transmitted data adopts the format of semi-structured data. Semi-structured data includes formats such as XML, JSON, and CSV. JSON is the most common among them. For simplicity, this paper represents the implementation and experimental verification of the proposed scheme using JSON format. Experimental results demonstrate the scheme's robustness against various typical attacks. Additionally, the proposed scheme can be easily extended to other typical semi-structured data formats, such as tabular data formats like Microsoft Excel or comma-separated values (CSV).

3.1. Data Anomaly Tracking Scheme

The power data involves some privacy information of power customers and labels added by the power company to identify specific transactions. As such, it falls under non-public data. After its formation, this data needs to circulate among various departments within the power company. Therefore, in the event of data tampering or leakage, it is crucial to track the anomalous data. This paper proposes a data anomaly tracking scheme utilizing zero-watermarking technology to achieve the identification of the data owner and facilitate tracking.

Figure 2 illustrates the schematic diagram of the proposed scheme. Before sending the data to the next circulating node, the original data owner generates a zero-watermark sequence containing identity information and associates it with their original data. This zero-watermark sequence is stored in a trusted third-party authentication entity or an equivalent entity. Since the watermark is independent of the data file itself, it does not affect the content of the file. Upon receiving the data, the next circulating node can request the zero-watermark sequence from the trusted third-party authentication entity or an equivalent entity and, in conjunction with the data, extract the watermark information to verify the data's source. After ensuring the legitimacy of the data source, the circulating node generates a zero-watermark sequence containing identity information for itself and the upper-level node and stores it in the trusted third-party authentication entity. Subsequently, the file continues to circulate to lower-level nodes.

During the data circulation process, it is possible to determine the nodes through which the data has passed by examining the zero-watermark sequences stored in a trusted third-party entity. In the event of data tampering or leakage onto the internet, all data owners can trace the origin of the current data by combining the leaked file with the zero-watermark sequence stored in the trusted third-party entity. This facilitates data anomaly tracking.

3.2. Preprocessing of Semi-Structured Data

Figure 3a presents an illustrative example of a JSON file. The JSON file adopts a hierarchical or parallel format for data storage. As depicted in Figure 3b, this paper represents the data hierarchy within the JSON using a tree structure. The received raw JSON-formatted power data is considered the root JSON object, and all data is stored in its leaf nodes. Elements in the JSON file can be classified into three types: JSON objects that store data hierarchically, JSON arrays that store elements in parallel, and JSON primitives directly storing data. Both JSON objects and JSON primitives consist of key-value pairs, while JSON arrays carry parallel data without having their own keys.

During the data preprocessing phase, this paper initially parses the raw power data JSON file (denoted as) as the provider of feature sequences. It is parsed into key-value pairs, which serve as the basic units for embedding watermark information in the subsequent scheme. The scheme initializes as an empty set and establishes a tree structure to represent hierarchical relationships. Traversing all nodes in the tree starting from, if a JSON object is encountered during the traversal, its key is appended to the end of the prefix, where the prefix initially is an empty string. Subsequently, an underscore "_" is appended at the end to signify the hierarchical relationship, and the traversal continues to the child nodes of this object. In case a JSON array is encountered during parsing, its elements are accessed in parallel. If a JSON primitive is encountered, its key is appended to the prefix.

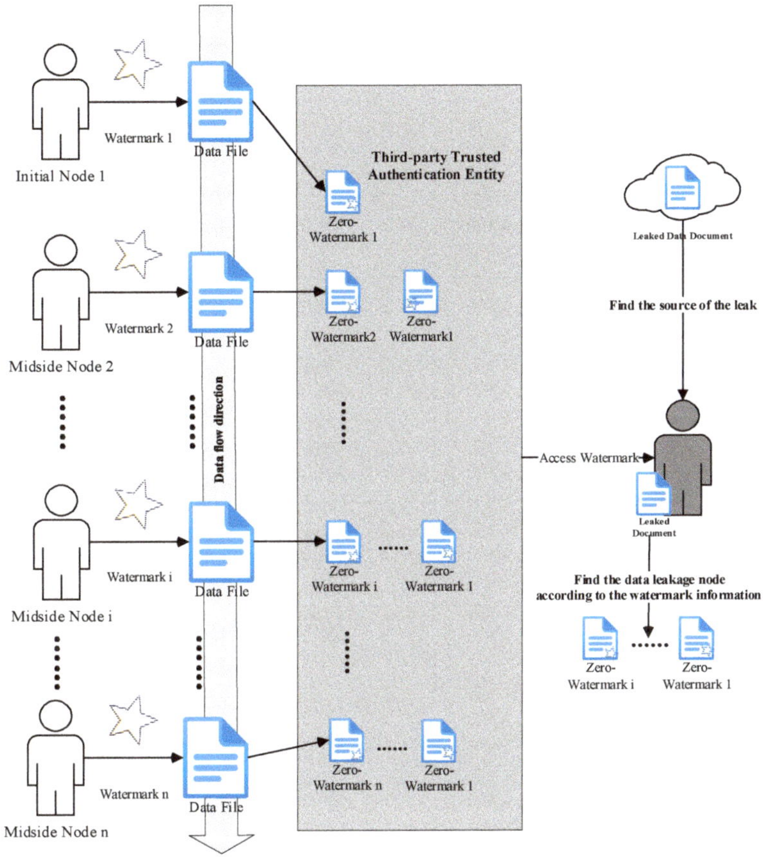

Figure 2. Data Anomaly Tracking.

The corresponding pairs for leaf nodes are represented as $p = \{prefix, value\}$, where the value is the value of the respective leaf node. Subsequently, the scheme performs backtracking and continues the traversal until all nodes have been visited. After parsing, the set of key–value pairs P is constructed, comprising all pairs formed by the leaf nodes of the tree. Let q denote the number of leaf nodes. Figure 3c illustrates the parsing result of the file depicted in Figure 3b.

In practical applications, power systems monitor and filter transmitted files using keyword filtering. However, for some plain text data, there may not be a comprehensive standard, leading to the possibility of synonymous substitutions within the text. In such cases, although the text may undergo synonymous substitutions, it essentially represents the same data. Consequently, the extracted feature sequences may exhibit expression differences. To address the aforementioned issues and considering that there might be variations in the representation of plain text data, particularly due to synonymous substitutions, this paper's approach exclusively embeds watermark data into feature sequences extracted from key-value pairs P_{num}, where the values consist solely of numerical data. This strategy is employed to mitigate potential semantic alterations resulting from changes in string-type data after the embedding of watermark information bits.

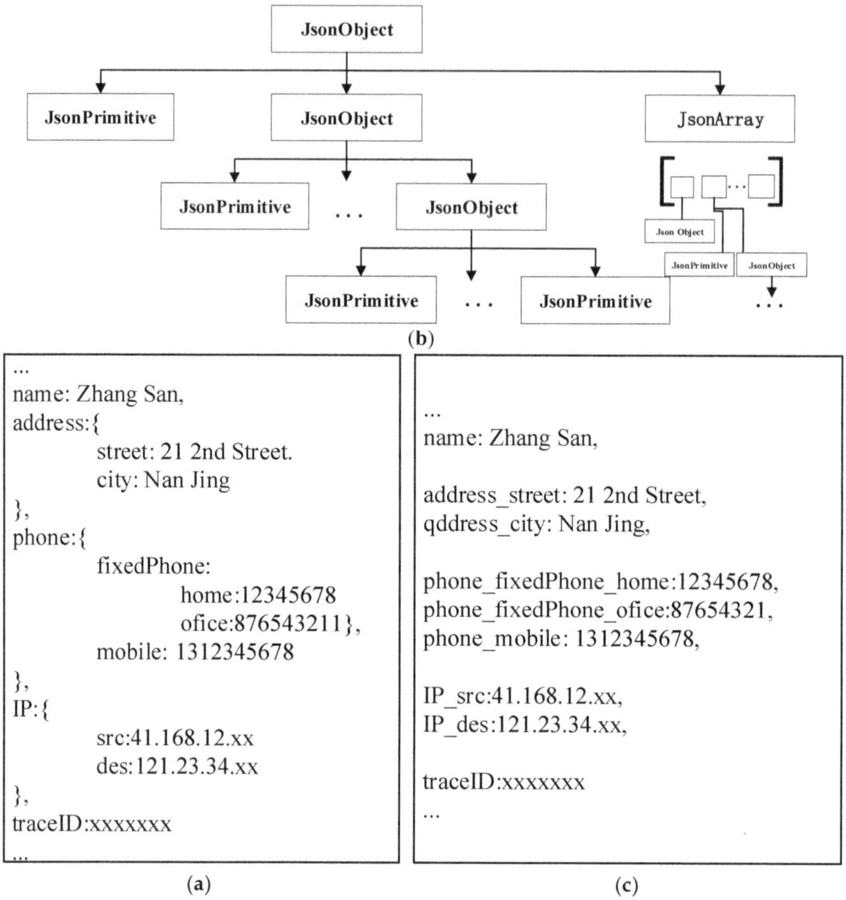

Figure 3. (**a**) JSON File Structure, (**b**) Raw JSON File, and (**c**) Parsed JSON Key-Value Pairs.

Furthermore, it is necessary to define a set of key–value pairs P_{ban} to be excluded from those eligible for watermark embedding. For instance, information such as phone numbers, IDs, or timestamps should be excluded, as they uniquely identify the data, making it easy to reverse-engineer the original content from the constructed feature sequence. This poses a risk of privacy data leakage. Hence, we exclusively utilize the remaining pairs $P' = P_{num} - P_{ban}$ to construct the feature sequence for embedding the watermark information. We denote the valid pairs as $p'_i P', i = \{1, 2, \ldots, n\}$, where n represents the size of P'.

Subsequently, we generate a set of sequences $S_{rand} = \{s_1, s_2, \ldots, s_n\}$, where each s_i is pseudo-randomly generated with a key as the seed. The elements in S_i fall within the range [0,1]. S_i determines the starting position for embedding watermark bits, and the key is shared among all parties involved in the power data flow while being kept confidential. This ensures that even if the zero-watermark is leaked, existing watermark information cannot be extracted, preventing attackers from adding a newly forged watermark.

Finally, the key–value pairs in P' are sorted in ascending order based on dictionary order, and the values of all valid key-value pairs are concatenated to form the watermark carrier feature sequence Q.

3.3. *Robust Zero-Watermark Embedding*

The watermark embedding process is illustrated in Figure 4.

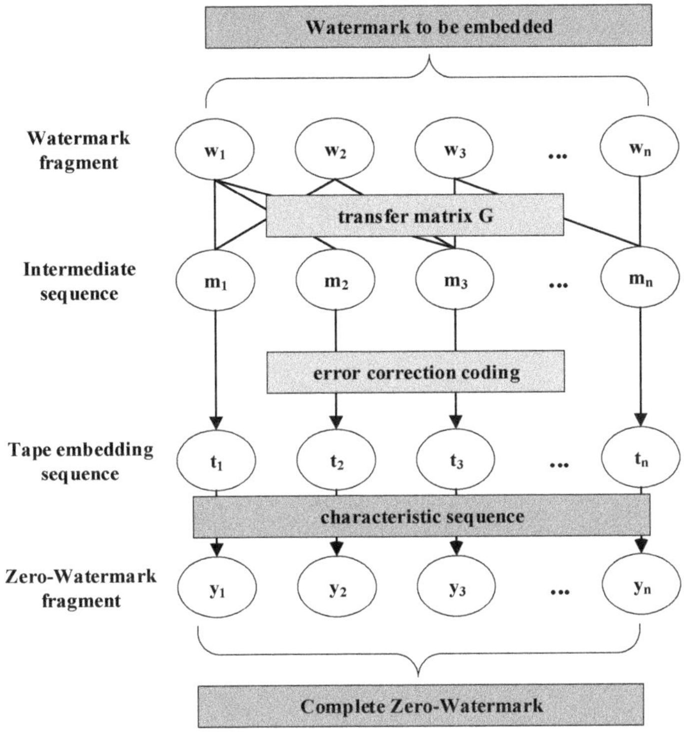

Figure 4. Watermark Embedding.

In the robust zero-watermark scheme proposed in this paper, the first step involves segmenting the watermark information and constructing an intermediate sequence $M = \{m_1, m_2, m_3, \ldots, m_n\}$ consisting of n segments. The length of each segment m_i is p.

Next, a transition matrix G is defined as follows:

$$G = \begin{pmatrix} g_{1,1} & \cdots & g_{1,n} \\ \vdots & \ddots & \vdots \\ g_{k,1} & \cdots & g_{k,n} \end{pmatrix} \tag{1}$$

In the above, G is a sparse matrix, where each $g_{i,j}$ takes values of 0 or 1. The construction of G is performed as follows: initially, the cumulative distribution function cdfRSD [21] of the robust soliton distribution is generated. Error Correction Codes (ECC) and Robust Soliton Distribution (RSD) are two critical concepts in the realm of digital communication and data encoding. ECC encompasses a set of techniques used to detect and rectify errors in transmitted data, ensuring its integrity and accuracy over noisy channels or unreliable storage. These codes, such as Reed–Solomon and Hamming codes, add redundant data to the original message, allowing for the correction of errors at the receiver's end. While ECC focuses on error correction within a fixed-size data block, RSD optimizes the transmission process in dynamic communication environments, making them both indispensable for reliable and efficient digital communications.

The probability density P_i of RSD is defined as follows:

$$P_i = \frac{\rho_i + \tau_i}{\sum_i(\rho_i + \tau_i)} \tag{2}$$

Here, ρi represents the ideal soliton distribution, and τi is defined as:

$$\tau_i = \begin{cases} \frac{R}{ik}, 1 \leq i \leq [k/(R-1)] \\ \frac{Rln(\frac{R}{\delta})}{k}, i = [k/R] \\ 0, others \end{cases} \tag{3}$$

where $R = c\sqrt{k}ln\left(\frac{k}{\delta}\right)$ represents the expected fluctuation size.

For the i-th column of G, this scheme converts a certain number of distinct $g_{j,i}$ indices from 0 to 1 based on the following algorithm:

$$\begin{cases} x_i = cdf_{RSD}(S_i[1]) \\ g_{j,i} = \begin{cases} 0, Uni(S_i[k]) mod n = 1 \\ 1, otherwise \end{cases} \end{cases} \tag{4}$$

Furthermore, we define the process of transferring W to M as:

$$M = W \bigoplus G \tag{5}$$

Here, ⊗ represents the XOR operation between matrices.

$$m_i = \sum_{j=1}^{k} w_j g_{i,j} \tag{6}$$

Then, the intermediate sequence M is generated. After processing, the original watermark information is transformed from k blocks to n blocks. During extraction, the original watermark information can be reconstructed from a subset of the new n blocks. For each intermediate data segment m_i, this paper also applies cyclic encoding as error correction to enhance the robustness of the generated watermark. The watermark information for embedding after cyclic encoding is denoted as $t_i = Cyc(m_i)$. After cyclic encoding, the length of t is denoted as $s(s > p)$.

Furthermore, this paper iteratively embeds t_i into the feature sequence Q extracted from the original semi-structured data. Split Q into n segments, forming the set $Q = \{x_1, x_2, \ldots, x_n\}$. The length q of each segment x_i should satisfy q>s. Subsequently, the processed watermark information t_i is embedded into each watermark carrier segment x_i. In this paper, the data format of Q is converted from numerical to string, and the least significant bit (LSB) of each character is XORed with each bit of t_i for data embedding. After embedding the watermark information t_i into x_i, it is represented as y_i.

To prevent zero-watermark leakage and thwart attackers attempting to extract and construct new forged watermarks, this paper, during data preprocessing, generates a sequence $S_{rand} = \{s_1, s_2, \ldots, s_n\}$ using a confidential key. s_i represents the initial position offset in bits when performing embedding. For instance, if the segment of the watermark carrier is denoted as X and the sequence to be embedded is a, according to s_i, $a[j]$ will be XORed with the $(s_i + j) mod\ len\ (X)$-th bit of X.

$$a[j] = mod(X[s_i + j], 2), j = 1, 2, \ldots, s \tag{7}$$

Finally, the robust zero-watermark embedding process yields n zero-watermark sequences denoted as $Y = \{y_1, y_2, \ldots, y_n\}$. Concatenating these n short sequences from Y results in the final robust zero-watermark. The data owner, after generating the robust zero-watermark by combining the original semi-structured data with watermark information identifying their own identity, uploads it to a trusted third-party certification authority or an entity with equivalent functionality.

3.4. Robust Zero-Watermark Extracting

When the data recipient obtains the semi-structured power data J*, slight changes may occur during the transmission process. However, due to the robustness of the data feature sequence extraction, the recipient can still request the corresponding zero-watermark Y* from a trusted third-party certification authority or an entity with equivalent functionality. This allows them to attempt to extract watermark information from the zero-watermark.

The flowchart of the extraction process is depicted in Figure 5. It is crucial to note that the data recipient needs to be aware of the key used for generating the random sequence in the zero-watermark embedding process; otherwise, watermark extraction cannot be performed.

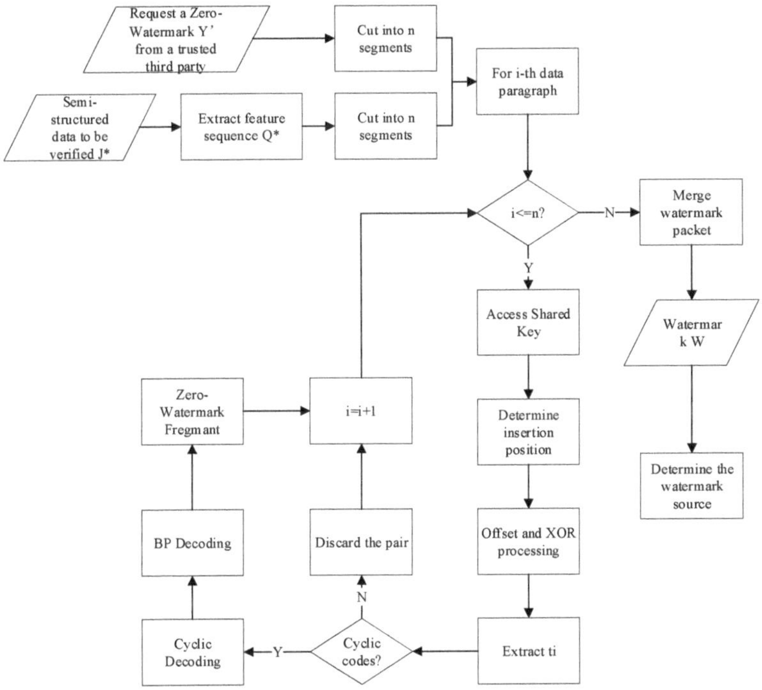

Figure 5. Robust Zero-Watermark Extraction.

The data recipient first performs preprocessing by generating a pseudo-random sequence $S_{rand} = \{s_1, s_2, \ldots, s_n\}$ using the key. Then, the recipient initializes G as an empty $n \times k$ matrix and begins the watermark extraction process. Then, Si[1] is utilized to obtain x_i, and $g_{j,i}$ is flipped using $[S_i[1]+1, \ldots, S_i[1]+x_i]]$, as described in Section 3.2. Subsequently, they obtain the precise transmission matrix G for data embedding.

Next, the valid key-value pairs in P* are sorted in ascending order based on dictionary order. The values of all valid key–value pairs are then concatenated to form the watermark carrier feature sequence $Q*$, which is divided into n segments, constituting the set $Q* = \{x'_1, x'_2, \ldots, x'_n\}$. Simultaneously, Y* is also split into n segments, forming the set $Y* = \{y'_1, y'_2, \ldots, y'_n\}$.

If the segment of the zero-watermark sequence to be extracted is represented as Y, and the segment to be extracted is denoted as a. According to s_i and $a[j]$ will be embedded into the $(s_i + j) mod\ len\ (Y)$ bit of Y. Therefore, the recipient obtains the watermark sequence using this formula:

$$a[j] = mod(Y[s_i + j], 2), j = 1, 2, \ldots, n \quad (8)$$

Utilizing the sequence t'_i with G, we need to perform cyclic decoding on t'_i to recover the intermediate sequence m'_i. If m'_i is not a valid cyclic code, the recipient considers the watermark information contained in this segment of the zero-watermark sequence to be tampered with. Therefore, the recipient will refrain from using this data packet to extract the complete watermark.

After discarding data packets with invalid cyclic codes, for the remaining valid n' data packets $\{m'_1, m'_2, \ldots, m'_{n'}\}(n' \leq n)$, the data recipient further employs the Belief Propagation (BP) algorithm [22–24] for decoding. Firstly, identify the intermediate data packets that are linked to only one segment of watermark information (i.e., degree of connectivity). After recovering these intermediate data packets, leverage them to reduce the connectivity of related data packets, subsequently enabling the recovery of intermediate data packets with low connectivity. Through iteration, all intermediate data packets can be decoded. Finally, extract the complete watermark information by connecting all recovered data packets.

4. Experimental Results and Analysis

To validate the robustness of the zero-watermark scheme, multiple experiments were conducted on a substantial number of JSON files in this study. The experimental dataset was provided by the Southern Division of the Customer Service Center of the State Grid Corporation of China. Binary random sequences were employed as digital watermarks during the testing process. The zero-watermark in this study is composed of feature sequences extracted from JSON data, ensuring that embedding the watermark does not modify the original data. The robustness of the zero-watermark against various attacks was tested, including typical attacks such as context truncation, modification, and redundant insertion.

The generation and extraction of zero-watermarks in this study were performed on a personal laptop with a 3.20 GHz CPU and 8.00 GB of RAM.

This study tested the robustness of semi-structured data watermarking against three types of attacks, applying varying degrees of typical attacks such as deletion, value erasure, and redundant insertion. The success rate of extracting the complete watermark from zero-watermarking was assessed, and a comparison was made with scenarios where watermark information was encoded without the use of erasure codes. For a fixed watermark size of 1000 bits, this paper conducted zero-watermark embedding and extraction tests using four different-sized JSON files: File 1, File 2, File 3, File 4, and File 5, each containing 100, 200, 800, 1500, and 3000 key-value pairs, respectively, after preprocessing and parsing. Multiple identical attacks were executed on each zero-watermark file. The success rates of watermark extraction under different attacks are presented in Table 1, where extractions with incorrectly retrieved bits are not considered successful. In the table, P_d, P_i and P_m, respectively, indicate the percentage of key-value pairs that were deleted, inserted, or manipulated in the file. The results demonstrate that the method proposed in this paper significantly enhances the robustness of the watermark, especially against numerical tampering attacks.

In addition, in the aforementioned File 3, File 4, and File 5, watermark information was embedded with bit sizes of 500, 1000, 1500, 2000, 2500, and 3000. The success rates of zero-watermark extraction were tested under three types of attacks: deletion, value tampering, and redundant insertion. In the tests, P_d, P_i and P_m were all set to 10%. The experimental results are illustrated in Figure 6.

Table 1. Extraction Success Rates of Semi-Structured Data under Different Attacks.

Type of Attack		Direct Extraction Success Rate/Extraction Success Rate Using Our Method				
		Document 1	Document 2	Document 3	Document 4	Document 5
No Attack		1.0/1.0	1.0/1.0	1.0/1.0	1.0/1.0	1.0/1.0
Deleted Attack	Pd = 5%	0.817/1.0	0.820/0.975	0.813/0.999	0.821/0.998	0.840/0.991
	Pd = 10%	0.610/0.957	0.554/0.995	0.653/0.997	0.541/0.950	0.687/0.981
	Pd = 20%	0.361/0.967	0.343/0.966	0.299/0.996	0.381/0.976	0.374/0.972
	Pd = 30%	0.121/0.958	0.201/0.984	0.176/0.976	0.141/0.992	0.187/0.981
Modified Attack	Pm = 5%	0.671/0.986	0.487/1.0	0.578/0.984	0.398/0.990	0.633/0.989
	Pm = 10%	0.321/0.997	0.241/0.987	0.322/0.988	0.178/0.991	0.452/0.988
	Pm = 20%	0.167/0.998	0.101/0.984	0.221/0.979	0.089/0.986	0.281/0.995
	Pm = 30%	0.076/0.996	0.009/0.990	0.067/0.995	0.004/0.996	0.079/0.976
Inserted Attack	Pi = 5%	0.876/0.999	0.859/1.0	0.778/0.998	0.862/0.996	0.856/0.998
	Pi = 10%	0.675/0.988	0.685/0.987	0.574/0.997	0.681/0.979	0.591/0.997
	Pi = 20%	0.471/0.987	0.461/0.980	0.310/0.986	0.444/0.990	0.297/0.979
	Pi = 30%	0.223/0.988	0.291/0.987	0.177/0.979	0.187/0.984	0.141/0.990

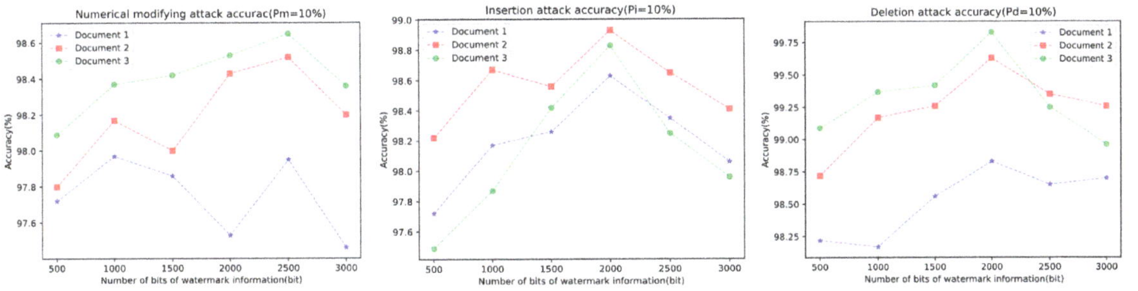

Figure 6. (**a**) Extraction accuracy of value modifying attacks, (**b**) extraction accuracy of insertion attacks, and (**c**) extraction accuracy of deletion attacks.

From the experimental results, it can be observed that the proposed zero-watermark generation and extraction scheme exhibit a certain level of robustness against all the mentioned attacks, even as the intensity of the attacks gradually increases. When the number of bits is too low, the robustness of the watermark after encoding is diminished. Additionally, files with more valid key-value pairs progressively demonstrate stronger robustness. The high robustness of this scheme is primarily attributed to the following reasons according to the algorithm analysis in this paper:

(1) For deletion attacks, the scheme can use the remaining valid key–value pairs to extract the remaining watermark information fragments, enabling complete watermark information recovery.

(2) For value tampering attacks, the scheme employs cyclic coding checks to identify the tampered positions and discards the tampered key–value pairs.

(3) For insertion attacks, it is challenging to extract meaningful data from the inserted pairs through cyclic coding checks; thus, they are also discarded.

In addition, from our experimental findings, it seems that a watermark bit size of around 2000 is most suitable for the method discussed in our paper. However, it is important to consider the capacity of the watermark carrier in practical applications, as it determines the size of the watermark information it can hold.

The proposed scheme also demonstrates robustness against combined attacks, as indicated in Table 2. All experimental results suggest that the scheme exhibits a certain level of reliability and is suitable for practical applications.

Table 2. Rate of successful extraction under different combination attacks.

Type of Attack	Direct Extraction Success Rate/Extraction Success Rate Using Our Method		
	Document 1	Document 2	Document 3
(Pd = 10%, Pm = 10%)	0.234/0.999	0.351/1.0	0.283/0.998
(Pd = 10%, Pi = 10%)	0.132/0.988	0.187/0.987	0.236/0.997
(Pm = 10%, Pi = 10%)	0.228/0.987	0.190/0.980	0.310/0.986

Furthermore, to enhance the security of this scheme, a key shared between the data owner and the data recipient is employed. Different keys lead to distinct starting embedding positions, aiding in preventing zero-watermark leakage and resisting collusion attacks. In other words, two data recipients cannot infer the embedding positions by comparing two identical files with different watermarks.

5. Conclusions

This study addresses data security concerns in the power industry and proposes a robust solitary wave distribution-based zero-watermark for semi-structured power data, enabling effective traceability in the event of localized changes in power data. Initially, feature sequences are extracted from semi-structured power data. Subsequently, these feature sequences serve as zero-watermark carriers, undergoing processing and segmentation into an equal number of blocks with the watermark body. Utilizing the robust solitary wave distribution in erasure codes and the theory of redundant error correction codes, an intermediate sequence is obtained through a transfer matrix and encoded. Finally, the error-correcting encoded watermark information is embedded into the feature sequences, generating a robust zero-watermark. During the data tracing process, effective identification and localization of abnormal data changes can be achieved by extracting and analyzing the robust zero-watermark of the traced data.

Through experimental and simulation verification, the proposed method not only ensures data security but also achieves a zero-watermark extraction success rate of over 98%. The outcomes of this study have significant practical applications in data monitoring and anomaly tracing in power systems.

Author Contributions: Conceptualization, L.Z.; methodology, L.Z.; writing—review and editing, L.Z. and Y.Z.; visualization, Q.S. and S.J.; supervision, Y.Y., Y.C., C.X. and W.S.; project administration, Y.M., Y.S. and Y.J. All authors have read and agreed to the published version of the manuscript.

Funding: This work was supported by the Science and Technology Project of State Grid Jiangsu Electric Power Co., Ltd. [5400-202318221A-1-1-ZN].

Data Availability Statement: We confirm that the data supporting the findings of this study are available within the article. Additional data that support the findings of this study are available from the corresponding author upon reasonable request.

Acknowledgments: We would like to express our gratitude to the Science and Technology Project of State Grid Jiangsu Electric Power Co., Ltd. [5400-202318221A-1-1-ZN] for their support. We would also like to acknowledge the collective efforts of all the authors in this study.

Conflicts of Interest: Author Wen Shen was employed by the company State Grid Smart Grid Research Institute Co., Ltd. The remaining authors declare that the research was conducted in the absence of any commercial or financial relationships that could be construed as a potential conflict of interest.

References

1. Liu, Z.; Chen, Z.; Yan, S. Design and Application of Marketing 2.0 Mobile Operation Platform Based on Dual Middleware Architecture. *Electr. Power Electr. Eng.* **2022**, *11*, 66–71.
2. Akoglu, L.; Tong, H.; Koutra, D. Graph based anomaly detection and description: A survey. *Data Min. Knowl. Discov.* **2015**, *29*, 626–688. [CrossRef]

3. Takeuchi, J.I.; Yamanishi, K. A unifying framework for detecting outliers and change points from time series. *IEEE Trans. Knowl. Data Eng.* **2006**, *18*, 482–492. [CrossRef]
4. Su, Y.; Zhao, Y.; Niu, C.; Liu, R.; Sun, W.; Pei, D. Robust anomaly detection for multivariate time series through stochastic recurrent neural network. In Proceedings of the 25th ACM SIGKDD International Conference on Knowledge Discovery & Data Mining, Anchorage, AK, USA, 4–8 August 2019; pp. 2828–2837.
5. Derakhshan, A.; Wang, Y.; Wang, Y.; Ortega Martín, J.L. Towards Innovative Research Approaches to Investigating the Role of Emotional Variables in Promoting Language Teachers' and Learners' Mental Health. 2023. Available online: https://hdl.handle.net/10481/84024 (accessed on 28 January 2024).
6. Panagiotelis, A.; Gamakumara, P.; Athanasopoulos, G.; Hyndman, R.J. Probabilistic forecast reconciliation: Properties, evaluation and score optimization. *Eur. J. Oper. Res.* **2023**, *306*, 693–706. [CrossRef]
7. Hendrycks, D.; Mazeika, M.; Dietterich, T. Deep anomaly detection with outlier exposure. *arXiv* **2018**, arXiv:1812.04606.
8. Ruff, L.; Vandermeulen, R.; Goernitz, N.; Deecke, L.; Siddiqui, S.A.; Binder, A.; Müller, E.; loftKloft, M. Deep one-class classification. In Proceedings of the International Conference on Machine Learning, Stockholm Sweden, 10–15 July 2018; pp. 4393–4402.
9. Lai, Z.; Zhang, D.; Zhu, X. Outlier Detection: A Survey. *Wiley Interdiscip. Rev. Data Min. Knowl. Discov.* **2021**, *11*, e1391.
10. Al-Maweri, N.A.A.S.; Ali, R.; Adnan, W.A.W.; Ramli, A.R.; Rahman, S.M.S.A.A. State-of-the-art in techniques of text digital watermarking: Challenges and limitations. *J. Comput. Sci.* **2016**, *12*, 62–80. [CrossRef]
11. Amrit, P.; Singh, A.K. Survey on watermarking methods in the artificial intelligence domain and beyond. *Comput. Commun.* **2022**, *188*, 52–65. [CrossRef]
12. Atallah, M.J.; McDonough, C.; Nirenburg, S.; Raskin, V. Natural Language Processing for Information Assurance and Security: An Overview and Implementations. In Proceedings of the 9th ACM/SIGSAC New Security Paradigms Workshop, Cork, Ireland, 18–21 September 2000; pp. 51–65.
13. Liang, B.; Li, H.; Su, M.; Bian, P.; Li, X.; Shi, W. Deep text classification can be fooled. *arXiv* **2017**, arXiv:1704.08006.
14. Atallah, M.J.; Raskin, V.; Hempelmann, C.F.; Karahan, M.; Sion, R.; Topkara, U.; Triezenberg, K.E. Natural language watermarking and tamperproofing. In *International Workshop on Information Hiding*; Springer: Berlin/Heidelberg, Germany, 2002; pp. 196–212.
15. Jalil, Z.; Mirza, A.M. A review of digital watermarking techniques for text documents. In Proceedings of the 2009 International Conference on Information and Multimedia Technology, Jeju Island, Republic of Korea, 16–18 December 2009; pp. 230–234.
16. Karanpartap, S.; Zou, J. New Evaluation Metrics Capture Quality Degradation due to LLM Watermarking. *arXiv* **2023**, arXiv:2312.02382.
17. Tsui, K.L.; Chen, V.; Jiang, W.; Yang, F.; Kan, C. Data mining methods and applications. In *Springer Handbook of Engineering Statistics*; Springer: London, UK, 2023; pp. 797–816.
18. Tekli, J. An overview on xml semantic disambiguation from unstructured text to semi-structured data: Background, applications, and ongoing challenges. *IEEE Trans. Knowl. Data Eng.* **2016**, *28*, 1383–1407. [CrossRef]
19. Wen, Q.; Sun, T.F.; Wang, S.X. Concept and Application of Zero-Watermarking. *J. Electron.* **2003**, *31*, 214.
20. Kamaruddin, N.S.; Kamsin, A.; Por, L.Y.; Rahman, H. A review of text watermarking: Theory, methods, and applications. *IEEE Access* **2018**, *6*, 8011–8028. [CrossRef]
21. Liu, F.; Li, J. Influence of System Parameters on the Distribution of Spatial Optical Solitons under Potential Well Modulation. *Optoelectron.·Laser* **2016**, *5*, 566–572.
22. Carleo, G.; Cirac, I.; Cranmer, K.; Daudet, L.; Schuld, M.; Tishby, N.; Vogt-Maranto, L.; Zdeborová, L. Machine learning and the physical sciences. *Rev. Mod. Phys.* **2019**, *91*, 045002. [CrossRef]
23. Blei, D.M.; Kucukelbir, A.; McAuliffe, J.D. Variational inference: A review for statisticians. *J. Am. Stat. Assoc.* **2017**, *112*, 859–877. [CrossRef]
24. Janai, J.; Güney, F.; Behl, A.; Geiger, A. Computer vision for autonomous vehicles: Problems, datasets and state of the art. *Found. Trends®Comput. Graph. Vis.* **2020**, *12*, 1–308. [CrossRef]

electronics

Article

Device Identity Recognition Based on an Adaptive Environment for Intrinsic Security Fingerprints

Zesheng Xi [1,2,3], Gongxuan Zhang [1], Bo Zhang [2,3,4,*] and Tao Zhang [2,3]

1 School of Computer Science and Engineering, Nanjing University of Science and Technology, Nanjing 210094, China; xizesheng@njust.edu.cn (Z.X.); gongxuan@njust.edu.cn (G.Z.)
2 State Grid Laboratory of Power Cyber-Security Protection and Monitoring Technology, Nanjing 210003, China; zhangtao@geiri.sgcc.com.cn
3 State Grid Smart Grid Research Institute Co., Ltd., Nanjing 210003, China
4 School of Cyber Science and Engineering, Shanghai Jiao Tong University, Shanghai 200240, China
* Correspondence: zhangbo@geiri.sgcc.com.cn

Abstract: A device's intrinsic security fingerprint, representing its physical characteristics, serves as a unique identifier for user devices and is highly regarded in the realms of device security and identity recognition. However, fluctuations in the environmental noise can introduce variations in the physical features of the device. To address this issue, this paper proposes an innovative method to enable the device's intrinsic security fingerprint to adapt to environmental changes, aiming to improve the accuracy of the device's intrinsic security fingerprint recognition in real-world physical environments. This paper initiates continuous data collection of device features in authentic noisy environments, recording the temporal changes in the device's physical characteristics. The problem of unstable physical features is framed as a restricted statistical learning problem with a localized information structure. This paper employs an aggregated hypergraph neural network architecture to process the temporally changing physical features. This allows the system to acquire aggregated local state information from the interactive influences of adjacent sequential signals, forming an adaptive environment-enhanced device intrinsic security fingerprint recognition model. The proposed method enhances the accuracy and reliability of device intrinsic security fingerprint recognition in outdoor environments, thereby strengthening the overall security of terminal devices. Experimental results indicate that the method achieves a recognition accuracy of 98% in continuously changing environmental conditions, representing a crucial step in reinforcing the security of Internet of Things (IoT) devices when confronted with real-world challenges.

Keywords: intrinsic security; device fingerprint; identity authentication; internet of things

1. Introduction

With the rapid development of the Internet of Things (IoT), the widespread application of various IoT devices has become an indispensable part of our daily lives. These devices play crucial roles in diverse fields, including industrial automation, smart homes, energy management, and many other application domains [1]. However, the data carried by these devices may include critical information related to device operations, control, and the privacy of users. Therefore, ensuring the security and authentication of these devices has become paramount.

The current realm of the IoT confronts primary security challenges that include the protection of data privacy, device authentication, and the defense against network attacks [2]. In recent years, the field of IoT security has witnessed significant advancements, encompassing the development of cutting-edge security protocols, encryption technologies, and intrusion detection systems [3–5].

Device intrinsic security fingerprint recognition, as an authentication method, has garnered considerable attention in the security domain. It relies on the unique hardware features of a device to authenticate users or devices. In comparison to traditional authentication methods, device intrinsic security fingerprint recognition utilizes the physical characteristics of a device, such as physical processor features and sensor performance parameters, to uniquely identify the device, providing a higher level of security for IoT terminals [6].

This method maximizes the use of hardware parameters, exploiting small variations present during the device production process and making the physical characteristics of each device unique. Consequently, device intrinsic security fingerprint recognition ensures the uniqueness of device identity, making it resistant to traditional security risks such as password leaks and identity spoofing attacks. By relying on physical characteristics, this technology provides more reliable and secure identity authentication for users and devices, offering an additional layer of protection for IoT terminals and enhancing the overall security of the system.

Despite its significant potential, device intrinsic security fingerprint recognition faces challenges, particularly in dynamic outdoor environments where factors such as dynamic physical conditions, noise, lighting variations, temperature changes, and other constantly changing elements may impact the accuracy and reliability of device intrinsic fingerprints. To overcome these challenges, an innovative approach is needed to address dynamic environmental changes and enhance the performance of device intrinsic security fingerprint recognition systems.

To address these issues and improve the accuracy and reliability of device intrinsic security fingerprint recognition in dynamic environments, this paper presents a novel method in the realm of IoT terminal device security and identity authentication. This method adapts to environmental uncertainties and noise fluctuations through the utilization of an aggregated hypergraph neural network architecture. This architecture processes the temporally changing physical features, allowing the system to acquire aggregated local state information from the interactive influences of adjacent sequential signals, constructing an adaptive environment-enhanced device intrinsic fingerprint recognition model.

The proposed method enhances the performance of intrinsic fingerprint recognition systems, meeting the stability and security demands for user identity authentication, even in dynamically changing environmental conditions. The main contributions of this paper are outlined as follows:

1. Real-time data collection in authentic outdoor environments, capturing the dynamic changes in physical features used to construct device intrinsic fingerprints;
2. Introduction of the Gramian angular field transformation, processing collected data to map it to a high-dimensional feature space, capturing the spatiotemporal characteristics of intrinsic fingerprints.
3. Design and application of a hypergraph neural network to extract and learn continuous spatiotemporal features of device intrinsic security fingerprints in real-world environments.

Experimental results demonstrate that the proposed adaptive environment-enhanced device intrinsic security fingerprint recognition system significantly improves accuracy and reliability in outdoor environments. The method effectively addresses the impact of constantly changing physical factors on device intrinsic fingerprints, presenting a breakthrough in the field of mobile device security and authentication. The comprehensive recognition accuracy of the proposed method reaches 98% in continuously changing environmental conditions.

The remainder of this paper is organized as follows: Section 2 provides an overview of the system. Section 3 introduces the extraction of the device's physical features and data processing methods. Section 4 details the construction process of the hypergraph neural network for building device intrinsic security fingerprints. Section 5 presents extensive experimental results to showcase system performance. Sections 6 and 7, respectively, introduce related works and summarize the paper.

2. System Overview

To address the impact of environmental physical noise fluctuations on the intrinsic security fingerprints within devices, this paper proposes the design of an adaptive environment-aware intrinsic security fingerprint recognition system. The overall system architecture is illustrated in Figure 1, comprising three main stages: model training, fingerprint generation, and identity recognition.

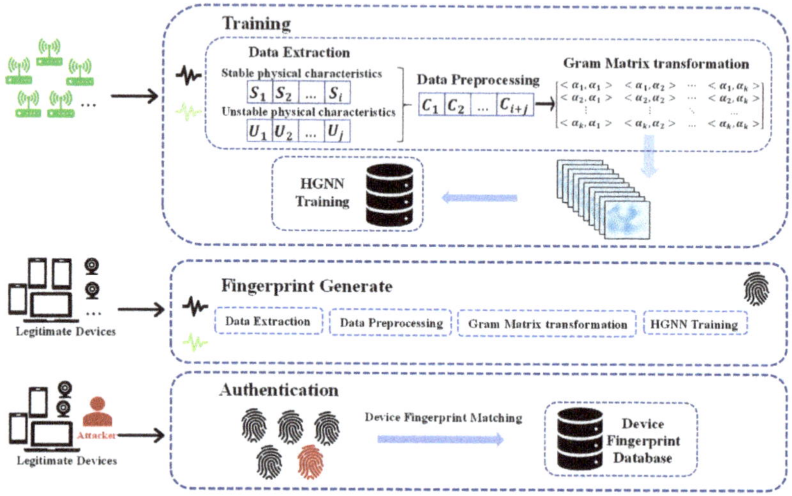

Figure 1. Overall architecture diagram.

2.1. Model Training

During the model training phase, the system initially records data in a real physical environment. The adaptive environment-aware intrinsic security fingerprint recognition system collects a series of continuous data on the terminal's physical features under different environmental conditions. These features include stable clock deviation information unaffected by time changes and channel state information susceptible to environmental interference and varying over time.

The system proceeds with feature extraction, employing the least squares fitting method to extract clock deviation information. Simultaneously, channel estimation is used to extract the amplitude values from the channel state information, and both are recorded to capture their temporal variations. In the data processing stage, the Gramian angular field [7] is introduced for feature transformation, converting temporal data into a two-dimensional format. This transformation provides richer input information to the neural network, enabling the model to consider the temporal changes in the terminal's physical features as crucial parameters. The two-dimensional data are then fed into the hypergraph neural network (HGNN) [8] for model construction, enhancing adaptability to environmental changes. The training phase of the model covers diverse real-world environmental data, ensuring robust performance under various conditions.

In the model evaluation phase, an independent test set is utilized to validate performance, with a particular focus on fingerprint recognition accuracy in outdoor environments. Through multiple rounds of adjustment and optimization, the model's high reliability in real environments is ensured. The goal is to construct an intrinsic fingerprint recognition model adaptable to diverse environments, ultimately improving fingerprint recognition accuracy in outdoor settings.

2.2. Fingerprint Generation

In the fingerprint generation phase, the system collects and records the physical features of multiple legitimate devices. Utilizing the pre-trained model, unique intrinsic security fingerprints representing each legitimate device are generated and stored in the device's intrinsic security fingerprint database.

2.3. Identity Recognition

In the identity recognition phase, the system, based on the physical features of a device attempting to connect to the system, extracts the intrinsic security fingerprint of that device. It then compares this fingerprint with the data in the device's intrinsic security fingerprint database to determine whether the device is an authenticated legitimate device. As legitimate devices cannot modify their own physical features, the intrinsic security fingerprint of legitimate devices cannot be forged. Illegitimate devices are thus identified, enhancing the security of identity recognition.

3. Extraction of Physical Device Features

In the feature extraction phase, we employed statistical analysis methods to extract signal clock deviation as a stable feature for the fingerprint. Simultaneously, we utilized time-series analysis methods to extract the temporal patterns of channel state information. In this way, we obtained a comprehensive set of features to fully capture the dynamic changes in the intrinsic security fingerprint of the device.

3.1. Clock Deviation Fingerprint

Device clock deviation is a physical characteristic that can be understood as the operation of a clock based on a crystal oscillator with a small but measurable speed deviation. It can serve as a unique identifier for a device and is resistant to forgery by attackers.

In ordinary computer clocks (and in the operation of TSF timers in Wi-Fi chipsets), the clock signal is generated by crystal oscillators. The frequency of crystal oscillators is determined by their manufacturing characteristics (such as cutting angle) and the type of crystal. Even crystals of the same model, series, and production date, due to the imperfect mechanical precision in the manufacturing process, will inevitably have inherent inaccuracies, such as slight variations in cutting angles and directions, leading to small changes in frequency.

Clock deviation is typically measured in parts per million (ppm). The clock c calculates time steps starting from some initial point i_c in real time. $R_c(t)$ denotes the timestamp reported by clock c at real time t, and it is given by $R_c(t) = t - i_c$. Let ex be the ideal clock under perfect conditions, and its reported timestamp is given by $R_{ex}(t) = t - i_{ex}$. However, since standard hardware does not use highly precise atomic clocks, there is an offset introduced, represented by $off_c(t) = R_c(t) - (t - i_c)$, and its absolute value increases over time. Clock deviation is the first derivative of the offset.

Due to clock deviation being based on the aforementioned crystal oscillator hardware characteristics, it is not easily manipulated or altered by attackers. Moreover, even for IoT devices of the same model, clock deviation fingerprints can exhibit differences. Therefore, clock deviation can uniquely identify hardware devices, and its value is less susceptible to external factors such as temperature and location, demonstrating a certain degree of stability. Hence, we aim to achieve reliable device recognition by utilizing clock deviation as a part of the intrinsic security fingerprint features.

When collecting clock deviation information, it is typically obtained from Beacon frames during device communication. Beacon frames are data frames used in wireless communication to transmit basic system information, including details about the network, channel, bandwidth, signal strength, and other critical information. Within Beacon frames, there is a TimeStamp field 8 bits in size that is used to synchronize client devices connected to the wireless network and measured in milliseconds. Besides the TimeStamp field being time-related, another time-related field can be obtained when capturing Beacon frames: the capture time. The generation of TimeStamp is mainly related to the hardware construction and drivers of IoT devices, while the capture time can be influenced by channel load. Both are time-related variables. The capture time of Beacon frames can be considered as the independent variable, and the TimeStamp field can be considered as the dependent variable. Using the least squares linear fit, the linear relationship between the capture time of Beacon frames and the TimeStamp field can be determined, which is also referred to as clock deviation.

Two mathematical methods are commonly used to estimate device clock deviation: the linear programming method (LPM) and the least squares fitting method (LSF). However, LSF is more sensitive to a small number of outliers compared to LPM. Therefore, when LSF is employed for clock deviation estimation and device identification, it exhibits higher sensitivity. In this paper, we adopt the least squares fitting method (LSF) to estimate device clock deviation.

For example, consider a set of data from a group of Beacon frames with a sliding window of size n: $(t_1, T_1), (t_2, T_2), \ldots, (t_i, T_i), \ldots, (t_n, T_n)$, where t_i represents the reception time of the i Beacon frame, and T_i represents the TimeStamp field in the i-th Beacon frame. When employing the least squares method to handle timestamps and the capture time of Beacon frames, in order to eliminate differences introduced by the time between each set of data, preprocessing is applied to these two attributes. The preprocessing methods are expressed as Formulas (1) and (2):

$$x_i = t_i - t_0 \tag{1}$$

$$y_i = T_i - T_0 \tag{2}$$

With each set having the corresponding timestamp and capture time variables (x_i, y_i), the least squares method is employed to extract the linear relationship for each set of corresponding (x, y) data. Assuming a linear relationship $y = \alpha x + \beta$, where α and β are the parameters to be determined, the objective is to minimize the sum of squared distances between this linear relationship and all (x_i, y_i) pairs. This is expressed in Formula (3):

$$\sum_{i=1}^{n} (y_i - \alpha t_i - \beta)^2 \tag{3}$$

The least squares fitting algorithm is used to calculate α and β.

Analyzing the clock deviation obtained through the least squares fitting computation for Beacon frames from different IoT devices reveals significant differences in clock deviation among various IoT devices. Moreover, the values of α and β for the same device are remarkably stable. Clock deviation emerges as a relatively stable discriminative fingerprint feature, minimally affected by external environmental factors. Only the capture time experiences slight fluctuations due to changes in channel load. Therefore, clock deviation can be considered one of the stable physical features of the intrinsic security fingerprint of a device.

3.2. Channel State Information

The wireless channel is an abstract representation of the communication link between the transmitter and receiver in wireless communication. Due to multipath propagation issues, the signal received in a wireless environment is, in reality, the sum of an infinite number of original transmitted signals, each subject to attenuation, delay, and phase shift. Interference occurs among the various delay paths. Additionally, the relative movement of mobile terminals and changes in the environment can alter the paths, leading to random fluctuations in signal amplitude and phase. These variations are user-specific, providing a valuable resource for physical layer security.

Furthermore, the wireless channel exhibits characteristics such as randomness, time variation, unpredictability, and uniqueness. The randomness of channel features is inherent to the channel itself. Time variation in the channel refers to rapid changes in channel state over time, resulting in independent channel characteristics within time intervals greater than the channel coherence time. Channel unpredictability arises from the random changes in the channel due to environmental variations. Channel uniqueness refers to the distinctiveness of channel features in different spatial locations.

These physical characteristics of the wireless channel serve as the foundation for research in physical layer security. In this study, we leverage the Channel State Information (CSI) of the wireless channel, comparing the estimated CSI of the current instance with the previous CSI as a part of the intrinsic security fingerprint. CSI is one of the features of the wireless channel, representing the frequency response of the wireless channel at the sampling points of each subcarrier in an Orthogonal Frequency Division Multiplexing (OFDM) system.

In OFDM systems, the CSI, composed of the fading, scattering, and transmission distance of subcarriers, can be utilized to depict the channel state between the transmitter and receiver [9]. Its frequency-domain model is represented as

$$Y = HX + N \tag{4}$$

In the frequency-domain model, where X is the transmitted signal, Y is the received signal, H is the channel frequency response, and N is Gaussian white noise.

The expression for the Channel Frequency Response (CFR) can be easily obtained through the pilot part of each OFDM symbol:

$$H = \sum_{k \in K} \|h_k\| \cdot e^{-j \cdot \varphi_k} \tag{5}$$

The magnitudes and phases of signals on each subcarrier are denoted as $\|h_k\|$ and φ_k, respectively.

Channel State Information (CSI) is typically acquired through channel estimation methods in wireless communication. In wireless transmission, signals emitted by the transmitter propagate along multiple wireless paths to reach the receiver, forming a wireless multipath channel utilized for device communication. CSI commonly refers to the Channel Frequency Response (CFR) of this wireless multipath channel. Thus, when the transmission frequency is f, CSI can be expressed as:

$$H(f) = \sum_{n}^{N} a_n e^{-j2\pi f \tau_n} \tag{6}$$

According to Equation (6), CSI reflects the overall amplitude attenuation and phase shift of the wireless channel. In practical wireless communication, each propagation path constituting the wireless channel experiences distinct amplitude attenuation and time delay. As wireless signals arrive at the receiver via different paths, signals with different amplitudes and phases superimpose to form the final received signal. CSI, in turn, reflects the amplitude attenuation and phase shift resulting from the superposition of multiple propagation paths.

In Orthogonal Frequency Division Multiplexing (OFDM) wireless networks, a set of CSI data is generated for each antenna pair. Each set of CSI data is an array with a length equal to the number of CSI values in the subcarriers of the OFDM mechanism. Each CSI value in the array represents the sampled value of the channel frequency response at the center frequency of the corresponding subcarrier, as expressed in the mathematical representation of each set of CSI data:

$$CSI_k = |csi_k| e^{-j\angle csi_k}, k = -i, \ldots, -1, 1, \ldots, i \tag{7}$$

where $|csi_k|$ represents the magnitude of the CSI value, and $\angle CSI_k$ represents the phase of the CSI value. This paper adopts the magnitude of CSI as the fingerprint feature.

To mitigate the negative impact of amplitude variations on fingerprint recognition performance, each CSI magnitude sequence undergoes maximum–minimum normalization.

When $(a_1, a_2, \ldots, a_k)$ represents a set of CSI magnitudes, let $a_{\max} = \max(a_1, a_2, \ldots, a_k)$, $a_{\min} = \min(a_1, a_2, \ldots, a_k)$. The maximum–minimum normalization method is then expressed as:

$$c_i = \frac{a_i - a_{\min}}{a_{\max} - a_{\min}}. \quad (8)$$

The normalized CSI magnitude sequence is denoted as CSI fingerprint; $CFP = [c_1, c_2, \ldots, c_k]$. The normalized CSI magnitude sequence exhibits smaller dispersion compared to the unprocessed CSI magnitude sequence.

4. Feature Transformation and Model Construction

There are numerous methods for extracting Channel State Information [10]. After a thorough comparison, we have opted to utilize Nexmon as our CSI extraction tool, owing to its more convenient extraction process and superior extraction efficiency [11].

In dynamic environments, the CSI (Channel State Information) fingerprints of devices exhibit temporal variations. These fluctuations, primarily due to environmental changes, necessitate a robust model capable of adapting to these variations. We address this challenge by employing an aggregated hypergraph neural network architecture.

The proposed model processes temporal CSI data by transforming it into a format suitable for hypergraph neural networks. This transformation involves the use of Gramian angular fields (GAF), a technique that converts time series data into a structured format. GAF represents the temporal relationships within CSI data, capturing the essence of its dynamic nature. Environmental factors such as temperature, humidity, and signal interference cause significant changes in CSI fingerprints. These changes are crucial in model construction as they directly affect the reliability of device identification. We analyze these factors, detailing how they influence CSI data over time and, consequently, the model's adaptation to these changes.

The hypergraph architecture excels in handling the localized information structure of CSI data. By aggregating local state information from adjacent sequential signals, the model adapts to the evolving nature of CSI fingerprints. This approach ensures that the intrinsic device fingerprint recognition remains reliable, even in fluctuating environmental conditions.

4.1. Gramian Angular Fields

Univariate time series, to some extent, may not adequately capture the commonality and latent states in the data. To address this limitation, a common approach involves employing transformation equations to map the original one-dimensional sequence into a high-dimensional form. However, most mapping methods tend to overlook the transformation of the time variable, which contains information about the timing and sequence of events. Consequently, after mapping, the temporal dependencies in the time series tend to disappear.

To better handle these extracted features, we introduce Gramian angular fields (GAFs) [12] for feature transformation. The use of Gramian angular fields enables the conversion of time series data into an image-like format, effectively capturing complex relationships between features and providing richer input information for subsequent hypergraph neural network models.

When encoding time series with Gramian angular fields, as time progresses, positions move from the upper-left corner to the lower-right corner, encoding the time dimension into the geometric structure of the matrix. This preserves temporal dependencies to the maximum extent. Therefore, in this study, we utilize Gramian angular fields to replace the original one-dimensional sequence with a more comprehensive representation. The

Gramian matrix is defined as the matrix composed of the pairwise inner products of any k vectors in n-dimensional Euclidean space:

$$\Delta(\alpha_1, \alpha_2, \cdots, \alpha_k) = \begin{bmatrix} \gamma(\alpha_1, \alpha_1) & \gamma(\alpha_1, \alpha_2) & \cdots & \gamma(\alpha_1, \alpha_k) \\ \gamma(\alpha_2, \alpha_1) & \gamma(\alpha_2, \alpha_2) & \cdots & \gamma(\alpha_2, \alpha_k) \\ \vdots & \vdots & \ddots & \cdots \\ \gamma(\alpha_k, \alpha_1) & \gamma(\alpha_k, \alpha_2) & \cdots & \gamma(\alpha_k, \alpha_k) \end{bmatrix} \tag{9}$$

Here, $\gamma(\alpha_i, \alpha_j)$ is a newly defined function used to calculate the relationship between vectors α_i and α_j. This relationship encompasses more than just the simple inner product; it includes the direction and magnitude of the vectors, as well as the angle information between them. When $\omega_{i,j}$ is the angle between the two vectors and assuming that all vectors in Equation (9) are unit vectors, we have

$$\Delta(\alpha_1, \alpha_2, \cdots, \alpha_k) = \begin{bmatrix} cos\omega_{1,1} & cos\omega_{1,2} & \cdots & cos\omega_{1,k} \\ cos\omega_{2,1} & cos\omega_{2,2} & \cdots & cos\omega_{2,k} \\ \vdots & \vdots & \ddots & \cdots \\ cos\omega_{k,1} & cos\omega_{k,2} & \cdots & cos\omega_{k,k} \end{bmatrix} \tag{10}$$

As evident from the above equation, the Gramian matrix is a positive semi-definite matrix. Conversely, every positive semi-definite matrix is the Gramian matrix of some vectors. The Gramian matrix encompasses the angles and orientation relationships between vectors. The collective term for GAFs includes Gramian Summation Angular Field (GASF) and Gramian Difference Angular Field (GADF). Equations (11) and (12), respectively, provide the definitions of GASF and GADF:

$$GASF = \begin{bmatrix} \eta(\theta_1, \theta_1) & \eta(\theta_1, \theta_2) & \cdots & \eta(\theta_1, \theta_k) \\ \eta(\theta_2, \theta_1) & \eta(\theta_2, \theta_2) & \cdots & \eta(\theta_2, \theta_k) \\ \vdots & \vdots & \ddots & \cdots \\ \eta(\theta_k, \theta_1) & \eta(\theta_k, \theta_2) & \cdots & \eta(\theta_k, \theta_k) \end{bmatrix} \tag{11}$$

$$GADF = \begin{bmatrix} \xi(\theta_1, \theta_1) & \xi(\theta_1, \theta_2) & \cdots & \xi(\theta_1, \theta_k) \\ \xi(\theta_2, \theta_1) & \xi(\theta_2, \theta_2) & \cdots & \xi(\theta_2, \theta_k) \\ \vdots & \vdots & \ddots & \cdots \\ \xi(\theta_k, \theta_1) & \xi(\theta_k, \theta_2) & \cdots & \xi(\theta_k, \theta_k) \end{bmatrix} \tag{12}$$

Here, η and ξ are new functions for the sum of angles and the difference of angles, respectively. They can be any suitable nonlinear functions, such as variants of the sine and cosine functions. These functions are capable of capturing complex patterns and features in time series data more effectively. In the feature extraction step, it is essential to extract features of the device over a specific period. A vector $V_i = [A, c_1, c_2, \ldots, c_k]$ is formed by combining the clock deviation feature value A extracted at time t_i with the processed CSI amplitudes. To meet the requirements of the model construction, a considerable amount of feature data is collected over a certain period, and the data is grouped into sets of n entries, which are then input into the Gramian angular field.

Before this, various processes such as normalization and quantization encoding are applied to the elements of V_i. Eventually, each element is transformed into a binary sequence of m bits, resulting in the formation of a vector $T_i = \left[b_1, b_2, \ldots, b_{m(k+1)}\right]$, where b_i equals either 0 or 1. The specific steps for temporal multi-dimensionalization of Gramian angular fields are outlined as follows:

Step 1: Normalization Processing:

Given a one-dimensional sequence $X = \{x_1, x_2, \ldots, x_n\}$, employ Equation (13) to perform min-max normalization on the sequence.

$$\tilde{x}_i = \frac{(x_i - max(X) + (x_i - min(X))}{max(X) - min(X)} \tag{13}$$

Step 2: Coordinate Transformation:

If the time units corresponding to the sequence are considered as radii, the time sequence in Cartesian coordinates can be transformed into a time sequence in polar coordinates:

$$\begin{cases} \omega = arccos\left(\tilde{x}_i\right), -1 \le \tilde{x}_i \le 1, \tilde{x}_i \in \tilde{X} \\ r = \frac{t_i}{N}, t_i \in N \end{cases} \tag{14}$$

where t_i represents a time point, and N is a constant polar coordinate span.

Step 3: Inner Product Calculation:

Define the inner product $< x,y >= f(x,y) = x \cdot y - \sqrt{1-x^2} \cdot \sqrt{1-y^2}$ and $< x,y >= \sqrt{1-x^2} \cdot y - x \cdot \sqrt{1-y^2}$. Substituting Equations (13) and (14) yields the Gram matrix $\left[< \tilde{x}_1, \tilde{x}_1 >\right]$:

$$G_{GASF} = \left[f(\theta_i + \theta_j)\right] \tag{15}$$

$$G_{GADF} = \left[g(\theta_i - \theta_j)\right] \tag{16}$$

G_{GASF} and G_{GADF} represent the relative relationships between different vectors in terms of superimposition and difference over time intervals, reflecting their temporal dependencies [12].

Further obtaining the input Gramian angular field (GAF) data as $< T_1, T_2, \ldots T_n >$, the Gram matrix for these n vectors is obtained as

$$\Delta(T_1, T_2, \cdots, T_k) = \begin{bmatrix} f(T_1,T_1) & f(T_1,T_2) & \cdots & f(T_1,T_k) \\ f(T_2,T_1) & f(T_2,T_2) & \cdots & f(T_2,T_k) \\ \vdots & \vdots & \ddots & \cdots \\ f(T_k,T_1) & f(T_k,T_1) & \ldots & f(T_k,T_k) \end{bmatrix} \tag{17}$$

Each element of the Gram matrix for these n vectors can be regarded as a pixel on the graph. Therefore, the generated Gram matrix can be used as training samples for the hypergraph neural network. By collecting a large amount of data samples and feeding them into the hypergraph neural network to generate the device's intrinsic security fingerprint model, the robustness and accuracy of the model can be improved.

Furthermore, to reduce the dimensionality of Gram Angular Fields (GAFs) and decrease computational complexity, we employ Piecewise Aggregation Approximation (PAA). This method calculates the piecewise aggregate average, preserving the trend-change characteristics of the sequence. In the context of continuously sampled Channel State Information (CSI) fingerprints, the integration of CSI into the GAF transformation is depicted as follows:

$$GAF_{CSI}(t) = \begin{bmatrix} cos(\theta_{t,t_1}) & \ldots & cos(\theta_{t,t_n}) \\ \vdots & \ddots & \vdots \\ cos(\theta_{t_n,t_1}) & \ldots & cos(\theta_{t_n,t_n}) \end{bmatrix} \tag{18}$$

where θ_{t_i,t_j} is the cumulative angular difference between $H(t_i)X(t_i) + N(t_i)$ and $H(t_j)X(t_j) + N(t_j)$. Here, $H(t)$ represents the channel frequency response at time t, $X(t)$ is the transmitted signal, and $N(t)$ is the noise. This function θ calculates the cumulative angular difference for the CSI fingerprints transformed through the channel response over time. This integrated approach provides a comprehensive view of how CSI data, influenced by channel characteristics and noise, is transformed into a meaningful GAF matrix, capturing the temporal dynamics essential for security fingerprint recognition.

4.2. Hypergraph Neural Networks

Next, we employ a hypergraph neural network (HGNN) for model construction [4], leveraging the open-source code provided in the referenced paper to process experimental data. In the realm of machine learning, especially in context-specific scenarios, handling complex data structures is often essential. In this study, the intricacies lie in the relationships between data points within the acquired two-dimensional graph structure and between adjacent graph-structured data. These relationships not only reflect the correlations among device physical features but also capture the dynamic changes in intrinsic security fingerprints over time in real-world environments—changes that are fundamental to defining intrinsic security fingerprints.

Particularly, the sensitivity of HGNN to specific fingerprint features, identified in the preceding section, plays a pivotal role in the training of the fingerprint model. This sensitivity allows HGNN to efficiently process and analyze fingerprint data, thereby enhancing the adaptability of the model to environmental changes. During the model training phase, it is crucial to include input samples that encompass continuous data from various real-world environments, ensuring the model's robustness under different conditions.

In practical scenarios, representing a group of intricately correlated objects merely as a graph model may be inadequate. To address this, Berge [13] introduced hypergraphs in 1970 as an extension of graph methods. Hypergraphs are adept at considering multiadic relations between objects, making them a suitable choice for modeling collaborative networks and complex interactions between data. This suitability is especially apparent in our application, where the hypergraph model effectively captures and processes the complex interactions inherent in device security fingerprint data.

According to Berge's hypergraph definition, let $\mathcal{V} = \{v_1, v_2, \ldots, v_N\}$ be a finite set. A hypergraph on v is defined by $\mathcal{E} = \left\{e_1, e_2, \ldots, e_{|\mathcal{E}|}\right\}$ of hyperedges. Each hyperedge e_i is a non-empty subset of v, satisfying

$$\bigcup_{i=1}^{|\mathcal{E}|} e_i = \mathcal{V}, \quad e_i \neq \varnothing \quad (i = 1, 2, \ldots, |\mathcal{E}|) \tag{19}$$

Incorporating clock deviation (CD), Channel State Information (CSI), and GAF parameters, the association matrix H and hyperedge weight equation $\omega(e)$ are redefined:

$$h(v_i, e_j; \delta_{CD}, \Theta_{CSI}, \gamma_{GAF}) = \begin{cases} 1 + \alpha \cdot \delta_{CD}(v_i) + \beta \cdot \Theta_{CSI}(v_i) + \gamma \cdot \gamma_{GAF}(v_i) \\ 0, \end{cases} \tag{20}$$

Here, γ_{GAF} represents the GAF parameters influencing the hypergraph structure. The weights α, β, and γ are adjustment factors for clock deviation, CSI, and GAF parameters, respectively. This formulation enables the hypergraph model to capture the intrinsic security fingerprints of devices more accurately, considering the influence of clock deviations, wireless channel responses, and GAF-transformed features.

Figure 2 illustrates the general framework of the hypergraph neural network, comprising two main modules: hypergraph modeling and hypergraph convolution.

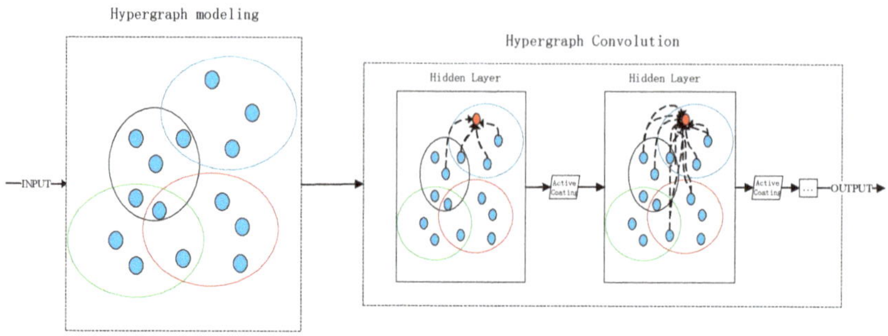

Figure 2. Schematic diagram of the hypergraph neural network model.

The hypergraph neural network also follows a neighborhood aggregation scheme, calculating the vector representation of the central node through recursive aggregation and transformation of the neighborhood node representations [14]. This process is accomplished by convolutional operators. In traditional neural networks, the convolutional kernel operates within an ordered, fixed-size neighborhood of nodes, as shown in Figure 3a. Hypergraph convolution, as illustrated in Figure 3b, aggregates the features of the red node and its neighborhood (i.e., nodes connected by dashed lines) through weighted aggregation. The neighborhood of nodes in the hypergraph is unordered and variable in size, making it challenging to obtain a unified convolutional kernel for convolutional operations.

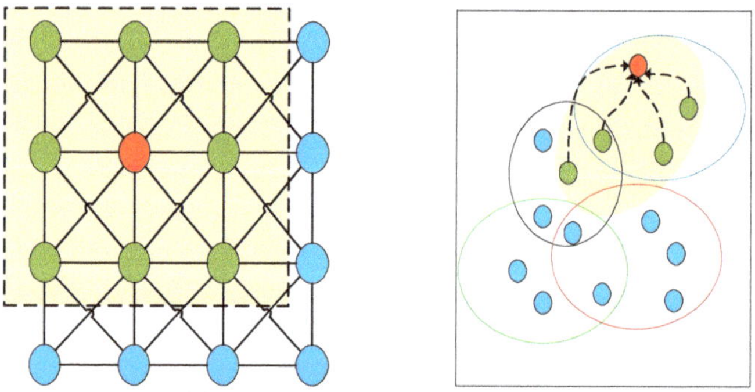

(**a**) (**b**)

Figure 3. Difference in convolution between regular data and hypergraph structure data. (**a**) Convolution on regular data in Euclidean space; (**b**) convolution on hypergraph.

Neural networks fundamentally possess the ability to learn from data, typically consisting of training and testing datasets. The network initially learns a model from the training set and then evaluates the practical predictive capability of the obtained model using the test data. Both hypergraph neural networks and traditional neural networks utilize forward propagation to compute output values and employ backward propagation to adjust weights and biases. During forward propagation, the input signals and their corresponding weights are multiplied, and an activation function is applied to the sum of these products to enhance the model's expressive power. Backward propagation enables the training of deep neural networks by first calculating the network's error, determining the gradients of the parameters through optimization methods, and finally updating parameter values in the opposite direction of the loss function gradient.

To ensure the robustness of the model under different environmental conditions, a specific time period T is defined. In this period, a novel approach is employed to handle the data points corresponding to adjacent graph structures collected at intervals of t. These n graphs are connected into a hyperedge, forming a hypergraph where nodes represent data points, and edges capture relationships between adjacent time points. Such a hypergraph structure within a specific time period T serves as a sample, providing a more comprehensive reflection of the temporal evolution of the data and the complex relationships between nodes.

Next, a hypergraph neural network (HGNN) is introduced to process and learn from the hypergraph. During the training phase, initial features are assigned to each node in the hypergraph, which may originate from the information obtained during the feature transformation step. Through hypergraph convolution layers, HGNN effectively considers higher-order relationships between nodes and the evolution between adjacent time points, thereby better capturing the dynamic characteristics of the data.

Emphasis is placed on the importance of adaptive training during the model training process, ensuring that the model exhibits robustness under different environmental conditions. This implies that our model needs to take as input hypergraphs composed of continuous data from various real-world environments, enhancing its adaptability to different environmental changes.

Ultimately, the trained HGNN model can be applied to various tasks, including predicting the states of nodes at future time points and learning higher-order relationships. This versatility demonstrates the strong potential of our approach in fields such as dynamic system modeling and time series prediction.

5. Experimental Conclusions

5.1. Experimental Setup and Evaluation Methods

During the model evaluation phase, an independent test set was utilized to validate the model's performance, with a specific focus on its fingerprint recognition accuracy in outdoor environments. By analyzing the model's output results, we assessed not only accuracy but also the model's robustness and stability. Based on the analysis outcomes, multiple rounds of model adjustments and optimizations were performed to ensure the model's high reliability in practical applications within real-world environments.

We employed two common performance metrics in machine learning, precision and recall, to evaluate the classification model. Precision and recall are defined as follows:

$$Precision = \frac{TP}{TP + FP} \tag{21}$$

$$Recall = \frac{TP}{TP + FN} \tag{22}$$

Precision refers to the proportion of samples predicted as positive by the model that are indeed positive. High precision indicates accurate positive predictions by the model.

Recall represents the proportion of actual positives that the model successfully predicted as positive. High recall indicates the model's ability to capture actual positives.

There is a trade-off between these two metrics. Improving precision may lead to a decrease in recall and vice versa. Therefore, to comprehensively consider both metrics, we used the F1 Score, which is the harmonic mean of precision and recall:

$$F1 = 2 \times \frac{Precision \times Recall}{Precision + Recall} \tag{23}$$

In this study, a diverse array of physical characteristics from various IoT devices was amassed in real-world settings for experimental analysis. Post data preprocessing, these attributes were input into a hypergraph neural network model. The implementation took place on a personal computing device running Ubuntu 20.04 and equipped with a 3.20 GHz CPU and 16.00 GB RAM. The device ensemble included wireless cameras, smart sockets, intelligent desk lamps, Raspberry Pi, and STM32 microcontrollers, among others, forming a broad spectrum of IoT and industrial control devices, as depicted in Figure 4. It is noteworthy that Figure 4 illustrates merely a subset of the devices engaged in this study.

Figure 4. Partial experimental devices.

The experimental setup incorporated meticulous environmental controls to simulate varying conditions. This was achieved through the deployment of humidifiers and heaters strategically positioned to modulate ambient temperature and humidity levels. These conditions were precisely monitored using hygrometers, ensuring a controlled yet dynamic experimental environment. Such measures were pivotal in evaluating the IoT devices' performance and resilience under different environmental scenarios.

In our experiment, the use of humidifiers and heaters was pivotal for creating specific environmental conditions. Humidifiers were set to maintain a relative humidity ranging from 50% to 70%, depending on the scenario, simulating conditions from moderately dry to extremely humid environments. Heaters, on the other hand, were used to create temperature variations from 10 °C to 30 °C, replicating both cool and hot conditions. For instance, to simulate a tropical environment, the humidifier was adjusted to maintain a humidity of approximately 65%, and the heater was set to 25 °C. The environmental conditions were continuously monitored using digital hygrometers, ensuring precise control. These settings were crucial to assess the functionality and resilience of IoT devices under varying climatic conditions.

5.2. Analysis of Experimental Results

In the context of our experimental paradigm, consistent environmental conditions were meticulously maintained. This included a controlled ambient temperature of 20 °C and a relative humidity of 70%. Critically, the duration for each Channel State Information (CSI) collection was set at 20s, aligning with our earlier discussion on the Gram–Schmidt process for CSI transformation. A series of trials were conducted across diverse electronic devices, rigorously evaluating the model's precision, recall, and F1 score metrics. The ensuing results are succinctly encapsulated in Table 1.

Table 1. Precision, recall, and F1 score for different devices.

Devices	Precision (%)	Recall (%)	F1
Device-1	97.8	97.8	0.978
Device-2	98.1	96.7	0.974
Device-3	98.0	97.5	0.97
Device-4	97.2	98.0	0.976
Device-5	97.3	97.1	0.972

The experiments indicate that our model demonstrates highly reliable performance in recognizing the intrinsic security fingerprints of devices amid the comprehensive challenges posed by physical noise fluctuations in the environment. The combined assessment of precision and recall highlights the model's outstanding accuracy and recall capabilities in recognizing device-specific intrinsic security fingerprints, particularly in outdoor environments. This underscores its adaptability to complex conditions in real-world settings.

Furthermore, this paper analyzes the ROC curves and AUC of the authentication results for Device 1 in three typical environments, as shown in Figure 5:

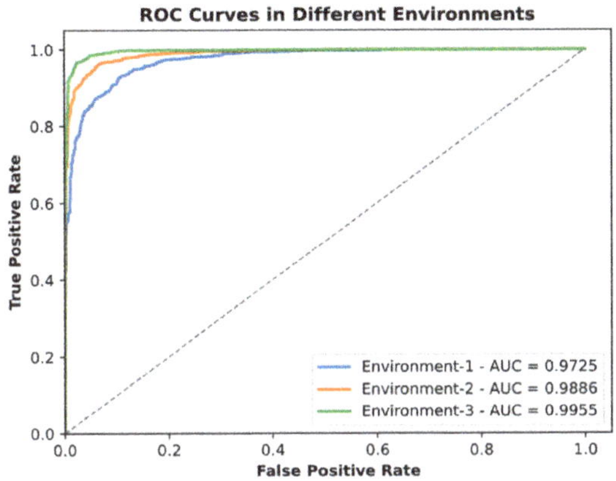

Figure 5. ROC curves in different environments.

In Figure 5, we explicate the ROC curves for Device 1 authentication across three carefully delineated environments. Environment 1, denoted by the blue line, illustrates a quintessential laboratory setting meticulously maintained at a constant temperature and shielded from electromagnetic disturbances, thereby providing a benchmark for optimal device performance. Environment 2, represented by the orange line, mimics an industrial milieu with prevalent electronic disruptions and thermal fluctuations, challenging the device's identification fidelity. Lastly, Environment 3, shown in green, embodies an outdoor landscape, subject to the whims of nature, with variable weather patterns and the potential for erratic signal interference, testing the limits of the device's discriminating abilities. The AUC values, alluding to proximity with unity, affirm the model's exceptional aptitude in distinguishing true positives from false positives within these multifarious conditions. This suggests the model's high efficacy for the classification task at hand.

The paper conducted recognition accuracy tests for device-specific intrinsic security fingerprints under different temperature and humidity conditions:

The experimental results depicted in Figure 6 articulate the model's recognition accuracy for device intrinsic security fingerprints under varying room temperatures and humidity conditions. The comparison table presented below contrasts these data with the accuracy obtained from traditional direct CSI fingerprint recognition methods. It highlights the superiority of the proposed model in terms of adaptability and robustness across diverse environmental scenarios, from cold and dry to hot and humid, offering robust support for real-world applications under fluctuating climatic conditions.

The bar chart in Figure 7 provides a detailed comparison of recognition accuracies for intrinsic security fingerprints between two methodologies: the direct Channel State Information (CSI) method (indicated by blue bars) and the enhanced model proposed by this research (represented by red bars).

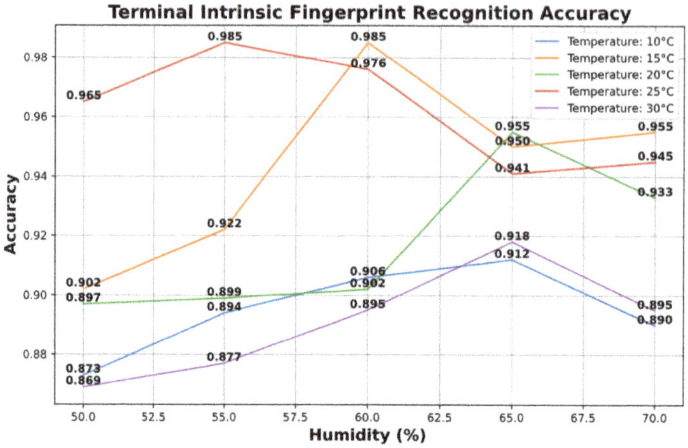

Figure 6. Recognition accuracy of device intrinsic security fingerprints.

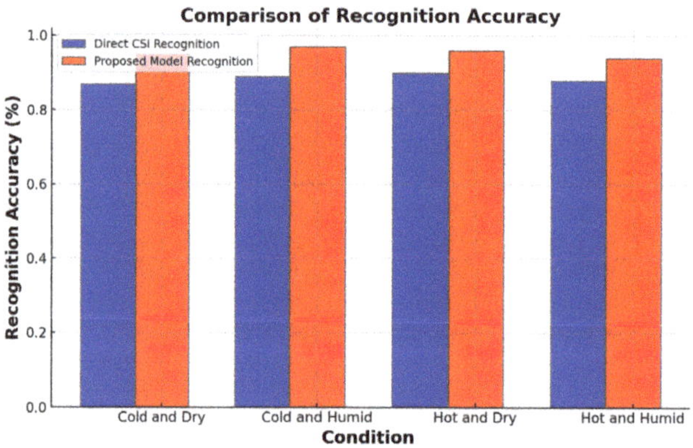

Figure 7. Fingerprint recognition accuracy under variable environmental conditions.

For 'Cold and Dry' conditions, the direct CSI method shows an accuracy of 87%, which is significantly improved to 95% by the proposed model. In 'Cold and Humid' scenarios, the direct CSI recognition stands at 89% accuracy, whereas the proposed model achieves a notable increase to 97%. The trend of improvement continues in 'Hot and Dry' conditions, where the direct CSI method records an accuracy of 90%, and the proposed model registers a higher accuracy of 96%. Lastly, under 'Hot and Humid' conditions, the direct CSI method's accuracy is 88%, while the proposed model demonstrates a marked improvement with an accuracy of 94%.

This comparative illustration clearly demonstrates the superior performance of the proposed model across all tested environmental conditions. The marked improvements in accuracy, particularly in extreme conditions, emphasize the robustness of the proposed model and its suitability for diverse operational scenarios.

To comprehensively evaluate the stability and reliability of our method in real-world environments, we conducted an extensive three-day continuous test using multiple devices, with device authentication being performed every 30 min. These devices were deployed across various IoT application scenarios to maximally simulate real-world environmental changes and interactions. Table 2 presents the performance of each device during the testing period, including metrics such as precision, recall, and F1 score. These indicators reflect the consistency and robustness of our method across different devices.

Table 2. Precision, recall, and F1 score for devices in a continuous test.

Devices	Precision (%)	Recall (%)	F1 (%)
Device-1	96.3	93.4	94.5
Device-2	94.0	92.1	93.0
Device-3	94.8	93.0	94.5
Device-4	97.1	95.0	96.0

Based on the above experimental results, it can be observed that we have constructed an endogenous fingerprint recognition model using a hypergraph neural network, which adapts well to diverse environments and improves fingerprint recognition accuracy in outdoor settings. The hypergraph network demonstrates significant advantages in endogenous security fingerprint feature recognition. Firstly, it effectively handles complex nonlinear correlations, capturing correlated high-order features in the inherent security fingerprints of devices. Secondly, the hypergraph network adapts to dynamic environments by capturing the interactive influences of adjacent sequential signals, thereby enhancing the accuracy and reliability of the fingerprint recognition system in practical environments. Lastly, the network handles high-dimensional data, aiding in capturing the spatiotemporal features of inherent security fingerprints, thus enhancing the system's adaptability to dynamic environments. Considering these advantages, the hypergraph network proves to be an effective tool for fingerprint feature recognition in dynamic environments.

The proposed solution in this paper constructs a robust and adaptable endogenous fingerprint recognition model in real environments. It not only performs exceptionally well under laboratory conditions but also, through multiple rounds of adjustments and optimizations, ensures high reliability in real-world applications.

6. Relate Works

Device intrinsic security fingerprint recognition is an identity verification method that utilizes the hardware features of mobile or terminal devices to identify and verify the identity of users or devices. As a component of intrinsic security, device intrinsic security fingerprint recognition is regarded as the practical application of intrinsic security strategies, embedding uniqueness and non-forgeability into the device itself.

The concept of intrinsic security was initially proposed by Jiang Weiyu and others [15]. Its objective is to reduce or eliminate dependence on external security measures and protect data and resources by constructing security within the system itself. In this field, there is a wealth of related research applied to the study of biometrics-based authentication methods, mobile device security, exploration of hardware security, investigation of device recognition and identity verification under dynamic environmental conditions, improvement of the performance of intrinsic fingerprint recognition systems using machine learning and deep learning methods, and research on enhancing the security of Internet of Things (IoT) devices [16].

Previous research primarily focused on the performance of intrinsic fingerprint recognition in static environments. These studies utilized traditional feature extraction and machine learning methods, typically tested and validated under controlled environmental conditions [17,18]. However, the performance of these methods may be affected when faced with dynamic environments, such as outdoor settings, fluctuations in temperature, changes in humidity, and variations in lighting conditions [19]. This is because intrinsic fingerprints often rely on device hardware features, which may change in continuously evolving environments.

To enhance the performance of intrinsic fingerprint recognition in dynamic environments, this paper adopts real-time data collection and introduces the Gram angle field transformation and hypergraph neural network to better capture the spatiotemporal characteristics of intrinsic fingerprints. The Gram angle field theory was initially proposed by Hungarian scientist, engineer, and physicist Dennis Gabor in 1946 [20]. The Gram angle field is a mathematical tool based on Gabor transformations used to analyze the texture and structural features of images. This method was initially employed in signal processing and communication fields and later became widely used in texture analysis, feature extraction, and image recognition tasks, especially in biometric recognition and image processing fields [21,22]. The Gram angle field is a local feature extraction method that uses kernel functions of different scales and directions, enabling it to capture features of different spatial frequencies and directions in sample data. It possesses a certain degree of rotation invariance, meaning it can recognize texture features with different orientations without being influenced by object rotation. The Gram angle field achieves a good balance between frequency and spatial domains, making it widely applicable in various applications.

Graph convolutional networks (GCN) and hypergraph neural networks are both branches of graph neural networks, with GCN providing the foundation for the development of hypergraph neural networks [23]. In graph theory and mathematics, a hypergraph is a generalized graph data structure used to represent relationships between sets. Unlike traditional graphs where edges connect two nodes, the edges (commonly referred to as hyperedges) of a hypergraph can connect multiple nodes. This flexibility allows hypergraphs to represent many-to-many relationships more effectively, making them suitable for modeling complex relationship networks. Hypergraph neural networks are a type of deep learning model designed to handle complex hypergraph data structures, not just traditional graph data [24]. Hypergraph neural networks extend the scope of traditional graph neural networks to accommodate the characteristics of hypergraph data.

7. Conclusions

This paper proposes an innovative approach that successfully constructs an adaptive device intrinsic security fingerprint recognition system capable of handling environmental changes through real-time data collection, Gram angle field transformation, and hypergraph neural networks. The system effectively extracts spatiotemporal features of device intrinsic security fingerprints in real outdoor environments, significantly improving the accuracy and reliability of device intrinsic security fingerprint recognition in dynamic settings. Experimental results demonstrate that the proposed method achieves satisfactory outcomes in outdoor environments, achieving a device intrinsic security fingerprint recognition accuracy of 99.5%. Through testing under different environmental conditions, the robustness of the model to temperature and humidity variations has been verified, providing strong support for practical applications.

The success of this study overcomes the challenges of device intrinsic security fingerprint recognition in dynamic environments, bringing significant advancements to the security and authentication of mobile and Internet of Things (IoT) devices. Future research directions may focus on further enhancing the model's performance and considering its application in broader scenarios. By continuously improving the robustness and performance of device intrinsic security fingerprint recognition systems, we aim to provide more trustworthy and secure means of identity verification for IoT terminal devices, addressing the continuously changing real-world environmental conditions.

Author Contributions: Conceptualization, Z.X.; methodology, Z.X.; writing—review and editing, Z.X. and B.Z.; visualization, T.Z.; supervision, G.Z.; project administration, T.Z. All authors have read and agreed to the published version of the manuscript.

Funding: This work was supported by the National Key R&D Program of China [2022YFB31043001].

Data Availability Statement: We confirm that the data supporting the findings of this study are available within the article Additional data that support the findings of this study are available from the corresponding author upon reasonable request.

Acknowledgments: We would like to acknowledge the collective efforts of all the authors in this study.

Conflicts of Interest: Zesheng Xi, Bo Zhang and Tao Zhang are employed by State Grid Smart Grid Research Institute Co., Ltd. The authors declare no conflicts of interest. The funders had no role in the design of the study; in the collection, analyses, or interpretation of data; in the writing of the manuscript; or in the decision to publish the results.

References

1. Kaur, B.; Dadkhah, S.; Shoeleh, F.; Neto, E.C.P.; Xiong, P.; Iqbal, S.; Lamontagne, P.; Ray, S.; Ghorbani, A.A. Internet of things (IoT) security dataset evolution: Challenges and future directions. *Internet Things* **2023**, *22*, 100780.
2. Jurcut, A.; Niculcea, T.; Ranaweera, P.; Le-Khac, N.A. Security considerations for Internet of Things: A survey. *SN Comput. Sci.* **2020**, *1*, 193.
3. Dean, A.; Agyeman, M.O. A study of the advances in IoT security. In Proceedings of the 2nd International Symposium on Computer Science and Intelligent Control, Stockholm, Sweden, 21–23 September 2018; pp. 1–5.
4. Malhotra, P.; Singh, Y.; Anand, P.; Bangotra, D.K.; Singh, P.K.; Hong, W.C. Internet of things: Evolution, concerns and security challenges. *Sensors* **2021**, *21*, 1809.
5. Rachit, B.S.; Ragiri, P.R. Security trends in Internet of Things: A survey. *SN Appl. Sci.* **2021**, *3*, 121.
6. Xu, K.; Fu, S.; Li, Q.; Liu, B.; Jiang, W.; Wu, B.; Feng, X. Research Progress on the Architecture of Endogenous Security System on the Internet. *J. Comput. Sci.* **2021**, *44*, 2149.
7. Garibo-i-Orts, Ò.; Firbas, N.; Sebastiá, L.; Conejero, J.A. Gramian angular fields for leveraging pretrained computer vision models with anomalous diffusion trajectories. *Phys. Rev. E* **2023**, *107*, 034138.
8. Feng, Y.; You, H.; Zhang, Z.; Ji, R.; Gao, Y. Hypergraph neural networks. In Proceedings of the AAAI Conference on Artificial Intelligence, Honolulu, HI, USA, 27 January–1 February 2019; Volume 33, pp. 3558–3565.
9. Zhang, D.; Wu, D.; Niu, K.; Wang, X.; Zhang, F.; Yao, J.; Jiang, D.; Qin, F. Practical issues and challenges in CSI-based integrated sensing and communication. In Proceedings of the 2022 IEEE International Conference on Communications Workshops (ICC Workshops), Seoul, Republic of Korea, 16–20 May 2022.
10. Gringoli, F.; Schulz, M.; Link, J.; Hollick, M. Free your CSI: A channel state information extraction platform for modern Wi-Fi chipsets. In Proceedings of the 13th International Workshop on Wireless Network Testbeds, Experimental Evaluation & Characterization, Los Cabos, Mexico, 25 October 2019; pp. 21–28.
11. Schulz, M.; Wegemer, D.; Hollick, M. Nexmon: Build your own wi-fi testbeds with low-level mac and phy-access using firmware patches on off-the-shelf mobile devices. In Proceedings of the 11th Workshop on Wireless Network Testbeds, Experimental Evaluation & Characterization, Snowbird, UT, USA, 20 October 2017; pp. 59–66.
12. Wang, J.; Li, S.; Ji, W.; Jiang, T.; Song, B. A T-CNN time series classification method based on Gram matrix. *Sci. Rep.* **2022**, *12*, 15731.
13. Berge, C. *Graphes*; Gauthier-Villars: Paris, France, 1983.
14. Yu, J.; Tao, D.; Wang, M. Adaptive hypergraph learning and its application in image classification. *IEEE Trans. Image Process.* **2012**, *21*, 3262–3272.
15. Jiang, W.; Liu, B.; Wang, C. Endogenous Security Network Architecture. *Telecommun. Sci.* **2019**, *35*, 20–28.
16. Yu, J.; Hu, A.; Li, G.; Peng, L. A robust RF fingerprinting approach using multisampling convolutional neural network. *IEEE Internet Things J.* **2019**, *6*, 6786–6799.
17. Christin, N.; Safavi-Naini, R. Financial cryptography and data security. In Proceedings of the 18th International Conference, Christ Church, Barbados, 3–7 March 2014.
18. Abbas, S.; Nasir, Q.; Nouichi, D.; Abdelsalam, M.; Abu Talib, M.; Abu Waraga, O.; Khan, A.U.R. Improving security of the Internet of Things via RF fingerprinting based device identification system. *Neural Comput. Appl.* **2021**, *33*, 14753–14769.
19. de Souza, C.A.; Westphall, C.B.; Machado, R.B.; Loffi, L.; Westphall, C.M.; Geronimo, G.A. Intrusion detection and prevention in fog based iot environments: A systematic literature review. *Comput. Netw.* **2022**, *214*, 109154.
20. Gabor, D. Electrical engineers-part III: Radio and communication engineering. *J. Inst.* **1946**, *93*, 39.
21. Tang, W.; Jia, F.; Wang, X. Image Large Rotation and Scale Estimation Using the Gabor Filter. *Electronics* **2022**, *11*, 3471.
22. Miao, Y.; Jeon, J.Y.; Kong, Y.; Park, G. Phase-based displacement measurement on a straight edge using an optimal complex Gabor filter. *Mech. Syst. Signal Process.* **2022**, *164*, 108224.
23. Vashishth, S.; Sanyal, S.; Nitin, V.; Talukdar, P. Composition-based multi-relational graph convolutional networks. *arXiv* **2019**, arXiv:1911.03082.
24. Jin, D.; Huo, C.; Dang, J.; Zhu, P.; Zhang, W.; Pedrycz, W.; Wu, L. Heterogeneous graph neural networks using self-supervised reciprocally contrastive learning. *arXiv* **2022**, arXiv:2205.00256.

electronics

Article

Secure Device-to-Device Communication in IoT: Fuzzy Identity from Wireless Channel State Information for Identity-Based Encryption

Bo Zhang [1,2,*], Tao Zhang [1], Zesheng Xi [1], Ping Chen [3], Jin Wei [3,4] and Yu Liu [3,4]

1 State Grid Smart Grid Research Institute Co., Ltd., Beijing 102201, China; zhangtao@geiri.sgcc.com.cn (T.Z.); xizesheng@geiri.sgcc.com.cn (Z.X.)
2 School of Cyber Science and Engineering, Shanghai Jiao Tong University, Shanghai 200240, China
3 Institute of BigData, Fudan University, Shanghai 200437, China; pchen@fudan.edu.cn (P.C.); jwei17@fudan.edu.cn (J.W.); yuliu21@m.fudan.edu.cn (Y.L.)
4 School of Computer Science, Fudan University, Shanghai 200433, China
* Correspondence: zhangbo@geiri.sgcc.com.cn

Abstract: With the rapid development of the Internet of Things (IoT), ensuring secure communication between devices has become a crucial challenge. This paper proposes a novel secure communication solution by extracting wireless channel state information (CSI) features from IoT devices to generate a device identity. Due to the instability of the wireless channel, the CSI features are fuzzy and time-varying; thus, we a employ locally sensitive hashing (LSH) algorithm to ensure the stability of the generated identity in a dynamically changing wireless channel environment. Furthermore, zero-knowledge proofs are utilized to guarantee the authenticity and effectiveness of the generated identity. Finally, the identity generated using the aforementioned approach is integrated into an IBE communication scheme, which involves the fuzzy extraction of channel state information from IoT devices, stable identity extraction for fuzzy IoT devices using LSH, and the use of zero-knowledge proofs to ensure the authenticity of the generated identity. This identity is then employed as the identity information in identity-based encryption (IBE), constructing the device's public key for achieving confidential communication between devices.

Keywords: Internet of Things; wireless channel state information; fuzzy identity; locally sensitive hashing; identity-based encryption; secure communication

1. Introduction

With rapid technological advancements, the Internet of Things (IoT) is undergoing a remarkable and swift expansion, emerging as a key driving force in today's digital era. The rapid proliferation and application of the IoT span diverse domains, ranging from smart homes and industrial automation to healthcare and urban infrastructure. This technology's dynamic growth plays a pivotal role in enhancing the quality of life, fostering industrial innovation, and building intelligent societies. The convergence of sensors, embedded devices, and interconnected networks enables various physical objects to exchange real-time information, creating an extensive ecosystem of data. The widespread collection and analysis of these data provide businesses, governments, and individuals with deeper insights and the foundation for intelligent decision making. From the development of smart cities to advancements in precision agriculture, the IoT is profoundly transforming the ways we live and work.

Despite the rapid technological advancements that bring unprecedented connectivity and intelligence, security communication remains a significant challenge in the IoT. The use of traditional Public Key Infrastructure (PKI) systems, especially in large-scale deployments of IoT devices, inevitably faces the daunting task of establishing massive Public Key

Certification Centers. Managing the identity information of a vast number of devices not only introduces complexity and cost challenges but also carries the potential risks of performance bottlenecks and single points of failure.

Adopting an identity-based encryption (IBE) solution for establishing communication systems presents unique challenges, even though IBE can avoid the implementation of massive Public Key Certification Centers. Since the physical information of IoT devices often exhibits fuzziness, traditional IBE struggles to directly construct a stable device identity based on these ambiguous physical features. This challenge involves maintaining the consistency of the device identity in a dynamically changing environment to ensure the feasibility of secure communication. In such a scenario, the solution requires an innovative combination of physical information extraction and secure communication technologies to address the complexity and security requirements of IoT device identity management.

In addressing the aforementioned challenges, we introduced a novel device-to-device communication solution for the Internet of Things (IoT). Firstly, by extracting the wireless channel state information (CSI) from IoT devices, we successfully generated stable physical features for these devices. Leveraging the wireless communication characteristics among devices, we established a device identity. Subsequently, addressing the issue of the fuzzy nature of physical features potentially causing disruptions and affecting the stability of device identity, we introduced a locally sensitive hashing (LSH) algorithm. Through LSH, we were able to generate stable identity representations for the fuzzy physical features. This process not only ensures the consistency of the device identity in dynamic environments but also provides a reliable foundation for establishing secure communication. Finally, we applied this stable identity representation to the identity-based encryption (IBE) framework, constructing device public keys. Through this innovative integration, we achieved confidential communication between devices, presenting a new paradigm to address challenges faced by existing Public Key Infrastructure (PKI) and traditional IBE solutions.

Our contributions are as follows:

1. We propose a novel device-to-device communication solution for the Internet of Things (IoT). By extracting the wireless channel state information from IoT devices, we successfully generated stable physical features for these devices and combined them with IBE to implement secret communication based on CSI.
2. We propose a method to generate a fixed identity identifier from the fuzzy device CSI. This method allows the generation of a unique identity identifier from a stable identity feature in a deterministic manner, which can be used as the device public key information in identity-based encryption (IBE).
3. We introduce an identity verification scheme based on zero-knowledge proofs. This scheme can prove that the identity information generated by the device is derived from its CSI without revealing the CSI itself, thus safeguarding the privacy of the device.

2. Related Work

2.1. Identity-Based Encryption

In the year 2001, Boneh and Franklin [1]; Sakai, Ohgishi, and Kasahara [2]; and Cocks [3], independently proposed three identity-based encryption (IBE) schemes, marking the initiation of a new era in identity-based cryptography research. Both the Boneh–Franklin and Sakai–Ohgishi–Kasahara schemes utilize pairings satisfying bilinear mappings. Boneh and Franklin, employing the random oracle model, demonstrated that their scheme achieves indistinguishability against an adaptive chosen identity and chosen ciphertext attacks (IND-ID-CCA). The widespread application of bilinear pairings in cryptographic scheme design was a result of their work, guiding the development of identity-based cryptography. Subsequent works have often adopted methods similar to the Boneh–Franklin method, utilizing pairings with bilinearity to construct IBE schemes. In 2005, Waters [4] designed an efficient IBE scheme that does not rely on a random oracle.

In recent years, many scholars have proposed various improvements to IBE. One major challenge in the real-world deployment of IBE is the key escrow problem. If the private key generator (PKG) is malicious, it can decrypt all messages. Khaleda Afroaz [5] proposed an IBE scheme based on anonymous identities, utilizing ring signatures to address this issue. In this process, identities are signed with ring signatures generated by a ring authority (RA) to mask the actual identity. Private keys are obtained from a key generation authority (KGA), preventing the KGA from knowing which key corresponds to which recipient. In the application of IBE schemes, V. Veeresh et al. [6] comprehensively overviewed the applications of IBE in cloud computing. Van-Quang-Huy Nguyen et al. [7] proposed a private identity-based encryption scheme for key management. Y. Liu et al. [8] introduced a hierarchical identity-based encryption scheme for key distribution in wireless sensor networks, reducing the computational time and saving storage space compared to IBE-based key distribution for wireless sensor nodes.

2.2. Channel State Information

In recent years, scholars both domestically and internationally have proposed numerous wireless device authentication schemes based on physical layer fingerprints. X. Wan et al. [9] employed the Received Signal Strength Indicator (RSSI) technique for device identification and monitoring. To enhance the spatial resolution and improve the accuracy of attack detection, multiple antennas were deployed at various landmarks to collect richer RSSI data. A. Mahmood et al. [10] introduced a distributed wireless device authentication method based on a Channel Impulse Response (CIR), enhancing the system detection accuracy through multipoint sensing technology. Q. Wu et al. [11] utilized Radio Frequency (RF) fingerprints for wireless device authentication, employing a Recursive Neural Network (RNN) to autonomously learn RF fingerprint features without manual intervention.

The RSSI, RSS, and CIR can be used to describe the characteristics of the wireless channel, but they provide limited channel information at a single frequency point. In contrast, CSI contains both amplitude and phase information for each OFDM subcarrier, offering more detailed wireless channel features and achieving a superior identification performance. To address this, R. Liao et al. [12] proposed a CSI-based device authentication scheme, employing a CNN as the recognition algorithm for physical layer fingerprints. Meanwhile, C. Shi et al. [13] utilized an SVM to identify user channel fingerprints. Ribouh et al. [14] designed a CSI-based key generation method for use in vehicular environments, treating the CSI values of each subcarrier as random sources and using a new QAM demodulation quantizer (QAM-Dem-Quan) to extract bit values for key generation. Ji et al. [15] proposed a key generation scheme combining adaptive link selection and a two-step decorrelation algorithm, leveraging CSI information. Wang et al. [16] combined CSI features with the static position of devices, constructing CSI data into CSI images. Through a deep learning-based recognition and authentication model, they learned the mapping relationship between CSI and the device identity, achieving device authentication. Wang et al. [17] introduced a physical layer authentication scheme based on Gaussian Process channel prediction. By establishing a mapping between historical CSI information and the sender's location information, they predicted the next legitimate CSI information for identity recognition. Additionally, they proposed a one-class authentication (OCA) scheme that does not require any channel information from attackers.

2.3. Zero-Knowledge Proof

Many researchers are concerned about privacy issues in data sharing and have proposed various data sharing schemes with privacy protection features. Lu et al. [18] introduced a novel approach based on federated learning and deep reinforcement learning to alleviate the transmission overhead and address the privacy concerns of data providers. The asynchronous federated learning mechanism, learning models from edge data, minimizes the total cost by selecting participating nodes and further enhances the efficiency of federated learning. To validate the authenticity of collected data and protect user privacy, a study [19] employs homomorphic encryption technology to construct a ciphertext space, ensuring the normal operation of data services under data encryption. Based on this ciphertext space, they propose an identity-based signature scheme and a two-tier batch signature verification scheme.

A zero-knowledge proof (ZKP) refers to the ability of a prover to convince a verifier of the correctness of a statement without revealing any useful information. This concept was introduced by S. Goldwasser and others [20]. The security of zero-knowledge proofs relies primarily on cryptographic assumptions related to challenging problems, such as discrete logarithms and elliptic curve problems. The zero-knowledge proof system is widely used for authentication because it has the following properties:

- Completeness: Referring to the assurance that anything valid generated by an honest prover can be successfully verified by an honest verifier.
- Soundness: Ensuring that for any prover without access to the secret, they cannot forge something that would pass verification.
- Honest verifier with zero knowledge: Ensuring that, for an honest verifier, apart from knowing the outcome of the proof (i.e., the known parameters mentioned above), no other information is revealed.

In recent years, ZKPs have been preliminarily applied and practiced in the context of IoT access security. Walshe et al. [21] proposed an IoT and sensor device authentication scheme based on non-interactive zero-knowledge proofs. Unlike traditional ZKP, the authors replaced the ZKP's NP-hard problem and used Merkle trees to create authentication challenges. The authors conducted simulations to evaluate the performance of non-interactive zero-knowledge proofs relative to traditional zero-knowledge proofs. Salleras et al. applied it to scenarios such as 5G services for user identity authentication [22]. Service providers can verify proofs and grant services without knowing the user's identity. Users can remain anonymous when using the service by proving the ownership of their signature without revealing any other information.

Zero-knowledge proofs have been applied as a privacy protection technology in various fields, such as traffic management, the crowdsourced IoT, identity management schemes in blockchain, and vehicular ad hoc networks [23]. However, with the exponential growth of IoT devices in various applications, ensuring the efficient, secure, and bidirectional authentication of relevant devices without leaking any information remains crucial.

3. Wireless Channel State Feature Extraction

3.1. *Multipath Effects*

Wireless signals typically propagate in environments characterized by complex electromagnetic wave scattering. In such environments, various objects along the signal propagation path from the transmitting device to the receiving device can induce electromagnetic wave scattering. These objects cause the signal to reflect along different paths, eventually reaching the receiving device. Due to the presence of these reflected paths, the signal received at the receiving device is the result of the superposition of multiple reflections, a phenomenon commonly referred to as multipath effects.The origins of multipath effects are diverse, including outdoor structures, terrain such as mountains, and densely packed objects in indoor environments, all contributing to varied electromagnetic wave reflections and refractions.

As the transmitted signal traverses different electromagnetic wave reflection or refraction paths, differences in the amplitude, phase, and arrival time occur during the transmission process. At the antenna position of the receiving device, multiple reflections or refractions with different phases may simultaneously superimpose. Therefore, under the influence of multipath effects, the signal response amplitude received at the antenna of the receiving device exhibits significant variations. This phenomenon is known as multipath fading.

3.2. Orthogonal Frequency Division Multiplexing

Orthogonal Frequency Division Multiplexing (OFDM) is a multi-carrier modulation technique widely employed in the field of wireless communication, particularly in high-speed data transmission environments. The core concept of OFDM involves dividing a high-speed data stream into multiple lower-speed substreams and concurrently transmitting these substreams on multiple carriers to enhance the overall data transmission efficiency.

OFDM subdivides the high-speed data stream into several lower-speed substreams and allocates these substreams to different orthogonal subcarriers. This allocation ensures mutual orthogonality among the subcarriers, reducing interference between spectral bands. Due to the orthogonality of the subcarriers, symbols on each subcarrier can be transmitted at different phases, achieving higher spectral efficiency within the same frequency band. This adaptability makes OFDM suitable for the demands of high-speed data transmission.

Assuming a carrier bandwidth of B, it can be divided into N orthogonal subcarriers with a bandwidth of $\Delta f = B/N$. If the center frequency of the first carrier is f_0, then the frequency of the nth carrier is given by the following:

$$f_n = f_0 + (n-1)\Delta f \tag{1}$$

Modulating the OFDM symbol P_n onto the subcarrier n results in the transmission symbol $P_n^{e^{j2\pi f_n t}}$. Summing up the signals across all N subcarriers yields the final transmitted signal:

$$f(t) = \sum_{n=1}^{N} P_n e^{j2\pi f_n t} = e^{j2\pi f_0 t} \sum_{n=1}^{N} P_n e^{j2\pi(n-1)\Delta f t} \tag{2}$$

Once the receiver obtains the signal, it can determine the OFDM symbol P_n transmitted over the subcarrier using the following formula:

$$\Delta f \int_0^{\frac{1}{\Delta f}} f(t) e^{-j2\pi f_n t} dt = P_n + \sum_{k \neq n} \Delta f \int_0^{\frac{1}{\Delta f}} P_k e^{j2\pi f_k t} e^{-j2\pi f_n t} dt = P_n \tag{3}$$

3.3. Channel State Information

In the same physical environment, different subcarriers experience varying fading and multipath effects in the wireless channel. The channel responses at different frequency positions of the subcarriers exhibit differences. To describe the subchannel response at each subcarrier frequency position, a set of data representing the features of the channel frequency response is required. These data enable the communication system at the receiving end to adapt to the actual conditions of the wireless channel, allowing the reconstruction of the effective original wireless signal received by the receiving antenna. This series of data describing the channel frequency response is commonly referred to as channel state information (CSI). CSI is a crucial data metric in wireless communication, encompassing various aspects of the radio waves between the terminals and enabling the real-time dataization and visualization of the electromagnetic wave status between the communicating parties.

The receiving device can recover the original signal based on the channel conditions described by CSI, facilitating signal transmission under the adaptation to the current channel conditions. This is vital for achieving robust communication in OFDM systems. The CSI is obtained through channel estimation in OFDM wireless communication systems. In OFDM communication transmission systems, the primary purpose of channel estimation is the selection of pilot information. As wireless channels may experience fading during transmission, continuous tracking of the channel is necessary, requiring the ongoing transmission of pilot information. Through the estimation of pilot information, the receiving terminal can acquire the CSI of the wireless communication channel from the other party.

CSI reflects the communication channel conditions between the transmitter and the receiver, manifesting on OFDM symbols as variations in the amplitude and phase of signals on each subcarrier. According to the signal system model, let H represent the channel frequency response, X be the transmitted signal, and N denote noise. The received signal Y can be expressed as follows:

$$Y = XH + N \tag{4}$$

In WiFi, OFDM technology is commonly employed, and CSI reflects the representation of the channel frequency response (CFR) on subcarriers. The expression of the CFR can be easily obtained through the pilot portion of each OFDM symbol:

$$H = \sum_{k \in K} \|h_k\| \times e^{-j\varphi_k} \tag{5}$$

In this context, $\|h_k\|$ and φ_k represent the amplitude and phase values of the signal on each subcarrier, respectively. The CFR can describe small-scale multipath effects and is widely utilized as a channel indicator. By adjusting the firmware, it is possible to obtain the CFR of multipath channel samples, i.e., the measured values of CSI, on existing wireless terminal devices, such as commercial IEEE 802.11a/g/n equipment.

CSI represents the sampling of the wireless channel frequency response at various subcarrier frequencies in OFDM. On each wireless channel, each antenna at the receiving end can generate a set of CSI data. Due to the presence of multipath effects and fading phenomena in the wireless channel environment, different subcarrier frequencies are affected to varying degrees. As a result, each subchannel possesses a unique gain. This implies that each subchannel has corresponding CSI values, reflecting its distinctive frequency response features. The CSI features of the wireless channel exhibit robustness, uniqueness, and irreproducibility.

3.4. Wireless Channel Features

The wireless channel possesses four features, reciprocity, time variability, short-term stationarity, and spatial sensitivity, which are descrived below:

1. Channel reciprocity: Channel reciprocity in a wireless channel refers to the symmetric propagation features between the transmitter and the receiver. In other words, if the propagation channel from the transmitter to the receiver is reciprocal, then the propagation channel from the receiver to the transmitter is also reciprocal. Reciprocity simplifies the analysis and modeling of wireless communication systems. However, in practical communication environments, various factors such as noise, channel variations, and environmental conditions may lead to incomplete consistency in the collected channel state data due to the asynchrony in signal reception times between communication parties.
2. Time variability: The propagation features of a wireless channel undergo changes over time. This time variability can be caused by various factors, including the movement of objects, changes in obstacles along the signal path, and variations in atmospheric conditions. Time variability is particularly crucial for mobile communication systems as it impacts the signal transmission quality and system performance.
3. Short-term stationarity: Despite the time variability of the wireless channel, it is often possible to approximate the channel as approximately stationary over short periods. This implies that within very short time intervals, the propagation features of the channel can be considered constant, simplifying the complexity of system design and signal processing.
4. Spatial sensitivity: The propagation features of a wireless channel are highly sensitive to spatial changes. Even within relatively small spatial ranges, significant variations in the channel's features may occur. This sensitivity is due to the signal's propagation through multiple paths, influenced by reflection, refraction, and scattering. Spatial sensitivity is particularly important in places with complex structures, such as indoor and urban environments, necessitating the adoption of appropriate antenna configurations and signal processing techniques to address it.

3.5. CSI Acquisition Module Based on Multipath Effects

3.5.1. CSI Acquisition

In general, CSI is often represented by the channel frequency response (CFR) in a wireless multipath channel environment. When the transmission frequency is denoted as f, the formula for CSI is given by the following:

$$H(f) = \sum_{n}^{N} a_n e^{-j2\pi f \tau_n} \quad (6)$$

In OFDM wireless networks, such as IEEE 802.11a/g/n, each pair of antenna channel propagations results in a set of CSI data. The length of each set of CSI data corresponds to the number of subcarriers, and the individual CSI values within the set are represented by the following formula:

$$CSI_{m,n} = [csi_{-i}, csi_{-i+1}, \ldots, csi_0, csi_1, \ldots csi_i] \quad (7)$$

In the above formula, m represents the index of the transmitting antenna, n denotes the index of the receiving antenna, and i represents the subcarrier index. When a device transmits data with a bandwidth of 20 MHz in the 2.4 GHz frequency band, the utilized channel will consist of 64 subcarriers. The measured CSI at the receiver will include the frequency response for each subcarrier, forming a 64-dimensional complex CSI vector. In a Multiple-Input Multiple-Output Orthogonal Frequency Division Multiplexing (MIMO-OFDM) wireless communication systems (assuming the system has V transmit antennas and G receive antennas), the CSI will be expanded into a three-dimensional complex matrix of size $V \times G \times 64$. This provides an alternative representation for the CSI:

$$\mathrm{CSI}_k = |csi_k| e^{-j\angle csi_k}, k = -i, \ldots, -1, 1, \ldots, i^{\circ} \quad (8)$$

where $|csi_k|$ represents the amplitude and $\angle csi_k$ represents the phase.

The majority of CSI amplitudes tend to stabilize within a relatively concentrated range, with only a portion of the data exhibiting discrete deviations. However, CSI phase data are characterized by an unstable pattern, displaying a distribution with random rotations. Additionally, significant discrepancies are observed in the CSI data between the receiving and transmitting ends at the same position.

3.5.2. Preprocessing of CSI

CSI data may have certain errors due to environmental noise. To eliminate these errors, preprocessing is applied. First, due to hardware errors, environmental factors, etc., there may be outliers or anomalous points in the data sequence. To reduce the impact of errors and enhance the robustness, an outlier detection method is employed. Secondly, normalization is used to reduce data dispersion. Finally, the samples undergo smoothing to eliminate the effects caused by environmental noise.

1. Outlier Handling

After obtaining CSI', the n samples are denoted as $^{-}\mathrm{CSI}'_n = c_n^1, c_n^2, \cdots, c_n^M (n = 1, 2, \cdots, N)$, where N represents the number of collected samples and M represents the number of available subcarriers collected (52 in this case). Let $L_m = (c_1^m, c_2^m, \cdots c_N^m)$ represent the average value of each subcarrier across all samples, where $m = 1, 2, \cdots, M$. The median window chosen in this paper is $C_{D,n}^I$ and the sample values within a range of $2l$ around it. The standard deviation for all samples is derived from the absolute deviation, as shown in the following formula:

$$\sigma_I^m = \frac{1}{\gamma} \mathrm{median}(|c_i^m - c_I^m|) \quad (9)$$

where c_I^m represents the median of the window, c_i^m represents the samples within the window, and $\gamma = \sqrt{2}\,\text{erfinv}(0.5)$. The removal of outliers in the samples is processed using the following formula:

$$c_i^m = \begin{cases} c_i^m & \left|c_i^m - c_I^m\right| \le \eta\sigma_I^m \\ c_I^m & \left|c_i^m - c_I^m\right| > \eta\sigma_I^m \end{cases} \tag{10}$$

2. Normalization

Due to environmental interference, the amplitude of CSI may exhibit certain variations over time, but, overall, it will have similar fluctuation trends. To reduce the adverse effects of amplitude fluctuations, the amplitude sequence of CSI is normalized using the following formula:

$$c_i = \frac{a_i - a_{\min}}{a_{\max} - a_{\min}} \tag{11}$$

After normalization, the amplitude sequence of CSI exhibits a smaller degree of dispersion while preserving the original shape information to a certain extent.

3. Smoothing

The smoothing process involves working solely on the amplitude values of each subcarrier, aiming to reduce temporal influences. The smoothing method is expressed as follows:

$$\tilde{c}_n^m = \frac{1}{w} \sum_{\max\left(0,n-\left\lfloor \frac{w}{2} \right\rfloor\right)}^{\min\left(N,n+\left\lfloor \frac{w-1}{2} \right\rfloor\right)} c_n^{m_0} \tag{12}$$

where w represents the length of the smoothing window.

4. Non-Interactive Channel Feature Similarity Comparison

4.1. Zero-Knowledge Proof

A zero-knowledge proof (ZKP) refers to the ability of a prover to convince a verifier of the correctness of a statement without revealing any useful information. This concept was introduced in the early 1980s by S. Goldwasser and others. The security of zero-knowledge proofs relies primarily on cryptographic assumptions related to challenging problems, such as discrete logarithms and elliptic curve problems. This paper focuses on the enhancement of Sigma Protocols in zero-knowledge proofs, grounded in the assumption of the difficulty of the discrete logarithm problem. The objective is to tailor Sigma Protocols to meet the specific requirements of certain industry applications while maintaining the security principles inherent in zero-knowledge proofs.

The Sigma Protocol is an interactive proof system consisting of a prover (P) and a verifier (V) in a three-step process. This system is based on the discrete logarithm problem and a commitment key (ck) generated with a security parameter λ. The commitment key ck is derived from the discrete logarithm problem and a random number $r \in \mathbb{Z}_q^*$, where represents a non-negative integer ring of order q. The prover can generate a commitment $Com_{ck}(c;r)$ for a secret c, representing a declaration of the secret c. Based on prior research results, it is known that, with negligible probability, this commitment uniquely binds to the secret c and does not leak information about c.

The Sigma Protocol process is described as follows:

1. The prover initiates the process by sending the commitment regarding the secret c to the verifier.
2. Upon receiving the commitment, the verifier randomly selects a challenge value $x \in \mathbb{Z}_q^*$ and sends it to the prover.
3. Based on the received challenge value x, the prover generates the corresponding response value z and sends it to the verifier.
4. These three steps constitute the proof by the prover for the secret c. With the known parameters, including the commitment key ck, commitment value $Com_{ck}(c;r)$, chal-

lenge value x, and response z, the verifier is capable of validating the legitimacy of the proof.

The intersection proof proposed in this paper is a modification of the aforementioned Sigma Protocol, based on the Pedersen commitment scheme. The properties of this commitment scheme are defined as follows:

Let $\mathbb{G}$ be a q-order cyclic group generated by the commitment key ck, with generators g and h. Given a random number $r \in \mathbb{Z}_q^*$, a Pedersen commitment based on the message c can be generated as follows:

$$Com_{ck}(c;r) = g^c \cdot h^r \in \mathbb{G} \tag{13}$$

The Pedersen commitment is a homomorphic commitment scheme that, under the discrete logarithm assumption, possesses two essential properties, hiding and binding:

- Concealment (hiding): For any adversary with a probabilistic polynomial time computational capability, if the adversary is unable to effectively distinguish between the commitments $Com_{ck}(c_0;r_0)$ and $Com_{ck}(c_1;r_1)$ corresponding to two distinct messages c_0 and c_1, then the commitment scheme is considered to possess concealment.
- Binding: For any adversary with a probabilistic polynomial time computational capability, given a known commitment $Com_{ck}(c_0;r_0)$, the task is to find another secret value $c_!$ such that their commitment values are equal, i.e., $Com_{ck}(c_0;r_0) = Com_{ck}(c_1;r_1)$. If the probability of successfully achieving this task is negligible, then the commitment scheme is deemed to exhibit binding characteristics.

4.2. *Interactive Similarity Matching*

Similar to fingerprint recognition, when collecting fingerprints from the same individual multiple times, various factors such as sweat, pressure variations, and other elements on the fingers can result in subtle differences in the collected fingerprints. Ensuring fuzzy identity recognition while maintaining both accuracy and fault tolerance in the presence of these subtle variations is a crucial consideration.

In the process of identity authentication, despite the preprocessing of channel state information (CSI), deviations from standard values may still occur during the quantification process. Therefore, it is necessary to enhance the tolerance of identity recognition without compromising accuracy. In this context, we introduce the concept of fuzziness to assess the similarity of fuzzy equations. The extracted CSI exhibits fuzzy characteristics, with the CSI collected by both parties not being entirely consistent but demonstrating a high degree of similarity. This paper, by comparing the similarity of CSI from both parties and obtaining the intersection, negotiates a shared channel key for communication. Simultaneously, the successful comparison of CSI similarity also signifies that the remote end possesses CSI highly similar to the local end, enabling dual-end authentication.

This paper employs a zero-knowledge proof based on the Sigma Protocol for conducting a Comparative Similarity Index (CSI) matching. Initially, the collected CSI information is quantified into a binary CSI vector. This binary vector serves as a representation of the CSI, and the similarity matching involves comparing the binary vectors held by both parties, leading to the determination of their binary vector intersection. Subsequently, by constructing an n-th order polynomial to express the binary vector, the similarity matching of binary vectors is transformed into the intersection operation of an n-th order polynomial. The intersection calculation is achieved by verifying the polynomial's zero points. This process substantiates the high degree of similarity between the binary vectors held by both parties, thereby facilitating the mutual authentication of the communicating entities.

For a binary string s owned by the communication party Alice, it is divided into n segments of a fixed length, represented as $(s_1, \ldots, s_n)$. The prover wishes to convince the verifier of possessing the secret vector $s = (s_1, \ldots, s_n)$ without disclosing any information. Similarly, after preprocessing, Bob obtains the set $s = (s'_1, \ldots, s'_n)$.

In the first place, we construct an n-degree polynomial $p(x) = (x - 1 \cdot s_1), \ldots, (x - n \cdot s_n) = x^n + a_{n-1}x^{n-1} + \cdots + a_1 x + a_0$. Clearly, the polynomial evaluates to 0 only when the input $x = i \cdot s_i (i \in [1, n])$. This property can be utilized for a prover to verify their possession of secrets without disclosing these secret values (including their corresponding values in the group field) to others. Based on this idea, the problem of similarity comparison can be transformed into a zero-knowledge similarity comparison problem: the prover needs to prove that they possess a polynomial $p(x)$, and the zeros of this polynomial can be verified by the verifier.

The similarity comparison relation is defined as follows:

$$R = \left\{ \begin{array}{ll} ck \leftarrow \text{Setup}(1^\lambda); P_i \in \mathbb{G}; a_i, r_i, x \in \mathbb{Z}_q^* & \sum_{i=1}^n P_i^{(s^i)} = \text{Com}_{ck}(0; r') \\ P_i = \text{Com}_{ck}(a_i; r_i)(i = 0, \ldots, n) & \text{where} \quad \text{s} \in 1 \cdot s_1, \ldots, n \cdot s_n \end{array} \right\} \quad (14)$$

Firstly, we define the variables required for the algorithmic flow description, based on the discrete logarithm problem. Let $\mathbb{G}$ be a cyclic group of order q, where q is a prime number. The generators of this group are denoted as $\mathbb{g}$ and $\mathbb{h}$, both belonging to $\mathbb{G}$. For an element x in the multiplicative group of q-order positive integers $\mathbb{Z}_q^*$, it holds that $\mathbb{g}^x \in \mathbb{G}$. Boldface notation such as $\boldsymbol{a}$ is used to represent vectors, for instance, $\boldsymbol{a} = (a_0, \ldots, a_n)$ denotes a vector composed of n numerical values. The prover can generate a corresponding Pederson commitment for their secret $\boldsymbol{a}$, denoted as $Com(\boldsymbol{a}; r)$, which can be succinctly expressed as $Com(\boldsymbol{a}; r) = \mathbb{g}^{\boldsymbol{a}} \cdot \mathbb{h}^r$.

The prover initially generates, for each secret value a_i, corresponding random numbers r_i, u_i, and v_i. The commitments $A_i = Com_{ck}(a_i; u_i)$ and $R_i = Com_{ck}(r_i; v_i)$ are computed and disclosed to the verifier. Subsequently, the verifier generates a random number x as the challenge value for the aforementioned commitments. The prover, in response to the verifier's challenge x, computes $f_i = a_i \cdot x + r_i$ and $z_i = u_i \cdot x + v_i$. Finally, the verifier performs validation on the proof, checking if the prover possesses the secret vector $\boldsymbol{a} = (a_0, \ldots, a_n)$ and confirming whether the subchannel characteristics are mutual. If the result corresponds to a commitment of 0 in the form $Com_{ck}(0; u')$, then the currently computed value s'_j is considered a shared secret between the communicating parties and is utilized in generating the final channel key.

Channel Key Computation

After the application of the feature extraction algorithm to the CSI information, a set of binary sequences is obtained. It is ensured that a significant portion of the binary sequences held by both Alice and Bob exhibit similarity, as illustrated in Figure 1.

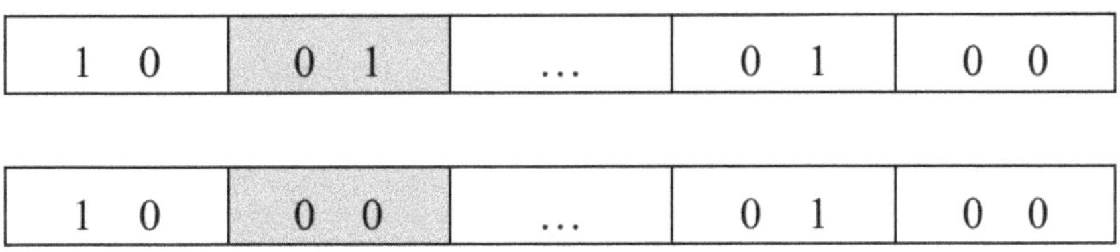

Figure 1. Quantized and segmented binary feature sequences.

In the proposed scheme, the sequence is divided into segments, and each segment is treated as a secret value s_i for verification purposes. The verifier only needs to sequentially compute the verification for each segmented secret value s'_j. If the equality holds, it can be inferred that the corresponding segments in the binary sequences of the communicating parties are identical, thereby establishing a common element. Ultimately, the verifier obtains the intersection of the secret value vectors $\boldsymbol{s}$ and $\boldsymbol{s}'$, denoted as $\boldsymbol{s} \cap \boldsymbol{s}'$. This intersection sequence serves as the shared channel key for the mutual authentication in the key negotiation process.

4.3. Non-Interactive Key Similarity Comparison

The aforementioned similarity comparison is observed to be interactive. In this context, apart from the commitment value initially transmitted, a challenge–response process must be completed between the prover and the verifier to execute the entire procedure. The interactive nature of this process may result in an increased execution time and potential resource waste or even incompatibility when deployed in certain protocols. This paper leverages the Fiat–Shamir transformation to convert the aforementioned three-step interactive similarity comparison into a non-interactive process requiring only one step. The principle of this transformation involves utilizing the hash value of the interactive data as the challenge for the second step of the Sigma Protocol and using this challenge value to compute the response in the third step. Finally, the commitment and response are sent together to the verifier.

Upon applying the Fiat–Shamir transformation, the non-interactive similarity comparison process is outlined as follows:

1. In the execution of the aforementioned Protocol 1, the prover randomly generates three sets of random vectors $(r_0, \ldots, r_n)$, $(u_0, \ldots, u_n)$, and $(v_0, \ldots, v_n)$, and produces the corresponding commitment values $(A_0, \ldots, A_n, R_0, \ldots, R_n)$.
2. The prover generates a challenge value for the data to be sent, where $x = H(ck, A_0, \ldots, A_n, R_0, \ldots, R_n)$ and $H(\cdot)$ denotes a hash function.
3. In accordance with the challenge value x, the secret vector $\boldsymbol{a} = (a_0, \ldots, a_n)$, random value vector $\boldsymbol{r} = (r_0, \ldots, r_n)$, $\boldsymbol{u} = (u_0, \ldots, u_n)$, and $\boldsymbol{v} = (v_0, \ldots, v_n)$. The prover computes the corresponding response vectors $\boldsymbol{f} = (f_0, \ldots, f_{n-1})$ and $\boldsymbol{z} = (z_0, \ldots, z_{n-1})$.
4. The final prover will transmit the proof, denoted as $Proof = (x, \boldsymbol{A}, \boldsymbol{R}, \boldsymbol{f}, \boldsymbol{z})$, to the verifier in a single instance.

5. Implementation

5.1. Locality-Sensitive Hashing

We employ the locality-sensitive hashing (LSH) algorithm to process bit sequences. LSH is an algorithm designed for similarity search in massive datasets. Essentially, LSH is a technique for data dimensionality reduction, aiming to map data points from the original high-dimensional space to a lower-dimensional space while attempting to preserve their similarity.

The LSH algorithm consists of two main parts. In the first part, we utilize the SimHash algorithm for data dimensionality reduction. It involves merging long bit sequences through weighted combination, merging, and dimensionality reduction steps, resulting in shorter bit strings. In the second part, we apply LSH to locally search for matching pairs among the short bit strings. The bit strings are hashed into hash buckets after being split, ultimately generating a unique identity for terminal devices.

The SimHash algorithm is primarily employed for text similarity detection, using Hamming distance to calculate similarity, making it suitable for the dimensionality reduction of long bit sequences. In the classical SimHash algorithm, text needs to be hashed and transformed into a binary string of 0s and 1s that can be measured using Hamming distance. The m = 6 SimHash algorithm is illustrated in the accompanying Figure 2.

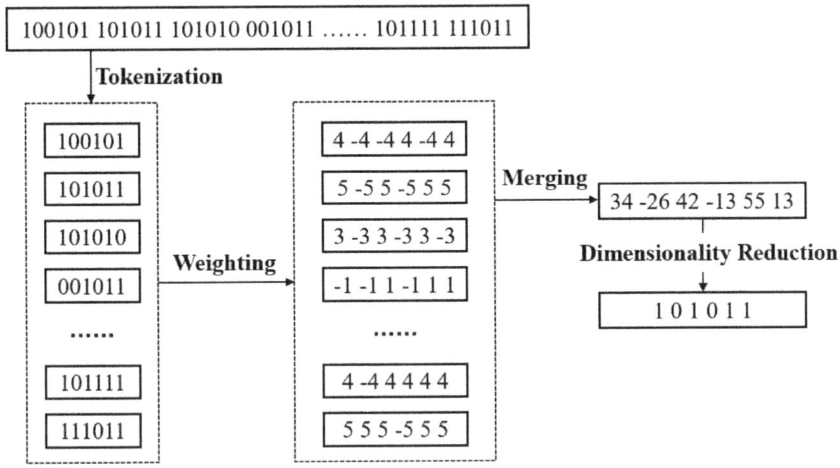

Figure 2. m = 6 SimHash algorithm.

The SimHash algorithm employed in this experiment is primarily divided into the following components:

1. Tokenization: The long bit sequence is segmented into multiple equidistant feature strings, each with a length of m bits.
2. Weighting: Each equidistant feature string is assigned a weight, based on its importance. Additionally, each bit in the feature string, whether 1 or 0, is transformed. For instance, for a feature string of length 6 bits, the assigned weight is 4, and the weighted representation becomes 4 −4 −4 4 −4 4.
3. Merging: The weighted feature strings are cumulatively added to obtain a final sequence string.
4. Dimensionality reduction: The merged sequence string undergoes dimensionality reduction. If a particular position in the sequence string is greater than 0, it is set to 1; otherwise, it is set to 0. The output is the signature corresponding to the long bit sequence. Multiple signatures are combined to produce the SimHash signature matrix.

After obtaining the SimHash signature, the locality-sensitive hashing (LSH) algorithm is employed to hash the signature matrix, aggregating the results into hash buckets. This facilitates local searching for matching pairs, with the hash bucket signature serving as the final identifier. During the hashing process, the algorithm further reduces the dimensionality of the input data, enabling unique and stable identity outputs for inputs with minor variations. The locality-sensitive hashing algorithm is depicted in Figure 3.

The specific steps of the locality-sensitive hashing (LSH) algorithm are as follows:

1. Initially, the signatures in the previously obtained signature matrix are divided into different bands, with each band containing a fixed number of rows.
2. Each band is hashed into a distinct hash bucket.
3. Identification is applied to each hash bucket, combining the identifiers of the buckets where each segment of the signature resides. The final result represents the output of the LSH algorithm.

These steps facilitate the segmentation of signatures into bands, followed by the hashing of each band into separate hash buckets. Subsequently, the identification of each hash bucket is performed, combining the identifiers of the buckets associated with each segment of the signature. The ultimate outcome constitutes the output of the LSH algorithm.

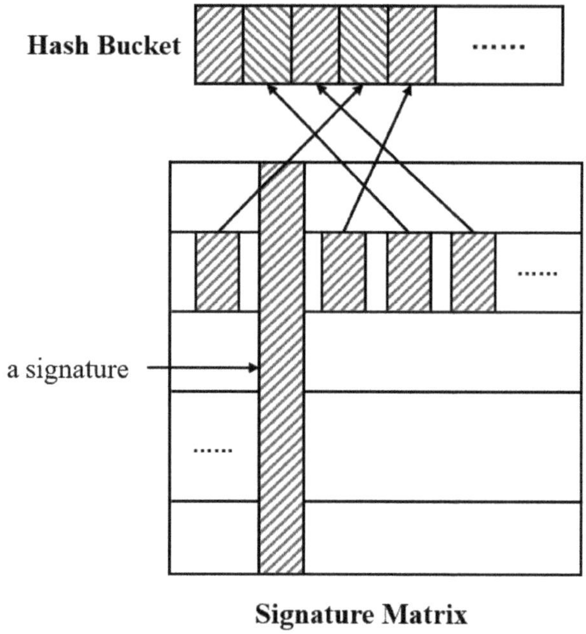

Figure 3. The locality-sensitive hashing algorithm.

5.2. CSI-Based IBE for IoT

We let k be the security parameter given to the setup algorithm.

Setup: (1) Choose a large prime p for some prime $q > 3$. Let E be the elliptic curve defined by $\cdot y^2 = x^3 + 1\cdot$ over $\cdot\mathbb{F}_p$. Choose an arbitrary $P \in E/\mathbb{F}_p\cdot$ of order q. (2) Pick a random $s \in \mathbb{Z}_q^*$ and set $P_{pub} = sP$. (3) Choose a cryptographic hash function $H : \mathbb{F}_{p^2} \rightarrow \{0,1\}^n$ for some n. Choose a cryptographic hash function $G : \{0,1\}* \rightarrow \mathbb{F}_p$.

The message space is $M = 0, 1^n$. The ciphertext space is $C = E/\mathbb{F}_p \times \{0,1\}^n$. The system parameters are $< p, n, P, P_{pub}, G, H >$. The master key is $s \in \mathbb{Z}_q^*$.

Extract: For a given string $ID \in \{0,1\}^*$, the algorithm builds a private key d as follows: (1) Map the ID to a point $Q_I D \in E/\mathbb{F}_p$ of order q. (2) Set the private key d_{ID} to be $d_{ID} = sQ_{ID}$ where s is the master key.

In the first step, we need to initially use the CSI Acquisition module in Section 3 to obtain the physical state information features of the device. Since in the actual environment these physical state information features are always fluctuating, it is necessary to use LSH to transform the steady-state features of the device into the same hash. Only in this way can they be used as identity identifiers in IBE, serving as public keys externally. In this process, it is also necessary to utilize the non-interactive channel feature similarity comparison in Section 4 to prove the effectiveness of mapping feature values to hash values through LSH and to maintain the privacy of the device's physical state features.

Encrypt: To encrypt $m \in M$ under the public key ID, take the following steps: map the ID into a point $Q_{ID} \in E/\mathbb{F}_p$ of order q. Then, choose a random $r \in \mathbb{Z}_q$, and set the ciphertext to be

$$C =< rP, m \oplus H(g_{ID}^r) > \tag{15}$$

where $g_{ID} = \hat{e}(Q_{ID}, P_{pub}) \in \mathbb{F}_{p^2}$.

Decrypt: Let $C = (U, V)$ be a ciphertext encrypted using the public key ID. If $U \in E/\mathbb{F}_p$ is not a point of order q, reject the ciphertext. Otherwise, to decrypt C using the private key d_{ID}, compute the following:

$$V \oplus H(\hat{e}(d_{ID}.U)) = m \tag{16}$$

6. Implementation and Experiment

6.1. Construction of a Key Exchange Module Testing System

6.1.1. Testing Environment

The testing environment for channel key negotiation based on channel fingerprints was established with distinct communication characteristics, namely, line-of-sight (LOS) and non-line-of-sight (NLOS) characteristics, as illustrated in Figures 4 and 5, respectively.

1. In the NLOS scenario, as illustrated in Figure 4, the communication devices of the two parties are positioned at distances of 3 m, 4 m, and 5 m, with the attacker at the closest proximity of 0.1 m.
2. In the LOS scenario illustrated in Figure 5, the devices of the communicating parties are situated at distances of 25 cm, 50 cm, and 75 cm, with the attacker positioned at a minimum proximity of 0.1 m.

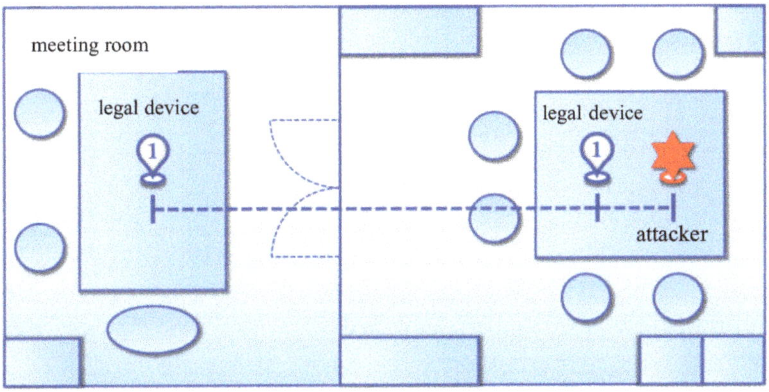

Figure 4. Illustration of key negotiation module testing scenario (non-line of sight).

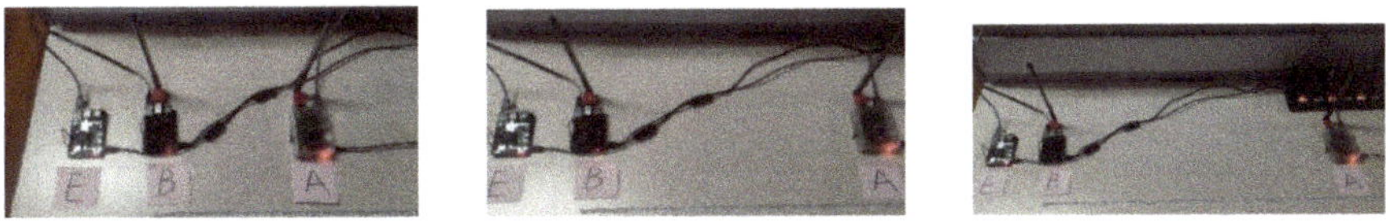

(**a**) A and B are 25 cm apart (**b**) A and B are 50 cm apart (**c**) A and B are 75 cm apart

Figure 5. Illustrative diagram of key exchange module testing scenario (within line of sight).

6.1.2. Testing Apparatus

In the channel key negotiation module testing, three Raspberry Pi devices (all Raspberry Pi 3 Model B+) were employed as the testing equipment, with the device information outlined in Table 1. The three Raspberry Pi devices assumed the roles of Alice (legitimate communication device (1)), Bob (legitimate communication device (2)), and Eve (illegitimate communication device, i.e., the attacker) during the testing. Specifically, Alice and Bob functioned as legitimate communicating parties, executing normal access requests, channel feature collection, identity authentication, key negotiation, and communication processes. Meanwhile, Eve played the role of an attacker, engaging in man-in-the-middle attacks and replay attacks during the identity authentication and key negotiation stages conducted by Alice and Bob.

Table 1. Device information for channel key negotiation module testing.

No.	Model of Device	Name of Device	Identity of Device
1	Raspberry Pi 3 Model B+	Alice	Legal equipment
2	Raspberry Pi 3 Model B+	Bob	Legal equipment
3	Raspberry Pi 3 Model B+	Eve	Attacker

6.1.3. Software and Hardware Parameters

All Raspberry Pi models utilized in this paper are Raspberry Pi 3 Model B+. The Wi-Fi chipset integrated into all Raspberry Pi devices is identified as BCM43455C0. The antennas employed for both transmission and reception are 2.4 GHz single-frequency antennas with a gain of 6 dBi. All experimental tests are conducted based on the wireless communication protocol IEEE 802.11n, utilizing channels 1–14 with a center frequency range of 2.412–2.472 GHz and a bandwidth of 20 MHz. The firmware version installed on the Wi-Fi chipset is 7_45_189, and the operating system deployed on the Raspberry Pi is the Raspberry Pi OS, with a kernel version of 4.19.

The software parameters for the LOS and NLOS test environments of the channel key negotiation module are configured as presented in Tables 2 and 3, respectively.

Table 2. Parameter configuration for non-line-of-sight indoor testing software.

No.	Communication Distance (m)	Minimum Distance to the Supplier (cm)	Packet Transmission Rate (pkts/s)	Number of Transmitted Packets (pkts)	Number of Channel Key Negotiation Iterations
1	3	10	500	50,000	5000
2	4	10	500	50,000	5000
3	5	10	500	50,000	5000

Table 3. Parameter configuration for line-of-sight testing software.

No.	Communication Distance (m)	Minimum Distance to the Supplier (cm)	Packet Transmission Rate (pkts/s)	Number of Transmitted Packets (pkts)	Number of Channel Key Negotiation Iterations
1	25	10	500	20,000	2000
2	50	10	500	20,000	2000
3	75	10	500	20,000	2000

After experimental verification, it has been demonstrated that there is a significant disparity in the modulus results between Alice and Bob compared to those of Eve. This observation elucidates the efficacy of the modulus operation in enhancing the distinguishability between attackers and legitimate devices. Following the modulus operation, the proportion of data variations across the three sets remains within the anticipated and reasonable range. Subsequent quantization processing further amplifies the observed distinctions.

6.2. *OFDM and CSI*

6.2.1. Testing Parameters

This paper selected a wireless network with a bandwidth of 20 MHz and 64 OFDM subcarriers, utilizing a wireless terminal with a single transmitter and receiver antenna as a sample. Upon receiving data packets, the receiver calculated the CSI using a channel estimation method, resulting in a matrix of size $1 \times 1 \times 64$. In the long training sequence, the amplitudes of 12 subcarriers are zero, numbered $-32, -31, -30, -29, -28, -27, 0, 27, 28, 29, 30$, and 31. This implies that the CSI data on these subcarriers is not obtained through channel estimation and is not associated with the wireless channel. After removing these data points, a matrix of size $1 \times 1 \times 52$, denoted as the complex sequence, was obtained, where each value corresponds to the amplitude and phase of a subcarrier.

In this scenario, if the above sequence is directly used for training and recognition, considering factors such as hardware errors and environmental interference, there may be outliers in the sample sequence, leading to the poor recognition performance of the trained model. Therefore, it is necessary to perform outlier handling, normalization, and smoothing on the obtained amplitude and phase sequences. This process is further explained in the following section, which discusses the preprocessing of CSI data.

6.2.2. Functional System Testing

This paper employed various wireless IoT devices of different types and brands, including Raspberry Pi, wireless cameras, smart lights, and smart plugs. These devices were connected to a router serving as an access point (AP) to create a simulated IoT network. All these IoT devices operated in the 2.4 GHz frequency band with a bandwidth of 20 MHz, and their communication data packets were captured. Nexmon was chosen as the CSI extraction tool because it offers support for larger bandwidths and a higher number of subcarriers compared to other tools.

This paper continuously recorded the changes in CSI amplitude curves for different IoT devices under four interference conditions, including scenarios with no human movement and individuals walking back and forth from distances of 1 m, 2 m, and 3 m from the terminal. A selection of typical IoT devices was chosen, and the CSI information varied among different devices. Even under interference conditions, the measured CSI amplitude curves maintained a similar shape, with an overall shift in amplitude occurring across all subcarriers. Further experiments indicated that, after processing, the differences in extracted device identities under various interference conditions were within the tolerance range of our algorithm.

6.3. *CSI and LSH*

Due to the inherent noise in the channel, signals inevitably degrade during transmission. The user identity used for encryption and decryption should be accurate. Therefore, channel state information (CSI) cannot be directly used as a user identity. Only through processing with locality-sensitive hashing (LSH), where the same segment of signal falls into the same hash bucket after stabilization, can CSI be used as a means of user identification. As illustrated in Figure 6, we transmitted 100 identical signal segments repeatedly. To simplify the problem, we calculate the average of the signal sequence in both amplitude and frequency dimensions. However, due to the inherent noise in the channel, the signals received by the actual receiver exhibit subtle differences in amplitude and frequency. These differences, amplified by the avalanche effect of cryptographic hash functions, result in completely different identity representations. Therefore, it is necessary to employ LSH to ensure that these 100 signal segments stably fall into the same hash bucket before they can be used for identity generation.

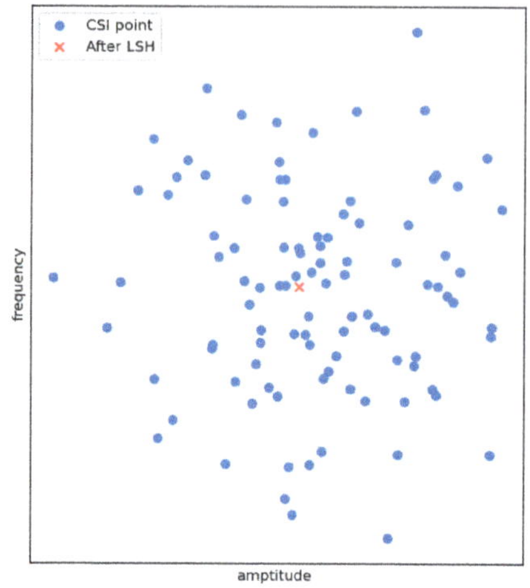

Figure 6. Stablity of LSH.

7. Discussion

7.1. Potential Attack and Security

In this section, we will discuss potential attacks that the methods described in this paper may face, as well as the security of the proposed solution.

7.1.1. Man-in-the-Middle Attack

The man-in-the-middle attack refers to the attacker inserting themselves between communicating parties to intercept or manipulate the information exchanged. Attackers can impersonate user identities through man-in-the-middle attacks. However, in the proposed solution in this paper, user identities rely on the physical characteristics of the user's device, specifically constructed through channel state information. Unlike traditional approaches that depend on specific message information submitted by users, the attacker cannot mimic the user's channel environment. Therefore, they are unable to impersonate users through man-in-the-middle attacks.

7.1.2. Replay Attack

The replay attack refers to the act of an attacker retransmitting previously intercepted communication data without modification, with the aim of deceiving the system to achieve unauthorized access or execute certain unauthorized operations. In this paper, on one hand, similar to a man-in-the-middle attack, attackers cannot mimic the channel state in which the user is located. On the other hand, in zero-knowledge proofs, a random freshness number is used as secret information. Therefore, attempting to impersonate a user through replaying messages cannot pass the zero-knowledge verification. Thus, in the discussed solution in this paper, it is not possible to impersonate a user through a replay attack.

7.1.3. Brute-Force Attack

The brute-force attack is a method of password cracking where attackers attempt all possible password combinations until the correct one is found. This method does not rely on pre-obtained information but systematically tries every possible password and is often automated using computer programs. It is a relatively straightforward but time-consuming attack, and its success typically depends on the strength and complexity of the password. In this paper, due to the difficulty of the discrete logarithm problem on elliptic curves, brute-force attacks are computationally infeasible. Meanwhile, attackers not only need to brute-force crack passwords but also attempt to brute-force crack the user's channel state. The attacker can only be successful if they find a channel that is equivalent to the one in which the user's device is located. However, the state of the channel itself is uncertain, making it impossible for attackers to brute-force crack the user's channel state.

7.2. Challenges

7.2.1. Channel Time Variability

Channel time variability refers to the phenomenon where the characteristics of a communication channel change over time. In wireless communication environments, factors such as multipath propagation and the movement of obstacles can cause variations in the channel. This time variability may result in signal fading, changes in multipath effects, and even a distortion of the channel. Due to the existence of channel time variability, the user identity generated based on CSI in this paper is also subject to time variations. Therefore, to ensure the effectiveness of the system, periodic updates of the channel state and user identity are necessary. This introduces an additional communication overhead and may reduce the system's availability. Addressing the time variability of the channel for efficient real-time updates is a direction for future research.

7.2.2. Location-Dependent Channel State

The location-dependent channel state refers to the characteristics of a communication channel that are influenced by the spatial position of communication devices, capturing how the channel changes based on the location and movement of the devices involved. The communication channel state describes the variations in the signal during the transmission process, encompassing changes such as fading, delay, and other effects caused by propagation paths, multipath effects, obstacles, and other influences. The position, movement, and environmental changes of devices can all have an impact on the channel state. Therefore, the solution discussed in this paper has limitations for general discussions about wireless mobile devices. The devices discussed in this paper are also fixed devices in specific scenarios. In Figure 7, we demonstrate the effect of user identity recognition when the device undergoes a position shift. We recorded the successful recovered number at the red cross, and it can be observed that after deviating a certain distance and angle, the device becomes unacceptable. The location dependency of the channel is also one of the directions for future research, which holds significant practical value for applications in wireless scenarios.

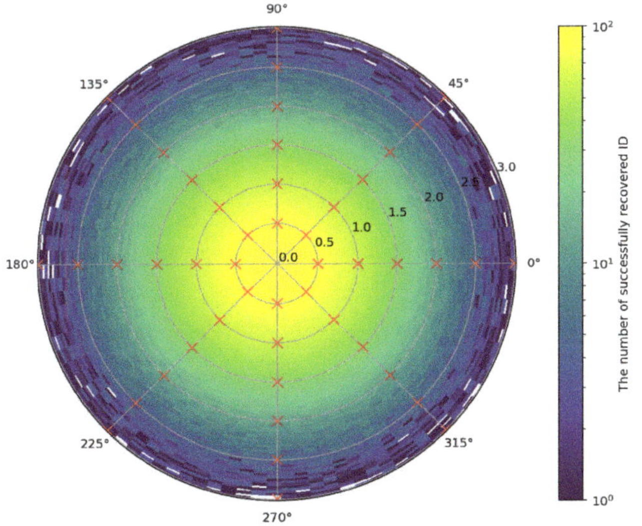

Figure 7. Location-dependent channel state and the number of successfully recovered IDs.

8. Conclusions

This paper introduces an innovative secure communication solution that leverages wireless channel state information (CSI) features from IoT devices for generating device identities. Given the inherent instability of wireless channels, the CSI features are inherently fuzzy and subject to time variations. To address this, we employ the locally sensitive hashing (LSH) algorithm, ensuring the stability of the generated identity within a dynamically changing wireless channel environment. Additionally, zero-knowledge proofs are incorporated to validate the authenticity and effectiveness of the generated identity. Subsequently, the identity produced through this approach is integrated into an identity-based encryption (IBE) communication scheme. This scheme encompasses the fuzzy extraction of channel state information from IoT devices, stable identity extraction for fuzzy IoT devices using LSH, and the application of zero-knowledge proofs to ensure the authenticity of the generated identity. The resultant identity serves as the basis for identity-based encryption, constructing the device's public key, and facilitating confidential communication among devices.

Author Contributions: Conceptualization, B.Z.; Methodology, B.Z. and Z.X.; Investigation, P.C.; Data curation, Y.L.; Writing—original draft, B.Z.; Writing—review & editing, T.Z. and Z.X.; Visualization, J.W.; Supervision, P.C.; Project administration, T.Z. All authors have read and agreed to the published version of the manuscript.

Funding: This work was supported by the National Key R&D Program of China [2022YFB3104300].

Data Availability Statement: Data are contained within the article.

Conflicts of Interest: Authors Bo Zhang, Tao Zhang and Zesheng Xi were employed by the company State Grid Smart Grid Research Institute Co., Ltd. The remaining authors declare that the research was conducted in the absence of any commercial or financial relationships that could be construed as a potential conflict of interest.

References

1. Boneh, D.; Franklin, M. Identity-based encryption from the Weil pairing. In *Annual International Cryptology Conference, Proceedings of the CRYPTO 2001, Santa Barbara, CA, USA, 19–23 August 2001*; Springer: Berlin/Heidelberg, Germany, 2001; pp. 213–229.
2. Sakai, R. Cryptosystems based on pairing over elliptic curve. In Proceedings of the Symposium on Cryptography and Information Security-SCIS'01, Orlando, FL, USA, 22–25 July 2001.
3. Cocks, C. An identity based encryption scheme based on quadratic residues. In Proceedings of the Cryptography and Coding: 8th IMA International Conference, Cirencester, UK, 17–19 December 2001; Proceedings 8; Springer: Berlin/Heidelberg, Germany, 2001; pp. 360–363.
4. Waters, B. Efficient identity-based encryption without random oracles. In Proceedings of the Advances in Cryptology–EUROCRYPT 2005: 24th Annual International Conference on the Theory and Applications of Cryptographic Techniques, Aarhus, Denmark, 22–26 May 2005; Proceedings 24; Springer: Berlin/Heidelberg, Germany, 2005; pp. 114–127.
5. Afroaz, K.; Rao, Y.S.; Rukma, R.N. A Key Escrow Free Anonymous Identity Based Encryption Scheme Using Ring Signatures. In Proceedings of the 2022 IEEE 11th International Conference on Communication Systems and Network Technologies (CSNT), Indore, India, 23–24 April 2022; IEEE: Piscataway, NJ, USA, 2022; pp. 596–600.
6. Veeresh, V.; Parvathy, L.R. Identity-based Encryption to Implement Anti-Collusion Information Sharing Schemes in Cloud Computing. In Proceedings of the 2023 2nd International Conference on Applied Artificial Intelligence and Computing (ICAAIC), Salem, India, 4–6 May 2023; IEEE: Piscataway, NJ, USA, 2023; pp. 1177–1182.
7. Ngo, D.H. Private Identity-Based Encryption For Key Management. In Proceedings of the 2020 7th NAFOSTED Conference on Information and Computer Science (NICS), Ho Chi Minh City, Vietnam, 26–27 November 2020; IEEE: Piscataway, NJ, USA, 2020; pp. 416–420.
8. Liu, Y.; Wu, X.; Chen, X. A scheme for key distribution in wireless sensor network based on Hierarchical Identity-Based Encryption. In Proceedings of the 2015 IEEE 12th International Conference on Networking, Sensing and Control, Taipei, Taiwan, 9–11 April 2015; IEEE: Piscataway, NJ, USA, 2015; pp. 539–543.
9. Wan, X.; Xiao, L.; Li, Q.; Han, Z. FHY-layer authentication with multiple landmarks with reduced communication overhead. In Proceedings of the 2017 IEEE International Conference on Communications (ICC), Paris, France, 21–25 May 2017; IEEE: Piscataway, NJ, USA, 2017; pp. 1–6.
10. Mahmood, A.; Aman, W.; Iqbal, M.O.; Rahman, M.M.U.; Abbasi, Q.H. Channel impulse response-based distributed physical layer authentication. In Proceedings of the 2017 IEEE 85th Vehicular Technology Conference (VTC Spring), Sydney, NSW, Australia, 4–7 June 2017; IEEE: Piscataway, NJ, USA, 2017; pp. 1–5.

11. Wu, Q.; Feres, C.; Kuzmenko, D.; Zhi, D.; Yu, Z.; Liu, X.; Liu, X. Deep learning based RF fingerprinting for device identification and wireless security. *Electron. Lett.* **2018**, *54*, 1405–1407. [CrossRef]
12. Liao, R.; Wen, H.; Pan, F.; Song, H.; Xu, A.; Jiang, Y. A novel physical layer authentication method with convolutional neural network. In Proceedings of the 2019 IEEE International Conference on Artificial Intelligence and Computer Applications (ICAICA), Dalian, China, 29–31 March 2019; IEEE: Piscataway, NJ, USA, 2019; pp. 231–235.
13. Shi, C.; Liu, J.; Liu, H.; Chen, Y. Smart user authentication through actuation of daily activities leveraging WiFi-enabled IoT. In Proceedings of the18th ACM International Symposium on Mobile ad Hoc Networking and Computing, Chennai, India, 10–14 July 2017; pp. 1–10.
14. Ribouh, S.; Phan, K.; Malawade, A.V.; Elhillali, Y.; Rivenq, A.; Al Faruque, M.A. Channel state information-based cryptographic key generation for intelligent transportation systems. *IEEE Trans. Intell. Transp. Syst.* **2020**, *22*, 7496–7507. [CrossRef]
15. Ji, Z.; Zhang, Y.; He, Z.; Yeoh, P.L.; Li, B.; Yin, H.; Li, Y.; Vucetic, B. Wireless secret key generation for distributed antenna systems: A joint space-time-frequency perspective. *IEEE Internet Things J.* **2021**, *9*, 633–647. [CrossRef]
16. Wang, S.; Huang, K.; Xu, X.; Zhong, Z.; Zhou, Y. Csi-based physical layer authentication via deep learning. *IEEE Wirel. Commun. Lett.* **2022**, *11*, 1748–1752. [CrossRef]
17. Wang, H.M.; Fu, Q.Y. Channel-prediction-based one-class mobile IoT device authentication. *IEEE Internet Things J.* **2021**, *9*, 7731–7745. [CrossRef]
18. Lu, Y.; Huang, X.; Zhang, K.; Maharjan, S.; Zhang, Y. Blockchain empowered asynchronous federated learning for secure data sharing in internet of vehicles. *IEEE Trans. Veh. Technol.* **2020**, *69*, 4298–4311. [CrossRef]
19. Niu, C.; Zheng, Z.; Wu, F.; Gao, X.; Chen, G. Trading data in good faith: Integrating truthfulness and privacy preservation in data markets. In Proceedings of the 2017 IEEE 33rd International Conference on Data Engineering (ICDE), San Diego, CA, USA, 19–22 April 2017; IEEE: Piscataway, NJ, USA, 2017; pp. 223–226.
20. Goldwasser, S.; Micali, S.; Rackoff, C. The knowledge complexity of interactive proof-systems. In *Providing Sound Foundations for Cryptography: On the Work of Shafi Goldwasser and Silvio Micali*; Association for Computing Machinery: New York, NY, USA, 2019; pp. 203–225.
21. Walshe, M.; Epiphaniou, G.; Al-Khateeb, H.; Hammoudeh, M.; Katos, V.; Dehghantanha, A. Non-interactive zero knowledge proofs for the authentication of IoT devices in reduced connectivity environments. *Ad Hoc Netw.* **2019**, *95*, 101988. [CrossRef]
22. Salleras, X.; Daza, V. SANS: Self-sovereign authentication for network slices. *Secur. Commun. Netw.* **2020**, *2020*, 8823573. [CrossRef]
23. Gabay, D.; Akkaya, K.; Cebe, M. A privacy framework for charging connected electric vehicles using blockchain and zero knowledge proofs. In Proceedings of the 2019 IEEE 44th LCN Symposium on Emerging Topics in Networking (LCN Symposium), Osnabrueck, Germany, 14–17 October 2019; IEEE: Piscataway, NJ, USA, 2019; pp. 66–73.

electronics

MDPI

Article

Signal Separation Method for Radiation Sources Based on a Parallel Denoising Autoencoder

Xusheng Tang [1,2,*] and Mingfeng Wei [1]

[1] School of Cyber Science and Engineering, Southeast University, Nanjing 211189, China; 220225887@seu.edu.cn
[2] Purple Mountain Laboratories, Nanjing 211111, China
* Correspondence: tangxsh@seu.edu.cn

Abstract: Radiation source signal sorting in complex environments is currently a hot issue in the field of electronic countermeasures. The pulse repetition interval (PRI) can provide stable and obvious parametric features in radiation source identification, which is an important parameter relying on the signal sorting problem. To solve the problem linked to the difficulties in sorting the PRI in complex environments using the traditional method, a signal sorting method based on a parallel denoising autoencoder is proposed. This method implements the binarized preprocessing of known time-of-arrival (TOA) sequences and then constructs multiple parallel denoising autoencoder models using fully connected layers to achieve the simultaneous sorting of multiple signal types in the overlapping signals. The experimental results show that this method maintains high precision in scenarios prone to large error and can efficiently filter out noise and highlight the original features of the signal. In addition, the present model maintains its performance and some robustness in the sorting of different signal types. Compared with the traditional algorithm, this method improves the precision of sorting. The algorithm presented in this study still maintains above 90% precision when the pulse loss rate reaches 50%.

Keywords: autoencoder; noise reduction; PRI; signal binning

1. Introduction

With the extensive use of radar signals in recent years, various types of interference and signal parameter spatial overlap phenomena have increased, creating a complex electromagnetic environment around the radar signal [1]. Signals in a complex environment are specifically characterized by certain measurement errors, more lost pulses, and false pulses, and these characteristics greatly interfere with the signals [2]. Therefore, radar radiation source sorting in complex environments has become a hot issue in the field of electronic countermeasures and other fields [3].

The traditional five-dimensional parameter method utilizes the pulse description word (PDW) of the signal, i.e., the five parameters of carrier frequency (RF), pulse amplitude (PA), pulse width (PW), direction-of-arrival (DOA), and time-of-arrival (TOA), for signal sorting and identification [4], and the errors generated in a complex environment cause the five-dimensional parameter method to be prone to parameter ambiguity and signal misjudgment, which greatly affects the sorting of the signal.

Among the five parameters of the pulse descriptor, the most stable is the TOA, and its first-level difference is called the pulse repetition interval (PRI), also known as re-frequency. The PRI parameter has a more obvious pattern [5]; so, it is a practical method with which to analyze the TOA parameter. Traditional signal sorting methods based on PRI include the difference histogram algorithm (CDIF) [6], the sequence difference histogram algorithm (SDIF) [7], the PRI transformation method, and its improved algorithm [8,9], etc. A common problem with these methods is that the accuracy of the algorithms is greatly reduced in the face of complex PRI pattern signals, as well as in scenarios with high false pulse rate or lost pulse rate, which cannot be sorted correctly.

For noise interference caused by a complex environment, the current main denoising processing methods include wavelet transform [10], singular value decomposition [11], and so on. However, due to the impulse representation of radar signals in the form of pulse description words, such traditional denoising methods cannot be used.

Aiming at the problem of there being more false pulses, lost pulses, and measurement errors that can interfere with the sorting task in real scenarios, as well as more signal overlapping, this paper proposes a parallel denoising autoencoder-based target sorting method, which can be used for multi-target parallel sorting tasks in complex environments.

The algorithm studied in this paper solves the problem presented by the currently used algorithms, which are generally sensitive to noise in the task of sorting key targets of radiation sources with known parameters; in fact, it can accurately and rapidly distinguish targets and has important applications in the fields of security, aviation, and so on. In the context of electronic countermeasures, the proposed algorithm can improve target identification accuracy, identify key signals to optimize electronic jamming strategies, and sort and summarize signal data to enhance electromagnetic situational awareness. Through these features, the proposed algorithm can improve the defense capability of electronic countermeasure systems.

The main contributions of this paper are as follows: (i) the incorporation of preprocessing operations in the form of binary encoding. The intercepted raw TOA data are preprocessed into binary sequences and then fed into the parallel denoising autoencoder network model for training. This operation facilitates the extraction and recognition of the data by the network model, highlights data features, and further improves the model recognition efficiency; (ii) the construction of a parallel denoising autoencoder network model. The described model contains multiple denoising autoencoders that can work in parallel, adapt to the strong noise environment, and realize the effective recognition and sorting of multi-target overlapping signals. The method described in this paper can realize the synchronous sorting of overlapping signals under the joint interference of lost pulse, false pulse, and measurement error, and the precision of sorting is improved compared with that of traditional algorithms.

2. Data Preprocessing

TOA (time-of-arrival) refers to the arrival time of a pulse, usually defined as the time at which the pulse front is received. In a single radiation source environment, the first-order difference of the TOA parameter is defined as the pulse repetitive interval (PRI), i.e., the re-frequency, which is the interval between two neighboring pulses [5]. According to the regular differences exhibited by the re-frequency characteristics, the inter-pulse modulation of radar signals can be classified into various types [12]. The most typical types include fixed re-frequency, periodic modulation re-frequency, and so on [13].

TOA data are a one-dimensional time series that can grow continuously, and the TOA sequence of a radar signal is usually expressed as

$$T = \{t_1, t_2, \cdots, t_n\}, \tag{1}$$

where n is the total number of data contained in the sequence.

When dealing with large-scale samples, there is a situation in which the value domain range of TOA sequences is too large, and the PRI range is relatively small, resulting in PRI data being difficult to capture and learn. The fitness of such data for neural networks is low. To address this problem, this work involved carrying out preprocessing operations on the acquired TOA sequences and input them into the network after transforming them into a data form suitable for machine model learning. The preprocessed data had a clear regularity, a simple format, and high adaptability to the neural network, allowing the effective recognition of the modulation type.

The preprocessing method in this paper is binary coding. It encodes the TOA sequence data into binary sequence data consisting of zeros and ones.

Typically, the arrival time of the first pulse of the signal is designated as zero. According to Equation (1), the timeframe of the entire TOA sequence can be determined as $[0, t_n]$. Introducing the variable t_{delta} as the unit time, this timeframe is segmented into equal intervals based on the unit time duration, with the number of segments represented by

$$N = \frac{t_n}{t_{delta}}. \tag{2}$$

The mathematical model of binary coding adopted in this paper is:

$$c_j = \begin{cases} 1, (j-1)\cdot t_{delta} < t_i \le j\cdot t_{delta} \\ 0, otherwise \end{cases}, j = 1, 2, \cdots, N; i = 1, 2, \cdots, n. \tag{3}$$

As shown in Equation (2), time segment j is denoted as $[(j-1)\cdot t_{delta}, j\cdot t_{delta}]$. If the acquired TOA data point t_i falls within time segment j, it is encoded as one, otherwise, it is encoded as zero. The resultant encoded TOA sequence is transformed into a fresh binary sequence denoted by

$$C = \{c_1, c_2, \cdots, c_N\}. \tag{4}$$

With an array of re-frequency values within a cycle, each type of re-frequency value cycles through according to the array. Assuming $t_{delta} = 20$ μs, an example is given to illustrate the coding logic of the TOA sequence and represent the coding sequences for the four modulation types.

As shown in Table 1, complex types of re-frequency features such as slip change are difficult to quickly and clearly extract from TOA sequences. However, upon conversion to binary sequences, the PRI laws become more apparent, as machines are better equipped to handle binary sequences than decimal numbers. Furthermore, employing the unit time for encoding initially helps mitigate certain measurement errors. This preprocessing step effectively accentuates the modulation law, enhances computational efficiency, and diminishes measurement errors in the TOA data, thereby facilitating subsequent training and sorting tasks.

Table 1. Representation of coding sequences for the four modulation types.

Modulation Types	Repetition Value (μs)	TOA Fragment (μs)	Coding Sequence
Fixed	[60]	[60, 120, 180, 240]	[0, 0, 1, 0, 0, 1, 0, 0, 1, 0, 0, 1]
Sliding	[40, 60, 80]	[40, 100, 180, 220]	[0, 1, 0, 0, 1, 0, 0, 0, 1, 0, 1]
Group	[50, 50, 70, 70]	[50, 100, 170, 240]	[0, 0, 1, 0, 1, 0, 0, 0, 1, 0, 0, 1]
Cyclic	[27, 84, 69]	[27, 111, 180, 207]	[0, 1, 0, 0, 0, 1, 0, 0, 1, 0, 1]

3. Methods

3.1. Model Introduction

Autoencoder (AE) [14] is an unsupervised learning neural network model that automatically learns the intrinsic laws within data without requiring pre-labeling. It is defined by its ability to reconstruct the input data as faithfully as possible in the output. The autoencoder consists of two components—encoder and decoder—each for two distinct phases—encoding and decoding. During encoding, the input data are compressed, while decoding entails the precise reconstruction of the data. Currently, the autoencoders primarily serve the purposes of data compression and feature extraction. By retaining the essential features and reducing data dimensionality, they effectively accentuate data patterns, thereby enhancing operational efficiency. Consequently, autoencoders are widely applied to anomaly detection and denoising tasks.

The denoising autoencoder (DAE) [15] represents a special category within the autoencoder family. While the fundamental structure of the denoising autoencoder remains largely unchanged compared to the basic autoencoder, it introduces artificial contamination to the input data. The deliberate addition of noise disrupts some regularities within the original data, compelling the model to acquire more robust denoising features. As a result, denoising autoencoders excel in preserving data information while effectively mitigating the impact of noise interference.

Due to the output characteristics of autoencoders, a single autoencoder model can only accommodate one type of signal. In practical scenarios, intercepted signals often comprise multiple distinct signals requiring classification. Repeatedly employing individual autoencoder networks or sequentially calling multiple autoencoder networks for training and sorting proves to be not only inefficient but also vulnerable to errors, and lacks robustness. To address these challenges, this paper introduces a parallel denoising autoencoder model aimed at enabling the simultaneous training and sorting of multiple modulation types of signals, leading to the concurrent acquisition of diverse binning results.

The workflow of the parallel denoising autoencoder is illustrated in Figure 1. Initially, the various TOA sequence data intended for training undergo preprocessing to encode them into corresponding binary sequences. During the pre-training phase, noise is added to the training binary sequences, followed by synchronous operation of denoising autoencoders to generate N network model files tailored to distinct modulation types. Subsequently, in the binning phase, the TOA sequences containing assorted radar signals are preprocessed into binary coded sequences. These binary sequences are then simultaneously inputted into the parallel denoising autoencoder network, utilizing the trained model files to yield multiple corresponding outputs. As noise presence may corrupt the PRI law of the signal and lead to errors in the output sequence during signal recovery, resulting in misclassification of radar signals, the model confirms the sorted types. Any instances of identical output types prompt further meticulous comparisons for precise identification. Ultimately, the network yields all the finalized binning results.

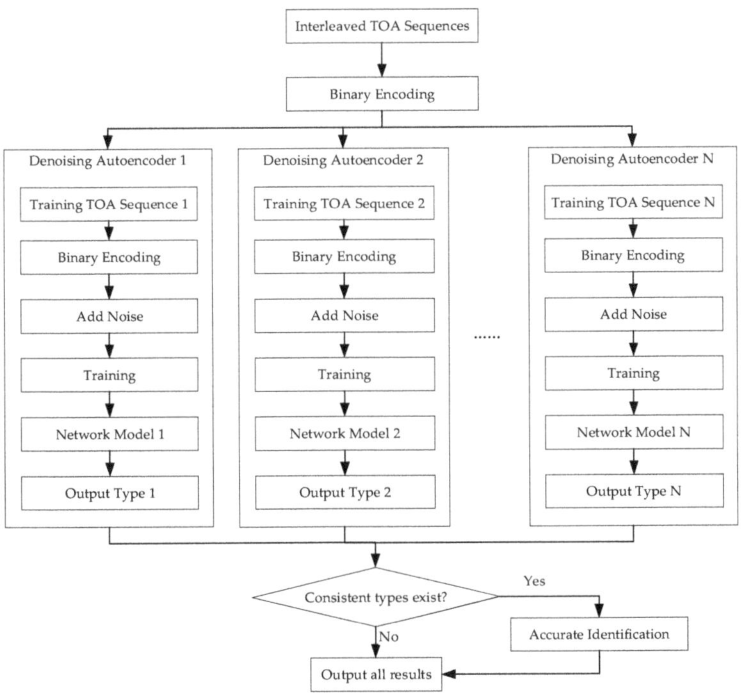

Figure 1. The workflow diagram of the parallel denoising autoencoder.

When conducting the sorting task, the parallel denoising autoencoder model synchronously activates multiple autoencoders to process the input aliased signals, generating multiple outputs simultaneously. This process incorporates specific error-correction mechanisms, thereby enhancing the efficiency and accuracy of signal sorting.

3.2. Architecture Design of the Model

The overall structure of the parallel denoising autoencoder model outlined in this paper is shown in Figure 2. In the coding sequence, solid circles represent the positions of signal pulses, with different colors denoting various signal types. Hollow circles signify the zeros within the coding sequence, while other circles mark the locations of assorted noise types. The model receives the aliased signals through a designated input port, and the signal sorting task is based on several relatively independent denoising autoencoder models operating in parallel. Each autoencoder network is responsible for sorting a specific signal type and is tasked with isolating the desired focal signal type from the binary encoded noisy aliased TOA sequence while removing the contained noise.

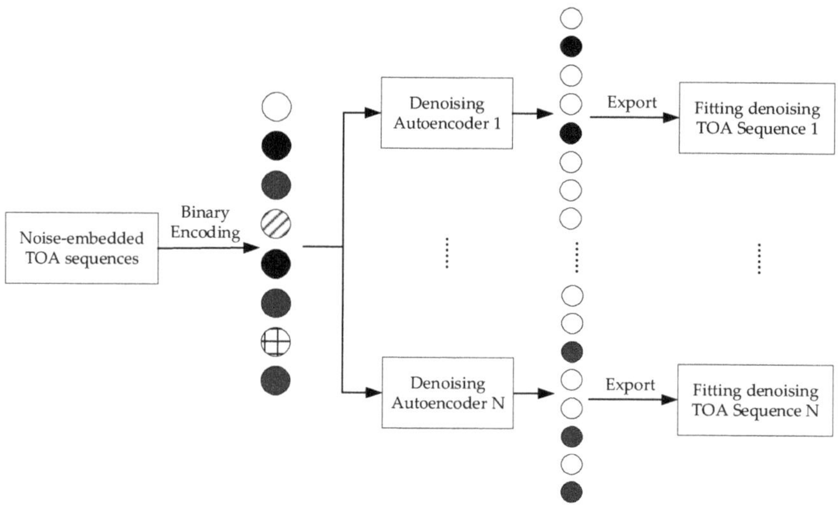

Figure 2. The model diagram of the parallel denoising autoencoder.

To ensure the generalizability of the entire model for various radar signal sorting tasks and the stability of the model itself, consistent structural design is maintained across all units. For clarity, use one unit as an example to elaborate on the network's structural design.

The network model of the denoising autoencoder unit is shown in Figure 3. In the coding sequence, solid circles denote the positions of signal pulses, hollow circles indicate zeros, and other circles illustrate the locations of various types of noise. After preprocessing the TOA data, noise is added to the resulting binary sequence as input to the denoising autoencoder. The noise addition process is represented as

$$y = h(x), \tag{5}$$

where x represents the encoded binary sequence, and $h(\cdot)$ denotes the noise addition function. When recognizing a specific focal signal type, other types are considered as noise.

The model comprises an encoder and a decoder, both consisting of multiple fully connected layers. A single fully connected layer is mathematically represented as

$$f(x) = g(Wx + b), \tag{6}$$

where x is the input, W denotes the layer's weight, b is the offset value, and $g(\cdot)$ represents the activation function. Since neural networks themselves are linear transformations, a linear model can only solve a limited set of problems. To introduce nonlinearity and enhance the model's effectiveness, activation functions are generally used. In this paper, all fully connected layers, except for the last one, employ the rectified linear unit (ReLU) activation function defined as:

$$g_{ReLU}(x) = max\{0, x\}. \tag{7}$$

The ReLU function outputs the greater value between zero and the input. It helps prevent the gradient vanishing problem and accelerates convergence during gradient descent. The last fully connected layer uses the Sigmoid function, which maps all output data to the range of zero to one:

$$g_S(x) = \frac{1}{1 + e^{-x}}. \tag{8}$$

Given that the final model output should be a binary sequence, a threshold ξ is set after the Sigmoid function. Numbers greater than or equal to ξ are assigned one, while numbers less than ξ are assigned zero. In this model, ξ is set to 0.5.

As seen in Figure 3, the encoding phase involves the noise-added data entering the input layer of the model and being mapped to multiple fully-connected hidden layers denoted as:

$$z = f^{(L_1)}(y) = \underbrace{f(\cdots f(y))}_{L_1}, \tag{9}$$

where L_1 represents the number of layers in the fully connected layer within the encoder, and y is the output of Equation (4), i.e., the binary sequence after adding various types of noise, which is substituted as an input variable into Equation (5) and mapped. The output z of the encoder typically has a much lower dimension than the input y, which aligns with its function of reducing data dimensionality. This compressed data z retains important features, facilitating effective network learning, reducing the risk of overfitting, and minimizing error data.

The processed data z are then fed into the decoder for reconstruction of the original data, denoted as

$$x' = f'^{(L_2)}(z) = \underbrace{f'(\cdots f'(z))}_{L_2}, \tag{10}$$

where L_2 denotes the number of fully connected layer layers within the decoder. The y in Equation (8) is the same class of signals containing different errors. Ideally, the only solution obtained by fitting y can only be the original binary sequence without noise, x. Based on this, the output of the decoder in Equation (9), x', is the sequence fitted to x, rather than reconstructing the noisy sequence, y. x' is kept in the same dimensionality as x, and is fitted as closely as possible to the eigenstructure of x.

The trained loss function measures the difference between the predicted result and the true value, and minimizing the loss function can make the output sequence of the autoencoder closer to the actual sequence. In this paper, where the input x and output x' are binary sequences, the binary cross-entropy function is chosen as the loss function, expressed mathematically, the model is presented in Equations (11) and (12):

$$\mathcal{L}(x, x') = \{l_1, \cdots, l_n\}^T, \tag{11}$$

$$l_i = -w_i[x_i \cdot \log x'_i + (1 - x_i) \cdot \log(1 - x'_i)], \tag{12}$$

where n denotes the number of training batches, x_i and x'_i represent the raw data and model output data corresponding to batch i, respectively, and w_i denotes the weights. The training begins with the initialization of weights W and the offset value b as random decimals between zero and one. The model is then trained in multiple batches, and the network parameters are adjusted using the error back propagation (BP) algorithm to minimize loss:

$$W_{all}, b_{all} = argmin\mathcal{L}(x, x'), \tag{13}$$

$$W' = W - \mu \frac{\partial l_i}{\partial W} \tag{14}$$

$$b' = b - \mu \frac{\partial l_i}{\partial b}', \tag{15}$$

where W' and b' denote the updated weights and offset values, respectively, and μ is the learning rate set for the model.

The training process continues until the model converges, reaching a state of stability. At this point, the model's parameters remain constant and can be further tested.

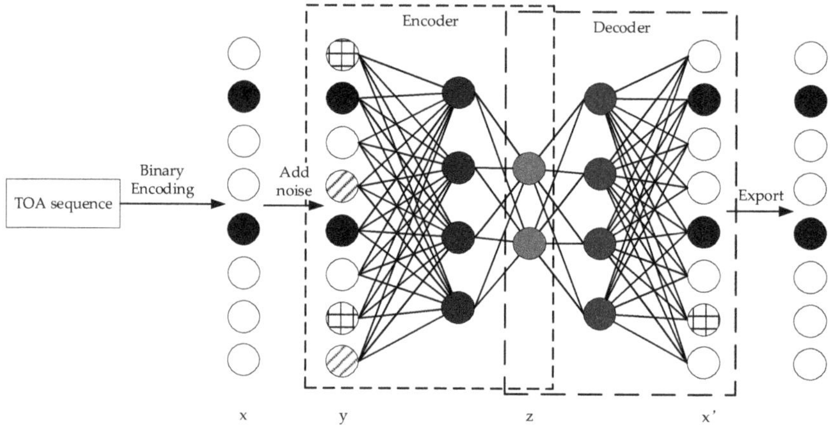

Figure 3. The model diagram of the denoising autoencoder unit.

4. Experiment

4.1. Experimental Data Simulation

4.1.1. Sample Simulation

For the sake of objectivity, this experiment selected four representative modulation types as experimental samples: fixed re-frequency, sliding re-frequency, pulse group re-frequency, and periodic modulation re-frequency. The original TOA sequences corresponding to these four types were generated using Matlab, with simulation parameters detailed in Table 2.

Table 2. The setting of sample data parameters.

Modulation Type	Cyclic Re-Frequency Value (μs)
Fixed Re-Frequency	[250]
Sliding Re-Frequency	[40, 70, 130, 160]
Pulse Group Re-Frequency	[90 × 4, 170 × 4, 240 × 4]
Periodic Modulation Re-Frequency	$[p = 50sin(\frac{\pi}{25}t) + 100]$

Each TOA data sequence was set to a length of 10 ms, and 2000 TOA sequences were generated as training samples for each type of modulation. During the preprocessing stage, the unit time t_{delta} was defined as 10 μs for this experiment. After encoding, the length of each binary data sequence was standardized to 1000.

4.1.2. Error Simulation

In order to simulate a realistic environment, this experiment introduces various types of errors into the data. After analysis and categorization, the errors impacting the radar signal were classified into three main categories: measurement errors, lost pulses, and fake pulses.

Due to the signal or the machine itself, a small deviation in the detected actual arrival time compared to the ideal arrival time of the signal, attributed to either the signal itself or the detection system, is referred to as a measurement error. Typically, following a Gaussian distribution, measurement errors were simulated in this experiment based on an ideal PRI sequence using the equation:

$$Er_j = \frac{P_j - \mu}{\sigma}, \tag{16}$$

where P_j denotes the value at index j in the sequence, Er_j corresponds to the measurement error, μ is the mean value of the sequence, and σ denotes the standard deviation. The TOA sequence is derived from the PRI sequence and can be expressed as:

$$T' = \{t_1, t_2{}', \cdots, t_{j+1}{}', \cdots, t_K{}'\}, \tag{17}$$

$$t_{j+1}{}' = t_1 + \sum_{1}^{j}(P_j + Er_j), \tag{18}$$

where t_1 is the initial value of the original TOA sequence, $t_{j+1}{}'$ represents the value at index $j+1$ in the noisy TOA sequence, and K signifies the total number of data points in the sequence.

Incomplete signal fragments that are not fully received or partial pulses with similar reception times that are mistakenly interpreted as a single TOA value can result in lost pulses. Signal disturbances caused by interference and pulse aliasing from other signals contribute to the occurrence of fake pulses. By considering the specified rates of lost pulses p_l and fake pulses p_f, the number of lost pulses is determined by:

$$N_l = K \cdot p_l, \tag{19}$$

and the number of fake pulses is expressed as

$$N_f = K \cdot p_f. \tag{20}$$

The final simulated noisy TOA sequence, incorporating all three types of errors, involves updating N_l ones to zeros and N_f zeros to ones in the binary sequence derived from the preprocessing of T'.

In this experiment, the measurement error rate p_e is within the [0, 10%] of the re-frequency value, the lost pulse rate p_l is between [0, 50%], and the fake pulse rate p_f is within [0, 70%]. During the training phase, these three parameters are randomly assigned values within specified ranges to generate diverse training data.

4.2. Network Parameter Setting

According to the sample setup of this experiment, a network model comprising four autoencoder units is established, with the parameter configurations of the unit model depicted in Figure 4.

The encoder within the unit model is structured with three fully connected layers containing 128, 64, and 32 neurons sequentially. Following each layer, the ReLU function is applied. Conversely, the decoder is composed of three fully connected layers with 32, 64, and 128 neurons sequentially. In this case, the ReLU function is used after the initial two layers, while the Sigmoid function is employed after the final layer.

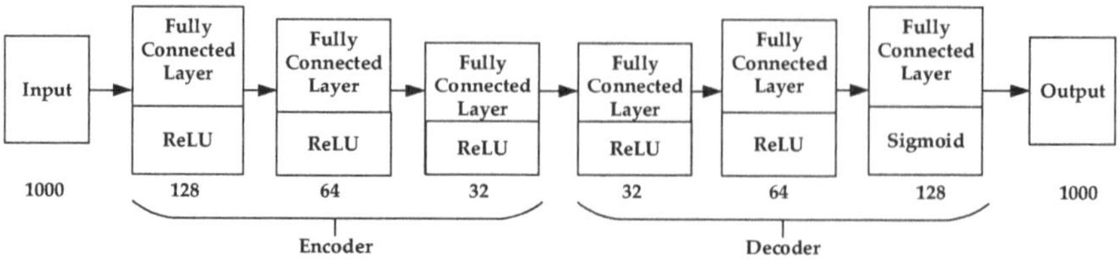

Figure 4. The parameter diagram of the autoencoder unit model.

The Pytorch framework is utilized in this experiment with a batch size of 128, a learning rate set at 0.0001, and a weight decay of 1×10^{-5}. Experimental results demonstrate that the model efficiently converges to a more optimal state within 20 cycles.

4.3. Description of The Training Process

Prior to testing, the model developed in this paper requires training. The training dataset is initially constructed by conducting preprocessing operations as detailed in Section 4.1, in order to convert the simulation data into binary form. Each of the four types in the dataset comprises 2000 binary data entries, with each piece of data having a length of 1000 and encompassing the PRI features of its corresponding type, along with randomly added errors falling within a specified range. Four denoising autoencoder units are established based on the parameters outlined in Section 4.2, and they are organized in parallel to construct the parallel denoising autoencoder model essential for this paper. During training, the model feeds the data from the training set into the denoising autoencoder units based on their respective type, with each unit processing data of only one type at a time. Throughout the training process, each unit autonomously completes the reconstruction of input data pertaining to its designated type. Employing a batch size of 128, the model achieves convergence within 20 cycles. Upon completion of training, the model file of the parallel denoising autoencoder is saved to capture the model structure after all four units have converged.

4.4. Analysis of Experimental Results

This paper comprehensively evaluates the algorithm's effectiveness using accuracy, precision, and recall. As shown in Table 3, the experimental results of the binary classification problem are classified into four types. TP represents data with positive predictions that align with the actual outcome, FP signifies data with positive predictions but contradicting actual negative outcomes, FN indicates data with negative predictions but actual positive outcomes, and TN denotes data with negative predictions matching the actual negative outcomes. Consequently, accuracy is denoted as:

$$Accuracy = \frac{TP + TN}{TP + FP + FN + TN}, \tag{21}$$

precision is denoted as

$$Precision = \frac{TP}{TP + FP}, \tag{22}$$

and recall is denoted as

$$Recall = \frac{TP}{TP + FN}. \tag{23}$$

Table 3. Table of binary classification results.

	Actual Positive Samples	Actual Negative Samples
Predicting positive samples	TP	FP
Predicting negative samples	FN	TN

4.4.1. Modulation Type Sorting Experiment

The test dataset still retains the modulation type and parameter configurations outlined in Table 2, with measurement errors within the [0, 10%] range and the random incorporation of fake pulses within the [0, 70%] range, added at random. The pulse loss rate was systematically increased from 0 to 50%, resulting in the generation of five distinct data sets. By overlaying the four types of TOA coding sequences at equivalent loss rates, five sets of test data comprising aliased signals with varying pulse loss rates were compiled, each set comprising 2000 binary coding sequences.

This experiment aims to assess the efficacy of the parallel denoising autoencoder model in categorizing the four types of modulated signals, with the test outcomes illustrated in Figure 5.

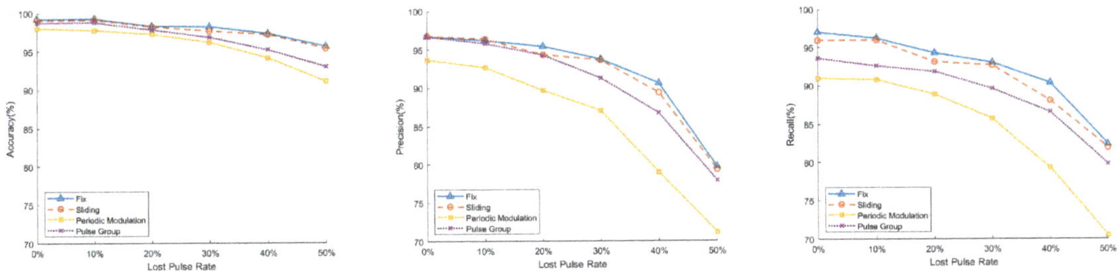

(a) (b) (c)

Figure 5. Sorting performance of the model for four types of signals with different pulse loss rates. Accuracy (**a**), precision (**b**), recall (**c**).

Figure 5 presents line plots depicting the three classification assessments at varying pulse loss rates, with (a) denoting the accuracy rate, (b) signifying the precision rate, and (c) indicating the recall rate. Observably, the model's overall performance in the classification task shows a declining trend as the lost pulse rate increases, attributed to the corruption of PRI features by lost pulses. The detrimental impact becomes more pronounced with higher lost pulse rates, and a substantial decrease in the model's classification performance is evident after the lost pulse rate exceeds 30% in Figure 5. A comparison of the plots (a), (b), and (c) reveals that the reduction in accuracy depicted in (a) is notably smaller than the trends observed in (b) and (c). This is due to the binary nature of the input network signals, which can be treated as a binary classification problem during assessment. Only the number 1 in the sequence represents the pulse, but the number 0 in the sequence also occupies a certain proportion, and the recognition results of both values are calculated into the accuracy rate, yielding a relatively high accuracy rate. Consequently, in this experiment, the accuracy rate can only partially reflect the model's performance and must be considered alongside the precision and recall rates. Notably, the model's classification performance across the four types of modulated signals exhibits a consistent trend, indicating its strong generalizability. Additionally, the representative nature of the four signal types used underscores the robustness of the parallel denoising autoencoder network model formulated in this paper, demonstrating its applicability to diverse signal classification tasks. Among these types, fixed and sliding re-frequencies consistently exhibit high values for all three criteria, while performing the poorest in the periodic modulated PRI sorting task. This is attributed to the relatively simple PRI patterns for fixed and sliding re-frequencies, which consist of repetitions of a single or a small set of digits easily captured and learned by the network. In contrast, the periodic modulation PRI type is more intricate, featuring changing PRI values over a period, posing challenges for the model to learn. Nonetheless, even in the most challenging scenario, the sorting accuracy in this experiment remains above 90%, with precision and recall rates exceeding 70%, affirming the parallel denoising autoencoder model's strong performance in signal sorting tasks.

4.4.2. Comparison Experiment

The traditional method of signal sorting, predominantly based on PRI, continues to be widely utilized. This includes enhancements to classical algorithms like SDIF and CDIF, as well as approaches that incorporate neural networks. Reference [16] proposes an enhanced SDIF algorithm that integrates the PRI transform method, representing an advancement over conventional techniques. Similarly, reference [17] presents a CRRNN algorithm, which leverages RNN networks and incorporates a residual network structure to achieve higher precision. To demonstrate the effectiveness of the method proposed in this paper, we conducted a comparative experiment. This experiment involved the improved SDIF algorithm, the CRRNN algorithm, and the parallel denoising autoencoder model developed in this study, focusing on the slip-variant PRI type as a case study. The data for this experiment were specifically configured to include lost pulses, but excluded fake pulses and measurement errors.

Figure 6 demonstrates the sorting performance of the three algorithms for slip variable PRI types at different pulse loss rates in terms of the precision rate. As the pulse loss rate increases, the precision of this paper's model remains consistently above 90%, showcasing its stability. In contrast, the precision of the enhanced SDIF algorithm shows a notable decline, dropping below 50% in the most severe case. This highlights the significant superiority of the model proposed in this paper over a traditional algorithm. Meanwhile, although the CRRNN algorithm demonstrates higher precision at a pulse loss rate below 20%, its performance noticeably deteriorates when the pulse loss rate exceeds 30%. This decline can be attributed to the autoencoder network's ability to reduce data dimensionality, which in turn enhances its capability for feature extraction in scenarios characterized by high error rates.

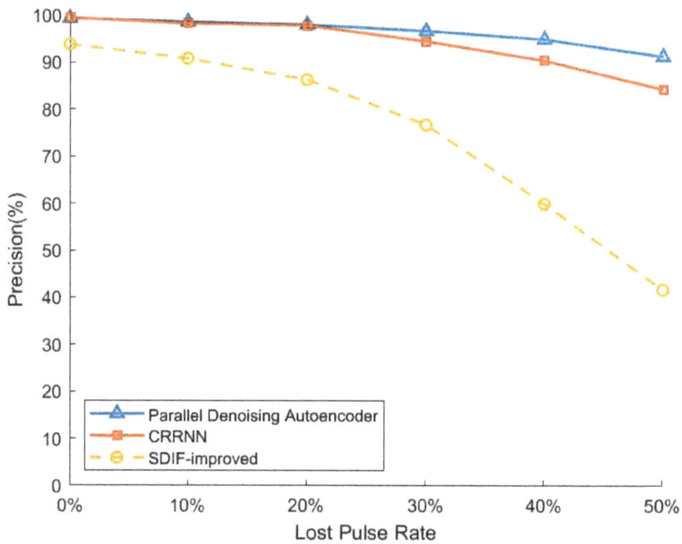

Figure 6. Comparison of algorithm performance at different pulse loss rates.

The experimental results discussed above convincingly demonstrate that the parallel denoising autoencoder network model excels in radar radiation source signal sorting, particularly when it comes to handling multiple signals in complex environments.

5. Conclusions

In this paper, we propose a parallel denoising autoencoder-based method for signal sorting. This method encodes known TOA sequences with preprocessing to amplify the PRI features of the signals. It efficiently segregates desired signal types from overlapping TOA sequences using a parallel denoising autoencoder network.

Comprehensive experimental results show that our algorithm exhibits remarkable adaptability in high error scenarios, maintaining high precision even as pulse loss rate increases. This adaptability makes it well-suited for sorting radiation source tasks in complex environments. In terms of algorithm performance, the algorithm in this paper demonstrates superior efficacy, maintaining an accuracy rate above 90% and a precision rate above 70%, even when the pulse loss rate reaches 50%. Regarding the algorithm's generalization capability, it exhibits a consistent trend and shows strong generalization capability, when facing the task of sorting various types of radiation source PRI signals.

Further analysis suggests that the advantage of the algorithm stems partly from the autoencoder's enhanced filtering ability, which effectively mitigates noise and other unfocused signals by reducing data dimensionality, thus proving to be more adaptable in complex environments. Additionally, the use of multiple repetition architectures, all built with fully connected layers, simplifies the complexity. This enables rapid sorting of extensive data and accommodates multiple sorting types.

Overall, the parallel denoising autoencoder model proficiently handles the classification of multiple signal types in challenging environments.

However, it is important to note that the algorithm performs optimally when the PRI features of the radiated source signal are distinct and the training data volume is adequate. In situations where errors, especially lost pulses, are prevalent, the autoencoder might extract incomplete PRI features, adversely affecting the sorting process. Future research will focus on enhancing the PRI features of the radiation source in extremely complex environments.

Author Contributions: Conceptualization, X.T.; methodology, X.T.; software, M.W.; validation, X.T. and M.W.; formal analysis, X.T.; investigation, M.W.; resources, M.W.; data curation, M.W.; writing—original draft preparation, M.W.; writing—review and editing, X.T.; visualization, X.T.; supervision, X.T.; project administration, X.T. All authors have read and agreed to the published version of the manuscript.

Funding: This research received no external funding.

Data Availability Statement: All data underlying the results are available as part of the article and no additional source data are required.

Acknowledgments: The authors would like to thank the editors and reviewers for their efforts to help with the publication of this work.

Conflicts of Interest: The authors declare no conflicts of interest.

References

1. Liu, Z.-M. Pulse Deinterleaving for Multifunction Radars with Hierarchical Deep Neural Networks. *IEEE Trans. Aerosp. Electron. Syst.* **2021**, *57*, 3585–3599. [CrossRef]
2. Li, X.; Liu, Z.; Huang, Z. Deinterleaving of Pulse Streams with Denoising Autoencoders. *IEEE Trans. Aerosp. Electron. Syst.* **2020**, *56*, 4767–4778. [CrossRef]
3. Dong, X.; Liang, Y.; Wang, J. Distributed Clustering Method Based on Spatial Information. *IEEE Access* **2022**, *10*, 53143–53152. [CrossRef]
4. Lang, P.; Fu, X.; Cui, Z.; Feng, C.; Chang, J. Subspace Decomposition Based Adaptive Density Peak Clustering for Radar Signals Sorting. *IEEE Signal Process. Lett.* **2022**, *29*, 424–428. [CrossRef]
5. Xiang, H.; Shen, F.; Zhao, J. Deep ToA Mask-Based Recursive Radar Pulse Deinterleaving. *IEEE Trans. Aerosp. Electron. Syst.* **2023**, *59*, 989–1006. [CrossRef]
6. He, Y.; Sang, X.; Li, Y.; Wang, J.; Guo, Q.; Wu, P. PRI-based radar signal binning algorithm and simulation implementation. In Proceedings of the 2023 IEEE 7th Information Technology and Mechatronics Engineering Conference (ITOEC), Chongqing, China, 15–17 September 2023; pp. 706–710. [CrossRef]

7. Sang, X.; He, Y.; Li, Y. Radar signal binning based on improved SDIF algorithm. In Proceedings of the 2023 IEEE 7th Information Technology and Mechatronics Engineering Conference (ITOEC), Chongqing, China, 15–17 September 2023; pp. 203–207. [CrossRef]
8. Liu, Y.; Zhang, Q. An improved method for deinterleaving radar signals and estimating PRI values. *IET Radar Sonar Navigat.* **2018**, *12*, 506–514. [CrossRef]
9. Xi, Y.; Wu, Y.; Wu, X.; Jiang, K. An improved SDIF algorithm for anti-radiation radar using dynamic sequence search. In Proceedings of the 2017 36th Chinese Control Conference (CCC), Dalian, China, 26–28 July 2017; pp. 5596–5601.
10. Wu, Y.; Gao, G.; Cui, C. Improved Wavelet Denoising by Non-Convex Sparse Regularization Under Double Wavelet Domains. *IEEE Access* **2019**, *7*, 30659–30671. [CrossRef]
11. Li, Y.; Yue, X.; Wu, X.; Zhang, L.; Zhou, Q.; Yi, X.; Liu, N. A Higher-Order Singular Value Decomposition-Based Radio Frequency Interference Mitigation Method on High-Frequency Surface Wave Radar. *IEEE Trans. Geosci. Remote Sens.* **2020**, *58*, 2770–2781. [CrossRef]
12. Han, J.-W.; Park, C.H. A Unified Method for Deinterleaving and PRI Modulation Recognition of Radar Pulses Based on Deep Neural Networks. *IEEE Access* **2021**, *9*, 89360–89375. [CrossRef]
13. Nuhoglu, M.A.; Alp, Y.K.; Ulusoy, M.E.C.; Cirpan, H.A. Image Segmentation for Radar Signal Deinterleaving Using Deep Learning. *IEEE Trans. Aerosp. Electron. Syst.* **2023**, *59*, 541–554. [CrossRef]
14. Min, B.; Yoo, J.; Kim, S.; Shin, D.; Shin, D. Network Anomaly Detection Using Memory-Augmented Deep Autoencoder. *IEEE Access* **2021**, *9*, 104695–104706. [CrossRef]
15. Lee, W.-H.; Ozger, M.; Challita, U.; Sung, K.W. Noise Learning-Based Denoising Autoencoder. *IEEE Commun. Lett.* **2021**, *25*, 2983–2987. [CrossRef]
16. Liu, Y.; Chen, Y.; Sun, S. A radar signal sorting algorithm based on PRI. In Proceedings of the 2019 19th International Symposium on Communications and Information Technologies (ISCIT), Ho Chi Minh City, Vietnam, 25–27 September 2019; pp. 144–149. [CrossRef]
17. Al-Malahi, A.; Almaqtari, O.; Ayedh, W.; Tang, B. Radar Signal Sorting Using Combined Residual and Recurrent Neural Network (CRRNN). In Proceedings of the 2021 18th International Computer Conference on Wavelet Active Media Technology and Information Processing (ICCWAMTIP), Chengdu, China, 17–19 December 2021; pp. 21–27. [CrossRef]

electronics

MDPI

Article

A Malicious Program Behavior Detection Model Based on API Call Sequences

Nige Li [1,2,*], Ziang Lu [1,2], Yuanyuan Ma [1,2], Yanjiao Chen [3] and Jiahan Dong [4]

1 State Grid Smart Grid Research Institute Co., Ltd., Nanjing 210003, China; luziang@geiri.sgcc.com.cn (Z.L.); mayuanyuan@geiri.sgcc.com.cn (Y.M.)
2 State Grid Laboratory of Power Cyber-Security Protection and Monitoring Technology, Nanjing 210003, China
3 College of Electrical Engineering, Zhejiang University, Hangzhou 310038, China; chenyanjiao@zju.edu.cn
4 State Grid Beijing Electric Power Research Institute, Beijing 100075, China; dongjiahan@bj.sgcc.com.cn
* Correspondence: linige@geiri.sgcc.com.cn

Abstract: To address the issue of low accuracy in detecting malicious program behaviors in new power system edge-side applications, we present a detection model based on API call sequences that combines rule matching and deep learning techniques in this paper. We first use the PrefixSpan algorithm to mine frequent API call sequences in different threads of the same program within a malicious program dataset to create a rule base for malicious behavior sequences. The API call sequences to be examined are then matched using the malicious behavior sequence matching model, and those that do not match are fed into the TextCNN deep learning detection model for additional detection. The two models collaborate to accomplish program behavior detection. Experimental results demonstrate that the proposed detection model can effectively identify malicious samples and discern malicious program behaviors.

Keywords: API call sequences; malicious programs; behavior detection

1. Introduction

Compared to traditional power systems, the structure of the new power system is more intricate. The integration of new energy sources, such as renewable energy, into the power system and the growing number of distributed power sources connected to the grid from the user's side are posing greater challenges to the stability and security of the power system. Edge-side applications in the new power system are those that directly interact with power equipment, sensors, controllers, and other components. These applications play a crucial role in collecting, processing, transmitting, and controlling power data, significantly influencing the operational status, fault diagnosis, and dispatch control of the power system. Abnormal or malicious behaviors in edge-side applications, such as data tampering, command errors, or cyber-attacks, can lead to failures, damage, or even paralysis of the power system, with potentially severe socio-economic repercussions [1]. Consequently, real-time behavior detection of edge-side applications is essential to detect and prevent such adverse behaviors, ensuring the safe and stable operation of the new power system.

There are two primary approaches to analyzing malicious programs: static analysis and dynamic analysis [2]. Static analysis does not involve executing the code; instead, it assesses whether a program is malicious based on code attributes, control flow diagrams, function call diagrams, system call sequences, and other characteristics [3–7]. While static analysis offers the benefits of rapid execution and high efficiency, its capacity for behavioral analysis is notably limited. It struggles to detect obfuscation and encryption techniques frequently employed by malicious programs, such as packing, modifications to the PE header, and code obfuscation. In contrast, dynamic analysis evaluates the behavior of an executable file by running it. This method's advantage lies in its resilience to code obfuscation, shelling, and polymorphism, providing the most authentic representation of the program's behavior [8].

Behavior detection technology is a form of dynamic analysis that involves monitoring a program's behavior during execution and determining its maliciousness based on this behavior. An Application Programming Interface (API) provides a means for applications to interact with the system. The sequences of API calls can reveal the functionality and behavioral traits of an application, making them a crucial element in the detection of malicious code [9].

At present, the dynamic features of malicious programs are usually based on API call sequences, with machine learning employed for their detection. However, traditional machine learning methods face challenges in feature selection and struggle to address the anomaly detection issue in high-dimensional massive network traffic, resulting in a high false detection rate. In the detection of malicious programs, rule matching is a commonly used method characterized by its simplicity and low false detection rate. However, it fails to capture the deep relationships within API call sequences and does not leverage the temporal nature of APIs, and the temporal nature of APIs is not utilized, which leads to low accuracy of the model. Deep learning models, known for their robust learning and classification capabilities, have found applications in power systems [10]. These models can automatically extract features and categorize them based on these features, leading to enhanced performance. Consequently, many researchers have explored using deep learning to address the analysis of malicious programs. To ensure the stable operation and data security of edge-side applications in new power systems and to reduce the false positive rate of malicious program detection, we propose a malicious program behavior detection model based on API call sequences by integrating rule matching and deep learning. Initially, the API call sequence is processed to complete the preprocessing of the dataset. Subsequently, the PrefixSpan algorithm is employed to mine frequent API call sequences and establish a rule base for malicious behavior sequences. Finally, the behavior sequence matching model and the TextCNN [11] deep learning detection model are jointly utilized to detect test API call sequences, achieving program behavior detection.

The contributions of this study can be summarized as follows:

- We used the PrefixSpan algorithm to mine the frequent API call sequences from various threads within a malicious program. These sequences serve as a foundation for directly discriminating for malignant API execution actions, obtaining malicious behavior sequences, and constructing a malicious behavior sequence rule base.
- We utilized two models, the behavior sequence matching model and the TextCNN deep learning detection model, to collaboratively detect the tested API call sequences. Firstly, the tested API call sequences are input into the behavior sequence matching model to compare them against the malicious behavior sequence rule base. If a match is found, the sequence is deemed malicious; otherwise, it is passed to the TextCNN neural network model for further analysis to obtain the detection results, thereby enhancing the accuracy of the detection.

2. Related Work

Malicious programs represent a significant security threat to the Internet, with attackers leveraging them for profit through remote control, private information theft, and occasionally targeting network infrastructures. Malware typically disseminates and infects susceptible systems via diverse propagation methods for nefarious purposes, including spam distribution, privacy compromise, system disruption, and denial-of-service attacks. Notable examples of malicious programs include Trojan horses, worms, viruses, ransomware, adware, and spyware [12,13].

On the Windows platform, program behaviors are predominantly executed through system API calls, making the use of APIs for dynamic analysis a focal point in malicious behavior detection research. API calls, whereby an application performs services by invoking functions provided by the operating system, encompass activities such as registry operations, process manipulation, accessing network resources, and file reading. Malicious code typically executes specific behaviors by calling a series of APIs, rather than a single API. Analysis of API call sequences reveals that malicious code often invokes fixed sequences to carry out destructive actions, with different malicious behaviors calling distinct sequences rarely used in normal programs [14]. Therefore, API call sequences provide a more accurate representation of program behavior, and malicious code can be identified by analyzing these sequences and extracting subsequence features that differentiate malicious from normal programs [15]. Modeling the API call behavior of malware and benign software, the actual relationship between API functions is represented as a semantic transformation matrix [16]. The author of [17] developed a malware detection model by integrating statistical, contextual, and graph mining features on API call sequences, bridging the gap of dynamic detection methods. The authors of [18] proposed a deep neural network-based malware detection method for the Windows platform, which learns parameter-enhanced API call sequences and employs rule-based and clustering-based classification methods to evaluate the sensitivity of the parameters of the API call sequences to malicious behavior. Kim [19] proposed a malware detection and classification system by generating a chain of behavioral sequences of some malware families and calculating the similarity between the chain of API behavioral sequences and the sequence of target processes. Dynamic malware detection methods like CTIMD [20] utilize Cyber Threat Intelligences (CTIs) to improve the learning of API call sequences with runtime parameters, offering better accuracy and efficiency compared to traditional methods. However, this approach depends on external threat knowledge and may have limited generalization capabilities.

With the ongoing advancements in natural language processing (NLP), API sequences can be viewed as semantically rich text, enabling the application of machine learning (ML) and deep learning techniques to analyze API call sequences [21–23]. K-nearest neighbor (KNN), naive Bayes (NB), decision tree (DT), and support vector machine (SVM) are widely used in the analysis of API sequences [24]. The authors of [25] propose an efficient malware detection system based on deep learning, which uses a reweighted class balance loss function in the final classification layer of the DenseNet model to significantly improve the performance of malware classification by addressing imbalanced data issues. Huang [26] proposed a hybrid visualization approach for malware that integrates static and dynamic analysis, transforming code into images and conducting malicious detection based on the VGG16 network, thereby improving the detection model's performance. However, due to the typically unbalanced distribution of malware and normal software, deep learning-based methods for detecting malicious programs still exhibit a high false detection rate and require further refinement.

A frequent sequence pattern is a subsequence that occurs more than a specified threshold in a sequence database, indicating a regular behavior or trend. PrefixSpan algorithm [27] is a prominent method for mining frequent sequence patterns from sequence data, which employs prefix projection and a depth-first search strategy to efficiently discover frequent patterns in sequence data. This algorithm is highly effective in various fields, including text processing, web log analysis, and bioinformatics. The core of the PrefixSpan algorithm lies in identifying frequent items in each prefix projection, adding them to the prefix to form a new prefix, and continuing this recursive projection and expansion until no further frequent items can be added [28]. Consequently, the PrefixSpan algorithm starts with frequent sequences of length 1, progressively generates longer frequent sequences, and ultimately obtains all frequent sequence patterns in the database. The advantage of the PrefixSpan algorithm is that it does not require generating candidate sequences, which reduces computational and storage requirements, and it leverages the prefix information of the sequence, minimizing unnecessary search space and enhancing efficiency.

3. Materials and Methods

3.1. Model Framework

In this paper, we propose a malicious program detection model based on API call sequences, and its architecture is shown in Figure 1. Initially, the API call sequences to be tested are extracted and subsequently preprocessed. The preprocessed API call sequences are then fed into the behavior sequence matching model for sequence matching. A successful match is denoted as 1, indicating a malicious sequence, while an unsuccessful match is denoted as 0, indicating a normal sequence. Sequences marked as 0 are subsequently input into the TextCNN model for detection, and the detection results from the TextCNN model are considered the final detection results, superseding the results from the behavior sequence matching model.

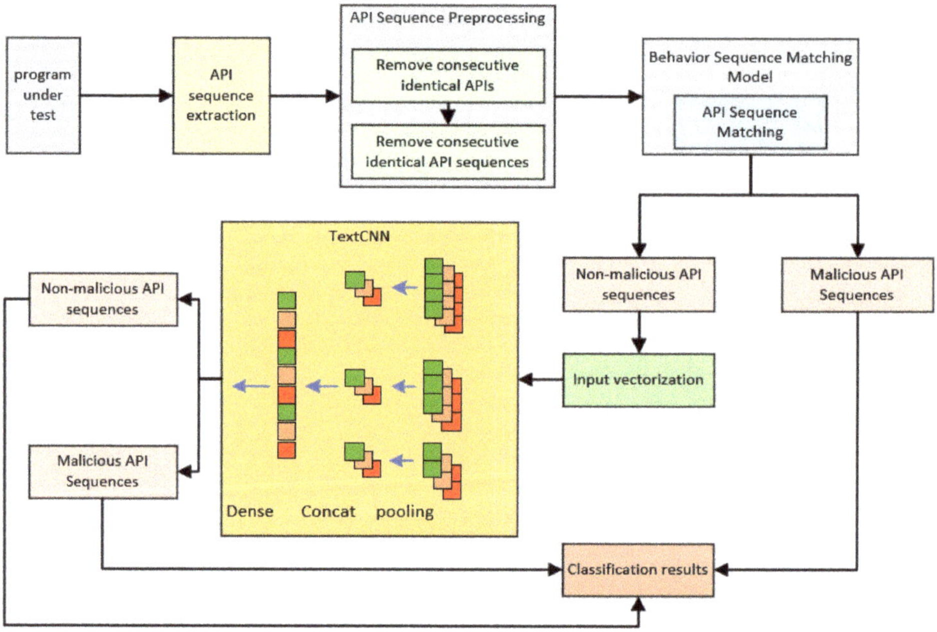

Figure 1. Malicious program detection model framework based on API call sequences.

3.1.1. Data Pre-Processing

Preprocessing API call sequences to remove redundant behavior is an important step in sequence mining. Malicious code frequently incorporates numerous redundant behaviors into normal behaviors, resulting in sequences characterized by multiple consecutive identical APIs or API sequence fragments. This increases the length and complexity of the sequences, leading to an increase in the time and space overhead of sequence mining. Moreover, it impacts the precision and interpretability of the mining process, making it difficult to identify the core behaviors of the malicious code.

In this paper, we deduplicate the sequence of API call sequences to reduce their complexity. The deduplication process involves retaining only one instance of APIs that are repeated consecutively within the sequence. The specifics of this process are outlined in Algorithm 1.

Algorithm 1: API deduplication algorithm

```
Input: API sequence set S, new API list
Output: new API sequence
foreach API seq in S do
    foreach API in API seq do
        if isEmpty(new API list) or API ≠ last(new API list) then
            Append(new API list, API)
    new API sequence = join(new API list, " ")
return new API sequence
```

3.1.2. Model Construction

Building a malicious program detection model based on the API call sequence is the key to this study. In the process of API sequence matching, we employ the PrefixSpan algorithm to mine frequent API call sequences and establish a rule base for malicious behavior sequences. This rule base, containing malicious behavior sequences, serves as the foundation for subsequent detection.

In this paper, we consider API call sequences from different processes of the same program. Initially, the PrefixSpan algorithm is employed to mine frequent API call sequences within each process of a malicious program, identifying key API call sequences for each program. Subsequently, the PrefixSpan algorithm is further applied to mine frequent sequences from the key API call sequences of all programs, yielding malicious API call sequences that are stored in the malicious behavior sequence repository. This repository is a collection of sequence sets that encapsulate the typical behavioral characteristics of various malicious programs and can be used to assess the behavior of unknown programs. By analyzing the API call sequences of different processes, we can more comprehensively capture the behavior patterns of malicious programs, enhancing the accuracy and interpretability of the detection model. Examples of malicious API call sequences are illustrated in Figure 2.

```
GetSystemTimeAsFileTime SetUnhandledExceptionFilter NtCreateFile NtCreateSection NtMapViewOfSection NtClose NtOpenKey NtQueryValueKey
NtClose CoInitializeEx CoInitializeSecurity CoCreateInstance GetSystemDirectoryW LdrLoadDll LdrGetProcedureAddress GetFileVersionInfoSizeW
GetFileVersionInfoW NtClose LoadStringW LookupPrivilegeValueW NtClose LdrGetDllHandle NtOpenKey NtQueryValueKey NtClose NtOpenKey
NtQueryValueKey NtClose NtOpenKey NtQueryValueKey NtClose NtOpenKey NtQueryValueKey NtClose CoCreateInstanceEx GetComputerNameW
CoCreateInstance CoGetClassObject IWbemServices ExecQuery NtOpenKey NtClose RegOpenKeyExW RegCloseKey RegOpenKeyExW
RegQueryValueExW RegCloseKey NtAllocateVirtualMemory NtOpenKey NtClose RegOpenKeyExW RegCloseKey RegOpenKeyExW
RegQueryValueExW RegCloseKey UuidCreate CoCreateInstance NtAllocateVirtualMemory LdrGetProcedureAddress RegOpenKeyExW
RegQueryValueExW RegCloseKey NtOpenDirectoryObject NtClose EnumWindows FindWindowExW EnumWindows FindWindowExW LoadStringW
GetFileType WriteConsoleW LdrUnloadDll CoUninitialize LdrGetDllHandle NtTerminateProcess NtClose NtUnmapViewOfSection NtClose
GetSystemTimeAsFileTime RegOpenKeyExW RegQueryInfoKeyW RegQueryValueExW RegCloseKey NtClose LdrGetProcedureAddress LdrUnloadDll
NtOpenKey NtQueryValueKey NtClose NtTerminateProcess,5
NtOpenDirectoryObject NtClose LdrLoadDll LdrGetProcedureAddress LdrLoadDll LdrGetProcedureAddress LdrLoadDll LdrGetProcedureAddress
NtProtectVirtualMemory NtAllocateVirtualMemory NtQuerySystemInformation NtProtectVirtualMemory NtAllocateVirtualMemory
NtFreeVirtualMemory LdrLoadDll LdrGetProcedureAddress LdrLoadDll LdrGetProcedureAddress NtProtectVirtualMemory NtFreeVirtualMemory
LdrLoadDll LdrGetProcedureAddress LdrLoadDll LdrGetProcedureAddress NtProtectVirtualMemory RegOpenKeyExA RegQueryValueExA
RegCloseKey FindFirstFileExW NtClose NtCreateMutant NtClose GetVolumePathNameW NtClose LdrLoadDll LdrGetProcedureAddress
GetSystemWindowsDirectoryW NtCreateFile NtCreateSection NtMapViewOfSection NtClose CreateDirectoryW GetFileAttributesW NtCreateFile
NtClose NtCreateFile NtClose DeleteFileW NtAllocateVirtualMemory CopyFileA CreateProcessInternalW NtClose NtFreeVirtualMemory
NtTerminateProcess NtClose LdrUnloadDll NtOpenKey NtQueryValueKey NtClose NtTerminateProcess,5
GetSystemTimeAsFileTime SetUnhandledExceptionFilter NtCreateFile NtCreateSection NtMapViewOfSection NtClose NtOpenKey NtQueryValueKey
NtClose CoInitializeEx CoInitializeSecurity CoCreateInstance GetSystemDirectoryW LdrLoadDll LdrGetProcedureAddress GetFileVersionInfoSizeW
GetFileVersionInfoW NtClose LoadStringW LookupPrivilegeValueW NtClose LdrGetDllHandle NtOpenKey NtQueryValueKey NtClose NtOpenKey
NtQueryValueKey NtClose NtOpenKey NtQueryValueKey NtClose NtOpenKey NtQueryValueKey NtClose CoCreateInstanceEx GetComputerNameW
CoCreateInstance CoGetClassObject IWbemServices ExecQuery NtOpenKey NtClose RegOpenKeyExW RegCloseKey RegOpenKeyExW
RegQueryValueExW RegCloseKey NtOpenKey NtClose RegOpenKeyExW RegCloseKey RegOpenKeyExW RegQueryValueExW RegCloseKey
UuidCreate CoCreateInstance NtAllocateVirtualMemory LdrGetProcedureAddress RegOpenKeyExW RegQueryValueExW RegCloseKey
NtOpenDirectoryObject NtClose EnumWindows FindWindowExW EnumWindows FindWindowExW NtAllocateVirtualMemory FindWindowExW
LoadStringW GetFileType WriteConsoleW LdrUnloadDll CoUninitialize LdrGetDllHandle NtTerminateProcess NtClose NtUnmapViewOfSection
NtClose GetSystemTimeAsFileTime RegOpenKeyExW RegQueryInfoKeyW RegQueryValueExW RegCloseKey NtClose LdrGetProcedureAddress
LdrUnloadDll NtOpenKey NtQueryValueKey NtClose NtTerminateProcess,5
NtDelayExecution gethostbyname socket connect closesocket setsockopt RegOpenKeyExA RegQueryValueExA RegCloseKey RegOpenKeyExA
RegQueryValueExA RegCloseKey LdrGetDllHandle send closesocket NtClose,5
```

Figure 2. Partial malicious API call sequences.

In this study, we employ regular expressions for sequence matching. Regular expressions utilize metacharacters, quantifiers, grouping, assertions, and additional grammatical constructs to formulate complex matching rules, catering to a wide range of matching requirements. Sequence matching is conducted on the API call sequences of the test set, using the malicious behavior sequence repository. This results in a label of 1 for successful matches, denoting a malicious sequence, and a label of 0 for unsuccessful matches, signifying a normal sequence.

After API sequence matching for the API call sequences to be tested, those sequences marked as 0 are further detected using the TextCNN model. The detection process of malicious programs in the neural network model is shown in Figure 3.

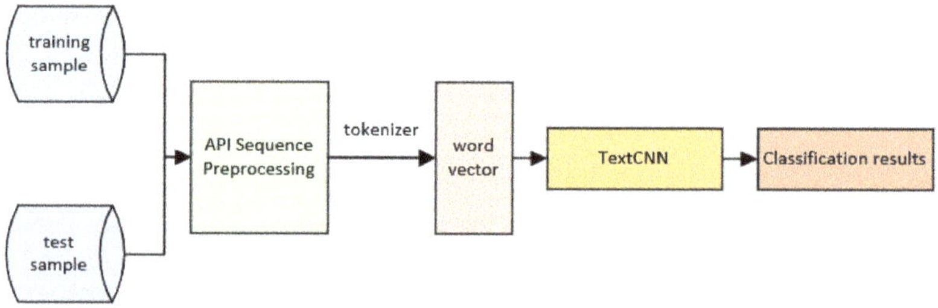

Figure 3. Neural network model malicious program detection process.

The specific steps for constructing the TextCNN malicious program detection model are as follows:

1. Data preprocessing: Remove redundant APIs that appear consecutively in the sequence, retaining only one instance of each API;
2. Data vectorization: The Keras toolkit is used for word vectorization. Treating the API sequence as text, the "fit_on_texts" method is employed to convert the text into integer sequences. Subsequently, the "texts_to_sequences" method transforms the integer sequences into vectors. Finally, the "pad_sequences" method is used to pad or truncate different-length text sequences to a uniform length, ensuring consistency in input data, with the length set to 5000;
3. Training model: The detailed structure of the TextCNN model is shown in Figure 4.

The training set data are input to the Input layer, and word embedding is performed in the Embedding layer to obtain the vector $X_i = \{x_1, x_2, \cdots, x_{5000}\}$ $(1 \leq i \leq n)$, where X_i denotes the vector representation of the ith API sequence, x_i denotes the vector represented by the ith API in a sample of API call sequences, and n denotes the number of samples in the training set. The vector X_i is input into the dropout layer to prevent overfitting, and then input to the TextCNN module. Firstly, feature extraction is performed by three convolutional modules with convolutional kernel sizes of 1, 3, and 5, and then MaxPooling1D is used for pooling, respectively, followed by Concat for feature fusion to obtain the vector $M_i = \{m_1, m_2, \cdots, m_{5000}\}$, and finally, the vector F_i is obtained by using the flatten layer for flattening.

The vector F_i is input into a dropout layer to obtain vector D_i, preventing over-fitting. The vector is then input into a dense layer.

Subsequently, the vector D_i is input into both a dropout layer and a dense layer. The softmax function is employed as the classifier to obtain the classification results.

The TextCNN configuration is shown in Table 1.

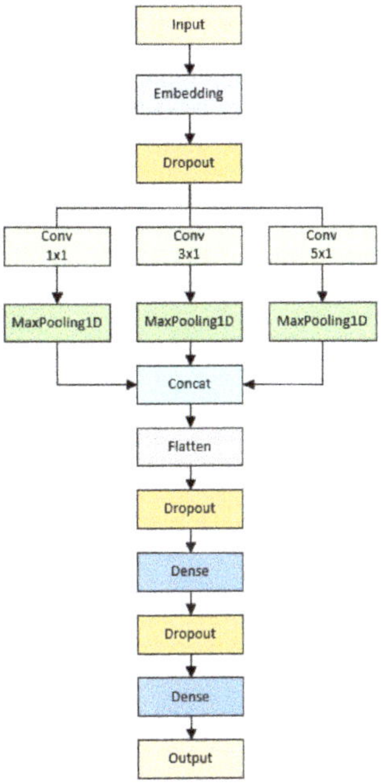

Figure 4. Detailed structure of TextCNN model.

Table 1. TextCNN configuration table.

Layer	Output Shape	Param	Connected to
input_1 (InputLayer)	(None, 5000)	0	
embedding (Embedding)	(None, 5000, 20)	6080	input_1
spatial_dropout1d (SpatialDropout)	(None, 5000, 20)	0	embedding
conv1d (Conv1D)	(None, 5000, 32)	672	spatial_dropout1d
conv1d_1 (Conv1D)	(None, 5000, 32)	1952	spatial_dropout1d
conv1d_2 (Conv1D)	(None, 5000, 32)	3232	spatia_dropout1d
max_pooling1d (MaxPooling1D)	(None, 2500, 32)	0	conv1d
max_pooling1d_1 (MaxPooling1D)	(None, 2500, 32)	0	conv1d_1
max_pooling1d_2 (MaxPooling1D)	(None, 2500, 32)	0	conv1d_2
concatenate(Concatenate)	(None, 2500, 96)	0	max_pooling1d max_pooling1d_1 max_pooling1d_2
flatten (Flatten)	(None, 240,000)	0	concatenate
dropout (Dropout)	(None, 240,000)	0	flatten
dense (Dense)	(None, 256)	61,440,256	dropout
dropout_1 (Dropout)	(None, 256)	0	dense
dense_1 (Dense)	(None, 8)	2056	dropout_1

3.2. Datasets

In this paper, we utilize the dataset of AliCloud Security Malicious Program Detection Challenge [29], and the data provided by the competition are derived from the API command sequence of the Windows binary executable program after simulated execution in a sandbox environment, with a total of 13,887 files and nearly 90 million call records, of which 4978 are normal files and 8909 are malicious files. There are a total of 7 types of malicious files, which are worms, infection viruses, Trojans, mining programs, ransomware, backdoor programs, and DDoS Trojans. The distribution of sample types and specific numbers are presented in Table 2.

Table 2. Experimental dataset.

Label	Type	Number
0	Normal sample	4978
1	Ransomware	502
2	Mining program	1196
3	DDoS Trojan	820
4	worm	100
5	infection virus	4289
6	backdoor program	515
7	Trojan	1487

The statistics of API sequence length before and after deduplication are shown in Figure 5.

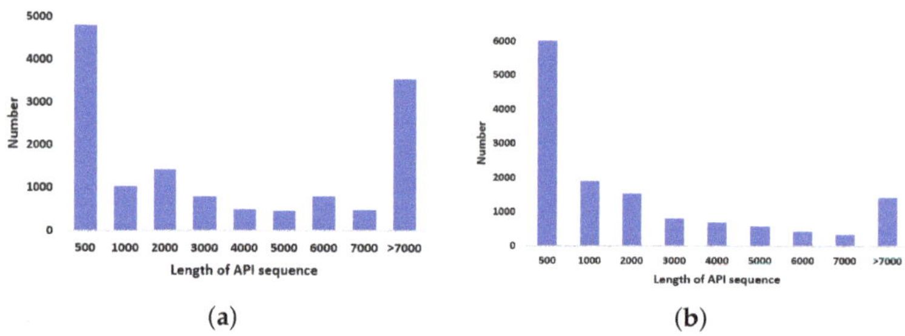

Figure 5. API sequence length statistics before and after deduplication. (**a**) API sequence length statistics before deduplication. (**b**) API sequence length statistics after deduplication.

We quantified the number of APIs in the samples before and after deduplication. As shown in the figure, before deduplication, 65% of the samples exhibitedhad an API sequence length of less than 5000. Following deduplication, this proportion increased to 83%. The deduplication process effectively shortened the length of the API sequence, thereby enhancing the efficiency of subsequent analyses.

3.3. Performance Metrics Used

For model evaluation, we employed Accuracy, Precision, Recall, F1-score, and execution time as metrics. The specific formula is as follows:

$$Accuracy = \frac{TP}{TP + TN + FP + FN}, \tag{1}$$

$$Precision = \frac{TP + TN}{TP + FP}, \tag{2}$$

$$Recall = \frac{TP}{TP + FN}, \tag{3}$$

$$F1\ score = \frac{2 \times Recall \times Precision}{Recall + Precision}, \tag{4}$$

where TP (True Positive) represents the number of instances that are actually positive and are correctly predicted as positive, TN (True Negative) represents the number of instances that are actually negative and are correctly predicted as negative, FP (False Positive) represents the number of instances that are actually negative but are predicted as positive, FN (False Negative) represents the number of instances that are actually positive but are predicted as negative. Accuracy represents the ratio of correctly classified samples to all samples; Precision represents the proportion of true positive instances among the instances predicted as positive in the classification model; Recall represents the proportion of correctly predicted positive instances among all positive instances; F1 score is the harmonic mean of Precision and Recall, which balances both precision and recall. A higher value of the metric indicates better classification performance.

4. Experimental Setup

Experiments were performed on a PC with an Intel Core i5-1240P CPU running at 1.70 GHz. We completed the experiment based on Python 3.8, Keras, Scikit-learn and Matplotlib. The experimental hyper-parameter settings for the TextCNN in this paper are shown in Table 3.

Table 3. Hyper-parameter settings for TextCNN.

Parameter	Value
Optimizer	Adam
Batch_size	1000
Epoch	100

5. Results

To verify the performance of the model, in the case of the same dataset, we conducted comparisons with the following models using the same dataset:

- TextCNN model: This model employs multiple convolutional kernels of different sizes (1, 3, 5) to extract key information from the program;
- Sequence Matching: We use the Prefixspan algorithm to mine the API call sequences of all malicious programs, obtaining the malicious API call sequences, and then perform sequence matching using these sequences;
- CNN model: We use Conv1D with convolutional kernel size 3 to extract local features by sliding the convolutional kernel over the input sequences;
- Our model: We initially employ the behavioral sequence matching model to match the API call sequences with malicious sequences, marking successful matches as 1 and unsuccessful matches as 0. Subsequently, sequences marked as 0 are input into the TextCNN model for detection. The detection result from the TextCNN model is considered the final detection result, overriding the outcome from the behavioral sequence matching model.

For the neural network model, this paper carried out 5-fold cross-validation on the training data, divided the training set into training and verification sets, and trained the model for each fold.

From the comparative results in Table 4, it can be observed that the Recall value of sequence matching is relatively high, indicating its effectiveness in capturing malicious samples. Utilizing a network with multiple convolutional layers allows for a more comprehensive extraction of API features, resulting in better detection performance compared to models with a single convolutional layer. Hence, the CNN model's performance is not as strong as the TextCNN model. By combining sequence matching and the TextCNN model, high values for Accuracy, Precision, Recall, and F1-score are achieved. However, since sequence matching is performed one by one using regular expressions, it results in a longer detection time. Our model, which combines sequence matching and a deep learning model, exhibits the longest execution time.

Table 4. Comparison of evaluation results of the models mentioned above.

Model	Accuracy	Precision	Recall	F1-Score	Execution Time (s)
TextCNN [11]	0.9279	0.9278	0.9280	0.9276	41.98
Sequence matching	0.8636	0.8681	0.9938	0.9267	292.3
CNN [30]	0.8779	0.8784	0.8779	0.8761	29.69
Our model	0.9288	0.9246	0.9993	0.9605	366.7

To obtain optimal classification performance, determining the appropriate size of the convolutional kernel in the TextCNN model is essential. The effectiveness of one-dimensional convolutional neural networks for text categorization lies in employing convolutional kernels of varying lengths to extract local features of the sequence. Utilizing multiple sizes of convolutional kernels allows for a more comprehensive capture of the information between APIs. In this paper, we fuse multiple convolutional kernels of different sizes to generate various TextCNN models. The experimental results are presented in Table 5.

Table 5. Comparison of evaluation results of the models mentioned above. The contents of the parentheses refer to the size of convolutional kernels.

Model	Accuracy	Precision	Recall	F1-Score
TextCNN (1 3 3 5 5)	0.9073	0.9057	0.9073	0.9047
TextCNN (1 3 5)	0.9279	0.9278	0.9280	0.9276
TextCNN (1 2 4)	0.9179	0.9173	0.9179	0.9163
TextCNN (2 3 4)	0.9165	0.9169	0.9165	0.9160

From the comparison results in the above table, it can be seen that the TextCNN model achieves its highest accuracy of 0.9279 when the convolutional kernel sizes are 1, 3, and 5. Therefore, in this paper, we choose the TextCNN model with the convolutional kernel sizes 1, 3, and 5 for the detection of malicious programs.

The confusion matrix of the TextCNN model (1, 3, 5) is shown in Figure 6.

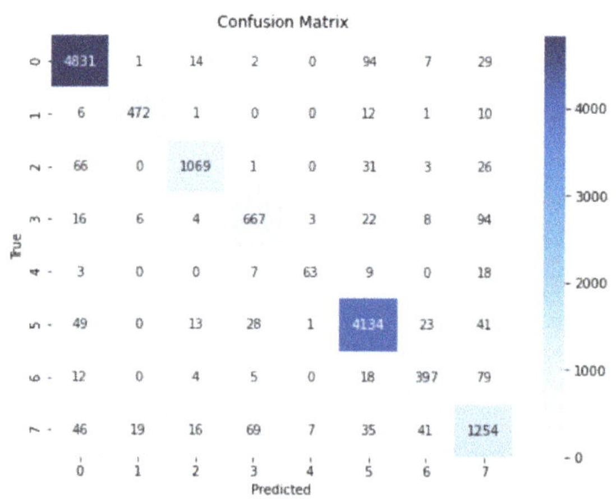

Figure 6. Confusion matrix of the TextCNN model (1, 3, 5).

The AUC value represents the area under the ROC curve. It serves as an evaluation metric to assess the quality of a classification model and effectively describes the model's overall performance. The ROC curves for each class of the TextCNN model with convolutional kernel sizes of 1, 3, and 5 are illustrated in Figure 7.

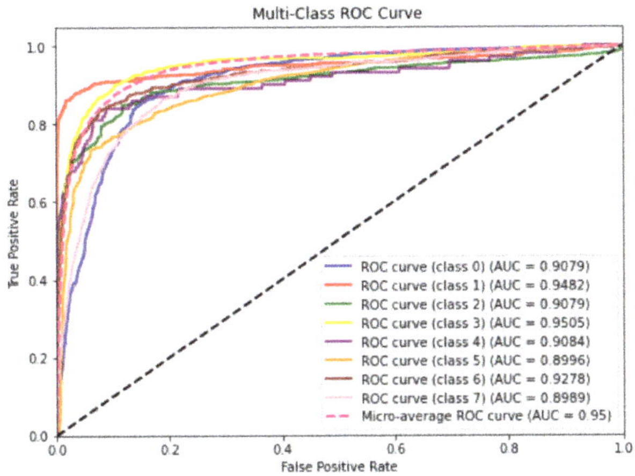

Figure 7. ROC curves for each class of TextCNN model (1, 3, 5).

Figure 8 shows the ROC curves of the four TextCNN models, from which it can be seen that the TextCNN model with convolutional kernel sizes 1, 3, and 5 exhibits the largest AUC value, indicating superior performance compared to the other models.

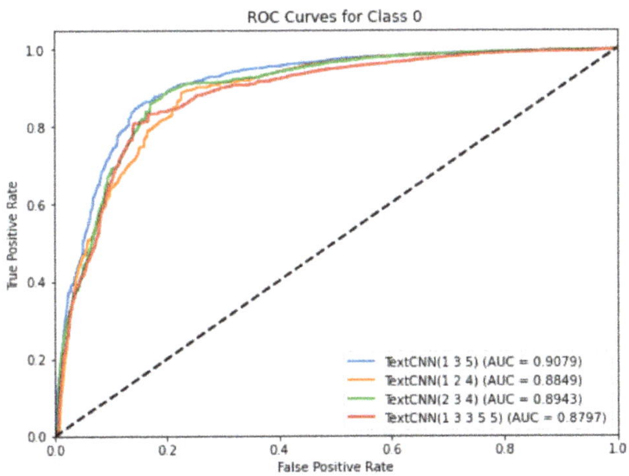

Figure 8. ROC curves of the four TextCNN models.

Furthermore, to validate the efficacy of deep learning, a machine learning algorithm is employed. The N-Gram algorithm is utilized for feature extraction of API call sequences, and the optimal size of n in the N-Gram algorithm must be determined to achieve the best classification performance. The value of n is set to 2, 3, and 4, and the random forest algorithm (the number of decision trees is set to 500), logistic regression and KNN algorithm are selected for model training.

The results of machine learning experiments with different values of n in the N-Gram algorithm are presented in Table 6.

Table 6. Results of machine learning experiments with different values of n in N-Gram.

Value of n	Model	Accuracy	Precision	Recall
2	Random Forest	0.9005	0.9022	0.9010
	Logistic Regression	0.8928	0.8950	0.8928
	KNN	0.8856	0.8856	0.8830
3	Random Forest	0.9028	0.9037	0.9048
	Logistic Regression	0.8938	0.8964	0.8959
	KNN	0.8882	0.8882	0.8902
4	Random Forest	0.8988	0.9029	0.9003
	Logistic Regression	0.8910	0.8933	0.8949
	KNN	0.8856	0.8882	0.8558

The detection results of each machine learning algorithm are shown in Figure 9.

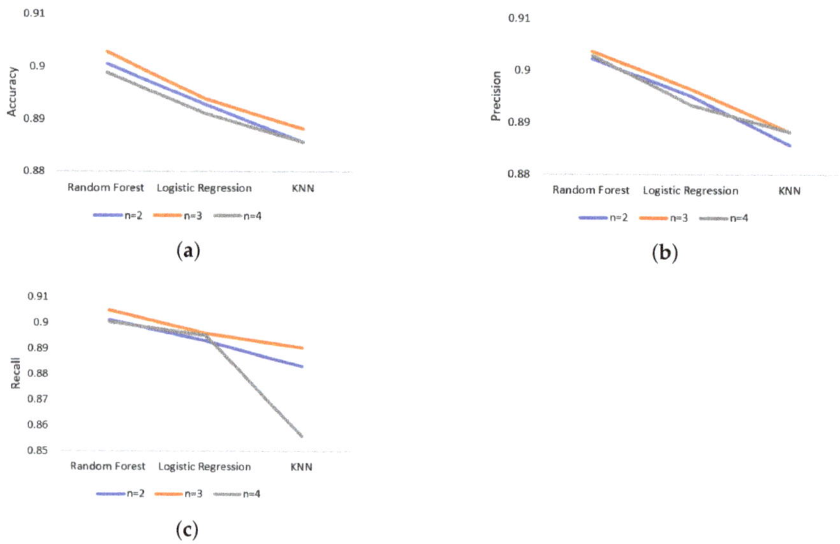

Figure 9. The detection results of three machine learning algorithms. (**a**) The statistical chart of Accuracy. (**b**) The statistical chart of Precision. (**c**) The statistical chart of Recall.

According to Figure 9 and Table 6, it can be seen that for the same value of n, the random forest algorithm outperforms logistic regression and KNN in terms of accuracy, precision and recall, and when n is taken as 3, the random forest algorithm achieves the highest performance in terms of Accuracy, Precision and Recall. All three algorithms exhibit slightly better detection results when $n = 3$, compared to when $n = 2$ or 4. However, their performance is still inferior to that of deep learning. The comparison chart of the detection results of machine learning algorithms and TextCNN and our model is shown in Figure 10.

According to Figure 10, it can be seen that the model we proposed outperforms other machine learning algorithms and TextCNN in terms of performance.

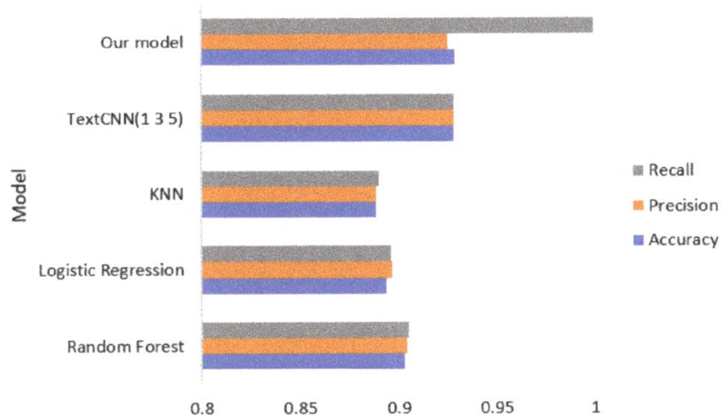

Figure 10. Comparison chart of performance metrics of different classifiers.

6. Discussion

In this paper, we use the public dataset from the AliCloud Malicious Program Detection Challenge. This dataset is derived from the API instruction sequence of Windows executable programs after sandbox simulation. The imbalance between categories exists in real-world scenarios, so an unbalanced dataset can better simulate the actual situation. However, the disparity between different categories and the relatively small size of this dataset compared to the expanding family of malicious code may impact detection results.

In this paper, we focus on dynamic API call sequences as the primary subject of study. However, dynamic analysis relies on the samples executing in the sandbox and producing an execution report. As malicious code countermeasures improve, anti-virtualization techniques used by malicious code can evade detection, preventing the samples from successfully executing in the sandbox. In the future, we consider employing static analysis for further feature extraction and combining both dynamic and static approaches for malicious code detection.

Although the malicious samples in the training set encompass various types of malicious code, their behavior remains constrained. In the future, a more comprehensive analysis of program behaviors can be conducted manually to uncover potential connections among multiple APIs. Enriching the behavioral dataset will be more conducive to the detection of malicious programs.

7. Conclusions

In this paper, we initially mitigate the impact of repetitive information in API call sequences, then analyze the API call sequences in the program to extract behavioral characteristics. Based on these characteristics, we employ a combination of rule matching and deep learning to detect malicious programs. Firstly, malicious sequences are filtered out using behavior sequence matching. Subsequently, the remaining sequences are examined using the TextCNN model. Finally, the detection results from the TextCNN model are used as the final outcomes, superseding the results from the behavioral sequence matching model, to achieve more effective detection of malicious sequences. Since this study only considers the names of the APIs, disregarding information such as parameters, a future direction is to incorporate API parameter information to enhance the accuracy of malicious program detection. In future work, we will continue to collect samples to balance the amount of data across categories. Moreover, we will further consider the parameters of API call sequences to augment their expressive capability. For instance, parameter information of API call sequences related to file operations could include file names, paths, sizes, permissions, etc. This information can aid in identifying potential malicious behaviors in the program, such as deleting, modifying, and hiding important files. Additionally, we will address the imbalance of dataset categories, which may lead to the model favoring categories with more data while overlooking the characteristics of categories with less data.

Author Contributions: Conceptualization, N.L., Z.L. and Y.M.; methodology, N.L., Z.L. and Y.M.; writing—review and editing, N.L., Z.L. and Y.M.; investigation, Y.C. and J.D.; software, Y.C. and J.D.; writing—original draft preparation, Y.C. and J.D.; validation: N.L., Z.L. and Y.M.; supervision: N.L. All authors have read and agreed to the published version of the manuscript.

Funding: This research was funded by the science and technology project of State Grid Corporation of China: "Research on Key Technologies of Multi-agent Trusted Interaction and Monitoring Response for New-type Power System User Side Business" (Grand No. 5108-202218280A-2-405-XG).

Data Availability Statement: The data presented in this study are available in this article.

Conflicts of Interest: The authors N.L., Z.L. and Y.M., were employed by State Grid Smart Grid Research Institute Co., Ltd. The author J.D., was employed by the State Grid Beijing Electric Power Research Institute. The remaining authors declare that the research was conducted in the absence of any commercial or financial relationships that could be construed as a potential conflict of interest.

References

1. Wang, B.; Zhang, J.; Luo, C.; Yang, L.; Chen, J.; Ma, H. Research on Deep Detection Technology of Abnormal Behavior of Power Industrial Control System. In Proceedings of the 2022 IEEE 6th Information Technology and Mechatronics Engineering Conference (ITOEC), Chongqing, China, 4–6 March 2022; Volume 6, pp. 1256–1261. [CrossRef]
2. Aboaoja, F.A.; Zainal, A.; Ghaleb, F.A.; Al-Rimy, B.A.S.; Eisa, T.A.E.; Elnour, A.A.H. Malware Detection Issues, Challenges, and Future Directions: A Survey. *Appl. Sci.* **2022**, *12*, 8482. [CrossRef]
3. Ghillani, D.; Gillani, D.H. A perspective study on Malware detection and protection, A review. *Authorea Prepr.* **2022** . [CrossRef]
4. Singh, J.; Singh, J. A survey on machine learning-based malware detection in executable files. *J. Syst. Archit.* **2021**, *112*, 101861. [CrossRef]
5. Gao, H.; Cheng, S.; Zhang, W. GDroid: Android malware detection and classification with graph convolutional network. *Comput. Secur.* **2021**, *106*, 102264. [CrossRef]
6. Cesare, S.; Xiang, Y.; Zhou, W. Control Flow-Based Malware VariantDetection. *IEEE Trans. Dependable Secur. Comput.* **2014**, *11*, 307–317. [CrossRef]
7. Hassen, M.; Chan, P.K. Scalable function call graph-based malware classification. In Proceedings of the Seventh ACM on Conference on Data and Application Security and Privacy, Scottsdale, AR, USA, 22–24 March 2017; pp. 239–248. [CrossRef]
8. Garcia, D.E.; DeCastro-Garcia, N. Optimal feature configuration for dynamic malware detection. *Comput. Secur.* **2021**, *105*, 102250. [CrossRef]
9. Muzaffar, A.; Hassen, H.R.; Lones, M.A.; Zantout, H. An in-depth review of machine learning based android malware detection. *Comput. Secur.* **2022**, *121*, 102833. [CrossRef]
10. Xu, P.; Duan, J.; Zhang, J.; Pei, Y.; Shi, D.; Wang, Z.; Dong, X.; Sun, Y. Active power correction strategies based on deep reinforcement learning—Part I: A simulation-driven solution for robustness. *CSEE J. Power Energy Syst.* **2021**, *8*, 1122–1133. [CrossRef]
11. Wang, Q.; Qian, Q. Malicious code classification based on opcode sequences and textCNN network. *J. Inf. Secur. Appl.* **2022**, *67*, 103151. [CrossRef]
12. Gopinath, M.; Sethuraman, S.C. A comprehensive survey on deep learning based malware detection techniques. *Comput. Sci. Rev.* **2023**, *47*, 100529. [CrossRef]
13. Faruk, M.J.H.; Shahriar, H.; Valero, M.; Barsha, F.L.; Sobhan, S.; Khan, M.A.; Whitman, M.; Cuzzocrea, A.; Lo, D.; Rahman, A.; et al. Malware detection and prevention using artificial intelligence techniques. In Proceedings of the 2021 IEEE International Conference on Big Data (Big Data), Orlando, FL, USA, 15–18 December 2021; pp. 5369–5377. [CrossRef]
14. Li, C.; Lv, Q.; Li, N.; Wang, Y.; Sun, D.; Qiao, Y. A novel deep framework for dynamic malware detection based on API sequence intrinsic features. *Comput. Secur.* **2022**, *116*, 102686. [CrossRef]
15. Lu, X.; Jiang, F.; Zhou, X.; Yi, S.; Sha, J.; Pietro, L. ASSCA: API sequence and statistics features combined architecture for malware detection. Computer Networks. *Comput. Netw.* **2019**, *157*, 99–111. [CrossRef]
16. Amer, E.; Zelinka, I. A dynamic Windows malware detection and prediction method based on contextual understanding of API call sequence. *Comput. Secur.* **2020**, *92*, 101760. [CrossRef]
17. Amer, E.; Zelinka, I.; El-Sappagh, S. A multi-perspective malware detection approach through behavioral fusion of api call sequence. *Comput. Secur.* **2021**, *110*, 102449. [CrossRef]
18. Chen, X.; Hao, Z.; Li, L.; Cui, L.; Zhu, Y.; Ding, Z.; Liu, Y. Cruparamer: Learning on parameter-augmented api sequences for malware detection. *IEEE Trans. Inf. Forensics Secur.* **2022**, *17*, 788–803. 10.1109/TIFS.2022.3152360. [CrossRef]
19. Kim, H.; Kim, J.; Kim, Y.; Kim, I.; Kim, K.J.; Kim, H. Improvement of malware detection and classification using API call sequence alignment and visualization. *Clust. Comput.* **2019**, *22*, 921–929. [CrossRef]

20. Chen, T.; Zeng, H.; Lv, M.; Zhu, T. CTIMD: Cyber threat intelligence enhanced malware detection using API call sequences with parameters. *Comput. Secur.* **2024**, *136*, 103518. [CrossRef]
21. Zhang, Z.; Qi, P.; Wang, W. Dynamic malware analysis with feature engineering and feature learning. In Proceedings of the AAAI Conference on Artificial Intelligence, New York, NY, USA, 7–12 February 2020; Volume 34, pp. 1210–1217. [CrossRef]
22. Kim, C.W. Ntmaldetect: A machine learning approach to malware detection using native api system calls. *arXiv* **2018**, arXiv:1802.05412. https://doi.org/10.48550/arXiv.1802.05412.
23. Lin, Z.; Xiao, F.; Sun, Y.; Ma, Y.; Xing, C.C.; Huang, J. A secure encryption-based malware detection system. In Proceedings of the KSII Transactions on Internet and Information Systems (TIIS), Online, 23 December 2018; Volume 12, pp. 1799–1818. [CrossRef]
24. Fan, M.; Liu, J.; Luo, X.; Chen, K.; Tian, Z.; Zheng, Q.; Liu, T. Android malware familial classification and representative sample selection via frequent subgraph analysis. *IEEE Trans. Inf. Forensics Secur.* **2018**, *13*, 1890–1905. [CrossRef]
25. Hemalatha, J.; Roseline, S.A.; Geetha, S.; Kadry, S.; Damaševičius, R. An efficient densenet-based deep learning model for malware detection. *Entropy* **2021**, *23*, 344. [CrossRef]
26. Huang, X.; Ma, L.; Yang, W.; Zhong, Y. A method for windows malware detection based on deep learning. *J. Signal Process. Syst.* **2021**, *93*, 265–273. [CrossRef]
27. Mane, R.V. A comparative study of Spam and PrefixSpan sequential pattern mining algorithm for protein sequences. In Proceedings of the International Conference on Advances in Computing, Communication and Control, Mumbai, India, 18–19 January 2013; pp. 147–155. [CrossRef]
28. Han, J.; Pei, J.; Mortazavi-Asl, B.; Pinto, H.; Chen, Q.; Dayal, U.; Hsu, M. Prefixspan: Mining sequential patterns efficiently by prefix-projected pattern growth. In Proceedings of the 17th International Conference on Data Engineering, Heidelberg, Germany, 2–6 April 2001; pp. 215–224. [CrossRef]
29. AliCloud Security Malicious Program Detection Dataset. Available online: https://tianchi.aliyun.com/dataset/dataDetail?dataId=137262 (accessed on 13 September 2022).
30. Ganesh, M.; Pednekar, P.; Prabhuswamy, P.; Nair, D.S.; Park, Y.; Jeon, H. CNN-based android malware detection. In Proceedings of the 2017 International Conference on Software Security and Assurance (ICSSA), Altoona, PA, USA, 24–25 July 2017; pp. 60–65. [CrossRef]

electronics

Article

Advancing User Privacy in Virtual Power Plants: A Novel Zero-Knowledge Proof-Based Distributed Attribute Encryption Approach

Ruxia Yang [1,2,*], Hongchao Gao [3], Fangyuan Si [3] and Jun Wang [4]

[1] State Grid Smart Grid Research Institute Co., Ltd., Nanjing 210003, China
[2] State Grid Laboratory of Power Cyber-Security Protection and Monitoring Technology, Nanjing 210003, China
[3] State Key Laboratory of Power Systems, Department of Electrical Engineering, Tsinghua University, Beijing 100084, China; hcgaoth@tsinghua.edu.cn (H.G.); sifangyuan@mail.tsinghua.edu.cn (F.S.)
[4] State Grid Shanghai Municipal Electric Power Company, Shanghai 200122, China; wangjun@sh.sgcc.com.cn
* Correspondence: yangruxia@geiri.sgcc.com.cn

Abstract: In virtual power plants, diverse business scenarios involving user data, such as queries, transactions, and sharing, pose significant privacy risks. Traditional attribute-based encryption (ABE) methods, while supporting fine-grained access, fall short of fully protecting user privacy as they require attribute input, leading to potential data leaks. Addressing these limitations, our research introduces a novel privacy protection scheme using zero-knowledge proof and distributed attribute-based encryption (DABE). This method innovatively employs Merkel trees for aggregating user attributes and constructing commitments for zero-knowledge proof verification, ensuring that user attributes and access policies remain confidential. Our solution not only enhances privacy but also fortifies security against man-in-the-middle and replay attacks, offering attribute indistinguishability and tamper resistance. A comparative performance analysis demonstrates that our approach outperforms existing methods in efficiency, reducing time, cost, and space requirements. These advancements mark a significant step forward in ensuring robust user privacy and data security in virtual power plants.

Keywords: zero-knowledge proof; attribute hiding; virtual power plant; privacy protection; attribute-based encryption

1. Introduction

In pursuit of carbon neutrality, China is undergoing a significant energy transformation, with a focus on integrating renewable energy sources within a robust smart grid framework [1,2]. This transformation involves the intricate coordination of generation, transmission, load, and storage systems, transitioning to both centralized and distributed generation models [1,3,4]. The envisioned power system aims to be sustainable, secure, adaptable, and efficient, heavily relying on new, cleaner energy sources [3,5–7].

Global electricity demands and environmental concerns highlight the inadequacies of traditional power generation. Renewable sources like wind and solar power have gained traction as sustainable alternatives. Yet, integrating these intermittent and distributed sources into the grid presents substantial challenges, notably in maintaining stable outputs and effective grid integration. Virtual power plants (VPPs) have emerged as a solution, orchestrating a myriad of distributed energy resources for improved renewable energy integration. This approach resonates with the comprehensive energy model encompassing generation, grid, load, and storage. However, existing VPP models are predominantly centralized in their management of information and transactions, creating vulnerabilities such as potential data manipulation and privacy breaches. Our research aims to tackle these issues through innovations in the realms of data security and privacy within VPP systems by leveraging advanced encryption and decentralized management methodologies.

As illustrated in Table 1, numerous domestic and international entities are actively investigating user data security within virtual power plants. In the United States, General Electric (GE) is pioneering the integration of blockchain technology with virtual power plants. This involves harnessing blockchain for the amalgamation of distributed energy generation and executing automated transactions via smart contracts, with the aim of achieving an equilibrium between supply and demand in the power grid. Another endeavor, SolarChange, is focused on developing a blockchain-based platform for energy interaction, targeting the energy balance challenge in virtual power plants and enhancing energy efficiency. In Japan, Kyocera is experimenting with the synergy of clean energy and energy storage systems in virtual power plants, utilizing blockchain as the foundational technology. Within China, a strategic partnership between Shanghai University of Electric Power and Shanghai Electric Power Company has been forged to expedite collaborative research in energy blockchain, including applications in virtual power plants. Additionally, the State Grid Corporation of China is leveraging its proprietary blockchain platform to streamline power trading, particularly in virtual power plant contexts.

Table 1. Application of blockchain technology in VPP at domestic and abroad.

Nation	Example	Technology Platform	Main Application Scenarios
America	TransActive Grid blockchain energy project	Ethereum blockchain	Virtual power plant distributed trading system and P2P trading
Australia	Ecochain	Ethereum blockchain	P2P trading system for PV surplus power
China	Energy blockchain lab	Hyperledger Fabric	Compressing costs in the virtual power plant trading and clearing process
Japan	Virtual power plant for solar and storage systems	LO3 Energy proprietary platform	Shared generation to reduce the burden on the grid
Spain	Blockchain tracking of the electricity distribution supply chain	TrustOS blockchain platform	Markets for renewable energy certification schemes
Estonia	Virtual power plant project based on power matchmaker	WePower platform	Promoting P2P interactions for clean energy
South Korea	Virtual power plant based on citizen sharing blockchain	Ethereum blockchain	Reduction of human error in record keeping

Despite these advancements, employing blockchain for user privacy protection in virtual power plants introduces several new challenges. Predominantly, existing methodologies facilitate only one-to-one data authorization and sharing. This necessitates the disclosure of one party's identity to the other with each data-sharing instance, potentially compromising both user privacy and system efficiency.

In response, researchers have explored the use of attribute-based encryption (ABE) to streamline data sharing and access between users and devices, as evidenced in the literature [8,9]. Hur and Noh [10] proposed a revocable attribute-based encryption system, utilizing a proxy for permission revocation, with the user list being publicly accessible to the proxy. Li et al. [11] applied scalable ABE in cloud computing for sharing personal health records. Khalil et al. [12] introduced a multi-authority ABE-based access control method, enabling IoT devices to interact with IoT gateways. While these solutions utilize ABE for data access control, they inadequately address the prevention of privacy breaches during data sharing. The concept of anonymous ABE [13] has been proposed to mitigate attribute privacy leakage. However, this approach only secures access policies and leaves user attributes exposed, thereby still posing a risk of privacy infringement.

This paper endeavors to tackle the challenge of user privacy protection in virtual power plants. By thoroughly analyzing user behavioral patterns and identifying diverse business scenarios, we propose a novel privacy protection scheme founded on zero-knowledge proofs. The primary contributions of this work are delineated as follows.

1. We introduce an innovative data protection strategy named attribute-hiding zero-knowledge proof (AH-ZKP). This approach effectively conceals user identities and attributes during authorization and verification processes, enhancing privacy and security.
2. Our model innovatively integrates distributed attribute-based encryption (DABE) with multiple attribute management nodes. This design achieves decentralized attribute management, mitigating risks associated with single-point failures and collusion attacks common in centralized systems. We also introduce a decentralized data sharing scheme that preserves the confidentiality of user attribute privacy and ciphertext access policies while also facilitating auditing capabilities.
3. The effectiveness of our scheme is demonstrated through its ability to maintain the confidentiality of data, attributes, and access policies. It addresses key privacy concerns in virtual power plants, ensuring secure and private data transactions.

The rest of this paper is organized as follows. Section 1 provides an overview of virtual power plants and zero-knowledge proofs. Section 2 establishes the system model of the proposed scheme. Section 3 analyzes the security of the scheme, and Section 4 conducts experimental simulations. Finally, Section 5 provides a brief summary.

2. Research Background

2.1. Virtual Power Plant

The virtual power plant (VPP), a concept dating back over two decades, represents a significant shift in energy management and distribution. Originating in Europe, with countries like Germany, the United Kingdom, France, and the Netherlands leading the way, VPPs have been the focus of numerous mature demonstration projects. These projects primarily centered on integrating distributed energy into the grid reliably and establishing robust business models within the electricity market [7,14–16]. In China, the VPP concept has garnered increasing attention in recent years, spurred by the evolution of the nation's power systems and market policies, leading to substantive demonstration practices [1,3,16,17].

A virtual power plant, while lacking the physical infrastructure typical of traditional power plants, performs similar functions. It not only generates electricity but also actively participates in energy markets, contributing to grid stability through peak shaving and frequency regulation [18–20]. At its core, a VPP employs advanced information technologies to integrate diverse energy resources, including generation, consumption, and storage. This integration is achieved through collaborative efforts with external centralized control systems and management platforms, facilitating coordinated control, optimization, and enabling comprehensive data analysis for strategic operational adjustments [20]. VPPs actively engage in energy trading with various market players, responding dynamically to fluctuations in market demands. The operational model of a VPP can be likened to a 'black box' that simulates the functionalities of a physical power plant. It can act as a 'positive power plant' by supplying power to the grid or as a 'negative power plant' by absorbing excess power. This 'black box' encompasses distributed energy sources such as renewable energy, diverse energy storage facilities, electric vehicles, controllable loads, and more [1,3]. However, the mere aggregation of these resources is not sufficient for effective energy management. A VPP necessitates a comprehensive set of technologies and systems for the intelligent aggregation and management of these resources.

The essence of a virtual power plant lies in its innovative electricity management approach. It aggregates a multitude of distributed energy devices, including solar panels, wind turbines, and energy storage units, through advanced interconnectivity technologies, creating a virtual energy generation system. This system employs state-of-the-art intelligent control technologies for the efficient dispatch and management of distributed energy resources. Such management optimizes energy generation and usage, enhances the reliability and stability of the power grid, and reduces operational and maintenance costs. Virtual power plants typically utilize cloud-based platforms for data aggregation and sophisticated analysis, thereby elevating the intelligence and efficiency of the power system. The continuous evolution of technologies like 5G, artificial intelligence, and cloud computing is expanding the application and potential of virtual power plants, promising a future of widespread global adoption and advancement in the energy sector.

2.2. Zero-Knowledge Proofs

Zero-knowledge proof (ZKP) is a cryptographic protocol enabling one party, the prover, to demonstrate the veracity of a proposition to another, the verifier, without divulging any additional information. This ensures the prover's privacy, safeguarding sensitive data from being inferred by the verifier during the proof process.

ZKP is characterized by three essential properties:

1. **Completeness**: Given correct evidence or a 'witness', the prover can convincingly demonstrate the truthfulness of the assertion to the verifier with high probability.
2. **Soundness**: A deceptive prover, lacking the correct witness, finds it implausibly challenging to convince the verifier of a false proposition.
3. **Zero-knowledge**: The verifier gains no additional information, apart from the proposition's validity, from the proof procedure.

ZKPs are classified into two types: interactive and non-interactive. Interactive ZKPs entail several rounds of communication between the prover and verifier, with the verifier posing random challenges and the prover responding accordingly. Conversely, non-interactive ZKPs require just a single communication round. Here, the prover sends a comprehensive message to the verifier, which diminishes communication complexity and enhances efficiency. The zero-knowledge succinct non-interactive argument of knowledge (zk-SNARK) is the non-interactive ZKP variant employed in this study.

We focus on the Groth16 algorithm [21] for zk-SNARK implementation, constructing pairing-based non-interactive zero-knowledge (NIZK) proofs within a quadratic arithmetic program (QAP) framework. Initially, we define the relation-generating element R, expressed as follows:

$$R = (p, G_1, G_2, G_T, e, l, \{u_i(X), v_i(X), w_i(X)\}_{i=0}^{m}, t(X)) \tag{1}$$

Here, $|p| = \lambda$, where p represents the size of the finite field, and λ is the security parameter. The degrees of u, v, and w are $n-1$, and of t is n. The relation R defines the domain Z_p, the statements $(a_1, \ldots, a_l) \in Z_p^l$, and the witnesses $(a_{l+1}, \ldots, a_m) \in Z_p^{m-l}$. These components ensure that, given $a_0 = 1$, for the $n-2$ degree quotient polynomial $h(X)$, the following equation holds:

$$\sum_{i=0}^{m} a_i u_i(X) \sum_{i=0}^{m} a_i v_i(X) = \sum_{i=0}^{m} a_i w_i(X) + h(X)t(X) \tag{2}$$

Building upon the zk-SNARK implementation via the Groth16 algorithm, we delineate the following pairing-based non-interactive zero-knowledge (NIZK) argument protocol:

Setup $(R) \rightarrow (\sigma, \tau)$:
Pick $\alpha, \beta, \gamma, \delta, x \leftarrow Z_p^*$.
Set $\tau = (\alpha, \beta, \gamma, \delta, x)$

$$\sigma = \begin{pmatrix} G^{\alpha}, G^{\beta}, H^{\beta}, H^{\gamma}, G^{\delta}, H^{\delta}, \{G^{x^i}\}_{i=0}^{n-1}, \{H^{x^i}\}_{i=0}^{n-1} \\ \{G^{\frac{\beta u_i(x)+\alpha v_i(x)+w_i(x)}{\gamma}}\}_{i=0}^{l}, \{G^{\frac{\beta u_i(x)+\alpha v_i(x)+w_i(x)}{\delta}}\}_{i=l+1}^{m}, \{G^{\frac{x^i t(x)}{\delta}}\}_{i=0}^{n-2} \end{pmatrix} \tag{3}$$

Prove $(R, \sigma, a_1, \ldots, a_m) \rightarrow \pi$:
Pick $r, s \leftarrow Z_p$.
Compute $\pi = (A, B, C)$ where
$A = G^{\alpha + \sum_{i=0}^{m} a_i u_i(x) + r\delta}$, $B = H^{\beta + \sum_{i=0}^{m} a_i v_i(x) + s\delta}$

$$C = G^{\frac{\sum_{i=l+1}^{m} a_i(\beta u_i(x)+\alpha v_i(x)+w_i(x))+h(x)t(x)}{\delta} + s\left(\alpha + \sum_{i=0}^{m} a_i u_i(x)\right) + \gamma\left(\beta + \sum_{i=0}^{m} a_i v_i(x)\right) - rs\delta}$$

Verify $(R, \sigma, a_1, \ldots, a_m) \rightarrow b$:
Compute a quadratic multi-variate polynomial, such that $\pi = (A, B, C)$ corresponds to the test.

$$e(A, B) = e(G^{\alpha}, H^{\beta}) e\left(G^{\frac{\sum_{i=l+1}^{m} a_i(\beta u_i(x)+\alpha v_i(x)+w_i(x))}{\gamma}}, H^{\gamma}\right) e(C, H^{\delta}) \tag{4}$$

Accept the proof if the test passes.

This protocol exemplifies a non-interactive zero-knowledge proof with complete and perfect zero-knowledge properties. It is among the fastest and most compact zk-SNARKs available, necessitating only three proof elements and featuring a straightforward verification equation. This ensures robust integrity and reliability under polynomial computation capabilities, making it an optimal choice.

3. User Attribute Hiding Model Based on Zero-Knowledge Proof

3.1. Problem Analysis

Virtual power plants (VPPs) epitomize the integration of diverse energy sources, encompassing conventional, renewable, and micro-energy systems. They play a pivotal role in balancing power generation with load demands by managing resources like energy storage, electric vehicles, and controllable loads. Moreover, VPPs engage in trading surplus energy, either to other VPPs or the public grid, optimizing electricity sale revenue and internal power balance while curbing operational costs. Consequently, safeguarding the privacy of VPP users becomes paramount.

Existing studies on data sharing in VPPs predominantly target the protection of data content. Attribute-based encryption (ABE) is employed for this purpose, offering several advantages:

1. ABE reduces encryption overhead as it does not necessitate individual encryption for each recipient, thereby streamlining the process.
2. It heightens data security. Even in scenarios of untrustworthy or compromised data servers, ABE ensures information confidentiality.
3. ABE supports fine-grained access control, enabling the creation of bespoke access structures tailored to specific scenarios and requirements.
4. The design of ABE thwarts collusion attacks by preventing the simultaneous use of different users' private keys.

However, the predominant focus of ABE methodologies on data content protection reveals inherent limitations. While encrypted data remain publicly accessible, malicious entities can exploit this visibility. Through record analysis, they can intercept the access policies of specific files or ascertain the attributes of particular users. Employing strategies like correlation and inference attacks or clustering analysis, these entities can potentially deduce sensitive user information or identities. Thus, it is imperative to extend protection beyond data security and traceability. Concealing user attributes, authorization relationships, and access policies is crucial to ensuring the sanctity of both data content and member privacy.

Table 2 in this paper elucidates the notations used in our discussion, aiding in a clearer understanding of these complex concepts.

This section combines the privacy attributes of virtual power plant users with different scenarios and utilizes distributed attribute-based encryption technology to propose an attribute hiding scheme.

Table 2. Symbol explanation.

Symbol	Meaning of Symbols
$RawData$	Raw data
$EncData$	Coded text
λ, G, P	Global parameters required by DABE
K_{prov}, K_{veri}	Proof keys and verification keys in zero-knowledge proofs
PK, SK	Public–private key pair
$addr$	User address
$AttrList$	List of properties used in DABE and zero-knowledge proofs
$AttrRoot$	Root node of the attribute Merkle tree
$attr_i$	User attributes
$K_{i,uid}$	DABE key corresponding to $attr_i$
r_{random}	Random number
PSF	Pseudo-random sorting function
CRH	Collision-resistant hash function
$COMM$	Non-interactive commitments
AH-ZKP	Zero-knowledge proofs of property hiding
$COMM_{attr}$	Non-interactive commitments generated by user attributes and random numbers
$COMM'_{attr}$	Non-interactive commitments generated from user attributes and addresses
$Cert_{veri}$	Certificates required to download data
$informariondownloader$	Information for data visitors

3.2. User Privacy Attributes

In the realm of virtual power plants (VPPs), user privacy data are multifaceted, informed by the data analysis of the VPP business system. These data encompass the following:

- Personal information: This includes the user's name, address, telephone number, email, and other identifying details.
- Power consumption data: Critical data such as real-time power usage, load profiles, and consumption timings.
- Electrical equipment data: Information on the user's electrical devices, including type, brand, model, and age.
- Behavioral data: Patterns and habits in electricity usage, like usage times and modes.

The sensitivity of these data points is evident; unauthorized access or breaches can lead to significant property losses or even physical safety risks. Hence, VPPs must implement rigorous data protection strategies to safeguard the confidentiality and integrity of user data.

3.3. Scene Analysis

The protection of user privacy data in VPPs spans multiple scenarios, each with its unique challenges:

- **Exchange and sharing scenarios**: Company data sharing, which is vital for analytics, auditing, or training, entails privacy risks. The de-identification of data is crucial to maintaining privacy integrity during internal exchanges.
- **Development and testing scenarios**: R&D and testing phases necessitate large volumes of raw data. To prevent privacy breaches, these data must undergo de-identification before being used in these environments.
- **External release scenarios**: The external dissemination of data, a key facet of the VPP data business, mandates stringent privacy safeguards. This includes the thorough analysis and de-identification of user data, ensuring no privacy leaks occur during external interactions or transactions.

This enhanced section underlines the criticality of protecting user privacy in diverse operational scenarios of VPPs, highlighting the need for specialized data handling practices to mitigate privacy risks.

3.4. System Model

This section intricately details a data sharing model within a virtual power plant ecosystem, leveraging an advanced zero-knowledge proof-based attribute hiding and policy protection mechanism. This sophisticated model interweaves cryptographic techniques and network entities, forming a bulwark for privacy and security in data sharing.

Our model addresses the three main privacy issues mentioned in the previous section. The system's architecture, illustrated in Figure 1, consists of seven integral entities at a logical level: registration and authentication node (RAN), multiple attribute management node (AMN), data uploader, data downloader, data center (DC), virtual power plant console (VPP), and review node (AN). Each entity is meticulously designed to fulfill critical functions in the data handling process, ensuring secure and private data management.

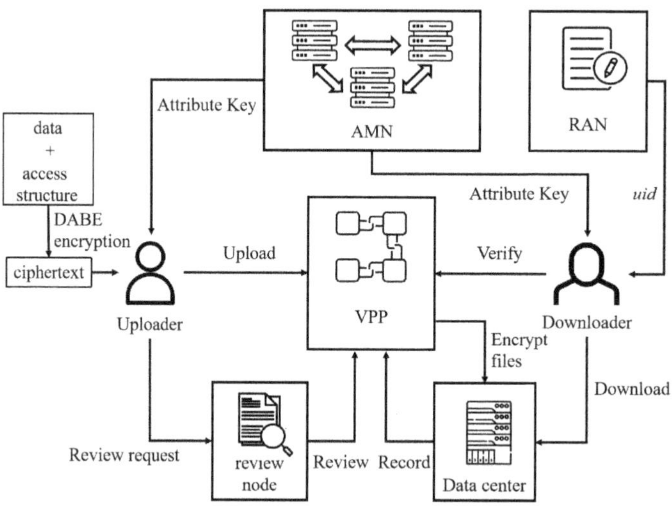

Figure 1. A user attribute privacy protection model based on zero-knowledge proof.

1. **Registration and authentication node (RAN):** This node is instrumental during the system's initialization. It generates a unique identity *uid* for each user, which is linked to a randomly generated value. This identity is crucial for user verification across

the system, and its one-time activation mechanism, coupled with its autonomy from central authorities, augments the system's security and reliability.

2. **Multiple attribute management nodes (AMNs):** These decentralized nodes are responsible for specific attribute domains. They generate private keys (SKs) for each attribute, binding these keys to the user's *uid*. This decentralized structure reduces the risks associated with centralized control, such as single-point failures and potential security breaches.
3. **Data uploader:** The uploader employs the distributed attribute-based encryption (DABE) algorithm for encrypting data. DABE is chosen for its efficiency in managing multiple attributes and its capability of enforcing granular access control policies. The uploader encrypts the data and then transmits the ciphertext to the smart contract, which in turn provides the data storage address.
4. **Data downloader:** Utilizing the attribute hiding zero-knowledge proofs (AH-ZKPs), this entity demonstrates compliance with access control policies without revealing specific attribute values. AH-ZKP is pivotal in preserving privacy while facilitating access to data storage addresses. The downloader decrypts the ciphertext using attribute keys, ensuring secure data retrieval.
5. **Data center (DC):** The DC is a nexus between the nodes and data storage. It receives encrypted data from the nodes, stores them, and returns the data storage address. For data retrieval, it verifies download requests through smart contracts and releases the encrypted data upon successful validation, adding an essential security layer.
6. **Virtual power plant console (VPP):** The VPP serves as an intermediary in data transmission. It handles encrypted files from uploaders, verifies attribute commitments against access control policies, and maintains access control lists (ACLs). These ACLs are crucial for tracking commitments and managing data storage, playing a significant role in the system's data governance.
7. **Review node (AN):** The AN is the system's audit and compliance overseer. In instances of data disputes or irregularities, the AN intervenes to provide an audit trail, ensuring transparency and accountability in data operations within the virtual power plant.

The elaborated model, with its emphasis on decentralization, zero-knowledge proofs, and attribute-based encryption, represents a state-of-the-art approach to data security and privacy in the context of virtual power plants. It addresses contemporary challenges in user privacy and data security with a comprehensive, innovative framework.

To safeguard the encrypted data stored in data centers, it is imperative to verify the data visitors' permissions against the access control list (ACL) before granting them the file's storage address. This section introduces a novel data access control strategy, the attribute-hiding zero-knowledge proof (AH-ZKP). AH-ZKP synergizes zero-knowledge proof with attribute-based encryption to enable attribute-hidden access control. This strategy surpasses the conventional attribute-based encryption methods by adding an extra layer of privacy, thereby validating user privileges without compromising the privacy of user attributes and access policies.

The implementation of AH-ZKP faces three primary challenges. Firstly, it requires a seamless integration of zero-knowledge proofs with user attributes to ensure robust privacy protection. Secondly, it involves utilizing zero-knowledge proofs for validating access policies, which are composed of user attributes, in a manner that circumvents potential security threats like re-entry and man-in-the-middle attacks. Lastly, deploying AH-ZKP within a virtual power plant setting demands careful consideration to maintain the trustworthiness of the validation results.

To address the outlined challenges, we introduce an attribute-based Merkle tree structure designed for the efficient aggregation of user attributes. Utilizing the Merkle root, we construct commitments within the zk-SNARK framework, enabling zero-knowledge proof verification. This approach ensures that verifiers ascertain compliance with access policy requirements without gaining insight into specific user attributes. Moreover, by storing only the Merkle tree's hash root, we achieve significant reductions in storage space and computational time.

Our design of zero-knowledge proofs incorporates attribute-based commitments. By linking attributes to user addresses, we strengthen the system's defense against man-in-the-middle and replay attacks. Figure 2 illustrates the AH-ZKP structure, encompassing elements like the collision-resistant hash function, pseudo-random sorting function, and the attribute Merkle tree, along with the attribute commitment (COMM) and NP declaration.

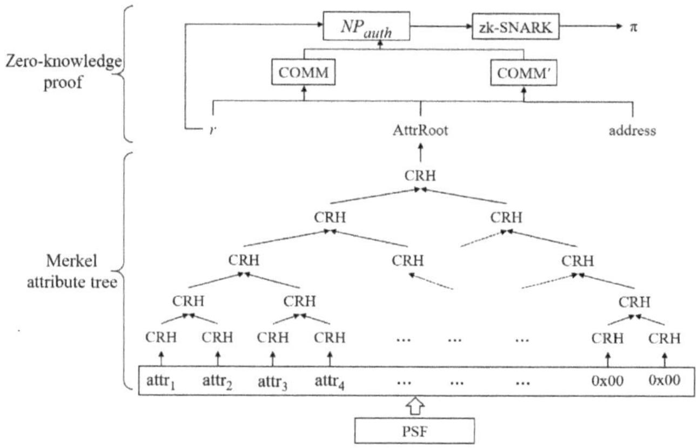

Figure 2. AH-ZKP structure emphasizing attribute hiding.

Key components of the AH-ZKP include the following:

1. Collision-resistant hash function (CRH): We employ the Pedersen hash, which is reliant on the discrete logarithm problem, to ensure anti-collision properties and compatibility with the R within a first-order constraint system (R1CS) required by AH-ZKP.
2. Pseudo-random sort function (PSF): This function is designed for anti-collision pseudo-randomness, ensuring distinct outputs for different inputs while maintaining consistency for identical inputs. The PSF plays a crucial role in obfuscating the attribute list ($AttrList$), including sorting and padding operations.
3. Attribute Merkle tree: Constructed using CRH, this tree provides a quick verification mechanism for attributes within $AttrList$. It stores the hash values of individual attributes in leaf nodes, with missing nodes filled with zero bytes, optimizing storage by retaining only the root hash value ($AttrRoot$).
4. Attribute commitment COMM: The value of $COMM_{attr}$ is computed by COMM based on the attribute root $AttrRoot$ and the random number r. $AttrRoot$ is the root of the attribute Merkle tree constructed from $AttrList$. In order to check the access rights, the data uploader and the data visitor need to generate the same value of $COMM_{attr}$. The data uploader should secretly send r_{random} to the data visitor in a secure channel. $COMM'_{attr}$ is computed by the COMM based on the attribute root $AttrRoot$ and the address $addr_{downloader}$ of the data visitor, thus associating the attribute root $AttrRoot$ with the address of the data visitor and preventing an attacker from using $COMM'_{attr}$ to impersonate a legitimate data visitor through a replay attack.
5. NP Statement: The earlier proposed NP_{auth} demonstrates that a data visitor possesses the requisite access rights. This statement includes a private input $AttrList$, public input $addr_{downloader}$, and r_{random}, leading to the generation of $COMM_{attr}$ and $COMM'_{attr}$ through non-interactive commitments.

The conversion of NP_{auth} into a relationship-generating meta R is expressed as

$$R = \left\{ \begin{array}{l} (addr_{downloader}, r_{random}, COMM_{attr}, COMM'_{attr}; AttrList) : \\ COMM_{attr} = COMM(AttrList, r_{random})\hat{}COMM'_{attr} \\ = COMM(AttrList, addr_{downloader}) \end{array} \right\} \quad (5)$$

We confine R within a first-order constraint system (R1CS), employing it to construct zk-SNARK commitments that underpin the aforementioned functionalities. This ensures that verifiers recognize the data visitor's compliance with access permissions without gaining knowledge of specific attributes possessed.

Our framework for attribute-hiding zero-knowledge proofs (AH-ZKPs) is meticulously architected to enable privacy-preserved authentication within virtual power plant systems. The process commences with an attribute list $AttrList$, strategically obfuscated via a pseudo-random sort function (PSF). We define f as an abbreviation for the collision hash function CRH. Each attribute $attr_i$ undergoes a cryptographic transformation through a collision-resistant hash (CRH) function, yielding hashed counterparts $leaf_i$:

$$CRH(attr_i) = leaf_i, \quad (6)$$

Subsequently, these leaf nodes are systematically aggregated to construct the Merkle tree, employing recursive hash pairings until the Merkle root $AttrRoot$ is derived, encapsulating the entirety of the user's attributes in a single hash value. The integrity of the Merkle tree is paramount, as it serves as the backbone for the zero-knowledge proof by succinctly summarizing the attribute set.

In the ensuing phase, we engender two commitments, $COMM$ and $COMM'$. These are formulated by intricately binding the $AttrRoot$ with a nonce r and the prover's address, expressed as

$$COMM = f(AttrRoot, r), \quad (7)$$

$$COMM' = f(AttrRoot, \text{address}), \quad (8)$$

Integral to the zero-knowledge aspect, these commitments lead to the generation of a non-interactive proof π within the zk-SNARK protocol. This proof robustly asserts the NP statement NP_{auth}, which allows the verifier to ascertain the authenticity of the attribute claims without gaining access to the attributes themselves:

$$NP_{auth} : \{(COMM, COMM'; AttrList) | \exists r, \text{address}\}. \quad (9)$$

A verifier, upon evaluating π, can confirm that the prover has satisfied the prescribed access policy. This process is executed without revealing any specific details of the attributes, thus upholding privacy. Our AH-ZKP framework is a testament to the harmonization of robust security protocols with the imperative of privacy, setting a new benchmark in the field of secure data access for virtual power plant systems.

The following will provide a detailed explanation of the specific steps for using AH-ZKP in conjunction with the plan.

3.5. Specific Steps

Our plan includes a system initialization process and five main steps: upload, verify, download, decdata, and audit. The main process is described as follows.

1. System initialization. We use data attribute-based encryption (DABE) to encrypt the raw data (RawData) and use AH-ZKP to protect attribute privacy. In DABE, the data are divided into multiple parts and are encrypted and stored on different distributed nodes. Each node only stores a portion of the data, and decryption of the data requires certain attribute conditions to be met. This design distributes data storage and management across multiple nodes, improving data security and reliability. The registration and authentication node (RAN) is used to initialize the public security parameters and keys required for DABE and AH-ZKP, while each

attribute management node (AMN) initializes and generates the corresponding public–private key pairs.

2. Upload. The data uploader uploads the file data after encrypting them using the DABE algorithm. During encryption, it is necessary to determine the file's access policy $AttrList$. We use a non-interactive commitment scheme COMM to generate commitments. This means that, given a random number r_{random} and the secret information $AttrList$, a commitment can be calculated. At the same time, others do not know the content of $AttrList$. When given the random number r_{random} and the secret information $AttrList$, anyone can verify and confirm their equality. The data uploader sends the commitments and encrypted data (EncData) to the virtual power plant. The system then sends the data to the data center and obtains a storage address. Subsequently, the storage address and the corresponding attribute commitments are sent to the access control list (ACL) to record the upload behavior. The storage address is then returned to the data uploader.
3. Verify. The data uploader uses AH-ZKP for permission verification. First, they need to generate attribute commitments $COMM_{attr}$ based on their own attributes. Then, the uploader also needs to calculate address commitments based on their own addresses, binding the attributes to the user's address. Finally, the uploader needs to prove the following NP authorization statement NP_{auth} to the terminal using AH-ZKP:
I have private inputs, an attribute list $AttrList$, $addr_{downloader}$, and a random number r_{random}, and have obtained $COMM_{attr}$ and $COMM'_{attr}$ through non-interactive commitment. We transform the above statement NP_{auth} into a relation generating element R and constrain it to R1CS. We use the Groth16 algorithm to generate the AH-ZKP proof of commitment. The data uploader then forwards it to the node to prove their possession of the relevant attributes. The system will verify the correctness and, upon successful verification, query the ACL to obtain the storage address corresponding to $COMM_{attr}$. Subsequently, the node will send the storage address of the encrypted data and the permission credentials for accessing the encrypted data to the data uploader and generate a permission authentication record. The data uploader can then obtain the encrypted data from the data center using the permission credentials.
4. Download. When a data accessor downloads data, they send the storage address, the hash value of their own address, and the verified credentials to the data center. Additionally, they also need to send the usage record encrypted with the data uploader's public key. This record combines the assessor's identity with their address. After the data center verifies the credentials (which prove that the accessor has the necessary permissions to access the address), the encrypted data (EncData) is returned to the data accessor, and a download record is sent.
5. DecData. After receiving the ciphertext, the data accessor sends the uid and attributes to the relevant attribute management node (AMN). Then, the AMN uses the secret key SK to generate the corresponding $K_{i,uid}$ for the attribute i and uid and returns it to the accessor. With sufficient $K_{i,uid}$, the accessor can then decrypt the ciphertext using the DABE algorithm and obtain the original data $RawData$.
6. Audit. When there is an anomaly with the data, the data uploader or relevant nodes can obtain the data download record by reviewing the nodes and decrypt it using the private key SK. Then, they conduct an operational review based on the record to determine the user responsible for the relevant operations.

4. Security Analysis

4.1. Security Model

Our security model for the virtual power plant system is underpinned by several crucial assumptions. Foremost is the trust in the registration and authentication nodes at the system's inception, ensuring the integrity of vital elements like the global parameters and the global identifier uid, which is essential for AH-ZKP and DABE.

The attribute management node (AMN) too plays a pivotal role during system initialization. It is not just about attribute distribution and key generation; the AMN is instrumental in reinforcing DABE's anti-collusion capabilities, preventing collusion attacks by disallowing the combination of attributes from different management sections to satisfy access policies.

We also rely on the robust anti-collision properties of the collision-resistant hash function (CRH) and pseudo-random sort function (PSF), which are the bedrock of our system's security.

However, certain threats remain:

Threat 1: The risk of unauthorized access to encrypted data.

Threat 2: The possibility of attackers decrypting original data from DABE-generated ciphertext.

Threat 3: The danger of attackers inferring private attribute data through analysis of data operation records.

Threat 4: The vulnerability to inference attacks that might expose file access policies.

Considering the security model of our DABE approach, we recognize the registration and authentication nodes, alongside the attribute management node, as trusted entities. Consequently, the DABE's encryption mechanism inherently safeguards against unauthorized data and privacy breaches. Specifically, only individuals possessing relevant attributes, directly countering Threat 2, can decrypt the original data.

In our data sharing and access control framework, user authentication via AH-ZKP is paramount. This process ensures that only verified users can retrieve data storage addresses, effectively addressing Threat 1 by restricting data access to intended recipients only.

Moreover, our system architecture necessitates fulfilling two critical security requirements: attribute indiscernibility and resistance to attribute tampering. These requirements, addressing Threat 3 (attribute privacy) and Threat 4 (access policy privacy), respectively, also substantiate the efficacy of AH-ZKP in our model.

We define our scheme $S = (Upload, Verify, Download, DecData, Audit)$ with the premise that, if it successfully meets both attribute indistinguishability and tamper resistance criteria, it is deemed secure.

We further elaborate on these two pivotal characteristics. They are conceptualized as interactive games between an adversary 'A' and a challenger 'C'. Within each game, the trusted entity operates a system model responding to various requests (upload, verify, download, decdata, and audit) through scheme S. 'A' issues query requests to 'C', who then facilitates these requests via S, ensuring responses are relayed back to 'A'. This process allows 'A' to comprehend query inputs and analyze corresponding responses, which is integral to maintaining the robustness of our security model.

Enhanced discussion on attribute indistinguishability (addressing Threat 3): In our secure system model, the adversary, denoted as A, is limited to accessing only publicly available information. This set includes the general public parameter (GP), the data visitor's address ($\text{addr}_{\text{downloader}}$), the attribute tree root (AttrRoot), non-interactive commitments ($\text{COMM}_{\text{attr}}$ and $\text{COMM}'_{\text{attr}}$), and a random number ($r_{\text{random}}$). The critical aspect of this model is its ability to maintain attribute privacy security. In a theoretical scenario, adversary A's capability to deduce a data visitor's attributes increases post-interaction with our scheme S. Assume A's initial guessing probability is p_1, which, following an adaptive query, improves to p_2. The scheme is deemed attribute indistinguishable when the probability difference, $\Pr[\text{Event}_{\text{Attr}}] = p_2 - p_1$, is negligible.

We define *attribute indistinguishability* via the game *GameI*, which is outlined as follows:

- Challenger C initializes the game by sampling a binary random number $b \in \{0, 1\}$ and setting up two schemes S_0 and S_1, with corresponding system models M_0 and M_1.
- C permits A to query both schemes S_0 and S_1, encompassing operations like upload, verify, download, decdata, and audit. The correspondence between the system models is revealed as $M_{\text{left}} := M_0$ and $M_{\text{right}} := M_1$, albeit in a randomized sequence. A's

objective is to ascertain whether the pairings match: $\left(M_{\text{left}}, M_{\text{right}}\right) = (M_0, M_1)$ for $b = 0$ or $\left(M_{\text{left}}, M_{\text{right}}\right) = (M_1, M_0)$ for $b = 1$.

In essence, our scheme S, encompassing operations (upload, verify, download, decdata, audit), attains attribute indistinguishability in *GameI* for polynomial orders of λ, satisfying the condition

$$\text{Adv}^{\text{I}}_{S,A}(\lambda) < \text{negl}(\lambda) \tag{10}$$

where $\text{Adv}^{\text{I}}_{S,A}(\lambda) = \Pr[\text{GameI}(S, A, \lambda) = 1]$ signifies the statistical advantage of adversary A in *GameI*. Here, $\text{negl}(\lambda)$ represents an inconsequential probability value on a polynomial scale of order λ.

Enhanced discussion on attribute tamper resistance (addressing Threat 4 in AH-ZKP). The concept of attribute tamper resistance is pivotal in ensuring the integrity and security of the AH-ZKP framework, particularly in virtual power plant environments. This resistance is crucial for preventing unauthorized modifications or the exploitation of access policies, thereby safeguarding the privacy of these policies and thwarting attempts by adversaries to misuse privileges. A typical scenario involves preventing an adversary from stealing a private key to decrypt a file without possessing the requisite attributes.

To rigorously define and evaluate this resistance, we introduce an interactive game, *GameII*. In this game, the challenger C initializes the AH-ZKP scheme S with the necessary parameters and engages with an adversary A.

The adversary's objective is to demonstrate the existence of an address addr*, which, while lacking the requisite attributes for file decryption, can still produce a valid zero-knowledge commitment $\pi_{attr} := \text{AH} - \text{ZKP}(\text{COMM}_{\text{attr}}, \text{COMM}'_{\text{attr}}, r, \text{addr}^*, \text{attr}_i)$, such that $\text{Validate}(\pi_{attr}, K_{veri}) := 1$. The adversary's success in this game would imply a breach in attribute tamper resistance; the scheme's resilience is demonstrated if A fails to accomplish this.

Further, the analysis of security and privacy in this scheme is dissected through two distinct proofs, each targeting one core aspect: attribute indistinguishability and attribute tamper resistance. These proofs collectively affirm the robustness of the scheme against both privacy invasion and unauthorized attribute modification, reinforcing the overall security framework of the system in virtual power plant contexts.

4.2. Proof of Attribute Indistinguishability

Theorem 1. *The scheme* $S = (Upload, Verify, Download, DecData, Audit)$ *demonstrates the property of indistinguishability in an adversarial setting, where adversary A is restricted to accessing only public parameters.*

Consider a simulation game G_{sim}, where adversary A interacts with challenger C in a manner akin to $Game_I$. Unlike $Game_I$, however, each response in G_{sim} to adversary A is independent of the binary variable b. Consequently, adversary A gains no advantage in G_{sim}, as its success probability remains at 0. This setup allows us to establish that any disparity in A's advantage between $Game_I$ and G_{sim} is, in fact, negligible.

Proof of Theorem 1. The simulation game G_{sim} unfolds as per the following protocol:

- Challenger C initializes the essential parameters and disseminates the public parameters to adversary A, ensuring the values are predetermined and consistent.
- In G_{sim}, the AH-ZKP key is initialized using $sim()$, in contrast to the standard $Set-up()$, underlining a fundamental divergence in the simulation process.
- Challenger C establishes instances of the scheme (S_0, S_1) for the subsequent interaction.

□

Subsequently, C presents two models, M_{left} and M_{right}, to adversary A. Adversary A then forwards two query types (Q, Q') to C, who responds in a manner contingent upon the query type. The intricate process is detailed below, emphasizing the crucial phases of upload, validation, and so forth.

In the upload phase, we assume Q and Q'.

$$\begin{aligned} Q &= \left(Upload; GP, RawData, PK_{downloader}, PK, addr_{uploader}, attr_i\right) \\ Q' &= \left(Upload; GP, RawData, PK_{downloader}, PK, addr_{uploader}, attr_i'\right) \end{aligned} \quad (11)$$

Challenger C modifies the computation method before returning the results to A. The revised calculation is explicated as follows:

(a) $AttrList = PSF(str_i)$: A random string of appropriate length is used to compute $AttrList$, diverging from the standard computation of $PSF(attr_i)$, where $attr_i$ represents an attribute required by the data visitor.

(b) $AttrRoot = BuildMerkleTree(str)$: Here, a random string str substitutes $AttrList$ in the computation of $AttrRoot$.

(c) $COMM_{attr} = CRH(str, r)$: A similar approach is adopted, where str, instead of $AttrRoot$, is used in the computation of $COMM_{attr}$.

This modified computational approach is also applied to request Q'.

In the validation phase, the response to Q is altered as follows:

(a) $AttrList = PSF(str_i)$: This step mirrors the upload phase, reinforcing the consistency across different phases of the simulation.

(b) $AttrRoot = BuildMerkleTree(str)$: Replicating the approach in the upload phase for computational consistency.

(c) $COMM_{attr} = CRH(str, r)$: Maintaining the established pattern of computation.

(d) $COMM'_{attr} = CRH(str, addr_{downloader})$: A deviation in the computation process by using str instead of $AttrRoot$.

(e) $\pi_{attr} = sim(COMM_{attr}, COMM'_{attr}, r, addr_{downloader}, attr_i)$: The simulation employs analog arithmetic instead of AH-ZKP for proof generation.

(f) $b_2 = sim(\pi_{attr})$: Analogous to the previous step, analog arithmetic substitutes the standard $Validate(\pi_{attr})$ process to generate judgments.

Challenger C applies identical calculations for request Q'.

The download, decryption, and review phases remain consistent with those in $Game_I$, ensuring uniformity across the entire simulation process.

To conclude, G_{sim}, defined above, is juxtaposed with the original *GameI*, termed G_{real}, to demonstrate that the responses in G_{sim} are independent of b, thereby rendering A's advantage in G_{sim} as zero. Proving the negligible difference in A's advantage between G_{sim} and G_{real} effectively substantiates the indistinguishability property of the scheme.

The following discusses the *GameI*-based modification games G_1, G_2, and G_3 played by challenger C and adversary A.

Define Adv_{G_i} as the advantage of A over G_{real} in the game G_i. We use q_{Up} and q_v to denote the number of upload and verification queries issued by opponent A and Num_{attr} as the number of attributes owned by the data visitor. Define Adv_{PFS} as the advantage of A in distinguishing between normal PSF and random input PSF, and Adv_{CRH} as the advantage of A in distinguishing between the normal CRH and the random input CRH.

The difference between G_{sim} and G_{real} is that PSF, AttrRoot, COMM, and AH-ZKP are different. Four progressive games will be used to demonstrate that A has a negligible advantage in discriminating attributes between G_{sim} and G_{real}.

(1) Game G_1. G_1 replaces the AH-ZKP process of G_{real} with a simulation calculation. Specifically, C uses $sim(\varphi)$ instead of $KeyGen(\varphi)$ to generate K_{prov} and K_{veri}. In the verification phase, C computes $\pi_{attr} := sim(info)$ instead of using the correct method. Since there is no regulation and AH-ZKP has perfect zero-knowledge, it is known that $\text{Adv}_{G_1} = 0$.

(2) Game G_2. G_2 changes the parameters used by G_1 in PSF by replacing the $attr_i$ of the input PSF with a random string str_i of appropriate length, i.e., $AttrList := PSF(str_i)$. Each $attr_i$ replacement will generate Adv_{PFS}. When the scope is extended to Num_{attr} attributes, q_{Up} upload queries, and q_V validation queries, the advantage difference between G_2 and G_1 is

$$|\mathrm{Adv}_{G_2} - \mathrm{Adv}_{G_1}| = (q_{Up} + q_V) * Num_{attr} * \mathrm{Adv}_{\mathrm{PSF}} \tag{12}$$

(3) Game G_3. G_3 changes the parameter used by G_2 in the *BuildMerkleTree* function by replacing the AttrList input to *BuildMerkleTree* with a random string *str* of suitable length, i.e., $AttrRoot := BuildMerkleTree(str)$. Since *BuildMerkleTree* is implemented with a CRH in this paper's scenario, each *AttrList* substitution will produce Adv_{CRH}. In this process, entropy smoothing and collision-resistance properties also play an important role. By replacing *AttrList* with a random string *str*, additional randomness is introduced, increasing the randomness and unpredictability of the output of the cryptographic algorithm, thereby achieving the effect of entropy smoothing. This helps to improve the security of the cryptographic algorithm, preventing the regularity of input data from affecting the randomness of the algorithm's output. At the same time, since a CRH is used as the hash function for building the Merkle tree, replacing *AttrList* each time will result in Adv_{CRH}. This indicates that replacing input parameters affects the output of the CRH, thereby influencing the construction process of the Merkle tree and the final hash value. Maintaining the collision-resistance property of the CRH is crucial to ensure that different input data will not produce the same hash value after hashing, thus ensuring data integrity and security. When the scope is extended to Num_{attr} attributes, q_{Up} upload queries and q_V validation queries, the advantage difference between G_3 and G_2 is

$$|\mathrm{Adv}_{G_3} - \mathrm{Adv}_{G_2}| = (q_{Up} + q_V) * (2 * Num_{attr} - 1) * \mathrm{Adv}_{\mathrm{CRH}} \tag{13}$$

(4) Game G_{sim} . G_{sim} changes the parameter used by G_3 in COMM by replacing the *AttrRoot* of the input COMM with a random string *str* of suitable length, i.e., $AttrList := COMM(str)$. Since *BuildMerkleTree* is implemented with a CRH in the scheme of this paper, each *AttrRoot* substitution will generate Adv_{CRH}, and the upload step will generate one time and the verification step will generate two times. When the scope is extended to q_{Up} upload queries and q_V validation queries, the advantage difference between G_{sim} and G_3 is as in Formula (14).

$$|\mathrm{Adv}_{G_{sim}} - \mathrm{Adv}_{G_3}| = (q_{Up} + 2 * q_V) * \mathrm{Adv}_{\mathrm{CRH}} \tag{14}$$

In summary, the advantage of adversary A in discriminating properties between G_{sim} and G_{real} is as in Formula (15).

$$\begin{aligned} |\mathrm{Adv}_{G_{real}} - \mathrm{Adv}_{G_{sim}}| &\leq \mathrm{Adv}_{G_1} + |\mathrm{Adv}_{G_2} - \mathrm{Adv}_{G_1}| \\ &+ |\mathrm{Adv}_{G_3} - \mathrm{Adv}_{G_2}| + |\mathrm{Adv}_{G_{sim}} - \mathrm{Adv}_{G_3}| \\ &= (q_{Up} + q_V) * Num_{attr} * \mathrm{Adv}_{\mathrm{PSF}} \\ &+ [(q_{Up} + q_V) * (2 * Num_{attr} - 1) + (q_{Up} + 2 * q_V)] * \mathrm{Adv}_{\mathrm{CRH}} \end{aligned} \tag{15}$$

Furthermore, due to the response value's independence from b in G_{sim}, its dominance is zero, which is deduced considering Equation (6).

$$\begin{aligned} \mathrm{Adv}^{\mathrm{I}}_{S,A}(\lambda) &\leq (q_{Up} + q_V) * Num_{attr} * \mathrm{Adv}_{\mathrm{PSF}} \\ &+ [(q_{Up} + q_V) * (2 * Num_{attr} - 1) + (q_{Up} + 2 * q_V)] * \mathrm{Adv}_{\mathrm{CRH}} \end{aligned} \tag{16}$$

Given the unidirectionality of PSF and CRH, both Adv_{PFS} and Adv_{CRH} are deemed negligible on a polynomial scale of order λ . Consequently, $Adv^{I}_{S,A}(\lambda)$ is also negligible at this scale, affirming the indistinguishability property of the scheme:

$$S = (Upload, Verify, Download, DecData, Audit) \tag{17}$$

4.3. Attribute Tamper Resistance Certification

Theorem 2. *Attribute tamper resistance. In the context of our proposed scheme for virtual power plant user data security, attribute tamper resistance is a pivotal property. It implies that an adversary A cannot significantly alter user attributes without detection. Formally, in GameII, a polynomial-*

size game of order λ, our scheme $S = (Upload, Verify, Download, DecData, Audit)$ is deemed tamper-resistant if the following inequality holds true:

$$\mathrm{Adv}_{S,A}^{\mathrm{II}}(\lambda) < \mathrm{negl}(\lambda) \tag{18}$$

Here, $\mathrm{Adv}_{S,A}^{\mathrm{II}}(\lambda) = \Pr[\mathrm{GameII}(S, A, \lambda) = 1]$ quantifies the probability of A's success in GameII, and $\mathrm{negl}(\lambda)$ denotes a negligible function in the polynomial scale of λ.

Proof of Theorem 2. We categorize the possible successful tampering events by A into disjoint categories to comprehensively argue the tamper resistance of our scheme.

(1) $EVENT_{addr}$: A wins *GameII* with an alternate address $addr'$ equating to the target $addr*$.

(2) $EVENT_{PSF}$: A wins *GameII* where $addr' \neq addr*$. For some attribute $attr_i'$ of $addr'$ and $attr*_i$ of $addr^*$, we have $AttrList' = PSF(attr_i')$ and $AttrList* = PSF(attr*_i)$, yet $AttrRoot' = AttrRoot*$.

(3) $EVENT_{root}$: A wins *GameII* with $addr' = addr*$ and $AttrRoot' \neq AttrRoot*$. Here, $COMM'_{\mathrm{attr}'} = CRH(AttrRoot', addr')$ and $COMM'_{\mathrm{attr}*} = CRH(AttrRoot*, addr*)$ are equivalent.

(4) $EVENT_{COMM}$: A wins *GameII* where $addr' \neq addr*$ and $AttrRoot' \neq AttrRoot*$, yet $COMM'_{\mathrm{attr}'} = COMM'_{\mathrm{attr}*}$ remains true. □

In summary, the adversary's advantage in *GameII* is represented as follows:

$$\begin{aligned}\mathrm{Adv}_{S,A}^{\mathrm{II}}(\lambda) = &\Pr[EVENT_{addr}] + \Pr[EVENT_{PSF}] \\ &+ \Pr[EVENT_{root}] + \Pr[EVENT_{COMM}]\end{aligned} \tag{19}$$

Thus, demonstrating that each event's probability is negligible on a polynomial scale of λ confirms the negligible nature of $\mathrm{Adv}_{S,A}^{\mathrm{II}}(\lambda)$, validating the tamper resistance of our scheme.

(1) **Probability of** $EVENT_{addr}$: Define $\varepsilon_1 = \Pr[EVENT_{addr}]$. In the context of our DABE scheme, ε_1 represents the probability that A can substitute an alternate address $addr'$ for the intended target $addr*$ undetected. Given the robust encryption and verification mechanisms of DABE, this probability is expected to be negligible.

(2) **Probability of** $EVENT_{PSF}$: Let $\varepsilon_2 = \Pr[EVENT_{PSF}]$. This event signifies A's success in finding an alternate address $addr'$ where the attribute lists generated by the pseudo-set function (PSF) for $addr'$ and $addr*$ collide, i.e., $AttrList' = AttrList*$. The negligible likelihood of such a collision, given the collision resistance of PSF, further asserts our scheme's resilience.

(3) **Probability of** $EVENT_{root}$: For this event, define $\varepsilon_3 = \Pr[EVENT_{root}]$. This occurs when A manages to generate a matching attribute root $AttrRoot\prime$ for a different set of attributes, thus defying the unique nature of Merkle tree constructions used in our DABE approach. The improbability of this event, given the cryptographic strength of Merkle trees and collision-resistant hash (CRH) functions, underscores the robustness of the scheme.

(4) **Probability of** $EVENT_{COMM}$: Finally, $\varepsilon_4 = \Pr[EVENT_{COMM}]$ assesses the chance of A successfully creating a collision in the commitment scheme, despite differing attribute roots and addresses. The commitment scheme's reliance on CRH ensures the minuscule probability of such an occurrence, reinforcing the security of our system.

Overall, these probabilities, being negligible on a polynomial scale of λ, validate the assertion that $\mathrm{Adv}_{S,A}^{\mathrm{II}}(\lambda)$ is negligible. Consequently, our DABE scheme ensures attribute tamper resistance, which is crucial for maintaining the integrity and confidentiality of user data in virtual power plants.

5. Experimental Simulation

To assess the efficacy of our proposed scheme, we established a simulation environment on a Lenovo desktop computer produced in Guangzhou, China, which is equipped with an Intel Core i5-10500T CPU @ 2.30GHz and 8GB RAM, operating under Ubuntu 18.04. We selected Java 1.8.0 for implementing the distributed attribute-based encryption (DABE) due to its robust security features and wide use in cryptographic applications. Similarly, the zero-knowledge proof component was developed using the Trust 1.38.0 nightly framework, which was chosen for its advanced cryptographic capabilities.

Our simulation infrastructure focuses on integrating DABE with zero-knowledge proofs within the AH-ZKP architecture, employing the bellman library for its comprehensive support of the rank 1 constraint system (R1CS). This choice facilitates the imposition of constraints on inputs, which are essential for converting the NP statement NP_{auth} (referenced in Section 3.4) into corresponding R1CS constraints.

Furthermore, AH-ZKP's attribute commitments $\{\pi_{attr}\}$ are disseminated across nodes via the web3 interface, promoting an efficient distribution mechanism. Following the architecture setup, the DABE algorithm was constructed using JDK to ensure compatibility and performance efficiency. The user interaction interface and the encryption/decryption modules were developed in Python and optimized for ease of use and versatility. The comprehensive structure of this simulation setup, including the integration of various components, is elucidated in Figure 3, providing a visual representation of the system's workflow and interconnections.

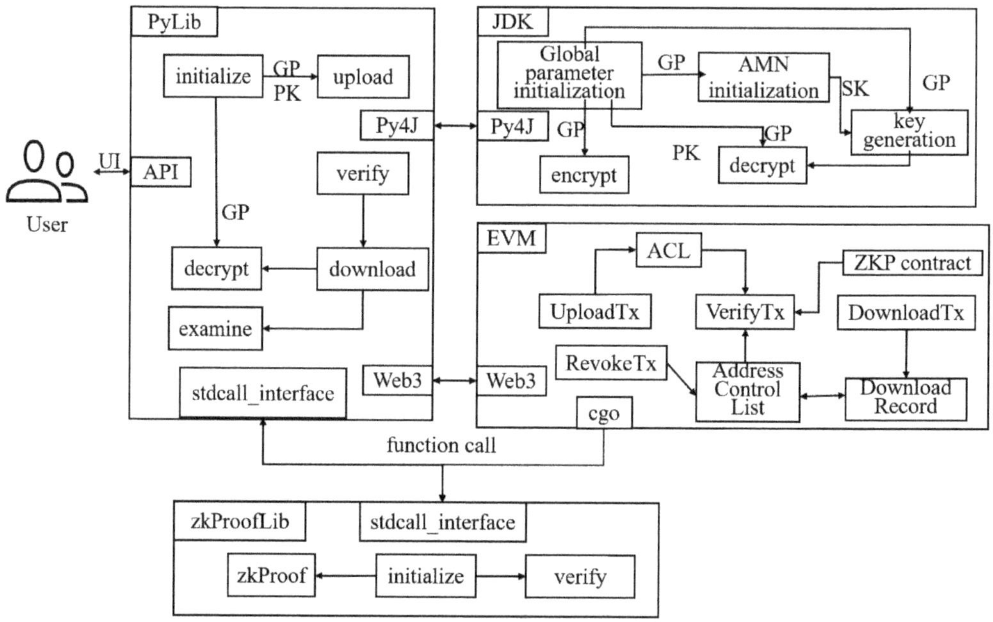

Figure 3. Implementation structure of the plan.

As depicted in Figure 4, an increase in user attributes leads to a corresponding rise in the time cost for both AH-ZKP and traditional DABE methods. However, it is notable that AH-ZKP maintains a significantly lower time cost compared to DABE, indicating enhanced efficiency.

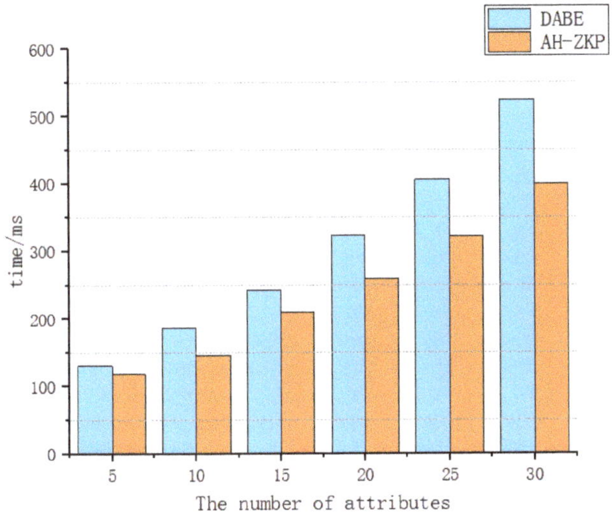

Figure 4. Comparison of time costs between DABE and AH-ZKP algorithms.

Further delving into the performance metrics, Table 3 presents a detailed analysis. Notably, the time efficiency in verifying AH-ZKP is considerably superior to that of any process in DABE, underscoring AH-ZKP's practical applicability in scenarios demanding swift data processing.

The simulation tests utilized two AMNs and five attributes. While the AH-ZKP initialization process incurs a time cost of approximately 6.7 s, it is a one-time process during system initialization. In contrast, DABE requires multiple runs of AMN initialization and key generation for each AMN and specific attributes. Consequently, the cumulative time of AH-ZKP processes, including proof generation and verification, is less than that of the DABE processes, which encompass encryption, key generation, and decryption. Furthermore, the total time cost of DABE escalates with the addition of attributes, thereby making AH-ZKP more time-efficient proportionally. Additionally, as detailed in Table 3, the time cost of other transactions is minimal, further reinforcing the efficiency of AH-ZKP.

Table 3. Time and space costs of each process in the program.

	Procedure	Time Cost	Space Cost
AH-ZKP	Initialization (run only once)	6.7359 s	Attribute parameter 1 KB
	Prove	0.7041 s	Attribute Proof 304 B
	Validate	0.0067 s	/
	Total time	0.7108 s	/
DABE	Global parameter initialization	0.4969 s	/
	AMN initialization (multiple runs required)	0.3518 s	Public key 1 KB Private key 787 B
	Key generation (multiple runs required)	0.0909 s	Attribute key 255 B
	Encryption	0.7602 s	Data size 3 KB
	Decryption	0.1115 s	/
	Total time	1.2351 s	/

In conclusion, the integration of zero-knowledge proofs for privacy protection within the proposed scheme introduces an acceptable overhead, validating its practical feasibility in real-world applications.

6. Conclusions

In this paper, we have developed an innovative privacy protection mechanism for virtual power plants, prioritizing user privacy in varied business contexts. Our approach integrates zero-knowledge proofs with distributed attribute-based encryption (DABE), enhancing both privacy and access control. The DABE framework facilitates file encryption, enabling granular access control while mitigating the risks associated with centralized attribute management through multiple attribute management nodes. This design significantly reduces the likelihood of unauthorized policy inference and ciphertext decryption. Central to our scheme is the attribute hiding zero-knowledge proof (AH-ZKP), which effectively conceals user attributes during verification and authorization. This method ensures the confidentiality of sensitive information, including user attributes and decryption prerequisites, across all transaction stages. We rigorously analyzed the security aspects of our scheme, confirming its robustness in providing attribute indistinguishability and resistance to attribute tampering. Comparative experimental analysis, as shown in our results, demonstrates the scheme's efficiency. Our tests reveal that the attribute-based encryption and zero-knowledge proof steps require approximately 1 s in total computation time, outperforming existing methods in terms of time and space efficiency. The proposed scheme excels in encrypted sharing, multi-party cooperation, collision resistance, verifiability, anonymity, and access policy protection. It proves particularly effective in securing user privacy across various application scenarios within virtual power plants, thereby addressing a critical need in the field.

Author Contributions: Conceptualization, R.Y.; methodology, H.G.; software, F.S.; validation, J.W. and R.Y.; formal analysis, H.G.; investigation, J.W.; resources, F.S.; data curation, H.G.; writing—original draft preparation, R.Y.; writing—review and editing, H.G.; visualization, F.S.; supervision, R.Y.; project administration, F.S.; funding acquisition, R.Y. All authors have read and agreed to the published version of the manuscript.

Funding: This work has been supported by the National Key Research and Development Program of China and Key Technologies for Aggregation and Interactive Control of Scalable and Flexible Virtual Power Plants under grant 2021YFB2401200.

Data Availability Statement: The data presented in this study are available in this article.

Conflicts of Interest: Author R.Y. was employed by the company State Grid Smart Grid Research Institute Co., Ltd. Author J.W. was employed by the company State Grid Shanghai Municipal Electric Power Company. The remaining authors declare that the research was conducted in the absence of any commercial or financial relationships that could be construed as a potential conflict of interest.

References

1. Hui, H.; Ding, Y.; Shi, Q.; Li, F.; Yan, J. 5G network-based Internet of Things for demand response in smart grid: A survey on application potential. *Appl. Energy* **2020**, *257*, 113–972. [CrossRef]
2. Zou, Y.; Yang, L. Synergetic dispatch models of a wind/PV/hydro virtual power plant based on representative scenario set. *Power Syst. Technol.* **2015**, *39*, 1855–1859. [CrossRef]
3. Lin, Y.; Miao, S.; Yang, W.; Yin, B.; Tu, Q.; Yw, C. Day-ahead optimal scheduling strategy of virtual power plant for environment with multiple uncertainties. *Electr. Power Autom. Equip.* **2021**, *41*, 143–150.
4. Liu, D.; Fan, Q.; You, H.; Dai, X.; Huang, Y.; Shao, Z. Research status and trends of virtual power plants under electrical Internet of Things. *Adv. Eng. Sci.* **2020**, *52*, 10.
5. Zhang, K.; Ding, G.; Wen, M.; Hui, H.; Ding, Y.; Zhu, J.; Xie, K.; Yu, C.; Zhang, L. Review of optimal dispatching technology and market mechanism design for virtual power plants. *Integr. Intell. Energy* **2022**, *44*, 60–72.
6. Fang, L.; Xu, Y.; Yang, X.; Li, L.; Fu, G.; Chai, Z. Multi-time scale coordinated operation strategy of virtual power plant clusters considering power interactive sharing. *Power Syst. Technol.* **2022**, *46*, 642–656.
7. Liu, S.; Ai, Q.; Zheng, J.; Wu, R. Bi-level coordination mechanism and operation strategy of multitime scale multiple virtual power plants. *Proc. CSEE* **2018**, *38*, 753–761.

8. Belguith, S.; Kaaniche, N.; Russello, G. Lightweight Attribute-based Encryption Supporting Access Policy Update for Cloud Assisted IoT. In Proceedings of the 2018 IEEE 11th International Conference on Cloud Computing (CLOUD) San Francisco, CA, USA, 2–7 July 2018, Volume 2, pp. 135–146.
9. Guan, Z.; Yang, W.; Zhu, L.; Longfei, W.U.; Wang, R. Achieving adaptively secure data access control with privacy protection for lightweight IoT devices. *Sci. China Inf. Sci.* **2021**, *64*, 14. [CrossRef]
10. Hur, J.; Noh, K.D. Attribute-Based Access Control with Efficient Revocation in Data Outsourcing Systems. *IEEE Trans. Parallel Distrib. Syst. Publ. IEEE Comput. Soc.* **2011**, *22*, 1214–1221. [CrossRef]
11. Li, M.; Yu, S.; Zheng, Y.; Ren, K.; Lou, W. Scalable and Secure Sharing of Personal Health Records in Cloud Computing Using Attribute-Based Encryption. *IEEE Trans. Parallel Distrib. Syst.* **2013**, *24*, 131–143. [CrossRef]
12. Khalil, A.; Mbarek, N.; Togni, O. IoT-MAAC: Multiple Attribute Access Control for IoT environments. In Proceedings of the 2020 IEEE 17th Annual Consumer Communications & Networking Conference (CCNC), Vegas, NV, USA, 10–13 January 2020.
13. Hayata, J.; Ishizaka, M.; Sakai, Y.; Hanaoka, G.; Matsuura, K. Generic Construction of Adaptively Secure Anonymous Key-Policy Attribute-Based Encryption from Public-Key Searchable Encryption. *IEICE Trans. Fundam. Electron. Commun. Comput. Sci.* **2020**, *E103.A*, 107–113. [CrossRef]
14. Li, J.; Ai, Q. Operation mode of virtual power plant considering peak regulation auxiliary service. *Electr. Power Autom. Equip.* **2021**, *41*, 7.
15. Zhu, Y.; Yi, Z.; Lu, Q.; Yang, Y.; Li, B.; Xu, Y. Collaborative pricing strategy of virtual power plant and distribution network considering typical scenes. *Electr. Power Constr.* **2019**, *40*, 74–85.
16. Zhong, Y.; Sun, Y.; Xie, D.; Zhai, S. Multi-scenario optimal dispatch of integrated community energy system with power-heating-gas-cooling subsys-tems. *Autom. Electr. Power Syst.* **2019**, *43*, 9.
17. Chen, W.; Sun, R.; Qiu, J.; Chai, Q. Profit allocation and frequency regulation bidding strategy of virtual power plant considering battery cycle life. *J. Glob. Energy Interconnect.* **2020**, *11*, 374–384.
18. Yi, Z.; Xu, Y.; Gu, W.; Wu, W. A Multi-Time-Scale Economic Scheduling Strategy for Virtual Power Plant Based on Deferrable Loads Aggregation and Disaggregation. *IEEE Trans. Sustain. Energy* **2020**, *11*, 1332–1346. [CrossRef]
19. Lv, M.; Lou, S.; Liu, J.; Wu, Y.; Wang, Z. Coordinated optimization of multi—Type reserve in virtual power plant accommodated high shares of wind power. *Proc. CSEE* **2018**, *38*, 9.
20. Qin, Y.; Ge, L.; Bo, W. Swarm intelligence collaborative control and optimiza-tion technology of Energy Internet. *Huadian Technol.* **2021** , *43*, 1–13. [CrossRef]
21. Groth, J. On the Size of Pairing-Based Non-interactive Arguments. In Proceedings of the Annual International Conference on the Theory and Applications of Cryptographic Techniques, Vienna, Austria, 8–12 May 2016.

electronics

MDPI

Article

Incorporating Entity Type-Aware and Word–Word Relation-Aware Attention in Generative Named Entity Recognition

Ying Mo and Zhoujun Li *

State Key Lab of Software Development Environment, Beihang University, Beijing 100191, China; moying@buaa.edu.cn
* Correspondence: lizj@buaa.edu.cn

Abstract: Named entity recognition (NER) is a critical subtask in natural language processing. It is particularly valuable to gain a deeper understanding of entity boundaries and entity types when addressing the NER problem. Most previous sequential labeling models are task-specific, while recent years have witnessed the rise of generative models due to the advantage of tackling NER tasks in the encoder–decoder framework. Despite achieving promising performance, our pilot studies demonstrate that existing generative models are ineffective at detecting entity boundaries and estimating entity types. In this paper, a multiple attention framework is proposed which introduces the attention of entity-type embedding and word–word relation into the named entity recognition task. To improve the accuracy of entity-type mapping, we adopt an external knowledge base to calculate the prior entity-type distributions and then incorporate the information input to the model via the encoder's self-attention. To enhance the contextual information, we take the entity types as part of the input. Our method obtains the other attention from the hidden states of entity types and utilizes it in self- and cross-attention mechanisms in the decoder. We transform the entity boundary information in the sequence into word–word relations and extract the corresponding embedding into the cross-attention mechanism. Through word–word relation information, the method can learn and understand more entity boundary information, thereby improving its entity recognition accuracy. We performed experiments on extensive NER benchmarks, including four flat and two long entity benchmarks. Our approach significantly improves or performs similarly to the best generative NER models. The experimental results demonstrate that our method can substantially enhance the capabilities of generative NER models.

Keywords: named entity recognition; attention; generative model

1. Introduction

Named entity recognition (NER) is a subtask of information extraction that seeks to locate and classify named entities mentioned in unstructured text into predefined categories, such as the entity types of person, organization, and location. NER is one of the fundamental research problems in natural language processing, which has been widely adopted in information retrieval and question-answering systems [1–3]. Previous works [4–9] have addressed NER tasks with task-specific token-level sequential labeling or span-level classification methods. In token-level sequential labeling methods, each token is assigned a label to represent its entity type. On the other hand, span-level classification methods enumerate all possible spans in the sentences and classify them into predefined entity types.

Recently, sequence-to-sequence (seq2seq) generative approaches [10,11] have gained attention in the NER community due to their ability to jointly model all NER tasks in a unified framework. Although these models have shown promising results across all three NER categories (flat NER, nested NER, and discontinuous NER), NER faces two limitations that require the proposal of suitable methods for addressing them. First, these generative models are ineffective at utilizing information about entity boundaries. For example, consider a seq2seq method tasked with identifying entities in a complex sentence; the model might successfully recognize "New York" as an entity but fail to discern the boundary between "New York" and "University" in the phrase "New York University". It incorrectly identifies the entire phrase as one entity instead of two separate entities: the location "New York", and the organization "University". This ineffectiveness stems from the autoregressive decoding process inherent in seq2seq models failing to capture the inter-word relationships within a sentence that are essential for identifying entity boundaries. Current seq2seq models generate coarse-grained entities and leverage context insufficiently, making a more precise and fine-grained approach required. Second, the seq2seq framework does not explicitly consider the effect of entity types on NER. While entity-type generation is based on the compounding tokens, the incorrect generation of these tokens from the decoder can lead to misguided entity-type mapping information. Access to prior knowledge from external entity databases aids the model in precisely determining entity types, and these entity types can in turn can shape the contextual learning of sentences, thereby improving the representation of entities. Therefore, it is crucial to incorporate entity-type mapping and entity boundary information into seq2seq NER models in order to overcome these limitations.

In this paper, we present a novel approach to address the limitations of existing seq2seq NER models. We propose a novel approach incorporating attention mechanisms built on the entity type and the word–word relation. Specifically, we leverage external knowledge bases such as Wikipedia to learn entity-type information, further improving entity-type mapping. We integrate entity-type distributions into the encoder. Within the decoder, we embed the entity type through self-attention and cross-attention mechanisms, improving the associative mapping between entities and their respective types. Furthermore, we integrate representations of word–word relations into the decoder in order to enhance the capability to distinguish entity boundaries.

Our proposed approach promotes the smooth incorporation of entity-type information and word pair relational knowledge into the seq2seq NER framework. The main contributions are summarized as follows:

- We propose a generative NER framework which merges entity-type embedding and word–word relation representation to improve named entity recognition performance.
- We leverage two novel attention mechanisms in the NER framework, namely, entity type-aware attention and word–word relation-aware attention, improving the interaction between entities, entity types, and word–word relations for better contextual information.
- We present a series of experiments demonstrating the effectiveness of our method against various baselines. Ablation studies further show the contribution of each component within our approach, confirming their individual effectiveness.

2. Related Work

2.1. Named Entity Recognition

Named entity recognition (NER) is a significant research area in natural language processing. Various methods have been proposed for named entity recognition. Traditional research on NER performed modeling as a sequence labeling task, primarily focusing on flat NER [4–6,12]. The focus later shifted to complex-structure NER [13–18], which is studied separately. Different approaches to NER include sequence labeling, span-based, hypergraph-based, and generative methods.

NER is typically treated as a sequence labeling problem which assigns a tag to each token and uses a sequence model [4,6,14,19–23] to predict labels of the sequences (e.g., BIO). Collobert et al. [20] introduce the linear-chain conditional random field (CRF) in convolutional neural networks (CNNs) and made the sequence labeling problem one of determining the respective likelihoods between adjacent tags. Strubell et al. [5] obtained features for the sentences via CNN. Following this work, Lample et al. [4] adopted bidirectional LSTM with CRF to obtain the token representations. A number of studies [24,25] have combined CNNs and RNNs to extract features and learn word representations. Ju et al. [26] used dynamically stacking flat NER layers in the LSTM model for nested NER. Tang et al. [27] extended BIO to the BIOHD label scheme for discontinuous NER. However, these methods primarily require the design of different tagging schemes, and do not effectively address structurally complex or longer sentences such as nested and long NER. In contrast, our generative model can simultaneously handle this issue. Furthermore, we incorporate entity-type embedding from external knowledge and the encoder, while, word–word relation representation is merged to enhance entity boundary information.

Span-based methods commonly tackle complex NER tasks, e.g., nested NER. Researchers have proposed various approaches to obtain reasonable spans. Wang et al. [28] proposed a model which allows for interaction between spans from different layers. Yu et al. [15] utilized bi-affine attention to measure the possibility as a mention of span. Tan et al. [29] first predicted the boundary and then performed classification over the span features. Ouchi et al. [30] built a feature space with similar entity spans. However, these span-based models must enumerate all possible spans, while our model directly generates the entities. Li et al. [9] and Zhang et al. [31] presented a similar NER model, treating it as a span-based machine reading comprehension task. These methods require the design of template-based questions and multiple accesses to models, however, which raises computational costs; our proposed framework is able to avoid these issues. Lin et al. [32] offered a method that first detects the type of an anchor word and then locates the entity's boundaries. Shen et al. [16] presented a two-stage object detection method for nested entities. In addition to the above issues, these models have problems with gaps or chaining errors in the results of different stages. This paper proposes a method that enables interaction between entity type and entity boundary information to directly generate entity sequences.

Hypergraph-based methods have been proposed to cover many possible mentions in a sentence effectively. Lu et al. [33] introduced a method for joint mention extraction and classification using hypergraphs, followed by similar work from Muis et al. [23,34], who utilized a multigraph representation to address overlapping NER. Katiyar et al. [35] developed a hypergraph representation for nested entities, leveraging features extracted from an RNN. Wang et al. [7,36] proposed the idea of neural segmental hypergraphs. However, these models have trouble dealing with long inputs or many entity categories, as their hypergraph structures become extremely complex. These methods additionally struggle with spurious structure and structural ambiguity during inference [37]. In this paper, we aim to further investigate a simple and efficient model that learns entity type and boundary information for NER.

Generative methods treat the entity span sequence as a generation task, aiming to generate entities and entity types directly without requiring unique design of the tagging schema or ways to enumerate spans. Seq2seq methods have been proposed that directly generate entity label sequences from the input [5]. Strakova et al. [14] proposed a seq2seq method for nested NER that directly outputs the label of each token, associating the relation between words and labels via hard attention. Yan et al. [10] presented a pointer-based model which splices the label's embedding with the token representation. Zhang et al. [11] offered data augmentation from a causal perspective to generate entities. However, generative models do not fully utilize the entity boundary information implicit in the entity itself, which is critical for named entity recognition.

2.2. Attention Mechanism

Attention mechanisms have been employed in machine translation, machine comprehension, named entity recognition, and related natural language processing tasks. Attention-based methods have achieved impressive results, in that attention mechanisms have a large amount of memory and can build cooperation between the sequence of input. In addition, attention mechanisms allow models to automatically concentrate on the essential parts of the information while ignoring the less relevant details, thereby enhancing the model's ability to process complex data. The transformer model, first introduced by Vaswani et al. [38], has revolutionized the field of named entity recognition with its self-attention and cross-attention mechanisms, allowing long-range dependencies within the data to be captured. Based on this, many works [39,40] have leveraged attention mechanisms to integrate features from various sources of information, such as character representations, word embeddings, and position embedding. These integrated approaches enable models to focus selectively on the most pertinent information and select valuable knowledge, facilitating more nuanced language understanding. Ren et al. [39] proposed using an attention-based architecture over the word embedding and character-level component to learn the same semantic features for each word. Tan et al. [40] directly utilized attention mechanisms to capture the global dependencies of the input in order to enhance the performance of Chinese NER. TENER [41] is an adapted encoder based on attention mechanisms to merge the character- and word-level features. FLAT [42] uses a variant of self-attention to leverage the relative span position encoding.

3. Generative NER Task Formulation

In this section, we define the problem of seq2seq named entity recognition. Given an input sentence of n tokens $X = \{x_1, x_2, \ldots, x_n\}$, the goal of seq2seq NER is to generate a target sequence $Y = \{s_{11}, f_{11}, s_{12}, f_{12}, \ldots, s_{1k}, f_{1k}, g_1, \ldots\ s_{i1}, f_{i1}, s_{i2}, f_{i2}, \ldots, s_{ij}, f_{ij}, g_i\}$. Here, s and f are the starting and ending indices of a span, k is the span index in an entity, and $g_i \in \{g_1, \ldots, g_N\}$ is the entity type, where N is the total number of possible entity types. The generated schematic can be shown in Figure 1.

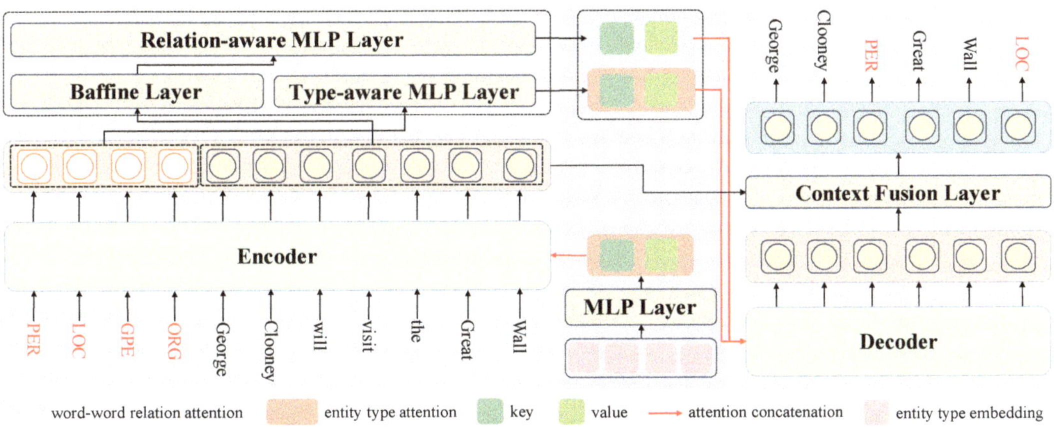

Figure 1. The architecture of our method, which contains both entity type-aware and word–word relation-aware attentions in the seq2seq framework. We incorporate the word–word relation-aware attention into the decoder and the entity type-aware attention into both the encoder and decoder. For the attention concatenation, refer to the process shown in the following sections.

4. Methodology

In this section, we introduce our proposed methodology. We outline the overall framework and describe the details of the modules (entity type-aware attention and word–word relation-aware attention) for implementing our method. The process in generative entities is introduced as well. Readers can expect a comprehensive overview of the supports that form the backbone of our framework.

4.1. Model Overview

Our model consists of an encoder that encodes the input sequence to its contextual embedding and a decoder that generates the output sequence with entity annotations. In addition to the entity generation task, we design a relation representation learning task over the token pairs to better capture the correlations among the entities. The entity token relation attention and entity type attention are introduced and fused into the encoder and decoder as shown in Figure 1. We present the details of each component separately in the following subsections.

4.2. Entity Type Aware Attention

Heterogeneous factors such as entity types and entity boundaries [15,43–45] greatly impact named entity recognition. In this section, we discuss the modeling of entity types in our seq2seq NER framework, allowing for interactions with the input sequences and guiding the model to learn more effective token representation. We merge the entity type-aware attention in the encoder and the decoder.

In the encoder, we incorporate entity types as part of the input, which are concatenated with the given sentence. To achieve better representations of entities, we try to obtain the entity type aware attention from an external entity base. Prior knowledge can be obtained to improve the NER task. Then, we feed the entity type-aware attention into the self-attention layers in the encoder.

As shown in Figure 2, the comprehensive representations of entity types are obtained from an external entity base incorporated into the encoder through entity type attention.

The representation of an entity type T is a weighted sum of the entity representations. For example, assuming that the entity label set is $G = \{person, location, organization\}$, as shown in Figure 2, if entity type $T = location$ contains entity set $C_T = \{Beijing, London, \ldots, New York\}$, the initial embedding of entity type T can be obtained as follows:

$$E_T = \theta_i E_{C_T^1} + \cdots + \theta_i E_{C_T^i} \tag{1}$$

where $E_{C_T^i} \in \mathbb{R}^{d_h}$ is the embedding of the i-th entity in the entity set C_T and θ_i is the weight of the entity, such as its frequency. Note that if the entity types are not in the external source, we may obtain entity type embeddings by random initialization or entity type tokens.

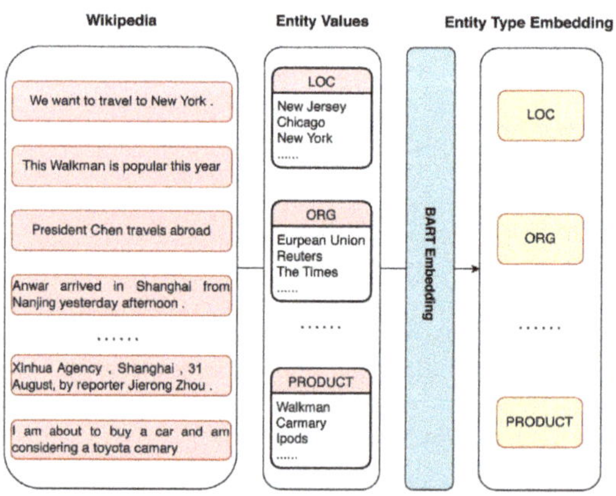

Figure 2. Entity type embedding from external entity knowledge.

To leverage the entity type information, we design an entity type-aware attention and integrate it into the corresponding self-attention layers. The vectors $K_E \in \mathbb{R}^{B \times N_h \times N \times d_k}$ and $V_E \in \mathbb{R}^{B \times N_h \times N \times d_k}$ represent the key and value of the entity type-aware attention, which are concatenated with the original key $K \in \mathbb{R}^{B \times N_h \times n \times d_k}$ and value $V \in \mathbb{R}^{B \times N_h \times n \times d_k}$ vectors in the encoder as follows:

$$R^*((K_E, V_E)) = \mathrm{MLP}_{type-aware}(E) \tag{2}$$

$$head^l = Attention(Q^l, (K_E^l \oplus K^l), (V_E^l \oplus V^l)) \tag{3}$$

where B is the batch size, N_h denotes the number of the heads, $head^l$ is the head representation of the l-th layer, K_E, V_E are obtained from the embedding E by an MLP layer [46], $E \in \mathbb{R}^{N \times d_h}$ is the embedding of entity types with N as the number of entity types, $Q \in \mathbb{Q}^{B \times N_h \times n \times d_k}$ denotes the query of the attention, and $\oplus$ means the concatenation. Figure 3 shows the merging of the entity type attention. The entity type-aware attention from the external entity knowledge base is only applied to self-attention layers in the encoder.

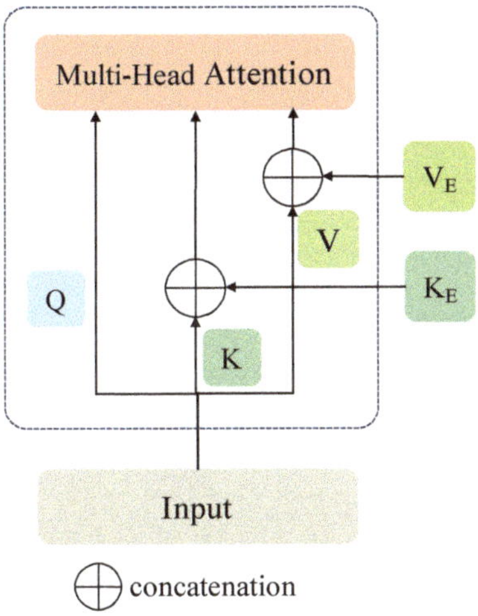

Figure 3. Concatenation in a self-attention layer. In the encoder, K_E and V_E are calculated from the entity type embedding of external entity knowledge via the type-aware MLP layer. In the decoder, K_E and V_E are calculated from the hidden states of entity type tokens in the encoder via the type-aware MLP layer.

In the decoder, E is from the hidden states of the entity type tokens, which are part of the input. Then, we use Equations (2) and (3) to apply the entity type-aware attention. In this process, we apply it to all self-attention and cross-attention layers.

4.3. Word–Word Relation-Aware Attention

Improving entity boundary detection is crucial for named entity recognition; therefore, we integrate information relevant to entity boundaries into our framework. We utilize word–word relation representations as feature information to learn about entity boundaries. Specifically, inspired by [45,47–49], which can be used to enhance relations between tokens in an entity for NER, we extract these word–word relation features to improve the representation of the predicted token in the decoder.

Given a sentence $X = \{x_1, \ldots, x_n\}$, we obtain the hidden representation $H = \{h_1 \ldots, h_n\}$ after the encoder layers. The word–word relation representation set $R\{r_{ij}|(i, j \in [1, n])\} \in \mathbb{R}^{n \times n \times d_h}$ in the sentence r_{ij} is the relation of word pair (x_i, x_j), and is obtained through the bi-affine layer.

$$\begin{aligned} s_i &= \text{MLP}(h_i), e_j = \text{MLP}(h_j) \\ r_{ij} &= s_i^\top W_1 e_j + W_2(s_i \oplus e_j) + b, \end{aligned} \tag{4}$$

where W_1, W_2, and b denote the trainable parameters and MLP is the fully connected layer.

The word–word relation representations r_{ij} reflect the entity boundary information and the syntactic structure of the sentence. These representations are valuable knowledge with which the model can perceive and learn entity boundaries more accurately, which plays a vital role in identifying entities. As the above r_{ij} cannot be directly used in our proposed word–word relation-aware attention mechanism, we feed the representations between words into an MLP layer to obtain useful features. Meanwhile, this process can generate keys and values that match the attention mechanism inherent in the seq2seq model itself. Finally, the obtained word–word relation-aware attention key $K_R \in \mathbb{R}^{B \times N_h \times M \times d_k}$ and value $V_R \in \mathbb{R}^{B \times N_h \times M \times d_k}$ matrices are concatenated with the original key $K \in \mathbb{K}^{B \times N_h \times n \times d_k}$ and value $V \in \mathbb{R}^{B \times N_h \times n \times d_k}$, respectively, in the cross-attention layers to enhance the model generation with regard to the entity boundaries. The entity relation-aware attention is defined as follows:

$$R^*((K_R, V_R)) = \text{MLP}_{relation-aware}(R) \tag{5}$$

$$head^l = Attention(Q^l, (K_R^l \oplus K_E^l \oplus K^l), (V_R^l \oplus V_E^l \oplus V^l)) \tag{6}$$

where B is the batch size, N_h denotes the number of heads, M is the length of the word–word relation-aware attention using the convolution operation, K_R^l and V_R^l are from K_R and V_R, respectively, and K_E^l and V_E^l are calculated from the entity type embedding described in the above section. However, the entity type embedding is the hidden state of the entity types as a part of the input sequence. Figure 4 shows the word–word relation-aware attention incorporated into the cross-attention layer.

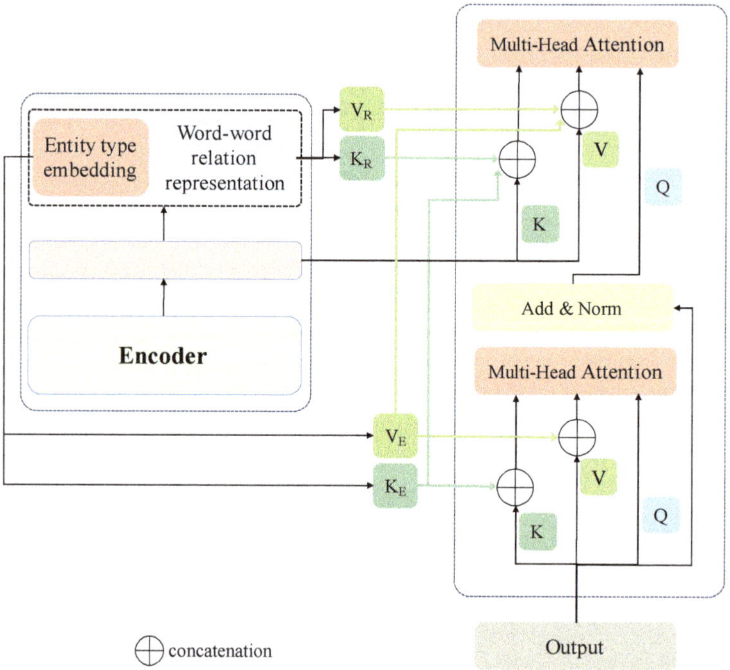

Figure 4. Concatenation in a self-attention and cross-attention layer. In the decoder, K_E and V_E are calculated from the hidden states of entity type tokens in the encoder by the type-aware MLP layer., while K_R and V_R are calculated from the word–word relation representations by the bi-affine and relation-aware MLP layer.

4.4. Entity Decoding

The decoder decodes the token embedding from the encoder to generate the entities. In particular, at step t, the decoder acquires the token embedding $h_t^d \in \mathbb{R}^{d_h}$ based on the encoder output and all the previous decoded tokens as follows:

$$h_t^d = Decoder(H^e, Y_{<t}^{\wedge}) \tag{7}$$

where $H^e \in \mathbb{R}^{n \times d_h}$, $Y^{\wedge}_{<t} = [y^{\wedge}_1, \ldots, y^{\wedge}_{t-1}]$ is the generated token sequence before t. To enhance the accuracy of the generated tokens, we introduce a context fusion layer to further decode the output. We join the entity type representations and hidden state of the tokens in the encoder to the respective hidden states of the output, which can help to improve the representation of context within the sentence:

$$\bar{h_t}^d = (H^e \otimes h_t^d) \oplus (E \otimes h_t^d) \tag{8}$$

where E is the entity type representation in the encoder and $\otimes$ denotes the dot product.

Finally, the output token index distribution P_t can be obtained by the function

$$P_t = Softmax(\bar{h_t}^d). \tag{9}$$

For a given sequence $X = \{x_1, x_2, \ldots, x_n\}$, we attempt to minimize the negative log-likelihood concerning the corresponding ground truth labels, which can be defined as

$$L = -\log p(Y|X). \tag{10}$$

5. Experiments

This experiments section provides our detailed experimental setup, including the NER datasets evaluated, the backbones with parameter settings, the evaluation metrics, and the baseline models for comparison. In addition, we discuss the main results of the datasets compared to the baselines. This section aims to provide readers with insight into the validation of the proposed method and its performance against the baselines.

5.1. Datasets

We evaluated NER on CoNLL 2003 [12] and OntoNotes 5.0 (https://catalog.ldc.upenn.edu/LDC2013T19 (accessed on 12 November 2023)) [50] in English, following the settings splits in prior works [4,15,51]. We performed further testing using OntoNotes 4.0 (https://catalog.ldc.upenn.edu/LDC2011T03 (accessed on 12 November 2023)) [52], MSRA [53], Weibo [54,55], and Resume [56] in Chinese.

To further validate the effectiveness of the model, we evaluated the long NER datasets EBM-NLP (https://github.com/bepnye/EBM-NLP/) (accessed on 12 November 2023) [57] and SemEval 2017 (https://scienceie.github.io/resources.html (accessed on 12 November 2023)) [58] as well. EBM-NLP annotates PICO spans, defining the Participants, Interventions, Comparisons, and Outcomes in a clinical trial paper [59]. We processed it following the works [60–62]. SemEval 2017 is a task involving extracting keyphrases and relations from documents with mention-level keyphrase identification (the types are PROCESS, TASK, and MATERIAL), mention-level keyphrase classification, and mention-level semantic relation extraction between keyphrases. We merged the first two subtasks as the NER task and prepared it following [58]. The statistics of the datasets are listed in Tables 1 and 2.

Table 1. Statistics of NER datasets other than SemEval 2017 and EBM-NLP.

	CoNLL 2003	Ontonotes 5.0	Ontonotes 4.0	MSRA	Resume	Weibo
#sentences	20,744	76,714	24,371	48,442	4759	1890
#entities	36,431	111,868	30,783	81,249	16,565	2677

Table 2. Statistics of the SemEval 2017 and EBM-NLP datasets.

	SemEval 2017	EBM-NLP
#entities	5730	63,693
#unique entities	1697	47,916
#single-word entities	18%	19%
#entities, word length ≥ 3	51%	51%
#entities, word length ≥ 5	22%	30%

5.2. Implementation Details

We adopted BART-Large as the backbone network. Following previous works [10,45], the encoder and decoder had twelve layers with 1024 dimensional embedding for our experiments. For the English datasets, we used the BART-Large model [63]. For the Chinese datasets, we used the BART-Large-Chinese model [64]. We used the AdamW [65] optimizer. We executed a grid search of the hyperparameters shown in Table 3 and selected the set of parameters that had the best performance on the validation set. The batch size was 32 for OntoNotes 5.0 and 16 for the others. Finally, we used 1×10^{-5} for the BART-Large model and 5×10^{-5} for the other components. When deriving the key K_E and value V_E of the self-attention from the entity type embedding, we employed multilayer MLP similar to the proj_down-proj_up structure [66], with down dim 512 and up dim 1024. For most baseline methods, the hyperparameters were set according to the experimental configurations in the original papers. However, there were a few variations; for the SemEval 2017 and EBM-NLP datasets, the batch size and max sequence length were the same as those used for our proposed method.

Table 3. Hyperparameters used to train our model.

Hyper-Parameters	Range	Final
Batch Size	[16, 32, 64]	16/32
Dropout	[0.2, 0.3, 0.5]	0.5
Learning Rate for Bart	[5×10^{-6} , 1×10^{-5}, 5×10^{-5}, 1×10^{-4}]	1×10^{-5}
Learning Rate for Other components	[5×10^{-6}, 1×10^{-5}, 5×10^{-5}, 1×10^{-4}]	5×10^{-5}
Weight Decay	[0, 0.01]	0.01
Warmup Ratio	[0, 0.01]	0.01
Max Sequence Length	[64, 128, 512]	128
Down_dim	[128, 256, 512]	512
Up_dim	[512, 768, 1024]	1024
MLP-hidden size	[128, 256]	128

5.3. Evaluation Metrics

An entity was considered to be correctly predicted if the entity label and boundary matched the ground truth. Following prior works [10,11,33], we computed the precision (P), recall (R), and F1 (F) scores for each dataset, utilizing the F1 score on the validation set as the criterion for selecting the optimal model. We ran each experiment five times and report the average metrics.

5.4. Comparative Baselines

We compared our method with several previous baselines:

- LSTM-CRF/Stack-LSTM [4] and ID-CNNs [5] offer iterated dilated convolutional neural networks.
- SH [7] propose the use of hypergraphs to address the NER task.
- Seq2Seq [14] obtains tokens with the labels in a sequence.
- BiaffineNER [15] offers a bi-affine module for span-based models to explore spans.
- BartNER [10] offers a unified NER model with a pointer generating the start–end indexes of entities and types.

- DebiasNER [11] designs data augmentation to eliminate incorrect biases from a causality perspective.
- W2NER [37] models the unified NER as word–word relation classification to tackle the different NER tasks.
- LatticeLSTM [56] probes a lattice LSTM encoding the characters and words matching a lexicon.
- TENER [41] uses an encoder to consider character, word, direction, relative distance, and unscaled attention.
- LGN [67] uses a lexicon-based graph neural network with global semantics to interact among characters, words, and sentence semantics.
- FLAT [42] is a flat-lattice model that converts the lattice structure into a flat structure.
- Lexicon [68] uses lexical knowledge in Chinese NER based on a collaborative graph network.
- LR-CNN [69] uses a CNN-based approach with lexicons via a rethinking mechanism.
- PLTE [70] uses the characters and matches lexical words in parallel via the transformer.
- SoftLexcion [71] merges the word lexicon into the character representations and adjusts the character representation layer.
- MECT [72] uses a multi-metadata embedding-based cross-transformer that fuses the characters' structural information.
- SciBERT [60], PubMedBERT [61], and VarMAE [62] are pretrained models based on BERT [73] focusing on the scientific and biomedical domains. Finally, TIAL_UM [58] ranks first on the SemEval 2017 keyphrase extraction leaderboard.

5.5. Results

We compared our model with seq2seq models [10,11,14], sequence labeling [4,5], span-based methods [15], hypergraph models [7], and more.

The results on all the datasets are shown in Tables 4–6. Several key observations can be made from the comparison results. Our model performs better than some sequence labeling, span-based, and generative models on most datasets. For CoNLL2003, our method outperforms sequence labeling [4], the span-based method [15], and the hypergraph-based method [7] by 2.6%, 1.02% and 3.04% in terms of F1 score. Compared with the seq2seq models (Seq2Seq [14], BartNER [10], and DebiasNER [11]), CoNLL 2003 shows increases of 0.56%, 1.02%, and 0.4%. For OntoNotes 5.0, our method improves the F1 score by 4.0% and 0.34% compared with the ID-CNNs [5] and W2NER [37] baselines. Compared with generative models BartNER and DebiasNER, there is an improvement of 0.46% and 0.42%, respectively, in terms of the F1 score. For the Chinese NER datasets, all demonstrate improvements in performance to varying extents. Compared to the generative method BartNER, our method shows increases of 5.99%, 0.76%, 2.75%, and 7.68%, respectively. For SemEval 2017 and EBM-NLP, the performance of our method shows significant improvement compared with both BartNER and W2NER. These experimental results validate our hypothesis that our approach can effectively model word–word relations, thereby improving entity decoding. Moreover, the entity type information incorporated into our method further boosts model performance.

The results of our approach show slight improvement overall compared to W2NER. The reason for this is that W2NER unites the position region-aware representation of the grid and the relation representation of token pairs to estimate entities. Although our model uses word–word relation representation, it has only coarse granularity and no directionality during inference.

Table 4. Results on the CoNLL2003 and OntoNotes 5.0 datasets; results are statistically significant with p-value < 0.005. The best scores are in bold, while the second-best scores are underlined.

Model	CoNLL2003			OntoNotes 5.0		
	P	R	F	P	R	F
LSTM-CRF/Stack-LSTM [4]	-	-	90.94	-	-	-
ID-CNNs [5]	-	-	90.65	-	-	86.84
SH [7]	-	-	90.50	-	-	-
Seq2Seq [14]	-	-	92.98	-	-	-
BiaffineNER [15]	92.91	92.13	92.52	90.01	89.77	89.89
BartNER [10]	92.61	**93.87**	93.24	89.99	90.77	90.38
DebiasNER [11]	92.78	93.51	93.14	89.77	91.07	90.42
W2NER [37]	92.71	93.44	93.07	90.03	90.97	90.50
Ours	**93.14**	93.65	**93.54**	**90.13**	**91.59**	**90.84**

Table 5. Results on the Chinese NER datasets; results are statistically significant with p-value < 0.005. The best scores are in bold, while the second-best scores are underlined.

MODEL	OntoNotes 4.0			MSRA			Resume			Weibo		
	P	R	F	P	R	F	P	R	F	P	R	F
LatticeLSTM [56]	76.35	71.56	73.88	93.57	92.79	93.18	94.81	94.11	94.46	53.04	62.25	58.79
TENER [41]	-	-	72.43	-	-	92.74	-	-	95.00	-	-	58.17
LGN [67]	76.40	72.60	74.45	94.50	92.93	93.71	95.37	94.84	95.11	57.14	66.67	59.92
FLAT [42]	-	-	81.82	-	-	96.09	-	-	95.86	-	-	68.55
Lexicon [68]	75.06	74.52	74.79	94.01	92.93	93.47	-	-	-	-	-	63.09
LR-CNN [69]	76.40	72.60	74.45	94.50	92.93	93.71	95.37	94.84	95.11	-	-	59.92
PLTE[BERT] [70]	79.62	81.82	80.60	94.91	94.15	94.53	96.16	96.75	96.45	**72.00**	66.67	69.23
SoftLexicon [71]	**83.41**	82.21	82.81	95.75	95.10	95.42	96.08	96.13	96.11	70.94	67.02	70.50
MECT[BERT] [72]	-	-	82.57	-	-	96.24	-	-	95.98	-	-	70.43
BartNER [10]	79.18	80.21	79.69	95.30	94.75	95.86	96.72	90.90	94.21	67.25	63.88	65.52
W2NER [37]	82.31	83.36	83.08	96.12	**96.08**	96.10	**96.96**	96.35	96.65	70.84	**73.87**	72.32
Ours	83.39	**87.92**	**85.68**	**96.26**	95.93	**96.62**	96.03	**96.85**	**96.96**	69.87	68.32	**72.68**

Table 6. Results on the Long NER SemEval 2017 and EBM-NLP datasets; results are statistically significant with p-value < 0.005. The best scores are in bold, while the second-best scores are underlined.

Model	SemEval 2017			EBM-NLP		
	P	R	F	P	R	F
SciBERT [60]	-	-	-	-	-	71.18
PubMedBERT [61]	-	-	-	-	-	**73.38**
VarMAE [62]	-	-	-	-	-	76.01
TIAL_UW [58]	-	-	44.00	-	-	-
BartNER [10]	38.36	47.92	42.16	51.22	47.84	40.96
W2NER [37]	49.92	44.68	47.16	**66.22**	38.84	48.96
Ours	**53.69**	**63.83**	**57.64**	63.16	**68.61**	71.89

It can be seen that the improvement of our model over the baselines on the EBM-NLP datasets is marginal compared to PubMedBERT [61]. The primary reason for this is that PubMedBERT is a domain-specific pre-trained language model utilizing biomedical data. Nonetheless, our model is capable of attaining comparable or superior performance.

6. Analysis and Discussion

In this analysis and discussion section, we analyze the results obtained from the various components within our method to show the performance of our proposed approach. Then, to assess our method's robust ability to process long sentences and long entities, we explore the implications of our approach and compare its performance with that of the baselines. Finally, by analyzing some instances of existing incorrect predictions, we aim to provide insights for potential future work. This section contextualizes our results, and we expect that the analysis will benefit future work.

6.1. Ablation Study

To estimate the impact of various components within our method, we conducted ablation studies by sequentially omitting each component, namely, word–word relation-aware attention (rel-att) and entity type-aware attention (type-att). In this section, we designate the seq2seq model devoid of "rel-att" and "type-att" as the "baseline". We refer to the model that includes word–word relation-aware attention as "+ rel-att". The same nomenclature applies to "+ type-att" and "+ rel-att & type-att".

The outcomes of the ablation studies are presented in Tables 7–9. The results indicate that our proposed method significantly outperforms the baseline when incorporating word–word relation attention (+ rel-att) or entity type attention (+ type-att). This validates the effectiveness of both word–word relation attention and entity type attention. Moreover, integrating word–word relation attention and entity type-aware attention into an NER framework yields the most promising results.

Table 7. Ablation studies on the CoNLL2003 and OntoNotes 5.0 datasets.

Model	CoNLL2003	OntoNotes 5.0
baseline	92.82	90.02
+ rel-att	93.19 ↑**0.37**	90.32 ↑**0.30**
+ type-att	93.39 ↑**0.57**	90.48 ↑**0.46**
+ rel-att & type-att	93.54 ↑**0.72**	90.84 ↑**0.82**

Table 8. Ablation studies on the Chinese NER datasets.

Model	OntoNotes 4.0	MSRA	Resume	Weibo
baseline	82.73	95.01	94.56	65.32
+ rel-att	83.97 ↑**1.24**	95.77 ↑**0.76**	95.73 ↑**1.17**	68.55 ↑**3.23**
+ type-att	84.81 ↑**2.08**	95.98 ↑**0.97**	96.34 ↑**1.78**	69.46 ↑**4.14**
+ rel-att & type-att	85.68 ↑**2.95**	96.62 ↑**1.61**	96.96 ↑**2.40**	72.68 ↑**7.36**

Table 9. Ablation studies on the Long NER SemEval 2017 and EBM-NLP datasets.

Model	SemEval 2017	EBM-NLP
baseline	52.55	66.15
+ rel-att	55.69 ↑**3.14**	69.61 ↑**3.46**
+ type-att	56.75 ↑**4.20**	70.24 ↑**4.09**
+ rel-att & type-att	57.64 ↑**5.09**	71.89 ↑**5.74**

The improvements have subtle differences considering the differences in the entity types, domains, and complexity of entities. For the Chinese NER datasets, the improvement is relatively significant. In addition to their simple structures, the external entity type embeddings mitigate the diverse and complex expressions of Chinese entities, leading to a closer representation of entities within the same type. For example, the entity types in Weibo have similarities, such as per.nam and per.nom, representing specific and general persons, respectively (i.e., "张三" is a per.nam, and "男人" is labeled as per.nom). Integrating external entities to construct the embedding of entity types can help to enhance the distinction between them. Furthermore, including the entity type as part of the input enhances the in-context learning within the sentence. Leveraging entity type-aware attention during decoding further reinforces the mapping between entity textual information and entity types. Additionally, given Chinese tokenization traits, introducing word pair relation representation helps to understand the entity boundary information. On the SemEval 2017 and EBM-NLP datasets, the performance of our proposed components is better compared with the baseline. Our method can generate various length sequences and learn more information from the entity type and word–word relation attention.

6.2. Effect on Long Sentences

In this section, we split the test set by sentence length in order to assess our method's ability to process long sentences. The results are shown in Figure 5. Specifically, we categorized the test sets into subsets based on sentence length (#words), with ranges set at [0–10, 10–20, 30–40, 50–60, ≥60]. It is obvious that our method provides the largest overall gain compared to the generative model on long sentences (≥60 words) [10]. Note that the amount of data with sentence lengths in [50–60, ≥60] is relatively tiny compared to other groups; thus, the evaluation is relatively high. Nonetheless, our model performs better than the baseline models, particularly in long-sentence scenarios.

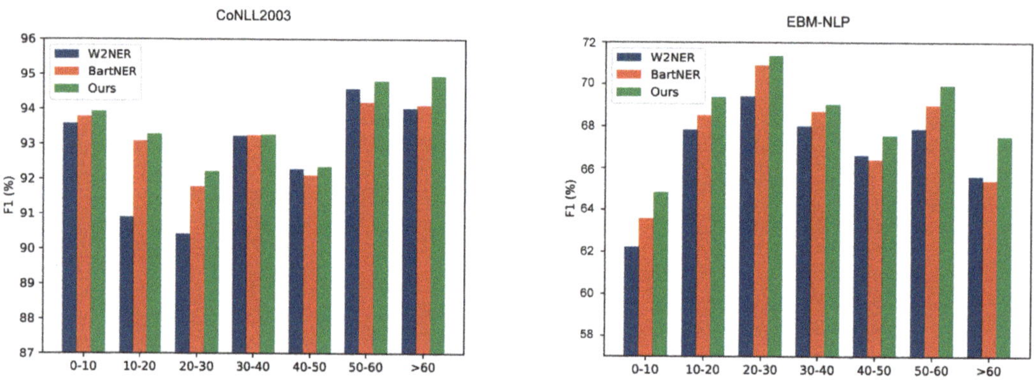

Figure 5. Results when sentence length changes (#words).

6.3. Effect on Long Entities

To verify the ability of our method to handle long entities, we report the experimental results in Figure 6. In this section, we selected BartNER and W2NER as baselines. Considering the number of long entities, we set the entity length in the range from 1 to 5 for CoNLL2003, 1 to 6 for SemEval 2017, and 1 to 8 for EBM-NLP. As can be observed, there is little change in the performance of the sets with a small length of entities. However, on CoNLL2003 with long entities (E(L) ≥ 5), the F1 score improves by up to 3%. For SemEval 2017, when the entity length is less than 5, the effect difference of each model is not noticeable; however, when it is greater than 5, the effect of our model is nearly 7% higher than the other models [10,37]. For EBM-NLP, our method provides the largest gain compared to the other models on long entities (E(L) ≥ 8).

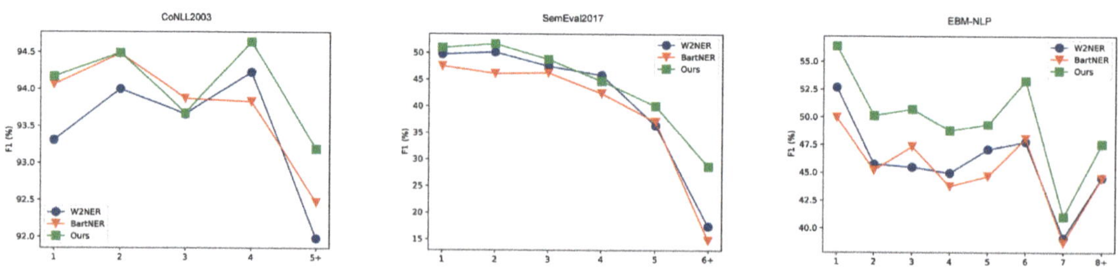

Figure 6. Results on various datasets when entity length changes.

6.4. Effectiveness for Entity Boundary

We ran experiments to analyze the effectiveness of entity boundary recognition, e.g., for Instance #1 in Table 10, the prediction "(中韩, gpe)" has an error in entity boundary detection even though the generated entity type is "gpe". In this analysis, we only consider the entity boundary metric and overlook whether the entity type is correct. The F1 scores of different models on the datasets are shown in Figure 7. It can be observed that our method has a positive impact on entity boundary detection. For CoNLL2003 and OntoNotes 4.0, our method performs slightly better than W2NER, which employs relative position representation and fine-grained token pair relation representation. For SemEval 2017, our proposed approach is significantly superior to the other models. These results are consistent with our expectation that leveraging the entity type-aware attention and word–word relation-aware attention into the generative NER framework can contribute to enhancing entity boundary detection performance.

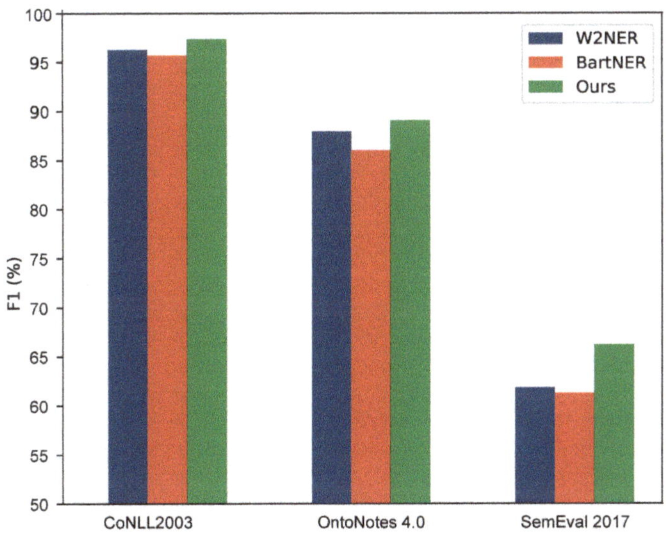

Figure 7. Results on entity boundary detection.

Table 10. Error analysis. Text in color indicates predicted entities that are incorrect.

Instance
instance #1: 中韩经贸研讨会即将在北京举行 **Pred:** (中韩, GPE), (北京, GPE) **Gold:** (中, GPE), (韩, GPE), (北京, GPE)
instance #2 : the Office of Fair Trade called for British Airways/American to allow third-party access to their joint frequent flyer programme where the applicant does not have access to an equivalent programme . **Pred:** (Office of Fair Trade, ORG), (British Airways American, ORG) **Gold:** (Office of Fair Trade, ORG), (British Airways American, ORG)
instance #3: These data were converted to standard triangulation language (STL) surface data as an aggregation of fine triangular meshes using 3D visualization and measurement software (Amira version X , FEI , Burlington , MA , USA). **Pred:** (standard triangulation language, Process), (triangular meshes, Material), (3D visualization, Process) **Gold:** (standard triangulation language, Process), (triangular meshes, Material), (3D visualization, Process), (Amira version X, Material)
instance #4: South Africa's trip to Kanpur for the third test against India has given former England test cricketer Bob Woolmer the chance of a sentimental return to his birthplace . **Pred:** (South Africa, LOC), (Kanpur, LOC), (India, LOC), (England, LOC), (Bob Woolmer, PER) (test cricketer, PER) **Gold:** (South Africa, LOC), (Kanpur, LOC), (India, LOC), (England, LOC), (Bob Woolmer, PER)

6.5. Case Study

We selected a number of instances for analysis to promote further future works in the field of NER. We have classified the incorrect entities into four classes, as shown in Table 10.

Incorrect Boundaries: As instance #1 shows, the generated entity has an incorrect boundary. This sentence of instance #1 in Chinese mentions two countries, which were misidentified as a single entity. In Chinese, the entity words denote abbreviations of the two countries, and the model did not learn this knowledge, which conveys the boundary difficulty of the entity. For multiple nested entities in sentences, the model is more prone to misjudgment. Therefore, enhancing the learning of entity boundary information can improve model performance.

Distract Context: As instance #2 shows, our model predicts the incorrect entity type because of the ambiguous contexts that may be expressed in a similar context or lacking the descriptive context. The same tokens may have different meanings in various semantic contexts. For accurate recognition of entity types, it is necessary for the model to learn a comprehensive understanding of sentence context and entity types in order to make the correct judgment.

Missing Entities: As instance #3 shows, the result misses an entity. This may be because the entity is rare or specific, caused by the unbalanced learning which makes the model tend to judge sentences with a similar context to high-frequency entities. For this type of error, improving the model's understanding of critical information in sentences can be achieved by enhancing the attention mechanisms and attempting data augmentation.

Extra Entities: As instance #4 shows, our model predicts extra entities that look right but are not in the gold set. The reason for this may be that the entity appears repeatedly in other sentences or the data are noisy. Combination with other tasks, such as entity boundary detection, entity linking, and entity disambiguation, can helpto prevent excessive entity recognition.

7. Conclusions

In this work, we have introduced a novel approach that merges entity type and word–word relation into the generative NER framework to achieve better performance.

Specifically, we combine entity type and word–word relation by attention mechanisms with the original attention in the backbone network, improving the model's ability to discriminate entity types and detect entity boundaries. We further take the entity types as special tokens and as part of the input for learning valuable knowledge from the context. Experiments on various benchmarks show the superior performance of our method. Integrating entity types as special tokens further enriches the model's context learning, allowing for more precise entity recognition. Furthermore, introducing entity type attention further strengthens the connection between entity tokens in the sentence and predefined entity types. We transform the information of the entity boundary to the relations of word pairs and merge it in the proposed framework via the attention mechanism, including the syntactic and semantic relationships between words to enhance the accuracy of entity boundary detection. However, there are weaknesses in the potential increase of model complexity and evaluation time. To address these issues, we will explore further approaches, such as non-autoregressive methods, which can speed up the decoding. Because our proposed method primarily relies on a large amount of annotated data, we will focus on generative NER models based on large language models in a low-resource setting and consider how to integrate resources such as images. The practical implications of our proposed approach extend to relation extraction, where accurate entity recognition is crucial. We are trying to use this method to improve knowledge graph construction.

Author Contributions: Y.M.: conceptualization, methodology, formal analysis, software, writing—original draft. Z.L.: supervision, writing—review and editing. All authors have read and agreed to the published version of the manuscript.

Funding: This research was funded by the National Natural Science Foundation of China (Grant Nos. 62276017, U1636211, 61672081) and the Fund of the State Key Laboratory of Software Development Environment (Grant No. SKLSDE-2021ZX-18).

Data Availability Statement: MDPI Research Data Policies at https://github.com/weizhepei/CasRel, (accessed on 15 September 2020).

Conflicts of Interest: The authors have no competing interests to declare that are relevant to the content of this article.

References

1. Aliod, D.M.; van Zaanen, M.; Smith, D. Named Entity Recognition for Question Answering. In *Proceedings of the ALTA 2006*; Cavedon, L., Zukerman, I., Eds.; Australasian Language Technology Association: Sydney, NSW, Australia, 2006; pp. 51–58.
2. Li, Q.; Ji, H. Incremental Joint Extraction of Entity Mentions and Relations. In Proceedings of the ACL 2014, Baltimore, MD, USA, 22–27 June 2014; pp. 402–412.
3. Zhong, Z.; Chen, D. A Frustratingly Easy Approach for Entity and Relation Extraction. In Proceedings of the NAACL-HLT 2021, Online, 6–11 June 2021; pp. 50–61.
4. Lample, G.; Ballesteros, M.; Subramanian, S.; Kawakami, K.; Dyer, C. Neural Architectures for Named Entity Recognition. In Proceedings of the NAACL HLT 2016, San Diego, CA, USA, 12–17 June 2016; pp. 260–270.
5. Strubell, E.; Verga, P.; Belanger, D.; McCallum, A. Fast and Accurate Entity Recognition with Iterated Dilated Convolutions. In Proceedings of the EMNLP 2017, Copenhagen, Denmark, 9–11 September 2017; pp. 2670–2680.
6. Panchendrarajan, R.; Amaresan, A. Bidirectional LSTM-CRF for Named Entity Recognition. In Proceedings of the PACLIC 2018, Hong Kong, China, 1–3 December 2018; Politzer-Ahles, S., Hsu, Y., Huang, C., Yao, Y., Eds.; Association for Computational Linguistics: Stroudsburg, PA, USA , 2018.
7. Wang, B.; Lu, W. Combining Spans into Entities: A Neural Two-Stage Approach for Recognizing Discontiguous Entities. In Proceedings of the EMNLP, Hong Kong, China, 3–7 November 2019; pp. 6215–6223.
8. Yu, B.; Zhang, Z.; Sheng, J.; Liu, T.; Wang, Y.; Wang, Y.; Wang, B. Semi-Open Information Extraction. In Proceedings of the WWW 2021, Online, 19–23 April 2021; pp. 1661–1672.
9. Li, X.; Feng, J.; Meng, Y.; Han, Q.; Wu, F.; Li, J. A Unified MRC Framework for Named Entity Recognition. In Proceedings of the ACL 2020, Virtual, 5–10 July 2020; pp. 5849–5859.
10. Yan, H.; Gui, T.; Dai, J.; Guo, Q.; Zhang, Z.; Qiu, X. A Unified Generative Framework for Various NER Subtasks. In *Proceedings of the 59th Annual Meeting of the Association for Computational Linguistics and the 11th International Joint Conference on Natural Language Processing (Volume 1: Long Papers)*; Association for Computational Linguistics: Kerrville, TX, USA, 2021; pp. 5808–5822.
11. Zhang, S.; Shen, Y.; Tan, Z.; Wu, Y.; Lu, W. De-Bias for Generative Extraction in Unified NER Task. In Proceedings of the ACL 2022, Dublin, Ireland, 22–27 May 2022; pp. 808–818.

12. Sang, E.F.T.K.; Meulder, F.D. Introduction to the CoNLL-2003 Shared Task: Language-Independent Named Entity Recognition. In Proceedings of the Seventh Conference on Natural Language Learning, CoNLL 2003, Held in cooperation with HLT-NAACL 2003, Edmonton, AB, Canada, 31 May– 1 June 2003; pp. 142–147.
13. Karimi, S.; Metke-Jimenez, A.; Kemp, M.; Wang, C. Cadec: A corpus of adverse drug event annotations. *J. Biomed. Inform.* **2015**, *55*, 73–81. [CrossRef] [PubMed]
14. Straková, J.; Straka, M.; Hajic, J. Neural Architectures for Nested NER through Linearization. In Proceedings of the ACL 2019, Florence, Italy, 28 July–2 August 2019; pp. 5326–5331.
15. Yu, J.; Bohnet, B.; Poesio, M. Named Entity Recognition as Dependency Parsing. In Proceedings of the ACL 2020, Virtual, 5–10 July 2020; pp. 6470–6476.
16. Shen, Y.; Ma, X.; Tan, Z.; Zhang, S.; Wang, W.; Lu, W. Locate and Label: A Two-stage Identifier for Nested Named Entity Recognition. In Proceedings of the ACL/IJCNLP, Bangkok, Thailand, 1–6 August 2021; pp. 2782–2794.
17. Dai, X.; Karimi, S.; Hachey, B.; Paris, C. An Effective Transition-based Model for Discontinuous NER. In Proceedings of the ACL, 2020, Virtual, 5–10 July 2020; pp. 5860–5870.
18. Li, F.; Lin, Z.; Zhang, M.; Ji, D. A Span-Based Model for Joint Overlapped and Discontinuous Named Entity Recognition. In *Proceedings of the 59th Annual Meeting of the Association for Computational Linguistics and the 11th International Joint Conference on Natural Language Processing (Volume 1: Long Papers)*; Association for Computational Linguistics: Kerrville, TX, USA, 2021; pp. 4814–4828.
19. Ratinov, L.; Roth, D. Design Challenges and Misconceptions in Named Entity Recognition. In Proceedings of the Thirteenth Conference on Computational Natural Language Learning, CoNLL 2009, Boulder, CO, USA, 4–5 June 2009; pp. 147–155.
20. Collobert, R.; Weston, J.; Bottou, L.; Karlen, M.; Kavukcuoglu, K.; Kuksa, P.P. Natural Language Processing (Almost) from Scratch. *J. Mach. Learn. Res.* **2011**, *12*, 2493–2537.
21. Metke-Jimenez, A.; Karimi, S. Concept Identification and Normalisation for Adverse Drug Event Discovery in Medical Forums. In Proceedings of the BMDID@ISWC, Kobe, Japan, 17 October 2016.
22. Chiu, J.P.C.; Nichols, E. Named Entity Recognition with Bidirectional LSTM-CNNs. *Trans. Assoc. Comput. Linguist.* **2016**, *4*, 357–370. [CrossRef]
23. Muis, A.O.; Lu, W. Learning to Recognize Discontiguous Entities. In Proceedings of the EMNLP 2016, Austin, TX, USA, 1–5 November 2016; pp. 75–84.
24. Ma, X.; Hovy, E.H. End-to-end Sequence Labeling via Bi-directional LSTM-CNNs-CRF. In Proceedings of the ACL 2016, Berlin, Germany, 7–12 August 2016.
25. Zhou, P.; Zheng, S.; Xu, J.; Qi, Z.; Bao, H.; Xu, B. Joint Extraction of Multiple Relations and Entities by Using a Hybrid Neural Network. In *Proceedings of the Chinese Computational Linguistics and Natural Language Processing Based on Naturally Annotated Big Data—16th China National Conference, CCL 2017, and 5th International Symposium, NLP-NABD 2017*; Lecture Notes in Computer Science; Springer: Berlin/Heidelberg, Germany, 2017 ; Volume 10565, pp. 135–146.
26. Ju, M.; Miwa, M.; Ananiadou, S. A Neural Layered Model for Nested Named Entity Recognition. In *Proceedings of the NAACL-HLT 2018*; Walker, M.A., Ji, H., Stent, A., Eds.; Association for Computational Linguistics: Kerrville, TX, USA, 2018; pp. 1446–1459.
27. Tang, B.; Hu, J.; Wang, X.; Chen, Q. Recognizing continuous and discontinuous adverse drug reaction mentions from social media using LSTM-CRF. *Wirel. Commun. Mob. Comput.* **2018**, *2018*, 2379208. [CrossRef]
28. Wang, J.; Shou, L.; Chen, K.; Chen, G. Pyramid: A Layered Model for Nested Named Entity Recognition. In Proceedings of the ACL 2020, Virtual, 5–10 July 2020; pp. 5918–5928.
29. Tan, C.; Qiu, W.; Chen, M.; Wang, R.; Huang, F. Boundary Enhanced Neural Span Classification for Nested Named Entity Recognition. In Proceedings of the AAAI 2020, New York, NY, USA, 7–12 February 2020; pp. 9016–9023.
30. Ouchi, H.; Suzuki, J.; Kobayashi, S.; Yokoi, S.; Kuribayashi, T.; Konno, R.; Inui, K. Instance-Based Learning of Span Representations: A Case Study through Named Entity Recognition. In Proceedings of the ACL 2020, Virtual, 5–10 July 2020; pp. 6452–6459.
31. Zhang, F.; Ma, L.; Wang, J.; Cheng, J. An MRC and adaptive positive-unlabeled learning framework for incompletely labeled named entity recognition. *Int. J. Intell. Syst.* **2022**, *37*, 9580–9597. [CrossRef]
32. Lin, H.; Lu, Y.; Han, X.; Sun, L. Sequence-to-Nuggets: Nested Entity Mention Detection via Anchor-Region Networks. In Proceedings of the ACL 2019, Florence, Italy, 28 July–2 August 2019; pp. 5182–5192.
33. Lu, W.; Roth, D. Joint mention extraction and classification with mention hypergraphs. In Proceedings of the EMNLP 2015, Lisbon, Portugal, 17–21 September 2015; pp. 857–867.
34. Muis, A.O.; Lu, W. Labeling Gaps Between Words: Recognizing Overlapping Mentions with Mention Separators. In Proceedings of the EMNLP 2017, Copenhagen, Denmark, 9–11 September 2017; pp. 2608–2618.
35. Katiyar, A.; Cardie, C. Nested Named Entity Recognition Revisited. In Proceedings of the NAACL-HLT 2018, New Orleans, LO, USA, 1–6 June 2018; pp. 861–871.
36. Wang, Y.; Yu, B.; Zhu, H.; Liu, T.; Yu, N.; Sun, L. Discontinuous Named Entity Recognition as Maximal Clique Discovery. In Proceedings of the ACL/IJCNLP 2021, Bangkok, Thailand, 1–6 August 2021; pp. 764–774.
37. Li, J.; Fei, H.; Liu, J.; Wu, S.; Zhang, M.; Teng, C.; Ji, D.; Li, F. Unified Named Entity Recognition as Word-Word Relation Classification. In Proceedings of the AAAI 2022, Virtual, 22 February–1 March 2022; pp. 10965–10973.

38. Vaswani, A.; Shazeer, N.; Parmar, N.; Uszkoreit, J.; Jones, L.; Gomez, A.N.; Kaiser, L.; Polosukhin, I. Attention is All you Need. In Proceedings of the Advances in Neural Information Processing Systems 30: Annual Conference on Neural Information Processing Systems 2017, Long Beach, CA, USA, 4–9 December 2017; pp. 5998–6008.
39. Rei, M.; Crichton, G.K.O.; Pyysalo, S. Attending to Characters in Neural Sequence Labeling Models. In Proceedings of the COLING 2016, Osaka, Japan, 11–16 December 2016; pp. 309–318.
40. Tan, Z.; Wang, M.; Xie, J.; Chen, Y.; Shi, X. Deep Semantic Role Labeling With Self-Attention. In Proceedings of the Thirty-Second AAAI Conference on Artificial Intelligence, (AAAI-18), the 30th Innovative Applications of Artificial Intelligence (IAAI-18), and the 8th AAAI Symposium on Educational Advances in Artificial Intelligence (EAAI-18), New Orleans, LO, USA, 2–7 February 2018; pp. 4929–4936.
41. Yan, H.; Deng, B.; Li, X.; Qiu, X. TENER: Adapting Transformer Encoder for Named Entity Recognition. *arXiv* **2019**, arXiv:1911.04474.
42. Li, X.; Yan, H.; Qiu, X.; Huang, X. FLAT: Chinese NER Using Flat-Lattice Transformer. In Proceedings of the ACL 2020, Virtual, 5–10 July 2020; pp. 6836–6842.
43. Fu, Y.; Tan, C.; Chen, M.; Huang, S.; Huang, F. Nested Named Entity Recognition with Partially-Observed TreeCRFs. *AAAI Conf. Artif. Intell.* **2021**, *35*, 12839–12847. [CrossRef]
44. Aly, R.; Vlachos, A.; McDonald, R. Leveraging Type Descriptions for Zero-shot Named Entity Recognition and Classification. In Proceedings of the ACL/IJCNLP 2021, Bangkok, Thailand, 1–6 August 2021; pp. 1516–1528.
45. Mo, Y.; Tang, H.; Liu, J.; Wang, Q.; Xu, Z.; Wang, J.; Wu, W.; Li, Z. Multi-Task Transformer with Relation-Attention and Type-Attention for Named Entity Recognition. In Proceedings of the ICASSP 2023, Rhodes Island, Greece, 4–10 June 2023; pp. 1–5.
46. Liu, R.; Li, Y.; Tao, L.; Liang, D.; Zheng, H.T. Are we ready for a new paradigm shift? A survey on visual deep mlp. *Patterns* **2022**, *3*, 100520. [CrossRef]
47. Mo, Y.; Yang, J.; Liu, J.; Wang, Q.; Chen, R.; Wang, J.; Li, Z. mCL-NER: Cross-Lingual Named Entity Recognition via Multi-view Contrastive Learning. *arXiv* **2023**, arXiv:2308.09073.
48. Shang, Y.; Huang, H.; Mao, X. OneRel: Joint Entity and Relation Extraction with One Module in One Step. In Proceedings of the AAAI 2022, Virtual, 22 February–1 March 2022; pp. 11285–11293.
49. Zhu, E.; Li, J. Boundary Smoothing for Named Entity Recognition. In Proceedings of the ACL 2022, Dublin, Ireland, 22–27 May 2022; pp. 7096–7108.
50. Pradhan, S.; Moschitti, A.; Xue, N.; Ng, H.T.; Björkelund, A.; Uryupina, O.; Zhang, Y.; Zhong, Z. Towards Robust Linguistic Analysis using OntoNotes. In Proceedings of the Seventeenth Conference on Computational Natural Language Learning, CoNLL 2013, Sofia, Bulgaria, 8–9 August 2013; pp. 143–152.
51. Pradhan, S.; Moschitti, A.; Xue, N.; Uryupina, O.; Zhang, Y. CoNLL-2012 Shared Task: Modeling Multilingual Unrestricted Coreference in OntoNotes. In Proceedings of the Joint Conference on Empirical Methods in Natural Language Processing and Computational Natural Language Learning—Proceedings of the Shared Task: Modeling Multilingual Unrestricted Conference in OntoNotes, EMNLP-CoNLL 2012, Jeju Island, Republic of Korea, 12–14 July 2012; pp. 1–40.
52. Weischedel, R.; Pradhan, S.; Ramshaw, L.; Palmer, M.; Xue, N.; Marcus, M.; Taylor, A.; Greenberg, C.; Hovy, E.; Belvin, R.; et al. *Ontonotes Release 4.0. LDC2011T03*; Linguistic Data Consortium: Philadelphia, PA, USA, 2011.
53. Levow, G.A. The third international Chinese language processing bakeoff: Word segmentation and named entity recognition. In Proceedings of the Fifth SIGHAN Workshop on Chinese Language Processing, Sydney, Australia, 22–23 July 2006; pp. 108–117.
54. He, H.; Sun, X. F-Score Driven Max Margin Neural Network for Named Entity Recognition in Chinese Social Media. In Proceedings of the 15th Conference of the European Chapter of the Association for Computational Linguistics, EACL 2017, Valencia, Spain, 3–7 April 2017; Volume 2: Short Papers, 2017; Association for Computational Linguistics: Kerrville, TX, USA, 2017; pp. 713–718.
55. Peng, N.; Dredze, M. Named entity recognition for chinese social media with jointly trained embeddings. In Proceedings of the EMNLP 2015, Lisbon, Portugal, 17–21 September 2015; pp. 548–554.
56. Zhang, Y.; Yang, J. Chinese NER Using Lattice LSTM. In Proceedings of the 56th Annual Meeting of the Association for Computational Linguistics, ACL 2018, Melbourne, Australia, 15–20 July 2018; Volume 1: Long Papers; Association for Computational Linguistics: Kerrville, TX, USA, 2018; pp. 1554–1564.
57. Nye, B.E.; Li, J.J.; Patel, R.; Yang, Y.; Marshall, I.J.; Nenkova, A.; Wallace, B.C. A Corpus with Multi-Level Annotations of Patients, Interventions and Outcomes to Support Language Processing for Medical Literature. In Proceedings of the 56th Annual Meeting of the Association for Computational Linguistics, ACL 2018, Melbourne, Australia, 15–20 July 2018; Volume 1: Long Papers; Association for Computational Linguistics: Kerrville, TX, USA, 2018; pp. 197–207.
58. Augenstein, I.; Das, M.; Riedel, S.; Vikraman, L.; McCallum, A. SemEval 2017 Task 10: ScienceIE - Extracting Keyphrases and Relations from Scientific Publications. In Proceedings of the 11th International Workshop on Semantic Evaluation, SemEval@ACL 2017, Vancouver, BC, Canada, 3–4 August 2017; pp. 546–555.
59. Kim, S.; Martínez, D.; Cavedon, L.; Yencken, L. Automatic classification of sentences to support Evidence Based Medicine. *BMC Bioinform.* **2011**, *12*, S5. [CrossRef]
60. Beltagy, I.; Lo, K.; Cohan, A. SciBERT: A Pretrained Language Model for Scientific Text. In Proceedings of the EMNLP-IJCNLP 2019, Hong Kong, China, 3–7 November 2019; pp. 3613–3618.

61. Gu, Y.; Tinn, R.; Cheng, H.; Lucas, M.; Usuyama, N.; Liu, X.; Naumann, T.; Gao, J.; Poon, H. Domain-Specific Language Model Pretraining for Biomedical Natural Language Processing. *ACM Trans. Comput. Health* **2022**, *3*, 2:1–2:23. [CrossRef]
62. Hu, D.; Hou, X.; Du, X.; Zhou, M.; Jiang, L.; Mo, Y.; Shi, X. VarMAE: Pre-training of Variational Masked Autoencoder for Domain-adaptive Language Understanding. In Proceedings of the EMNLP Findings 2022, Abu Dhabi, United Arab Emirates, 7–11 December 2022; pp. 6276–6286.
63. Lewis, M.; Liu, Y.; Goyal, N.; Ghazvininejad, M.; Mohamed, A.; Levy, O.; Stoyanov, V.; Zettlemoyer, L. BART: Denoising Sequence-to-Sequence Pre-training for Natural Language Generation, Translation, and Comprehension. *arXiv* **2019**, arXiv:1910.13461.
64. Shao, Y.; Geng, Z.; Liu, Y.; Dai, J.; Yang, F.; Zhe, L.; Bao, H.; Qiu, X. CPT: A Pre-Trained Unbalanced Transformer for Both Chinese Language Understanding and Generation. *arXiv* **2021**, arXiv:2109.05729.
65. Loshchilov, I.; Hutter, F. Decoupled Weight Decay Regularization. In Proceedings of the ICLR 2019, New Orleans, LA, USA, 6–9 May 2019.
66. Li, X.L.; Liang, P. Prefix-Tuning: Optimizing Continuous Prompts for Generation. In *Proceedings of the 59th Annual Meeting of the Association for Computational Linguistics and the 11th International Joint Conference on Natural Language Processing (Volume 1: Long Papers)*; Association for Computational Linguistics: Kerrville, TX, USA, 2021; pp. 4582–4597.
67. Gui, T.; Zou, Y.; Zhang, Q.; Peng, M.; Fu, J.; Wei, Z.; Huang, X. A Lexicon-Based Graph Neural Network for Chinese NER. In Proceedings of the EMNLP-IJCNLP 2019, Hong Kong, China, 3–7 November 2019; pp. 1040–1050.
68. Sui, D.; Chen, Y.; Liu, K.; Zhao, J.; Liu, S. Leverage Lexical Knowledge for Chinese Named Entity Recognition via Collaborative Graph Network. In Proceedings of the EMNLP-IJCNLP 2019, Hong Kong, China, 3–7 November 2019; pp. 3828–3838.
69. Gui, T.; Ma, R.; Zhang, Q.; Zhao, L.; Jiang, Y.; Huang, X. CNN-Based Chinese NER with Lexicon Rethinking. In Proceedings of the IJCAI 2019, Macao, China, 10–16 August 2019; pp. 4982–4988.
70. Xue, M.; Yu, B.; Liu, T.; Zhang, Y.; Meng, E.; Wang, B. Porous Lattice Transformer Encoder for Chinese NER. In Proceedings of the COLING 2020, Online, 8–13 December 2020; pp. 3831–3841.
71. Ma, R.; Peng, M.; Zhang, Q.; Wei, Z.; Huang, X. Simplify the Usage of Lexicon in Chinese NER. In Proceedings of the ACL 2020, Virtual, 5–10 July 2020; pp. 5951–5960.
72. Wu, S.; Song, X.; Feng, Z. MECT: Multi-Metadata Embedding based Cross-Transformer for Chinese Named Entity Recognition. In Proceedings of the ACL/IJCNLP 2021, Bangkok, Thailand, 1–6 August 2021; Association for Computational Linguistics: Kerrville, TX, USA, 2021; pp. 1529–1539.
73. Devlin, J.; Chang, M.; Lee, K.; Toutanova, K. BERT: Pre-training of Deep Bidirectional Transformers for Language Understanding. *arXiv* **2018**, arXiv1810.04805.

electronics

MDPI

Article

Knowledge Graph Multi-Hop Question Answering Based on Dependent Syntactic Semantic Augmented Graph Networks

Songtao Cai [1], Qicheng Ma [1], Yupeng Hou [1] and Guangping Zeng [1,2,*]

[1] School of Computer & Communication Engineering, University of Science and Technology Beijing, Beijing 100083, China; b20180322@xs.ustb.edu.cn (S.C.); d202110388@xs.ustb.edu.cn (Q.M.); d202210392@xs.ustb.edu.cn (Y.H.)
[2] Beijing Key Laboratory of Knowledge Engineering for Materials Science, University of Science and Technology Beijing, Beijing 100083, China
* Correspondence: zgp@ustb.edu.cn

Abstract: In the rapidly evolving domain of question answering systems, the ability to integrate machine comprehension with relational reasoning stands paramount. This paper introduces a novel architecture, the Dependent Syntactic Semantic Augmented Graph Network (DSSAGN), designed to address the intricate challenges of multi-hop question answering. By ingeniously leveraging the synergy between syntactic structures and semantic relationships within knowledge graphs, DSSAGN offers a breakthrough in interpretability, scalability, and accuracy. Unlike previous models that either fall short in handling complex relational paths or lack transparency in reasoning, our framework excels by embedding a sophisticated mechanism that meticulously models multi-hop relations and dynamically prioritizes the syntactic–semantic context.

Keywords: question answering; knowledge graph-based multi-hop QA; knowledge graph embedding; deep learning

1. Introduction

In the dynamic landscape of service mining and analytics, knowledge-based question answering (KBQA) systems, as outlined by Xiao et al. [1], have garnered significant interest across both academic and commercial sectors. These systems, designed to deduce precise target entities in response to queries posed in natural language, leverage extensive knowledge bases (KBs) as delineated by Bin et al. [2]. The core of KBQA's efficacy lies in its adeptness at interpreting complex semantic nuances inherent in natural language and pinpointing accurate responses within vast, structured knowledge repositories. A notable subset within this domain is knowledge graph question answering (KGQA), highlighted in studies by Hao et al. [3] and Michael et al. [4], which specifically employs knowledge graphs (KGs) for its knowledge repository. This approach, further explored by Bin et al. [2] and Yunshi et al. [5], capitalizes on the distinct organizational structure of KGs and their proficient querying mechanisms, offering users expedited access to deep, actionable insights encapsulated within KGs, thereby enhancing the overall user experience.

In the evolving landscape of multi-hop question answering (QA), the quest for sophisticated models capable of navigating complex information development across multiple documents has led to the development of specialized datasets like OpenBookQA [6], NarrativeQA [7], MultiRC [8], WikiHop [9], CommonsenseQA [10], and HotpotQA [11]. These platforms are designed to challenge the abilities of QA systems to perform intricate reasoning, with tasks ranging from identifying the correct answer from a set of options in WikiHop to locating specific answer snippets within paragraphs in HotpotQA.

Initial strategies focused on leveraging recurrent neural networks (RNNs) equipped with attention mechanisms to distill and extract pertinent information from texts, as seen in the early query-focused extractor (QFE) method by Nishida et al. [11] and the DecompRC approach by Min et al. [12], which simplifies complex multi-hop questions into more manageable sub-questions. Subsequent innovations have explored the selection of relevant document paragraphs and the utilization of chain reasoning, as demonstrated by the Dynamically Fused Graph Network (DFGN) by Qiu et al. [13] and hierarchical memory network models proposed by Jiang and Bansal [14], reflecting a growing sophistication in tackling multi-hop QA tasks. Recent advancements have embraced attention-based mechanisms and adaptive reinforcement learning, notably improving performance on complex QA tasks, as evidenced by the work of Zhao et al. [15] and the adaptive reinforcement learning (ARL) framework by Zhang et al. [16]. These developments underscore a shift towards more detailed and adaptive QA systems.

Simultaneously, the integration of graph neural networks (GNNs) has emerged as a pivotal innovation, enhancing the representation of complex entity relationships essential for multi-hop QA. The introduction of methods like multi-task prompting for graph neural networks highlights the potential of leveraging pre-trained models across various graph tasks, effectively bridging the gap between general graph knowledge and specific application needs [17]. The exploration of hypergraph representation for sociological analysis emphasizes the richness of social interactions and environments, providing a novel approach to understanding complex sociological phenomena through data mining techniques [18]. The factor-mixed Hawkes process (FMHP) for event-based incremental recommendations introduces a nuanced understanding of event generation, considering intrinsic, external, and historical intensities, thereby enhancing recommendation systems [19]. Furthermore, graph-masked autoencoders (GMAEs) represent a significant step forward in learning graph representations, adopting a self-supervised, transformer-based model that addresses the challenges of training deep transformers from scratch [20]. The novel recommendation model based on graph diffusion and the Ebbinghaus curve offers insights into users' evolving online interests, incorporating a graph diffusion method and neural network inspired by the Ebbinghaus curve to capture long-term and short-term tastes [21].

In the field of multi-hop QA, GNN-based models, such as those developed by Kipf and Welling [22] and Veličković et al. [23], have shown significant promise as well. Coref-GRU by Dhingra et al. [24], MHQA-GRN by Song et al. [25], and the breadth first reasoning graph (BFR-Graph) by Huang and Yang [26] exemplify the integration of entity recognition and graph construction to facilitate deeper information analysis. Moreover, the from easy to hard (FE2H) model by Li et al. [27] and the bidirectional recurrent graph neural network (BRGNN) by Zhang et al. [28] illustrate the ongoing evolution of graph-based reasoning in multi-hop QA, highlighting efforts to minimize errors and leverage relational patterns for improved QA performance.

However, as user queries become more complex, especially in multi-hop QA tasks that require synthesizing information from multiple knowledge points, the limitations of existing QA frameworks have become more pronounced. This includes challenges such as data sparsity, the difficulty of mapping complex queries to specific knowledge graph nodes and edges, and the need to dynamically update the knowledge base to incorporate the latest information. These issues highlight the need for adaptive, robust, and context-aware models that can navigate intricate knowledge graph structures with greater accuracy and comprehension.

In confronting these challenges, our paper introduces the Dependent Syntactic Semantic Augmented Graph Network (DSSAGN), an architecture designed to revolutionize QA systems' approach to multi-hop relational reasoning. To address the identified limitations, DSSAGN integrates external knowledge graphs to enrich the model with relevant entities, thereby providing a richer context for answering complex queries. Furthermore, by incorporating graph convolutional networks (GCNs) alongside dependency syntax analysis, DSSAGN significantly boosts the semantic understanding and interpretation of queries. These approaches not only facilitate a deeper comprehension of the relationships and entities within the knowledge graph, but also mirror the cognitive processes involved in human reasoning and comprehension.

Specifically, we present innovations in the realm of knowledge graph-based question answering, encapsulating our novel architecture, the DSSAGN. Our contributions are manifold, incorporating dependent syntactic analysis for a refined understanding of questions, graph convolutional networks (GCNs) for capturing intricate entity relationships, a KG Embedding Generator for advanced entity and relation embeddings, and an Answer Scoring Module for precise answer identification and ranking. These elements collectively propel DSSAGN beyond the current state-of-the-art, showcasing superior performance in multi-hop reasoning tasks through a synergistic approach that marries syntactic clarity with semantic depth and graph-based insights. The detailed source code is available at https://github.com/USTBSCCE1028/DSSAGN (accessed on 6 April 2024).

2. Materials and Methods

2.1. Materials

2.1.1. Dataset and Settings

In the experimental setup, two benchmark datasets are utilized to evaluate the performance of knowledge graph question answering tasks, which include CommonsenseQA [10] and OpenbookQA [6]. Success in these tests demands a deep grasp of world knowledge that surpasses mere textual comprehension. CommonsenseQA challenges users with a requirement for diverse kinds of commonsense reasoning. It generates its questions using elements from ConceptNet, aiming to explore the underlying complex relationships among these elements within ConceptNet's framework. OpenBookQA adopts the structure of an open-book test to evaluate an individual's grasp of a subject. Accompanying the queries are 1326 points of scientific knowledge tailored for elementary school education. Around 6000 crafted questions aim to test the comprehension of these knowledge points and their adaptability in unfamiliar situations. The data set in the experiment was divided as shown in Table 1.

Table 1. Partitioning of the data set in the experiment.

Dataset	Training Set	Test Set	Validation Set
CommonsenseQA	9741	1140	1221
OpenbookQA	4957	500	500

In addition, our evaluation uses ConceptNet, a knowledge graph across multiple domains proposed by Speer et al. [29], as an external knowledge base to assess the model's ability to utilize structured knowledge sources.

The initial configuration for training neural network models employs several key parameters designed to optimize performance and efficiency. Central to these settings is the use of the Adam optimizer, which is popular in deep learning applications due to its adaptive learning rate feature. The learning rate is set to 5×10^{-4}, a value that balances the risk of rapid convergence and minimization of the overshooting loss function. The batch size is set to 128, which is large enough to ensure that each batch captures representative samples of the dataset's diversity and thus stabilizes the gradient update. The training process was designed to run continuously for 30 epochs. This predetermined length of training time allows the model enough time to learn from the data and adjust the weights to effectively minimize the loss function. The discard rate is set to 0.3, a technique that prevents the network from over-relying on any one neuron, thus reducing model redundancy. Finally, BatchNorm (batch normalization) is enabled. It reduces internal covariance bias by normalizing the inputs of each layer, thereby increasing the learning rate, reducing the model's sensitivity to initialization, and ultimately speeding up the training process.

2.1.2. Experimental Environment

In this study, the DSSAGN model was built using the deep learning framework PyTorch, a Python3.7-based scientific computing library that provides highly flexible deep learning tools that support dynamic computational graphs and static computational graphs. The experimental environment and parameter settings are shown in Table 2 below.

Table 2. Experimental platform and environmental parameters.

Computer Information	Operating System	Windows 10 64-bit
	CPU	Intel(R) Core (TM) i5-8265U CPU @ 1.60 GHz (8 CPUs) ~1.8 GHz
	GPU	RTX 3060
	RAM	16 GB
Toolkit	Python 3.7	Numpy 1.21.5
		Scikit_Learn 1.0.2
		Pandas 0.25.1
		Torch 1.12.0
		Matplotlib 3.5.2

2.2. Methods

This section presents the details of the DSSAGN framework designed for knowledge graph question answering (KGQA) tasks, as illustrated in Figure 1. The framework incorporates various components and strategies, including a feature extractor, dependent syntactic analysis, graph neural network, graph embedding generator, and an answer scoring module.

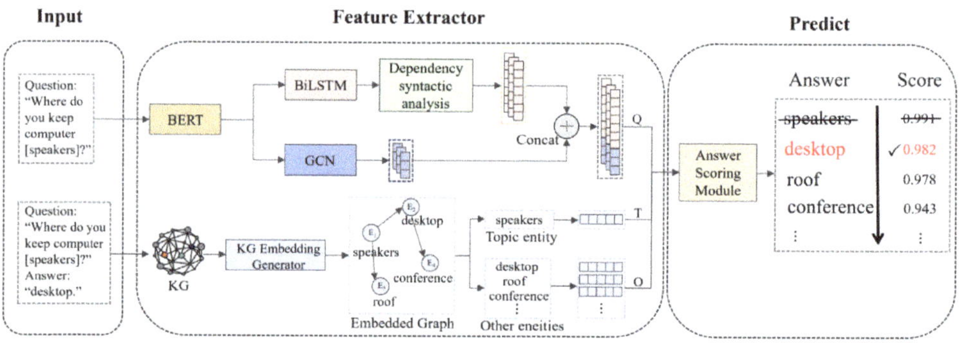

Figure 1. Overview of the proposed framework.

The initialization vectors of the question text are extracted using the BRET pre-training model [30], which is a popular word embedding learning method that incorporates local contextual information to learn word vectors. The Q&A text is fed into the KG to extract the entities associated with the text. BiLSTM works by reading an input sequence forward and backward twice to obtain context-sensitive hidden states at each time step. Specifically, for the input sequence $\{x_1, x_2, x_3, \ldots, x_n\}$ (where n is the number of words in the sequence), BiLSTM will generate a series of hidden states, $H = \{h_1, h_2, h_3, \ldots, h_n\}$. The GCN network [22] leverages the structure of the graph to capture the relationships between nodes by aggregating and passing information across the nodes within the graph. Within the structure of $G = (V, E)$, where each vertex, v, is endowed with a feature, x, the graph convolutional network (GCN) is employed to construct a representational vector, h, for every vertex. The updating mechanism of each vertex's representation leverages both the features of the vertex itself and the representations of its neighboring vertices. By iterating this mechanism, the representations of the vertices are progressively enriched to encapsulate the local and global attributes of $G = (V, E)$.

2.2.1. KG Embedding Generator

In our study, inspired by the outstanding results demonstrated in previous work, especially those of EmbedKGQA [31] and Rce-KGQA, proposed by Jin et al. [32], we explore the use of knowledge graph (KG) embedding techniques to solve some problems that are difficult to cope with through traditional methods, such as the inference of implicit relations and the handling of subgraph localization. We found that by embedding the global relational knowledge and structural information of KG into a continuous low-dimensional space, we can not only simplify the processing flow of KG, but also expect to improve the overall accuracy of the question answering process.

In this work, we adopt the method of mapping entities and relations in KG into a low-dimensional continuous vector space to obtain a sparse representation of these elements. In particular, we employ the Complex Embeddings model [33], which maps entities and relations into a complex vector space, in conjunction with considering semantic associations between elements. Compared to previous KG embedding techniques such as TransE [34] and its variants, semantic matching models such as ComplEx typically provide superior performance.

In the initialization phase of the embedding, the vector representations of all KG elements are randomly selected from a uniform distribution. The embedding dimensions of entities and relations are usually set to be no less than 100, and 200 dimensions are chosen in this study to be consistent with related studies. The training process involves extracting positive example fact triples of real-world relations from the KG while introducing false fact triples in the negative example generation step through negative sampling, i.e., randomly replacing tail entities or relations. This method helps the model learn to distinguish between true and false relationships.

Further analysis by Trouillon et al. points out that increasing the number of negative samples usually improves model performance. An appropriate ratio of positive to negative samples of about 1:50 balances both inference accuracy and training overhead. This empirical setting was followed in this study. For each relational triple $T, O \in \varepsilon$ and $Q \in \mathrm{R}$, our embedding method assigns it to a representation $v_T, v_Q, v_O \in Cd$ in the d-dimension complex vector space, and the scoring function is computed according to the following definition:

$$\begin{aligned} \varnothing(T,Q,O) &= Re(< v_T, v_Q, v_O >) \\ &= Re\left(\sum_{k=1}^{d} v_T^{(k)} v_Q^{(k)} v_O^{(k)}\right) \end{aligned} \tag{1}$$

$$\varnothing(T,Q,O) > 0\, \forall \{T,Q,O\} \in A \tag{2}$$

$$\varnothing(T,\overline{Q},\overline{O}) < 0\, \forall \left\{T,\overline{Q},\overline{O}\right\} \notin A \tag{3}$$

where $Re(\cdot)$ denotes the real portion of a complex number, while $\overline{v_O}$ indicates the complex conjugate of a specified target entity, v_O. Moreover, Q' and O' are used to denote sets of alternative triples; these are generated by selecting incorrect relations or tail entities at random, respectively. $\{T, Q, O\}$ refers to a relational triple composed of entities T, O and relation Q. Set A aggregates all the triples that reflect real-world knowledge.

Our goal is to optimize specific formulas to reduce the scores of false triples with negative values, while increasing the scores of true triples with positive values. This optimization process can be smoothly executed in each training round by stochastic gradient descent (DAD) or the Adam optimizer. In this way, the initial structural and relational information in the knowledge graph (KG) is preserved in the learned vectors, which effectively supports the execution of various downstream applications.

2.2.2. Dependent Syntactic Analysis Module

The feature vectors output from BiLSTM are fed into the dependency syntactic analysis module to obtain new feature representations. Dependency syntactic analysis is used to parse natural language sentences with the aim of revealing the dependencies between words. Specifically, a dependency tree is constructed, where each node represents a vocabulary word and each edge represents a syntactic dependency between words, forming a structured sentence representation. Its core objective can be expressed by the following formula:

$$L = \sum_{(i,j)\in E} \log P\left(r_{ij} \middle| w_i, w_j, \theta\right) \tag{4}$$

where L symbolizes the log-likelihood of a sentence's dependency tree, with E representing the collection of edges where each edge (i,j) signifies a dependency from word i to word j. Here, r_{ij} is defined as the relationship type between word i and word j, while w_i and w_j correspond to the lexical representations of word i and word j, respectively. θ denotes the parameters of the model.

The analysis process starts with the identification of the main verb of the sentence, progressively identifies the words directly associated with it (e.g., subject, object), and so on, until every word in the sentence is fully parsed. This process relies on a set of predefined grammatical rules and patterns that are based on a large amount of corpus data and in-depth linguistic theory.

2.2.3. Graph Convolutional Network

After obtaining the vector representations of BERT, we further input these vectors as node features into the graph neural network. The graph neural network can efficiently process graph structure data by iteratively updating the node representations to capture the dependencies between nodes and the global structure of the entire graph. In this process, the features of each node not only contain the semantic information of the original text, but also incorporate the information of other nodes connected to it, resulting in a new node representation that synthesizes the text content and graph structure information.

We employ a typical GNN variant, the graph convolutional network (GCN), for node feature updating. For every node within the graph, the updated feature representation is derived through a weighted aggregation of its features combined with those of its adjacent nodes. This process is mathematically depicted as:

$$H^{(l+1)} = \sigma\left(\tilde{D}^{-\frac{1}{2}}\tilde{A}\tilde{D}^{-\frac{1}{2}}H^{(l)}W^{(l)}\right) \tag{5}$$

where $H^{(l)}$ is the node identity matrix of layer l, $\tilde{A} = A + I_N$ is the adjacency matrix A of the graph plus the unit matrix I_N, $\tilde{D}$ is the diagonal node degree matrix, $W^{(l)}$ is the weight matrix of the layer, and σ is the activation function.

2.2.4. Answer Scoring Module

In this study, we employ a scoring mechanism that aims to rank each potential answer, t, based on a combined score of all possible knowledge graph (KG) entity pairs (i.e., topic entities and relationships). The formula is as follows:

$$Rank(O) = \begin{cases} \max(\varnothing(T,Q,O)),\ \forall O \in A \\ \min(\varnothing(T,Q,O)),\ \forall O \notin A \end{cases} \tag{6}$$

This process utilizes the complex scoring function proposed by Trouillon et al. [33], which seeks to optimize the model such that the likelihood of a positive sample t being included in set A is increased, while simultaneously reducing the score for any negative sample t' (not included in A). Here, A denotes the set comprising all real-world knowledge triples. It is crucial to note that to preserve the stability of the pre-trained knowledge graph entity embeddings, these embeddings are not altered during the model training phase.

Our approach doesn't just seek a balance between accuracy and recall; it implements a strategy that initially filters answers by setting a threshold of n (options are 5, 10, and 15). This is aimed at identifying candidate answers with high recall but moderate scores. In the inference phase, we assign a likelihood score to each candidate answer to reflect its credibility as the correct answer and screen out those top-ranked n but centered scoring candidates for further relational chain inference analysis.

The design of this method takes into account the adaptability of the actual relational properties and ensures that the model can efficiently process and analyze complex knowledge while progressively optimizing the model.

3. Results

This section presents the outcomes of comparative experiments, highlighting the efficacy of the DSSAGN framework. Additionally, an ablation study is conducted to assess the performance of each newly introduced architecture detailed within this document.

To enhance clarity and comprehension for our readers, we introduce a comprehensive overview of the evaluation metrics employed in our study. The metrics are as follows:

Accuracy (Acc.): This metric calculates the percentage of questions for which the model identified the correct answer out of the total questions posed. Given the task's emphasis on precise answer retrieval, accuracy serves as a primary indicator of the model's performance in correctly leveraging the knowledge graph for question answering.

Interpretability Index (II): A novel metric introduced in this study, measuring the ease with which the reasoning process of the model can be understood by human observers. The II is crucial for evaluating how well the model's decision-making process can be traced and comprehended, reflecting our research's objective to not only improve answer accuracy but also enhance transparency in reasoning.

3.1. Comparative Experiments

For a rigorous assessment of performance, various baseline models were chosen for benchmarking in comparative experiments against our proposed model. The selected baseline models are outlined as follows:

The R-GCN framework [35] is proposed for link prediction and entity classification tasks. It introduces parameter sharing and enforces sparsity constraint techniques to apply R-GCN to multi-graphs with a large number of relations.

The GconAttn framework [36] utilizes a combination of techniques for external knowledge to improve the performance of leaderless intelligence problems in scientific problem domains.

KagNet [37] is a textual reasoning framework designed to handle common sense-based queries that enables an interpretable reasoning process by integrating an external structured commonsense knowledge graph.

MHGRN [38] provides a new knowledge-aware approach that performs multi-hop multi-relational reasoning on subgraphs extracted from external knowledge graphs.

Rce-KGQA [26] has been introduced to discern inferential connections between topical entities and their answers within a knowledge graph (KG), leveraging both the explicit relation chains presented in user-posed questions and the implicit relation chains embedded within the structured KGs.

The results of the comparison experiments between the proposed model and other models are shown in Table 3.

In summary, the DA model framework demonstrated superior performance over the standard benchmark model. Specifically, within the CommonsenseQA dataset, the DA model enhanced the accuracy of answering knowledge graph-based questions by approximately 2% more than competing models, with validation set accuracy increasing by around 1.7% and test set accuracy by roughly 2.1%. When applied to the OpenbookQA dataset, the DA model framework showed an improvement in Q&A accuracy related to knowledge graphs by about 1% over alternative models. These outcomes underscore the DSSAGN framework's effectiveness in elevating performance across knowledge graph Q&A challenges. Most importantly, the BERT model is able to capture rich contextual information, and the design and combination with the dependent syntax approach and the GCN allow the model to more thoroughly understand the semantic information in the problem text. In this way, our framework not only utilizes the powerful representational capabilities of BERT, but also obtains a deeper understanding of the semantics through dependent syntax and GCN, making full use of the representational capabilities of the entire model. The KG Embedding Generator utilizes an external KG to embed related entities into a continuous low-dimensional space method, facilitating the inference of implicit relationships that may not be directly observed in the data. Additionally, the embedding process simplifies the identification and processing of relevant subgraphs in the KG. This is important for focusing on specific parts of the knowledge graph that are relevant to the query, thus improving the efficiency and accuracy of the response. In addition, the answer scoring module keeps the knowledge graph entity embeddings unchanged during the model training process, which helps to maintain the stability of the model and the validity of the pre-trained embeddings and improves the accuracy of question answering by more precisely identifying the most likely correct answer with comprehensive scoring and ranking of all potential answers.

Table 3. Performance of comparative experiments.

Model	CommonsenseQA		OpenbookQA	
	IHdev-Acc. (%)	IHtest-Acc. (%)	Dev-Acc. (%)	Test-Acc. (%)
R-GCN * [35]	56.72 (±0.42)	53.90 (±0.62)	63.51 (±1.81)	61.83 (±1.60)
GconAttn * [36]	56.37 (±0.72)	53.64 (±0.78)	62.62 (±1.07)	61.21 (±2.14)
KagNet * [37]	55.77 (±0.50)	56.39 (±0.53)	64.77 (±1.17)	61.83 (±2.05)
MHGRN * [38]	60.12 (±0.33)	56.93 (±0.72)	67.40 (±1.33)	66.15 (±1.45)
Rce-KGQA * [32]	61.52 (±0.42)	59.18 (±0.63)	67.72 (±1.13)	66.45 (±1.29)
DSSAGN framework *	63.22 (±0.20)	62.35 (±0.45)	68.52 (±0.93)	67.38 (±1.05)

All asterisks (*) denote results run on the local machine. For the CommonsenseQA dataset, we used the results of the evaluations performed on the internal development set (IHdev) and the test set (IHtest) based on the data partitioning defined by Lin et al. [37]. This includes the average accuracy of the four runs and their standard deviations.

Additionally, we conducted a comparative experiment on training time and testing time, comparing our model with the current advanced models. The purpose of this experiment was to evaluate not only the accuracy and effectiveness of each model in processing and answering questions based on knowledge graphs, but also the efficiency in terms of computational resources and time required for training. This is shown in Table 4.

Table 4. Efficiency of comparative experiments.

Model	CommonsenseQA		OpenbookQA	
	Training Time (min)	Testing Time (min)	Training Time (min)	Testing Time (min)
R-GCN * [35]	25.90	6.23	24.85	4.66
GconAttn * [36]	24.66	5.68	23.60	4.08
KagNet * [37]	22.05	4.88	19.55	3.26
MHGRN * [38]	21.25	4.45	19.03	3.05
Rce-KGQA * [32]	19.30	3.85	17.26	2.43
DSSAGN framework *	21.21	4.33	17.21	2.12

All asterisks (*) denote results run on the local machine.

In terms of efficiency, the DSSAGN framework performs slightly differently in terms of training and testing time on the two datasets. On the OpenbookQA dataset, which has the shortest testing time, DSSAGN is the most efficient, while on the CommonsenseQA dataset, DSSAGN has the second highest efficiency and has a similar training time as the fastest model, Rce-KGQA. This small difference highlights the robustness and adaptability of the DSSAGN framework across different datasets and tasks. It emphasizes the framework's ability to maintain a balance between computational efficiency and accuracy, not only ensuring fast processing times but also maintaining a high level of accuracy. This balance is crucial for real-world applications where both accuracy and computational efficiency in answering knowledge graph-based questions are critical.

3.2. Ablation Study

This section outlines a set of ablation studies designed to ascertain the discrete impact of each component on the overall efficacy of the proposed model. The objective of these experiments is to assess the utility of different modules when configured as follows:

Model 1: Excludes the dependent syntax module, relying solely on the features generated by BiLSTM combined with the outputs from GCN. This setup allows for a direct comparison with variants incorporating the dependency syntax approach.

Model 2: The answer scoring module is replaced with a fully connected layer as a predictor. In this configuration, we can compare it with the version that employs the answer scoring module strategy.

Model 3: Omits the GCN module, utilizing only the outputs from the dependent syntax module in tandem with the representations produced by EERT. This allows for evaluation against configurations that include the GCN component.

Based on the data presented in Table 5 for both the CommonsenseQA and OpenbookQA datasets, several key observations can be made:

Table 5. Ablation experiments for the proposed model.

Model	CommonsenseQA		OpenbookQA	
	IHdev-Acc. (%)	IHtest-Acc. (%)	Dev-Acc. (%)	Test-Acc. (%)
Model 1	61.35 (±0.38)	60.52 (±0.73)	66.40 (±1.64)	65.65 (±1.88)
Model 2	61.58 (±0.42)	61.88 (±0.67)	66.90 (±1.35)	65.91 (±1.47)
Model 3	62.67 (±0.25)	61.93 (±0.36)	67.89 (±1.03)	66.31 (±1.21)
DSSAGN framework	63.22 (±0.20)	62.35 (±0.45)	68.52 (±0.93)	67.38 (±1.05)

Firstly, eliminating the dependent syntax module significantly impacts the accuracy of the KGQA task, leading to a reduction in the overall accuracy for the CommonsenseQA dataset by approximately 2% and a similar decrease of about 2% for the OpenbookQA dataset. Furthermore, substituting the answer scoring module with a fully connected prediction layer results in a decline of roughly 1.5% in the overall accuracy for CommonsenseQA and about a 1.6% decrease for OpenbookQA. Lastly, the removal of the GCN module causes a decrease in overall accuracy by around 0.5% for CommonsenseQA and about 0.8% for OpenbookQA. Dependency syntax plays a more crucial role in the model's understanding of semantic information. The model interprets the intention of the sentence more accurately by revealing the dependency relationship between words, and the constructed dependency tree provides a structured representation of the sentence, which enables the model to better understand the deeper meanings and complex structures of the sentence. The answer scoring module also has a significant effect on the model's performance. It reduces the interference of low-quality answers by setting the screening threshold and preliminary filtering of candidate answers and keeps the knowledge graph entity embeddings unchanged during the model training process, which helps to maintain the stability of the model and the effectiveness of the pre-trained embeddings. In addition, the removal results of the GCN module show that graph convolutional networks play an important role in combining textual semantic information and graph structural information, further enhancing the accuracy and robustness of the Q&A system.

In summary, these experiments not only validate the importance of individual modules in enhancing the model's ability to handle complex Q&A tasks, but also emphasize the synergies of these components with each other, which together form an efficient and accurate Q&A framework.

4. Discussion

This study provides insights into the performance of our proposed DSSAGN framework and the contribution of its individual modules to the performance of the knowledge graph quizzing (KGQA) task through a series of comparative and ablation experiments. The experimental results clearly show that the DSSAGN framework outperforms the current baseline model. Furthermore, the removal of the dependent syntactic analysis module, the answer scoring module, and the graph convolutional network (GCN) module all lead to significant degradation of the model's performance, which attests to their importance in improving the model's understanding of complex Q&A tasks.

The enhanced interpretability of the DSSAGN framework is a pivotal advancement over existing approaches, primarily attributed to its unique integration of syntactic and semantic analysis within the knowledge graph domain. The core of this advancement lies in the dependency syntactic analysis module, which provides a systematic extraction and representation of syntactic dependencies between words. This explicit representation facilitates a deeper comprehension of the query structure, enabling the model to map textual queries to their semantic equivalents within the knowledge graph with high precision and transparency.

In particular, the dependency syntax analysis module enhances the model's understanding of deeper meanings and complex structures of sentences by revealing dependencies between words. The answer scoring module effectively improves answer accuracy and system robustness by comprehensively scoring and ranking candidate answers, while the GCN module further enhances the performance of the Q&A system by combining the semantic information of the text and the structural information of the knowledge graph.

Moreover, the synergy between the dependency syntactic analysis and the graph convolutional networks within DSSAGN further enriches the model's interpretability. The graph convolutional layers, informed by the structured syntactic representation, are adept at capturing the intricate relationships between entities within the knowledge graph. This dual-layered approach—combining syntactic clarity with semantic depth—provides a clear and coherent framework for understanding how the model navigates through the knowledge graph to arrive at an answer. DSSAGN enriches its model by integrating external knowledge graphs, a design that allows the model to adapt to and utilize larger or more comprehensive external knowledge graphs to enhance its performance. As the external knowledge graph expands, DSSAGN is able to access richer information and relationships to more accurately understand and answer complex queries. As a result, DSSAGN has the potential to demonstrate superior performance on both existing datasets and larger datasets that may emerge in the future. This approach based on the integration of external knowledge graphs ensures the scalability and flexibility of the model in dealing with diverse and complex problems and is a key factor in its ability to maintain high performance on different datasets.

In addition, DSSAGN demonstrates its uniqueness in dealing with knowledge graph problems compared to larger language models, such as LLaMA. DSSAGN achieves efficient computation through a smaller number of model parameters, which reduces the demand for computational resources to a certain extent and makes it more suitable for resource-limited environments. In addition, DSSAGN directly integrates with an external knowledge base, a design that allows the model to utilize the rich knowledge graph information to enhance the accuracy and depth of question answering, especially in scenarios that require multi-hop reasoning and complex relationship understanding. A clear advantage of DSSAGN over approaches such as LLaMA, which rely on massive amounts of data and complex network structures to improve model performance, is the time-efficiency of its training and inference processes. With a smaller number of parameters, DSSAGN is more flexible and faster in updating and optimizing.

In summary, through the in-depth analysis and validation of the key components in the DSSAGN framework, this study clearly demonstrates the importance and effectiveness of these components for enhancing the performance of knowledge graph Q&A, providing valuable insights and methodologies for further optimizing the Q&A system.

5. Conclusions

In summary, our proposed DSSAGN framework demonstrates significant effectiveness and innovation in handling knowledge graph question-answering tasks. Through a well-designed combination of modules, such as dependent syntactic analysis, answer scoring, and graph convolutional networks, the framework not only improves the depth and breadth of question comprehension, but also significantly enhances the accuracy of the quiz and the robustness of the system. The results of the ablation experiment further validate the importance of each module and the synergistic effect between them, providing valuable insights for future research and development in complex Q&A systems.

This study also demonstrates the importance of combining textual semantic information and knowledge graph structural information, proving the effectiveness of this combination in improving the performance of Q&A systems. Moreover, with the continuous expansion and enrichment of external knowledge graphs, DSSAGN is expected to further improve its performance and realize deeper semantic understanding and more accurate information retrieval. In addition, as technology advances and knowledge domains expand, larger and more comprehensive knowledge graphs are expected to emerge, providing DSSAGN with richer information sources. This will enable DSSAGN to not only provide more accurate answers, but also to understand and answer more complex multi-hop quizzing tasks. With the rapid development of knowledge graphs in various domains, we believe that the methodology and findings presented in this study will provide important references and insights for future research and applications of knowledge graph Q&A tasks.

Author Contributions: Conceptualization, S.C.; methodology, S.C. and Q.M.; software, S.C. and Y.H.; validation, S.C., Y.H. and Q.M.; formal analysis, S.C.; investigation, G.Z.; resources, S.C.; data curation, Y.H. and Q.M.; writing—original draft preparation, S.C., Q.M. and Y.H.; writing—review and editing, G.Z.; visualization, Q.M. and Y.H.; supervision, G.Z.; project administration, G.Z.; funding acquisition, G.Z. All authors have read and agreed to the published version of the manuscript.

Funding: This research was funded by the National Natural Science Foundation of China (General Program), grant number 62072031, and the Second Department, Second Institute of China Aerospace Science and Industry Corporation, grant number classified.

Data Availability Statement: The data presented in this study are available upon request from the corresponding author.

Conflicts of Interest: The authors declare no conflict of interest.

References

1. Huang, X.; Zhang, J.; Li, D.; Li, P. Knowledge Graph Embedding Based Question Answering. In Proceedings of the Twelfth ACM International Conference on Web Search and Data Mining, Melbourne, Australia, 30 January 2019; ACM: Melbourne, VIC, Australia, 2019; pp. 105–113.
2. Fu, B.; Qiu, Y.; Tang, C.; Li, Y.; Yu, H.; Sun, J. A Survey on Complex Question Answering over Knowledge Base: Recent Advances and Challenges. *arXiv* **2020**, arXiv:2007.13069.
3. Hao, Y.; Zhang, Y.; Liu, K.; He, S.; Liu, Z.; Wu, H.; Zhao, J. An End-to-End Model for Question Answering over Knowledge Base with Cross-Attention Combining Global Knowledge. In Proceedings of the 55th Annual Meeting of the Association for Computational Linguistics (Volume 1: Long Papers), Vancouver, BC, Canada, 30 July–4 August 2017; pp. 221–231.
4. Petrochuk, M.; Zettlemoyer, L. SimpleQuestions Nearly Solved: A New Upperbound and Baseline Approach. *arXiv* **2018**, arXiv:1804.08798.

5. Lan, Y.; He, G.; Jiang, J.; Jiang, J.; Zhao, W.X.; Wen, J.-R. A Survey on Complex Knowledge Base Question Answering: Methods, Challenges and Solutions. *arXiv* **2021**, arXiv:2105.11644.
6. Mihaylov, T.; Clark, P.; Khot, T.; Sabharwal, A. Can a Suit of Armor Conduct Electricity? A New Dataset for Open Book Question Answering. *arXiv* **2018**, arXiv:1809.02789.
7. Kočiský, T.; Schwarz, J.; Blunsom, P.; Dyer, C.; Hermann, K.M.; Melis, G.; Grefenstette, E. The NarrativeQA Reading Comprehension Challenge. *Trans. Assoc. Comput. Linguist.* **2017**, *6*, 317–328. [CrossRef]
8. Khashabi, D.; Chaturvedi, S.; Roth, M.; Upadhyay, S.; Roth, D. Looking Beyond the Surface: A Challenge Set for Reading Comprehension over Multiple Sentences. In Proceedings of the 2018 Conference of the North American Chapter of the Association for Computational Linguistics: Human Language Technologies, Volume 1 (Long Papers), New Orleans, LO, USA, 1–6 June 2018; pp. 252–262.
9. Welbl, J.; Stenetorp, P.; Riedel, S. Constructing Datasets for Multi-Hop Reading Comprehension Across Documents. *TACL* **2018**, *6*, 287–302. [CrossRef]
10. Talmor, A.; Herzig, J.; Lourie, N.; Berant, J. CommonsenseQA: A Question Answering Challenge Targeting Commonsense Knowledge. *arXiv* **2019**, arXiv:1811.00937.
11. Yang, Z.; Qi, P.; Zhang, S.; Bengio, Y.; Cohen, W.W.; Salakhutdinov, R.; Manning, C.D. HotpotQA: A Dataset for Diverse, Explainable Multi-Hop Question Answering. *arXiv* **2018**, arXiv:1809.09600.
12. Min, S.; Zhong, V.; Zettlemoyer, L.; Hajishirzi, H. Multi-Hop Reading Comprehension through Question Decomposition and Rescoring. *arXiv* **2019**, arXiv:1906.02916.
13. Qiu, L.; Xiao, Y.; Qu, Y.; Zhou, H.; Li, L.; Zhang, W.; Yu, Y. Dynamically Fused Graph Network for Multi-Hop Reasoning. In Proceedings of the 57th Annual Meeting of the Association for Computational Linguistics, Florence, Italy, 28 July–2 August 2019; pp. 6140–6150.
14. Jiang, Y.; Bansal, M. Self-Assembling Modular Networks for Interpretable Multi-Hop Reasoning. *arXiv* **2019**, arXiv:1909.05803.
15. Zhao, C.; Xiong, C.; Rosset, C.; Song, X.; Bennett, P.; Tiwary, S. Transformer-xh: Multi-evidence reasoning with extra hop attention. In Proceedings of the International Conference on Learning Representations, Addis Ababa, Ethiopia, 30 April 2020.
16. Zhang, Q.; Weng, X.; Zhou, G.; Zhang, Y.; Huang, J.X. ARL: An Adaptive Reinforcement Learning Framework for Complex Question Answering over Knowledge Base. *Inf. Process. Manag.* **2022**, *59*, 102933. [CrossRef]
17. Sun, X.; Cheng, H.; Li, J.; Liu, B.; Guan, J. All in One: Multi-Task Prompting for Graph Neural Networks. In Proceedings of the 29th ACM SIGKDD Conference on Knowledge Discovery and Data Mining, ACM, Long Beach, CA, USA, 6 August 2023; pp. 2120–2131.
18. Sun, X.; Cheng, H.; Liu, B.; Li, J.; Chen, H.; Xu, G.; Yin, H. Self-Supervised Hypergraph Representation Learning for Sociological Analysis. *IEEE Trans. Knowl. Data Eng.* **2023**, *35*, 11860–11871. [CrossRef]
19. Cui, Z.; Sun, X.; Pan, L.; Liu, S.; Xu, G. Event-Based Incremental Recommendation via Factors Mixed Hawkes Process. *Inf. Sci.* **2023**, *639*, 119007. [CrossRef]
20. Zhang, S.; Chen, H.; Yang, H.; Sun, X.; Yu, P.S.; Xu, G. Graph Masked Autoencoders with Transformers. *arXiv* **2022**, arXiv:2202.08391.
21. Cui, Z.; Sun, X.; Chen, H.; Pan, L.; Cui, L.; Liu, S.; Xu, G. Dynamic Recommendation Based on Graph Diffusion and Ebbinghaus Curve. *IEEE Trans. Comput. Soc. Syst.* **2024**, *11*, 2755–2764. [CrossRef]
22. Kipf, T.N.; Welling, M. Semi-Supervised Classification with Graph Convolutional Networks. *arXiv* **2017**, arXiv:1609.02907.
23. Veličković, P.; Cucurull, G.; Casanova, A.; Romero, A.; Liò, P.; Bengio, Y. Graph Attention Networks. In Proceedings of the 6th ICLR 2018, Vancouver, BC, Canada, 30 April–3 May 2018.
24. Dhingra, B.; Jin, Q.; Yang, Z.; Cohen, W.W.; Salakhutdinov, R. Neural Models for Reasoning over Multiple Mentions Using Coreference. *arXiv* **2018**, arXiv:1804.05922.
25. Song, L.; Wang, Z.; Yu, M.; Zhang, Y.; Florian, R.; Gildea, D. Exploring Graph-Structured Passage Representation for Multi-Hop Reading Comprehension with Graph Neural Networks. *arXiv* **2018**, arXiv:1809.02040.
26. Huang, Y.; Yang, M. Breadth First Reasoning Graph for Multi-Hop Question Answering. In Proceedings of the 2021 Conference of the North American Chapter of the Association for Computational Linguistics: Human Language Technologies, Online, 6–11 June 2021; pp. 5810–5821.
27. Li, X.-Y.; Lei, W.-J.; Yang, Y.-B. From Easy to Hard: Two-Stage Selector and Reader for Multi-Hop Question Answering. In Proceedings of the ICASSP 2023—2023 IEEE International Conference on Acoustics, Speech and Signal Processing (ICASSP), Rhodes Island, Greece, 4 June 2023; pp. 1–5.
28. Zhang, G.; Liu, J.; Zhou, G.; Xie, Z.; Yu, X.; Cui, X. Query Path Generation via Bidirectional Reasoning for Multihop Question Answering from Knowledge Bases. *IEEE Trans. Cogn. Dev. Syst.* **2023**, *15*, 1183–1195. [CrossRef]
29. Speer, R.; Chin, J.; Havasi, C. ConceptNet 5.5: An Open Multilingual Graph of General Knowledge. In Proceedings of the Thirty-First AAAI Conference on Artificial Intelligence, San Francisco, CA, USA, 4–9 February 2017; Volume 31. [CrossRef]
30. Devlin, J.; Chang, M.-W.; Lee, K.; Toutanova, K. BERT: Pre-Training of Deep Bidirectional Transformers for Language Understanding. *arXiv* **2019**, arXiv:1810.04805.
31. Saxena, A.; Tripathi, A.; Talukdar, P. Improving Multi-Hop Question Answering over Knowledge Graphs Using Knowledge Base Embeddings. In Proceedings of the 58th Annual Meeting of the Association for Computational Linguistics, Online, 5–10 July 2020; pp. 4498–4507.

32. Jin, W.; Zhao, B.; Yu, H.; Tao, X.; Yin, R.; Liu, G. Improving Embedded Knowledge Graph Multi-Hop Question Answering by Introducing Relational Chain Reasoning. *Data Min. Knowl. Disc.* **2023**, *37*, 255–288. [CrossRef]
33. Trouillon, T.; Welbl, J.; Riedel, S. Complex Embeddings for Simple Link Prediction. *Proc. Mach. Learn. Res.* **2016**, *48*, 2071–2080.
34. Bordes, A.; Usunier, N.; Garcia-Duran, A.; Weston, J.; Yakhnenko, O. Translating Embeddings for Modeling Multi-Relational Data. In Proceedings of the Advances in Neural Information Processing Systems 26, Lake Tahoe, NV, USA, 5–10 December 2013.
35. Gangemi, A.; Navigli, R.; Vidal, M.-E.; Hitzler, P.; Troncy, R.; Hollink, L.; Tordai, A.; Alam, M. (Eds.) *The Semantic Web: 15th International Conference, ESWC 2018, Heraklion, Crete, Greece, 3–7 June 2018*; Lecture Notes in Computer Science; Springer International Publishing: Cham, Switzerland, 2018; Volume 10843, ISBN 978-3-319-93416-7.
36. Wang, X.; Kapanipathi, P.; Musa, R.; Yu, M.; Talamadupula, K.; Abdelaziz, I.; Chang, M.; Fokoue, A.; Makni, B.; Mattei, N.; et al. Improving Natural Language Inference Using External Knowledge in the Science Questions Domain. *AAAI* **2019**, *33*, 7208–7215. [CrossRef]
37. Lin, B.Y.; Chen, X.; Chen, J.; Ren, X. KagNet: Knowledge-Aware Graph Networks for Commonsense Reasoning. *arXiv* **2019**, arXiv:1909.02151.
38. Feng, Y.; Chen, X.; Lin, B.Y.; Wang, P.; Yan, J.; Ren, X. Scalable Multi-Hop Relational Reasoning for Knowledge-Aware Question Answering. *arXiv* **2020**, arXiv:2005.00646.

electronics

MDPI

Article

Design and Development of Knowledge Graph for Industrial Chain Based on Deep Learning

Yue Li, Yutian Lei *, Yiting Yan, Chang Yin and Jiale Zhang

School of Computer Science and Technology, Donghua University, Shanghai 201620, China; frankyueli@dhu.edu.cn (Y.L.); 2222843@mail.dhu.edu.cn (Y.Y.); 2222779@mail.dhu.edu.cn (C.Y.); 2222748@mail.dhu.edu.cn (J.Z.)

* Correspondence: 2222849@mail.dhu.edu.cn

Abstract: This paper aims to structure and semantically describe the information within the industrial chain by constructing an Industry Chain Knowledge Graph (ICKG), enabling more efficient and intelligent information management and analysis. In more detail, this paper constructs a multi-domain industrial chain dataset and proposes a method that combines the top-down establishment of a semantic expression framework with the bottom-up establishment of a data layer to build an ICKG. In the data layer, a deep learning algorithm based on BERT-BiLSTM-CRF is used to extract industry chain entities from relevant literature and reports. The results indicate that the model can effectively identify industry chain entities. These entities and relationships populate a Neo4j graph database, creating a large-scale ICKG for visual display and aiding cross-domain applications.

Keywords: industrial chain; knowledge graph; information extraction; entity recognition; NLP

1. Introduction

The industrial chain is one of the cornerstones of the modern economic system, describing the entire process of products and services from the starting point of raw materials to the final consumer. Currently, many scholars are dedicated to constructing and refining industry chains in various sectors. Among them, Lou et al. [1] proposed a framework for the traditional Chinese medicine industry chain, which includes upstream, midstream, and downstream segments. Lu et al. [2] conducted an in-depth analysis of the technical efficiency and influencing factors of the energy industry chain in China. Yang et al. [3] explained how studying the carbon footprint in the industry chain would promote hydrogen development in specific sectors. Song et al. [4] highlighted the importance and challenges of the rice industry chain. The authors of [5] emphasized the comprehensive industry chain perspective on mineral resource security, highlighting the importance of industry chains in safeguarding the supply of strategic mineral resources and sustainable development.

A knowledge graph is a technological means capable of mining, organizing, and efficiently managing knowledge from massive data, providing qualitative improvement for information services, and offering users more intelligent and personalized services [6]. In various fields, knowledge graphs have shown a wide range of application prospects, including search engine optimization in medical care [7–12] intelligent recommendation systems [13–15], intelligent transportation and urban planning, financial risk management [16–21], etc. Knowledge graphs can integrate scattered information within the industrial chain, establish comprehensive entity relationships, achieve efficient sharing and management of information, and thereby break information silos. Utilizing knowledge graphs can intelligently analyze the relationships between various links in the industrial chain, helping to deepen the understanding of business processes and optimize decisions. Knowledge graphs can also integrate data from multiple sources, enabling real-time monitoring and prediction of potential risks in the industrial chain, thereby improving the accuracy and efficiency of risk management. Based on knowledge graph-based data analysis, more comprehensive and accurate information support can be provided for decision-making in the industrial chain, helping managers make wiser decisions.

The current industrial chain is becoming increasingly complex, covering multiple stages including raw material procurement, manufacturing, logistics, inventory management, and sales channels, with participants including manufacturers, suppliers, and logistics companies [22]. However, these participants typically use different information systems and data formats, leading to information asymmetry and inefficient processes [23–25]. Existing industrial chain datasets have limited coverage [26], are outdated, and struggle to handle unstructured data. Traditional industrial chains also face issues such as information asymmetry, supply chain risks, and inefficiencies [27]. Particularly when dealing with complex texts, traditional entity recognition algorithms and relationship extraction rules may encounter difficulties [28]. Texts often contain noise and ambiguity, making entity recognition and relationship extraction even more complex.

To address these challenges, this research aims to construct a cross-disciplinary, comprehensive industrial chain dataset by integrating data from multiple sources with strong real-time capabilities and various dimensions. This integration aims to enhance the comprehensive understanding of industrial chains and provide decision support. Simultaneously, the introduction of knowledge graphs into industrial chains aims to promote digital transformation, improve overall operational efficiency and management levels, and achieve efficient sharing and management by eliminating information silos. In order to extract knowledge more accurately, we plan to optimize the entity recognition algorithm and relationship extraction rules and use deep learning and natural language processing technology to process unstructured data to improve the quality of data extraction. This comprehensive strategy aims to address current challenges and promote the intelligent and informatized development of industrial chains.

This paper collected a large amount of structured data and unstructured text related to the industry chain and preprocessed these sample data to construct a comprehensive industry chain dataset covering multiple domains. Based on this comprehensive dataset, the study investigated a deep learning-based method for industry chain entity recognition, comparing the effectiveness of different deep learning algorithms on the industry chain dataset to obtain the best method for industry chain entity recognition. The experiments showed that the BERT-BiLSTM-CRF model significantly improved the efficiency of industry chain entity recognition. Finally, the extracted standard data were stored in the Neo4j graph database, successfully constructing a large-scale ICKG. This knowledge graph provides strong support for cross-domain applications, including knowledge retrieval, intelligent question answering, smart decision-making, intelligent marketing, and intelligent recommendation systems. The main contributions of our research are as follows:

- This paper integrated structured data (such as Shenwan Industry, Shenzhen Stock Exchange, Shanghai Stock Exchange, etc.) and unstructured data (such as encyclopedias, news, annual reports, etc.) to build a comprehensive industry chain dataset. This comprehensive dataset helps provide more comprehensive and multidimensional industry information and knowledge;
- The entity recognition algorithm based on the BERT-BiLSTM-CRF model proposed in this paper performed excellently on the industry chain dataset. The macro-F1, macro-P, and macro-R of the BERT-BiLSTM-CRF model were 97.10%, 96.80%, and 96.95%, respectively, showing the best performance among the three models. The macro-F1 of this model is 0.44% higher than that of the BERT model and 24.78% higher than that of the BERT-CRF model;
- This paper proposes a method of combining top-down and bottom-up approaches to construct an ICKG. This ICKG serves as a core resource for cross-domain applications, providing extensive and robust support for various fields, including knowledge retrieval, intelligent question answering, smart decision-making, intelligent marketing, and intelligent recommendation systems.

The remaining sections of the paper are arranged as follows: Section 2 outlines the relevant research on entity recognition and relation extraction. Section 3 introduces the concept and overall architecture of the ICKG. Sections 4 and 5, respectively, discuss the construction and improvement of the model layer and data layer of the ICKG. Section 6 employs various deep learning models to perform entity recognition on the industrial chain dataset and thoroughly analyze the experimental results. Finally, we summarize the findings of the study and propose directions for future research.

2. Related Work

Named entity recognition (NER) is a technique used to identify entities from a large amount of text [29]. NER can be mainly categorized into three types [28]. The first type is rule-based or knowledge-based methods [30], which have the advantages of strong interpretability and good adaptability in specific domains. Due to their reliance on manually designed rules and domain expert knowledge, these methods do not require a large amount of annotated data. However, their generalization ability is limited, making it difficult to handle different languages and complex grammars, and the maintenance cost is high when facing new domains or changes. Rule-based methods may perform poorly in processing long texts or complex contexts due to their relatively weak capability of handling contextual dependencies and complex grammars. The second type is learning-based methods [31], which utilize machine learning algorithms, such as deep learning models, to learn patterns for identifying named entities from text through a large amount of annotated data. Their advantages lie in their strong adaptability, the ability to handle diverse language structures, and the absence of manual rule design. The third type is neural network methods based on feature inference [32], which infer named entities by learning features from the text. Their advantages include efficient utilization of contextual information, adaptation to diverse language structures, and no need for manual feature design. However, they depend heavily on a large amount of annotated data, have higher model complexity, are relatively difficult to interpret, and require more computational resources.

The goal of entity relation extraction models is to identify relationships between entities from text [33]. Commonly used methods for entity relation identification include rule-based methods [34,35], pattern-based methods [36], machine learning-based methods [37,38], and deep learning-based methods [39,40].

After a comprehensive analysis of relevant research work, this paper addresses the following issues when constructing an ICKG: how to deal with data scarcity and labeling difficulties; how to improve the model's domain adaptability and generalization ability; and explore how to more effectively utilize contextual information. This paper constructs a comprehensive industrial chain dataset, and the proposed BERT-BiLSTM-CRF-based model can significantly improve the efficiency of industrial chain entity recognition.

3. The Overall Architecture of the ICKG

The industrial chain refers to the entire production and delivery process of a product, from the production of raw materials, processing and manufacturing, and distribution to the final consumer. The industrial chain is typically divided into three parts: upstream, midstream, and downstream. Upstream refers to the part of the industrial chain responsible for providing raw materials, components, and primary processing. Midstream is the part of the industrial chain responsible for processing, manufacturing, and assembly. Downstream is the part of the industrial chain responsible for product distribution, sales, and final consumption. Upstream provides raw materials and basic substances; midstream processes and manufactures products; and downstream interacts with end-users, driving product flow to the market. This division helps to understand and analyze the entire industrial chain, thereby optimizing decisions related to supply chain management, product design, and market positioning.

This paper employs data processing and structured extraction techniques to successfully construct a comprehensive dataset of the industrial chain. Entity recognition methods based on BERT-BiLSTM-CRF models and rule-based methods are utilized for knowledge extraction, and the data are stored in the Neo4j graph database, forming a large-scale ICKG. This knowledge graph provides powerful support for cross-disciplinary applications, covering various aspects such as knowledge retrieval, intelligent question-answering, intelligent decision-making, intelligent marketing, and intelligent recommendation. The overall architecture design is illustrated in Figure 1.

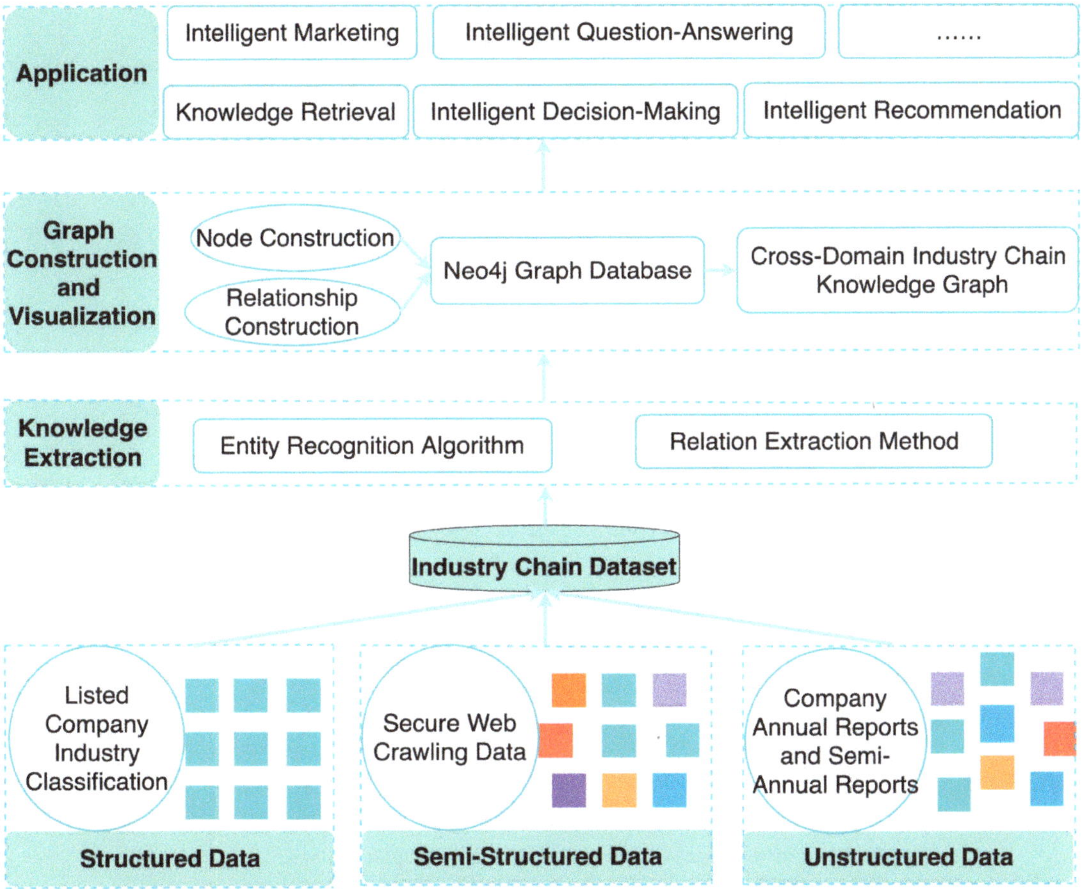

Figure 1. Framework for constructing the ICKG.

The construction of the ICKG adopts a combined approach of top-down and bottom-up methodologies, as illustrated in Figure 2, depicting the basic process of constructing the pattern layer and data layer. The top-down construction of the pattern layer provides a theoretical framework and abstract model, guiding the construction of the knowledge graph. The bottom-up construction of the data layer ensures the authenticity and practicality of the knowledge graph through the extraction and integration of actual data. The integration of top-down and bottom-up approaches, through modeling and validation from multiple perspectives, enhances the accuracy and credibility of the knowledge graph. This enables it to meet the requirements of different domains and scenarios, flexibly applying it to various practical situations.

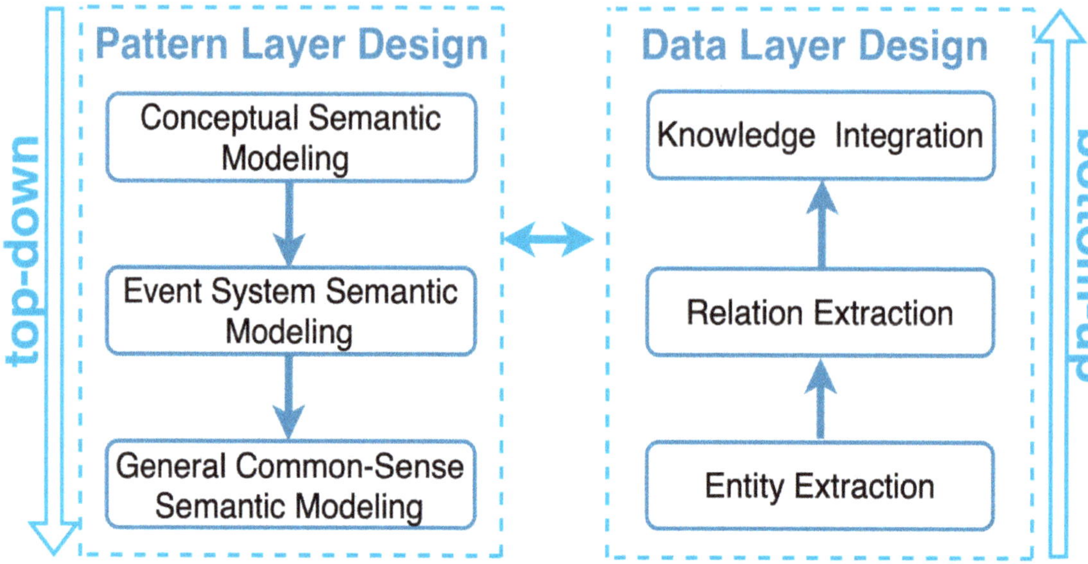

Figure 2. Basic process of constructing the pattern layer and data layer of the ICKG.

4. Construction of the Pattern Layer of the ICKG

This paper constructs the pattern layer of the ICKG through three steps: conceptual semantic modeling, event semantic modeling, and general common-sense semantic modeling. Conceptual semantic modeling aims to define and establish key concepts, entities, relationships, and their logic within the business domain. Event semantic modeling follows conceptual semantic modeling, relying on the defined conceptual model to derive semantic relationships between events, actions, or processes. General common-sense semantic modeling builds upon the first two steps, relying on the models of conceptual and event semantics to add more universal concepts and relationships to the system's knowledge base. By top-down construction of the pattern layer of the ICKG through conceptual, event, and general common-sense semantic modeling, comprehensive modeling and logical derivation of key concepts, events, and universal relationships in the industrial chain are achieved, enhancing the richness and universality of the knowledge graph.

4.1. Conceptual Semantic Modeling

The first layer of conceptual semantic modeling in the pattern layer aims to associate entities with relevant concepts, with the goal of describing and representing concepts, entities, and their relationships in the real world to better understand, analyze, and process complex information and data. It helps organize complex concepts and information into a structured format for knowledge sharing, automated reasoning, and data integration. In the context of the industrial chain, conceptual semantic modeling involves modeling industry standards, domain-specific terminology, and so on. As depicted in Figure 3, the conceptual model adopts a hierarchical tree-like classification system and forms a concept dictionary by hierarchically encoding the concept tree. The benefit of this design is that when renaming concepts, only the concept dictionary information needs to be updated without the need to update the data of indexes or relationships. Since concepts are associated with many entities, any change in a concept will involve changes throughout the tree. Using a concept dictionary effectively addresses this issue.

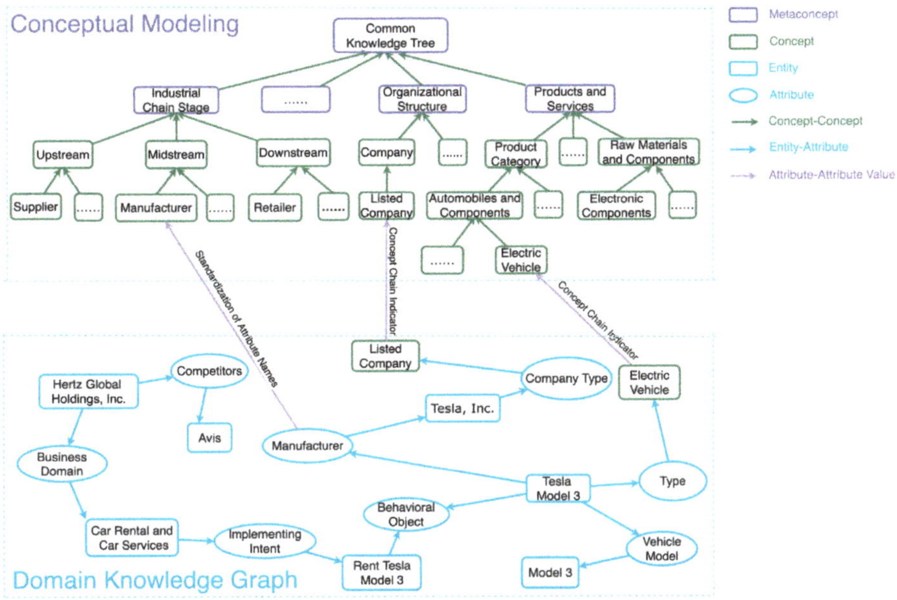

Figure 3. Conceptual semantic modeling.

4.2. Event Semantic Modeling

The second layer of semantic modeling in the pattern layer focuses on defining and modeling events, determining relationships between events, and associating events with entities to capture dynamic information in the knowledge graph. In the ICKG, this involves defining and modeling events within the industrial chain, such as market changes and company mergers.

The industrial chain encompasses numerous types of events, including supply chain event modeling, market event modeling, environmental event modeling, marketing and sales modeling, as well as service and after-sales modeling. Introducing each new event type necessitates designing a new schema, which adds complexity to knowledge extraction and management. To streamline this process, this paper establishes a set of standardized event modeling specifications, as shown in Table 1. This standardized event modeling framework defines uniform modeling patterns for different event types, categorizing event attributes into different categories such as basic elements, temporal elements, spatial elements, subject elements, and object elements.

Table 1. Industrial chain event schema model.

Element Type	Attribute Name	Attribute Type	Value Examples
Basic Elements	Type	String	Product Launch, Mergers and Acquisitions, Supply Chain Disruption
	Description	Text	New Model Launch, Company Acquisition, Supplier Bankruptcy
	Level	String	High, Medium, Low
Temporal Elements	Occurrence_Time	Datetime	15 January 2023 10:00:00
	Duration	Integer	2, 5, 10 (units in days)
	Deadline	Datetime	28 February 2023 23:59:59

Table 1. *Cont.*

Element Type	Attribute Name	Attribute Type	Value Examples
Spatial Elements	Location	String	Shanghai, Beijing, Shenzhen
	Impact_Area	String	Global, Regional, Local
	Coordinates	Geographical Coordinates	(31.2304° N, 121.4737° E)
Subject Elements	Subject	String	Company, Individual, Government
	Participant	String	Investor, Supplier, Customer
	Responsible_Party	String	Manufacturer, Distributor, Government Agency
Object Elements	Product_Model	String	Tissue Paper
	Raw_Material	String	Steel, Semiconductor
	Transaction_Amount	Currency	500,000

4.3. General Common-Sense Semantic Modeling

The third layer of the pattern layer focuses on general common-sense semantic modeling, which involves modeling the association, attributes, and events of general common sense with specific industrial chains. This allows the system to better understand and infer various relationships within the industrial chain. Such models can cover multiple aspects, including industry interrelations, supply-demand relationships, market trends, and more, ensuring that the knowledge graph not only relies on domain-specific information but also comprehends a broader context.

This paper first determines the scope and objectives of modeling, clarifying the common-sense knowledge content that the system needs to acquire and understand, including the involved industrial chain links, related entities, events, etc. Next, it collects and organizes common-sense knowledge within the industrial chain, including industry standards, expert knowledge, document materials, case analyses, historical data, and other sources. Knowledge is extracted and integrated from various sources and organized into a form that the system can comprehend and utilize. Finally, based on the extracted and integrated common-sense knowledge, a general common-sense model is established.

5. Construction of the Data Layer of the ICKG

This paper constructs the data layer of the ICKG from the bottom up through three steps: entity relationship modeling, entity recognition and relation extraction, and knowledge fusion. Entity relationship modeling is the process of defining and modeling entities and their relationships within the industrial chain. This step clarifies the connections between various entities in the industrial chain, establishing a clear framework for subsequent entity recognition and relation extraction, making them more targeted and accurate. The second step involves identifying specific entities and relationships from text. Through this step, textual information is transformed into structured data, enriching the content of the ICKG. Finally, knowledge fusion integrates and combines knowledge obtained from different sources to make the knowledge graph more complete and comprehensive. Knowledge fusion helps address the limitations of a single data source, improving the accuracy and credibility of the knowledge graph.

5.1. Entity Relationship Modeling

Entity relationship modeling defines and models entities in the knowledge graph, determines their relationships, and specifies entity attributes. Its aim is to create a structured representation of things and their relationships in the real world to better organize and understand complex data structures. The main goal is to represent complex real-world data structures in a clear and maintainable manner for data storage, querying, and analysis.

The schema architecture in the knowledge graph plays a role in defining and delineating entities, attributes, and relationships. It abstracts and standardizes the data model within the domain, providing the foundation for constructing and applying the knowledge graph. By using types and properties, the schema specifies feasible categories and constraints, enabling the knowledge graph to organize, query, and utilize domain knowledge more effectively. The enterprise schema model is defined in Table 2.

Table 2. Enterprise schema definition.

Attribute Name	Attribute Type	Attribute Value
Id	String	4873
Code	String	300636
City	String	Jiangxi Province
Fullname	String	China Jiangxi Tonghe Pharmaceutical Co., Ltd.
Location	String	Shenzhen Stock Exchange
Comp_Name	String	Tonghe Pharmaceutical
Reg_Capital	Numeric	350 million
Setup_Date	Datetime	31 March 2017

As shown in Figure 4, the ICKG encompasses five types of entities: products, companies, industries, supply chains, and customers. It defines ten types of entity relationships, including upstream material, higher-level industry, downstream product, product subcategory, core product, business sector, purchase relationship, service relationship, procurement relationship, and partnership relationships.

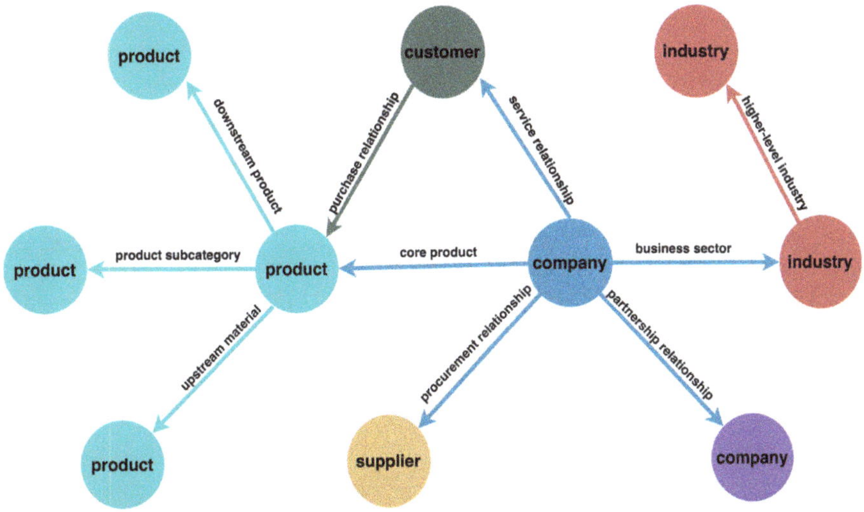

Figure 4. Entity and relationship definitions.

5.2. Entity Recognition Methods

NER is the process of identifying named entities with specific meanings from text and classifying them into predefined categories. This section analyzes and compares various deep learning algorithms' applications in entity recognition in the industrial chain context from three aspects: semantic representation, context awareness, and sequence labeling.

5.2.1. Semantic Representations

The role of semantic representations is to convert textual data into vector representations with semantic information. Its main function is to map natural language text into a high-dimensional vector space, where texts with similar semantics are represented closer to each other in the vector space. In these models, each word or subunit is mapped to a vector, and the entire text is represented by the combination of these vectors.

This paper utilizes the Bidirectional Encoder Representations from Transformers (BERT) model to learn semantic representations of textual data. The BERT model employs bidirectional transformer encoders, which can consider context information simultaneously during the pre-training phase, thereby better capturing the context and semantics of words. This architecture can effectively capture long-distance dependencies, which is advantageous for processing longer text sequences. During pre-training, BERT performs two tasks simultaneously: the Masked Language Model (MLM) and Next Sentence Prediction (NSP). This multi-task learning approach helps the model learn richer semantic representations.

5.2.2. Context-Aware Models

Context-aware models refer to models or components used to capture contextual information from textual data. Their main function is to consider the context of textual data before and after, enabling a more comprehensive understanding of the text content. The role of context-aware models is to not only consider the current word or sentence when processing textual data but also take into account the context before and after, leading to more accurate understanding and processing.

This paper utilizes the Bidirectional Long Short-Term Memory (BiLSTM) model to study its application effectiveness in entity recognition in the industrial chain context. Long Short-Term Memory (LSTM) is a variant of Recurrent Neural Network (RNN) that effectively addresses the vanishing gradient and exploding gradient problems in traditional RNNs by introducing internal gate mechanisms, thus better capturing long-term dependencies. BiLSTM extends LSTM by considering both past and future context information at each time step. BiLSTM consists of two LSTMs, one responsible for extracting information from the forward sequence and the other for extracting information from the backward sequence. Their outputs are then concatenated to obtain richer contextual information.

5.2.3. Sequence Tagger

The main function of a sequence tagger is to label input sequence data by assigning a label or category to each element in the input sequence (such as words, characters, etc.). Conditional Random Field (CRF) is a probabilistic graphical model commonly used for sequence tagging tasks. CRF models the label sequences in the sequence, considering the dependency relationships between labels, thereby improving the accuracy of sequence tagging. In industrial entity recognition, CRF models can utilize previously extracted features (such as word embeddings, part-of-speech tagging, character-level features, etc.) to predict the label for each word while considering the transition probabilities between labels, thus ensuring the consistency and rationality of the recognition results.

5.3. Relation Extraction

The ICKG constructed in this paper includes five main entity types, including product, company, industry, supplier, and customer. It defines ten types of entity relationships. Firstly, focusing on the industry relationships of listed companies, based on publicly available results of industry classification for listed companies, we construct the business sector of listed companies. These relationships demonstrate clear associations with the industries in which companies operate, providing an important foundation for the establishment of the ICKG. Secondly, according to the latest industry classification table, we establish higher-level industry relationships between industries. These relationships describe the hierarchical structure between different industries, revealing the hierarchical relationships between industries and aiding in better understanding and analyzing the structure and hierarchy of the entire industrial chain. Additionally, by formulating corresponding rules and applying the method of rule pattern matching, we successfully extract rich relationship information from the semi-annual and annual reports published by companies each year. This information provides detailed descriptions of companies' main businesses, the association between products and raw materials, the connections between products and downstream products, and the subdivision of product categories, among other aspects, thereby providing important information and perspectives for a deeper understanding of the interactions between various links in the industrial chain.

5.4. Knowledge Fusion

The ICKG integrates information from different data sources to eliminate duplicates, consolidate identical entities, and ensure the completeness and accuracy of the information in the knowledge graph. Different descriptions of the same entity exist across different data sources, and knowledge fusion eliminates this heterogeneity, thus unifying entity information in the knowledge graph. Various links, entities, and relationships within the industrial chain need to be comprehensively considered, and knowledge fusion helps integrate information from multiple domains or stages to achieve a holistic view of the entire industrial chain. This paper primarily conducts knowledge fusion on industrial chain data from two aspects: semantic knowledge fusion and entity fusion.

5.4.1. Semantic Knowledge Fusion

Semantic knowledge fusion in the industrial chain mainly involves semantic mapping and ontology fusion, which can enhance the consistency of data across different stages of the industrial chain. For instance, when constructing a knowledge graph covering the electronic product supply chain, it includes data such as different suppliers, part information, production stages, and market demands from multiple sources. These data employ different terminologies and standards to describe the same concepts. Supplier A may describe a component as an "aluminum bracket", while Supplier B may describe the same component as an "aluminum support frame". Through semantic mapping, these two descriptions are mapped to a unified semantic model, ensuring consistent descriptions of the components in the knowledge graph and establishing their associations. In the electronic product supply chain, different stages may use different ontologies or knowledge representation models to describe product specifications, production processes, quality standards, etc. Production stages in the supply chain use a specific set of terms and concepts to describe the manufacturing process and technical requirements, while sales stages use different terms. Through ontology fusion, these different ontologies are integrated to establish a common ontology representation model, ensuring consistent and interrelated descriptions of product manufacturing and sales stages in the knowledge graph.

5.4.2. Entity Fusion

Entity fusion refers to identifying the correspondence between descriptions of the same entity in different data sources and aligning them with the same entity. This includes resolving differences in entity names, eliminating multiple descriptions of the same entity, and associating dispersed entity information to ensure consistency of entities in the knowledge graph. For example, in the aviation industry, there are multiple similar entities, such as airlines, aerospace engineering organizations, aviation logistics service providers, and aviation maintenance service providers. These entities describe different aspects of the same industry, but they may differ in naming and description. In the process of constructing the ICKG, it is necessary to standardize entity names, unify naming formats, or use consistent naming conventions, such as unifying "aviation logistics service" and "aviation cargo transportation" into "aviation logistics". Next, text similarity algorithms are used to analyze the descriptions of these entities to determine their degree of similarity. Entities with high similarity in descriptions are identified and associated with the same entity, indicating that they refer to the same domain or service. Finally, integrate other attribute information about these entities, such as service scope, technical characteristics, customer base, etc., to ensure they are associated with the same entity. Such entity alignment and linking processes ensure the consistency of entities in relevant domains of the knowledge graph, providing a consistent and reliable entity information foundation for comprehensive analysis of the industrial chain. Table 3 below shows entity fusion between some similar industries when constructing the ICKG.

Table 3. Schematic representation of closely related industries.

Industry	Related Industry
Solar Cells	Wind Power Generation, Hydroelectric Power Generation
Medical Devices	Pharmaceutical Manufacturing, Medical Equipment Components
Artificial Intelligence (AI)	Machine Learning, Deep Learning
Catering Industry	Fast Food Chain, Bar, and Entertainment
E-commerce	Internet Finance, Online Payment
Environmental Technology	Waste Management, Renewable Energy
Aviation Industry	Aerospace Engineering, Air Logistics
Human Resources (HR)	Training and Development, Recruitment Services

6. Experiment

This section discusses the application of deep learning algorithms to entity recognition within industrial chains. Through deep learning models, the automatic identification and extraction of entity information relevant to specific industrial chains from text data are achieved, laying the foundation for constructing an ICKG.

6.1. Experimental Data and Experimental Environment

We utilized web crawling technology to collect various data sources related to industrial chains, including structured data from industries such as the Shenwan Industry Index, the Shenzhen Stock Exchange, and the Shanghai Stock Exchange, as well as unstructured data extracted from sources like encyclopedias, news, and annual reports. Our dataset contains structured information from 9300 companies, including fields such as comp_name, ts_code, chairman, manager, secretary, reg_capital, setup_date, province, city, website, email, office, employees, etc. Additionally, we obtained unstructured text data from these companies, including introductions, business scopes, main businesses, and company essentials, totaling 37,200 texts. We conducted experiments using the Python language and employed the BIO annotation method to label the positions of entity names such as companies and products in the text. In the BIO labeling method, 'B' is used to mark the beginning word of an entity, 'I' is used to mark words inside the entity, and 'O' is used to mark words that do not belong to any entity. We manually annotated 108,462 sentences from the crawled unstructured text, randomly selecting 80% as the training set, 10% as the validation set, and 10% as the test set.

The experimental environment utilized a computational server equipped with NVIDIA GeForce RTX 4090 and NVIDIA GeForce RTX 4060 GPUs sourced from NVIDIA Corporation, located in Santa Clara, CA, USA. TensorFlow 2.5.0, a deep learning framework, and the Python 3.8.17 programming language were used for entity extraction experiments.

In industrial chain entity recognition experiments, adjusting experimental parameters is aimed at optimizing model performance and training process efficiency. These parameters include the learning rate, number of iterations, maximum sequence length, and batch size. The learning rate controls the speed of parameter updates, and an appropriate learning rate can accelerate model convergence and improve performance. The choice of iteration number depends on factors such as dataset size, model complexity, and training time. Typically, increasing the number of epochs can enhance model performance but may also increase the risk of overfitting. The maximum sequence length limits the length of input sequences, helping to save computational resources and avoid inefficiencies in handling excessively long sequences. Batch size determines the number of training samples in each iteration. With the initial learning rate set to 2×10^{-5}, the maximum sequence length set to 10, and the batch size set to 16, by iteratively adjusting these parameters, the goal is to enhance the accuracy and training speed of the model in entity recognition tasks to achieve optimal results while avoiding resource waste and overfitting risk.

6.2. Deep Learning Method Selection and Model Evaluation Criteria

BERT, as a base model, possesses strong language representation capabilities and excels in natural language processing tasks, effectively addressing named entity recognition tasks. CRF and BiLSTM-CRF, as commonly used sequence labeling models, demonstrate excellent performance in named entity recognition tasks, effectively considering contextual information and entity relationships. By combining BERT with CRF or BiLSTM-CRF, one can fully leverage BERT's understanding of contextual nuances and the modeling capabilities of sequence labeling models to enhance the accuracy and robustness of entity extraction. This paper selects three models, namely BERT, BERT-CRF, and BERT-BiLSTM-CRF, to investigate the application effectiveness of deep learning algorithms in industrial chain named entity recognition tasks. Through multiple rounds of comparative experiments, a thorough evaluation of different models' performance in industrial chain named entity recognition is conducted. The selection and framework of entity extraction models are shown in Figure 5.

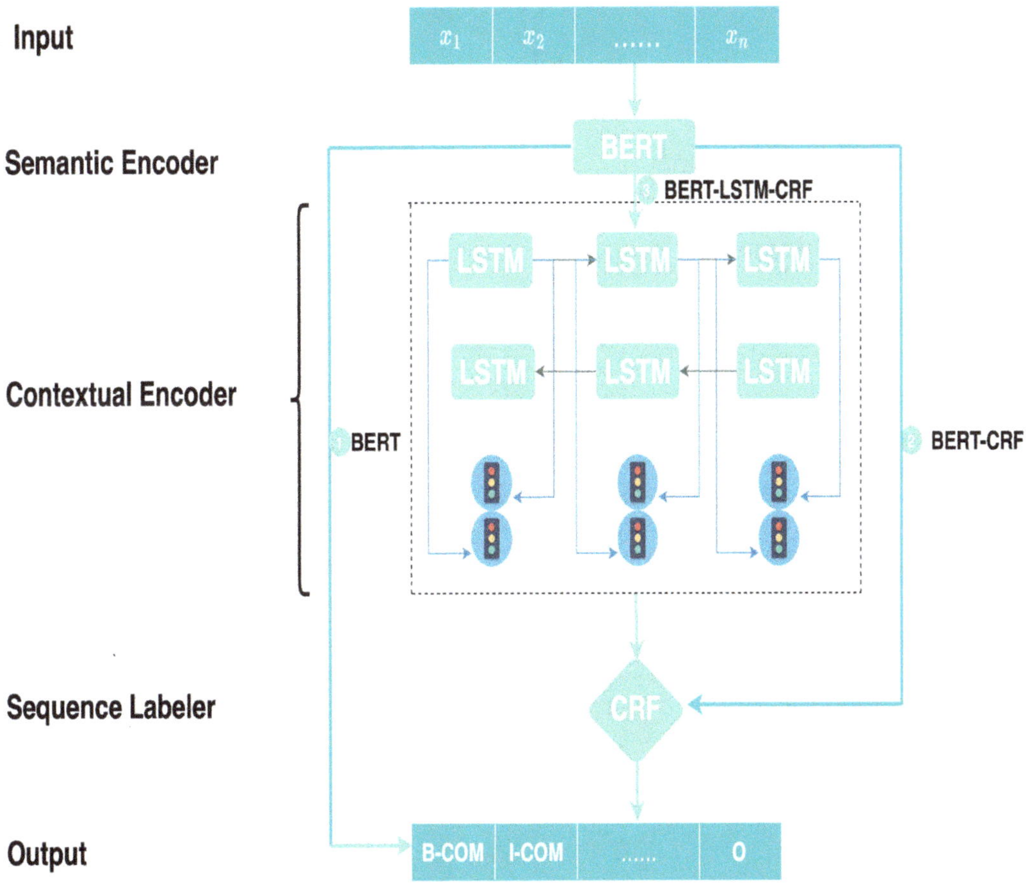

Figure 5. Model selection and framework.

This study selects macro-averaging as the evaluation metric for the industrial chain entity recognition experiments. Macro-averaging balances the influence of different categories by considering the performance of each category and averaging them. In this multi-classification problem, macro-averaging can independently evaluate the performance of each category, providing a better understanding of the performance of each category. The evaluation metrics include macro-average F1 score (Macro-F1), macro-average precision (Macro-P), and macro-average recall (Macro-R). Where Macro-P, Macro-R, and Macro-F1 are, respectively, the arithmetic averages of Precision (P), Recall (R), and F1-score ($F1$). The formulas for calculating P, R, and $F1$ are as follows (Equations (1)–(3)):

$$P = \frac{TP}{TP + FP} \quad (1)$$

$$R = \frac{TP}{TP + FN} \quad (2)$$

$$F1 = \frac{2 * R * P}{R + P} \quad (3)$$

Among them, TP refers to the number of samples that the model correctly identifies as positive examples, that is, the number of positive samples for which the entity recognition is correct. FP refers to the number of samples in which the model incorrectly identifies negative examples as positive examples, that is, the number of positive samples that the model misjudges. FN refers to the number of samples in which the model incorrectly identifies positive examples as negative examples, that is, the number of positive samples that the model misses.

6.3. Experimental Results and Discussion

This paper conducted comparative experiments among BERT, BERT-CRF, and BERT-BiLSTM-CRF and obtained the experimental results shown in Table 4 after multiple parameter adjustments. Based on the experimental results in the table, we can draw the following conclusions:

Using different learning rates, the performance of the BERT model does not vary significantly, but overall performance is good, with macro-F1 scores ranging from 0.9666 to 0.9695. macro-P and macro-R scores of the BERT model both remain at a high level. The BERT-CRF model, which combines BERT with CRF, performs significantly lower in the F1 score compared to the pure BERT model. The BERT-BiLSTM-CRF model further extends the BERT-CRF model by adding BiLSTM and fine-tuning the learning rate of CRF. This model achieves a macro-F1 score of 0.9710, an increase of 0.44% compared to the BERT model and 24.78% compared to the BERT-CRF model. However, there is a slight decrease in macro-P and macro-R compared to the pure BERT model, although they still remain at a high level.

Table 4. Experimental results of entity recognition for different models.

Model	Macro-F1	Macro-P	Macro-R	Learning Rate	Epoch	Maxlen	Batch_Size
BERT	0.9674	0.9735	0.9709	3×10^{-5}	3	10	16
	0.9695	0.9735	0.9715	4×10^{-5}	3	10	16
	0.9666	0.9693	0.9679	5×10^{-5}	3	10	16
BERT-CRF	0.7232	0.7658	0.8611	5×10^{-5} (bert), 3×10^{-3} (crf)	3	10	16
BERT-BiLSTM-CRF	0.9710	0.9680	0.9695	2×10^{-5} (bert), 3×10^{-3} (crf)	3	10	16
	0.9710	0.9671	0.9690	3×10^{-5} (bert), 3×10^{-3} (crf)	3	10	16

Overall, the BERT-BiLSTM-CRF model achieves the best performance, with an F1 score higher than the other two models, and it also performs well in terms of precision and recall, making it suitable for the entity recognition task of industrial chain naming addressed in this paper. In this model, BERT learns bidirectional contextual relationships between words to generate word-level contextual representations. BiLSTM has two directions of hidden states, one for reading sequences from left to right and the other for reading sequences from right to left, which enables capturing semantic information over longer distances.

CRF is a sequence labeling model that, based on the output of the BiLSTM layer, labels the entire sequence and considers dependencies between labels, thereby improving the accuracy of labeling.

The advantages of the BERT-BiLSTM-CRF model in the task of entity name recognition in the industrial chain mainly include the following points: First, because the industrial chain involves multiple fields and professional terms, the semantic representation learned by BERT during pre-training can better understand the terms and relationships in specific fields, thereby improving the accuracy of entity name recognition, especially when dealing with proprietary terms and abbreviations in the industrial chain. Secondly, BiLSTM can capture the influence of context on entity names, while BERT provides a more comprehensive understanding of context, further enhancing the precision of entity recognition. In addition, the CRF model globally models the labeled sequences, considering the dependency relationships between entity labels, thus improving consistency and accuracy, especially when dealing with complex entity relationships in the industrial chain. Finally, the BERT-BiLSTM-CRF model has strong versatility and generalization ability, adapting to entity name recognition tasks in different industrial chain scenarios and providing robust performance.

7. ICKG Instance Display

Through complex data processing and extraction work, a large-scale knowledge graph has been successfully established, with data stored in the graph database, Neo4j. This knowledge graph encompasses hundreds of thousands of entities and their relationships within the industrial chain and has been visualized. A partial display of the ICKG is shown in Figure 6.

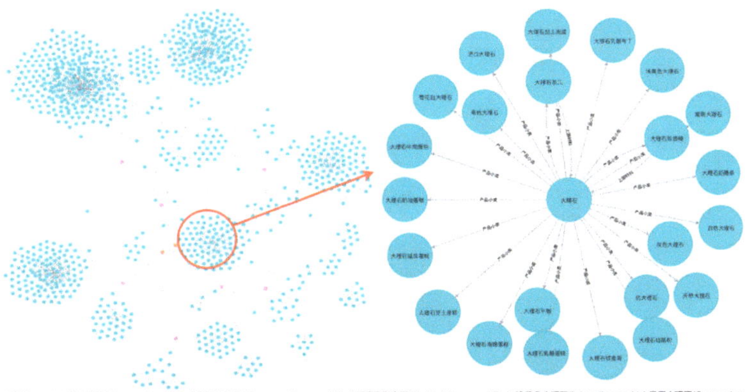

大理石(marble); 进口大理石(Imported marble); 大理石加工而成(Processed from marble); 大理石乳酪布丁(Marbled cheese pudding); 浅黄色大理石(light yellow marble);常用大理石(Commonly used marble);
大理石奶酪条(marble cheese sticks); 白色大理石(white marble); 天然大理石(natural marble); 大理石结晶粉(marble crystal powder); 大理石纹曲奇(Marbled Cookies); 大理石乳酪蛋糕(marble cheesecake);
大理石海绵蛋糕(Marble Sponge Cake); 大理石芝士蛋糕(Marble cheesecake); 大理石戚风蛋糕(Marble chiffon cake); 大理石奶油蛋糕(Marble Cream Cake); 大理石平板(marble slab); 仿大理石(imitation marble);
雪花白大理石(snowflake white marble); 高档大理石(High-grade marble); 大理石茶几(marble coffee table); 大理石垃圾桶(Marble trash can); 灰色大理石(gray marble); 大理石牛角面包(Marble croissant);
产品小类(product subcategory); 上游材料(upstream material).

Figure 6. Cross-domain knowledge graph (partial).

The query statement is entered in the graph database Neo4j, and the ICKG system queries the entity information through the semantic network built in the knowledge graph and visually displays the knowledge structure of this type. Figure 7 displays all the main products of China Chongqing Xinda Zheng Property Group Co., Ltd. Information about the main products can be used in various internal applications of the enterprise, such as marketing, product development, and supply chain management. Understanding a company's main products helps analyze its market position, competitive advantages, and product positioning, providing support for business decisions.

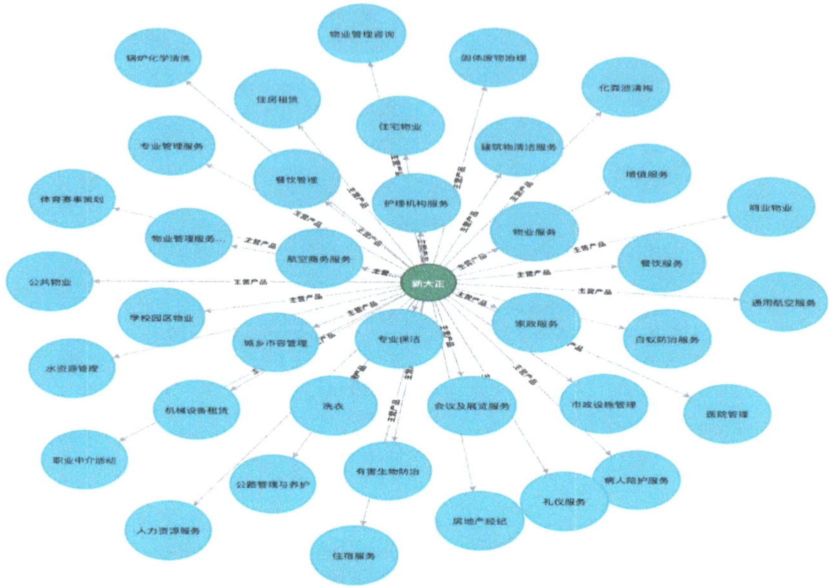

新大正(Xinda Zheng); 锅炉化学清洗(Boiler chemical cleaning); 物业管理咨询(Property management consulting); 固体废物治理(solid waste management); 化粪池清掏(Septic tank cleaning); 专业管理服务(Professional management services); 住房租贷(housing rental loan); 住宅物业(residential property); 建筑物清洁服务(building cleaning services); 增值服务(Value-added services); 体育赛事策划(Sports event planning); 餐饮管理(Catering management); 护理机构服务 (nursing facility services); 物业服务 (commercial service); 商业物业 (commercial property); 公共物业 (public property); 物业管理服务 (Property management services); 航空商务服务(Aviation business services); 餐饮服务(Catering Services); 水资源管理(water resources management); 学校园区物业 (School campus property); 城乡市容管理(Urban and rural city appearance management); 专业保洁(Professional cleaning); 家政服务(Housekeeping); 白蚁防治服务(Termite control services); 通用航空服务(General aviation services); 职业中介活动(Employment agency activities); 机械设备租赁(Machinery and equipment rental); 洗衣(Laundry); 会议及展览服务(Conference and exhibition services); 市政设施管理(Municipal facilities management); 医院管理(hospital management); 人力资源服务(Human resources services); 公路管理与养护(Highway management and maintenance); 有害生物防治(pest control); 住宿服务 (Accommodation services); 房地产经纪(Real estate brokerage); 礼仪服务(ceremonial service); 病人陪护服务(Patient escort service); 主营产品(core product)

Figure 7. ICKG query display.

8. Conclusions

This paper utilized both structured data from sources like the Shenwan Industry Index, Shenzhen Stock Exchange, Shanghai Stock Exchange, etc., and unstructured data from sources like encyclopedias, news articles, annual reports, etc., to construct a comprehensive dataset for the industrial chain. Through data processing and structured extraction techniques, we built a comprehensive industrial chain dataset. After analyzing the performance of various deep learning algorithms in industrial chain NER, we selected an entity recognition algorithm based on BERT-BiLSTM-CRF and rule-based relationship extraction for industrial chain knowledge extraction. Regarding graph generation and visualization, we constructed the framework as shown in the figure through node and relationship construction and stored the data in the Neo4j graph database, successfully creating a comprehensive ICKG. This knowledge graph provides strong support for cross-disciplinary applications, including knowledge retrieval, intelligent question answering, smart decision-making, intelligent marketing, and recommendations.

Despite constructing a full-scale ICKG and providing support for cross-disciplinary applications, there are still some shortcomings and areas for further improvement. The following aspects are considered for improvement in future work:

- Enhancing Precision: Further optimize the entity recognition algorithm and relationship extraction rules to improve the recall and precision of knowledge extraction. Enhance its generalization ability to adapt to entity and relationship extraction tasks in different contexts.
- Data Completeness and Updates: Ensure the completeness of knowledge graph data and regularly update it. Continuously collect the latest data and promptly incorporate it into the knowledge graph to maintain its timeliness and comprehensiveness.

- Optimization of Intelligent Application Functions: Further develop and optimize intelligent application functions based on the knowledge graph to enhance the intelligence level in areas such as knowledge retrieval, intelligent question answering, decision support, marketing, and recommendations.
- User Experience and Interface Optimization: Design user-friendly interfaces and interactive experiences to make it easier for users to access and utilize the information and functionalities provided by the knowledge graph.

Author Contributions: Conceptualization, Y.L. (Yue Li) and Y.L. (Yutian Lei); methodology, Y.L. (Yue Li), Y.L. (Yutian Lei) and Y.Y.; software, Y.L. (Yutian Lei) and Y.Y.; validation, Y.L. (Yutian Lei) and J.Z.; formal analysis, J.Z.; investigation, J.Z.; data curation, Y.L. (Yue Li) and Y.L. (Yutian Lei); writing—original draft preparation, Y.L. (Yutian Lei); writing—review and editing, Y.L. (Yue Li), Y.Y. and C.Y.; visualization, Y.L. (Yutian Lei); supervision, Y.L. (Yue Li). All authors have read and agreed to the published version of the manuscript.

Funding: This research was supported in part by the Natural Science Foundation of Shanghai (Grant No. 22ZR1400200) and the Fundamental Research Funds for the Central Universities (No. 2232023Y-01).

Data Availability Statement: The datasets presented in this article are not readily available because the data are part of an ongoing study.

Conflicts of Interest: The authors declare no conflicts of interest.

References

1. Lou, Q.; Xin, T.Y.; Song, J.Y. Application of DNA barcoding technology in the whole industrial chain of traditional Chinese medicine. *Acta Pharm. Sin.* **2020**, *12*, 1784–1791.
2. Lu, H.; Peng, J.; Lu, X. Do Factor Market Distortions and Carbon Dioxide Emissions Distort Energy Industry Chain Technical Efficiency? A Heterogeneous Stochastic Frontier Analysis. *Energies* **2022**, *15*, 6154. [CrossRef]
3. Yang, Y.; Tong, L.; Yin, S.; Liu, Y.; Wang, L.; Qiu, Y.; Ding, Y. Status and Challenges of Applications and Industry Chain Technologies of Hydrogen in the Context of Carbon Neutrality. *J. Clean. Prod.* **2022**, *376*, 134347. [CrossRef]
4. Song, H.; Lu, B.; Ye, C.; Li, J.; Zhu, Z.; Zheng, L. Fraud Vulnerability Quantitative Assessment of Wuchang Rice Industrial Chain in China Based on AHP-EWM and ANN Methods. *Food Res. Int.* **2021**, *140*, 109805. [CrossRef] [PubMed]
5. Haizhong, A.N.; Huajiao, L.I. Theory and Research Advances in Whole Industrial Chain of Strategic Mineral Resources. *Resour. Ind.* **2022**, *24*, 8.
6. Chen, X.; Jia, S.; Xiang, Y. A Review: Knowledge Reasoning over Knowledge Graph. *Expert Syst. Appl.* **2020**, *141*, 112948. [CrossRef]
7. Fu, D.; Zhou, S.; Shen, B.; Chen, Y. Enhancing Semantic Search of Crowdsourcing IT Services Using Knowledge Graph. In Proceedings of the International Conference on Software Engineering and Knowledge Engineering, Lisbon, Portugal, 10 July 2019.
8. Sarrafzadeh, B.; Vechtomova, O.; Jokic, V. Exploring Knowledge Graphs for Exploratory Search. In Proceedings of the 5th Information Interaction in Context Symposium, Regensburg, Germany, 26 August 2014.
9. Fernández, M.; Cantador, I.; López, V.; Vallet, D.; Castells, P.; Motta, E. Semantically Enhanced Information Retrieval: An Ontology-Based Approach. *J. Web. Semant.* **2011**, *9*, 434–452. [CrossRef]
10. Wang, Q.; Li, M.; Wang, X.; Parulian, N.; Han, G.; Ma, J.; Tu, J.; Lin, Y.; Zhang, R.H.; Liu, W.; et al. COVID-19 Literature Knowledge Graph Construction and Drug Repurposing Report Generation. In Proceedings of the 2021 Conference of the North American Chapter of the Association for Computational Linguistics: Human Language Technologies: Demonstrations, Online, 6–11 June 2021.
11. Yu, T.; Li, J.; Yu, Q.; Tian, Y.; Shun, X.; Xu, L.; Zhu, L.; Gao, H. Knowledge Graph for TCM Health Preservation: Design, Construction, and Applications. *Artif. Intell. Med.* **2017**, *77*, 48–52. [CrossRef] [PubMed]
12. Shi, L.; Li, S.; Yang, X.; Qi, J.; Pan, G.; Zhou, B. Semantic Health Knowledge Graph: Semantic Integration of Heterogeneous Medical Knowledge and Services. *BioMed Res. Int.* **2017**, *2017*, 1–12. [CrossRef] [PubMed]
13. Guo, Q.; Zhuang, F.; Qin, C.; Zhu, H.; Xie, X.; Xiong, H.; He, Q. A Survey on Knowledge Graph-Based Recommender Systems. *IEEE Trans. Knowl. Data Eng.* **2022**, *34*, 3549–3568. [CrossRef]
14. Wang, H.; Zhang, F.; Wang, J.; Zhao, M.; Li, W.; Xie, X.; Guo, M. RippleNet: Propagating User Preferences on the Knowledge Graph for Recommender Systems. In Proceedings of the 27th ACM International Conference on Information and Knowledge Management, Torino, Italy, 22–26 October 2018.
15. Wang, H.; Zhao, M.; Xie, X.; Li, W.; Guo, M. Knowledge Graph Convolutional Networks for Recommender Systems. In Proceedings of the World Wide Web Conference, San Francisco, CA, USA, 13–17 May 2019.
16. Tan, J.; Qiu, Q.; Guo, W.; Li, T. Research on the Construction of a Knowledge Graph and Knowledge Reasoning Model in the Field of Urban Traffic. *Sustainability* **2021**, *13*, 3191. [CrossRef]

17. Ahmed, U.; Srivastava, G.; Djenouri, Y.; Lin, J.C.W. Knowledge Graph Based Trajectory Outlier Detection in Sustainable Smart Cities. *Sustain. Cities Soc.* **2022**, *78*, 103580. [CrossRef]
18. Luettin, J.; Monka, S.; Henson, C.; Halilaj, L. A Survey on Knowledge Graph-Based Methods for Automated Driving. In Proceedings of the Knowledge Graphs and Semantic Web, Madrid, Spain, 21–23 November 2022.
19. Miao, R.; Zhang, X.; Yan, H.; Chen, C. A Dynamic Financial Knowledge Graph Based on Reinforcement Learning and Transfer Learning. In Proceedings of the 2019 IEEE International Conference on Big Data (Big Data), Los Angeles, CA, USA, 9–12 December 2019.
20. Zehra, S.; Mohsin, S.F.M.; Wasi, S.; Jami, S.I.; Siddiqui, M.S.; Syed, M.K.U.R.R. Financial Knowledge Graph Based Financial Report Query System. *IEEE Access* **2021**, *9*, 69766–69782. [CrossRef]
21. Yang, B.; Liao, Y. Research on Enterprise Risk Knowledge Graph Based on Multi-Source Data Fusion. *Neural Comput. Appl.* **2022**, *34*, 2569–2582. [CrossRef]
22. Gundlach, G.T.; Bolumole, Y.A.; Eltantawy, R.A.; Frankel, R. The Changing Landscape of Supply Chain Management, Marketing Channels of Distribution. *Logist. Purchasing. J. Bus. Ind. Mark.* **2006**, *21*, 428–438. [CrossRef]
23. Mao, D.; Wang, F.; Hao, Z.; Li, H. Credit Evaluation System Based on Blockchain for Multiple Stakeholders in the Food Supply Chain. *Int. J. Environ. Res. Public Health* **2018**, *15*, 1627. [CrossRef] [PubMed]
24. Agrawal, T.K.; Kumar, V.; Pal, R.; Wang, L.; Chen, Y. Blockchain-Based Framework for Supply Chain Traceability: A Case Example of Textile and Clothing Industry. *Comput. Ind. Eng.* **2021**, *154*, 107130. [CrossRef]
25. Nasar, Z.; Jaffry, S.W.; Malik, M.K. Named Entity Recognition and Relation Extraction: State-of-the-Art. *ACM Comput. Surv.* **2021**, *54*, 20:1–20:39. [CrossRef]
26. Avinadav, T.; Shamir, N. The Effect of Information Asymmetry on Ordering and Capacity Decisions in Supply Chains. *Eur. J. Oper. Res.* **2021**, *292*, 562–578. [CrossRef]
27. Peck, H. Reconciling Supply Chain Vulnerability, Risk and Supply Chain Management. *Int. J. Logist. Res. Appl.* **2006**, *9*, 127–142. [CrossRef]
28. Al-Moslmi, T.; Gallofré Ocaña, M.L.; Opdahl, A.; Veres, C. Named Entity Extraction for Knowledge Graphs: A Literature Overview. *IEEE Access* **2020**, *8*, 32862–32881. [CrossRef]
29. Sun, J.; Liu, Y.; Cui, J.; He, H. Deep Learning-Based Methods for Natural Hazard Named Entity Recognition. *Sci. Rep.* **2022**, *12*, 4598. [CrossRef] [PubMed]
30. Gallofré Ocaña, M.; Opdahl, A. Supporting Newsrooms with Journalistic Knowledge Graph Platforms: Current State and Future Directions. *Technologies* **2022**, *10*, 68. [CrossRef]
31. Evtimova-Gardar, M.; Mellouli, N. An Overview of Methods and Tools for Extraction of Knowledge for COVID-19 from Knowledge Graphs. In Proceedings of the Pattern Recognition and Artificial Intelligence, Paris, France, 1–3 June 2022.
32. Braşoveanu, A.M.P.; Andonie, R. Integrating Machine Learning Techniques in Semantic Fake News Detection. *Neural Process. Lett.* **2021**, *53*, 3055–3072. [CrossRef]
33. Shi, P.; Lin, J. Simple BERT Models for Relation Extraction and Semantic Role Labeling. *arXiv* **2019**, arXiv:1904.05255.
34. Stapley, B.J.; Benoit, G. Biobibliometrics: Information retrieval and visualization from co-occurrences of gene names in Medline abstracts. In Proceedings of the Biocomputing 2000, Honolulu, HI, USA, 4–9 January 2000.
35. Jenssen, T.K.; Lægreid, A.; Komorowski, J.; Hovig, E. A Literature Network of Human Genes for High-Throughput Analysis of Gene Expression. *Nat. Genet* **2001**, *28*, 21–28. [CrossRef] [PubMed]
36. Bunescu, R.; Ge, R.; Kate, R.J.; Marcotte, E.M.; Mooney, R.J.; Ramani, A.K.; Wong, Y.W. Comparative Experiments on Learning Information Extractors for Proteins and Their Interactions. *Artif. Intell. Med.* **2005**, *33*, 139–155. [CrossRef] [PubMed]
37. Raychaudhuri, S.; Chang, J.T.; Sutphin, P.D.; Altman, R.B. Associating Genes with Gene Ontology Codes Using a Maximum Entropy Analysis of Biomedical Literature. *Genome Res.* **2002**, *12*, 203–214. [CrossRef] [PubMed]
38. Leonard, J.E.; Colombe, J.B.; Levy, J.L. Finding Relevant References to Genes and Proteins in Medline Using a Bayesian Approach. *Bioinformatics* **2002**, *18*, 1515–1522. [CrossRef] [PubMed]
39. Choi, S.P. Extraction of Protein–Protein Interactions (PPIs) from the Literature by Deep Convolutional Neural Networks with Various Feature Embeddings. *J. Inf. Sci.* **2018**, *44*, 60–73. [CrossRef]
40. Zhao, Z.; Yang, Z.; Lin, H.; Wang, J.; Gao, S. A Protein-Protein Interaction Extraction Approach Based on Deep Neural Network. *IJDMB* **2016**, *15*, 145. [CrossRef]

electronics

MDPI

Article

Optimizing Network Service Continuity with Quality-Driven Resource Migration

Chaofan Chen [1,2,†], Yubo Song [1,2,*,†], Yu Jiang [1,2,†] and Mingming Zhang [3,†]

1 School of Cyber Science and Engineering, Southeast University, Nanjing 211151, China; 220215466@seu.edu.cn (C.C.); jiangyu@seu.edu.cn (Y.J.)
2 Purple Mountain Laboratories, Nanjing 211189, China
3 State Grid Jiangsu Electric Power Co., Ltd., Information & Telecommunication Branch, Nanjing 210024, China; zhangmms@hotmail.com
* Correspondence: songyubo@seu.edu.cn
† These authors contributed equally to this work.

Abstract: Despite advances in security technology, it is impractical to entirely prevent intrusion threats. Consequently, developing effective service migration strategies is crucial to maintaining the continuity of network services. Current service migration strategies initiate the migration process only upon detecting a loss of service functionality in the nodes, which increases the risk of service interruptions. Moreover, the migration decision-making process has not adequately accounted for the alignment between tasks and node resources, thereby amplifying the risk of system overload. To address these shortcomings, we introduce a Quality-Driven Resource Migration Strategy (QD-RMS). Specifically, QD-RMS initiates the migration process at an opportune moment, determined through an analysis of service quality. Subsequently, it employs a method combining Pareto optimality and the simulated annealing algorithm to identify the node most suitable for migration. This approach not only guarantees seamless service continuity but also ensures optimal resource distribution and load balancing. The experiments demonstrate that, in comparison with conventional migration strategies, QD-RMS achieves superior service quality and an approximate 20% increase in maximum task capacity. This substantiates the strategic superiority and technological advancement of the proposed strategy.

Keywords: service continuity; resource migration; Pareto optimality; load balancing

1. Introduction

As networking technologies rapidly advance, significant enhancements in network security have strengthened the defenses of network infrastructure against malicious intrusions. Nonetheless, the dynamic nature of cyber threats makes the complete evasion of intrusion risks impractical [1]. Even the most robust security measures may fall short in fully deterring hackers who employ increasingly complex tactics. The "WannaCry" ransomware incident serves as a pertinent example; it exploited system vulnerabilities, affecting vital services globally like hospitals and banks, and resulted in extensive service disruptions and data encryption despite stringent security. Hence, the advent of intrusion tolerance technology is pivotal, designed not merely to counter attacks but, more crucially, to ensure the ongoing operation of essential services during cyber incidents. This is vital for users, as the continuity and reliability of services profoundly impact their perception of the network system's performance [2,3]. In the realm of cybersecurity challenges, maintaining service continuity is central to users' assessment of network service quality.

Thus, the development of effective service migration strategies has become a subject of significant interest within the intrusion tolerance domain [4], garnering substantial attention and investigation from scholars worldwide. Wang et al. [5] proposed a polymorphic heterogeneous security architecture, which is grounded in an intrusion tolerance mechanism. This architecture permits the migration of services from one executor to another in the event of a system attack. Such a migration mechanism is instrumental in preserving system continuity and reliability, thereby bolstering the system's capabilities to tolerate network attacks. The efficacy of this method in delivering a high recovery rate has been validated through experiments, which also highlighted its advantages of quicker execution and reduced costs in link mapping. Kang et al. [6] introduced a primary-backup Virtual Network Function (VNF) placement model, predicated on an availability schedule. This model treats the service migration challenge as an integer linear programming problem, aiming primarily to optimize the least count of continuous available time slots across all service function chains. This objective inherently seeks to mitigate service disruptions attributable to node unavailability. Zhao et al. [7] introduced a Fault-Tolerant Redundant Path Service Migration (FRSM) approach, utilizing a sliding window-based model for pinpointing potential service migration paths. This method integrates re-submission and replication mechanisms to enhance fault tolerance. By opting for several redundant paths, it devises an edge service migration strategy, significantly bolstering the migration's reliability and efficiency. Ma et al. [8] introduced a Predictive, Reliability-Assured Service Migration Path Selection Method (PTSM), which integrates user movement trajectory prediction with the reliability needs of service migration to optimize migration paths. This integration aims to guarantee uninterrupted service and optimal performance. The PTSM method is particularly effective in minimizing service disruptions and upholding service quality.

In the domain of research and implementation concerning service migration strategies, two main obstacles are encountered. First, the majority of existing strategies are only triggered in the event of a node losing its service provision capability or when a specific metric surpasses a preset static threshold. This approach fails to adequately predict or rectify potential decreases in service quality, resulting in prolonged service interruptions and a notable degradation in user experience. Second, current research predominantly focuses on evaluating the volume of task loads on nodes to inform migration decisions, often neglecting the compatibility between tasks and node resources during the migration process. As a consequence, services may be moved to nodes that are close to or have exceeded their capacity, thereby increasing the likelihood of system overloads.

This article presents the Quality-Driven Resource Migration Strategy (QD-RMS), which focuses on a migration timing decision approach influenced by service quality and a node selection algorithm that prioritizes load balancing. QD-RMS utilizes a comprehensive Service Migration Index (SMI) for the accurate assessment of service migration requirements. By employing SMI for evaluation, QD-RMS strategically initiates migration to ensure uninterrupted service continuity. In terms of node selection after determining migration timing, QD-RMS combines Pareto optimality theory with a simulated annealing algorithm to select the most suitable node for migration. This methodology not only facilitates effective service migration but also optimizes resource allocation and achieves load balance, resulting in improved task support after migration and enhanced overall system performance. The contributions of this paper are as follows.

1. Quality-guided migration timing decision: QD-RMS introduces a Service Migration Index (SMI) for the holistic evaluation of node service quality, aiding in the prediction of migration propensities. This index amalgamates crucial indicators like the average distance between users and base stations, service throughput, and node resource utilization. Continual SMI monitoring allows QD-RMS to proactively discern the necessity for service migration, facilitating an immediate assessment of service status. Upon the SMI hitting or surpassing a dynamic threshold, the system interprets this as an indicator of deteriorating service quality, thereby initiating the migration process and adaptively recalibrating the threshold to align with current node conditions. If the SMI remains below this threshold, the service shifts into a dormant state, pending subsequent evaluation. This approach preemptively triggers migration to

avert significant service quality decline, effectively stabilizing service quality levels and curtailing both service downtime and the duration required for migration.

2. Optimize the load through Pareto optimality theory: QD-RMS starts by merging node resources and task loads to evaluate the load status of potential migration nodes, leading to the development of a multi-objective optimization model. This model, utilizing Pareto optimality theory, gauges the load quality of these nodes and is efficiently resolved through the simulated annealing algorithm, facilitating the identification of superior candidate nodes promptly. Distinct from conventional load balancing methods, QD-RMS accentuates the compatibility of resources between tasks and nodes, thereby circumventing the selection of nodes at the brink of resource saturation, minimizing overload risks, and fostering a more sophisticated load-balancing regime.
3. Effective experimental validation: Comprehensive empirical tests were carried out on QD-RMS to assess its effectiveness in real-world applications, particularly in terms of service quality and maximum task capacity at nodes. By simulating four different service requests on a virtual machine platform, we compared the performance of QD-RMS with that of conventional reference strategies in service migration, illustrating their service quality in comparative graphs. The results highlighted QD-RMS's significant advantage in maintaining service quality, evidenced by more stable service performance and smaller fluctuation ranges. Additionally, the load-balancing performance of QD-RMS was evaluated, with experimental data confirming that, under similar hardware configurations, QD-RMS improved the maximum task capacity by approximately 20% compared to traditional load-balancing algorithms.

2. Related Work

Service migration, driven by user mobility and the limited nature of server resources, is an unavoidable component within the realm of mobile intrusion tolerance. The selection of appropriate timing for service migration is crucial, as it directly influences the duration of service interruptions. Notably, the length of these interruptions significantly affects the user's experience of the service.

Traditionally, the decision to migrate services is triggered by monitoring the utilization rate of a system's static resources, initiating migration when this rate meets a predefined threshold [9]. Kulshrestha et al. [9] have refined this approach by introducing a three-parameter Exponential Weighted Moving Average (EWMA3) model, aimed at detecting overload situations in hosts within cloud data centers. Conversely, Yang et al. [10] developed a resource transaction model for determining the optimal timing for migration, albeit with the limitation of considering only bandwidth as the measure for migration thresholds, thus narrowing its applicability. These studies primarily focused on the static utilization rate of server resources. However, in distributed systems with constrained resources and stringent Quality of Service (QoS) demands, such as Mobile Edge Computing (MEC), relying solely on static thresholds for service migration is deemed inappropriate [11].

Beyond server load considerations, the dynamic nature of user mobility and request patterns also plays a pivotal role in service migration strategies. X. Chen et al. [12] emphasized the real-time monitoring of network conditions and user demands to dynamically initiate service migration, aiming to minimize latency and enhance service continuity. E. Bozkaya et al. [13] leveraged digital twin models to simulate user mobility and the MEC environment, facilitating dynamic predictions of service migration needs and timing. H. Wang et al. [14] adopted deep reinforcement learning to optimize the timing of service migration with a focus on reducing user access delays and network costs. This approach dynamically adapts to user mobility patterns and network status changes. Z. Liang [15] et al. explored user mobility support within the mobile edge computing context, employing an optimization-based method to dynamically determine the optimal timing for service migration based on user mobility trajectories and edge network resource status. MoDEMS [16] predicts user future locations and mobility patterns by analyzing mobility data, enabling the system to make proactive migration decisions to ensure service continuity and quality as users move to new geographical locations.

This body of research on service migration timing highlights the challenges posed by the high heterogeneity of mobile edge networks and the specificity of applications, making rapid service migration without compromising user experience a challenging endeavor.

In the domain of intrusion tolerance, service migration trust and security garner significant attention. The proximity of edge nodes to end-users in mobile intrusion-tolerant networks, coupled with the limited computational and storage resources available at edge servers, introduces higher security risks compared to traditional cloud computing. Edge nodes are vulnerable to network attacks, and the control of a service node by malicious attackers can lead to severe security threats such as data theft and privacy breaches. Yi Xu et al. [17] employed three-way decision theory in service migration strategies, enhancing decision-making flexibility and predictability by considering the necessity and timing of migration, thereby avoiding unreliable migration nodes. Le et al. [18] developed a trust score-based algorithm for migration node selection, combining EigenTrust and RLIoT reputation systems with dynamic distance algorithms to provide credible choices. Chunlin Li et al. [19] demonstrated how SDN architecture supports granular network management and security policy enforcement, offering real-time insights into network traffic and node behavior to indirectly improve trust management in migration nodes. An Du et al. [20] applied reinforcement learning to dynamically adjust service deployment in response to user mobility, balancing the trade-off between service migration response times and quality maintenance. PreGAN [21] aims to predict edge nodes likely to fail, facilitating preemptive service migration to minimize security vulnerabilities and data loss risks.

In addition to the "trust and security" concerns at the terminals and server levels, ensuring the "capability security" within edge networks emerges as a critical aspect. The inherently uneven distribution of tasks across the MEC system, driven by user mobility and task randomness, underscores the necessity for load balancing on edge network servers. This balancing act not only safeguards the servers' "capability security" but also forms a foundational element of service migration's overall security framework. Through the dispersion of task processing across devices, X. Dai et al. [22] have effectively alleviated the burden on edge servers, facilitating a more equitable allocation of resources. Moon et al. [23] introduced a novel approach by advocating for the subdivision of tasks into multiple subtasks for parallel processing across several servers. This strategy, aimed at load equilibrium, entails reallocating subtasks from overloaded to under- or adequately-loaded MECs, based on prevailing load disparities. Addressing the challenge of load balancing within the MEC from a novel angle, Zhao et al. [24] conceptualized it as a dual objective of minimizing energy consumption and reducing queue redundancy, subsequently applying the Lyapunov optimization technique as a resolution mechanism. Similarly, Liu et al. [25] ventured into the domain of game theory for load-balancing solutions, initially framing the issue as a population game model before introducing two evolutionary dynamics and protocol modification-based algorithms for load equilibrium. Song S and colleagues [26] refined the task offloading process to diverse edge nodes, ensuring cost-efficiency while averting the risk of overloading individual nodes, thereby promoting a harmonious distribution of workload.

The realm of intrusion-tolerant service migration research is rapidly expanding, yet it is not devoid of limitations in existing studies. Predominantly, the exploration into the timing of service migration has been marked by a narrow focus on singular factors, such as service node overload scenarios or the proximity between users and service nodes, neglecting the multifaceted nature of service quality indicators. Furthermore, the discourse on the security of service nodes within intrusion-tolerant services remains comparatively underexplored, especially against the backdrop of terminal security, with the applicability and scope of trust models in evaluating service nodes presenting certain constraints. Drawing from these observations, the discourse on intrusion-tolerant service migration has garnered extensive attention and undergone significant evolution in recent years. Nonetheless, there remains a pressing need for deeper inquiries into aspects of migration timing and node security. Anchored in the objectives of enhancing security and efficiency within intrusion-tolerant service migration, this paper aspires to align with and contribute to the vanguard of ongoing research trajectories in this field.

3. Preliminaries

3.1. Service Migration

Service migration refers to the process of transferring services from the original server to a new server within a different geographical region when users move beyond the service coverage or when server resources are insufficient to support the services. The process is shown in Figure 1. The goal of service migration is to ensure the uninterrupted operation of computing services for users during their movement. To achieve this, the following points must be addressed:

1. Service continuity: If a user moves to another location, the services associated with that user must remain available.
2. Service mobility: Services must be capable of being migrated to new servers when needed.
3. User state mobility: The data associated with user services must be moved along with the services.

The transfer of user context information is crucial during the service migration process, as it determines whether users can seamlessly continue using the current services. Context can be categorized into the following four types:

1. System context: This includes any information related to computing and communication systems.
2. User context: This refers to any context information associated with user characteristics.
3. Environmental context: This encompasses any context information related to the physical environment, excluding system and user context.
4. Temporal context: This defines any context information related to time.

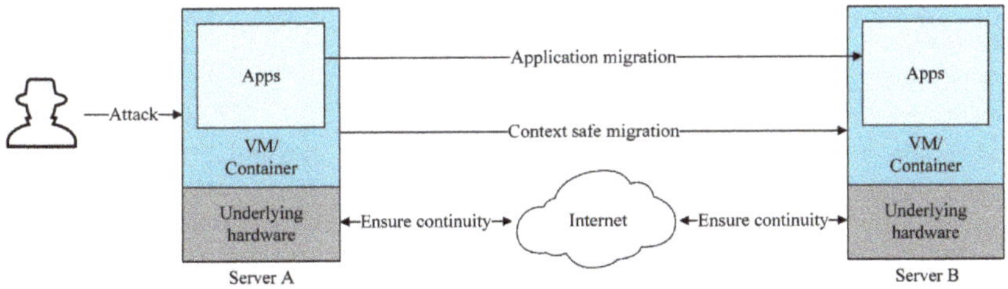

Figure 1. Schematic diagram of data transfer in service migration.

Furthermore, service migration presents security-related challenges, as different enterprises operate servers. If data are sent from a trusted source server to a destination server that is in a compromised state, it may potentially give rise to security issues. Hence, the security of the servers should also be taken into consideration during the service migration process.

3.2. Load Balancing

Load balancing is a cost-effective mechanism for expanding network equipment bandwidth, enhancing data throughput and processing capabilities, and bolstering network robustness, all without the need for additional hardware investment. Its central principle involves evenly distributing tasks across all servers to ensure the efficient operation of all devices. As a key apparatus for achieving this goal, load balancers disperse inbound requests across multiple servers, maintaining balanced loads and preventing network bottlenecks and single points of failure. Additionally, load balancing facilitates automatic failover, fault tolerance, and redundancy backup to ensure continuous system operation in emergencies. Common load balancing algorithms include the following:

1. Random Algorithm: Random algorithms distribute incoming requests by selecting servers at random. These methods do not account for the server's load or response metrics, relying solely on random selection.
2. Round Robin Algorithm: Requests are distributed to servers in a sequential, rotating order. Despite its simplicity, it does not account for performance differences between servers, which can lead to inefficient resource allocation.
3. Least Connection Algorithm: Requests are assigned based on the current number of connections to each server, aiming for balanced task distribution. However, this can still result in unbalanced resource utilization when server performance varies significantly.

3.3. Pareto Optimality

Pareto optimality, introduced by Italian economist Vilfredo Pareto, is a seminal concept in welfare economics and is predominantly applied in the context of multi-objective optimization problems. The core of Pareto optimality is to find a solution that facilitates the optimal trade-off among various conflicting objectives, such as cost, efficiency, and environmental impact. The set of solutions that achieves this optimality forms the "Pareto frontier" or the "Pareto boundary". At any point along this frontier, enhancing one objective necessitates compromising another.

This concept is grounded in the principle of Pareto efficiency. This principle posits that in a system with two objectives, labeled A and B, and under conditions of fixed total resources without the possibility of additional investments, enhancing one objective invariably leads to the diminution of the other. Pareto efficiency is the state in which no further improvements can be made to any objective without diminishing the others. In practical terms, Pareto optimality is achieved by formulating and adhering to specific constraints. Decision-makers can delineate the objective function and constraints to explore all viable solutions within the solution space, thereby identifying the set of Pareto optimal solutions.

4. Methodology

4.1. Active Migration Timing Based on Service Quality

In recent years, within the field of intrusion tolerance, studies have proposed the concept of "active migration" in service migration, as opposed to the earlier default "passive migration" (where migration occurs only when a service node is unable to continue providing service due to certain factors or when a user completely exits the coverage area of the service node). The comparative analysis of active versus passive migration is presented in Table 1. Active migration ensures a better service experience. Active migration refers to the process during which, to safeguard user service experience, decisions on service migration are made based on operational factors such as the load on service nodes, the distance between users and service nodes, service quality, etc. This occurs while the service node remains in normal operation; thus, it is termed as active migration.

Table 1. Comparison between active migration and passive migration.

	Active Migration	Passive Migration
Service node status during migration	Running	Suspended
Factors affecting the timing of migration	Quality of users and status of service node	Availability of services
Purpose of migration	Ensure high-quality services	Ensure continuous services

This paper introduces a Quality-Driven Resource Migration Strategy, rooted in the concept of active migration, which significantly enhances the intrusion tolerance mechanism by enabling migration through anticipatory resource management and optimizing the load on network resources. This strategy not only minimizes service disruptions caused by migration but also ensures service continuity and security through rapid resource reorganization in response to network security threats, thereby strengthening the system's self-protective capabilities following an intrusion.

Following a review of existing research, it is evident that current studies on active migration predominantly determine migration timing based on the resource utilization of service nodes or user locations [9], often overlooking the service quality of these nodes. However, significantly compromised service quality, resulting from various factors, can severely impact the user experience. Therefore, QD-RMS recognizes service quality as a critical metric for determining the timing of active migration and initially introduces a method for this determination in this section.

4.1.1. Service Migration Index

In order to quantify the migration trend of services, the Service Migration Index (SMI) is introduced, as shown in Equation (1):

$$SMI = \frac{D \cdot Q}{f(R)} \tag{1}$$

where D is the average distance between all session users and the service node, Q is the total throughput of all session instances, and R is the resource utilization of the service node. Since resource utilization rates do not necessarily have an inverse proportional relationship with the SMI, Equation (1) employs a function $f(R)$ in the denominator. The function $f(R)$ illustrates that the impact of resource utilization rates on the Service Migration Index decreases first and then increases, with a peak value at 70%. This implies that when the resource utilization rate reaches 70%, the service node is in an optimal state in terms of resource utilization for the Service Migration Index. We can efficiently calculate $D, Q, R,$ and $f(R)$ as follows.

$$D = \frac{\sum_{i=1}^{n} d_i}{n} \tag{2}$$

$$Q = \sum_{i=1}^{n} q_i \tag{3}$$

$$R = \frac{W_1 \cdot r_1^{norm} + W_2 \cdot r_2^{norm} + W_3 \cdot r_3^{norm} + W_4 \cdot r_4^{norm}}{\sum_{j=1}^{4} W_j} \tag{4}$$

$$f(R) = -50R^2 + 50R \tag{5}$$

where d_i is the distance between user i and the service node; q_i is the throughput of a particular session instance i; n is the total number of users; and W_i and r_i^{norm} represent the weight and the normalized utilization rate of a specific resource i, respectively.

Due to varying degrees of resource requirements by different applications running on service nodes, it is necessary to assign different weights to various resources based on the type of application. For instance, in Internet of Things (IoT) networks, an intelligent metering application aggregating utility meter readings may have a higher weight assigned to disk storage resources, whereas a high-definition video streaming application may prioritize network resources for enhanced defense mechanisms. Furthermore, in environments with multiple types of resources, each resource may exhibit distinct scales and units. Standardization ensures that when resources are allocated, weighting factors are applied appropriately according to application requirements, thereby reducing scale differences among resources. Consequently, the efficiency of resource utilization is evaluated through standardized and normalized metrics. For instance, CPU utilization can be described in millions of instructions per second (MIPS), memory utilization in megabytes (MB), network bandwidth utilization in megabits per second (Mbps), and disk utilization in gigabytes (GB). Resource utilization is standardized so that all metrics, such as CPU, memory, disk, and network bandwidth utilization rates, are represented on a uniform scale ranging from 0 to 100%. The r_i^{norm} of a specific resources i can be determined by employing Equation (6).

$$r_i^{norm} = \frac{r_i - r_{min}}{r_{max} - r_{min}} \tag{6}$$

where r_i denotes the utilization rate of a specific resource i, while r_{max} and r_{min} represent the maximum and minimum utilization rates observed across all resources, respectively.

4.1.2. Service Monitoring

The concept of the Service Migration Index was introduced in the preceding text. To calculate the Service Migration Index, the monitoring of service programs is necessary, including measuring metrics such as throughput and resource utilization rates. The combination of Prometheus and exporters is considered for monitoring service programs. The metrics and methods for data collection are encapsulated in Table 2.

Table 2. The metrics and methods for data collection.

Data	Collection Method	Collection Cycle
Throughput (queries_per_second)	Exposing exporter	1 (s)
CPU Utilization (node_cpu_seconds_total)	Exposing exporter	1 (s)
Memory Utilization (node_memory_MemTotal_bytes)	Exposing exporter	1 (s)
Storage Utilization (node_disk_io_time_second)	Exposing exporter	1 (s)
Network Activity (node_netstat_Tcp_(Active | Passive)Opens)	Exposing exporter	1 (s)
Average user session distance	Provided by base station	Determined by base station

Prometheus is a service monitoring software that encompasses four common metric types:

1. Counter: An incrementing counter used for tracking request counts, task completion counts, and similar metrics.
2. Gauge: A metric that can take on arbitrary values, suitable for metrics like CPU utilization, memory usage, and other numerical data.
3. Histogram: Categorizes a set of observations into multiple bins and exposes the number of bins and the respective observation value ranges.
4. Summary: An extension of Histogram that aggregates data (sums, counts) and provides metrics like mean and sample standard deviation.

Exporter is a tool designed to export metric data from existing applications or systems. Exporter is often an essential component in Prometheus monitoring systems as it feeds monitoring data to Prometheus. Common exporters include the following:

1. Node Exporter: For Linux/Unix systems, providing data on CPU, disk, network, memory, and more.
2. Blackbox Exporter: For probing network ports, HTTP, DNS, ICMP, and other network services to assess service statuses.
3. Redis Exporter: For monitoring the performance of Redis databases and exporting metric data to Prometheus.

The operational principle of Prometheus and exporters involves each exporter exposing an HTTP interface to Prometheus. Periodically, Prometheus calls the metrics data interface provided by the exporter to retrieve data. The exporter gathers data from the target system and transforms it into a format supported by Prometheus. Due to its independent process nature, the exporter can seamlessly integrate with any application or system. Hence, it is feasible to deploy the required exporter for monitoring service programs on individual service nodes via Kubernetes, deploy Prometheus on a management platform, and establish connections with the exporters on the service nodes, thus enabling the monitoring of service programs on each node, as illustrated in Figure 2.

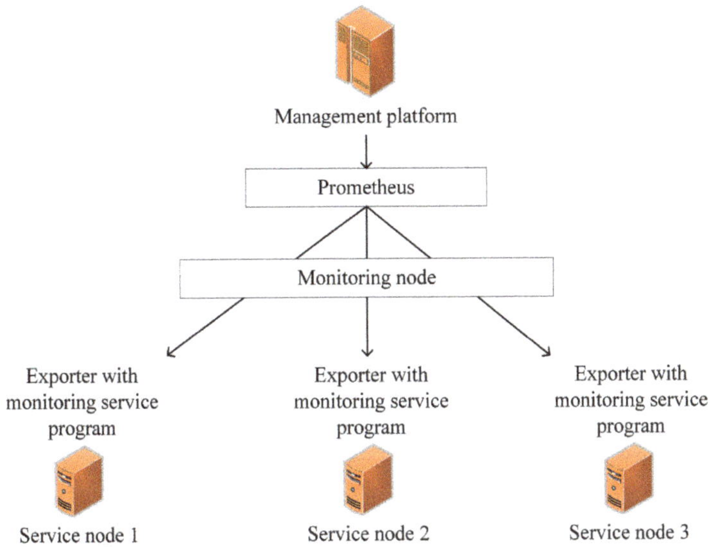

Figure 2. Service monitoring method.

4.1.3. Active Migration Process

Initiating service migration prematurely may result in the underutilization of the host's resources. Conversely, delayed migration can adversely affect user experience. Thus, optimal timing for service migration hinges on setting an appropriate migration threshold; migration should be triggered when the Service Migration Index hits this threshold. This section introduces a proactive migration strategy guided by the Service Migration Index and migration threshold, determining the optimal juncture for transferring service operations. This strategy encompasses three phases: index monitoring, service migration, and threshold updating. The detailed procedure is depicted in Figure 3.

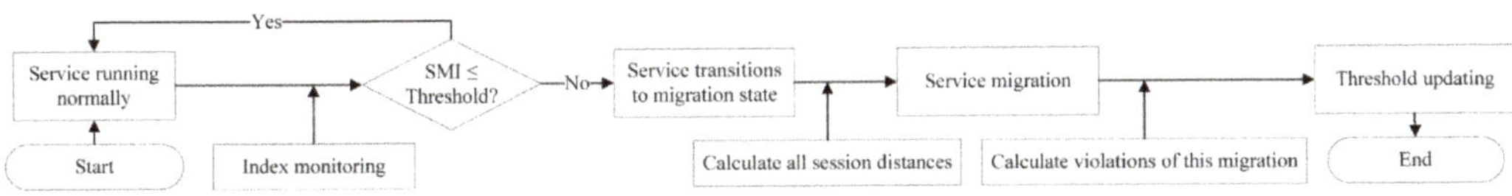

Figure 3. Active migration process.

1. Index Monitoring Module: This module monitors the status of applications on service nodes using monitoring software. It calculates the Service Migration Index SMI in real-time based on relevant parameters and compares it with the migration threshold to determine the migration trend for the service. The primary objective of the monitoring program is to monitor and compute parameters. As shown in Algorithm 1, this module calculates the real-time SMI by continuously collecting data on the current service's resource utilization, the average distance of all session users, and the total throughput of all session instances Q. If the SMI is less than the set threshold (SMI-T) for the current round, the system will sleep for a period before resuming the process. If the SMI is greater than or equal to the SMI-T threshold, the service status is changed to migration mode, the loop is terminated, and the service migration module is invoked.

Algorithm 1 Index monitoring

Input: Application APP, Resource weight W, Threshold $SMI\text{-}T$
Output: Application state app_status
$app\_status \leftarrow normal$
while $app\_status == normal$ **do**
$f(R) \leftarrow calculate\_f(R)(APP, W)$
$D \leftarrow calculate\_D(APP)$
$Q \leftarrow calculate\_Q(APP)$
$SMI \leftarrow calculate\_SMI(f(R), D, Q)$
if $SMI < SMI\text{-}T$ **then**
Wait some time
else
$app\_status \leftarrow migration\_trend$ /*Application enters migration state*/
end if
end while
run Service migration
return app_status

2. Service Migration Module: Initially, all session instances within the service are scanned and sorted based on the distance of each user from the nodes, and users are sequentially moved to a migration queue for migrating instances starting with users farthest from the nodes. This process continues until the SMI drops below the migration threshold, at which point migration stops. During this process, violations by migrating users are monitored and recorded. The service migration program primarily selects session instances for migration based on the SMI. It iterates through all current session instances, calculates the distance of each user from the service nodes, adds this information to a distance queue, and then proceeds to migrate users in order of their distance from the service nodes until the SMI falls below the set threshold ($SMI\text{-}T$), at which point the loop stops, and the threshold update module is called. Algorithm 2 demonstrates the procedure of a service migration.

Algorithm 2 Service migration

Input: Application APP, Service migration index SMI
Output: otal number of service violations $sla\_violations\_count$
while $SMI \geq SMI\text{-}T$ **do**
for all $instance$ **do**
$Distance[] \leftarrow [d[instance_1] \ldots d[instance_n]]$
Sort $Distance[]$
$MI \leftarrow \arg\max(d[instance_i])$
migration MI
$max.sla\_violations \leftarrow calculate\_sla(MI)$ /* Calculate the maximum number of violation incidents about MI*/
if $max.sla\_violations$ **then**
$sla\_violations\_count+ = max.sla\_violations$
end if
end for
end while
run Threshold updating
return $sla\_violations\_count$

3. Threshold Updating Module: This module compares the product of distance and average waiting delay with a predefined base value to evaluate the reasonableness of the threshold. A violation value of 0 indicates an appropriately set threshold for migration in the current context, and a slight random increase in the threshold can enhance the utilization of service nodes. If the violation value is greater than 0, it

signifies that the threshold set is too high, causing multiple violations by the time the SMI reaches the threshold. In such cases, a small random decrease in the threshold is necessary. The threshold update program first calculates the current migration round for the service. If the migration rounds are relatively low, such as equal to or less than 5, the $SMI\text{-}T$ is randomly adjusted based on violations, with the adjustment value correlated to the violation severity. For higher migration rounds, the module takes the $SMI\text{-}T$ and average waiting delay into account, using the method of least squares to fit a function. The computation determines the maximum value of the independent variable for which the fitted function equals 0, providing a new $SMI\text{-}T$ value. The threshold update strategy is shown in Algorithm 3.

Algorithm 3 Threshold updating

Input: Application APP, Distance D, Average waiting delay $delay$, Migration round $migration\_round$, Total number of service violations $sla\_violations\_count$
Output: updated threshold $SMI\text{-}T$
  if $migration\_round \leq 5$ **then**
    if $sla\_violations\_count == 0$ **then**
      $SMI\text{-}T$ increase small random number
    else
      $SMI\text{-}T$ descend small random number
    end if
  else
    $f(x) \leftarrow polyfit(D, delay)$ /*Using least squares method for function fitting*/
  end if
  $X \leftarrow \arg\max_{f(x)==0} x$ /*Calculating the maximum value of the independent variable when the fitted function f equals 0*/
  $SMI\text{-}T \leftarrow X$
  return $SMI\text{-}T$

4.2. Node Selection Algorithm Based on Load Balancing

Following the determination of the need for migration as outlined in Section 4.1, the ensuing critical task is to strategically select the optimal target node to manage the migration. In this section, we present a migration node selection algorithm designed to enhance migration decisions through load balancing, aiming to improve system performance and maintain stability across the network. The essence of load balancing is to evenly distribute various tasks across each server in the network as much as possible, allowing these servers to share the workload and enabling all network devices to operate efficiently. Neglecting server loads during the migration process may result in some servers bearing a heavy burden of tasks while others remain idle. This imbalance can lead to overloaded servers or even server crashes, along with the wastage of resources on many idle servers. Therefore, when allocating tasks to servers, it is essential to strive for a balanced distribution, ensuring that the load on each server is close to equilibrium, thus maximizing the utilization of the computational and storage resources provided by the servers.

Figure 4 illustrates an uneven load distribution within a service area. From the depicted load states in the figure, it is evident that the load distribution across the servers is uneven. For instance, servers S_2, S_4, and S_6 are already experiencing high levels of load, whereas S_1 and S_5 remain at relatively low load levels. As analyzed earlier, an uneven load distribution significantly decreases the operational efficiency of servers and results in wastage of computational and storage resources.

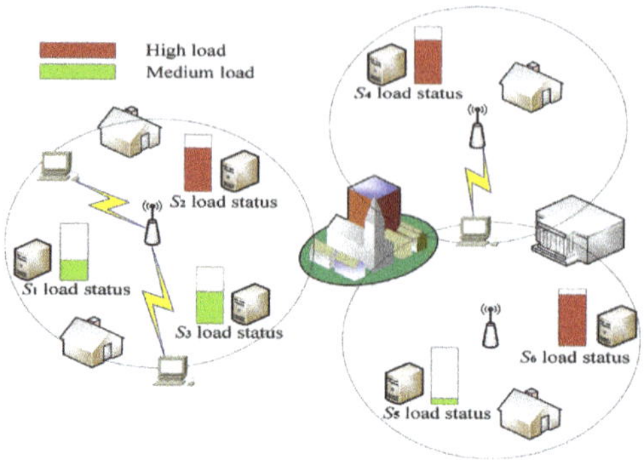

Figure 4. Imbalanced load distribution.

Figure 5 depicts a schematic diagram illustrating the load status at each server after load-balancing adjustments. By appropriately distributing tasks to balance the workload among servers, load balancing aims to enhance the operational efficiency among servers.

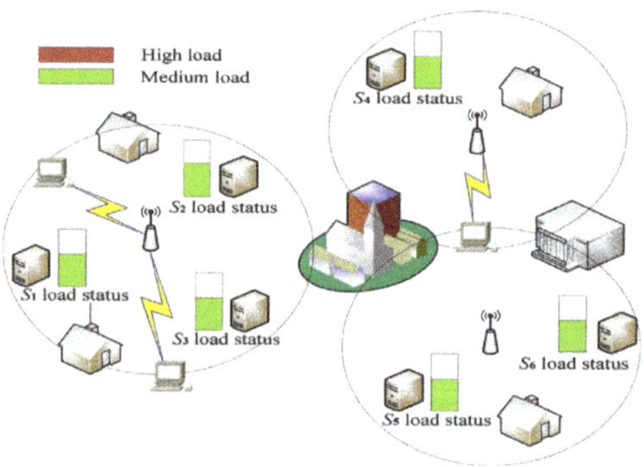

Figure 5. Balanced load distribution.

Currently, there has been extensive research in the field of load balancing. Classic load-balancing approaches are implemented using random algorithm, round-robin scheduling, and least-connection algorithm. Additionally, there are new explorations into load-balancing issues. For example, P. Zhao et al. [24] initially framed load balancing in MEC (Multi-access Edge Computing) as a problem of minimizing energy consumption and queue redundancy. Then, they applied Lyapunov algorithms to solve such optimization problems. L. Liu et al. [27] considered forcing an overloaded server to randomly select two servers from a group of adjacent servers and then unload to the one with the smallest load. However, this approach leads to redirecting a large number of tasks to originally lightly loaded servers, causing them to become overloaded, thus failing to address the issue of load imbalance. Abedin et al. [28] used game theory to solve load-balancing problems by formulating the problem of minimizing costs as a transportation problem and employing the Vogel approximation method to compute the optimal solution. Similarly, D. Liu et al. [25] considered introducing game theory to solve load-balancing problems. They initially formulated the load-balancing problem as a population game model and proposed two load-balancing algorithms based on evolutionary dynamics and modified protocols.

However, the aforementioned studies mainly focus on balancing the number of tasks among servers, neglecting a consideration of the sizes of tasks themselves. Assuming that the computational resource requirements for Task A are several times greater than Task B, treating Tasks A and B as equivalent tasks and allocating server resources based solely on task quantity may not fully utilize server resources. Therefore, this section further advances the existing load-balancing algorithms by incorporating considerations for matching task resource demands with server resource capacities, proposing a migration node selection algorithm based on load balancing to more effectively utilize the computational resources of service nodes.

4.2.1. Resource-Based Load Balancing

Considering the existence of a cluster of n servers $S = (S_1, S_2, S_3, \ldots, S_n)$, for a server S_i, its total resource content is a resource vector R_i^{init}, as shown in Equation (7):

$$R_i^{init} = (C, M, H, B) \tag{7}$$

where C, M, H, and B represent the CPU, memory, disk, and network bandwidth resource, respectively. Additionally, the vector of remaining available resources at the current moment t is the following:

$$R_i^t = (C_t, M_t, H_t, B_t) \tag{8}$$

where C_t, M_t, H_t, and B_t represent the remaining available resources of the CPU, memory, disk, and network bandwidth resource at the current moment t, respectively.

A closer ratio of R_i^{init} to R_i^t to ω $(0 < \omega < 1)$ suggests a higher level of resource utilization equality. This indicates that the resources are being used more efficiently and effectively. When the two resource vectors are not proportional, this indicates a deviation from the optimal utilization of resources. τ represents the cosine similarity between two resource vectors, serving to quantify the degree of deviation in resource utilization.

$$\tau = \cos\left(R_i^t, R_i^{init}\right) \tag{9}$$

If the allocated tasks can correct the deviation in resource utilization rate, it can be considered as beneficial for the load balancing of server resources.

Let the resource vector required for the user's task at time t be denoted as D_i^t. The remaining resource vector after accepting the task $\dot{R}_i^t$ can be calculated using Equation (10). We can then determine the deviation in resource utilization following the acceptance of task $\dot{\tau}$ using Equation (11).

$$\dot{R}_i^t = R_i^t - D_i^t \tag{10}$$

$$\dot{\tau} = \cos\left(\dot{R}_i^t, R_i^{init}\right) \tag{11}$$

If $\sigma = \dot{\tau} - \tau > 0$, it indicates that the task can contribute to improving the balance of resource utilization in the server.

4.2.2. Task-Based Load Balancing

For the server S_i, the vector of total resource content and remaining available resources at the current moment t is denoted by Equations (7) and (8). The load level on each resource can be calculated using the following equations:

$$LB_C = \frac{C_t}{C} \tag{12}$$

$$LB_M = \frac{M_t}{M} \tag{13}$$

$$LB_H = \frac{H_t}{H} \tag{14}$$

$$LB_B = \frac{B_t}{B} \tag{15}$$

where LB_C, LB_M, LB_H, and LB_B represent the load level on CPU, memory, disk, and network bandwidth resource, respectively.

Furthermore, ω is the load level of the server S_i, which can be calculated using Equation (16). The average load on the server cluster $\bar{\omega}$ is given by Equation (17).

$$\omega = \frac{LB_C + LB_M + LB_H + LB_B}{4} \tag{16}$$

$$\bar{\omega} = \frac{\sum_{i=1}^{n} \omega_i}{n} \tag{17}$$

Finally, the variance value of the average load on the server cluster $\dot{\omega}$ can be calculated by Equation (18), which reflects the load balancing of tasks undertaken by individual servers in the server cluster.

$$\dot{\omega} = \sum_{i=1}^{n} (\omega_i - \bar{\omega})^2 \tag{18}$$

4.2.3. Migration Node Selection Algorithm Based on Task-Resource Matching

The preceding two subsections analyzed the balance of server resources and the load balancing of task quantities across servers. Therefore, the consideration of load balancing on nodes in the candidate server pool during task migration can be transformed into optimization problems concerning the aforementioned two metrics. This issue fundamentally constitutes a multi-objective optimization problem. Due to the heterogeneity of user devices and the diversity of user tasks, optimizing one metric inevitably impacts another. Introducing Pareto optimality theory measures superior load balancing solution nodes. The concept of Pareto optimality refers to a state of resource allocation where modifying the allocation status does not compromise any objective function, while benefiting at least one objective function. If no further allocation changes can be made in this manner, the solution is considered one of the Pareto optimal solutions. Thus, the consideration of load balancing aims to achieve Pareto optimal status for the two aforementioned metrics. However, given the need for service continuity in the data center, excessive time spent seeking Pareto optimal solutions may lead to a misplaced emphasis, thereby compromising the original objective of efficient and high-quality migrations. Hence, in this scenario, considerations should be made regarding the magnitude of service nodes, delineating different scenarios. When the number of candidate nodes does not exceed a specific threshold (subject to real-world conditions), comprehensive screening is conducted, wherein each node undergoes Pareto adjustments to find the optimal solution.

Considering that the search latency of Algorithm 4 would become unmanageable with a large number of nodes, the adoption of Algorithm 5 with a simulated annealing approach is contemplated for expedited exploration, aiming to identify a set of superior solutions within an acceptable timeframe.

Algorithm 4 Comprehensive screening of Pareto optimal nodes

Input: Server nodes ID, User demand resource vector
Output: Set of servers that achieves Pareto optimality μ

```
for i ∈ n do
    Calculate the resource balance degree τ̇ − τ after server i accepts the task
    Calculate the load balancing degree ω̇ after server i accepts the task
end for
for i ∈ n do
    for y ∈ n do
        if (τ̇_y ≥ τ̇_i and ω̇_y ≥ ω̇_i) and (τ̇_y ≥ τ̇_i or ω̇_y ≥ ω̇_i) then
            Replace node i with node y
            Record the serial number of node i
        end if
    end for
    σ ← σ ∪ y
    Delete all recorded nodes from n
end for
```

Algorithm 5 Simulated annealing searches for Pareto optimal nodes

Input: Serialized server nodes ID, User demand resource vector
Output: Set of servers that achieves Pareto optimality σ
  for $i \in n$ **do**
    Calculate the resource balance degree $\dot{\tau} - \tau$ after server i accepts the task
    Calculate the load balancing degree $\dot{\omega}$ after server i accepts the task
    Perform range perturbation $Rand(i \pm \epsilon)$ to generate new solutions
    Calculate the degree of equilibrium
    if $new > old$ **then**
      Accept and record new optimal
    else
      Accept with a certain probability according to metropolis guidelines
    end if
    Iterate for multiple times
    Terminate gradually according to annealing temperature
  end for

5. Evaluation

5.1. Active Migration Based on Service Quality

In our research, we evaluated passive and active migration strategies across four service program types. The outcomes for the passive migration algorithm are depicted in Figure 6, with the experiment's duration plotted on the x-axis in seconds. The left y-axis indicates the number of request sessions, represented by blue bars in the graph. The right y-axis calculates the product of average distance D and average request waiting time AWT, in milliseconds, offering a composite measure of spatial and temporal efficiency in service delivery. This product, $D \times AWT$, acts as a service quality index SQ, where the distance D reflects the spatial component related to transmission delay.

The red line in the figure denotes the benchmark for desirable service quality, preset in this experiment. In contrast, the green curve shows the actual performance of the service program. The threshold represented by the red line is adaptable, allowing for customization based on various operational scenarios and requirements. For this experiment, the threshold was set at 50 ms, indicating a higher standard of service quality. Any segment of the green curve surpassing the red line signals a period when the service quality dips below the established threshold.

Passive migration is initiated when the resources for a service program are depleted or when users exit the service area, rendering continued service impossible. Consequently, services may remain active but suffer from diminished quality. As demonstrated in Figure 6, for matrix calculation, video service, and website service, the green curve, indicative of service demand, escalates swiftly with increasing service requests. When session numbers escalate to a certain threshold, the latency, represented by the green curve, substantially exceeds the established benchmark for superior service quality, subjecting users to excessive delays and a substandard service experience. Notably, in game service, approaching 150 session requests triggers passive migration due to resource depletion at the node. This leads to the migration of about half the session processes from the node, causing a decline in the green curve to below the threshold, which corresponds to an enhancement in service quality. The analysis of passive migration experiments illustrates the challenge in selecting the optimal timing for passive migration, crucial for maintaining service quality at edge nodes across various scenarios.

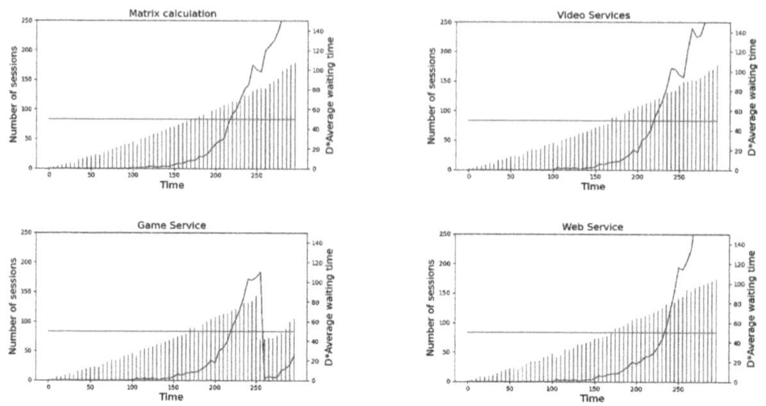

Figure 6. Results of passive transfer experiment.

Figure 7 presents the experimental results of proactive migration based on static resource utilization rates. The decision to migrate is contingent upon reaching a predetermined threshold of resource utilization at the service node, meaning that migration occurs when the node's resource utilization hits this predefined limit.

The experimental findings indicate that, compared to passive migration, proactive migration based on static resource utilization can, to some extent, ensure a higher quality of service. For instance, in the experiment involving matrix calculation, migration was initiated once the session count hit 100, effectively reducing latency to below the baseline. However, the performance in video and web service applications was less than ideal. In the video service scenario, despite the latency significantly exceeding the baseline, migration was not executed because the resource utilization had not met the established threshold. A similar situation occurred with the web service application, where migration was delayed until the session count neared 150, reaching the resource utilization ceiling, by which point the latency had already significantly exceeded the baseline, indicating severely compromised service quality. Conversely, in the game service, migration was triggered even though the actual latency had not yet reached the baseline, leading to the underutilization of the service node's resources.

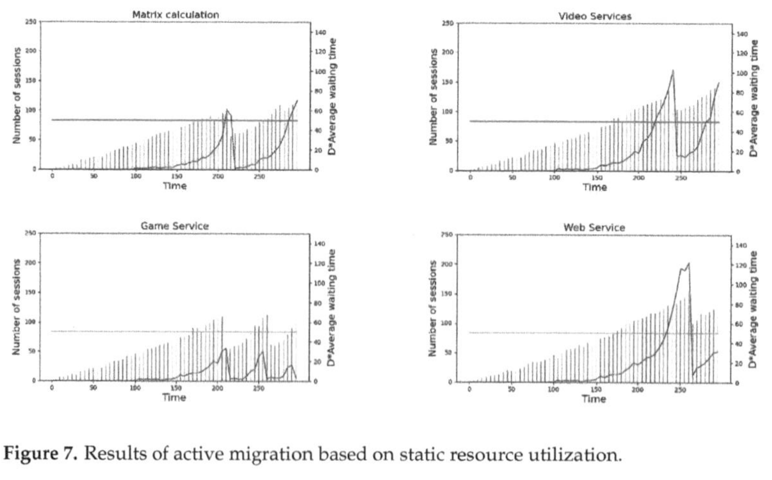

Figure 7. Results of active migration based on static resource utilization.

Further expanding on this, we present the findings based on the service quality of proactive migration. As depicted in Figure 8, across the four service programs tested, migration is instantaneously triggered when the green curve (representing real-time service quality metrics) surpasses the red line (the set threshold), subsequently maintaining a position almost equivalent to the red line. This effectiveness stems from the algorithm's dynamic threshold-updating mechanism, where the Service Migration Index Threshold (SMI-T) is adjusted according to the deviation from the standard Service Quality (SQ) value. This adjustment enables the green curve to precisely gauge the SMI's upper boundary in the experiments. In comparison to passive migration and proactive migration based on static resource utilization, the service quality-based proactive migration strategy proposed herein optimizes the timing of migration, thereby maximizing the utilization of service node resources without compromising on service quality.

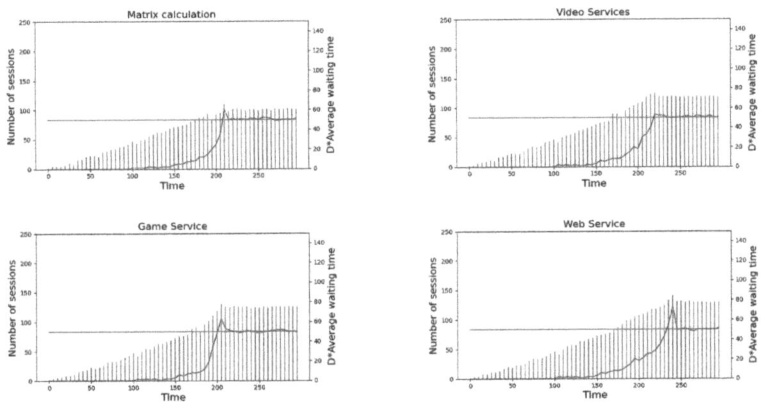

Figure 8. Results of active migration based on quality of service.

5.2. Migration Node Selection for Task-Resource Matching

To assess the effectiveness of our migration node selection algorithm based on task-resource matching, we conducted several tests across diverse scenarios and compared the results of our algorithm with those of the random algorithm, round robin algorithm, and least connection algorithm in the same situation. First, we simulated a user who sends 30 task requests to the load balancer. Figure 9 shows the tasks assigned to each server where the x-axis is the server serial number, and the y-axis is the number of tasks assigned. Figure 10 shows the resource deviation of service system nodes after load balancer allocation. It can be seen from the results of the Figures 9 and 10 that the four algorithms have little difference in the number of tasks assigned, but there is a significant difference in the degree of resource deviation. Since the traditional random algorithm, round robin algorithm, and least connection algorithm do not consider the problem of resource matching between tasks and servers, it can be seen from the experimental results that the resource deviation of the service node is large. This also means that the resource utilization of service nodes is not balanced, and the full capacity of the server is not fully utilized. The task resource matching algorithm proposed in this paper can ensure lower resource deviation and allocate different types of tasks to appropriate service nodes more reasonably.

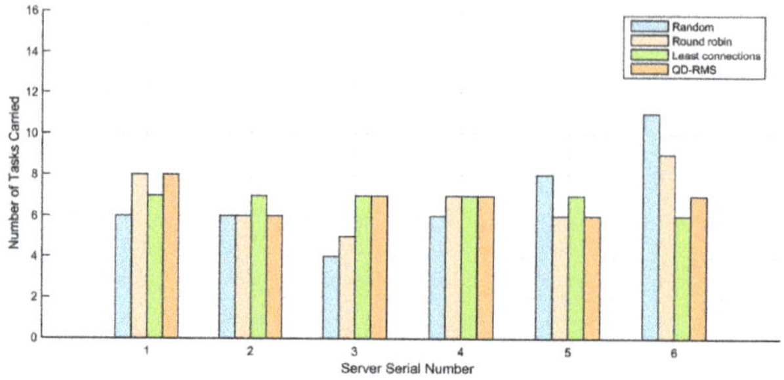

Figure 9. Results of 30 assignment requests.

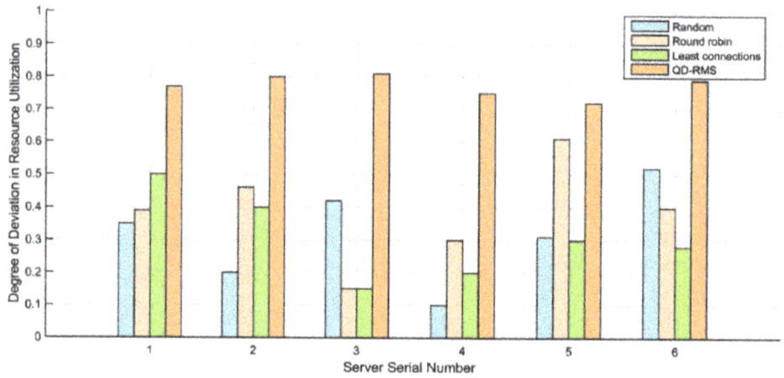

Figure 10. Resource deviation degree of a service node after 30 tasks are assigned.

Second, we simulated users who apply for tasks from the load balancer indefinitely until a resource on the server is exhausted. Figure 11 shows the tasks assigned to each server and Figure 12 shows the degree of deviation in resource utilization τ (as the value approaches 1, resource utilization becomes more balanced; see Equation (9)) of service nodes after an unlimited number of tasks are assigned. It can be seen from the results that under the infinite number of task requests, the QD-RMS proposed in this paper has a significant improvement in the number of tasks carried out and still maintains a good performance in the resource deviation.

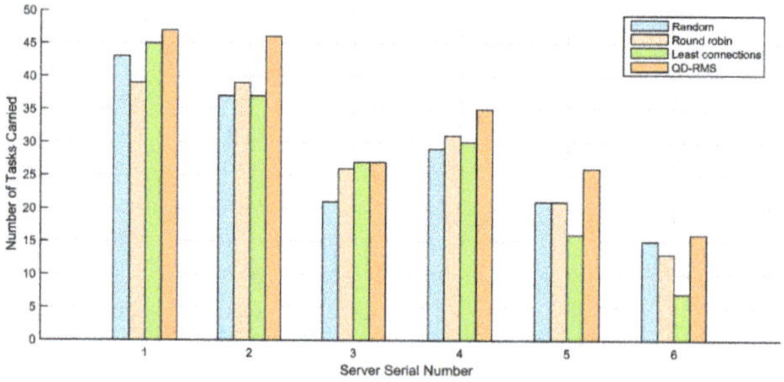

Figure 11. Results of an unlimited number of task requests.

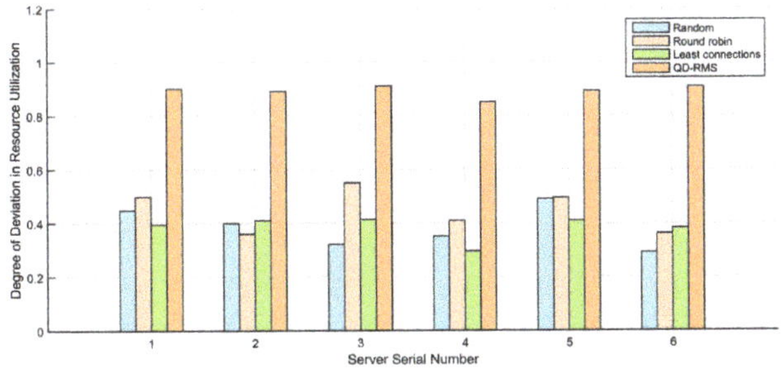

Figure 12. Resource deviation degree of a service node after an infinite number of tasks are assigned.

Lastly, we compare the maximum task carrying capacity of various algorithms, that is, the total number of tasks carried out by all service nodes. As shown in Figure 13, the algorithm proposed in this paper can make full use of the resources of service nodes because it takes into account the matching degree between the resources required by different task types and the server resources. Under the same equipment conditions, the maximum task load is increased by about 20%.

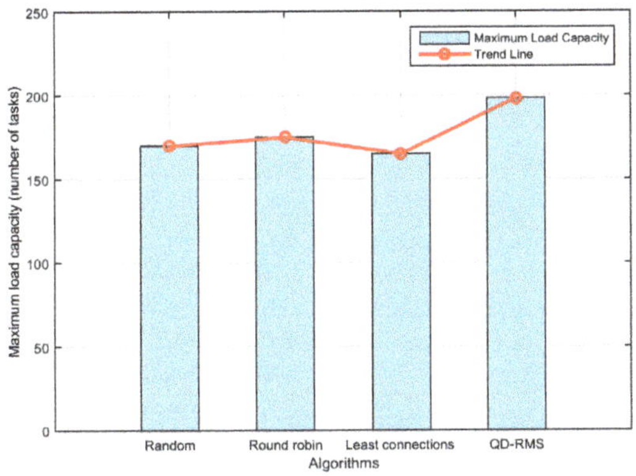

Figure 13. Comparison of Maximum Task Capacity

6. Conclusions

In conclusion, this research introduces the Quality-Driven Resource Migration Strategy (QD-RMS), a policy focused on optimizing resource allocation and enhancing decision making in service migration, guided by service quality metrics. QD-RMS proactively triggers resource migration prior to any decline in service quality through a service migration index and a dynamic threshold mechanism, thereby ensuring uninterrupted migration and significantly mitigating fluctuations in service quality. Moreover, leveraging Pareto optimization and the simulated annealing algorithm, this strategy efficiently selects the optimal node for migration within a feasible computational timeframe, optimizing resource utilization and load balancing.

QD-RMS effectively mitigates the delayed response of conventional migration strategies to potential service quality declines. Through the continuous monitoring of the Service Migration Index (SMI), it facilitates the real-time assessment of service status, allowing for the early activation of migration processes before significant degradation in service quality, thus diminishing variability in service quality and minimizing service downtime. Additionally, QD-RMS employs a multi-objective optimization model that amalgamates node resources and task load, enhancing the load-balancing process and preventing service migration to nodes at the risk of resource overutilization, consequently reducing system overload risks.

To ascertain QD-RMS's efficacy, a series of experiments were conducted, simulating varied service requests on a virtual machine platform to benchmark QD-RMS against conventional resource migration strategies. The experimental results indicate that QD-RMS not only maintains service quality but also reduces service fluctuation and increases the maximum task capacity by approximately 20%, thereby validating its superior performance and advanced load-balancing capabilities in real-world settings.

Beyond ensuring continuous network services, QD-RMS extends its utility to optimizing resource scheduling within networks. It dynamically reallocates resources by harnessing service quality metrics and load data, thereby adapting to ever-evolving network demands and traffic flows. Nevertheless, its centralized decision-making framework is not without drawbacks. It can lead to transmission bottlenecks as the scale of resources expands. To mitigate this, forthcoming enhancements will pivot toward a distributed framework, aiming to distribute the responsibilities of resource management and migration decisions across multiple units. This shift will alleviate the load on central management nodes and enhance overall efficiency.

Author Contributions: Y.S. and Y.J. primarily handled conceptualization and methodology; C.C. carried out software development and implementation; Y.J. conducted the experimental validation; C.C. was responsible for data collection and management; Y.S. and C.C. prepared the initial draft of the manuscript; Y.S., Y.J. and M.Z. performed the review and editing of the manuscript. All authors have read and agreed to the published version of the manuscript.

Funding: This research was funded by the Research on Intrusion Tolerance and Protection Technology of Power Data Center (Grand No. 5700-202218185A-1-1-ZN).

Data Availability Statement: The data presented in this study are available on request from the corresponding author due to privacy and ethical considerations.

Conflicts of Interest: Author Mingming Zhang was employed by the company "State Grid Corporation of China". The remaining authors declare that the research was conducted in the absence of any commercial or financial relationships that could be construed as a potential conflict of interest. The authors declare that this study received funding from the project "Research on Intrusion Tolerance and Protection Technology of Power Data Center" (Grand No. 5700-202218185A-1-1-ZN). The funder was not involved in the study design; the collection, analysis, or interpretation of the data; the writing of this article; or the decision to submit it for publication.

References

1. Wu, J. Cyberspace Endogenous Safety and Security. *Engineering* **2022**, *15*, 179–185. [CrossRef]
2. Tan, K.H.; Lim, H.S.; Diong, K.S. Modelling and Predicting Quality-of-Experience of Online Gaming Users in 5G Networks. *Int. J. Technol.* **2022**, *13*, 1035–1044. [CrossRef]
3. Lu, H.; Li, M.; Zhang, Y. Research on optimization method of computer network service quality based on feature matching algorithm. *Proc. J. Phys. Conf. Ser.* **2021**, *1982*, 012005. [CrossRef]
4. Flora, J. Improving the security of microservice systems by detecting and tolerating intrusions. In Proceedings of the 2020 IEEE International Symposium on Software Reliability Engineering Workshops (ISSREW), Coimbra, Portugal, 12–15 October 2020; pp. 131–134.
5. Wang, Z.; Jiang, D.; Wang, F.; Lv, Z.; Nowak, R. A polymorphic heterogeneous security architecture for edge-enabled smart grids. *Sustain. Cities Soc.* **2021**, *67*, 102661. [CrossRef]
6. Kang, R.; He, F.; Oki, E. Virtual network function allocation in service function chains using backups with availability schedule. *IEEE Trans. Netw. Serv. Manag.* **2021**, *18*, 4294–4310. [CrossRef]
7. Zhao, J.; Dai, M.; Xia, Y.; Ma, Y.; He, M.; Peng, K.; Li, J.; Li, F.; Fu, X. FRSM: A Novel Fault-Tolerant Approach for Redundant-Path-Enabled Service Migration in Mobile Edge Computing. In *Proceedings of the International Conference on Web Services*; Springer: Cham, Switzerland, 2022; pp. 1–12.
8. Ma, Y.; Dai, M.; Shao, S.; Xia, Y.; Li, F.; Shen, Y.; Li, J.; Li, Y.; Peng, H. A Performance and Reliability-Guaranteed Predictive Approach to Service Migration Path Selection in Mobile Computing. *IEEE Internet Things J.* **2023**, *10*, 17977–17987. [CrossRef]
9. Kulshrestha, S.; Patel, S. An efficient host overload detection algorithm for cloud data center based on exponential weighted moving average. *Int. J. Commun. Syst.* **2021**, *34*, e4708. [CrossRef]

10. Yang, L.; Yang, D.; Cao, J.; Sahni, Y.; Xu, X. QoS Guaranteed Resource Allocation for Live Virtual Machine Migration in Edge Clouds. *IEEE Access* **2020**, *8*, 78441–78451. [CrossRef]
11. Velrajan, S.; Sharmila, V. QoS Aware Service Migration in Multi access Edge Compute Using Closed Loop Adaptive Particle Swarm Optimization Algorithm. *J. Netw. Syst. Manag.* **2023**, *31*, 17. [CrossRef]
12. Chen, X.; Bi, Y.; Chen, X.; Zhao, H.; Cheng, N.; Li, F.; Cheng, W. Dynamic Service Migration and Request Routing for Microservice in Multicell Mobile-Edge Computing. *IEEE Internet Things J.* **2022**, *9*, 13126–13143. [CrossRef]
13. Bozkaya, E. Digital twin-assisted and mobility-aware service migration in Mobile Edge Computing. *Comput. Netw.* **2023**, *231*, 109798. [CrossRef]
14. Wang, H.; Li, Y.; Zhou, A.; Guo, Y.; Wang, S. Service migration in mobile edge computing: A deep reinforcement learning approach. *Int. J. Commun. Syst.* **2023**, *36*, e4413. [CrossRef]
15. Liang, Z.; Liu, Y.; Lok, T.M.; Huang, K. Multi-Cell Mobile Edge Computing: Joint Service Migration and Resource Allocation. *IEEE Trans. Wirel. Commun.* **2021**, *20*, 5898–5912. [CrossRef]
16. Kim, T.; Chen, S.; Im, U.; Zhang, X.; Ha, S.; Joe-Wong, C. MoDEMS: Optimizing Edge Computing Migrations for User Mobility. *IEEE J. Sel. Areas Commun.* **2023**, *41*, 675–689. [CrossRef]
17. Xu, Y.; Zheng, Z.; Liu, X.; Yao, A.; Li, X. Three-way decisions based service migration strategy in mobile edge computing. *Inf. Sci.* **2022**, *609*, 533–547. [CrossRef]
18. Le, V.T.; Ioini, E.; Barzegar, H.R.; Pahl, C. Trust Management For Service Migration Multi-access Edge Computing environments. *Comput. Commun.* **2022**, *194*, 167–179. [CrossRef]
19. Li, C.; Zhu, L.; Li, W.; Luo, Y. Joint edge caching and dynamic service migration in SDN based mobile edge computing. *J. Netw. Comput. Appl.* **2021**, *177*, 102966. [CrossRef]
20. Du, A.; Jia, J.; Chen, J.; Guo, L.; Wang, X. Online two-timescale service placement for time-sensitive applications in MEC-assisted network: A TMAGRL approach. *Comput. Netw.* **2024**, *244*, 110339. [CrossRef]
21. Tuli, S.; Casale, G.; Jennings, N.R. PreGAN: Preemptive Migration Prediction Network for Proactive Fault-Tolerant Edge Computing. In Proceedings of the IEEE INFOCOM 2022—IEEE Conference on Computer Communications, London, UK, 2–5 May 2022; pp. 670–679.
22. Dai, X.; Xiao, Z.; Jiang, H.; Alazab, M.; Lui, J.C.S.; Dustdar, S.; Liu, J. Task Co-Offloading for D2D-Assisted Mobile Edge Computing in Industrial Internet of Things. *IEEE Trans. Ind. Inform.* **2023**, *19*, 480–490. [CrossRef]
23. Moon, S.; Lim, Y. Task Migration with Partitioning for Load Balancing in Collaborative Edge Computing. *Appl. Sci.* **2022**, *12*, 1168. [CrossRef]
24. Zhao, P.; Tao, J.; Rauf, A.; Jia, F.; Xu, L. Load balancing for energy-harvesting mobile edge computing. *IEICE Trans. Fundam. Electron. Commun. Comput. Sci.* **2021**, *104*, 336–342. [CrossRef]
25. Liu, D.; Hafid, A.; Khoukhi, L. Workload Balancing in Mobile Edge Computing for Internet of Things: A Population Game Approach. *IEEE Trans. Netw. Sci. Eng.* **2022**, *9*, 1726–1739. [CrossRef]
26. Song, S.; Ma, S.; Zhao, J.; Yang, F.; Zhai, L. Cost-efficient multi-service task offloading scheduling for mobile edge computing. *Appl. Intell.* **2022**, *52*, 4028–4040. [CrossRef]
27. Liu, L.; Chan, S.; Han, G.; Guizani, M.; Bandai, M. Performance modeling of representative load sharing schemes for clustered servers in multiaccess edge computing. *IEEE Internet Things J.* **2018**, *6*, 4880–4888. [CrossRef]
28. Abedin, S.F.; Bairagi, A.K.; Munir, M.S.; Tran, N.H.; Hong, C.S. Fog load balancing for massive machine type communications: A game and transport theoretic approach. *IEEE Access* **2018**, *7*, 4204–4218. [CrossRef]

electronics

MDPI

Article

Integration of Semantic and Topological Structural Similarity Comparison for Entity Alignment without Pre-Training

Yao Liu [1] and Ye Liu [2,*]

[1] School of Computer Science and Technology, Beihang University, Beijing 100191, China; ly0708@buaa.edu.cn
[2] School of Instrumentation and Optoelectronic Engineering, Beihang University, Beijing 100191, China
* Correspondence: lylyzyq1314@buaa.edu.cn

Abstract: Entity alignment (EA) is a critical task in integrating diverse knowledge graph (KG) data and plays a central role in data-driven AI applications. Traditional EA approaches rely on entity embeddings, but their effectiveness is limited by scarce KG input data and representation learning techniques. Large language models have shown promise, but face challenges such as high hardware requirements, large model sizes and computational inefficiency, which limit their applicability. To overcome these limitations, we propose an entity-alignment model that compares the similarity between entities by capturing both semantic and topological information to enable the alignment of entities with high similarity. First, we analyze descriptive information to quantify semantic similarity, including individual features such as types and attributes. Then, for topological analysis, we introduce four conditions based on graph connectivity and structural patterns to determine subgraph similarity within three hops of the entity's neighborhood, thereby improving accuracy. Finally, we integrate semantic and topological similarity using a weighted approach that considers dataset features. Our model requires no pre-training and is designed to be compact and generalizable to different datasets. Experimental results on four standard EA datasets validate the effectiveness of our proposed model.

Keywords: entity alignment; knowledge graph; description information; topological structure

1. Introduction

The entity-alignment (EA) [1,2] task involves matching and aligning entities from various data [3] sources or Knowledge graphs (KGs) [4–6]. Its objective is to establish associations between entities that share the same semantic meaning. This enables accurate correspondence when performing operations such as data integration [7], querying [8] and analysis [9] across different data sources. EA plays a crucial role in natural language processing, information extraction [10], intelligent question-answering systems [11] and social network analysis [12].

In the field of EA, knowledge-representation methods are primarily employed to obtain the vector information of entities for alignment purposes. Existing EA methods can be broadly categorized into three groups: translation-based methods, graph neural network (GNN)-based methods and other approaches. Translation-based methods, such as MTransE [13] and BootEA [14], use the TransE [15] framework to transform individual elements in the KG into semantically rich vector representations. This facilitates tasks such as semantic relevance reasoning, entity relationship reasoning and knowledge graph applications. GNN-based methods [16], represented by models such as GCN-Align [17], RDGCN [18] and Dual-AMN [19], generate entity embeddings by aggregating neighborhood information using graph neural networks. These models effectively capture structural information and learn entity embeddings. Other GNN-based methods, such as TEA-GNN [20], TREA [21] and STEA [22], further improve performance by incorporating temporal features. Other approaches, including Fualign [23], Simple-HHEA [24] and BERT-INT [25], address the challenge of heterogeneity in KGs by exploiting side information.

However, these three types of EA methods have significant limitations. They rely heavily on the performance of the Knowledge Representation Learning (KRL) model and the quality of the datasets used. Additionally, when different data sources have distinct mapping spaces within the KRL model, performing similarity comparisons becomes challenging.

Recently, large-scale language models (LLMs) [26] have demonstrated exceptional performance in various natural language processing tasks, including XLNet [27], GPT [28], Transformer-XL [29] and RoBERTa [30]. These transformer-based models take advantage of rich contextual information from large corpora and have proven to be highly effective in improving entity-related tasks in KGs. As a result, EA models based on LLMs have emerged, such as LLMEA [7], ChatEA [31] and BERT-INT [25], which effectively leverage the semantic and ancillary information provided by LLMs to perform entity-alignment (EA) tasks. However, it is important to recognize that while LLMs trained on large-scale textual data have rich linguistic patterns and statistical information, they may have limitations when dealing with ambiguity and polysemy. In such cases, LLMs tend to favor the most frequent or common meanings, potentially overlooking other possible interpretations in the given context. This limitation [32] becomes particularly significant in entity-alignment tasks, where a precise understanding of contextual information is crucial for accurately defining an entity. Alignment accuracy depends directly on this understanding, and therefore the limitations of LLMs can affect overall alignment performance.

In this paper, we present our entity-alignment model, which integrates semantic and structural information without the need for pre-training. The descriptive information of an entity, e.g. Beijing, the capital and largest city of China, with geographic coordinates (39°54′ N, 116°23′ E). Beijing holds significant political, cultural, and educational importance as the center of China.... Utilizing this descriptive information, we compare entities for semantic similarity. However, entities in the graph not only have semantic attributes but also exhibit structural characteristics, including attributes and features of neighboring nodes. To capture these characteristics, we propose a structure-based similarity-comparison module. This module takes into account the features of neighboring nodes and attributes of edges to determine whether entities in different graphs share similar structural features, employing conditional comparisons. Finally, the contributions of the two modules are effectively fused by employing a weighted sum approach, which takes into consideration the characteristics of the dataset. We evaluate the effectiveness of our approach on several EA datasets, including the traditional DBP15K (EN-FR) and DBP-WIKI datasets, as well as the more challenging and practical ICEWS-WIKI and ICEWS-YAGO datasets. These datasets exhibit a high degree of KG heterogeneity and complexity in capturing correlations between KGs. Through extensive experiments, we demonstrate that our method outperforms existing state-of-the-art EA models. Our contributions can be summarized as follows:

- We propose a novel EA model that employs both semantic and structural similarity comparisons. The entities are enhanced through the integration of semantic and structural information, thereby achieving highly accurate alignment. Furthermore, weighting factors are introduced to effectively balance the contributions of the two models, ensuring optimal alignment across different dataset features.
- We conduct EA task-based experiments on four datasets, and the results of these experiments demonstrate the effectiveness of our model.

The remainder of the paper is structured as follows: Section 2 provides a comprehensive explanation of our model. Section 3 presents the experimental setup. Section 4 shows the results and thoroughly analyzes these results. Section 5 concludes the paper.

2. Methods

This section describes the details of our approach. The overall framework is shown in Figure 1. Our model consists of three primary modules: semantic-based similarity comparison, topology-based similarity comparison and fusion of semantic and structural similarity comparison.

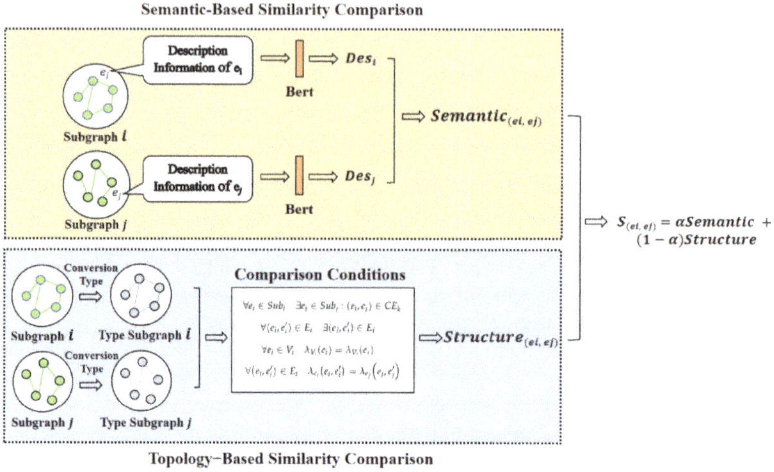

Figure 1. An overview of our model. The framework of our model consists of three components: Semantic-based Similarity Comparison, Structural-based Similarity Comparison and Fusion of Semantic and Structural Similarity Comparison. The Semantic-based Similarity Comparison module employs Bert to quantify the descriptive information of entities from different KGs and calculates their similarity using the cosine function. The Topological-based Similarity Comparison module determines the similarity of two subgraphs based on four specific conditions. Finally, the results of the two comparisons are integrated.

2.1. Preliminaries

Knowledge graph (KG). We define a KG as $\mathcal{G} = \{\mathcal{E}, \mathcal{R}\}$, where $\mathcal{E}$ represents the set of entities and $\mathcal{R}$ represents the set of relations. In a KG, a fact or edge is represented as a triple (h, r, t), where $h \in \mathcal{E}$ denotes the head entity, $t \in \mathcal{E}$ denotes the tail entity and $r \in \mathcal{R}$ denotes the relation between them. The embedding vectors for h, r and t are denoted by $\mathbf{h}$, $\mathbf{r}$, and $\mathbf{t}$, respectively, using bold characters.

Entity alignment (EA). EA is a crucial task in KG research. Given two KGs, $\mathcal{G}_1 = (\mathcal{E}_1, \mathcal{R}_1)$ and $\mathcal{G}_2 = (\mathcal{E}_2, \mathcal{R}_2)$, the goal is to determine the identical entity set $S = \{(e_i, e_j) | e_i \in \mathcal{E}_1, e_j \in \mathcal{E}_2\}$. In this set, each pair (e_i, e_j) represents the same real-world entity but exists in different KGs.

2.2. Semantic-Based Similarity Comparison

To semantically measure whether two entities are similar, we quantify the descriptive information of the entities using Bert, and then test the quantified similarity. Specifically, consider the entities $e_i \in G_i$, $e_j \in G_j$, e_i descriptive information labeled as Des_{e_i} and e_j descriptive information labeled as Des_{e_j}. The Bert employs the Transformer architecture, which is capable of processing longer text sequences and enabling better understanding of contextual information.

The vectors $\mathbf{Des_{e_i}}$ and $\mathbf{Des_{e_j}}$ are obtained after quantization by Bert. To test the similarity between the two vectors, we employ cosine similarity, which offers several advantages: simplicity, efficiency and independence of length and dimension in measuring vector similarity. These advantages align well with the experimental needs of our study. The cosine-based vector similarity calculation is:

$$Semantic_{(e_i, e_j)} = \frac{\mathbf{Des}_{e_i} \cdot \mathbf{Des}_{e_j}}{||\mathbf{Des}_{e_i}|| \, ||\mathbf{Des}_{e_j}||} \tag{1}$$

where $Semantic_{(e_i, e_j)}$ represents the similarity between e_i and e_j, $\cdot$ denotes the dot product of vectors and $||\mathbf{Des}_{e_i}||$ and $||\mathbf{Des}_{e_j}||$ denote the norms of the vectors $\mathbf{Des}_{e_i}$ and $\mathbf{Des}_{e_j}$ respectively.

2.3. Topology-Based Similarity Comparison

An entity in a KG contains not only its semantic information, but also additional information such as topology. Entities in different KGs often share similarities in their links and relations. For example, an entity classified as person may have relations such as co-worker, colleague and more. These relations also connect to entity types that share similarities. Consequently, even when dealing with different KGs, the relations and associated entity types tend to have similarities. Leveraging this insight allows us to achieve entity alignment across different KGs.

We employ K-means to group entities based on their quantized descriptive information, allowing us to label entities in the same cluster as belonging to the same type. For example, consider the triple (Beijing, belongs_to, China), where both Beijing and China belong to the geography category. After clustering, these entities are assigned to cluster CE_0. Similarly, the relationship 'belongs_to' is assigned to cluster CR_1. Therefore, the type of the triple can be represented as (CE_0, CR_1, CE_0).

We consider the entities and relations within three hops of the neighbor of the target entity to form a subgraph. The similarity between these subgraphs is then determined by evaluating their isomorphism.

Given two entities $e_i \in G_i$ and $e_j \in G_j$ with corresponding subgraphs $Sub_i = (V_i, R_i)$ and $Sub_j = (V_j, R_j)$ respectively, where V is the set of entities and R is the set of relations. The isomorphism between these two subgraphs can be determined based on the following conditions.

Condition 1:

$$\forall e_i \in Sub_i \quad \exists e_j \in Sub_j : (e_i, e_j) \in CE_k \tag{2}$$

where CE_k is the kth cluster. It is required that both e_i and e_j are of the same type.

Condition 2:

$$\forall (e_i, e_i') \in E_i \quad \exists (e_j, e_j') \in E_j \tag{3}$$

where e' denotes the neighborhood of node e. (e, e') denotes the edge connected between e and e'. The formula indicates that the edge present in the subgraph Sub_i are also present in Sub_j.

Condition 3:

$$\forall e_i \in V_i \quad \forall e_j \in V_j \quad \lambda_{V_i}(e_i) = \lambda_{V_j}(e_j) \tag{4}$$

where V_i denotes the set of nodes in Sub_i and V_j denotes the set of nodes in Sub_j. $\lambda_{V_i}(e_i)$ denotes the type of neighboring nodes of e_i, where the nodes all belong to V_i. This condition indicates that the types of all connected nodes of $e_i \in Sub_i$ and the types of the nodes connected to $e_j \in Sub_j$ should be similar.

Condition 4:

$$\forall (e_i, e_i') \in E_i \quad \forall (e_j, e_j') \in E_j \quad \lambda_{E_i}(e_i, e_i') = \lambda_{E_j}\left(e_j, e_j'\right) \tag{5}$$

where E_i denotes the set of edges in Sub_i, while E_j denotes the set of edges in Sub_j. $\lambda_{E_i}(e_i, e_i')$ denotes the type of neighboring edge of e_i, where the edges all belong to E_i. This condition indicates that the types of all connected edges of $e_i \in Sub_i$ and the types of all edges connected to $e_j \in Sub_j$ should be similar.

The two graphs can be considered isomorphic if and only if all of the above conditions are satisfied simultaneously.

2.4. Fusion of Semantic and Structural Similarity Comparison

In real-world scenarios, certain datasets are incomplete, resulting in a sparse structure. Therefore we introduce a parameter $\alpha \in [0, 1]$ to balance the semantic and structural information. The formula is defined as follows:

$$S_{(e_i,e_j)} = \alpha \times (Semantic_{(e_i,e_j)}) + (1 - \alpha) \times (Structure_{(e_i,e_j)}), \alpha \in [0, 1] \tag{6}$$

where $Structure_{(e_i,e_j)}$ denotes the structural similarity, which is calculated on the basis of the degree of coverage of the four conditions. For example, the third condition, $e_i \in Sub_i$ has approximately 80% of the number of nodes of the same type as $e_j \in Sub_j$. Therefore, the structural similarity can be defined by the following formula:

$$Structure_{(e_i,e_j)} = \alpha_1 \times (\#Edge) + \alpha_2 \times (\#Type_{node}) + \alpha_3 \times (\#Type_{edge}) \\ \alpha_1 + \alpha_2 + \alpha_3 = 1 \tag{7}$$

where $\#Edge$ denotes the number of identical edges (i.e., Condition 2), $\#Type_{node}$ denotes the number of neighbors of the same type (i.e., Condition 3) and $\#Type_{edge}$ denotes the number of neighboring edges of the same type (i.e., Condition 4). The symbols α_1, α_2 and α_3 denote the weights of the three conditions. These parameters are defined in a predetermined manner, and when the similarity between entities e_i and e_j, denoted as $S_{(e_i,e_j)}$, exceeds a certain threshold (e.g., $S_{(e_i,e_j)} > 0.9$), it indicates a high degree of similarity. Based on this similarity measure, entities e_i and e_j can be determined to be the same entity.

3. Experiment Setting

We conduct comparison experiments on the EA task using four standard datasets. Furthermore, we perform ablation studies to evaluate the specific contributions of two modules in our model. The effect of hyper-parameters on model performance is evaluated. The experiments are conducted on an Ubuntu 18.04.4 environment with 62 GB of RAM and a 60 GB GPU.

3.1. Datasets

We conduct experiments on four entity-alignment datasets. The statistics of these selected datasets are summarized in Table 1.

Table 1. The detailed statistics of the datasets. Temporal denotes whether the dataset contains temporal information.

Dataset		#Entities	#Relations	#Facts	Density	#Anchors	Temporal
DBP15K(EN-FR)	EN	15,000	193	96,318	6.421	15,000	No
	FR	15,000	166	80,112	5.341		No
DBP-WIKI	DBP	100,000	413	293,990	2.940	10,000	No
	WIKI	100,000	261	251,708	2.517		No
ICEWS-WIKI	ICEWS	11,047	272	3,527,881	319.352	5058	Yes
	WIKI	15,896	226	198,257	12.472		Yes
ICEWS-YAGO	ICEWS	26,863	272	4,192,555	156.072	18,824	Yes
	YAGO	22,734	41	107,118	4.712		Yes

DBP15K(EN-FR) and DBP-WIK [33] are two simple EA datasets, which share a similar structure for their KG pairs, with an equivalent number of entities. Furthermore, the structural features, such as the number of facts and density, of these two datasets closely align. ICEWS-WIKI and ICEWS-YAGO [24] are two complex EA datasets. Here, the KG pairs exhibit significant heterogeneity, differing not only in the number of entities but also in structural features. Notably, the quantity of anchors does not equal the number of entities. Consequently, aligning these complex datasets poses greater challenges.

To ensure consistency, we standardized the average length of descriptive information for entities across all datasets to 800 words. In cases where entities had insufficient descriptive information, we utilize ChatGPT [28] to supplement and enhance the available information.

3.2. Baselines

We select a set of state-of-the-art EA methods. These methods encompass a wide range of input features. Among the selected methods, we included translation-based approaches such as MTransE [13] and BootEA [14]. Additionally, we incorporated GNN-based techniques such as GCN-Align [17], RDGCN [18] and Dual-AMN [19]. Each baseline model has unique characteristics and high performance that make them suitable for evaluating the effectiveness of our proposed method.

3.3. Hyper-Parameters

To determine the optimal hyperparameters for each dataset, we perform a grid search. The optimal experimental setup includes the following hyperparameters:

For DBP15K(EN-FR): $\alpha - 0.6$, $\alpha_1 - 0.4$, $\alpha_2 - 0.3$, $\alpha_3 - 0.3$. For DBP-WIKI: $\alpha - 0.6$, $\alpha_1 - 0.3$, $\alpha_2 - 0.4$, $\alpha_3 - 0.3$. For ICEWS-WIKI: $\alpha - 0.4$, $\alpha_1 - 0.2$, $\alpha_2 - 0.4$, $\alpha_3 - 0.4$. For ICEWS-YAGO: $\alpha - 0.4$, $\alpha_1 - 0.2$, $\alpha_2 - 0.4$, $\alpha_3 - 0.4$.

3.4. Evaluation Metrics

In line with widely adopted evaluation methods in EA research, we use two metrics for evaluation:

(1) Hits@k, measuring the percentage of correct alignments within the top $k(k = 1, 10)$ matches. It is computed by $1/|\mathcal{S}|\sum_{i=1}^{|\mathcal{S}|} I(\mathrm{rank}_i < n)$, where $\mathbb{I}(\cdot)$ is the indicator function.

(2) Mean Reciprocal Rank (MRR), reflecting the average inverse ranking of correct results. It is computed by average of the reciprocal ranks $1/|\mathcal{S}|\sum_{i=1}^{|\mathcal{S}|} \frac{1}{\mathrm{rank}_i}$, where rank_i, $i \in \{1, \ldots, |\mathcal{S}|\}$ is a set of ranking results.

Higher values in Hits@k and MRR indicate superior performance in EA.

4. Results and Discussion

4.1. Performance Comparison

Tables 2 and 3 show our results on the four datasets. It can be concluded from the results:

Table 2. Main experiment results on the four datasets. Bold: the best result; underline: the runner-up result.

Models		DBP15K(EN-FR)			DBP-WIKI	
	Hits@1	Hits@10	MRR	Hits@1	Hits@10	MRR
MTransE	0.247	0.577	0.360	0.281	0.520	0.363
BootEA	0.653	0.874	0.731	0.748	0.898	0.801
GCN-Align	0.411	0.772	0.530	0.494	0.756	0.590
RDGCN	0.873	0.950	0.901	0.974	0.994	0.980
Dual-AMN	**0.954**	**0.994**	**0.970**	**0.983**	**0.996**	**0.991**
Ours	0.901	0.980	0.962	0.980	0.993	0.981

Table 3. Main experiment results on the four datasets. Bold: the best result; underline: the runner-up result.

Models		ICEWS-WIKI			ICEWS-YAGO	
	Hits@1	Hits@10	MRR	Hits@1	Hits@10	MRR
MTransE	0.021	0.158	0.068	0.012	0.084	0.040
BootEA	0.072	0.275	0.139	0.020	0.120	0.056
GCN-Align	0.046	0.184	0.093	0.017	0.085	0.038
RDGCN	0.064	0.202	0.096	0.029	0.097	0.042
Dual-AMN	**0.083**	0.281	0.145	0.031	0.144	0.068
Ours	0.081	**0.285**	**0.148**	**0.033**	**0.146**	**0.071**

- In Table 2, which shows the test results of our model on two non-temporal upper datasets, the results show that our model performs consistently at a high level for most of the evaluation parameters, closely following the Dual-AMN model.
- Table 3 presents the evaluation results of our method on the time series dataset. The results clearly show that our method outperforms the other baseline models. Compared to the Dual-AMN model, our method achieves an average improvement of 0.03 in Hit@1, Hits@10 and MRR, which highlights the effectiveness and superiority of our model.
- The results clearly show that our method has a significant advantage on the temporal dataset. This advantage is due to the use of temporal features, which act as identifiers during entity alignment, enabling us to accurately determine the same entities. Analyzing the parameters α_1, α_2, α_3 and α, we observe that the structure-based information is

more useful in datasets with higher graph density (e.g., ICEWS-WIKI, ICEWS-YAGO). On the other hand, descriptive information of entities tends to be more advantageous in cases where the graph structure is sparser (e.g., DBP15K(EN-FR), DBP-WIKI), while alignment using semantic information proves to be more effective.

4.2. Parameter Sensitivity

We perform parameter sensitivity tests on the model, specifically analyzing the effect of the α parameter on the performance of the model. The performance of the model is evaluated using MRR. The results are shown in Figure 2. We can conclude that:

- As shown in the figure, the analysis reveals a clear trend. It is evident that each dataset has an optimal α value, beyond which the performance of the model either converges or even tends to decrease. This finding suggests that there is a critical threshold for the α parameter, beyond which further tuning may not significantly improve model performance.
- When evaluating the DBP15K(EN-FR) and DBP-WIKI datasets, we observed that the model's MRR initially increases with increasing α values, but eventually starts to decrease. Here, α represents the weight of semantic information, indicating that increased emphasis on semantic information leads to improved performance in the early stages. However, in the later stages, the pronounced decrease in performance suggests that overemphasis on semantic information may lead to diminishing returns.
- When evaluating the ICEWS-WIKI and ICEWS-YAGO datasets, we observe a consistent trend in the performance of the model. The MRR peaks at a α value of 0.4 for these datasets, while the best overall performance for the DBP15K(EN-FR) and DBP-WIKI datasets is achieved at a α value of 0.6. This observation suggests that the ICEWS-WIKI and ICEWS-YAGO datasets have a higher dependence on the structural information of the model. This higher dependence on structural information can be attributed to the higher density and number of triples present in these datasets. Consequently, comparing structures in these datasets provides more valuable information.
- In summary, structural information is advantageous in densely structured datasets because it provides richer information about neighboring nodes and links. On the contrary, in sparsely structured datasets, semantic information is particularly helpful to compensate for the lack of structural information and to provide semantic information about characterized entities.

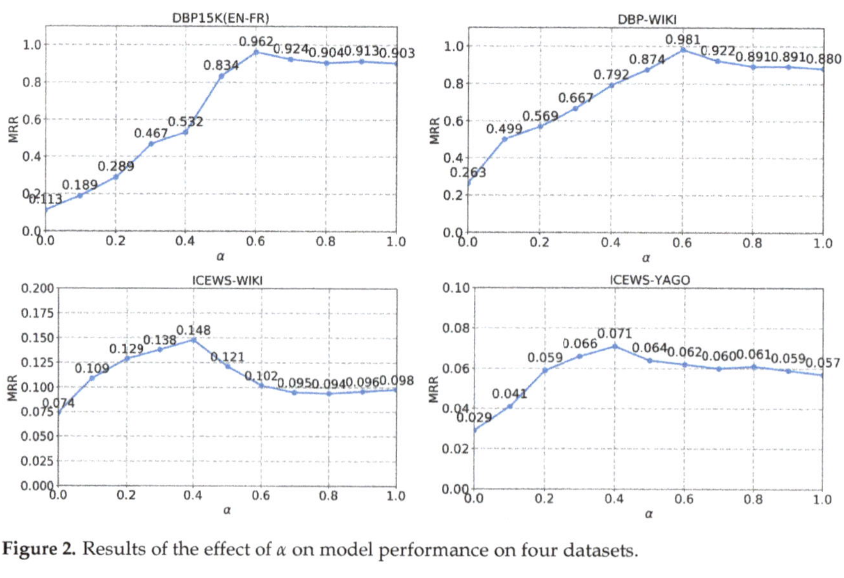

Figure 2. Results of the effect of α on model performance on four datasets.

4.3. Ablation Studies

We perform an ablation study using four datasets to evaluate the contribution of the two modules in the model. The symbol (+SSC) indicates the Semantic-based Similarity Comparison module, and the symbol (+TSC) indicates the Topology-based Similarity Comparison module. From the results, we can conclude that:

- Table 4 presents the performance of both the DBP15K(EN-FR) and DBP-WIKI datasets, demonstrating that the SSC module contributes significantly more than the TSC module to these two datasets. The SSC module exhibited a greater impact on the datasets, with an average increase of 0.318 in Hits@1, 0.244 in Hits@10 and 0.258 in MRR compared to the TSC module. This suggests that the semantic similarity module is a more effective approach for these two datasets.
- Table 5 presents the performance of the ICEWS-WIKI and ICEWS-YAGO datasets, indicating that the TSC module exhibits a significant contribution to both datasets compared to the SSC module. On average, Hits@1 improves by 0.0235, Hits@10 improves by 0.0865 and MRR improves by 0.0455. These results suggest that employing the structural similarity module is more effective for these two datasets.
- The results presented above shows that both modules contribute to the overall performance of our model. However, it is important to note that each module shows different contributions based on the KG characteristics.

Table 4. Results of ablation studies on DBP15K(EN-FR) and DBP-WIKI. Bold: the best result; underline: the runner-up result.

Models	DBP15K(EN-FR)			DBP-WIKI		
	Hits@1	Hits@10	MRR	Hits@1	Hits@10	MRR
SSC	<u>0.793</u>	<u>0.810</u>	<u>0.892</u>	<u>0.849</u>	<u>0.930</u>	<u>0.890</u>
TSC	0.560	0.678	0.692	0.445	0.574	0.573
SSC+TSC	**0.901**	**0.980**	**0.962**	**0.980**	**0.993**	**0.981**

Table 5. Results of ablation studies on ICEWS-WIKI and ICEWS-YAGO. Bold: the best result; underline: the runner-up result.

Models	ICEWS-WIKI			ICEWS-YAGO		
	Hits@1	Hits@10	MRR	Hits@1	Hits@10	MRR
SSC	0.034	0.121	0.086	0.022	0.091	0.032
TSC	<u>0.073</u>	<u>0.245</u>	<u>0.141</u>	<u>0.030</u>	<u>0.140</u>	<u>0.068</u>
SSC+TSC	**0.081**	**0.285**	**0.148**	**0.033**	**0.146**	**0.071**

5. Conclusions

This paper presents a novel entity-alignment module that combines semantic and structural comparisons. The descriptive information of an entity provides various features, semantics and characteristics, which we quantify to measure semantic similarity. Additionally, for graphs with higher structural density, we introduce a structure-based similarity-comparison module. This module assesses similarity by comparing the types of neighboring nodes and link attributes of entities across different graphs. Finally, we fuse the comparison results from both modules. Experimental results on four datasets demonstrate the effectiveness of our method. In future work, our future research aims to capture more distinguishable features for entity alignment.

Author Contributions: Conceptualization, Y.L. (Yao Liu) and Y.L. (Ye Liu); Methodology, Y.L. (Yao Liu) and Y.L. (Ye Liu); Validation, Y.L. (Yao Liu) and Y.L. (Ye Liu); Formal analysis, Y.L. (Yao Liu) and Y.L. (Ye Liu); Investigation, Y.L. (Yao Liu) and Y.L. (Ye Liu); Resources, Y.L. (Yao Liu) and Y.L. (Ye Liu); Data curation, Y.L. (Yao Liu) and Y.L. (Ye Liu); Writing – original draft, Y.L. (Yao Liu) and Y.L. (Ye Liu); Writing – review & editing, Y.L. (Yao Liu) and Y.L. (Ye Liu); Visualization, Y.L. (Yao Liu) and Y.L. (Ye Liu); Supervision, Y.L. (Yao Liu) and Y.L. (Ye Liu); Project administration, Yao Liu. All authors have read and agreed to the published version of the manuscript.

Funding: This research received no external funding.

Data Availability Statement: No new data were created or analyzed in this study. Data sharing is not applicable to this article.

Conflicts of Interest: The authors declare no conflicts of interest.

References

1. Yan, Z.; Peng, R.; Wu, H. Similarity propagation based semi-supervised entity alignment. *Eng. Appl. Artif. Intell.* **2024**, *130*, 107787. [CrossRef]
2. Yang, L.; Chen, J.; Wang, Z.; Shang, F. Relation mapping based on higher-order graph convolutional network for entity alignment. *Eng. Appl. Artif. Intell.* **2024**, *133*, 108009. [CrossRef]
3. Ranaldi, L.; Pucci, G. Knowing knowledge: Epistemological study of knowledge in transformers. *Appl. Sci.* **2023**, *13*, 677. [CrossRef]
4. Cao, J.; Fang, J.; Meng, Z.; Liang, S. Knowledge graph embedding: A survey from the perspective of representation spaces. *ACM Comput. Surv.* **2024**, *56*, 1–42. [CrossRef]
5. Ge, X.; Wang, Y.C.; Wang, B.; Kuo, C.C.J. Knowledge Graph Embedding: An Overview. *Apsipa Trans. Signal Inf. Process.* **2024**, *13*, 1–51. [CrossRef]
6. Wang, Y.; Lipka, N.; Rossi, R.A.; Siu, A.; Zhang, R.; Derr, T. Knowledge graph prompting for multi-document question answering. *AAAI Conf. Artif. Intell.* **2024**, *38*, 19206–19214. [CrossRef]
7. Yang, L.; Chen, H.; Wang, X.; Yang, J.; Wang, F.Y.; Liu, H. Two Heads Are Better Than One: Integrating Knowledge from Knowledge Graphs and Large Language Models for Entity Alignment. *arXiv* **2024**, arXiv:2401.16960.
8. Chen, C.; Zheng, F.; Cui, J.; Cao, Y.; Liu, G.; Wu, J.; Zhou, J. Survey and open problems in privacy-preserving knowledge graph: Merging, query, representation, completion, and applications. *Int. J. Mach. Learn. Cybern.* **2024**, 1–20. [CrossRef]
9. Chen, J.; Yang, L.; Wang, Z.; Gong, M. Higher-order GNN with Local Inflation for entity alignment. *Knowl.-Based Syst.* **2024**, *293*, 111634. [CrossRef]
10. Luo, S.; Yu, J. ESGNet: A multimodal network model incorporating entity semantic graphs for information extraction from Chinese resumes. *Inf. Process. Manag.* **2024**, *61*, 103524. [CrossRef]
11. Chen, Z.; Zhang, Y.; Fang, Y.; Geng, Y.; Guo, L.; Chen, X.; Li, Q.; Zhang, W.; Chen, J.; Zhu, Y.; et al. Knowledge Graphs Meet Multi-Modal Learning: A Comprehensive Survey. *arXiv* **2024**, arXiv:2402.05391.
12. Huber, M.N.; Angst, M.; Fischer, M. The Link Between Social-Ecological Network Fit and Outcomes: A Rare Empirical Assessment of a Prominent Hypothesis. *Soc. Nat. Resour.* **2024**, 1–18. [CrossRef]
13. Chen, M.; Tian, Y.; Yang, M.; Zaniolo, C. Multilingual knowledge graph embeddings for cross-lingual knowledge alignment. *arXiv* **2016**, arXiv:1611.03954.
14. Sun, Z.; Hu, W.; Zhang, Q.; Qu, Y. Bootstrapping entity alignment with knowledge graph embedding. In Proceedings of the Twenty-Seventh International Joint Conference on Artificial Intelligence IJCAI-18, Stockholm, Sweden, 9–19 July 2018; Volume 18.
15. Bordes, A.; Usunier, N.; Garcia-Duran, A.; Weston, J.; Yakhnenko, O. Translating Embeddings for Modeling Multi-relational Data. In *Advances in Neural Information Processing Systems 26*; Curran Associates Inc.: Glasgow, UK, 2013.
16. Kipf, T.N.; Welling, M. Semi-supervised classification with graph convolutional networks. *arXiv* **2016**, arXiv:1609.02907.
17. Wang, Z.; Lv, Q.; Lan, X.; Zhang, Y. Cross-lingual Knowledge Graph Alignment via Graph Convolutional Networks. In Proceedings of the 2018 Conference on Empirical Methods in Natural Language Processing, Brussels, Belgium, 31 October–4 November 2018; pp. 349–357.
18. Chen, Z.; Wu, Y.; Feng, Y.; Zhao, D. Integrating manifold knowledge for global entity linking with heterogeneous graphs. *Data Intell.* **2022**, *4*, 20–40. [CrossRef]
19. Mao, X.; Wang, W.; Wu, Y.; Lan, M. Boosting the speed of entity alignment 10*: Dual attention matching network with normalized hard sample mining. In *WWW '21: Proceedings of the Web Conference 2021*; Association for Computing Machinery: New York, NY, USA, 2021.
20. Xu, C.; Su, F.; Lehmann, J. Time-aware graph neural networks for entity alignment between temporal knowledge graphs. *arXiv* **2022**, arXiv:2203.02150.
21. Xu, C.; Su, F.; Xiong, V.; Lehmann, J. Time-aware Entity Alignment using Temporal Relational Attention. In Proceedings of the ACM Web Conference 2022 (WWW '22), Barcelona, Spain, Online, 26–29 June 2022; Association for Computing Machinery: New York, NY, USA, 2022; pp. 788–797.
22. Cai, L.; Mao, X.; Ma, M.; Yuan, H.; Zhu, J.; Lan, M. A simple temporal information matching mechanism for entity alignment between temporal knowledge graphs. *arXiv* **2022**, arXiv:2209.09677.
23. Wang, C.; Huang, Z.; Wan, Y.; Wei, J.; Zhao, J.; Wang, P. FuAlign:Cross-lingual entity alignment via multi-view representation learning of fused knowledge graphs. *Inform. Fusion* **2023**, *89*, 41–52. [CrossRef]
24. Jiang, X.; Xu, C.; Shen, Y.; Su, F.; Wang, Y.; Sun, F.; Li, Z.; Shen, H. Rethinking gnn-based entity alignment on heterogeneous knowledge graphs: New datasets and a new method. *arXiv* **2023**, arXiv:2304.03468.
25. Tang, X.; Zhang, J.; Chen, B.; Yang, Y.; Chen, H.; Li, C. BERT-INT: A BERT-based Interaction Model For Knowledge Graph Alignment. *Interactions* **2020**, *100*, e1.
26. Chang, Y.; Wang, X.; Wang, J.; Wu, Y.; Yang, L.; Zhu, K.; Chen, H.; Yi, X.; Wang, C.; Wang, Y.; et al. A survey on evaluation of large language models. *ACM Trans. Intell. Syst. Technol.* **2024**, *15*, 1–45. [CrossRef]

27. Yang, Z.; Dai, Z.; Yang, Y.; Carbonell, J.; Salakhutdinov, R.; Le, Q.V. Xlnet: Generalized autoregressive pretraining for language understanding. In *Advances in Neural Information Processing Systems 32*; Curran Associates Inc.: Glasgow, UK, 2019.
28. Radford, A.; Narasimhan, K.; Salimans, T.; Sutskever, I. Improving Language Understanding by Generative Pre-Training. Preprint. 2018. Available online: https://paperswithcode.com/paper/improving-language-understanding-by (accessed on 20 May 2024).
29. Dai, Z.; Yang, Z.; Yang, Y.; Carbonell, J.; Le, Q.V.; Salakhutdinov, R. Transformer-xl: Attentive language models beyond a fixed-length context. *arXiv* **2019**, arXiv:1901.02860.
30. Liu, Y.; Ott, M.; Goyal, N.; Du, J.; Joshi, M.; Chen, D.; Levy, O.; Lewis, M.; Zettlemoyer, L.; Stoyanov, V. Roberta: A robustly optimized bert pretraining approach. *arXiv* **2019**, arXiv:1907.11692.
31. Jiang, X.; Shen, Y.; Shi, Z.; Xu, C.; Li, W.; Li, Z.; Guo, J.; Shen, H.; Wang, Y. Unlocking the Power of Large Language Models for Entity Alignment. *arXiv* **2024**, arXiv:2402.15048.
32. Lynch, C.J.; Jensen, E.; Munro, M.H.; Zamponi, V.; Martinez, J.; O'Brien, K.; Feldhaus, B.; Smith, K.; Reinhold, A.M.; Gore, R. GPT-4 Generated Narratives of Life Events using a Structured Narrative Prompt: A Validation Study. *arXiv* **2024**, arXiv:2402.05435.
33. Sun, Z.; Zhang, Q.; Hu, W.; Wang, C.; Chen, M.; Akrami, F.; Li, C. A benchmarking study of embedding-based entity alignment for knowledge graphs. *arXiv* **2020**, arXiv:2003.07743.

electronics

MDPI

Article

Cross-Social-Network User Identification Based on Bidirectional GCN and MNF-UI Models

Song Huang [1], Huiyu Xiang [1,*], Chongjie Leng [1] and Feng Xiao [2]

[1] School of Computer and Artificial Intelligence, Beijing Technology and Business University, Beijing 100048, China; 2230601007@st.btbu.edu.cn (S.H.); lengchongjie@163.com (C.L.)
[2] Cyberspace Security Department, Beijing Electronic Science & Technology Institute, Beijing 102627, China; xiaofrank777@163.com
* Correspondence: xianghy@th.btbu.edu.cn

Abstract: Due to the distinct functionalities of various social network platforms, users often register accounts on different platforms, posing significant challenges for unified user management. However, current multi-social-network user identification algorithms heavily rely on user attributes and cannot perform user identification across multiple social networks. To address these issues, this paper proposes two identity recognition models. The first model is a cross-social-network user identification model based on bidirectional GCN. It calculates user intimacy using the Jaccard similarity coefficient and constructs an adjacency matrix to accurately represent user relationships in the social network. It then extracts cross-social-network user information to accomplish user identification tasks. The second model is the multi-network feature user identification (MNF-UI) model, which introduces the concept of network feature vectors. It effectively maps the structural features of different social networks and performs user identification based on the common features of seed nodes in the cross-network environment. Experimental results demonstrate that the bidirectional GCN model significantly outperforms baseline algorithms in cross-social-network user identification tasks. The MNF-UI (multi-network feature user identification) model can operate in situations with two or more networks with inconsistent structures, resulting in improved identification accuracy. These two user identification algorithms provide technical and theoretical support for in-depth research on social network information integration and network security maintenance.

Keywords: user identification; cross-social network; bidirectional GCN; MNF-UI; network embeddedness

1. Introduction

In the era of rapid mobile internet development, social networks have become an integral part of daily life, increasingly recognized for their importance [1]. Various social network platforms vie for user registration by leveraging their unique core functionalities, allowing users to experience these specific features. However, this trend poses significant challenges to the management of user accounts uniformly. In response, multi-social-network user identification technology has emerged, aiming to identify accounts of the same individuals across different social network platforms, thus enabling cross-platform data integration [2]. This technology has profound impacts on user recommendation systems, network security, and public opinion monitoring. Currently, the field of social network user identification employs various methods, mainly categorized into three types: based on user attributes, based on user relationships (i.e., the topology of social networks), and based on user behavior information [3].

Firstly, methods based on user attributes rely on personal information such as age, gender, occupation, and other static information for identification. These methods are popular for their simplicity and ease of data acquisition. For instance, Zeng W et al. proposed a method for user identification across online social networks by integrating multi-dimensional information such as personal profiles, social relationships, and online behaviors, achieving efficient cross-platform user identity recognition [4]. Çoban Ö explored a username-based method for identifying users across online social networks, using usernames to match accounts belonging to the same user, showing that the learning function constructed by binary classification outperformed similarity methods, reaching an optimal F-score of 0.921 without feature selection and expansion [5]. Li Y investigated a social network user identification method based on usernames and display names (UISN-UD), demonstrating the possibility of matching user accounts by comparing display names or usernames with limited online data, providing practical support for building better user profiles [6]. Solanki P and Harwood A discussed a method for cross-platform user identification using personal profiles and posting patterns on social network sites. Their study developed an algorithm by analyzing personal information such as interests and professions to match and identify the same user on different social network platforms [7]. Secondly, methods based on user relationships utilize the web of relationships in social networks, i.e., the interactions and social circles forming the topology. These methods reflect users' social activities and preferences well, with easier and more authentic network structure acquisition. For example, Qu Y and his team proposed a friendship-based identification method (FBI) by analyzing and learning the friendship link patterns of users on different social networks [8]. Kojima K et al. explored a method based on the similarity of friends' location distributions across online social networks, assuming that users' social circles have certain similarities even on different networks. By comparing and analyzing the location distribution of users' friends, the study proposed an innovative identification strategy that effectively identifies the same user across platforms [9]. Ahmad W and Ali R introduced a method for user identification across multiple online social networks, relying on cross-link attributes and network relationships, developing an algorithm to identify and link the same user on different platforms [10]. Qu Y et al. introduced a method for cross-social network user identification by utilizing users' friendship networks. This approach matches and identifies user identities based on their social relationships across different platforms, demonstrating the potential of leveraging structural information of social networks in user identification [11]. Lastly, methods based on user behavior information focus on the behavior patterns on social platforms, such as topics of posts and activity times. These methods capture dynamic characteristics of users, providing a richer dimension for user identification. Xing L et al. focused on identifying users across platforms by their behavior habits in social networks, based on the key observation that despite different activities, users' behavior habits and patterns have certain consistencies. By analyzing and comparing users' behavior habits, such as posting frequency, active time slots, and interaction preferences, the research team developed a novel identification algorithm [12]. Solanki P and Harwood A explored a method using user profiles and posting patterns for cross-social-network site user identification, proposing an innovative algorithm that considers both personal profile information and posting behavior patterns on different social networks [7]. Lei T and colleagues proposed a user identification method based on machine learning. This method effectively improves the accuracy of identification by analyzing users' behaviors and social relationships across different platforms. This work not only offers a new technical approach for cross-social- network user identification, but also opens new possibilities for research and applications in related fields [13]. In recent years, graph neural networks (GNNs) have made significant progress in processing graph-structured data, finding wide applications in social network analysis, recommendation systems, bioinformatics, and other fields. However, existing GNN methods still face numerous challenges when dealing with complex graph structures and large-scale data. To improve the performance and efficiency of GNNs, researchers have proposed a series of enhancement methods, including APGVAE (adaptive disentangled representation learning with the graph-based structure information) and injective aggregation techniques. APGVAE is a novel adaptive graph variational autoencoder method that aims to improve the performance of GNNs by incorporating graph structure information for disentangled representation learning [14]. This method not only learns more interpretable representations, but also enhances representation learning by adaptively integrating graph structure information. However, the complexity and computational resource requirements of the APGVAE method present challenges when processing large-scale graph data. Another study proposed improving GNN performance and efficiency through injective aggregation techniques [15]. Injective aggregation ensures that the aggregation function uniquely maps different input sets, thereby better capturing the complex dependencies in graph data. This approach has shown significant performance improvements in practical applications, but it also faces challenges related to the increased implementation complexity and computational resource demands. Despite achievements in addressing user identification issues, challenges remain due to specific reasons, summarized as follows:

1. Missing user attributes. The absence or inaccuracy of user attribute information primarily stems from three aspects. First, users often only provide the most basic mandatory information when filling in personal details, due to concerns over privacy protection or to avoid the hassle. Secondly, as privacy awareness increases, more and more users opt to set their personal information to limited visibility, such as visible only to friends or completely confidential, making direct access to user information more challenging. Lastly, some users may fill in incorrect or false personal details due to reluctance to disclose true information. Therefore, traditional methods based on user attribute matching significantly lose effectiveness under these circumstances, urgently necessitating the exploration of more effective user identification techniques.

2. Heterogeneity of data structures. Different social network platforms, due to their unique functional requirements, lead to diverse rules that users follow when submitting information at the time of registration. This results in a variety of data formats. For example, Facebook allows the collection of diverse information including usernames, nicknames, addresses, interests, etc., while Twitter mainly limits data collection to basic information. Meanwhile, the representation of user relationships across social networks also varies, such as the bilateral friend relationships in WeChat versus the unilateral following mechanism in Weibo. These differences increase the complexity of cross-platform user identification.

3. Incompleteness of user matching. Usually, users on social networking platforms do not correspond completely. That is, some users may be active on one platform, but not exist on others. Therefore, effective user identification requires finding corresponding user accounts across multiple social networks, a process that considers many factors aiming to ensure high accuracy and precision, constituting a challenge.

In response to the limitations observed in current user identification methods across social networks, which predominantly rely on user attributes, we conducted a comprehensive analysis of data from multiple social networking platforms. This analysis particularly focused on friend relationship data in social networks to devise an innovative user identification algorithm. Our paper introduces a cross-social-network user identification model based on bidirectional graph convolutional networks (GCNs), addressing the deficiencies of traditional attribute-dependent methods. This model represents a significant advance in neural network applications by leveraging node classification technology within GCNs to identify the same user across multiple social networks. Key contributions include:

1. Innovative model design: we propose a cross-social-network user identification model that utilizes bidirectional GCNs. This model innovates by initializing user node feature vectors, which allow each node in the network to aggregate information from neighboring nodes. This aggregation process generates a new, enhanced node representation, thereby significantly boosting the model's performance through iterative training.

2. Application to multi-social-network scenarios: our model addresses the challenge of user identification in environments where multiple social networks are involved, and there is a scarcity of user attribute information. Unlike traditional methods, our model, termed MNF-UI, is designed to operate effectively regardless of the number of networks and the variance in their topology structures. This adaptability enhances the applicability and accuracy of the model, setting a new standard in the field.

This paper aims to fill the gap in existing methods by providing a robust solution to user identification across multiple social network platforms without relying on direct user attribute data, using advanced computational techniques in neural networks. Through our proposed models—particularly the MNF-UI—we demonstrate the feasibility of cross-social-network user identification, significantly advancing the field's current methodologies. The technical roadmap of this paper, as shown in Figure 1, and the subsequent work of this paper are as follows: Section 2 details the cross-social-network user identification model based on bidirectional GCN, describing its design and implementation and validating the effectiveness of the proposed model through a series of experiments. Section 3 focuses on the multi-social-network user identification model based on MNF-UI, outlining the overall design of the model framework, delving into the specific implementation of the multi-social-network user identification model based on MNF-UI, and verifying the model's performance through experiments. Section 4 concludes the paper, aiming to summarize the work presented.

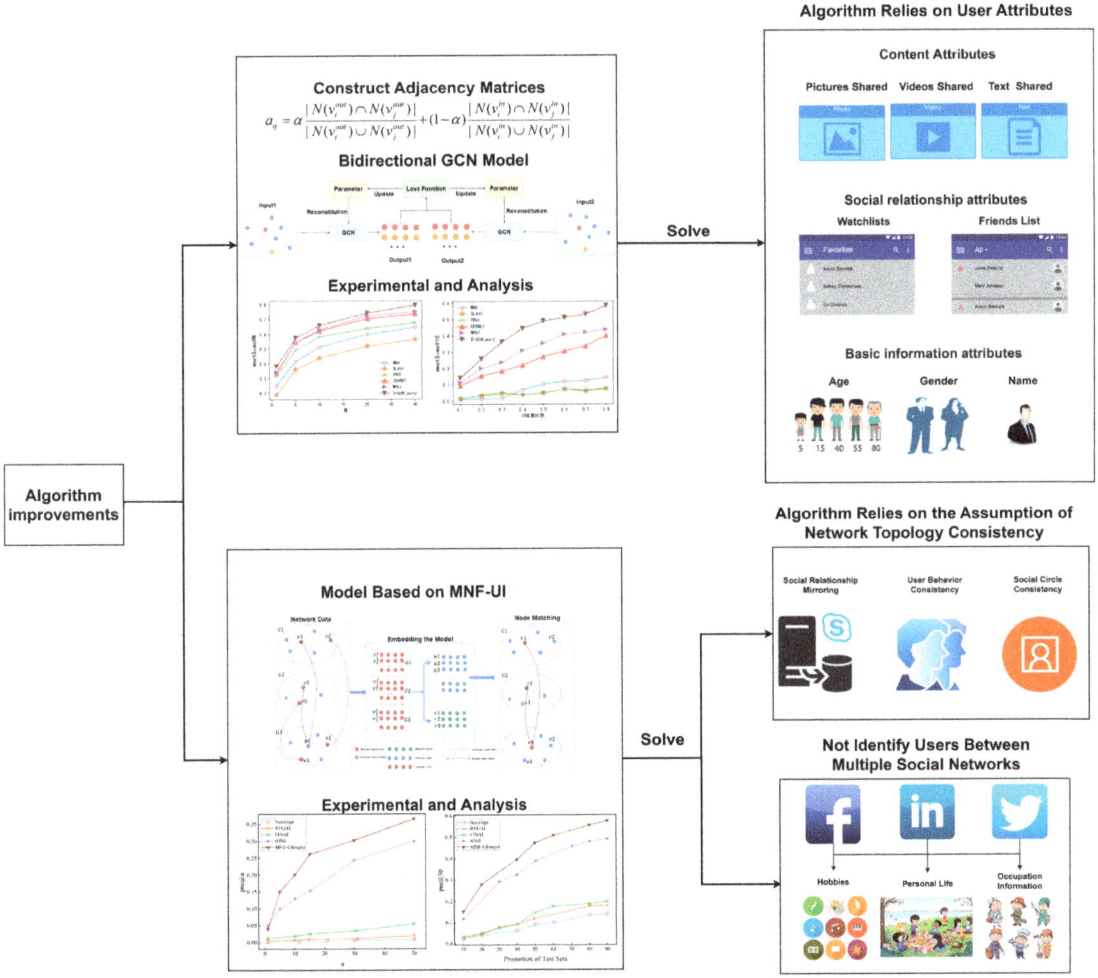

Figure 1. Technical roadmap.

2. Cross-Social-Network User Identification Model Based on Bidirectional GCN

In social networks, each node possesses not only basic attribute information but also embeds complex social connections, such as "friendship relations" of varying scales that construct a sophisticated social network system [16,17]. Against this backdrop, accurately identifying the same users in the real world has become a hot research topic in the field of social network analysis. Traditional identification methods mainly rely on user attribute information, network structural information, or a comprehensive application of both. However, with the increasing awareness of user privacy protection, obtaining users' attribute information has become increasingly difficult, directly leading to a decline in the accuracy of traditional methods for user identification. Methods that rely solely on network structure lack in-depth analysis of individual user characteristics, thereby affecting the precision of identification. To address this issue, this paper develops a bidirectional graph convolutional network (GCN) model that ingeniously circumvents the negative impact caused by missing user attribute information through random initialization of user attributes. Compared to traditional methods that depend solely on user social relationships, our model achieves a significant improvement in identification accuracy. This innovation not only makes up for the deficiencies of existing methods, but also offers a new perspective and technical path for user identification research in social networks.

2.1. Problem Definition and Model Framework

(1) Problem definition

Graphs are the optimal way to represent network information, where users and their relationships within social networks can be represented by a graph $G = (V, E)$, with V representing the set of all user nodes in the graph and E representing the set of all user relationship links within the graph. The following definitions are necessary for the identification of users across multiple social networks:

Definition 1. *User identification can be defined as the process of identifying accounts belonging to the same real-world user across two distinct social networks $G^X(V^X, E^X)$ and $G^Y(V^Y, E^Y)$. This involves identifying user pairs (v_i^X, v_j^Y) representing the same real-world user, where $v_i^X \in V^X$ and $v_j^Y \in V^Y$.*

Definition 2. *Seed nodes are defined as users who have already been identified across different social networks as the same user. They are represented by (s_i^X, s_i^Y), where $s_i^X \in V^X$ and $s_i^Y \in V^Y$ correspond to the same user in the real world, with i being the index of the seed node. The set of seed nodes is called the seed set, represented by $S = \{(s_1^X, s_1^Y), (s_2^X, s_2^Y), \cdots, (s_n^X, s_n^Y)\}$.*

The network topology can be represented by an adjacency matrix $A \in R^{N*N}$, and the features of the nodes can be represented by a feature matrix $H \in R^{N*F}$, where R is the set of real numbers, N is the number of nodes, and F is the number of features per node. As illustrated in Figure 2, the problem to be solved in the identification of users across multiple social networks is to determine whether a user v_i^X in social network G^X and a user v_j^Y in social network G^Y are the same user.

(2) Model framework

Graph convolutional networks (GCN) are a neural network architecture designed specifically for graph data. The core idea is to use the edge and node information within a graph for comprehensive aggregation, thus producing updated node representations [18]. A key aspect of this architecture is that, through the learning changes of the convolutional factors (see Equation (1)) between layers, it achieves the aggregation of surrounding node information and generates new node representations, where H represents the feature matrix, A is the adjacency matrix, and W is the weight matrix. Given that the adjacency matrix itself does not include self-loops, making it incapable of integrating self-information, self-loops are typically added during the node self-update process to incorporate the node's own information, thereby achieving a comprehensive update of a node's features and its neighbors'. In social networks, the degree of each node varies and, without normalization, nodes with higher degrees may have disproportionately large feature values which could affect feature extraction and model convergence. To address this issue, this study optimizes for the limitation of not considering self-information using the Laplacian matrix and normalizes the feature vectors by performing a square root inverse operation on the degree matrix of the adjacency matrix, as shown in Equation (2), where $\hat{A} = A + I$, A is the network adjacency matrix, and I is the identity matrix, $\hat{D}$ is the degree matrix of $\hat{A}$. Based on this, the activation function σ is where the GCN model employs the ReLU function, as described in Equation (3). The basic implementation process of GCN is illustrated in Figure 3, where graph data are processed and transformed into the graph's adjacency matrix, degree matrix, and node feature matrix, among other forms, to be input into the GCN model. After transformation by the convolutional factors, an updated feature matrix is output.

$$H^{(l+1)} = \sigma(AH^{(l)}W^{(l)}) \tag{1}$$

$$H^{(l+1)} = \sigma(\hat{D}^{-\frac{1}{2}}(\hat{D} - \hat{A})\hat{D}^{-\frac{1}{2}}H^{(l)}W^{(l)}) \tag{2}$$

$$relu(x) = \max(0, x) \tag{3}$$

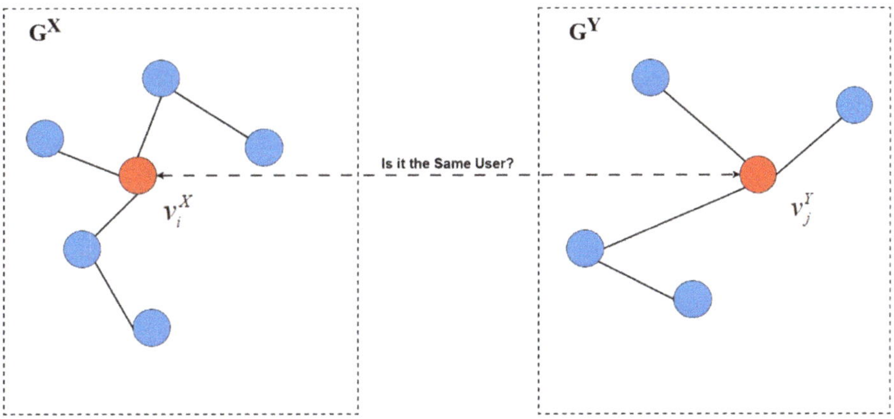

Figure 2. Identifying problems across social network users.

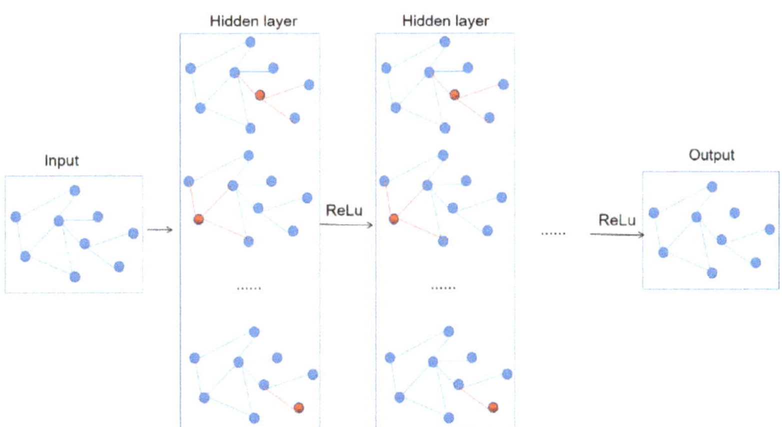

Figure 3. Basic implementation of GCN.

2.2. Model Building

In the field of network science, the adjacency matrix is widely used to describe the topological structure of a network. In this matrix, the value of elements indicates the connectivity between nodes in the graph, with a conventional practice of setting the value between connected nodes to 1 and between unconnected nodes to 0. However, in the context of social networks, the intimacy between users is not uniformly the same. For example, in the friendship relations formed by user node v_1 with user nodes v_2 and v_3, the intimacy between v_1 and v_2 is significantly higher than that between v_1 and v_3. This phenomenon manifests in social networks as the co-occurrence probability between user node v_1 and v_2 being higher than that between v_1 and v_3. Clearly, representing the degree of intimacy between nodes merely with binary values of 0 and 1 would result in the loss of a considerable amount of critical information. To address this issue, this study adopts the Jaccard coefficient to quantify the intimacy between users. The calculation formula for element a_{ij} in the adjacency matrix is shown in Equation (4), where $N(v)$ represents the set of neighbor nodes of user v. Given that most user relationships in social networks are unidirectional, forming directed graphs, such as the "follow" and "be followed" relationships on Weibo. Among all social activities of users, active following and passive being followed reflect different user behaviors, which reveal users' preferences and social circles. Based on this, this study proposes a new method to measure the intimacy between users using the Jaccard coefficient, as detailed in Equation (5). Here, $(v_i, v_j) \in E$, $N(v^{out}))$ and $N(v^{in})$ represent the set of neighbor nodes of user's out-links and in-links, respectively. Furthermore, in social networks, there exists a special mutual following relationship, i.e., $(v_i, v_j) \in E$ and $(v_j, v_i) \in E$, for which the adjacency matrices of the two graphs can be calculated separately using the aforementioned method.

$$a_{ij} = \frac{|N(v_i) \cap N(v_j)|}{|N(v_i) \cup N(v_j)|} \tag{4}$$

$$a_{ij} = \alpha \frac{\left|N(v_i^{out}) \cap N(v_j^{out})\right|}{\left|N(v_i^{out}) \cup N(v_j^{out})\right|} + (1-\alpha) \frac{\left|N(v_i^{in}) \cap N(v_j^{in})\right|}{\left|N(v_i^{in}) \cup N(v_j^{in})\right|} \tag{5}$$

The core logic of identifying users across social networks is based on the assumption that, if two nodes belonging to different social networks exhibit similar attribute characteristics and close topological structures, then, these two accounts are very likely to belong to the same real-world user [19]. Given the difficulty in directly obtaining node attributes, studies commonly generate users' feature vectors through random initialization methods and, then, based on the connections between users, calculate structural similarity to identify the same user across different social networks [20,21]. Based on this, this study proposes a cross-social-network user identification model based on bidirectional graph convolutional networks (GCN).

The architecture of the model is shown in Figure 4, where Input1 and Input2 represent the comprehensive input information generated by the adjacency matrix construction method and node feature matrix initialization technique mentioned above, respectively. After processing by the graph convolutional network (GCN), the model outputs the node feature matrix. Subsequently, the model optimizes the weight matrix W by minimizing the loss function based on the average distance between corresponding seed nodes in the feature matrices of two social networks (see Equation (6)) and iteratively updates the GCN until the loss function converges. Finally, the output feature matrix is used for further analysis. In this process, n represents the number of seed nodes, d represents the feature dimension of each seed node, v_i^1 and v_i^2 represent the i-th seed node in social networks G^1

and G^2, respectively, and H^1, H^2 are the feature matrices output by the GCN for G^1 and G^2, respectively.

$$f(n, d, v_i^1, v_i^2) = \frac{\sum_{i,j}(H_{i,j}^1 - H_{i,j}^2)}{n} \tag{6}$$

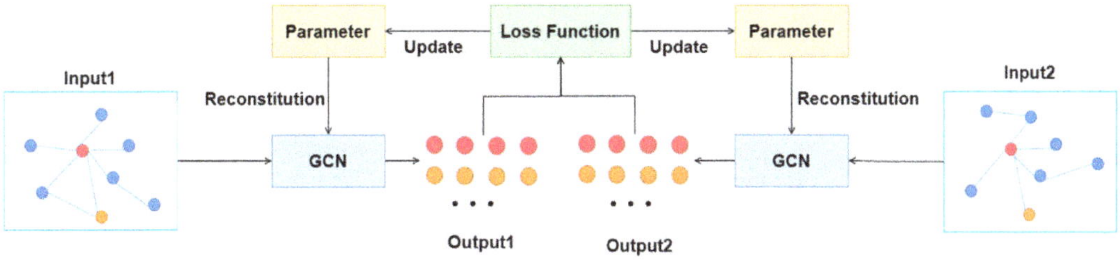

Figure 4. Bidirectional GCN multi-social-network user model.

By applying a finely trained graph convolutional network (GCN) model, this study successfully learned the vector representations of user nodes. For any given two user nodes $v_i^X \in V^X$ and $v_j^Y \in V^Y$, the distance between them is calculated using Equation (7). This research is based on a core assumption: the spatial distance between pairs of seed nodes should be as small as possible, while the spatial distance between pairs of non-seed nodes should be as large as possible. To achieve this goal, the model adopts an optimization strategy, the specifics of which are described in Equation (8). Here, C^{-1} represents the set of negative examples, γ is a parameter used to adjust the distance between positive and negative examples, and $[x]_+ = \max(0, x)$ defines a non-negative activation function. For the objective function proposed, this study employs the stochastic gradient descent (SGD) method for optimization, with the gradient update rule detailed in Equation (9).

$$d(v_i, v_j) = ||v_i - v_j|| \tag{7}$$

$$J = \sum_{(c_i, c_j \in C)} \sum_{(c_i^-, c_j^- \in C^-)} [d(c_i, c_j) + \gamma - d(c_i^-, c_j^-)]_+ \tag{8}$$

$$\theta = \theta - \eta \cdot \nabla_\theta J(\theta; x^{(i)}; y^{(i)}) \tag{9}$$

2.3. *Experiments and Result Analysis*

(1) Experimental datasets

The models in this chapter were tested on real-world datasets, including the Stanford Twitter Dataset, LiveJournal–MySpace, Facebook Social Circles Data, and LinkedIn API, validating the effectiveness of the model. Detailed information about these four social networks is presented in Table 1.

Table 1. Information about the dataset used in the experiment.

Social Networks	Number of Users	Number of Relationships	Number of Seed Nodes
Twitter	4572	154,921	1703
MySpace	4716	93,725	
Facebook	4039	88,234	1097
LinkedIn	3718	63,528	

(2) Evaluation criteria and experiments

In this project, *mostSims@N* was selected as the primary evaluation metric for assessing model performance, as defined in Equation (10). Here, *RightCount@N* represents the number of correct matches among the top N most similar users for each user in the test set, with the correctness of a match indicated by the subscript. *TestAnchors* represents the total number of correct seed node pairs in the test set. An improvement in the *mostSims@N* value directly reflects better identification results. For this project's model, the parameter settings were as follows: the number of negative samples was set to five to maintain a balance between positive and negative samples, the gap parameter $\gamma = 1$, the dimension of the user node feature vector was 100, and the user closeness coefficient $\alpha = 0.9$. This parameter configuration was designed to optimize model performance and ensure maximum precision.

$$mostSims@N = \frac{RightCount@N_{XY} + RightCount@N_{YX}}{TestAnchors \times 2} \tag{10}$$

(3) Analysis of experimental results

Table 2 shows the benchmark algorithm selected in this paper.

Table 2. Benchmark algorithms.

Algorithm	Description
MAH [22]	Based on the traditional network topology, the semi-supervised learning model realizes user identification across two social networks through a small number of seed nodes, and efficiently uses a small amount of annotated data.
DLAUI [23]	Through the in-depth modeling of friendship and the introduction of manifold alignment framework, user information is mapped to low-dimensional space, which significantly reduces the computational complexity and simplifies the calculation process of user identification.
FRUI [24]	The user similarity is measured by using the information between the known nodes and the nodes to be matched, and the user identification is carried out through the node similarity, which simplifies the identification process.
COSNET [25]	Starting from the research of energy model, the energy level difference is used to distinguish different structure matching modes, and the energy model is optimized by the subgradient algorithm, and the lowest energy is the optimal matching result.
WHUI [9]	By comprehensively considering the network friendship and other information shared by users, such as interest group affiliation, etc., the similarity is calculated by using weighted supergraphs, and the threshold pruning is set to improve the accuracy and efficiency of recognition.

In experiments conducted on the Twitter–MySpace dataset, multiple evaluation metrics (*mostSims@N*) were used to measure the performance of the proposed model. As shown in Table 3, the model proposed in this study significantly outperformed several existing algorithms on all evaluated metrics, including MAH, DLAUI, FRUI, COSNET, and WHUI, especially noting that the performance of the COSNET and WHUI algorithms is close to that of the model proposed in this research. This is further illustrated in a detailed comparison in Figure 5, where the x-axis represents the top N most similar nodes selected from the test set, and the y-axis represents the probability of correctly matching nodes between two networks among these top N nodes. Figure 5 reveals an important phenomenon: as N increased from 0 to 5, there was a noticeable improvement in the model's identification performance. However, as N continued to increase, the rate of performance improvement gradually diminished. This phenomenon mainly resulted from sorting the similarity of seed nodes awaiting matching, with seed nodes ranked higher being more easily matched correctly. This analysis not only highlights the effectiveness of the model in processing social network structural information, but also provides potential directions for further optimizing model performance in future research.

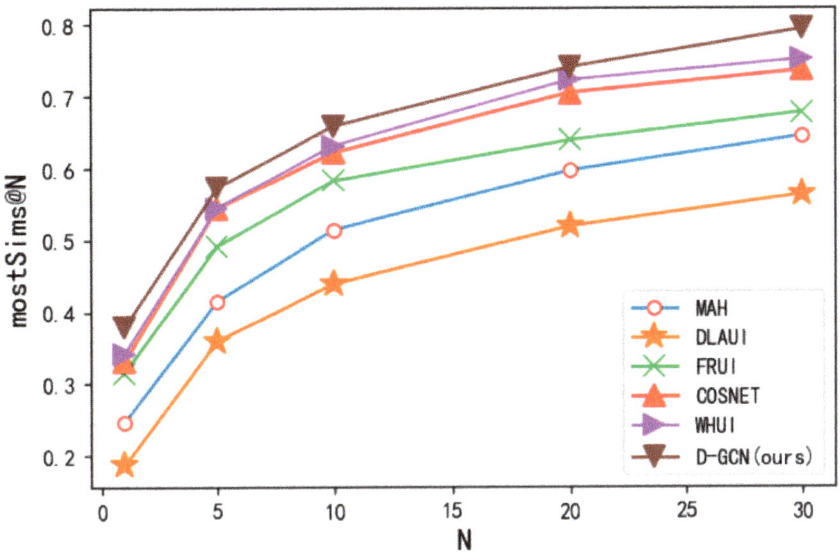

Figure 5. Comparison of the optimal *mostSims@N* of each algorithm.

Table 3. Different recognition effects are set for each algorithm on the Twitter–MySpace dataset.

Algorithm	*mostSims@1*	*mostSims@5*	*mostSims@10*	*mostSims@20*	*mostSims@30*
MAH	0.2468	0.4145	0.5139	0.5962	0.6444
DLAUI	0.1865	0.3593	0.4388	0.5183	0.5626
FRUI	0.3152	0.4906	0.5822	0.6381	0.6771
COSNET	0.3314	0.5433	0.6213	0.7041	0.7351
WHUI	0.3419	0.5444	0.6311	0.7219	0.7505
D-GCN(ours)	0.3787	0.5721	0.6582	0.7396	0.7929

This study demonstrates that our model can achieve significant identification performance solely through the structure of social networks. This effectiveness is primarily attributed to the differences between our model and algorithms such as N-GCN, MAH, and DLAUI. The latter rely solely on the superficial information of friendships, without delving into the underlying aspects of these relationships, such as whether users follow the same influencers or share the same idol preferences, leading to their limited identification accuracy. In contrast, the FRUI algorithm shows advancement in calculating node similarity by considering successfully identified pairs of seed nodes. Its advantages are mainly in two aspects: first, the FRUI model believes that the joint representation of a node and its neighboring nodes can provide more comprehensive information for user identification; second, the model can calculate the network similarity between nodes in different networks, effectively reducing the impact of different network structures. However, the FRUI algorithm does not fully consider the heterogeneity between nodes, making its identification accuracy inferior to the WHUI algorithm. The WHUI algorithm, by introducing a hypergraph structure that considers additional information beyond friendships, more accurately reflects the actual situation. However, due to its fixed weight settings, which require manual configuration and lack the ability to adaptively adjust according to actual conditions, its identification performance is somewhat lacking compared to the N-GCN algorithm.

In this paper, the N-GCN algorithm, catering to the needs of real-world application scenarios, not only considers friendships, but also delves into the intimacy between friends by reconstructing the adjacency matrix through the Jaccard coefficient, revealing deeper information behind friendships. Thanks to the natural advantage of GCN in processing graph data, namely representing nodes with new feature vectors after learning information from neighboring nodes, this model can integrate more factors and align more closely with actual situations, thus improving the accuracy of the experiments. As shown in Table 3, with the increase in N in the evaluation metric $mostSims@N$, the identification performance of each model has been improved.

After extensive benchmark model comparisons, this study further evaluated the performance of the $D-GCN$ model and its various versions on the Facebook–LinkedIn dataset, specifically including $D-GCN_{nor}$, $D-GCN_{in\_Jaccard}$, $D-GCN_{out\_Jaccard}$, and $D-GCN$. These versions represent the use of traditional adjacency matrices, out-degree neighbor Jaccard coefficient matrices, in-degree neighbor Jaccard coefficient matrices, and the adjacency matrix construction method proposed in this research, respectively. The research results (see Table 4) show that the closeness between users significantly affected the performance of cross-social-network user identification. Specifically, the D-GCN model proposed in this study significantly improved the accuracy of user identification by effectively utilizing the close relationships between users to construct and learn adjacency matrices.

Table 4. Performance statistics of the Facebook–LinkedIn dataset for each variant.

Algorithm	*mostSims@1*	*mostSims@15*	*mostSims@30*
$D-GCN_{nor}$	0.3136	0.6331	0.7692
$D-GCN_{in\_Jaccard}$	0.3432	0.6627	0.7751
$D-GCN_{out\_Jaccard}$	0.3609	0.6746	0.7870
$D-GCN$	0.3719	0.6937	0.7916

To explore the relationship between model performance and training sample size, this study conducted a comparative analysis of the $mostSims@10$ metric of each algorithm under different training set sizes. By gradually increasing the proportion of the training set, the study meticulously examined the precision performance of different models. The specific experimental results are displayed in Figure 6, where the brown downward triangle curve represents the $D-GCN$ model, the purple rightward triangle curve represents the WHUI model, the red upward triangle curve represents the COSNET model, the green star-shaped line represents the FRUI model, the yellow star-shaped line represents the DLAUI model, and the white circular curve represents the MAH model. The x-axis represents the proportion of the training set, and the y-axis represents the $mostSims@10$ metric at different training set proportions. In this experiment, the training set proportion of the Facebook–LinkedIn dataset was gradually increased from 10% to 80%, while keeping the testing set proportion at 10%. The experimental results indicate that, regardless of the size of the training set, as long as friendship relations were considered, our model significantly outperformed other models. This advantage stems from our model not only incorporating additional information, especially in the reconstruction of adjacency matrices and application of the GCN model, but also presenting, compared to other models, weight adjustments that are automatically optimized based on outcomes, thereby achieving higher identification accuracy.

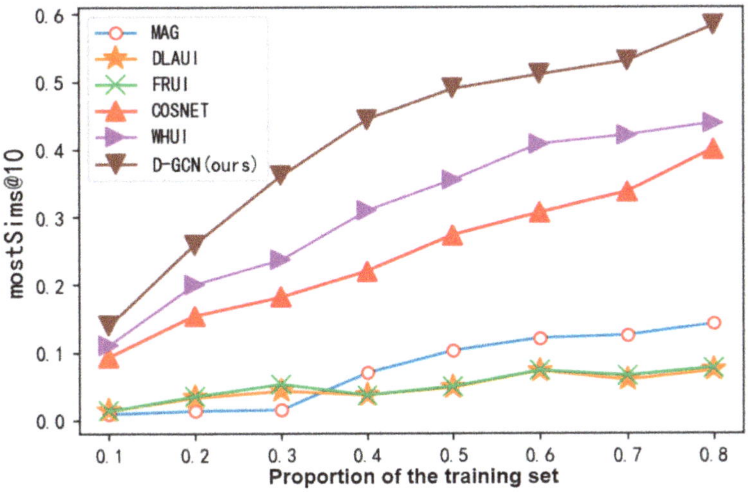

Figure 6. Comparison of the optimal *mostSims@10* at different training set ratios.

3. Multi-Social-Network User Identification Model Based on MNF-UI

With the rapid growth of information diversity, various social networking media such as Weibo, Kuaishou, and Zhihu have emerged. Currently, users commonly participate in multiple different types of social network platforms, revealing two pieces of information: on the one hand, each social network can map out the unique topological structure of the relationships formed by its users; on the other hand, there are the same users across different social networks, thereby having the potential to interconnect various networks through user relationships. Although multiple related networks may share the same user group, they are often isolated in different social network platforms without clear interconnecting links. Facing this challenge, our goal is to utilize multi-network fusion technology to explore and reveal the unknown links between these different social networks, thereby achieving the identification work of the same user across social networks.

3.1. Problem Definition and Model Framework

(1) Problem definition

In the following definitions, we assume that the edges are unweighted and that all edges are directed, as an undirected edge can be converted into two directed edges.

Definition 3. *(Multi-network matching): define a set of networks* $G = ((G^1, G^2, \cdots, G^N), (A^{(1,2)}, A^{(1,3)}, \cdots, A^{(N-1,N)}))$ *as matching networks, where* $G_i, i \in \{1, 2, \cdots, N\}$ *represents the i-th network in G, N is the number of related networks.* $A^{(i,j)}, i, j \in \{1, 2, \cdots, N\}$ *represents the set of seed linkages between* G^i *and* G^j*. We define each network as* $G^i = (V^i, E^i)$*, where* V^i *is the set of nodes, and* E^i *is the set of edges.*

Definition 4. *(Seed linkage): for two networks, we define a seed linkage* $(v_k^i, v_k^j) \in A^{(i,j)}$*, where* v_k^i, v_k^j *are the seed nodes in the two social networks, respectively. If* $(v_k^i, v_k^j) \in A^{(i,j)}$ *and* $(v_k^i, v_k^h) \in A^{(i,h)}$*, then* $(v_k^j, v_k^h) \in A^{(j,h)}$*. For ease of notation, nodes with the same subscript in different networks are referred to as known seed nodes.*

Definition 5. *(Multi-network matching problem): given a set of partially known seed linkages between multiple social networks, the problem is to discover unknown or potential seed linkages. It is noteworthy that the social networks are partially matched, meaning that not all nodes have corresponding nodes in other social networks, and the seed nodes follow a one-to-one matching constraint.*

(2) Model framework

As shown in Figure 7, the overall structural framework of the MNF-UI model mainly consists of three core components: network data representation, multi-network embedding, and node matching tasks. First, for the network data representation part, the MNF-UI model views social networks as a topological structure graph, where nodes symbolize users on social networks and edges represent social relationships between users, such as friendship links on Twitter or follow relationships on Weibo. In this context, different accounts of the same real-world individual are defined as seed node pairs. Specifically, identified seed node pairs are collectively referred to as the seed node pair set. Subsequently, the design of the multi-network embedding part aims to map two different social networks into a unified, low-dimensional vector space through the seed node pair set. In this space, since the seed node pairs represent already matched node pairs, their relative distances in the vector space will be closer, while those unmatched node pairs will be further apart. Our goal was to minimize the distance between seed node pairs as much as possible in this embedding space, while maximizing the distance between non-seed node pairs. By stripping away the interference of the network environment, we can obtain the internet vector, which can effectively be used for node matching like seed nodes. Finally, the node matching part calculates the relative distance between two nodes using cosine similarity and identifies seed node pairs by setting a certain threshold. Those seed node distances greater than the threshold will be ranked and selected to find the matching seed node pairs with the smallest distance, while those below the threshold are considered unsuccessfully matched seed nodes and are excluded.

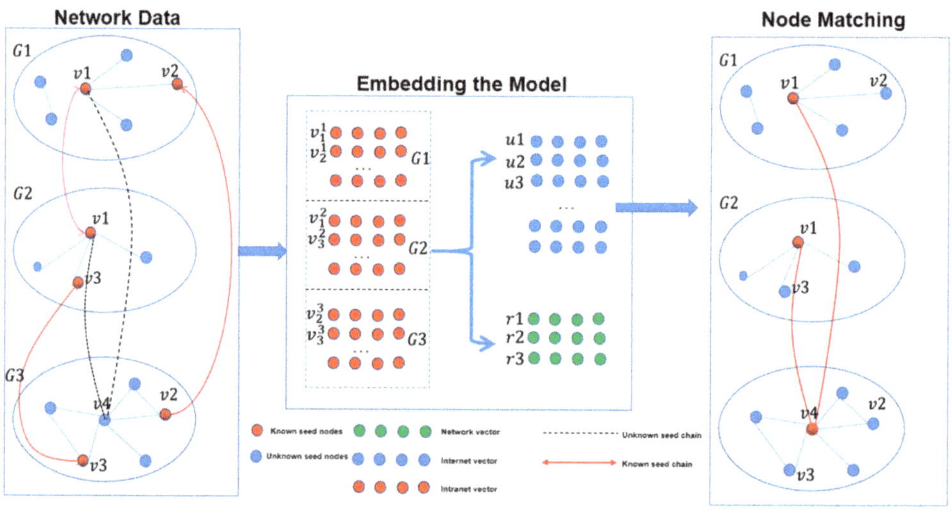

Figure 7. Overall framework of the MNF-UI model.

3.2. Model Building

In different network structures, seed nodes exhibit varying patterns of interaction behavior. As shown in Figure 7, seed node v_1 presents different connection patterns in networks G^1 and G^2. As the embodiment of the same entity in the real world, seed nodes maintain some common characteristics across networks. For example, if it is known that node v^4 in network G^3 corresponds to node v^1 in networks G^1 and G^2, we observe that seed node v^1 tends to interact with nodes v^2 or v^3 within each network. Based on this, we infer that, in selected networks, seed nodes can not only display structural characteristics similar to their corresponding nodes, but also exhibit different connection patterns due to different network environments. These common characteristics between seed nodes are crucial for user identification. Therefore, this study introduces the internet vector to capture the common characteristics between seed nodes. Through the training process, we expect an unknown seed node's internet vector to approximate the vectors of its corresponding nodes across all network environments. However, due to the lack of direct connections between unknown seed nodes, training to obtain the corresponding vectors poses a significant challenge, such as the lack of a direct connection between node v_1 in v_4 and node v_4 in G^3. Thus, it is necessary to learn the internet vector indirectly. Through network fusion methods, it is intuitive to extract the structural characteristics of nodes, referred to as the intranet vector in our MNF-UI model. Due to differences in network environments, this vector simultaneously contains the commonality between seed nodes and the specific connection characteristics within their networks. Only by eliminating the influence of network environments can we apply the internet vector to the problem of multi-social network user identification. For this purpose, we constructed Formula (11) to establish the relationship among the intranet vector, internet vector, and network vector:

$$v_i^k = u_i + r^k \tag{11}$$

In network G^k, the intranet vector (v_i^k) of node v_i is easy to learn, while the internet vector (u_i) of node v_i shares this vector with its known corresponding seed nodes; r^k represents the network vector formed by extracting the structural characteristics of G^k, reflecting the global differences between networks. Therefore, by training based on the composite intranet vector, we can indirectly learn the internet vector of seed nodes. Taking Figure 7 as an example for further elaboration, by observing seed node v_1, one can find commonalities between the two networks, which can be represented through the internet vector. Meanwhile, due to G^1 and G^2 being different networks, v_1's local links also differ due to network structural differences. Based on Formula (11), we can define the intranet vector for node v_1 in G^1 and G^2, as shown in Formula (12).

$$\begin{aligned} v_1^1 &= u_1 + r^1 \\ v_1^2 &= u_1 + r^2 \end{aligned} \tag{12}$$

Firstly, by jointly training the intranet vector, the shared u_1 can store complementary information between two networks. For instance, v_1 might establish connections with both v_2 and v_3. Secondly, considering the information conveyed in u_1 is consistent, and r^1 and r^2 can reveal the global differences between the two networks, the intranet vector of node v_4 in network G^3 can be expressed as Formula (13). By learning the network structure information in G^3, v_4^3 might include features similar to v_1^1 or v_1^2, for example, v_4 might also tend to interact with nodes v_2 and v_3. Since there are other known seed linkages between G^3 and other networks, r^3 can reflect the specific structural characteristics of G^3. Therefore, by eliminating the influence of network structural differences, $u_4 = v_4^3 - r^3$, the internet vector u_4 can exhibit features more similar to u_1, thereby inferring that v_4 and v_1 form a pair of seed nodes. On this basis, this paper introduces the transformation matrix W, to align u across different dimensions. Equation (11) is thus rewritten as Formula (14), where U^{d_1} and R^{d_2} represent different vector spaces of dimensions d_1 and d_2, respectively. W, u_i, and r^k are parameters to be learned in the MNF-UI model. From the above discussion, theoretically, the more networks involved, the higher the accuracy of node matching. Therefore, we propose a total objective function for joint training across all networks, as shown in Formula (15), where J^k is the objective function for each network G^k, capable of preserving the structural information of each node in G^k. For every directed edge (v_i^k, v_j^k) in network G^k, we define the conditional probability of generating v_j^k from v_i^k as Formula (16). The objective function for each network G^k can be defined as Formula (17).

$$v_4^3 = u_4 + r^3 \tag{13}$$

$$v_i^k = Wu_i + r^k, u_i \in U^{d_1}, v_i^k \in R^{d_2} \tag{14}$$

$$J = \sum_{k} J^k \tag{15}$$

$$p(v_j^k \middle| v_i^k) = \frac{\exp((Wu_i + r^k) \cdot (Wu_j + r^k))}{\sum_{v_z^k \in v^k} \exp((Wu_i + r^k) \cdot (Wu_z + r^k))} \tag{16}$$

$$J^k = \sum_{(v_j^k, v_i^k) \in E^k} p(v_j^k \middle| v_i^k) \tag{17}$$

During the training process, the known seed nodes will play their utmost role, passing structural information through the shared internet vector u, ensuring this vector captures the commonality between seed nodes. Meanwhile, with Formula (16), the intranet vector v of each seed node can maintain its local structural features in different networks, thus allowing the network vector r^k to extract and identify the global structural features of the network itself. For each unknown seed node v_i^k, although we cannot establish a direct connection with the corresponding network, the composite vector, i.e., the intranet vector, can identify some similar features in other networks. By eliminating the influence of network structure r^k, the internet vector will exhibit features similar to those of seed nodes, something which is highly effective for node matching.

After training, we will be able to obtain the internet vector for each node, representing the common information between different seed nodes. In the problem of multi-social network user identification, a basic approach is to calculate the similarity between nodes. We use cosine similarity to measure the distance between two nodes and set a threshold. Node pairs with a similarity above this threshold are sorted by similarity, and the pair with the highest similarity is selected as the successfully identified seed node pair. Nodes below the threshold are discarded, indicating that the corresponding seed node pair was not identified in this match.

3.3. Experiments and Analysis of Results

We conducted a series of experiments aimed at validating the effectiveness of our proposed multi-network fusion for user identification (MNF-UI) model. By comparing our model with several leading methods in the field of multi-social-network user identification, we demonstrated the advantages and application potential of our approach.

(1) Experimental datasets

To validate the effectiveness of the MNF-UI model, this study selected widely recognized public datasets in the field of multi-social-network user identification for experimentation. Specifically, the first dataset chosen was based on the data from the 2013 World Athletics Championships which divided the Twitter dataset into three independent networks: Twitter-RT, Twitter-MT, and Twitter-RE through behaviors such as retweeting, mentioning, and replying. This dataset contains 88,804 nodes, 210,250 edges, and 55,362 seed links. The second dataset encompasses four real social network platforms: Twitter, MySpace, Facebook, and LinkedIn. Detailed information about this dataset is provided in Section 2.3 and its summary information is also presented in Table 5. The selection of these two datasets aimed to comprehensively assess the MNF-UI model's ability to identify users in different social network environments and the model's adaptability and effectiveness in processing different types of network structural information.

Table 5. Twitter–MySpace–Facebook–LinkedIn dataset information.

Social Networks	Number of Users	Number of Relationships	Number of Seed Nodes
Twitter	4572	154,921	653
MySpace	4716	93,725	
Facebook	4039	88,234	
LinkedIn	3718	63,528	

(2) Evaluation indexes and experimental settings

To validate the effectiveness of our proposed method in solving the problem of multi-social-network user identification, this study adopted an approach that solely utilizes network structural information and compared it with four different baseline methods, as detailed in Table 6.

Table 6. Four baseline methods.

Name of Method	Algorithm Description	Type
NetAlign [26]	The messaging algorithm is used to identify social network users in unsupervised mode and explore the potential correspondence between network structures.	Unsupervised
REGAL [27]	The similarity-based graph vector representation is extracted, and the same user across multiple social networks is identified by comparing these learned embedding vectors.	Unsupervised
FINAL [28]	From the perspective of optimization, according to the principle of network consistency, supplemented by attribute information, the same user across multiple social networks is accurately identified through a series of attribute recognition algorithms.	Unsupervised
IONE [29]	Node vectors, including the input vectors and output vectors of nodes, are used to jointly define the representation of user nodes. This representation strategy effectively maintains the mapping of the relationship between the concerned and the followed between users in the network in the embedded space.	Semi-oversight

To further explore the performance differences between the MNF-UI model and existing methods in the field of multi-social network user identification, this study conducted experimental validations using two different datasets. The first dataset was based on the 2013 World Athletics Championships and divided Twitter data into three independent networks through actions such as retweeting, mentioning, and replying. The second dataset spanned Twitter, MySpace, Facebook, and LinkedIn, providing a diversified social network environment. To ensure the fairness of the experiments, all embedding-based methods adopted the same node dimension setting, i.e., $d = 100$. In the MNF-UI model, we specifically set $d_1 = 100$ and $d_2 = 100$ and, to accelerate the training process, the number of negative samples was set to 1. In the multi-social-network user identification task, we utilized the internet vector as a key tool. For experimental design, we randomly selected 50% of the seed links as the test set, with the remainder used as the training set. Moreover, we compared the identification accuracy of the MNF-UI model with several other models.

In this study, we adopted the widely recognized evaluation standard in the field of multi-social-network user identification, i.e., $pre@\alpha$, as the key indicator to assess the performance of our model. The design goal of $pre@\alpha$ is to quantify the accuracy of seed node identification between two networks G^i and G^j. The calculation formula for this evaluation metric is as described in Formula (18), where $UnMappedAnchors^{(i,j)}$ represents the number of seed node links that were not successfully matched, including both correct and incorrect matches, $RightNodes^{(i,j)}@\alpha$ refers to the number of seed node links that were correctly matched. Further, the specific expression of this evaluation metric can be referred to in Formula (19), where N represents the total number of networks:

$$pre^{(i,j)}@\alpha = \frac{\left|\mathrm{Right}Nodes^{(i,j)}@\alpha\right|}{\left|UnMappedAnchors^{(i,j)}\right|} \tag{18}$$

$$pre@\alpha = \frac{1}{N(N-1)}\sum_{i}\sum_{j\neq i} pre^{(i,j)}@\alpha \tag{19}$$

(3) Analysis of experimental results

First, we set the proportion of the training set to 50% and adjusted the value of parameter α. Based on this, we conducted a comprehensive comparison of several algorithms on two different datasets. As shown in Figure 8, the x-axis represents the number of top α similar nodes selected from the test set, while the y-axis reflects the probability of correctly matching nodes between different networks among the top α nodes. By gradually increasing the value of α in intervals of 10, it can be clearly observed in Figure 8a,b that both MNF-UI and IONE demonstrated superior performance in relation to the two datasets. In contrast, unsupervised learning methods such as NetAlign, REGAL, and FINAL performed poorly relative to all datasets examined. The fundamental reason for this phenomenon is that the structure of each social network does not strictly adhere to the topological structure consistency principle assumed by these algorithms, leading to their identification effects being far inferior than that of the model we proposed.

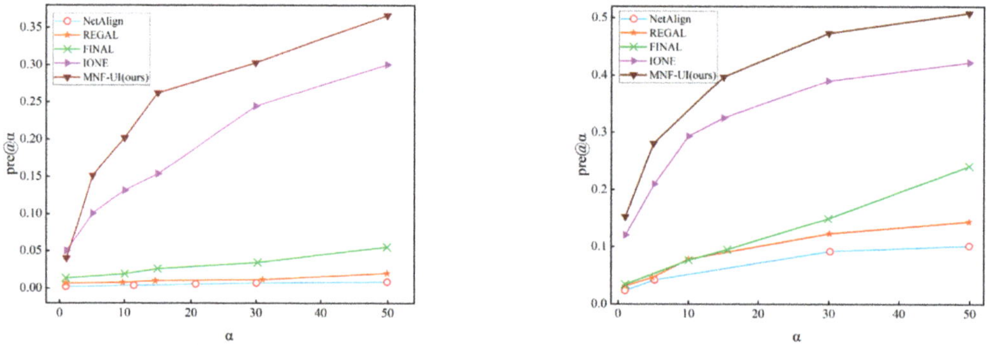

(**a**) The first dataset (**b**) The second dataset

Figure 8. Change the experimental results of α.

From the analysis of Figure 8a,b, it is evident that the model proposed in this study significantly outperformed the other benchmark models with respect to the vast majority of training sets. Notably, even under conditions of extremely limited training data, our model still demonstrated certain effectiveness. This experimental result proves that our method can still function even in situations where seed link information is scarce, something which is very common in practical application scenarios. Although the network embedding-based IONE method can achieve good identification results on various datasets, it only considers pairwise learning of two networks, thus ignoring the complementary information between many networks. At the same time, this method does not fully consider the characteristics of the network structure, leading to ineffective matching of seed nodes where structural local differences exist. Therefore, the recognition effect of the IONE method is limited in scenarios with small structural differences between networks. For example, in the Twitter dataset, because the dataset is divided into retweet, mention, and reply sub-networks based on the same event, these three networks show a similar global structure, and the distribution of seed nodes is relatively uniform, thus IONE performed well on this dataset. Especially when the training set ratio was 50% and $\alpha = 1$, the recognition effect of IONE was better than our model. However, as the training set ratio increased, our model gradually demonstrated a recognition performance that surpassed that of other models by integrating the collective learning ability of all networks.

Setting the parameter α to 30 and adjusting the proportion of the training set, we compared the performance of various algorithms using two different datasets. The results are shown in Figure 9. The x-axis represents the selected test set proportion, while the y-axis indicates the probability of successfully matching the top 30 nodes with the target node in the test set. The proportion of the test set starts at 0.1 and increases in increments of 0.1 to 0.9 to evaluate the two datasets. The results show that MNF-UI and IONE performed well under different test set proportions, while methods such as NetAlign, REGAL, and FINAL exhibited a relatively mediocre performance across all test proportions. Part of the reason for this phenomenon is that these social network structures do not follow the assumed topological structure consistency, leading to significant local structural differences of the same users in different networks. Therefore, even when the training set proportion reached 0.9, these methods still failed to achieve significant effects. Although IONE performed better than the other three methods under different test proportions, since it only involves pairwise learning among multiple networks without fully exploiting the potential complementary information among multiple networks, its effectiveness was still inferior to that of our proposed model.

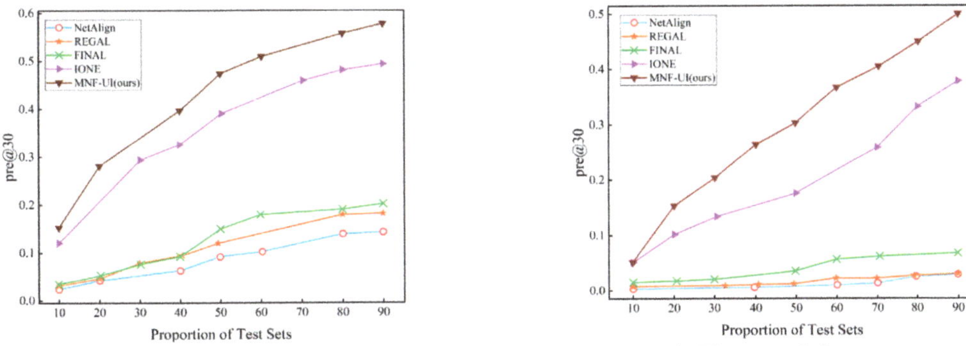

(**a**) The first dataset (**b**) The second dataset

Figure 9. Experimental results adjusted for the scale of the test set.

On the Twitter–MySpace–Facebook–LinkedIn dataset, the IONE method did not achieve better recognition results due to significant structural differences among these four social networks. IONE is limited to pairwise learning of matching information between two networks and lacks the ability to handle structural differences among multiple networks. In contrast, our proposed model, through joint learning of four networks, can not only effectively integrate cross-network information, but also mitigate the impact of network structural differences to a certain extent. This characteristic significantly enhances the model's efficiency and accuracy in user identification across multi-network environments, thereby achieving superior recognition results relative to this dataset.

To explore the specific impact of dimension parameters on experimental effects, we conducted detailed experimental research on the dimension parameters d_1 and d_2 for two key vectors—internet vector and intranet vector. Initially, we set both d1 and d2 to 100 as the baseline parameters. During the experiments, we tested the impact of parameter changes on the experimental results by fixing one parameter while changing the other. The experiments were conducted on the Twitter–MySpace–Facebook–LinkedIn dataset, with the training set proportion set to 50% and parameter α set to 30. According to the experimental results (as shown in Figure 10a,b), the following phenomena can be observed: as the dimension of d_1 increased, the model's performance significantly improved. This indicates that increasing the dimension of the internet vector effectively enhanced the model's ability to capture network structural information, thereby improving the accuracy of user identification. However, when d_2 exceeded a certain threshold, performance tended to stabilize, and this threshold appears to be related to the scale of the network. Specifically, on the Twitter–MySpace–Facebook–LinkedIn dataset, performance gains tended to plateau when d_1 exceeded 200. Meanwhile, the impact of the d_2 dimension on model performance was relatively limited. This finding suggests that adopting a smaller value strategy for d_2 can not only save computational resources, but also optimize model performance to some extent, under the premise of ensuring model efficiency. Therefore, selecting appropriate values for d_1 and d_2 is of great significance for resource optimization and performance enhancement. For instance, setting d_1 to 300 and d_2 to 500 can ensure model performance while being more resource-efficient.

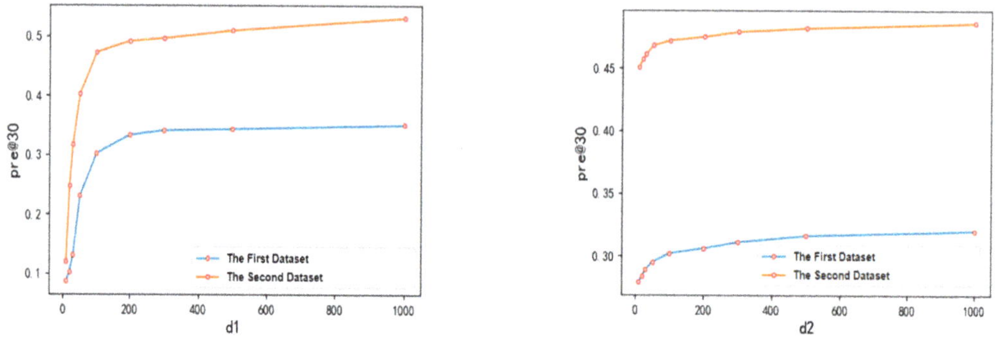

(**a**) experimental result d1 (**b**) experimental result d2

Figure 10. Effect of dimensions on the recognition effect of MNF-UI model.

4. Conclusions

With the rapid development of internet technology, various social networking platforms with different functionalities have emerged one after the other. While people enjoy the convenience brought by these platforms, it also exerts certain impacts on network security. Therefore, the problem of social network user identification holds significant research importance. It can integrate user information across multiple social networks, which is crucial for user recommendation, network security, and public opinion supervision. This paper first introduces the background and significance of multi-social-network user identification, analyzes the current research status, clarifies the challenges faced by multi-social-network user identification, and points out the problems existing in current research methods and the directions for improvement. To address the issues in multi-social-network user identification, this paper proposes two methods. The main research contents are as follows:

1. This paper applies graph convolutional networks to the task of cross-social-network user identification and proposes a cross-social-network user identification model based on bidirectional GCN. First, we propose a user intimacy measurement method based on the Jaccard coefficient which reflects the degree of intimacy between social network users in the adjacency matrix. Secondly, we reconstruct the adjacency matrix of social networks. Finally, we randomly initialize user features to address the problem of unobtainable user attributes. Experimental results show that our model significantly outperforms the baseline models.

2. In response to the current methods' over-reliance on the assumption of network topological structure consistency and the inability to identify users across multiple social networks, we propose a multi-social network user identification model based on MNF-UI. Our model defines a network feature vector representing the structural features of each social network which can reflect the global structural differences between social networks. It represents each seed node's vector as the sum of the cross-network common features inherent in the seed node and the network features of the network where the seed node is located. Then, it uses the cross-network common features inherent in the seed node for user identification, successfully solving the problems existing in current methods. Moreover, our model achieved better recognition effects on two datasets compared to baseline models.

In summary, based on existing user identification methods, this paper innovatively combines the advantages of graph convolutional networks, network embedding, and data mining to conduct a deeper study on the algorithm for multi-social network user identification. Finally, it proposes two algorithms that can be used for multi-social-network user identification, providing technical and theoretical support for in-depth research on social network information fusion and network security maintenance.

Author Contributions: Software, C.L.; Validation, F.X.; Writing—original draft, S.H.; Writing—review & editing, H.X. All authors have read and agreed to the published version of the manuscript.

Funding: This research received no external funding.

Data Availability Statement: Data are contained within the article.

Conflicts of Interest: The authors declare no conflict of interest.

References

1. Van Dülmen, C.; Klärner, A. Places that bond and bind: On the interplay of space, places, and social networks. *Soc. Incl.* **2022**, *10*, 248–261. [CrossRef]
2. Xing, L.; Deng, K.; Wu, H.; Xie, P.; Zhao, H.V.; Gao, F. A survey of across social networks user identification. *IEEE Access* **2019**, *7*, 137472–137488. [CrossRef]
3. Zahra, K.; Azam, F.; Butt, W.H.; Ilyas, F. User identification on social networks through text mining techniques: A systematic literature review. In *Information Science and Applications 2018*; Springer Nature: Singapore, 2019; pp. 485–498.
4. Zeng, W.; Tang, R.; Wang, H.; Chen, X.; Wang, W. User identification based on integrating multiple user information across online social networks. *Secur. Commun. Netw.* **2021**, *2021*, 5533417. [CrossRef]
5. Çoban, Ö.; Ali, İ.; Ozels, A. Your username can give you away: Matching turkish OSN users with usernames. *Int. J. Inf. Secur. Sci.* **2021**, *10*, 1–15.
6. Li, Y.; Peng, Y.; Zhang, Z.; Yin, H.; Xu, Q. Matching user accounts across social networks based on username and display name. *World Wide Web* **2019**, *22*, 1075–1097. [CrossRef]
7. Solanki, P.; Harwood, A. User identification across social networking sites using user profiles and posting patterns. In Proceedings of the 2021 International Joint Conference on Neural Networks (IJCNN), Shenzhen, China, 18–22 July 2021; IEEE: New York, NY, USA, 2021; pp. 1–8.
8. Qu, Y.; Yu, S.; Zhou, W.; Niu, J. FBI: Friendship learning-based user identification in multiple social networks. In Proceedings of the 2018 IEEE Global Communications Conference (GLOBECOM), Abu Dhabi, United Arab Emirates, 9–13 December 2018; IEEE: New York, NY, USA, 2018; pp. 1–6.
9. Kojima, K.; Ikeda, K.; Masahiro, T. Short Paper: User Identification across Online Social Networks Based on Similarities among Distributions of Friends' Locations. In Proceedings of the 2019 IEEE International Conference on Big Data (Big Data), Los Angeles, CA, USA, 9–12 December 2019; IEEE: New York, NY, USA, 2019; pp. 4085–4088.
10. Ahmad, W.; Ali, R. User identification across multiple online social networks using cross link attribute and network relationship. *J. Interdiscip. Math.* **2020**, *23*, 205–214. [CrossRef]
11. Qu, Y.; Xing, L.; Ma, H.; Wu, H.; Zhang, K.; Deng, K. Exploiting user friendship networks for user identification across social networks. *Symmetry* **2022**, *14*, 110. [CrossRef]
12. Xing, L.; Deng, K.; Wu, H.; Xie, P.; Gao, J. Behavioral habits-based user identification across social networks. *Symmetry* **2019**, *11*, 1134. [CrossRef]
13. Lei, T.; Ji, L.; Liu, S. Investigation of Cross-Social Network User Identification. In Proceedings of the 2021 International Conference on Advanced Computing and Endogenous Security, Nanjing, China, 21–22 April 2022; IEEE: New York, NY, USA, 2022; pp. 1–7.
14. Ke, Q.; Jing, X.; Woźniak, M.; Xu, S.; Liang, Y.; Zheng, J. APGVAE: Adaptive disentangled representation learning with the graph-based structure information. *Inf. Sci.* **2024**, *657*, 119903. [CrossRef]
15. Dong, W.; Wu, J.; Zhang, X.; Bai, Z.; Wang, P.; Woźniak, M. Improving performance and efficiency of Graph Neural Networks by injective aggregation. *Knowl. Based Syst.* **2022**, *254*, 109616. [CrossRef]
16. Lavanya, R.; Saksena, A.; Singh, A. Effective networking on social media platforms for building connections and expanding E-commerce business by analyzing social networks and user's nature and reliability. In *Artificial Intelligence Techniques for Advanced Computing Applications: Proceedings of ICACT 2020*; Springer: Singapore, 2021; pp. 503–514.
17. Yang, D.; Qu, B.; Yang, J.; Cudré-Mauroux, P. Lbsn2vec++: Heterogeneous hypergraph embedding for location-based social networks. *IEEE Trans. Knowl. Data Eng.* **2020**, *34*, 1843–1855. [CrossRef]
18. Pei, H.; Wei, B.; Chang KC, C.; Lei, Y.; Yang, B. Geom-gcn: Geometric graph convolutional networks. *arXiv* **2020**, arXiv:2002.05287.
19. Lei, T.; Ji, L.; Wang, G.; Liu, S.; Wu, L.; Pan, F. Transformer-Based User Alignment Model across Social Networks. *Electronics* **2023**, *12*, 1686. [CrossRef]
20. Ma, T.; Guo, L.; Wang, X.; Qian, Y.; Tian, Y.; Al-Nabhan, N. Friend closeness based user matching cross social networks. *Math. Biosci. Eng.* **2021**, *18*, 4264–4292. [CrossRef] [PubMed]
21. Ding, X.; Zhang, H.; Ma, C.; Zhang, X.; Zhong, K. User identification across multiple social networks based on naive Bayes model. *IEEE Trans. Neural Netw. Learn. Syst.* **2024**, *35*, 4274–4285. [CrossRef] [PubMed]
22. Qu, Y.; Ma, H.; Wu, H.; Zhang, K.; Deng, K. A Multiple Salient Features-Based User Identification across Social Media. *Entropy* **2022**, *24*, 495. [CrossRef] [PubMed]

23. Zhou, F.; Liu, L.; Zhang, K.; Trajcevski, G.; Wu, J.; Zhong, T. Deeplink: A deep learning approach for user identity linkage. In Proceedings of the IEEE INFOCOM 2018-IEEE Conference on Computer Communications, Honolulu, HI, USA, 16–19 April 2018; IEEE: New York, NY, USA, 2018; pp. 1313–1321.
24. Shu, K.; Wang, S.; Tang, J.; Zafarani, R.; Liu, H. User identity linkage across online social networks: A review. *Acm Sigkdd Explor. Newsl.* **2017**, *18*, 5–17. [CrossRef]
25. Zhang, Y.; Tang, J.; Yang, Z.; Pei, J.; Yu, P.S. Cosnet: Connecting heterogeneous social networks with local and global consistency. In Proceedings of the 21th ACM SIGKDD International Conference on Knowledge Discovery and Data Mining, Sydney, Australia, 10–13 August 2015; ACM: New York, NY, USA, 2015; pp. 1485–1494.
26. Huang, X.; Chen, D.; Ren, T.; Wang, D. A survey of community detection methods in multilayer networks. *Data Min. Knowl. Discov.* **2021**, *35*, 1–45. [CrossRef]
27. Heimann, M.; Shen, H.; Safavi, T.; Koutra, D. Regal: Representation learning-based graph alignment. In Proceedings of the 27th ACM International Conference on Information and Knowledge Management, Torino, Italy, 22–26 October 2018; ACM: New York, NY, USA, 2018; pp. 117–126.
28. Bhowmick, S.; Bell, P.; Taufer, M. A Survey of Graph Comparison Methods with Applications to Nondeterminism in High-Performance Computing. *Int. J. High Perform. Comput. Appl.* **2023**, *37*, 306–327. [CrossRef]
29. Liu, L.; Cheung, W.K.; Li, X.; Liao, L. Aligning Users across Social Networks Using Network Embedding. In Proceedings of the Twenty-Eighth International Joint Conference on Artificial Intelligence (IJCAI-16), New York, NY, USA, 9–15 July 2016; IJCAI: New York, NY, USA, 2016; pp. 1774–1780.

electronics

MDPI

Article

A Bayesian-Attack-Graph-Based Security Assessment Method for Power Systems

Lu Chen [1,2,*], Tao Zhang [1,2], Yuanyuan Ma [1,2], Yong Li [1,2], Chen Wang [1,2], Chuan He [1,2], Zhuo Lv [3,4] and Nuannuan Li [3,4]

1 State Grid Smart Grid Research Institute Co., Ltd., Nanjing 210003, China; zhangtao@geiri.sgcc.com.cn (T.Z.); mayuanyuan@geiri.sgcc.com.cn (Y.M.); liyong@geiri.sgcc.com.cn (Y.L.); wangchen@geiri.sgcc.com.cn (C.W.); hechuan@geiri.sgcc.com.cn (C.H.)

2 State Grid Laboratory of Power Cyber-Security Protection and Monitoring Technology, Nanjing 210003, China

3 State Grid Henan Electric Power Research Institute, Zhengzhou 450000, China; lvzhuo@ha.sgcc.com.cn (Z.L.); linuannuan@ha.sgcc.com.cn (N.L.)

4 State Grid Henan Electric Power Company, Zhengzhou 450000, China

* Correspondence: chenluchina@aliyun.com

Abstract: In today's highly advanced information technology environment, modern network and communication technologies are widely used in monitoring and controlling power systems. These technologies have evolved significantly. They now form a high-performance digital system known as the cyber–physical power system. However, vulnerabilities in communication networks present growing threats to these systems. This paper seeks to enhance the accurate assessment of the security posture of cyber-physical power systems by inferring attackers' intentions. A threat modeling approach based on Bayesian attack graphs is presented, employing Bayesian networks to define and evaluate potential threats that attackers could pose to different system infrastructures. The paper initially conducts a qualitative analysis of the system's threats, constructing a directed graph structure and establishing conditional probability tables among nodes based on prior knowledge. Subsequently, methods are developed to compute the threat levels at different system nodes using real-time detected attack events. Further analysis methods and security assessment metrics are also developed to identify attack paths and quantify system security. Finally, a Bayesian attack graph is constructed in accordance with the system's structure. In practical scenarios, the attack path analysis method can predict the most vulnerable attack paths, while the absolute values of the security assessment metrics indicate the overall risk level of the system.

Keywords: cyber–physical systems; Bayesian attack graph; threat modelling; power system security; vulnerability assessment

1. Introduction

Modern power grids are critical infrastructure, and any threats to them could significantly impact national security and economic stability. Integrating modern network communication technology into power systems enhances monitoring and control functions [1]. However, this incorporation increases the likelihood of cyber threats, raising the risk of catastrophic failures. If the vulnerabilities of the system are attacked, it will threaten the safe and stable operation of the power systems and cause serious consequences [2]. The new generation of power systems, which intertwine traditional power grids with modern network communication technologies, are regarded as highly interconnected and interdependent infrastructure [3–5]. Any component failure can significantly affect the entire power system [6].

Standardized communication protocols reveal vulnerabilities. These vulnerabilities affect power systems significantly, allowing attackers to gain unauthorized access and control over assets [7]. These new power systems comprise both traditional power grid infrastructure and communication networks for monitoring and control. Substations communicate with regional control centers using Ethernet protocols, while control centers exchange information via inter-control center protocols and communicate with transmission operators through Ethernet routers. In this context, intruders can exploit vulnerabilities in control centers or substations to gain administrator privileges over human–machine interfaces. With this access, they can manipulate control commands to operate circuit breakers in the physical power system, leading to imbalances between power generation and load that cause grid instability [8].

For example, the Stuxnet attack in 2010 exploited programmable logic controllers that controlled centrifuges, causing equipment failures and severely damaging Iran's nuclear facilities. In 2015, a coordinated cyberattack caused a massive power outage in Ukraine, affecting hundreds of thousands of people. These incidents took advantage of vulnerabilities in firewalls and communication protocols within power systems. Due to their critical positions and weak defense mechanisms, these network vulnerabilities are attractive to hackers and pose significant risks to the safe and stable operation of power grids. Therefore, assessing and analyzing the vulnerabilities of cyber–physical power systems under cyberattacks is essential, enabling the effective identification of weak nodes and the rational allocation of defense resources.

In recent years, researchers worldwide have explored this issue and proposed various assessment methods. Wu [9] designed a network attack selection model based on attack costs. By analyzing these costs, they identified network attacks with higher probabilities of success and provided corresponding countermeasures, reducing cybersecurity risks. However, their method overlooked the attack gains those attackers consider in practice. Sun [10] combined Markov chains and attack graphs to assess network risks, quantifying atomic attack success probabilities based on vulnerability disclosure status, available attack methods, and tools. They calculated node risk values accordingly. Hu [11] converted attack graphs into absorbing Markov chains and quantified state transition probabilities using the CVSS vulnerability scoring system, thereby determining node probabilities. Although these methods are feasible, they overlook that attackers are intelligent decision-makers who consider both attack costs and gains. Additionally, as these methods do not account for the impact of detected attack events on node probabilities, they can only provide static assessments and cannot dynamically evaluate risks.

Xie [12] considered attack events while analyzing network security with Bayesian networks but did not calculate the posterior probabilities of nodes with observed attack events. Poolsappasit [13] used observed node states in Bayesian networks as attack evidence to compute posterior probabilities, dynamically assessing network risk and providing administrators with real-time security insights. Chen [14] used observed attack events to deduce the probability of specific attacks but only discussed the impact of observed attack events on the posterior probabilities of directly affected nodes, neglecting the influence on related nodes. Gao [15] comprehensively considered the effect of attack events on posterior probabilities when assessing network risk using Bayesian attack graphs but did not analyze how attack costs and benefits affected node probabilities. Ma [16] quantified node probabilities based on attack pressure and unknown threats, improving assessment accuracy, but overlooked cases where node relationships are "OR".

Risk analysis involves inherent uncertainties that incorporate aspects such as the complexity of the system, parameter randomness, the risk model applied, and human subjectivity [17]. Based on the above principles, this paper introduces a novel threat modeling approach tailored for power system infrastructures. Unlike typical methods that overlook the economic motivations behind attacks, our model innovatively incorporates the importance of assets and the cost implications of launching attacks. This dual consideration allows for a more realistic estimation of an attacker's probability of initiating an attack, directly addressing the gap in existing approaches that often simplify attacker behavior to technical factors alone.

Further advancing the field, we have developed a method that dynamically calculates the threat level on different system nodes using real-time detected attack events. This approach enhances the adaptability of security assessments, allowing for real-time updates and more accurate risk evaluations compared to static models that fail to capture the fluid nature of cyber threats.

Additionally, our work enhances traditional risk assessments by introducing attack path analysis methods and security evaluation metrics that provide quantifiable indicators following the completion of risk analysis, enabling a detailed evaluation of system vulnerabilities and defenses. These innovations not only help in identifying high-risk attack paths but also facilitate a deeper understanding of systemic vulnerabilities through the comparison of security assessment values based on prior and posterior probabilities. By integrating these elements, the proposed method significantly refines the accuracy and relevance of security assessments, providing a comprehensive tool for power system protection.

The primary application of the Bayesian attack graph methodology developed in this paper is to enhance the security assessment of cyber–physical power systems. These systems, integral to the infrastructure of modern power grids, are increasingly susceptible to sophisticated cyberattacks that can disrupt their operation and stability.

Our approach utilizes Bayesian attack graphs to model potential attack paths and quantify the likelihood of successful exploits, enabling system operators to predict and mitigate the most probable threats. By integrating this model into regular security assessments, operators can dynamically evaluate the system's vulnerability to various attack scenarios. This proactive analysis helps in prioritizing security measures and allocating resources more effectively to protect critical infrastructure components.

The Bayesian attack graph method offers a systematic way to assess risk by considering both the likelihood of attack vectors and the potential impact of successful breaches. This dual focus is crucial for maintaining not just the operational integrity but also the safety of power systems which are essential for national security and economic stability.

The remainder of this paper is organized as follows. Section 2 discusses the technical methods involved in the proposed approach. Section 3 describes the novel power system model used for threat analysis. Section 4 provides a detailed simulation of the proposed solution's results. Finally, Section 5 concludes this paper.

2. Power System Cyber Security Analysis and Modelling

Malicious cyberattacks targeting power systems typically progress through multiple stages, with each stage exploiting vulnerabilities in various system assets. Beyond the initial attack, subsequent stages depend on successfully compromising specific assets within the system. This dependence implies that network intrusions can be modeled using directed graphs, where nodes represent assets and attack actions, and directed edges signify the dependencies between them. Thus, by analyzing the topology and vulnerabilities of the system, a corresponding Bayesian attack graph can be constructed. The process for constructing a Bayesian attack graph for a specific system is illustrated in the diagram. The lowest layer consists of the physical entities, including primary electrical equipment such as generators, transformers, transmission lines, and loads. These components are electrically interconnected within the physical layer, forming the backbone of the power system that directly handles the generation, transmission, and distribution of electrical energy.

As shown in Figure 1, this illustrates the process of constructing a Bayesian attack graph. The first step involves analyzing the network topology and vulnerability information of the system to establish the structure of the Bayesian attack graph. Subsequently, by integrating CVSS metrics and expert knowledge, the probabilities of vulnerability exploitation and attack execution are assessed, resulting in the conditional probability distribution of the nodes. Once the quantification of node information is completed, a complete Bayesian attack graph is obtained.

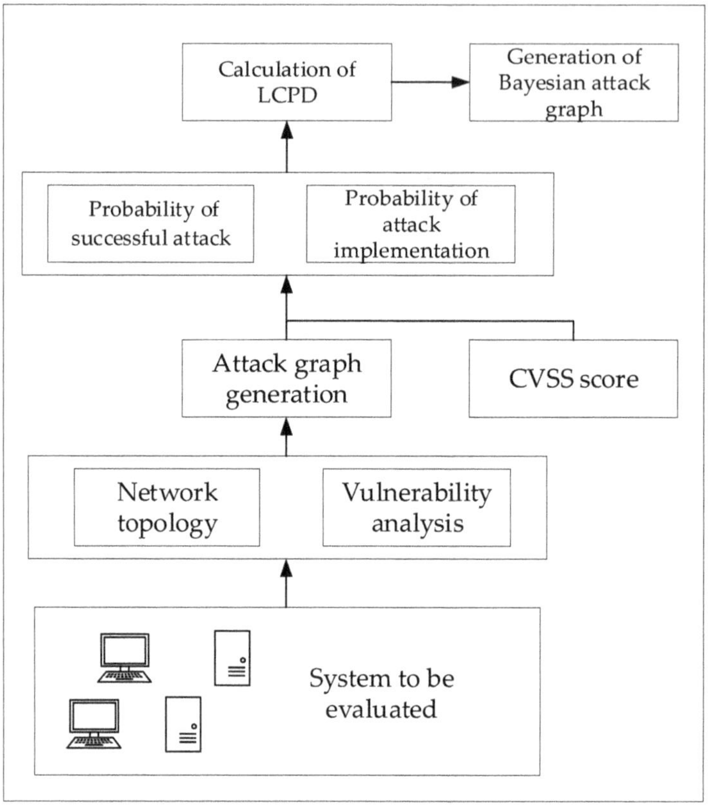

Figure 1. Bayesian attack graph generation framework.

Therefore, this section will conduct a cybersecurity analysis of the electrical power system, introducing the types of cyberattacks that may exist within the system. Following this, the basic definition of the Bayesian attack graph for the targeted power system is provided. Finally, a node information quantification method based on CVSS scoring metrics is proposed, facilitating the construction of the Bayesian attack graph.

2.1. Power System Network Security Analysis

Modern power grids are exemplary cyber–physical systems (CPSs), intricately weaving together electrical infrastructure and communication technology. As depicted in Figure 2, the hierarchical structure of the power CPS is meticulously outlined from the control centers to the physical devices.

At the topmost layer are the control centers, encompassing distribution main stations, SCADA servers, and Management Information System (MIS) servers [18]. These centers form the neural network of the power CPS, responsible for processing and managing data across the entire grid, monitoring the operational status, and ensuring the stability and security of the power supply.

Beneath this is the power communication network layer, composed of various communication devices and protocols, such as routers, smart meters, and actuators. This layer facilitates the transmission of data, including measurement information and control commands, between the control centers and distributed substations, ensuring seamless communication within the system.

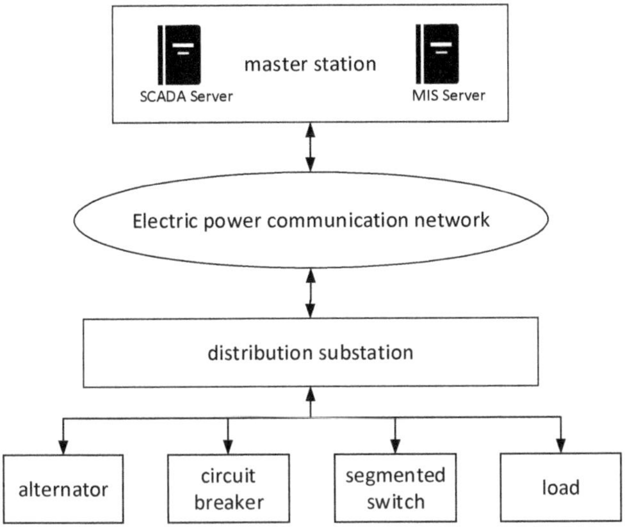

Figure 2. Hierarchical structure of the power CPS.

Further down is the distributed substation layer, equipped with secondary devices like Remote Terminal Units (RTUs) and Feeder Terminal Units (FTUs). These units act as the interface between the physical and information layers, collecting real-time data from the grid and executing control commands from the information layer, playing a crucial role in regulating the operation of the power system.

The lowest layer consists of physical entities, including primary electrical equipment such as generators, transformers, transmission lines, and loads. These components are electrically interconnected within the physical layer, forming the backbone of the power system that directly handles the generation, transmission, and distribution of electrical energy.

Building upon the integrated communication technologies within the power CPS, the system is a multi-layered distributed network, where each subsystem interacts and coordinates through fiber optic communications and wireless transmission methods. Sensors embedded within primary power equipment continuously sample operational data from the power system. These data are digitized by measuring and control units and transmitted up the communication network to the main station's measurement data management system. The central station servers then perform real-time online calculations based on the received grid operational data and issue control commands to regulate power generation equipment. These control commands are relayed through the communication network to specific devices, where intelligent control units execute operations according to the instructions provided.

Network attacks on power CPS systems can be divided into WAN and NAN attacks. Wide Area Network (WAN) communication has a broad coverage (up to 100 km), with a data transmission frequency ranging from 10 Mbit/s to 1 Gbit/s. It supports real-time monitoring and protection in power systems and provides a communication pathway between NANs and control centers, thus serving as the backbone of smart grid networks. Power applications like SCADA telemetry, EMMS energy management, WAMS phasor measurement unit (PMU) data processing, and data exchange between substations and control centers rely on WAN communication [19]. Typical WAN attack targets include generation and control equipment. In substation automation, WAN attacks can occur via VPNs, dial-up networks, wireless networks, remote login programs, or Trojan programs on unidentified devices. Infiltration methods include repetitive dialing, scanning, communication monitoring, and password cracking. Such attacks could lead to the loss or tampering of system information, causing secondary equipment misoperation or failure, potentially resulting in equipment damage, line overloads, load losses, and system instability. In extreme cases, this could trigger large-scale cascading failures, leading to severe economic losses [20].

Neighborhood Area Networks (NANs) support data exchange between WANs and users within a range of approximately 10 km, with data transmission rates from 100 kbit/s to 10 Mbit/s. NANs facilitate bidirectional data transmission between user devices and data concentrators or substations, enabling services like remote metering, usage control, and field equipment monitoring through the metering network. Typical NAN attack targets include power substations and distribution centers, and attacks can be carried out directly through substations or secure access gateways. Since NANs connect users to WANs, their network security is crucial to the entire smart grid. NAN network attack detection can leverage intrusion detection systems based on support vector machines and artificial intelligence methods [21]. Scholars also suggest adopting more sophisticated authentication mechanisms to reduce NAN network attack risks.

Furthermore, on the user side of power systems, attackers can reverse-engineer easily accessible user-side equipment (e.g., smart meters and communication hardware) to identify vulnerabilities for targeted attacks. Strengthening authentication mechanisms is also an effective preventive measure against these attacks.

In power systems, network attacks primarily exploit security vulnerabilities to infiltrate information devices, gaining control over functional nodes and progressively compromising the information system to disrupt the normal operation of intelligent electronic devices. This could ultimately cause system failures and disrupt the power grid's normal functioning, thereby achieving cross-domain attacks from the information to the physical domain. As new applications and smart devices increasingly connect to power CPS systems, substations and distribution centers face more NAN network attacks. Therefore, this paper mainly investigates network attacks on substation control center local area networks.

2.2. *Definition of Bayesian Attack Graphs*

Probabilistic graphical models effectively and succinctly represent relationships between variables and offer powerful tools for reasoning under uncertainty. They have become a popular research area in artificial intelligence and machine learning in recent years. Currently, probabilistic graphical models have been successfully applied in various fields, including image analysis, biomedical studies, and computer science. To perform uncertain reasoning using probabilistic graphical models, one must first construct the model using domain knowledge. Probabilistic graphical models combine graph theory and probability theory to compactly describe multivariate statistical relationships. Different representations exist, such as Bayesian networks, Markov networks, chain graphs (CGs), temporal models (TMs), and probabilistic relational models (PRMs). Although these representations vary, they all aim to factorize joint probability distributions by assuming conditional independence, simplifying the representation and inference process. Due to their ability to reflect the uncertainty of attack behaviors effectively, Bayesian networks are commonly used to model and detect distributed threats in threat modeling.

Bayesian networks consist of nodes and directed edges. The directed edges indicate dependencies between nodes, which may represent logical relationships such as causality. A directed edge from node 1 to node 2 indicates that the probability distribution of node 2 is influenced by node 1. If no path exists between two nodes, they are considered probabilistically independent. In threat modeling, nodes represent resources and attacks, while directed edges illustrate causal relationships. A directed edge from an attack node to a resource node suggests that the resource may be at risk of this attack, meaning it could be compromised if the attack is launched.

To model vulnerabilities in power CPS systems using Bayesian attack graphs, we assume that attackers have one or multiple potential targets, such as compromising the confidentiality, integrity, or availability of certain system resources. Various smart devices within power CPS systems contain exploitable vulnerabilities, some of which can be directly leveraged by attackers while others require a certain level of privilege [22]. Thus, in constructing a Bayesian network, resource nodes may not represent a complete device but rather a specific privilege within a device. Attacking this privilege implies that the corresponding vulnerability is being exploited. We assume that the probability of launching an attack depends on its difficulty and potential rewards, while its success rate relies on how easily a vulnerability can be exploited. The attack initiation probabilities constitute the local conditional probability distribution (LCPD) tables of attack nodes, while the attack success probabilities form the LCPD tables of resource nodes.

To quantify threats using Bayesian attack graphs, one must first establish a structural model based on information such as the power network environment, terminal assets, network connectivity, and threat information. Next, a risk assessment system is constructed, and conditional probability tables are provided for each node, forming a complete Bayesian network. Finally, based on the prior probabilities of threat nodes and the conditional probability tables of each node, one can compute the potential changes in core assets resulting from any given threat.

A Bayesian network is a directed acyclic graph with conditional probability tables, defined as a five-tuple $B_{AG} = \{S,\ A,\ E,\ R,\ T\}$ with specific meanings as follows.

1. $S = S_{ext} \cup S_{int} \cup S_{ter}$, S is the set of resource nodes, comprising external attack initiation nodes S_{ext}, attribute state nodes S_{int}, and final attribute state nodes S_{ter}. The nodes have binary values (true/false, 1/0). When false, the attacker lacks specific attack resources or access privileges; when true, the attacker has such resources or privileges. For a node S_i, $P(S_i)$ denotes its accessibility probability, indicating the likelihood that the node has been compromised.
2. $A = \{A_i | i = 1,\ 2, \ldots, n\}$ is the set of attacks in the graph, representing exploitation of asset vulnerabilities. Both parent and child nodes of an attack node are resource nodes. Attack nodes also have binary values. For an attack node A_i, $P(A_i)$ indicates the probability of launching this attack.
3. $E = \{E_i | i = 1,\ 2, \ldots, n\}$ is the set of directed edges in the graph, representing dependencies between nodes. An edge from an asset to an attack node indicates that the attack depends on its parent resource node. An edge from an attack to a resource node indicates that the attack exploits a specific vulnerability of the asset.
4. R represents the dependency of any node with its set of parent nodes. The relations can be either AND (all parents must be true) or OR (at least one parent is true).
5. T is the node's local conditional probability distribution (LCPD) table. Attack node tables depend on attack initiation probabilities, and resource node tables depend on the probability of successful exploitation of their vulnerabilities.

2.3. *Quantification of Node Information*

After constructing the Bayesian network, it is essential to generate conditional probability tables for each intermediate node and calculate the prior probabilities for the initial attack nodes. With these tables and Bayes' theorem, we can compute the conditional probabilities of each node, thereby assessing the network's risk values and predicting potential attack behaviors in advance. Since the Bayesian network in this study is constructed based on the exploitation relationships between vulnerabilities, the network edges represent the vulnerabilities exploited to achieve the attacks. Thus, the conditional probability tables of the Bayesian attack graph are derived from the relevant vulnerability information.

Conditional probability is the likelihood of event B occurring given that event A has already happened. In a Bayesian network, the conditional probability of a node indicates the likelihood of an attack happening, provided that certain attack conditions are met. A vulnerability's severity affects the probability of it being exploited. If the vulnerability level is high, exploitation is more challenging, and thus, less likely. Conversely, if the vulnerability is easily exploited, the success probability of the attack increases. In this study, the Common Vulnerability Scoring System (CVSS) is used to assess vulnerabilities [23], converting these scores into probabilities.

Exploitability, the CVSS sub-item is defined as follows:

$$Exploitability = 8.22 \cdot AV \cdot AC \cdot PR \cdot UI \tag{1}$$

In the CVSS (Common Vulnerability Scoring System) framework, the Attack Vector (AV) metric assesses how a vulnerability can be exploited remotely; a higher score indicates that an attacker can exploit the vulnerability from a more remote location. The Attack Complexity (AC) metric evaluates the complexity of the attack; a higher score signifies that the attack is easier to perform. The Privileges Required (PR) metric determines the level of privileges necessary for an attack; a higher score means lower privileges are needed. The User Interaction (UI) metric measures the degree of user interaction required for an attack; a higher score indicates less user interaction is necessary. Table 1 lists the values of these metrics at different levels.

Table 1. Evaluation Indicators for Basic Metrics Groups.

Norm	Hierarchy	Score
Access Vector	Physical/Local/Adjacent Network/Network	0.2/0.55/0.62/0.85
Access Complexity	High/Low	0.44/0.77
Privileges Required	High/Low/None	0.5/0.68/0.85
User Interaction	Required/None	0.62/0.85

The sub-item "Exploitability" in the CVSS metrics involves calculating the product of the individual scores for Attack Vector (AV), Attack Complexity (AC), Privileges Required (PR), and User Interaction (UI), and then multiplying this product by a constant factor of 8.22. We can refer to it to define the vulnerability exploitability probability. However, considering the definition of probability, which must fall within the interval [0, 1], it is necessary to adjust this constant to fit within these bounds.

To accommodate this requirement, the vulnerability exploitability probability (the attack success probability) can be defined as follows:

$$P_e = 2 \cdot AV \cdot AC \cdot PR \cdot UI \tag{2}$$

For the attacker, the probability of attacking a node depends on the ratio of the attack cost to the attack benefit. The cost is related to the difficulty of exploiting the node's vulnerability, and it is characterized using the base metrics group. The benefit depends on the value the attacker gains from compromising the asset. The attack benefit is defined in Table 2.

Table 2. Attack Gain.

Metric	Value
information leakage	0.3
remote registration	0.55
Authentication bypass	0.65
limited access	0.85
full competence	1

Considering both attack costs and benefits, the probability of an attack occurring is defined as follows:

$$P_a = AC \cdot AV \cdot Value \tag{3}$$

3. Design of the Security Assessment Methodology

In the specific context of power systems, after generating a Bayesian attack graph, it is essential to calculate the conditional probability tables for each node based on prior knowledge to quantify node information. Furthermore, this chapter introduces a static risk analysis method based on prior probabilities and a dynamic risk analysis method based on posterior probabilities. To better understand the attacker's estimated intent and evaluate the overall risk status of the system, an attack path analysis method and security assessment metrics are proposed.

3.1. Static Risk Analysis

Security risk refers to the potential that a specific threat could exploit asset vulnerabilities, leading to damage or disruption. Threat risk assessment is foundational for providing threat feedback and implementing security measures. This study proposes a probabilistic graph-based threat risk assessment algorithm using a Bayesian network model. By analyzing the initial values of threat nodes and the topology of attack paths, the algorithm calculates the probability of each resource node entering a risky state, along with other related information. The results can vary depending on the focus of the system's security goals, with each boundary threat node's value determined by the system's actual conditions.

If no active attack is detected in the system but exploitable vulnerabilities exist in the network, risk quantification of network assets and the overall network environment can be achieved by evaluating the likelihood of vulnerability exploitation and the importance of assets. Based on the quantified risk values, one can predict which targets attackers are most likely to pursue, allowing security personnel to take appropriate defensive measures.

Upon completing the construction of the Bayesian network structure and calculating the conditional probabilities using prior knowledge, it is only necessary to specify the probability of an initial attack node launching an attack to compute the prior probabilities of all nodes. This prior probability represents either the probability of the resource represented by the node being compromised by an attacker or the probability of the attack being initiated by the node. In our designed Bayesian attack graph, the parent node of a resource node is always an attack node, and the parent node of an attack node is always a resource node. Therefore, we need to discuss separately the methods for calculating the prior probabilities of these two types of nodes. For any resource node S_k, assume it has n parent attack nodes, denoted as e_i for convenience. Further, $P(e_i)$ represents the probability of the attacker launching that attack, and Pei is the probability of the attack being successful, which is the exploitability probability defined earlier. The calculation formula for the prior probability of the node depends on its dependency relationship R with its parent nodes. The formulas for calculating the prior probability of the resource nodes under different dependency relationships are as follows:

$$P(S_k) = \begin{cases} \prod_{i=1}^{n} P_{ei} \cdot P(e_i), R = AND \\ 1 - \prod_{i=1}^{n} [1 - P_{ei} \cdot P(e_i)], R = OR \end{cases} \quad (4)$$

This formula uses the prior probabilities of the parent nodes, which are the attack nodes. The prior probability of an attack node A_h is dependent on the prior probabilities of its parent resource nodes. For any attack node A_h, assume it has m parent resource nodes, denoted as a_j for convenience. Further, $P(a_j)$ represents the probability of the attacker compromising that resource node, and Paj is the probability of the attacker launching further attacks after occupying that resource, which is the attack occurrence probability defined earlier. The formula for calculating the prior probability of the attack node depends on its dependency relationship R with its parent nodes. The formulas for calculating the prior probabilities of attack nodes under different dependency relationships are as follows:

$$P(A_h) = \begin{cases} \prod_{i=1}^{n} P_{aj} \cdot P(a_j), R = AND \\ 1 - \prod_{i=1}^{n} [1 - P_{aj} \cdot P(a_j)], R = OR \end{cases} \quad (5)$$

The steps to use the Bayesian network model for threat risk assessment are as follows:

Input: Attack graph $AG = (S, A, E, R, T)$, as previously defined;

Output: Static risk assessment probabilistic graph $SAG = (S, A, E, R, T, P_1)$, where P_1 is the set of prior probabilities for each node.

Step 1: Initialize the parameters in the static risk assessment graph and copy the components from the attack graph to the static risk assessment graph.

Step 2: Calculate the probabilities of occurrence and success for each threat node using prior knowledge.

Step 3: For each node:

- If it is an attack node, calculate its conditional probability table based on the probability of the attack occurring.
- If it is a resource node, calculate its conditional probability table based on the success probability of the attacks targeting it.

Step 4: Use the conditional probability tables and the prior probabilities of the initial attack nodes to calculate the prior probabilities of the resource nodes.

Step 5: Copy the calculated prior probabilities to the static risk assessment graph.

After obtaining the local conditional probability values of each state node, traverse the graph. All nodes (except the initial attack nodes) can derive their joint probability distributions based on prior knowledge and their parent nodes' influence. This distribution provides the probability of a state node transitioning to different risk states. Since attackers can sequentially gain various permissions for a host by exploiting vulnerabilities, changes in attacker permissions result in changes in the host's state. Therefore, the risk value calculation for a host requires summing up the probabilities of it transitioning to each risk state. To simplify the graph's structure, consider representing a particular vulnerability or permission as a resource node, with its value being either true or false to indicate whether the asset has been compromised.

This algorithm is generally used to assess potential risks in target networks that are not yet in use. Once the probabilistic graph model is constructed, the risk assessment results are fixed unless the prior knowledge is adjusted, giving each node a static risk value. However, security conditions and factors in operational systems constantly change over time. Therefore, dynamic factors must be considered for accurate risk assessment. In this context, the accuracy of prior-probability-based risk assessments decreases because reality does not always match prior knowledge. By incorporating real-time security incidents to update the attribute state nodes' probability distribution in the static risk assessment graph, security risks under dynamic conditions can be more accurately evaluated.

3.2. Dynamic Risk Analysis

The following steps outline how to derive a dynamic risk assessment probabilistic graph using both the static risk assessment probabilistic graph and real-time security incidents.

Input: Static risk assessment probabilistic graph $SAG = (S, A, E, R, T, P_1)$;

Output: Dynamic risk assessment probabilistic graph $DAG = (S, A, E, R, T, P_1, P_2)$, where P_2 is the set of posterior probabilities for each node.

Step 1: Initialize the parameters in the dynamic risk assessment probabilistic graph DAG. Copy all components from the static risk assessment graph SAG to the dynamic risk assessment graph DAG.

Step 2: Identify the resource nodes corresponding to a detected attack incident in the static risk assessment graph, selecting the nodes to be updated in the Bayesian network.

Step 3: For each selected resource node S_j in the static risk assessment graph, adjust its posterior probability based on its current detected state, such that $P(S_j = 1) = 1$.

Step 4: For each parent node $S_k \in Par(S_j)$ of the attribute node S_j, update its reachability probability using the conditional probability table, and copy the results to P_2. Repeat this step until all parent nodes have been calculated.

Step 5: Remove S_k from the parent node set $P_{ar}(S_j)$ and treat it as a child node. Repeat Step 4 to update the state of its parent nodes.

Step 6: Continue updating the parent node set $P_{ar}(S_j)$ until the root parent node (initial attack node) is reached.

Step 7: Based on the posterior probability of the root node, calculate and update the posterior probabilities of nodes not in the same path as the update nodes. Update the static risk assessment attack graph accordingly.

Step 8: For each detected attack incident, repeat Steps 2–7, combining different attack events to achieve real-time assessment of network security risks.

The dynamic risk assessment method based on the Bayesian attack graph addresses the lack of consideration for the dynamic impact of ongoing attack incidents on attribute nodes in the graph. It dynamically updates the risk values of each state node and host based on intrusion detection system (IDS) information, enabling the timely prediction of attackers' targets and attack paths. This method aligns more closely with real-world network environments than static risk assessment methods, allowing security personnel to implement different defense strategies based on varying alerts. As the risk of nodes in the graph changes, the total risk also changes. Monitoring these changes helps security personnel keep track of overall network security trends in different scenarios.

3.3. Attack Paths and Security Assessment Indicators

When attackers attempt to breach a system, they navigate through various nodes to reach the final target node, resulting in multiple possible attack paths. To better predict which path the attacker will likely use, it is crucial to identify potential attack paths. For a Bayesian network based on a directed acyclic graph, we can use the Depth-First Search (DFS) algorithm. The basic steps are as follows:

Step 1: Initialize an empty path list to store all identified paths;

Step 2: Start from the initial node and add it to the current path;

Step 3: If the initial node matches the target node, add the current path to the path list, indicating a successful path discovery;

Step 4: If the initial node is not the target node, iterate through each neighboring node. If a neighboring node is not in the current path, recursively call the DFS algorithm, treating this neighbor as the new starting node while keeping the same target node and path list, but using a copy of the current path;

Step 5: After the recursive call returns, remove the starting node from the current path to explore other paths;

Step 6: Repeat Steps 4 and 5 until all possible paths have been traversed;

Step 7: Return the path list containing all paths between the starting and target nodes.

For instance, in Figure 3a, there are two attack paths from the initial attack node S_1 to node S_4: {S1, S2, S4} and {S1, S3, S4}. If the intrusion detection system detects that S_2 has been compromised, we can deduce that the attacker used the first attack path. In practice, Bayesian network models are often more complex than this illustration. To determine which attack path the attacker is most likely to use, or which path poses the highest risk to the assets, consider multiplying the probabilities of all compromised assets along the path to obtain the path reachability probability.

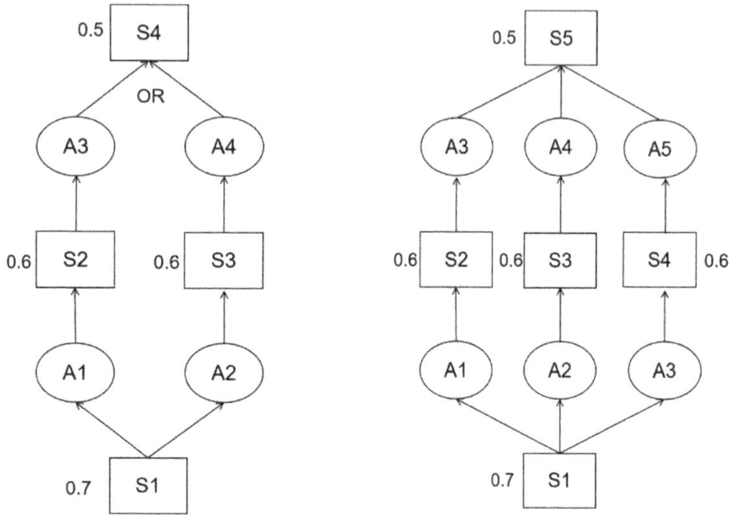

(a) (b)

Figure 3. Comparison of two probability plots with different numbers of paths. (**a**) AG_1; (**b**) AG_2.

For any path, if the nodes on the path are denoted as Sj, then the reachability probability of this path is defined as follows:

$$P(path) = \prod P(S_j) \tag{6}$$

Given an initial and target node, the DFS algorithm can identify all possible paths between them. Using the above formula, the reachability probabilities of each path can be calculated, revealing which attack path is most likely to be exploited.

Due to the scale and complexity of real-world networks, their Bayesian networks can also be substantial. Comprehensive and targeted security assessment metrics are needed to evaluate the system's overall risk. Probabilistic graphs possess both graph structure and node probabilities, allowing for combined design metrics.

The Mean of Path Probability (MPP) is the arithmetic mean of all path probabilities in a probabilistic graph. The mean involves the entire probabilistic graph, and any path change may affect the average path probability. Thus, in some cases, the MPP can reflect changes in network security. The formula for calculating MPP is as follows:

$$MPP(AG) = \frac{\sum_{i=1}^{n} s(p_i)}{NP(AG)} \tag{7}$$

where

NP(AG): The number of paths in the probabilistic graph AG;

$s(p_i)$: Cumulative probability of all nodes in the attack path p_i.

Generally, the higher the MPP value, the lower the network security. The MPP indicator can capture the overall security level of the system. If the cumulative node probability for any path exceeds the MPP value, it indicates significant danger, and timely defensive strategies should be deployed.

However, the MPP does not always reflect the impact of path quantity on security. For example, Figure 3 shows that probabilistic graph AG1 has two attack paths with a cumulative probability of 1.8, while AG2 has three paths with a cumulative probability of 1.8. Evaluating these graphs using the MPP yields an average path probability of 1.8 for both. When each attack path has the same reachability probability, the graph with more attack paths is riskier, which is not reflected in the MPP-based assessment. Thus, to account for the difference in the number of paths, the Normalized Mean of Path Probability (NMPP) is used:

$$NMPP(AG) = \frac{\sum_{i=1}^{n} s(p_i)}{\sqrt{MPP(AG)}} \tag{8}$$

Evaluating Figure 3 using NMPP:

$$NMPP(AG1) = \frac{3.6}{\sqrt{1.8}} = 2.68$$

$$NMPP(AG2) = \frac{5.4}{\sqrt{1.8}} = 4.02$$

The risk assessment results of probabilistic graphs AG1 and AG2 are 2.68 and 4.02, respectively. The results show that NMPP(AG1) < NMPP(AG2), meaning that AG2 is riskier, which aligns with expectations.

4. Simulation and Results

Using the threat modeling method designed above, it is possible to quantitatively describe the new business scenarios of power systems. Moreover, the risk assessment methods, attack path analysis methods, and security assessment metrics designed above can quantify both local and overall risk states of the system, identify potential attack paths, and calculate the likelihood of these paths being exploited.

To compare the effectiveness of static risk assessment based on prior knowledge with dynamic risk assessment based on real-time security incidents, and to test the efficacy of the attack path analysis method and security metrics, a typical interactive scenario in new power system business is chosen. This scenario is modeled using a Bayesian network, and the conditional probability tables and exploitation probabilities for nodes are quantified according to the methods discussed above.

This study considers a typical small-scale local area network structure of a power system, as shown in Figure 4. In this simulated topology, the power system's LAN is divided into an internal network and an external network. Users can directly access the external network via a gateway, and also access the internal network through a relay server and video platform.

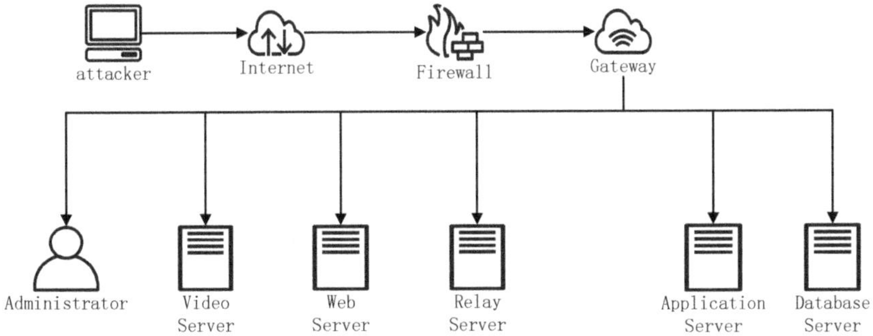

Figure 4. Network Environment Topology Diagram.

Nessus is used to scan host vulnerabilities in different network areas, and the detected vulnerability data are aggregated. The vulnerability information is shown in Table 3.

Furthermore, based on vulnerability information and network topology, a preliminary Bayesian attack graph can be constructed, as shown in Figure 5. In the figure, node relationships with multiple parent nodes are all OR.

Table 3. Vulnerability Information.

Hosts	Vulnerability Information	CVE-Number Vulnerability Number	Asset Number	Atomic Attack Number
Switch	Access Restriction Bypass	CVE-2015–8467	S2	A1
Relay Server	Buffer Cross-border Access	CVE-2012–4707	S3	A2
Video Server	Remote Code Execution	CVE-2015–1635	S4	A3
Administrator	Remote Code Execution	CVE-2004–0840	S5	A4
Administrator	IIS FTP Service Heap BOF	CVE-2010–3972	S5	A5
Database Server	Remote Code Execution	CVE-2013–4465	S6	A6
Video Server	Port Scanning	CVE-2015–1635	S7	A7
Application Server	Flooding Attack	CVE-2014–1446	S8	A8

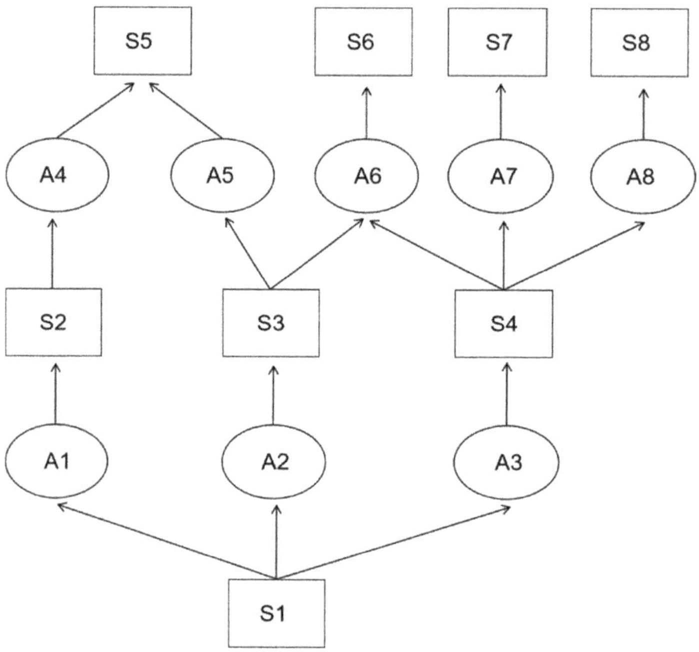

Figure 5. Bayesian network model based on simulated experimental environment.

Based on a quantitative analysis of the vulnerabilities on each host in the system, the attacker's probability of launching an attack and exploiting a vulnerability successfully is calculated. Using the vulnerabilities and their exploitation relationships and probabilities, a Bayesian network model is constructed. Each attack node in the diagram corresponds to a vulnerability, and the attack success probability is the vulnerability exploitation success probability. To simplify the model, the node values are defined as 1 or 0 (logical true or false). If the attack succeeds, the resource node pointed to by the attack node is taken over by the attacker, and the corresponding random variable is set to 1, allowing the attacker to continue attacking further. If the attack fails and the asset remains unoccupied, the random variable is set to 0, preventing further attacks.

The conditional probability tables for each node can be derived by combining each attack node's success probability with the logical relationships between nodes. Thus, by initializing the initial attack node S_1 with an attack probability of 0.7, the prior probabilities of all resource nodes in the graph can be calculated using the static threat risk assessment algorithm based on prior knowledge. This will provide the prior probabilities for all resource nodes being in a risky state.

To assess vulnerabilities using CVSS metrics and calculate the exploitation and initiation probabilities, we refer to Equations (2) and (3) defined above. The calculation results are shown in Table 4. Since the accuracy of static risk assessment based on prior knowledge depends on the accuracy of the prior information, it does not always reflect the actual state of the system. When the intrusion detection system identifies an attack that successfully occurs, the corresponding resource node becomes an observed sample with a definite value rather than a random variable. As a result, the probabilities of other resource nodes falling into risky states will also change.

Table 4. Attack Initiation and Success Probabilities.

Attack Action	A1	A2	A3	A4	A5	A6	A7	A8
probability of launch	0.48	0.55	0.48	0.65	0.42	0.37	0.65	0.57
probability of success	0.69	0.55	0.41	0.76	0.61	0.54	0.95	0.69

However, static risk analysis methods cannot effectively adjust assessment results based on real-time attack detection. Therefore, by incorporating real-time attack data, the posterior probabilities of resource nodes in risky states can be calculated. This gives a probability that more accurately reflects the system's state under a specific attack event. For instance, if the relay server detects attack event A2, the posterior probabilities of other resource nodes in risky states can be computed using the dynamic threat risk assessment method under the assumption that A2 has occurred. Therefore, we assume that the attack represented by A2 is detected and calculate the probability based on this. The calculation results of prior and posterior probabilities are shown in Figure 6.

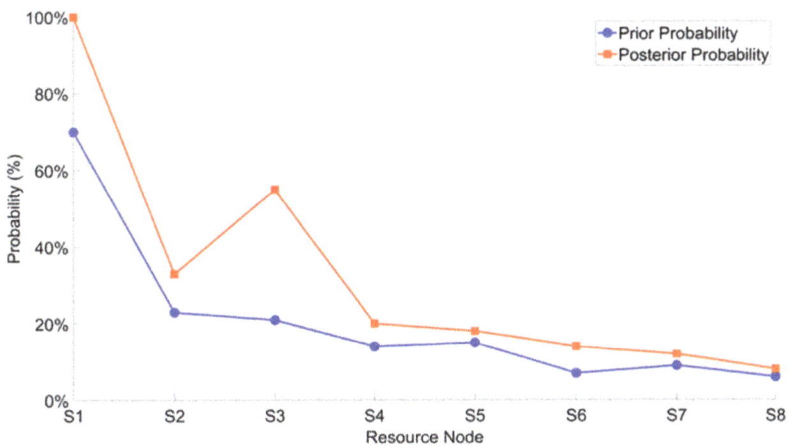

Figure 6. Prior and posterior probabilities of each node.

Using the relationships between nodes in the Bayesian network and the vulnerability status in the simulated environment, the prior probabilities of each attribute node are calculated using the static risk assessment algorithm. Suppose an intrusion detection system captures attack event A2 in the simulated environment. In that case, the dynamic risk assessment algorithm updates the probabilities of attribute nodes in the static attack graph, yielding posterior probabilities.

1. Attack Path Analysis

Based on the attack path analysis methods and security assessment metrics introduced earlier, security risk assessment results can be obtained under real-time attack scenarios. Six attack paths are identified in Figure 5: {S1, S2, S5}, {S1, S3, S5}, {S1, S3, S6}, {S1, S4, S6}, {S1,

S4, S7}, and {S1, S4, S8}. These are labeled as Path 1–6, and their reachability probabilities are calculated using Equation (6). The calculation results are shown in Figure 7.

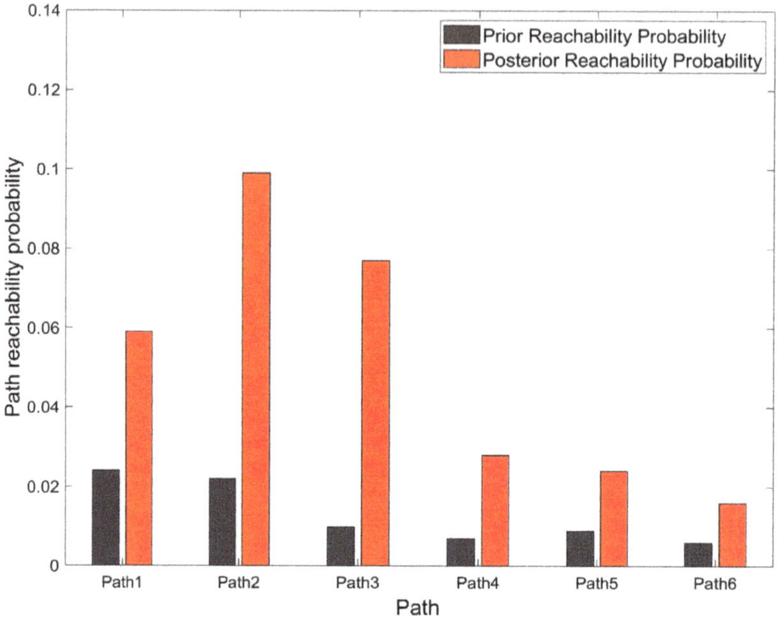

Figure 7. Path reachability probabilities.

The results indicate a key point. Regardless of whether prior or posterior probabilities are used, Path 2 has a relatively high reachability probability. This is because the nodes in Path 2 have higher vulnerability exploitation probabilities and valuable nodes, making the path highly attractive for attackers. Therefore, defensive strategies should focus on protecting assets along Path 2.

When attack event A2 is detected, the overall reachability probabilities of all attack paths increase, suggesting that every path is now riskier. Paths containing event A2, like Path 2 and Path 3, see the largest increase in reachability probabilities, indicating the attacker's intention. The data show that once the attacker's intent is known, the system's risk state changes. The posterior probabilities calculated using the dynamic risk assessment method more accurately reflect the system's actual risk at that moment.

2. Security Assessment Metrics

Bayesian networks in real-world scenarios often have large-scale and complex structures. To quickly visualize the system's overall security risk status, security assessment metrics specific to Bayesian networks are needed. The normalized mean of path probability (NMPP) is designed to capture the overall security risk by reflecting both node probabilities and path structures.

Before calculating the NMPP, the cumulative probabilities of all paths need to be calculated, which is the sum of the probability values of all resource nodes on the paths. Therefore, based on the previously mentioned environment, the prior cumulative probabilities and posterior cumulative probabilities of all paths are calculated separately, and the results are shown in Table 5.

Table 5. Path cumulative probability.

Path	Priori Cumulative Probability	Posterior Cumulative Probability
Path1	1.08	1.51
Path2	1.06	1.73
Path3	0.98	1.69
Path4	0.91	1.34
Path5	0.93	1.32
Path6	0.9	1.28

Based on the above calculation results and Equations (7) and (8). The calculation is as follows:

$$MPP_{pr} = \frac{\sum s(p_i)}{NP(AG)} = \frac{1.08 + 1.06 + 0.98 + 0.91 + 0.93 + 0.9}{6} = 0.978$$

$$MPP_{po} = \frac{\sum s(p_i)}{NP(AG)} = \frac{1.51 + 1.73 + 1.69 + 1.34 + 1.32 + 1.28}{6} = 1.478$$

Further,

$$NMPP_{pr} = \frac{\sum s(p_i)}{\sqrt{MPP_{pr}}} = \frac{1.08 + 1.06 + 0.98 + 0.91 + 0.93 + 0.9}{\sqrt{0.978}} = 5.93$$

$$NMPP_{po} = \frac{\sum s(p_i)}{\sqrt{MPP_{po}}} = \frac{1.51 + 1.73 + 1.69 + 1.34 + 1.32 + 1.28}{\sqrt{1.478}} = 7.29$$

The results show that $NMPP_{pr} < NMPP_{po}$, meaning that the NMPP calculated based on posterior probabilities is higher than that calculated based on prior probabilities. When a specific attack event is detected, the initial attack node is certainly 1 (attacker has initiated the attack). The occurrence of security event A2 raises the overall risk, reflected in the increase of the normalized mean of path probability.

The absolute value of NMPP indicates the overall risk level at a given moment. Higher NMPP values indicate higher security risk, calling for immediate defensive measures. By continuously monitoring the occurrence of security incidents, the system's risk level over time can be calculated to understand overall risk trends.

5. Conclusions

With modern networking and communication technologies widely integrated into monitoring and controlling power systems, vulnerabilities in communication networks expose highly interconnected power grids to new threats. Defenders must proactively identify network intrusions targeting power grids, determine potential attack paths, and deploy appropriate defense strategies. To address this issue, this paper proposes a Bayesian attack graph-based security assessment method for power systems.

Compared to existing studies, this paper quantifies Bayesian network node information by considering both the importance of assets and the cost of launching an attack to calculate the attacker's initiation probability. Additionally, it determines the probability of attack success based on the difficulty of exploiting vulnerabilities. Using these calculations, prior probabilities for each node are derived, reflecting the likelihood of assets being threatened based on past experiences.

Furthermore, this paper introduces a security assessment method that calculates the posterior probabilities of associated nodes based on real-time detected attack incidents. Posterior probabilities indicate the likelihood of threats to each node under specific conditions, and the system's security state changes accordingly with each detected attack event.

Additionally, an attack path analysis method and security assessment metrics are developed to assess the overall system risk status. Experimental results verify the effectiveness of the proposed risk analysis methods and security assessment metrics.

Author Contributions: Conceptualization, L.C. and T.Z.; methodology, L.C.; software, T.Z.; validation, L.C., Y.M. and Y.L.; formal analysis, Y.M.; investigation, C.W.; resources, C.H.; data curation, C.H.; writing—original draft preparation, T.Z.; writing—review and editing, L.C. and Z.L.; visualization, Y.M. and N.L.; supervision, C.W. and Z.L.; project administration, Y.L.; funding acquisition, N.L. All authors have read and agreed to the published version of the manuscript.

Funding: This work is supported by the Science and Technology Project of State Grid Corporation of China. (Research on Flexible Secure Access and Unknown Attack Awareness Technology for New-type Business Terminals, 5108-202218280A-2-232-XG).

Data Availability Statement: All data are unavailable due to privacy restrictions.

Acknowledgments: We express our heartfelt gratitude to the reviewers and editors for their meticulous work.

Conflicts of Interest: Author Lu Chen, Tao Zhang, Yuanyuan Ma, Yong Li, Chen Wang, and Chuan He are employed by State Grid Smart Grid Research Institute Co., Ltd. Author Zhuo Lv and Nuannuan Li are employed by State Grid Henan Electric Power Company. The remaining authors declare that the research was conducted in the absence of any commercial or financial relationships that could be construed as a potential conflict of interest. The funders had no role in the design of the study; in the collection, analyses, or interpretation of data; in the writing of the manuscript; or in the decision to publish the results.

References

1. Liu, C.; Stefanov, A.; Hong, J.; Panciatici, P. Intruders in the Grid. *IEEE Power Energy Mag.* **2012**, *10*, 58–66. [CrossRef]
2. Liu, F.; Zhang, S.; Ma, W.; Qu, J. Research on Attack Detection of Cyber Physical Systems Based on Improved Support Vector Machine. *Mathematics* **2022**, *10*, 2713. [CrossRef]
3. Abdelmalak, M.; Venkataramanan, V.; Macwan, R. A Survey of Cyber-Physical Power System Modeling Methods for Future Energy Systems. *IEEE Access* **2022**, *10*, 99875–99896. [CrossRef]
4. Zhang, Y.; Ni, M.; Sun, Y. Fully Distributed Economic Dispatch for Cyber-physical Power System with Time Delays and Channel Noises. *J. Mod. Power Syst. Clean Energy* **2022**, *10*, 1472–1481. [CrossRef]
5. Dong, Z.; Tian, M.; Ding, L. A Framework for Modeling and Structural Vulnerability Analysis of Spatial Cyber-Physical Power Systems from an Attack–Defense Perspective. *IEEE Syst. J.* **2021**, *15*, 1369–1380. [CrossRef]
6. Wang, W.; Yang, S.; Hu, F.; Stanley, H.E.; He, S.; Shi, M. An Approach for Cascading Effects within Critical Infrastructure Systems. *Phys. A Stat. Mech. Its Appl.* **2018**, *510*, 164–177. [CrossRef]
7. Lau, P.; Wang, L.; Liu, Z.; Wei, W.; Ten, C.W. A Coalitional Cyber-Insurance Design Considering Power System Reliability and Cyber Vulnerability. *IEEE Trans. Power Syst.* **2021**, *36*, 5512–5524. [CrossRef]
8. Zhang, Y.; Wang, L.; Xiang, Y.; Ten, C. Power System Reliability Evaluation with SCADA Cybersecurity Considerations. *IEEE Trans. Smart Grid* **2015**, *6*, 1707–1721. [CrossRef]
9. Wu, H.R.; Qin, J.; Zheng, B.J. Anti-attack ability based on costs in complex networks. *Comput. Sci.* **2012**, *39*, 224–227.
10. Sun, F.; Pi, J.; Lv, J. Network security risk assessment system based on attack graph and Markov chain. *J. Phys. Conf. Ser.* **2017**, *910*, 012005. [CrossRef]
11. Hu, H.; Liu, Y.L.; Zhang, H.Q. Route prediction method for network intrusion using absorbing Markov chain. *J. Comput. Res. Dev.* **2018**, *55*, 831–845.
12. Xie, P.; Li, J.H.; Ou, X. Using bayesian networks for cyber security analysis. In Proceedings of the 2010 IEEE/IFIP International Conference on Dependable Systems and Networks (DSN), Chicago, IL, USA, 28 June–1 July 2010; pp. 211–220.
13. Poolsappasit, N.; Dewri, R.; Ray, I. Dynamic security risk management using bayesian attack graphs. *IEEE Trans. Dependable Secur. Comput.* **2012**, *9*, 61–74. [CrossRef]
14. Chen, X.J.; Fang, B.X.; Tan, Q.F. Inferring attack intent of malicious insider based on probabilistic attack graph model. *Chin. J. Comput.* **2014**, *37*, 62–72.
15. Gao, N.; Gao, L.; He, Y.Y. Dynamic security risk assessment model based on bayesian attack graph. *J. Sichuan Univ.* **2016**, *48*, 111–118.
16. Ma, C.G.; Wang, C.H.; Zhang, D.H. A dynamic network risk assessment model based on attacker's inclination. *J. Comput. Res. Dev.* **2015**, *52*, 2056–2068.
17. Yazdi, M.; Zarei, E.; Adumene, S.; Abbassi, R.; Rahnamayiezekavat, P. Chapter Eleven—Uncertainty Modeling in Risk Assessment of Digitalized Process Systems. *Methods Assess Manag. Process Saf. Digit. Process Syst.* **2022**, *6*, 389–416.
18. Zhang, Y.; Ni, M. Security-Oriented Cyber-Physical Risk Assessment for Cyberattacks on Distribution System. *Appl. Sci.* **2023**, *13*, 11569. [CrossRef]
19. He, R.; Yang, S.; Deng, J.; Feng, T.; Lai, L.L.; Shahidehpour, M. Reliability Analyses of Wide-Area Protection System Considering Cyber-Physical System Constraints. *IEEE Trans. Smart Grid* **2021**, *12*, 3458–3467. [CrossRef]

20. Ten, C.W.; Liu, C.C.; Manimaran, G. Vulnerability assessment of cybersecurity for SCADA systems. *IEEE Trans Power Syst.* **2008**, *23*, 1836–1846. [CrossRef]
21. Zhang, Y.C.; Wang, L.F.; Sun, W.Q. Distributed intrusion detection system in a multi-layer network architecture of smart grid. *IEEE Trans Smart Grid* **2011**, *2*, 796–808. [CrossRef]
22. Qin, H.; Liu, D. Risk Assessment in Distribution Networks Considering Cyber Coupling. *Int. J. Electr. Power Energy Syst.* **2023**, *145*, 108650. [CrossRef]
23. Lagerström, R.; Ekstedt, M.; Franke, U. Can the Common Vulnerability Scoring System Be Trusted? A Bayesian Analysis. *IEEE Trans. Dependable Secur. Comput.* **2018**, *15*, 1002–1015.

electronics

MDPI

Article

UDIS: Enhancing Collaborative Filtering with Fusion of Dimensionality Reduction and Semantic Similarity

Hamidreza Koohi [1,*], Ziad Kobti [1], Tahereh Farzi [2] and Emad Mahmodi [2]

1 School of Computer Science, University of Windsor, Windsor, ON N9B-3P4, Canada; kobti@uwindsor.ca
2 Computer Engineering Department, Shomal University, Amol 4616184596, Iran; tahereh.farzi@shomal.ac.ir (T.F.); emad.mahmodi@alumni.um.ac.ir (E.M.)
* Correspondence: koohi@uwindsor.ca

Abstract: In the era of vast information, individuals are immersed in choices when purchasing goods and services. Recommender systems (RS) have emerged as vital tools to navigate these excess options. However, these systems encounter challenges like data sparsity, impairing their effectiveness. This paper proposes a novel approach to address this issue and enhance RS performance. By integrating user demographic data, singular value decomposition (SVD) clustering, and semantic similarity in collaborative filtering (CF), we introduce the UDIS method. This method amalgamates four prediction types—user-based CF (U), demographic-similarity-based (D), item-based CF (I), and semantic-similarity-based (S). UDIS generates separate predictions for each category and evaluates four different merging techniques—the average, max, weighted sum, and Shambour methods—to integrate these predictions. Among these, the average method proved most effective, offering a balanced approach that significantly improved precision and accuracy on the MovieLens dataset compared to alternative methods.

Keywords: recommender systems; fuzzy C-means; clustering; collaborative filtering; singular value decomposition; semantic similarity; demographic information

1. Introduction

In today's digital age, where choices are abundant, recommender systems (RS) serve as vital tools to help individuals navigate the overwhelming array of options. Individuals encounter a multitude of choices daily, with an extensive range of options available. The vast volume of information presents a significant challenge in selecting preferred goods and services, often complicating decision-making. Recommender systems (RS) are employed to aid in these decisions. These systems have been extensively utilized since the 1990s to automate providing personalized goods and service offers. As a personalization technology for information filtering, RS predict the likelihood of a user finding a specific information object useful and identify the N objects of most significant interest to that user [1].

Collaborative filtering (CF) has emerged as one of the most widely used techniques in developing RS, owing to its ability to generate personalized recommendations [1]. In CF, the user–item rating domain is represented in a vector space. However, these vectors are often very high-dimensional and contain redundancy. The inefficiency of CF algorithms in large, distributed databases has prompted researchers to explore dimensionality reduction techniques. A significant challenge in CF RS is data sparsity, because most users are only interested in and rate a limited subset of items. Consequently, user–item matrices contain many empty values. To address this issue, many researchers have employed dimensionality reduction techniques, primarily based on Matrix Factorization (MF) [2].

SVD is a key dimensionality reduction tool that decomposes large, sparse user–item matrices into smaller, interpretable components, enhancing RS efficiency by uncovering latent structures [3]. While SVD can significantly improve recommendation accuracy, it often involves high computational costs. However, when applied to datasets like movie ratings, SVD-based CF methods can outperform other approaches, making them a valuable asset in addressing data sparsity issues [4].

Research indicates that clustering methods yield effective results in CF. Clustering algorithms are employed in RS to identify groups of users with similar characteristics. Fuzzy C-means (FCM) [5] is a widely used clustering technique in which data points can belong to more than one cluster. This differs from traditional non-fuzzy (or hard) clustering methods, where data are separated into distinct clusters, with each data point belonging to only one cluster. In this fuzzy method, the degree of belonging of each element in each cluster is determined by membership coefficients between 0 and 1, and their sum for one element is one. FCM clusters m data points, $Z = \{Z_1, \ldots, Z_m\}$, into a group of n clusters, $N = \{N_1, \ldots, N_n\}$ [6,7].

Item-based algorithms in CF address scalability challenges found in user-based models. These algorithms generate predictions by utilizing item similarities and various knowledge sources, including semantic structural information about the items. The system can infer a user's interest in exploring specific item sets by integrating semantic similarities with those based on ratings or usage. Additionally, leveraging semantic similarities enables the system to provide reasonable recommendations even when information is sparse or items are unrated [8].

As previously discussed, SVD, FCM clustering, and semantic techniques have individually demonstrated promising results in various aspects of CF. Each of these methods addresses specific weaknesses in CF algorithms, leading us to explore alternative approaches for RS. To overcome these deficiencies, we investigated whether combining these methods could enhance the performance of RS. We integrated user demographic information, item semantic similarity, and SVD within an FCM clustering framework to generate more accurate recommendations. The primary objectives of this paper are outlined as follows:

- Integrate user demographic information, semantic similarity, and SVD methods within an FCM clustering framework to enhance the RS and provide appropriate recommendations.
- Reduce the sparsity problem by using SVD to improve the accuracy and precision of the generated predictions.
- Suggest items to users based on their characteristics by employing demographic-similarity-based predictions.
- Explore approaches for integrating user-based and item-based predictions.

The remainder of the paper is organized as follows: Section 2 offers a review of the literature on previous research into related studies. Section 3 presents the novel approach proposed in this study. Section 4 presents the experimental data and methodologies employed. Finally, Section 5 outlines the study's conclusions.

The UDIS methodology enhances recommendation accuracy and precision by integrating collaborative filtering (CF), singular value decomposition (SVD), fuzzy C-means (FCM) clustering, and semantic similarity. This multimodal approach addresses data sparsity and supports scalable recommendation systems through dimensionality reduction. By incorporating demographic and semantic data, UDIS provides personalized recommendations, making it suitable for diverse user contexts.

However, UDIS has certain limitations. It currently uses only basic demographic features (age and gender), which may limit personalization. Additionally, its semantic analysis is restricted to genre-based attributes, which may not fully capture item nuances. While flexible, the linear combination of predictions may not reveal complex relationships that advanced methods could uncover. Finally, UDIS's effectiveness can vary depending on the chosen clustering method, suggesting a need for further optimization for specific applications.

2. Background

The following introduces the key components of the proposed approach: CF, FCM clustering, SVD, semantic approach, and demographic information.

2.1. Collaborative Filtering

CF is widely adopted in RS, as it efficiently generates personalized recommendations using similar users' preferences. CF predictions are derived from the data of neighbors of the target user or item. CF encompasses two primary methods: user-based and item-based [7,9].

In user-based CF, the predicted rating of an item is determined by the preferences of similar users, i.e., users who have rated similar items. The following formula is used in user-based CF prediction.

$$p_{z,a} = \overline{r}_z + \left[\frac{\sum_{u'=1}^{g} (r_{z',a} - \overline{r}_{z'}) \times sim(z, z')}{\sum_{z'=1}^{g} sim(z, z')} \right] \quad (1)$$

where $p_{u,x}$ is the predicted rating of item a by user z, $\overline{r}_z$ is the average of all ratings given by user z to all items, z' is the neighbor user of user z, $r_{z',a}$ is the rating given by user z' to item a, $\overline{r}_{z'}$ is the average of all ratings given by user z' to all items, g is the number of selected neighbors, and $sim(z, z')$ is the similarity between user z and user z'.

In contrast, item-based CF predicts ratings based on the similarity between items rather than users. The following formula is used in item-based CF prediction.

$$p_{z,a} = \overline{r}_a + \left[\frac{\sum_{b=1}^{g} (r_{z,b} - \overline{r}_b) \times sim(a, b)}{\sum_{b=1}^{g} sim(a, b)} \right] \quad (2)$$

where $p_{z,a}$ is the predicted rating of test item a by test user z, $\overline{r}_a$ is the average of all ratings of item a, b is the neighbor item of item a, $r_{z,b}$ is the rating given by user z to item b, $\overline{r}_b$ is the average of all ratings given to item b, g is the number of selected neighbors, and $sim(a, b)$ is the similarity between item a and item b [10].

2.2. Demographic Recommendation Systems

Demographic RS analyze user characteristics, such as age, gender, language, and location, to provide personalized recommendations. These systems operate on the assumption that individuals with different demographic profiles tend to have distinct preferences. As a result, they recommend items to users based on demographic similarities. Also, demographic information is used to identify users who like a particular product. This approach describes the connection between an item and the type of users who want that item. Unlike conventional CF, this approach is beneficial because it does not require prior user ratings. Instead, it classifies users based on personal characteristics and makes recommendations accordingly.

2.3. Semantic Similarities

Today, semantic measures are widely employed to compare the meanings or relatedness of items rather than relying solely on user interactions or ratings. Semantic knowledge encompasses various aspects. Take the example of oranges: we understand them as citrus fruits, recognize their characteristic orange color, and acknowledge their high vitamin C content. This multifaceted understanding constitutes our knowledge about the concept of oranges. However, studies on semantic knowledge frequently rely on singular sources of information, such as word associations or textual distribution within extensive corpora. Yet, it is improbable that these diverse sources of information uniformly correlate with all aspects of semantic knowledge. In general, assessing the degree of semantic similarity between semantic entities is a semantic measure and is expressed as a numerical value [11].

2.4. The Jaccard Binary Similarity Coefficient

The Jaccard binary similarity coefficient is utilized to evaluate the similarity between the two sample sets, and it is equal to the intersection of the two sets divided by their union. If we have two binary vectors, X and Y, we apply Formula (3) to calculate their Jaccuard similarity. In this formula, $H_{1,0}$ is the number of all attributes X has, but Y does not. $H_{0,1}$ is the number of all attributes that X does not have but Y has, and, $H_{1,1}$ is the number of attributes that both X and Y have [12,13].

$$Jacquard\ (X,Y) = \frac{|X \cap Y|}{|X \cup Y|} = \frac{H_{1,1}}{H_{0,1} + H_{1,0} + H_{1,1}} \tag{3}$$

The Jaccard similarity is particularly useful when working with binary vectors, as it allows us to focus on the presence or absence of features rather than the magnitude of values.

2.5. Singular Value Decomposition in RS

The SVD method can be utilized to estimate missing data. For instance, [14] employs SVD outcomes to populate vacant ratings and utilizes item-based CF to forecast ratings for unrated items, addressing the challenges of accuracy, scalability, and data sparsity. Similarly, the model proposed in [15] employs SVD smoothing within CF to alleviate data sparsity issues. SVD effectively generates recommendations by decomposing a user–item matrix into lower-dimensional matrices, which helps uncover latent relationships between users and items.

The SVD technique has been shown to enhance the performance of existing filtering algorithms. For example, in [4], a hybrid CF algorithm incorporating SVD and k-means clustering was introduced to improve recommendation accuracy while addressing scalability and cold-start issues. This approach clusters similar users, reduces dimensions, and identifies the most similar users to improve RS performance and address issues like sparsity, cold starts, and scalability.

Similarly, [16] optimized an item-based hybrid CF model for privacy preservation and high performance. This method uses SVD to optimize the number of neighbors used in the recommendation process, ensuring an appropriate balance between accuracy and privacy.

Additionally, [17] conducted a comparison of three MF algorithms—SVD, SVD++ (singular value decomposition plus), and NMF (Nonnegative Matrix Factorization)—for restaurant recommendation tasks. The study shows that SVD achieves the lowest Root Mean Square Error (RMSE), while SVD++ achieves the lowest Mean Absolute Error (MAE), reinforcing SVD's effectiveness in recommendation tasks.

2.6. Demographic Information in RS

Utilizing the SVD method for data beyond the conventional user–item rankings can yield significant effectiveness. In [18], SVD is applied to reduce the dimensionality of either the user–item matrix or the demographic matrix, leveraging the complementary information found in demographic data. The study demonstrated that SVD could be seamlessly integrated and amalgamated with filtering methods by utilizing existing demographic data.

Clustering users based on demographic information helps define neighborhood ranges, which can be used to predict ratings. Predictions derived from demographic data are often integrated with other prediction sources in these methods. For instance, [19] incorporated demographics and transactional and genre information, calculating user or item similarities to obtain three types of predictions, which were then combined using a weighted approach to mitigate challenges like new items or user cold starts.

Similarly, [20] utilized user ratings, item details (e.g., genre), and demographic data, employing biased MF on an extended rating matrix for prediction. Moreover, [21] merged collaborative, content-based, and demographic filtering in financial planning, leveraging TF-IDF and Markov chains to enhance recommendation quality. Pereira and Varma [22] combined demographic filtering with collaborative and content-based methods to suggest doctors to patients, employing an adaptive algorithm to establish a doctor rating function. In [23], the semantic similarity between users and items is calculated based on their profiles linked to an ontology to predict unknown values in the original matrix. Furthermore, [24] introduced a switching-based hybrid model, combining collaborative and content- and demographic-based approaches for book recommendations. This model adjusts between a weighted combination model and demographic information utilization depending on user type to effectively address the cold start issue.

2.7. Fuzzy C-Means Clustering in RS

FCM clustering is a prevalent clustering technique [5]. In methods such as those in [6] and [25], FCM is integrated with other optimization algorithms to enhance recommendation systems. For example, [25] combines FCM with a genetic algorithm, where users are clustered based on item rating data, and the genetic algorithm is then used to compute similarity functions for recommendations.

Conversely, in [6], FCM is paired with bat optimization to address scalability issues in collaborative RS. This approach clusters users with FCM and uses the bat algorithm to refine the cluster centers, optimizing the recommendation process. Similarly, in [25], FCM is utilized for user classification based on ratings, while the gray wolf optimization is employed to identify initial clusters and reduce features. In [26], FCM clustering and supervised learning models are proposed to tackle the cold-start problem. In this method, FCM clustering is utilized to construct user and item membership vectors, aiming to enhance algorithm performance and mitigate the impact of data sparsity.

2.8. Item-Based and User-Based RS

In the method outlined in [27], user clustering and item clustering are combined to address scalability and sparsity challenges in CF RS. The k-means algorithm is used for both user and item clustering, which helps reduce the dimensionality of the user–item matrix, making it denser and more manageable for prediction tasks. User clustering is employed to estimate missing values in the user–item matrix, thereby improving the accuracy of predictions.

Similarly, [28] proposes an approach where user clustering is performed in the preprocessing stage. This method initially reduces data sparsity by using case-based reasoning and average filling, and it then applies clustering techniques like the Self-Organizing Map (SOM) optimized by a genetic algorithm (GA) to further refine the prediction process. This method effectively addresses scalability issues by narrowing the scope of item-based CF to the most relevant cluster.

In [29], a multi-criteria CF RS method is introduced to enhance prediction accuracy and alleviate sparsity issues. This system integrates an item-based ontological semantic filter with user-based demographic information to create a hybrid model, leading to more precise recommendations using multiple data sources.

Similarly, the authors of [3] employ a movie ontology for items in their proposed method. However, their approach differs. In [3], item and user clustering are initially performed using the Expectation-Maximization (EM) algorithm, followed by the application of SVD to each cluster. This method leverages item-based and user-based similarities based on SVD and item semantic similarity derived from the movie ontology.

The model outlined in [9] diverges significantly from other methods, exploring various techniques to merge user-based and item-based CF predictions to minimize prediction errors. This includes combining Support Vector Regression (SVR) and Multiple Linear Regression (MLR) to demonstrate the superiority of merging methods over single-technique approaches.

Conversely, [30] introduces a modified CF method that integrates user-based and item-based CF. This method accounts for positive and negative correlations among neighbors, using a weighting mechanism to optimize the balance between user- and item-based predictions.

2.9. Trustworthy Neighbors for CF RS

The primary objective of RS is to help users efficiently navigate extensive product selections to find relevant items. However, recent years have seen an increased focus on the potential hazards these systems face, such as malicious attacks, excessive noise, and bias, leading researchers to recognize that accuracy alone is insufficient for a reliable recommendation system. As a result, there has been a shift from accuracy-centric systems to the development of trust-based RS (TRS) [10,31–33].

In the research conducted in [34], the authors argue that traditional user similarity calculations are insufficient for selecting trustworthy neighbors in CF, leading to suboptimal recommendations. To address this issue, they propose a two-layer neighbor selection model for CF to enhance recommendation accuracy. Users are chosen based on influence and trustworthiness to recommend to the target user.

Similarly, [35] leverages user social trust information and implicit feedback to alleviate sparsity in tensor factorization for context-aware RS. By incorporating trust into the recommendation process, this method has outperformed traditional techniques like BiasTF in terms of accuracy.

Furthermore, [36] investigates the trust levels between pairs of social network users using factorization matrices. This approach allows for calculating both positive and negative trust scores, providing a more nuanced understanding of user relationships. The results show the effectiveness of using trust in real-world recommendation scenarios, highlighting its importance in building robust RS.

3. Proposed Method

In this paper, we leverage user demographic information alongside SVD in clustering and semantic similarity within CF to enrich the RS, thus offering tailored user recommendations. As a result, we introduce the UDIS method, aimed at bolstering the performance of the RS and crafting suitable recommendations. This method integrates four prediction types: user-based CF prediction (U), demographic-similarity-based prediction (D), item-based CF prediction (I), and semantic-similarity-based prediction (S). This approach combines these techniques in a structured manner to leverage their strengths, ultimately improving the recommendation accuracy and user experience. The UDIS method framework is depicted in Figure 1; a detailed elaboration is provided in the following sections.

1. Preprocess the dataset to obtain the user–item matrix.

The dataset used in this study is initially preprocessed to construct a user–item matrix, where each entry represents a user's rating for an item.

2. Apply the FCM clustering algorithm to the user–item matrix, considering both users and items.

Given this matrix's sparse nature, clustering is essential to reduce dimensionality and identify patterns. The FCM clustering algorithm is employed, enabling data points to belong to multiple clusters with varying degrees of membership. FCM was chosen over traditional clustering methods, such as k-means, due to its flexibility in handling the fuzzy boundaries often present in user preference data.

For each cluster generated by FCM, an SVD-based similarity matrix is calculated, allowing for dimensionality reduction and the identification of latent user preferences and item features.

3. Utilize SVD for dimensionality reduction within each cluster, generating similarity matrices based on SVD parameters for each cluster.

SVD is applied to the clustered data to address sparsity and improve computational efficiency. SVD decomposes the user–item matrix into three matrices, allowing us to represent users and items in a reduced dimensional space. This not only captures the latent structure in the data but also improves scalability. For instance, in a cluster where users' item ratings are missing, SVD approximates these missing values based on existing data, which is critical for enhancing recommendation quality.

4. Construct a user similarity matrix using demographic information.

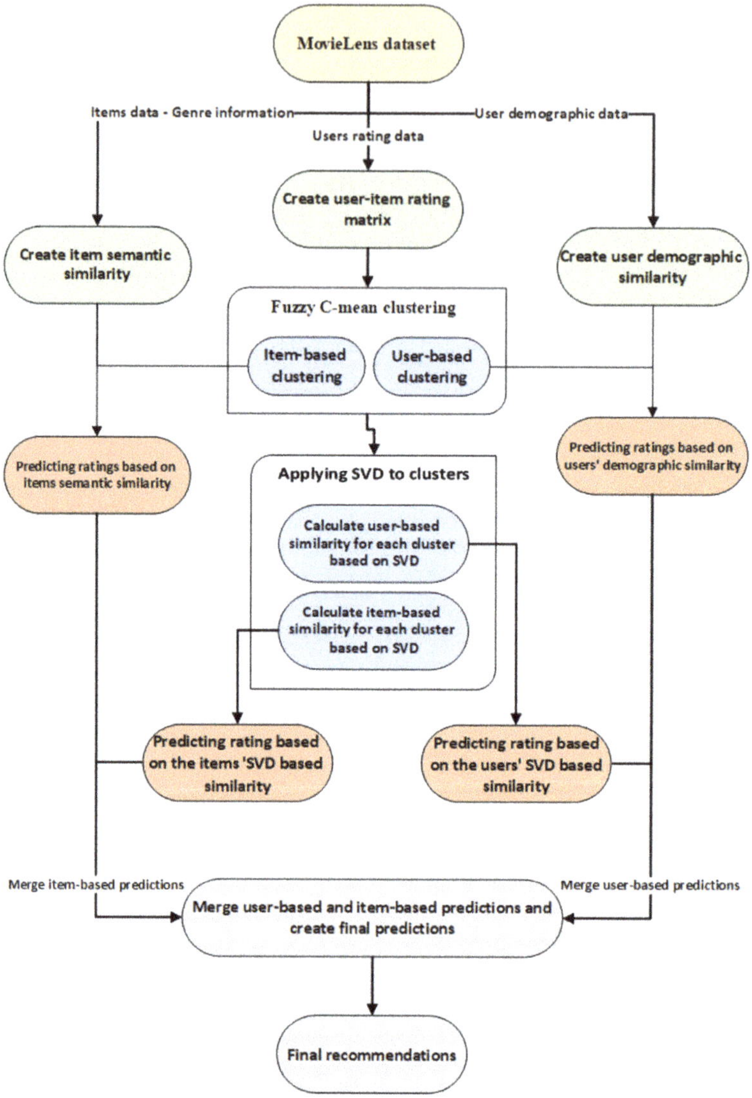

Figure 1. Architecture of the proposed UDIS.

We calculate demographic similarity by using the cosine similarity metric to incorporate demographic information into the recommendation process. Each user is represented by a binary vector that includes demographic attributes such as age and gender. These vectors are then compared using cosine similarity to generate a demographic similarity matrix. By including demographic data, the model can tailor recommendations to align more closely with users' intrinsic characteristics, leading to more personalized suggestions.

For example, users within the same age group or with similar interests are likely to have correlated preferences, which can be used to recommend items more effectively.

5. Calculate item similarity based on semantic similarity derived from movie genres.

Items are represented by a set of features indicating their semantic properties. This study uses the Jaccard similarity coefficient to measure the semantic similarity between items based on their genre attributes. Each item is represented as a binary vector where the presence or absence of a genre is marked. The Jaccard coefficient then calculates the similarity between any two items, creating an item similarity matrix based on semantic attributes. This process allows the system to make informed predictions even when users have not rated certain items.

6. Utilize the semantic similarity, SVD-based similarity, and user demographic similarity matrices to determine neighborhood ranges for users and items, facilitating recommendation calculation.

After calculating the user-based, item-based, demographic, and semantic predictions, we merge them to generate a comprehensive recommendation. We explored four merging techniques:

The Shambour Method: This rule-based approach selects predictions based on specific conditions, offering a structured integration based on the availability of certain prediction types.

The Average Method: This method calculates the average of all predictions, which was ultimately selected as the primary merging technique due to its simplicity and robust performance.

The Max Method: This approach chooses the highest prediction value among the four sources, providing a conservative estimate emphasizing the strongest recommendation.

The Weighted Sum Method: Here, predictions are combined with adjustable weights, allowing for prioritization based on prediction confidence.

7. Generate four distinct predictions and merge them into a final prediction. Evaluate the four merging methods and select the most effective one.

8. Compare the obtained results with other similar methods for performance assessment.

3.1. Semantic Similarity

To calculate the semantic similarity between items, we consider each item a binary vector $\overrightarrow{F} = (f_{a,1}, f_{a,2}, \ldots, f_{a,m})$. Each binary variable $f_{a,p}$ is a movie genre, and a value of one is obtained if the item belongs to category p, and a value of zero is obtained if it does not belong to category p. Each movie can have different genres simultaneously. There are 19 genres: unknown, film-noir, action, drama, adventure, children, comedy, fantasy, crime, documentary, horror, musical, mystery, animation, romance, trailer, sci-fi, and Western. After creating the binary vector for each item, the semantic similarity between items 'a' and 'b' is calculated using the Jaccard binary similarity coefficient. In the end, an item–item semantic matrix containing the semantic similarity of all items is obtained. This similarity ranges from 0 to 1. Zero means two items are not similar, and one means two are completely similar.

3.2. Demographic Similarity

To calculate similar users based on the demographic approach, we employ the cosine similarity coefficient. This calculation begins by creating a binary vector to represent the demographic information of each user. Each element of this vector is assigned a value of either zero or one based on the user's demographic characteristics. Specifically, the vector comprises elements for gender and age. For gender, which is stored as character data, we convert it to integer data. Here, males are represented by a zero, while females are represented by a one. Age categories are defined as follows: younger than 12 years, between 12 and 17 years, between 18 and 34 years, between 35 and 44 years, between 45 and 54 years, and older than 55 years. Subsequently, a demographic matrix is constructed for all users, wherein cosine similarity is employed to calculate the demographic similarity between any two users based on Formula (4). The resulting user matrix is depicted in Table 1, where 'm' represents the number of users.

$$cos(\theta) = \frac{d_1 \cdot d_2}{|d_1||\ d_2|} \tag{4}$$

$$d_1 \cdot d_2 = x_{11}x_{21} + x_{12}x_{22} + x_{13}x_{23} + \ldots + x_{1z}x_{2z} \tag{5}$$

$$|d_1| = \left(x_{11}^2 + x_{12}^2 + x_{13}^2 + \ldots + x_{1z}^2 \right)^{1/2} \tag{6}$$

$$|d_2| = \left(x_{21}^2 + x_{22}^2 + x_{23}^2 + \ldots + x_{2z}^2 \right)^{1/2} \tag{7}$$

Table 1. User demographic matrix.

			Age Range					
		Gender	Less than 12 Years	Between 12 and 17 Years	Between 18 and 34 Years	Between 35 and 44 Years	Between 45 and 54 Years	More than 55 Years
Users	1	1	0	0	1	0	0	0
	2	0	1	0	0	0	0	0
	3	1	0	0	0	0	0	1
	4	1	0	0	0	1	0	0
	m	0	0	1	0	0	0	0

In these formulas, $d_1 = (\ x_{11}\ ,\ x_{12}\ ,\ x_{13}\ ,\ \ldots\ ,\ x_{1z}\ )$ and $d_2 = (\ x_{21}\ ,\ x_{22}\ ,\ x_{23}\ ,\ \ldots\ ,\ x_{2z}\ )$ are user demographic vectors, and z is the number of user demographic vector elements equal to 7.

3.3. SVD-Based Similarity

After clustering users and items, SVD is applied to each cluster, yielding decomposition matrices for each cluster. Consequently, parameters U, S, and V are obtained for each cluster. The similarity between cluster components is then calculated based on the SVD. To achieve this, we utilize the first two columns of the U and V matrices, disregarding the remaining columns. This approach aims to uncover hidden relationships between users and items, effectively reducing both users and items to a two-dimensional space.

After clustering and applying SVD, we calculate user similarity within user-based clusters by utilizing only the first two columns of the U matrix. Each row of this matrix represents a user within that cluster, effectively projecting users into a two-dimensional space. We then employ Pearson's similarity to calculate the similarity between users.

Similarly, we use only the first two columns of the V matrix for item-based clustering. Each row of this matrix represents an item within that cluster, projecting items into a two-dimensional space. We then use cosine similarity to determine the similarities and differences between items.

During the testing phase, we use Formula (8) to determine the two-dimensional position of the target user and Formula (9) to ascertain the two-dimensional position of the new item. Furthermore, to handle missing data, we employ the SVD method proposed by [3].

$$newuser_{2D} = newuser \times V_2 \times S_2^{-1} \tag{8}$$

$$newitem_{2D} = newitem \times U_2 \times S_2^{-1} \tag{9}$$

3.4. Integrating Predictions

In this research, we generate four types of predictions: item-based CF prediction, item-based prediction using semantic similarity, user-based CF prediction, and user-based prediction using demographic similarity. These predictions are merged into a single comprehensive prediction. Initially, item-based predictions and user-based predictions are merged separately. Subsequently, the two resulting predictions are combined. Four different methods for merging these predictions are evaluated. After comparing the results (as discussed below), the average method, which has demonstrated superior performance (as shown in Figures 2 and 3), is selected as the primary method for combination.

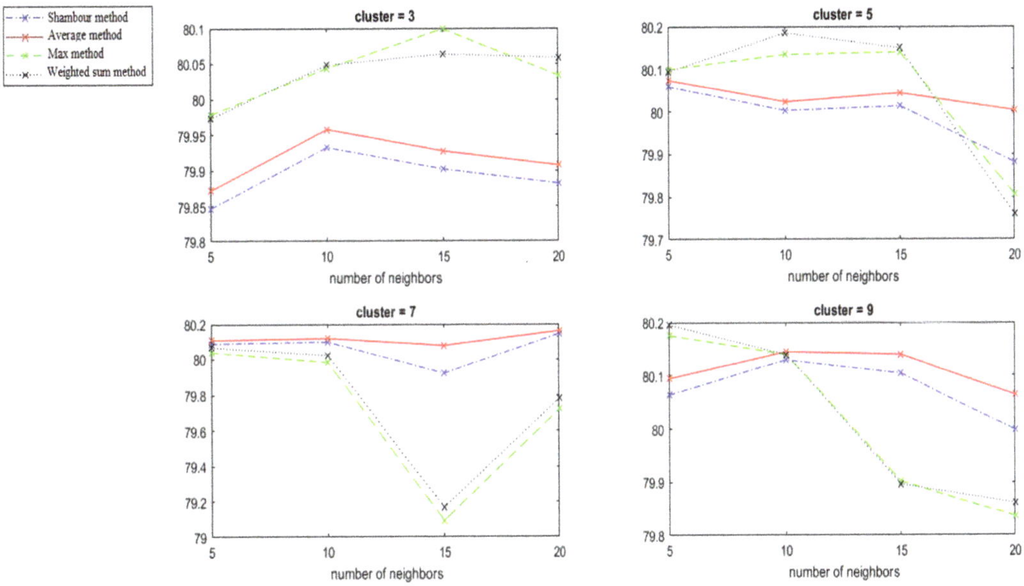

Figure 2. Comparison results of four different integration methods in the accuracy measures.

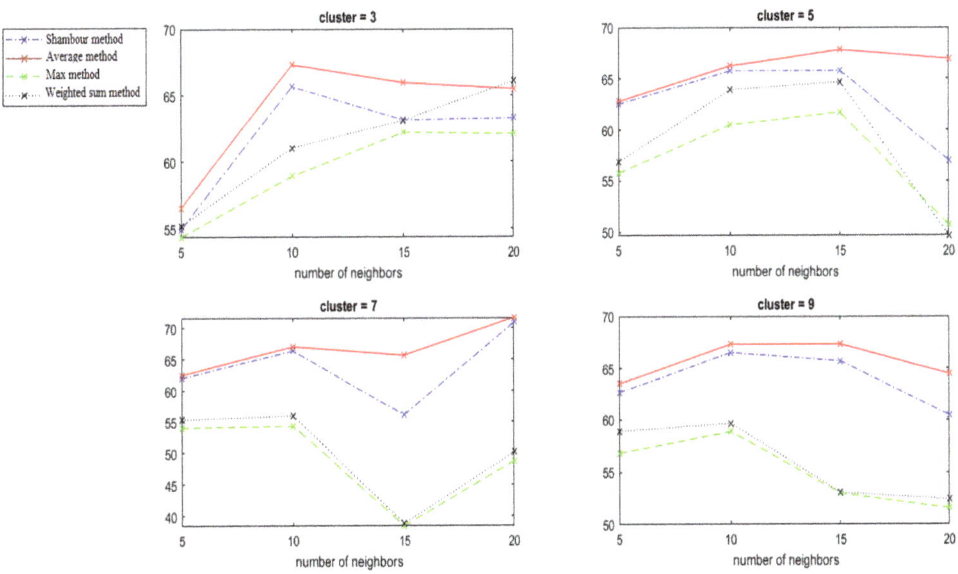

Figure 3. Comparison results of four different integration methods in precision measures.

The Shambour Method: This method uses Formula (10) [37] to integrate item-based predictions and user-based predictions.

$$r = \begin{cases} 0 & if\ r_1 = 0,\ r_2 = 0 \\ r_1 & if\ r_2 = 0 \\ r_2 & if\ r_1 = 0 \\ \frac{2 \times r_1 \times r_2}{r_1 + r_2} & \text{otherwise} \end{cases} \tag{10}$$

For example, to predict item-based ratings, r_1 and r_2 are the item-based CF prediction and item-based prediction using semantic similarity.

The Average Method: In this method, the average of the predictions is considered.

The Max Method: In this method, the highest prediction is considered as the final prediction.

The Weighted Sum Method: This method uses a weighted sum (linear combination), as used in the [19] method, which combines the rating prediction results according to Formula (11). In this formula, r_1 and r_2 are the predictions we want to integrate, and α and β are the weights of each of these predictions.

$$r_{final} = \alpha \times r_1 + \beta \times r_2 \tag{11}$$

The proposed UDIS method advances beyond a simple overlay of existing techniques by integrating four distinct prediction approaches: user-based collaborative filtering, demographic-similarity-based, item-based collaborative filtering, and semantic-similarity-based predictions. This combination leverages the unique strengths of each approach within a structured framework, thereby enhancing recommendation accuracy and more effectively addressing challenges such as data sparsity.

Notably, UDIS employs fuzzy C-means (FCM) clustering in conjunction with singular value decomposition (SVD) for dimensionality reduction within clusters, which enables the system to capture and adapt to complex user preferences with greater precision. This method of combining demographic and semantic similarities with collaborative filtering techniques distinguishes UDIS from conventional hybrid recommender systems.

Additionally, UDIS explores and evaluates four prediction merging techniques—average, max, Shambour, and weighted sum—ultimately identifying the average method as the most effective. This comprehensive evaluation and selection process further highlights the approach's novelty. By empirically testing these integration methods, UDIS establishes a structured and empirically validated method for combining predictions, enhancing the accuracy and precision of recommendations.

4. Experimental Evaluation

This research used the MovieLens dataset to evaluate the proposed method. The MovieLens dataset is widely recognized and frequently used in education, research, and industry, with thousands of downloads annually, underscoring its popularity [38]. This dataset, collected by GroupLens Research, comprises 100,000 ratings (ranging from 1 to 5) from 943 users on 1682 movies. Additionally, it includes basic demographic information for users, such as age, gender, occupation, and zip code.

The evaluations for the UDIS method were conducted using the MovieLens dataset in 2024. For comparison, this study referenced recent research conducted primarily within the past 3 to 5 years, focusing on contemporary RS techniques.

This paper presents the comparison results of the four different integration methods regarding accuracy and precision, as shown in Figures 2 and 3. Additionally, we compared the UDIS method, which employs FCM clustering, with the UDIS method using k-means clustering, the Self-Organizing Map (SOM), and the Expectation-Maximization (EM) clustering techniques. The results of this comparison are illustrated in Figures 4 and 5. These figures examine accuracy and precision across various numbers of clusters (3, 5, 7, and

9) and different neighborhood sizes (5, 10, 15, and 20). Formulas 12 and 13 were used to calculate the accuracy and precision, respectively.

$$\text{Accuracy} = \frac{\sum \textit{True Positive} + \sum \textit{True Negative}}{\sum \textit{Total Population}} \quad (12)$$

$$\text{Precision} = \frac{\sum \textit{True Positive}}{\sum \textit{Test Outcome Positive}} \quad (13)$$

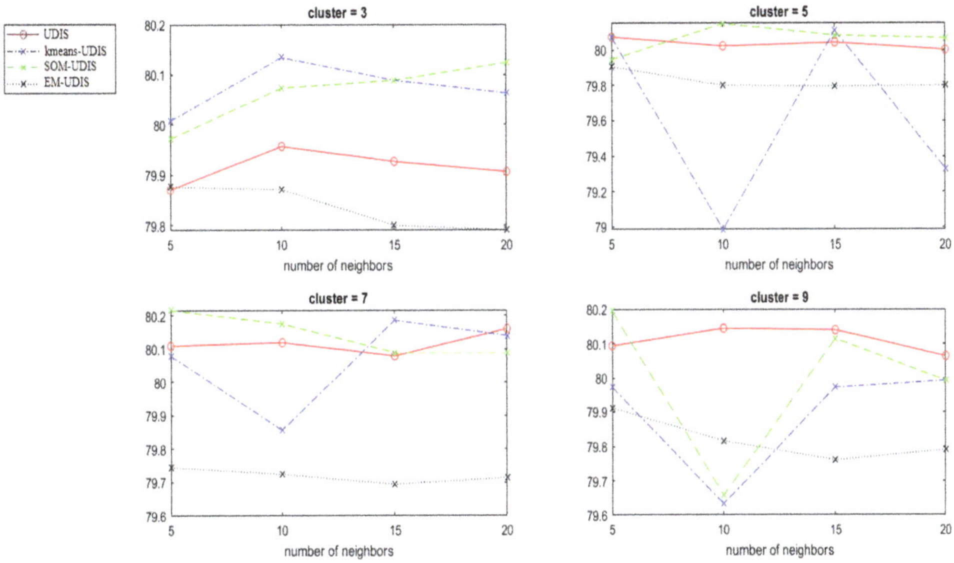

Figure 4. Comparison of UDIS method based on FCM clustering with k-means, SOM, and EM methods in the accuracy measure.

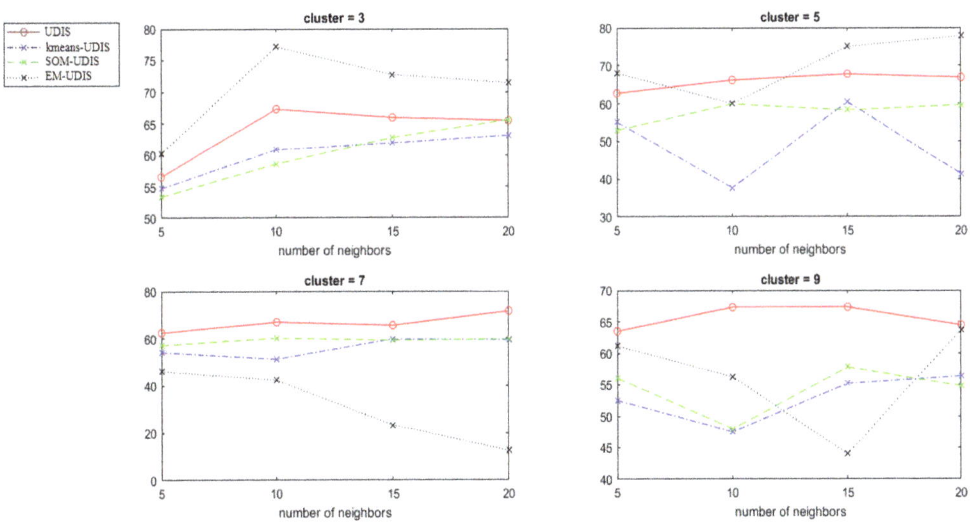

Figure 5. Comparison of UDIS method based on FCM clustering with k-means, SOM, and EM methods in the precision measure.

As shown in Figure 2, when the number of clusters was 3 or 5, the max and weighted sum methods demonstrated superior results, maintaining their performance even as the number of neighbors increased. At this stage, the average method performed better than the Shambour method but fell short in accuracy compared to the max and weighted sum methods. However, as the number of clusters increased to 7 or 9, the accuracy of the Shambour and average methods surpassed that of the max and weighted sum methods, with the average method outperforming the Shambour method.

According to Figure 3, the average method consistently achieved better precision than the other three methods as the number of neighbors and clusters increased. An exception occurred when the number of clusters was 3 and the number of neighbors was 20, where the precision of the weighted sum method slightly exceeded that of the average method. Generally, the Shambour method outperformed the max and weighted sum methods. While the max and weighted sum methods often yielded similar results, the weighted sum method typically exhibited better precision.

Figures 2 and 3 show that the average method consistently outperformed the Shambour method in all diagrams. The max and weighted sum methods showed close results; however, the weighted sum method generally performed better. The accuracy of the average method surpassed that of the other three methods in all cases. As the number of clusters and neighbors increased, the average method's performance improved further, surpassing the other methods in both accuracy and precision measures. Thus, the average method achieved the best overall results, considering both accuracy and precision.

These findings indicate that while the max and weighted sum methods can perform well in specific configurations, the average method offers a more balanced and reliable approach across different clustering scenarios. This makes it particularly suitable for the UDIS framework, where accuracy and precision are critical.

The effectiveness of the UDIS method was also compared using various clustering techniques: FCM, k-means, SOM, and EM. Figures 4 and 5 present the results across different cluster and neighborhood configurations.

As shown in Figure 4, with three clusters, the accuracy of k-means-UDIS and SOM-UDIS surpassed that of UDIS and EM-UDIS, with UDIS outperforming EM-UDIS. After increasing the number of clusters to five, UDIS's accuracy became comparable to SOM-UDIS, though SOM-UDIS still maintained a slight edge. Meanwhile, the accuracy of k-means-UDIS and EM-UDIS remained lower than that of UDIS. As the number of clusters rose, UDIS's accuracy improved, aligning with k-means-UDIS and SOM-UDIS. When the number of clusters reached nine, UDIS achieved better accuracy than the other clustering methods, and this improvement held steady as the number of neighbors increased.

As shown in Figure 5, when the number of clusters was set to three, EM-UDIS exhibited the highest precision, significantly outperforming the other three methods. In this scenario, UDIS demonstrated better precision than both k-means-UDIS and SOM-UDIS, though UDIS and SOM-UDIS showed equal precision when the number of neighbors reached 20. With five clusters, EM-UDIS maintained superior precision, except when the number of neighbors was 10, where UDIS surpassed EM-UDIS, k-means-UDIS, and SOM-UDIS in terms of precision.

At seven clusters, EM-UDIS's precision sharply declined and decreased as the number of neighbors increased, resulting in lower precision than all three other methods. Conversely, UDIS achieved higher precision than the other methods across all neighbor counts. When the number of clusters reached nine, UDIS again outperformed the other three methods in terms of precision. At the same time, EM-UDIS showed better precision than k-means-UDIS and SOM-UDIS, except when the number of neighbors was 15.

Overall, Figure 5 illustrates that increasing both the number of clusters and neighbors improved the precision of the proposed UDIS method with FCM clustering. In all cases, UDIS exhibited better precision than the k-means-UDIS and SOM-UDIS methods. These comparisons suggest that while k-means and SOM can be effective in smaller configurations, FCM clustering provided the most consistent performance improvements in both accuracy and precision as the number of clusters increased. This validates the selection of FCM in the UDIS method for achieving superior recommendation quality across different user scenarios.

In summary, the experimental results demonstrate that the average merging method, combined with FCM clustering, consistently outperforms other techniques in terms of both accuracy and precision across varying dataset configurations. This combination addresses data sparsity and adapts well to different user and item characteristics, offering enhanced scalability and personalization in recommendations. The UDIS approach, integrating demographic and semantic data, proves particularly robust and effective, making it highly applicable for domains with diverse user preferences.

5. Conclusions

Recommendation systems have been widely developed to provide automated personalized product and service offerings. In our work, we improved the quality of recommendations through the UDIS method, which integrates FCM clustering and SVD dimensionality reduction techniques. UDIS enhances RS by incorporating demographic information to calculate user demographic similarity and utilizing genre information to determine the semantic similarity of items.

The experimental results demonstrated that this method, in most cases, outperformed other approaches regarding accuracy and precision. Specifically, including user demographic similarity and the semantic similarity of items alongside rating information yielded superior results. Furthermore, by evaluating four merging techniques, we identified the average method as the most effective, significantly improving the accuracy and precision of the MovieLens dataset compared to other approaches. These results demonstrate that incorporating multiple prediction types can effectively address data sparsity, leading to more accurate and personalized recommendations.

This study identified some limitations and areas for future exploration. Currently, UDIS uses only age and gender as demographic features, which may not fully capture user preferences. Future research will consider additional attributes such as occupation and location to enrich demographic similarity. Likewise, using genre as the sole semantic feature limits the depth of item analysis. Employing Natural Language Processing (NLP) could allow for extracting more detailed semantic information from item descriptions and reviews, thereby improving recommendation relevance.

Additionally, while UDIS employs a simple linear combination for merging predictions, future work will explore advanced methods like deep learning and Artificial Neural Networks (ANNs). These methods could allow UDIS to learn and adapt to more complex relationships, potentially enhancing accuracy and personalization in diverse recommendation scenarios.

The broader implications of UDIS suggest its applicability in domains where user preferences are varied, such as e-commerce, streaming services, and social media. By tailoring recommendations to both demographic and semantic factors, UDIS has the potential to elevate user experiences in fields like movie or music recommendations. Expanding UDIS's features and integrating advanced techniques could refine its effectiveness and adaptability in these contexts.

Author Contributions: Conceptualization, H.K. and T.F.; methodology, H.K. and T.F.; software, T.F. and E.M.; validation, H.K., Z.K. and E.M.; formal analysis, H.K. and Z.K.; data curation, T.F. and E.M.; writing—original draft preparation, T.F. and E.M; writing—review and editing, H.K. and Z.K; visualization, T.F. and E.M.; supervision, H.K.; project administration, H.K. and Z.K. All authors have read and agreed to the published version of the manuscript.

Funding: This research received no external funding.

Data Availability Statement: The authors will make the raw data supporting this article's conclusions available upon request.

Acknowledgments: We sincerely thank the reviewers and editors for their meticulous work.

Conflicts of Interest: The authors declare no conflicts of interest.

Abbreviations

Artificial Neural Networks	ANNs
Collaborative filtering	CF
Expectation-Maximization	EM
Fuzzy C-means	FCM
Matrix Factorization	MF
Mean Absolute Error	MAE
Multiple Linear Regression	MLR
Natural Language Processing	NLP
Nonnegative Matrix Factorization	NMF
Recommender systems	RS
Root Mean Square Error	RMSE
Self-Organizing Map	SOM
Singular value decomposition	SVD
Support Vector Regression	SVR
Trust-based RS	TRS
User-based CF (U), demographic-similarity-based (D), item-based CF (I), and semantic-similarity-based (S)	UDIS

References

1. Campana, M.G.; Delmastro, F. Recommender Systems for Online and Mobile Social Networks: A Survey. *Online Soc. Netw. Media* **2017**, *3*, 75–97. [CrossRef]
2. Sarwar, B.; Karypis, G.; Konstan, J.; Riedl, J. Application of Dimensionality Reduction in Recommender System A Case Study. *Comput. Sci. Eng. Dept. Univ. Minn.* **2000**. Available online: http://files.grouplens.org/papers/webKDD00.pdf (accessed on 14 October 2024).
3. Nilashi, M.; Ibrahim, O.; Bagherifard, K. A Recommender System Based on Collaborative Filtering Using Ontology and Dimensionality Reduction Techniques. *Expert. Syst. Appl.* **2018**, *92*, 507–520. [CrossRef]
4. Zarzour, H.; Al-Sharif, Z.; Al-Ayyoub, M.; Jararweh, Y. A New Collaborative Filtering Recommendation Algorithm Based on Dimensionality Reduction and Clustering Techniques. In Proceedings of the 2018 9th International Conference on Information and Communication Systems, ICICS 2018, Irbid, Jordan, 3–5 April 2018; 2018; pp. 102–106.
5. Koohi, H.; Kiani, K. User Based Collaborative Filtering Using Fuzzy C-Means. *Measurement* **2016**, *91*, 134–139. [CrossRef]
6. Vellaichamy, V.; Kalimuthu, V. Hybrid Collaborative Movie Recommender System Using Clustering and Bat Optimization. *Int. J. Intell. Eng. Syst.* **2017**, *10*, 38–47. [CrossRef]
7. Koohi, H.; Kobti, Z.; Nazari, Z.; Mousavi, J. Enhancing Recommender System Performance through the Fusion of Fuzzy C-Means, Restricted Boltzmann Machine, and Extreme Learning Machine. *Multimed. Tools Appl.* **2024**, *83*, 63095–63119. [CrossRef]
8. Mobasher, B.; Jin, X.; Zhou, Y. Semantically Enhanced Collaborative Filtering on the Web. In *Proceedings of the European Web Mining Forum*; Springer: Berlin/Heidelberg, Germany, 2003; pp. 57–76.
9. Thakkar, P.; Varma, K.; Ukani, V.; Mankad, S.; Tanwar, S. Combining User-Based and Item-Based Collaborative Filtering Using Machine Learning. In *Proceedings of the Information and Communication Technology for Intelligent Systems*; Springer Science and Business Media Deutschland GmbH: Berlin/Heidelberg, Germany, 2019; pp. 173–180.
10. Barzegar Nozari, R.; Koohi, H. A Novel Group Recommender System Based on Members' Influence and Leader Impact. *Knowl. Based Syst.* **2020**, *205*, 106296. [CrossRef]
11. Harispe, S.; Ranwez, S.; Janaqi, S.; Montmain, J. Semantic Similarity from Natural Language and Ontology Analysis. In *Synthesis Lectures on Human Language Technologies*; Springer: Cham, Switzerland, 2015; Volume 8, pp. 1–256. [CrossRef]
12. Yan, Z.; Wu, Q.; Ren, M.; Liu, J.; Liu, S.; Qiu, S. Locally Private Jaccard Similarity Estimation. In *Proceedings of the Concurrency and Computation: Practice and Experience*; John Wiley and Sons Ltd.: Hoboken, NJ, USA, 2019; Volume 31.
13. Koohi, H.; Kiani, K. A New Method to Find Neighbor Users That Improves the Performance of Collaborative Filtering. *Expert. Syst. Appl.* **2017**, *83*, 30–39. [CrossRef]
14. Gong, S.; Ye, H.; Dai, Y. Combining Singular Value Decomposition and Item-Based Recommender in Collaborative Filtering. In Proceedings of the 2009 2nd International Workshop on Knowledge Discovery and Data Mining, WKKD 2009, Moscow, Russia, 23–25 January 2009; pp. 769–772.
15. Ren, Y.; Gong, S. A Collaborative Filtering Recommendation Algorithm Based on Svd Smoothing. In Proceedings of the Third International Symposium on Intelligent Information Technology Application, Nanchang, China, 21–22 November 2009; Volume 2, pp. 530–532.

16. Sahoo, A.K.; Pradhan, C.; Mishra, B.S.P. SVD Based Privacy Preserving Recommendation Model Using Optimized Hybrid Item-Based Collaborative Filtering. In Proceedings of the 2019 IEEE International Conference on Communication and Signal Processing, ICCSP 2019, Chennai, India, 4–6 April 2019; pp. 294–298.
17. Al-Nafjan, A.; Alrashoudi, N.; Alrasheed, H. Recommendation System Algorithms on Location-Based Social Networks: Comparative Study. *Information* **2022**, *13*, 188. [CrossRef]
18. Vozalis, M.G.; Margaritis, K.G. Using SVD and Demographic Data for the Enhancement of Generalized Collaborative Filtering. *Inf. Sci.* **2007**, *177*, 3017–3037. [CrossRef]
19. Tiwari, S.K.; Shrivastava, S.K. An Approach for Recommender System by Combining Collaborative Filtering with User Demographics and Items Genres. *Int. J. Comput. Appl.* **2015**, *128*, 16–24. [CrossRef]
20. Valdiviezo-Díaz, P.; Bobadilla, J. A Hybrid Approach of Recommendation via Extended Matrix Based on Collaborative Filtering with Demographics Information. In *Proceedings of the International Conference on Technology Trends*; Springer: Cham, Switzerland, 2018; Volume 895, pp. 384–398.
21. Pereira, N.; Varma, S.L. Financial Planning Recommendation System Using Content-Based Collaborative and Demographic Filtering. In *Proceedings of the Advances in Intelligent Systems and Computing*; Springer Verlag: Berlin/Heidelberg, Germany, 2019; Volume 669, pp. 141–151.
22. Waqar, M.; Majeed, N.; Dawood, H.; Daud, A.; Aljohani, N.R. An Adaptive Doctor-Recommender System. *Behav. Inf. Technol.* **2019**, *38*, 959–973. [CrossRef]
23. Chew, L.-J.; Haw, S.-C.; Subramaniam, S. A Hybrid Recommender System Based on Data Enrichment on the Ontology Modelling. *F1000Res* **2021**, *10*, 937. [CrossRef] [PubMed]
24. CK, R.; Srikantaiah, K.C. Switching Hybrid Model for Personalized Recommendations by Combining Users Demographic Information. *J. Theor. Appl. Inf. Technol.* **2022**, *100*, 825–835.
25. Katarya, R.; Verma, O.P. Recommender System with Grey Wolf Optimizer and FCM. *Neural Comput. Appl.* **2018**, *30*, 1679–1687. [CrossRef]
26. Duan, L.; Wang, W.; Han, B. A Hybrid Recommendation System Based on Fuzzy C-Means Clustering and Supervised Learning. *KSII Trans. Internet Inf. Syst.* **2021**, *15*, 2399–2413.
27. Gong, S. A Collaborative Filtering Recommendation Algorithm Based on User Clustering and Item Clustering. *J. Softw.* **2010**, *5*, 745–752. [CrossRef]
28. Kumar, N.P.; Fan, Z. Hybrid User-Item Based Collaborative Filtering. *Proc. Procedia Comput. Sci.* **2015**, *60*, 1453–1461. [CrossRef]
29. Ranjbar Kermany, N.; Alizadeh, S.H. A Hybrid Multi-Criteria Recommender System Using Ontology and Neuro-Fuzzy Techniques. *Electron. Commer. Res. Appl.* **2017**, *21*, 50–64. [CrossRef]
30. Yue, W.; Wang, Z.; Liu, W.; Tian, B.; Lauria, S.; Liu, X. An Optimally Weighted User- and Item-Based Collaborative Filtering Approach to Predicting Baseline Data for Friedreich's Ataxia Patients. *Neurocomputing* **2021**, *419*, 287–294. [CrossRef]
31. Barzegar Nozari, R.; Koohi, H. Novel Implicit-Trust-Network-Based Recommendation Methodology. *Expert. Syst. Appl.* **2021**, *186*, 115709. [CrossRef]
32. Wang, S.; Zhang, X.; Wang, Y.; Ricci, F. Trustworthy Recommender Systems. *ACM Trans. Intell. Syst. Technol.* **2024**, *15*, 1–20. [CrossRef]
33. Barzegar Nozari, R.; Koohi, H.; Mahmodi, E. A Novel Trust Computation Method Based on User Ratings to Improve the Recommendation. *Int. J. Eng.* **2020**, *33*, 377–386. [CrossRef]
34. Zhang, Z.; Liu, Y.; Jin, Z.; Zhang, R. Selecting Influential and Trustworthy Neighbors for Collaborative Filtering Recommender Systems. In Proceedings of the 2017 IEEE 7th Annual Computing and Communication Workshop and Conference, CCWC 2017, Las Vegas, NV, USA, 9–11 January 2017.
35. Zhao, J.; Wang, W.; Zhang, Z.; Sun, Q.; Huo, H.; Qu, L.; Zheng, S. TrustTF: A Tensor Factorization Model Using User Trust and Implicit Feedback for Context-Aware Recommender Systems. *Knowl. Based Syst.* **2020**, *209*, 106434. [CrossRef]
36. De Meo, P. Trust Prediction via Matrix Factorisation. *ACM Trans. Internet Technol.* **2019**, *19*, 1–20. [CrossRef]
37. Shambour, Q.; Lu, J. A Hybrid Multi-Criteria Semantic-Enhanced Collaborative Filtering Approach for Personalized Recommendations. In Proceedings of the 2011 IEEE/WIC/ACM International Conference on Web Intelligence, WI 2011, Lyon, France, 22–27 August 2011; Volume 1, pp. 71–78.
38. Harper, F.M.; Konstan, J.A. The Movielens Datasets: History and Context. *ACM Trans. Interact. Intell. Syst.* **2015**, *5*, 1–19. [CrossRef]

electronics

MDPI

Article

Multiloss Joint Gradient Control Knowledge Distillation for Image Classification

Wei He [1], Jianchen Pan [1], Jianyu Zhang [2], Xichuan Zhou [1], Jialong Liu [1], Xiaoyu Huang [1] and Yingcheng Lin [1,*]

[1] The School of Microelectronics and Communication Engineering, Chongqing University, Chongqing 400044, China
[2] China Railway Design Corporation, Tianjin 300450, China
* Correspondence: linyc@cqu.edu.cn

Abstract: Knowledge distillation (KD) techniques aim to transfer knowledge from complex teacher neural networks to simpler student networks. In this study, we propose a novel knowledge distillation method called Multiloss Joint Gradient Control Knowledge Distillation (MJKD), which functions by effectively combining feature- and logit-based knowledge distillation methods with gradient control. The proposed knowledge distillation method discretely considers the gradients of the task loss (cross-entropy loss), feature distillation loss, and logit distillation loss. The experimental results suggest that logits may contain more information and should, consequently, be assigned greater weight during the gradient update process in this work. The empirical findings on the CIFAR-100 and Tiny-ImageNet datasets indicate that MJKD generally outperforms traditional knowledge distillation methods, significantly enhancing the generalization ability and classification accuracy of student networks. For instance, MJKD achieves a 63.53% accuracy on Tiny-ImageNet for the ResNet18 MobileNetV2 pair. Furthermore, we present visualizations and analyses to explore its potential working mechanisms.

Keywords: knowledge distillation; deep learning; image classification; transfer learning

1. Introduction

Deep convolution neural networks (CNNs) have been the predominant design paradigm for numerous computer vision tasks over the past few decades [1,2]. However, high-capacity models typically necessitate massive architectures, resulting in substantial computational and memory requirements. The deployment of state-of-the-art models into resource-constrained embedded systems remains a significant challenge. As the demand for low-cost networks on embedded systems continues to increase, there is an urgent need for more compact networks with reduced computational and memory requirements while maintaining performance comparable to their larger counterparts.

To address these issues, numerous techniques have been developed for compact neural networks, including knowledge distillation (KD) [3], network pruning [4–6], and quantization [7–9]. In this study, we focused on knowledge distillation due to its efficacy and potential for robust model compression capabilities. Knowledge distillation functions as a methodology for guiding the training of "student" neural networks through the encoding and propagation of knowledge from previously trained "teacher" networks. KD methods can be categorized into two primary classifications: logit-based and feature-based.

The original logit-based KD method introduced by Hinton [3] operates by minimizing the KL-divergence between the predicted logits of the teacher and student models. In comparison with logit-based methods, feature distillation demonstrates superior performance across various tasks, prompting numerous researchers to focus on investigating feature-based distillation methods [10–15]. To enhance the transfer of deep feature knowledge from intermediate layers to lightweight student networks, feature-based distillation methods such as FitNets [16] were proposed. FitNets initially addressed the issue of intermediate representation mismatches between the student and teacher networks through intermediate layer mapping, thus enabling feature-based knowledge distillation. Building on the FitNet method, AT [12] achieves further optimization by redefining the attention of convolutional neural networks to transfer knowledge through attention maps of features. In addition, the PKT [10] models the intermediate layer features of both the teacher and student as probability distributions, thereby facilitating a more effective knowledge transfer from the teacher. CRD [11] employs contrastive learning to transfer the deep knowledge of convolutional networks. Due to their outstanding performance and improved interpretability, feature-based distillation has long been a focus of research in knowledge distillation. However, recent perspectives suggest that logit-based distillation also holds significant potential, as the features from the final layer of the network may encapsulate comprehensive information about the entire model. DKD [17] effectively decouples the classical KD loss, achieving state-of-the-art performance in classification and detection tasks across various datasets solely using logit distillation. Furthermore, Hao et al. [18] have observed that the classical KD method can also achieve leading performance in numerous cases, particularly with larger datasets and extended distillation training periods. This observation underscores the simplicity and efficiency of logit-based distillation methods. Additionally, the LD [19] method highlights that the output features from the network's final layer may also contain information related to target localization, further underscoring the potential of output feature-based distillation. From the perspective of deep learning optimizers, DOT [20] addresses the trade-off between the two losses in logit-based methods by employing a momentum buffer, thereby further enhancing the performance of logit-based distillation methods. Indeed, logits, as the final output of the network, encapsulate the overall network information and hold a comparably significant position alongside feature-based methods.

The aforementioned methods primarily focus on either feature-based or logit-based aspects. A more effective combination of the strengths of both methods can significantly enhance the students' assimilation of knowledge, thereby improving their performance. However, merely combining these two methods does not substantially enhance the effectiveness of distillation. To address this issue, we propose a novel knowledge distillation method called Multiloss Joint Gradient Control Knowledge Distillation (MJKD). Inspired by recent advancements in deep learning optimizers [20], our method integrates the task loss (cross-entropy loss) between the student network outputs and the labels, feature distillation loss, and logit distillation loss with gradient control. The feature distillation loss and logit distillation loss were derived from the previous works, [10] and [17], respectively. In contrast to traditional methods, we control the proportions of different losses by adjusting the momentum of each loss independently, thus fully utilizing each component's loss to achieve superior student model performance. The primary contributions of this study are as follows:

- We present a novel method for independently controlling the momentum of task loss, feature distillation loss, and logit distillation loss. This innovation facilitates a more effective transfer of knowledge, resulting in enhanced student network performance.
- We empirically validate the efficacy of the proposed MJKD method on two widely used image classification datasets, CIFAR-100 and Tiny-ImageNet. The empirical results demonstrate that training the student network using the MJKD distillation method achieves superior performance compared with traditional knowledge distillation methods. Our findings indicate that logits may contain richer network information. Furthermore, the robustness and efficiency of MJKD has been substantiated.
- We provide a comprehensive analysis of the MJKD method, including visualizations of loss landscapes and correlation matrices between student and teacher logits. These insights offer a more profound understanding of the mechanisms underlying the improved performance of student networks trained with MJKD.

The remainder of this paper is organized as follows. In Section 2, we describe the primary methods employed in our study, focusing on feature distillation loss, logit distillation loss, and multiloss joint gradient control. Section 3 details the implementation of our experiments, including descriptions of the datasets and experimental setup. We present the main results, including motivation validation, comparative results, and visualization analysis. Finally, in Section 4, we summarize our research and briefly discuss the practical significance of MJKD.

2. Main Methods

In this section, we delineate the three key components of our knowledge distillation method. First, we define the feature distillation loss for our distillation method. Subsequently, we introduce distillation loss. Finally, we present a detailed explanation of the core component of our method, the multiloss joint gradient control mechanism.

2.1. Feature Distillation Loss

Feature distillation loss refers to the supervision derived from the intermediate layers of the teacher network, which is used to guide the intermediate layers of the student network. To facilitate the student model's effective assimilation of the teacher model's features, it is imperative to characterize the geometric structure of the feature spaces of both networks for each batch of data. Specifically, the joint probability density between any two data points within the network's feature space can be utilized to calculate the distance between them. The objective is to minimize the discrepancy in joint density between the student probability distribution S and the teacher probability distribution T. Kernel Density Estimation (KDE) [21] provides an efficacious method to estimate these joint density probability functions as follows:

$$s_{ij} = s_{i|j}s_j = \frac{1}{N}K(\mathbf{x}_i, \mathbf{x}_j; 2\sigma_t^2), \tag{1}$$

and

$$t_{ij} = t_{i|j}t_j = \frac{1}{N}K(\mathbf{y}_i, \mathbf{y}_j; 2\sigma_s^2), \tag{2}$$

where $\mathbf{x}_i$ and $\mathbf{y}_i$ denote the output representations of the student model and teacher model, respectively, for the i-th class. N represents the number of classes in the dataset. $K(\mathbf{x}_i, \mathbf{x}_j; 2\sigma_s^2)$ is a symmetric kernel with width $2\sigma_s^2$. Additionally, since the conditional probability distribution can represent the similarity between data within each batch [22], employing the conditional probability distribution allows for a more precise description of the local regions between samples [10]. Consequently, the joint probability density function can be substituted with the conditional probability distribution of the samples. For both the teacher model and the student model, the conditional probability distribution is defined as follows:

$$s_{i|j} = \frac{K(\mathbf{x}_i, \mathbf{x}_j; 2\sigma_t^2)}{\sum_{k=1,k\neq j}^{N} K(\mathbf{x}_k, \mathbf{x}_j; 2\sigma_t^2)} \in [0,1], \tag{3}$$

and

$$t_{i|j} = \frac{K(\mathbf{y}_i, \mathbf{y}_j; 2\sigma_t^2)}{\sum_{k=1,k\neq j}^{N} K(\mathbf{y}_k, \mathbf{y}_j; 2\sigma_s^2)} \in [0,1]. \tag{4}$$

In this study, we employ an approach that utilizes an affinity metric based on cosine similarity. The similarity metric employed is defined as follows:

$$K_{cosine}(\mathbf{x}_i, \mathbf{x}_j) = \frac{1}{2}\left(\frac{\mathbf{x}_i^T\mathbf{x}_j}{||\mathbf{x}_i||_2||\mathbf{x}_j||_2} + 1\right) \in [0,1]. \tag{5}$$

Cosine metrics often demonstrate superior performance compared with Euclidean metrics, particularly in high-dimensional spaces [23], by utilizing cosine similarity as the kernel metric, enabling a more accurate computation of affinity. we employ the Kullback–

Leibler (KL) divergence. Given that the distributions S and T can only be estimated through a finite number of data points, the feature distillation loss is defined as follows:

$$\mathcal{L}_{feature} = \sum_{i=1}^{N} \sum_{j=1, i \neq j}^{N} s_{j|i} \log\left(\frac{s_{j|i}}{t_{j|i}}\right). \tag{6}$$

2.2. *Logit Distillation Loss*

"Logit" refers to the raw output of a model, which is converted into class probabilities through the application of a "softmax" output layer. The logit distillation loss represents the supervision from the teacher model's logits over the student model's logits. Within each batch, the classification probabilities for a training sample belonging to the t-th class are represented as $\mathbf{n} = [n_1, n_2, \ldots, n_t, \ldots, n_D] \in \mathbb{R}^{1\times D}$, where n_i denotes the probability of the i-th class, and D is the total number of classes. Given that z_i represents the logits of the i-th class, the softmax function can be formally written as

$$n_i = \frac{\exp(z_i)}{\sum_{k=1}^{D} \exp(z_k)}. \tag{7}$$

The softmax function can be decoupled into two components. Excluding the t-th class, the probabilities are represented by $\hat{\mathbf{n}} = [\hat{n}_1, \ldots, \hat{n}_{t-1}, \hat{n}_{t+1}, \ldots, \hat{n}_D] \in \mathbb{R}^{1\times(D-1)}$, which independently models probabilities among nontarget classes. Each element is computed as follows:

$$\hat{n}_i = \frac{\exp(z_i)}{\sum_{k=1, k\neq t}^{D} \exp(z_k)}. \tag{8}$$

Subsequently, we define the binary probabilities as $\mathbf{c} = [c_t, 1 - c_t] \in \mathbb{R}^{1\times 2}$, where c_t represents the probability of the target class, and $1 - c_t$ represents the probability of all other non-target classes. The specific calculation is as follows:

$$c_t = \frac{\exp(z_t)}{\sum_{k=1}^{D} \exp(z_k)}. \tag{9}$$

Thus, the logit distillation loss can be defined as

$$\mathcal{L}_{logits} = \alpha \mathrm{KL}(\mathbf{c}^{\mathcal{T}} || \mathbf{c}^{\mathcal{S}}) + \beta \mathrm{KL}(\hat{\mathbf{n}}^{\mathcal{T}} || \hat{\mathbf{n}}^{\mathcal{S}}). \tag{10}$$

Here, $\mathrm{KL}(\cdot)$ denotes the KL divergence. $\mathrm{KL}(\mathbf{c}^{\mathcal{T}} || \mathbf{c}^{\mathcal{S}})$ represents the Target Class Knowledge Distillation (TCKD) component, which measures the similarity between the teacher and student models' binary probabilities for the target class. Concurrently, $\mathrm{KL}(\hat{\mathbf{n}}^{\mathcal{T}} || \hat{\mathbf{n}}^{\mathcal{S}})$ represents the NonTarget Class Knowledge Distillation (NCKD) component, which measures the similarity between the teacher and student models' probabilities of the nontarget classes. Following the approach in [17], this study sets the values of α and β to 1 and 8, respectively.

2.3. *Multiloss Joint Gradient Control*

The primary contribution of this paper is the introduction of multiloss joint gradient control, which enables the independent regulation of multiple loss functions by updating the gradients of each loss separately and storing them in distinct momentum buffers. This approach facilitates the management of the optimization process for each individual loss component.

Prior to elucidating the specifics of updating gradient control, it is necessary to provide an introduction to Stochastic Gradient Descent (SGD). The SGD optimizer is currently a widely utilized method for training in deep learning. SGD with momentum updates the network parameters using both the current gradient and historical gradients. This is denoted as $g = \nabla_{\theta}\mathcal{L}(\theta)$, where θ represents the network parameters. Specifically, SGD maintains a "momentum buffer" to store gradients for network parameter updates. For each training batch, the momentum buffer update in SGD can be expressed as follows:

$$v \leftarrow g + \mu v, \tag{11}$$

Here, $\boldsymbol{v}$ and $\boldsymbol{\mu}$ represents the momentum buffer and the momentum coefficient. Subsequently, the model parameters $\boldsymbol{\theta}$ will be updated according to the gradient descent rule with the learning rate γ:

$$\boldsymbol{\theta} \leftarrow \boldsymbol{\theta} - \gamma \boldsymbol{v}, \tag{12}$$

Subsequently, we introduce Multiloss Joint Gradient Control Knowledge Distillation (MJKD). For each batch of input data, MJKD initially computes three distinct types of losses, then independently updates the momentum buffers, and finally updates the student network parameters.

As illustrated in Figure 1, Figure 1a depicts the classical knowledge distillation (KD) method, while Figure 1b presents an overview of the MJKD approach. The KD method employs the Stochastic Gradient Descent (SGD) update mechanism, wherein different loss terms are numerically summed directly. The gradient of the total loss is then computed and stored in a momentum buffer, followed by backpropagation to update the model parameters. In contrast to the SGD optimizer, MJKD independently computes the gradients for the task loss, logit distillation loss, and feature distillation loss. Subsequently, it utilizes a hyperparameter Δ to individually control the gradient of each loss, storing them separately in their respective momentum buffers. Finally, the parameters of the student network are updated accordingly.

To further investigate the differences between this method and the SGD optimizer, the mathematical formulation of the update process will be analyzed. These three momentum buffers are denoted as v_{task}, v_{logits}, and v_{feature}, respectively. MJKD introduces a hyperparameter Δ and employs $\mu + \Delta_1$, $\mu + \Delta_2$, and $\mu + \Delta_3$ to update the momentum buffers v_{task}, v_{logits}, and v_{feature}, respectively. The specific formulas are as follows:

$$\begin{aligned} v_{\text{task}} &\leftarrow g_{\text{task}} + (\mu + \Delta_1) v_{\text{task}}, \\ v_{\text{logits}} &\leftarrow g_{\text{logits}} + (\mu + \Delta_2) v_{\text{logits}}, \\ v_{\text{feature}} &\leftarrow g_{\text{feature}} + (\mu + \Delta_3) v_{\text{feature}}. \end{aligned} \tag{13}$$

The parameters of the student network are updated based on the sum of three momentum buffers:

$$\boldsymbol{\theta} \leftarrow \boldsymbol{\theta} - \gamma (v_{\text{task}} + v_{\text{logits}} + v_{\text{feature}}). \tag{14}$$

To further examine the differences between the two updating approaches, we begin by analyzing the momentum buffer formulation for SGD, given as follows:

$$v_{\text{sgd}} = g_{\text{task}} + g_{\text{logits}} + g_{\textbf{feature}} + \mu (v_{\text{task}} + v_{\text{logits}} + v_{\text{feature}}), \tag{15}$$

For MJKD, the updated momentum buffer is

$$\begin{aligned} v_{\text{mjkd}} &= g_{\text{task}} + g_{\text{logits}} + g_{\text{feature}} \\ &\quad + (\mu + \Delta_1) v_{\text{task}} + (\mu + \Delta_2) v_{\text{logits}} + (\mu + \Delta_3) v_{\text{feature}} \\ &= g_{\text{task}} + g_{\text{logits}} + g_{\text{feature}} \\ &\quad + \mu (v_{\text{task}} + v_{\text{logits}} + v_{\text{feature}}) + \Delta_1 v_{\text{logits}} + \Delta_2 v_{\text{task}} + \Delta_3 v_{\text{feature}}, \end{aligned} \tag{16}$$

Contrasting Equations (15) and (16), the differences between the two methods are as follows:

$$\begin{aligned} v_{\text{diff}} &= v_{\text{mjkd}} - v_{\text{sgd}} \\ &= \Delta_1 v_{\text{logits}} + \Delta_2 v_{\text{task}} + \Delta_3 v_{\text{feature}} \end{aligned} \tag{17}$$

MJKD can enhance the impact of each branch of loss on the gradient updates by adjusting Δ_1, Δ_2, and Δ_3. Furthermore, when $\Delta = 0$, the update mechanism of MJKD is equivalent to traditional SGD.

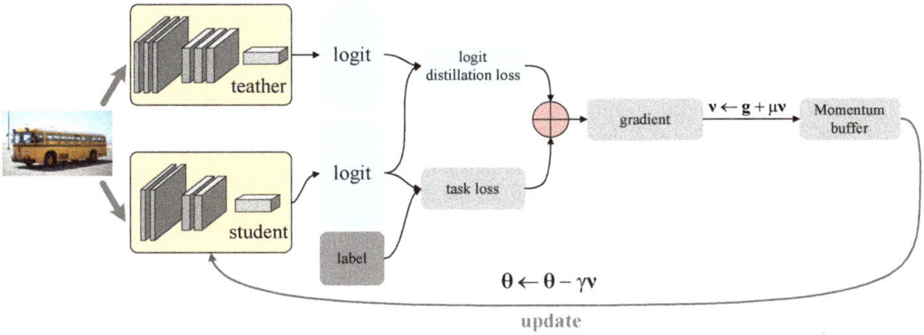

(a) Knowledge Distillation (KD).

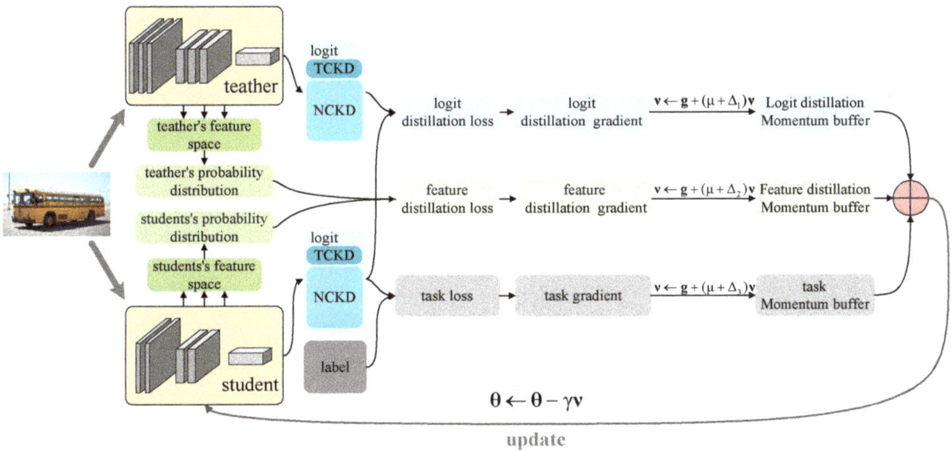

(b) Multi-Loss Joint Gradient Control Knowledge Distillation (MJKD).

Figure 1. The figure illustrates the concept of knowledge distillation [3] alongside our proposed Multiloss Joint Gradient Control Knowledge Distillation (MJKD) approach. In MJKD, the gradients associated with the task loss, logit distillation loss, and feature distillation loss are computed independently and subsequently utilized to update their respective momentum buffers.

3. Experiments and Discussion

In this part, we first detail the experimental settings of two datasets. Subsequently, we empirically validate our hypotheses and discuss the primary results on widely used image classification benchmarks. We also provide analyses, including visualizations, for further insights.

3.1. Dataset and Experimental Setup

To ensure the reliability of the experimental results, unless otherwise specified, all data are presented as the mean ($\pm$standard deviations) of five independent experiments. The values in bold within the table indicate the highest values in the context of the presented comparisons. We conduct experiments on two image classification datasets, CIFAR-100 [24] and Tiny-ImageNet [25].

We start with the CIFAR-100 dataset to evaluate our method. CIFAR-100 is a well-known image classification dataset, containing 32 × 32 images of 100 categories. Training and validate sets are composed of 50 k and 10 k images. For CIFAR-100, we train all models for 240 epochs with learning rates decayed by 0.1 at the 150th, 180th, and 210th epochs. The batch size is 64 for all models. We use SGD with 0.9 momentum and 0.0005 weight decay as the optimizer.

Tiny-ImageNet consists of 200 classes and the image size is 64 × 64. The training set contains 100 k images and the validation contains 10 k images. ImageNet-1k is a large-scale classification dataset that consists of 1 k classes. The training set contains 1.28 million images and the validation set contains 50 k images. All images are cropped to 224 × 224. For Tiny-ImageNet, all the models are trained for 200 epochs with learning rates decayed by 0.1 at the 60th, 120th, and 160th epochs. The initial learning rate is 0.05 for a 64-batch size. We use SGD with 0.9 momentum and 0.0005 weight decay as the optimizer.

3.2. *Main Results*

3.2.1. Motivation Validations

The verification of our conjectures and hypotheses constitutes a critical experiment. We initially investigated three questions: (1) Is the effectiveness of independent gradient control genuinely substantiated? (2) Among task loss, logit distillation loss, and feature distillation loss, which plays a more critical role? (3) Is it possible to improve distillation performance solely by adjusting the relative contributions of different loss functions without independent gradient control?

To address the first question, we initially investigated the impact of Δ_1, Δ_2, and Δ_3 on model performance. Δ_1, Δ_2, and Δ_3 are the momentum buffer update parameters for the task loss, logit distillation loss, and feature distillation loss, respectively. A positive Δ indicates that the corresponding loss receives a greater update weight. Utilizing ResNet32x4 as the teacher network and ResNet8x4 as the student network, we conducted distillation training on the CIFAR-100 dataset. As illustrated in Table 1, we observe that the performance of the student network is significantly influenced by the values of Δ_1, Δ_2, and Δ_3. When these parameters are set to −0.05, 0.05, and −0.05, respectively, the model achieves the optimal validation accuracy of 76.52%, indicating that the logit distillation loss, with $\Delta_2 > 0$, plays a crucial role in enhancing performance. This finding suggests that increasing the weight of the logit distillation loss allows it to contribute more substantially to the overall optimization, resulting in improved knowledge transfer between the teacher and student networks. This configuration outperforms the others. Therefore, the subsequent experiments will continue to maintain the configuration where $\Delta_2 > 0$.

Table 1. Different Δ values on CIFAR-100 validation. The teacher network is ResNet32x4 and the student network is ResNet8x4.

Δ_1 Δ_2 Δ_3	−0.05 −0.05 0.05	−0.05 0.05 −0.05	0.05 −0.05 −0.05
Top-1	75.41 ± 0.21	**76.52 ± 0.37**	75.26 ± 0.29
Δ_1 Δ_2 Δ_3	−0.05 0.05 0.05	0.05 −0.05 0.05	0.05 0.05 −0.05
Top-1	76.08 ± 0.20	74.64 ± 0.22	75.47 ± 0.33

To further examine whether the effectiveness of independent gradient control is not due to meticulous hyperparameter tuning, we investigated the impact of varying Δ values in MJKD. As shown in Table 2, setting $\Delta = 0$ (i.e., training all losses with the same momentum, equivalent to SGD) results in a top-1 accuracy of 75.78%. In contrast, introducing controlled multiloss joint gradient control significantly improves performance. For example, when Δ_1, Δ_2, and Δ_3 are set to −0.0375, 0.0375, and −0.0375, respectively, the model achieves the highest top-1 accuracy of 76.44%. Under all other parameter configurations, the model's accuracy consistently exceeded that observed in the case where

$\Delta = 0$. This demonstrates the effectiveness of independent gradient control in improving model performance without requiring meticulous hyperparameter tuning.

Table 2. Different Δ values on CIFAR-100 validation under logit distillation loss dominance. The teacher network is ResNet32x4 and the student network is ResNet8x4.

Δ_1 Δ_2 Δ_3	0.00 0.00 0.00	−0.0125 0.0125 −0.0125	−0.025 0.025 −0.025	−0.0375 0.0375 −0.0375
Top-1	75.78 ± 0.37	76.17 ± 0.31	76.15± 0.12	**76.44 ± 0.23**
Δ_1 Δ_2 Δ_3	−0.05 0.05 0.05	−0.0625 0.0625 −0.0625	−0.0750 0.0750 −0.0750	−0.0875 0.0875 −0.0875
Top-1	76.42 ± 0.26	76.33 ± 0.27	76.15 ± 0.19	75.29 ± 0.13

Based on the results above, it can be observed that amplifying the dominance of logit distillation loss in gradient updates contributes to improving the student network's performance. This raises the second question: What is the relationship between task loss, logit distillation loss, and feature distillation loss, and which plays a more critical role? To investigate this issue, we conducted a series of experiments employing ResNet32x4 as the teacher network and ResNet8x4 as the student network on the CIFAR-100 dataset. Additionally, we utilized the ResNet18-MobileNetV2 teacher–student pair for experiments on the Tiny-ImageNet dataset. For simplicity, in our subsequent experiments, we set the parameters Δ_1, Δ_2, and Δ_3 to −0.05, 0.05, and −0.05, respectively.

We plot the training loss in Figure 2, where the left Figure 2a represents results on the CIFAR-100 training set, and the right Figure 2b represents results on the Tiny-ImageNet training set. In these figures, the baseline refers to training using only the task loss (i.e., cross-entropy loss), while MJKD without gradient control refers to the case of MJKD with equal momentum (i.e., $\Delta = 0$). MJKD with $\Delta_1 = -0.05$ implies that the task loss receives a smaller update momentum, which would typically impede the task loss from converging to a lower level. However, the results suggest that reducing the supervision of the task loss while enhancing the role of the logit loss may be more advantageous for knowledge transfer. As demonstrated in Figure 2, the final performance of MJKD (depicted by blue lines) on the CIFAR-100 dataset is comparable to that of the cross-entropy baseline (represented by black lines), with a slight improvement over MJKD without gradient control (shown by green lines). Furthermore, MJKD consistently achieves a lower task loss on Tiny-ImageNet datasets compared with both baseline and MJKD without gradient control.

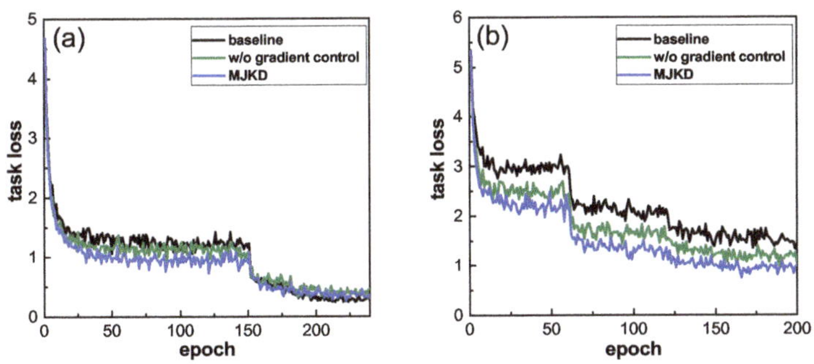

Figure 2. Task loss on CIFAR-100 (**a**) and Tiny-ImageNet (**b**).

This phenomenon can be attributed to the fact that the information carried by the labels is not readily assimilated by the student network. Utilizing independent gradient control allows the logit distillation loss from the teacher network to dominate the updates. Furthermore, the label information carried by the logit distillation loss, after being processed by the teacher network, is more readily assimilated by the student network, thus more effectively guiding it to achieve enhanced model performance.

Subsequently, we investigate the relationship between the logit distillation loss and feature distillation loss. As shown in Figure 3, "MJKD without feature loss" and "MJKD without logits loss" indicate that these losses are excluded from the backpropagation process, contributing only their computed values to the results. We adopt a warm-up strategy for the distillation loss, gradually increasing it over the first 20 epochs. Consistent with the previous analysis, the left Figure 3a and Figure 3c represent results on the CIFAR-100 training set, while the right Figure 3b and Figure 3d represent results on the Tiny-ImageNet training set. The network and parameter settings remain consistent with those previously mentioned.

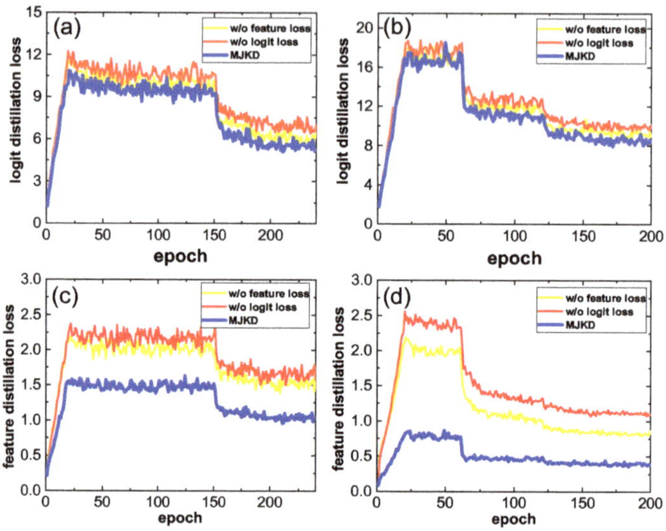

Figure 3. Distillation Loss on CIFAR-100 (**a**,**c**) and Tiny-ImageNet (**b**,**d**).

In Figure 3, it is evident that the blue MJKD curve is the lowest in both the logit distillation loss and feature distillation loss diagrams. This demonstrates that utilizing both logits and feature distillation losses concurrently is beneficial for enhanced knowledge transfer from the teacher network, leading to improved student network performance. Omitting either distillation loss results in performance degradation. However, it is noteworthy in Figure 3c and Figure 3d that the absence of logit distillation loss leads to a higher feature distillation loss compared with the absence of feature distillation loss. This indicates that the "logits" of the fully connected output contain overall feature information of the network. Nevertheless, this phenomenon may not occur with other distillation configurations, as we employed specific methods for calculating the logit loss and feature loss. Consequently, the absence of supervision from the logit distillation loss hinders the student network's ability to effectively learn feature information from the teacher network. However, the absence of feature distillation loss results in a decrease in student network performance. Although the role of feature distillation loss is relatively secondary, it remains significant. Feature-based distillation methods provide a more precise representation of intermediate network layer characteristics and have consistently demonstrated robust distillation performance. These methods have long been a central focus in knowledge distillation research. However, recent studies have revealed the substantial potential of logit-based methods, which has not been fully realized due to certain limiting factors [17,19]. The information contained in the logit distillation loss from the teacher network encompasses, to some extent, the comprehensive information present in the feature distillation loss. Consequently, logit distillation loss should assume a primary role in our distillation training.

Nevertheless, the third question arises as to whether it is possible to improve distillation performance solely by adjusting the relative contributions of different loss functions, without employing independent gradient control. To address this question, we introduced a weight parameter α to regulate the proportion of each loss, without utilizing gradient control. The logit distillation loss is multiplied by the coefficient α, while the task loss and feature distillation loss are multiplied by the coefficient $1-\alpha$. A larger α value amplifies the influence of logit distillation loss on optimization and diminishes the influence of task loss and feature distillation loss.

Tables 3 and 4 present the experimental results with varying weightings of α on the CIFAR-100 and Tiny-ImageNet datasets, respectively. As demonstrated, regardless of the value of α, the top-1 accuracy achieved with different weightings is consistently lower than that obtained with the MJKD method. For CIFAR-100, the best accuracy of 76.42% is achieved with MJKD, whereas the highest accuracy obtained with any α setting is 75.14%. Similarly, for Tiny-ImageNet, the MJKD method achieves a top-1 accuracy of 63.53%, while the highest accuracy with any α setting is 60.98%. MJKD significantly outperformed the method of only adjusting the relative contributions of different loss functions without employing independent gradient control on both datasets.

Table 3. Different weight (α) results on CIFAR-100 validation.

α	0.1	0.25	0.5	0.75	0.9	MJKD
top1	74.88 ± 0.19	75.14 ± 0.39	74.87 ± 0.20	75.01 ± 0.15	74.93 ± 0.23	$\mathbf{76.42 \pm 0.26}$

Table 4. Different weight (α) results on Tiny-ImageNet validation.

α	0.1	0.25	0.5	0.75	0.9	MJKD
top1	60.25 ± 0.31	60.98 ± 0.24	60.78 ± 0.22	60.47 ± 0.05	59.97 ± 0.16	$\mathbf{63.53 \pm 0.26}$

Figure 4 illustrates the impact of different α values on the three types of loss during training and compares them with the MJKD method. The upper three subfigures are derived from experiments using the CIFAR-100 dataset, while the lower three subfigures are based on the Tiny-ImageNet dataset. The MJKD method generally demonstrates a consistent ability to achieve the lowest loss, indicating that employing independent momentums to control different loss weights is both necessary and effective. These results indicate that adjusting α alone does not attain the performance level of MJKD, and the final student network performance is substantially inferior to that of the MJKD method, highlighting the importance of gradient control in achieving superior model performance.

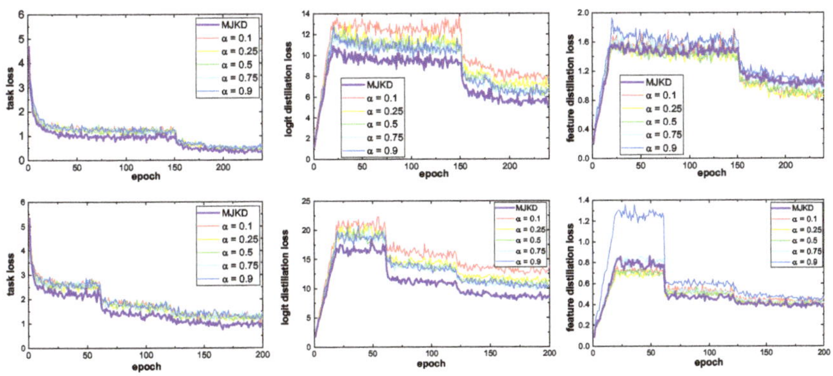

Figure 4. Illustration of loss for weighing α on CIFAR-100 and Tiny-ImageNet.

3.2.2. Comparative Results

For CIFAR-100 image classification, Table 5 presents a comparative analysis of our proposed MJKD method with other widely used knowledge distillation. The evaluation includes teacher–student pairs involving both identical and heterogeneous network architectures. It is evident that our MJKD consistently achieves superior performance, yielding the highest validation accuracy across all configurations. This demonstrates the robustness and generalizability of our method, which maintains high accuracy across various architectures. For example, when using ResNet32x4 as the teacher and ResNet8x4 as the student, our MJKD method achieves a validation accuracy of 76.42%, surpassing other advanced techniques such as AT, DKD, and PKT, which reach 73.61%, 76.06%, and 74.10%, respectively. In a similar manner, when utilizing MobileNet-V2 as the student network in conjunction with VGG13 as the teacher, the MJKD approach demonstrates a performance improvement of nearly 1% over classical DKD, underscoring its efficacy in addressing teacher–student pairs involving heterogeneous network architectures. These results validate the effectiveness and robustness of our method under diverse teacher–student framework configurations.

Table 5. Results on the CIFAR-100 validation.

Teacher	**ResNet32x4 79.42**	**VGG13 74.64**	**VGG13 74.64**	**WRN-40-2 75.61**	**ResNet50 79.34**	**ResNet32x4 79.42**	**ResNet32x4 79.42**
Student	**ResNet8x4**	**VGG8**	**MobileNet-V2**	**WRN-16-2**	**MobileNet-V2**	**ShuffleNet-V1**	**ShuffleNet-V2**
	73.06 ± 0.16	**70.94 ± 0.24**	**65.85 ± 0.22**	**73.50 ± 0.25**	**65.85 ± 0.22**	**72.40 ± 0.38**	**73.80 ± 0.22**
AT [12]	73.61 ± 0.26	71.76 ± 0.17	60.42 ± 0.47	74.30 ± 0.17	58.06 ± 1.44	73.57 ± 0.34	73.66 ± 0.24
VID [26]	72.98 ± 0.12	71.00 ± 0.30	65.72 ± 0.53	73.87 ± 0.15	65.77 ± 0.47	72.78 ± 0.23	73.84 ± 0.38
FITNET [16]	73.71 ± 0.17	71.48 ± 0.32	64.44 ± 0.99	73.61 ± 0.21	64.33 ± 0.56	74.39 ± 0.35	75.09 ± 0.15
PKT [10]	74.10 ± 0.35	73.36 ± 0.13	68.34 ± 0.18	75.12 ± 0.18	68.59 ± 0.82	75.71 ± 0.35	76.10 ± 0.20
KD [3]	73.70 ± 0.37	73.31 ± 0.22	68.02 ± 0.27	75.07 ± 0.23	68.50 ± 0.42	74.88 ± 0.24	75.35 ± 0.12
RKD [14]	72.72 ± 0.16	71.71 ± 0.39	65.97 ± 0.29	73.82 ± 0.09	65.95 ± 0.52	73.84 ± 0.23	74.87 ± 0.37
DKD [17]	76.06 ± 0.25	74.66 ± 0.17	67.11 ± 0.51	75.40 ± 0.19	68.23 ± 0.43	74.34 ± 0.21	76.97 ± 0.46
MJKD	**76.42 ± 0.26**	**74.75 ± 0.23**	**68.76 ± 0.69**	**75.52 ± 0.23**	**69.78 ± 0.55**	**76.38 ± 0.09**	**77.25 ± 0.43**

For Tiny-ImageNet classification, Table 6 presents results in terms of both top-1 and top-5 accuracy. Here, we conducted experiments comparing MJKD to other distillation methods, with ResNet18 as the teacher network and either MobileNet-V2 or ShuffleNetV2 as the student networks. The results clearly demonstrate that MJKD achieves superior performance across all metrics. When MobileNet-V2 is the student, MJKD improves the top-1 accuracy by approximately 2% over DKD, achieving 63.53% compared with DKD's 61.17%. Similarly, for ShuffleNetV2 as the student, MJKD attains a significant accuracy boost, with top-1 accuracy reaching 57.68%, outperforming DKD's 56.09%. Furthermore, MJKD also excels in top-5 accuracy, achieving 84.64% for MobileNet-V2 and 80.80% for ShuffleNetV2, confirming the effectiveness of the proposed method.

Table 6. Results on the Tiny-ImageNet validation.

	Teacher	**Student**	**AT** [12]	**KD** [3]	**PKT** [10]	**DKD** [17]	**MJKD**
			ResNet18 as the teacher, MobileNet-V2 as the student				
Top-1	63.74	55.51 ± 0.48	57.20 ± 0.44	57.26 ± 0.25	57.43 ± 0.16	61.17 ± 0.22	**63.53 ± 0.26**
Top-5	83.55	79.76 ± 0.21	80.91 ± 0.24	80.80 ± 0.37	81.37 ± 0.22	83.55 ± 0.19	**84.64 ± 0.18**
			ResNet18 as the teacher, ShuffleNetV2 as the student				
Top-1	63.74	51.65 ± 0.36	53.56 ± 0.11	52.32 ± 0.42	52.50 ± 0.45	56.09 ± 0.18	**57.68 ± 0.23**
Top-5	83.55	76.67 ± 0.30	78.16 ± 0.21	77.31 ± 0.23	77.40 ± 0.37	79.96 ± 0.13	**80.80 ± 0.27**

3.2.3. Visualization Analysis

To further illustrate the superiority of the proposed knowledge distillation method, we visualized the model's loss landscapes and the differences in correlation matrices between the student and teacher logits. Three knowledge distillation methods were employed for comparative analysis: KD, which represents the classical knowledge distillation approach; DKD, indicating the current state-of-the-art framework of knowledge distillation; and MJKD, which is the knowledge distillation method proposed by us. We used the ResNet18-MobileNetV2 teacher–student pair on the Tiny-ImageNet dataset. As shown in Table 6, the experimental top-1 accuracies for the KD, DKD, and MJKD methods are 57.43%, 61.17%, and 63.53%, respectively.

Leveraging three distinct types of loss can flatten the loss convergence minima of a student network. A well-established hypothesis posits that the flatness of the loss convergence minima is related to the generalization capability of the neural networks [27]. Networks with flatter minima exhibit enhanced robustness and generalization ability [28–30]. Due to the inherent bias between the training and testing datasets, the model's optimal parameters for peak performance may exhibit slight variations. In instances where the minima are sharp, even minor differences in the model's parameters can result in significant fluctuations in accuracy. Conversely, flatter minima offer greater flexibility, as small changes in parameters do not substantially impact performance. Consequently, flatter minima demonstrate increased resilience to stochastic perturbations in the loss landscape, which mitigates the sensitivity to these parameter shifts and effectively reduces the generalization error.

Utilizing the work of Li et al. [31] to visualize the loss landscape can facilitate the observation of loss convergence in models after knowledge distillation, thus providing enhanced insights into their operational mechanisms. To further investigate the impact of our MJKD method on model generalization, we visualized the loss landscapes of the converged student networks after training. As shown in Figure 5, the left Figure 5a employ the KD method, and Figure 5b utilize the DKD method, while Figure 5c depicts the corresponding landscapes when the student networks are trained using our proposed MJKD method. The primary area of interest in the figure is the size of the purple region at the center of the loss landscapes, which indicates the flatness of the loss minima. The comparative analysis of these loss landscapes reveals that the loss functions of student networks trained with MJKD exhibit significantly flatter minima compared with those obtained with KD and DKD. This enhanced flatness of minima suggests that our method encourages the convergence of the task loss to smoother and broader regions in the parameter space. This enhanced flatness of minima suggests that our method encourages the convergence of the task loss to smoother and broader regions in the parameter space, which explains the generalization performance observed in the student networks.

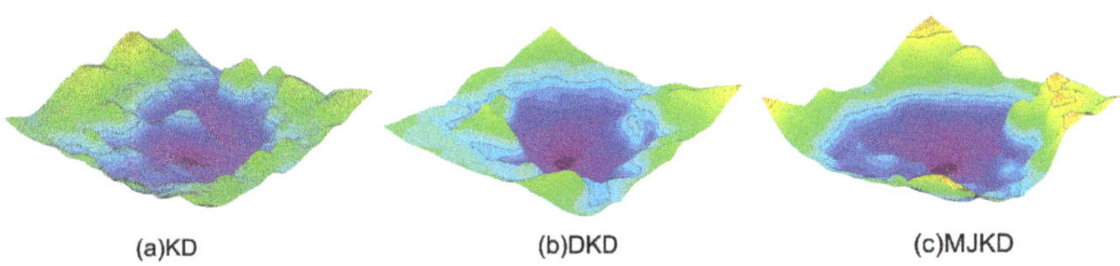

Figure 5. Loss landscapes of (**a**) KD, (**b**) DKD, and (**c**) MJKD on the Tiny-ImageNet dataset.

In addition, we visualized the differences in correlation matrices between the logits generated by the student networks and those produced by the teacher networks. This analysis provides a more comprehensive understanding of how effectively the student networks learn to replicate the behavior of the teacher networks. In Figure 6, the subfigures represent the differences in correlation matrices when utilizing KD(a), DKD(b), and MJKD(c) on Tiny-ImageNet datasets. The comparison elucidates that, in contrast to KD, the MJKD method enables the student networks to produce logits that are more closely aligned with those of the teacher. Although the disparity is less pronounced compared with the advanced DKD method, the student networks trained with MJKD still produce logits that align more closely with those of the teacher, demonstrating a subtle improvement. This greater similarity in the logits indicates that MJKD significantly enhances the distillation process by enabling the student to more effectively emulate the output distributions of the teacher network. This improved alignment between the student and teacher logits contributes to the enhanced performance of MJKD.

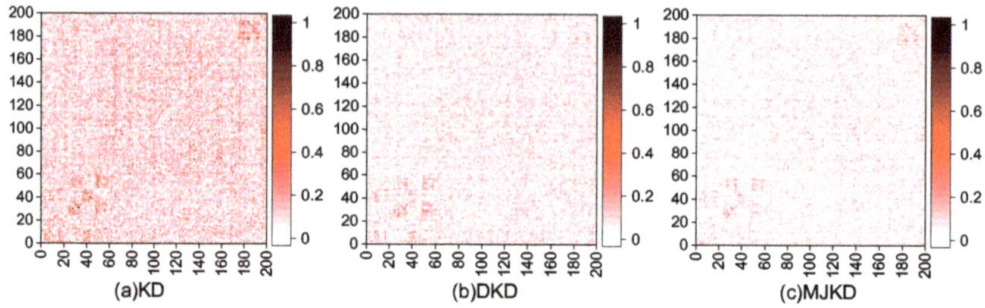

Figure 6. Difference in the correlation matrices of student and teacher logits on the Tiny-ImageNet dataset.

4. Conclusions

In this study, we propose a novel knowledge distillation method called Multiloss Joint Gradient Control Knowledge Distillation (MJKD) to enhance the performance of student networks by effectively combining feature-based and logit-based knowledge distillation with gradient control. Our approach introduces independent gradient control for task loss, feature distillation loss, and logit distillation loss, which facilitates a more efficient and effective knowledge transfer from teacher to student networks.

The introduction of independent gradient control for the three loss components is a critical innovation of our method. A detailed theoretical analysis of the proposed method was conducted, followed by several experiments to evaluate the knowledge distillation approach. The experimental results suggest that logits may encapsulate substantial information about the model's overall architecture. Our empirical evaluation of the proposed method on the CIFAR-100 and Tiny-ImageNet datasets demonstrated significant improvements over the classical knowledge distillation methods. By independently controlling the gradients of task loss, feature distillation loss, and logit distillation loss, the MJKD method consistently achieves higher validation accuracies across various teacher–student network pairs, regardless of whether the architectures are identical or diverse. For instance, MJKD achieves a validation accuracy of 76.42% with the ResNet32x4–ResNet8x4 pair. On Tiny-ImageNet, MJKD reaches 63.53% for the ResNet18–MobileNet-V2 pair. Our experiments validated the robustness and effectiveness of the MJKD method, confirming its potential for broader application in various image classification tasks. Furthermore, we present visualizations and analyses to explore the potential working mechanisms of our method by examining the model's loss landscapes and the differences in correlation matrices between the student's and teacher's logits.

The practical implications of our research are significant for the development of efficient and high-performance neural networks for real-world applications. The MJKD method enables the deployment of lightweight student networks that maintain high accuracy, making it suitable for resource-constrained environments such as mobile devices and edge computing.

Author Contributions: Conceptualization, W.H. and X.Z.; methodology, W.H. and X.Z.; software, J.P.; validation, J.P., J.Z. and X.H.; formal analysis, J.Z.; investigation, J.P. and X.H.; resources, X.Z.; data curation, J.P.; writing—original draft preparation, J.P.; writing—review and editing, W.H. and Y.L.; visualization, J.Z. and X.H.; supervision, X.Z. and Y.L.; project administration, J.L.; funding acquisition, Y.L. All authors have read and agreed to the published version of the manuscript.

Funding: This work was funded by the Class A key project of China Railway Design Corporation, grant number 2023A0203602.

Data Availability Statement: The data presented in this study are available on request from the corresponding author.

Conflicts of Interest: Author Jianyu Zhang was employed by the company China Railway Design Corporation. The remaining authors declare that the research was conducted in the absence of any commercial or financial relationships that could be construed as a potential conflict of interest.

References

1. He, K.; Zhang, X.; Ren, S.; Sun, J. Deep residual learning for image recognition. In Proceedings of the IEEE Conference on Computer Vision and Pattern Recognition, Las Vegas, NV, USA, 27–30 June 2016; pp. 770–778.
2. Krizhevsky, A.; Sutskever, I.; Hinton, G.E. ImageNet classification with deep convolutional neural networks. *Commun. ACM* **2017**, *60*, 84–90. [CrossRef]
3. Hinton, G.; Vinyals, O.; Dean, J. Distilling the knowledge in a neural network. *arXiv* **2015**, arXiv:1503.02531.
4. Anwar, S.; Hwang, K.; Sung, W. Structured pruning of deep convolutional neural networks. *ACM J. Emerg. Technol. Comput. Syst.* **2017**, *13*, 1–18. [CrossRef]
5. Liu, Z.; Sun, M.; Zhou, T.; Huang, G.; Darrell, T. Rethinking the value of network pruning. *arXiv* **2018**, arXiv:1810.05270.
6. Han, S.; Pool, J.; Tran, J.; Dally, W. Learning both weights and connections for efficient neural network. *Adv. Neural Inf. Process. Syst.* **2015**, *28*, 1135–1143.
7. Courbariaux, M.; Bengio, Y.; David, J.P. Binaryconnect: Training deep neural networks with binary weights during propagations. *Adv. Neural Inf. Process. Syst.* **2015**, *28*, 3123–3131.
8. Jacob, B.; Kligys, S.; Chen, B.; Zhu, M.; Tang, M.; Howard, A.; Adam, H.; Kalenichenko, D. Quantization and training of neural networks for efficient integer-arithmetic-only inference. In Proceedings of the IEEE Conference on Computer Vision and Pattern Recognition, Salt Lake City, UT, USA, 18–23 June 2018; pp. 2704–2713.
9. Rastegari, M.; Ordonez, V.; Redmon, J.; Farhadi, A. Xnor-net: Imagenet classification using binary convolutional neural networks. In Proceedings of the European Conference on Computer Vision, Amsterdam, The Netherlands, 11–14 October 2016; Springer: Berlin/Heidelberg, Germany, 2016; pp. 525–542.
10. Passalis, N.; Tzelepi, M.; Tefas, A. Probabilistic Knowledge Transfer for Lightweight Deep Representation Learning. *IEEE Trans. Neural Netw. Learn. Syst.* **2021**, *32*, 2030–2039. [CrossRef]
11. Tian, Y.; Krishnan, D.; Isola, P. Contrastive Representation Distillation. In Proceedings of the International Conference on Learning Representations, Addis Ababa, Ethiopia, 26–30 April 2020.
12. Zagoruyko, S.; Komodakis, N. Paying more attention to attention: Improving the performance of convolutional neural networks via attention transfer. *arXiv* **2016**, arXiv:1612.03928.
13. Peng, B.; Jin, X.; Liu, J.; Li, D.; Wu, Y.; Liu, Y.; Zhou, S.; Zhang, Z. Correlation congruence for knowledge distillation. In Proceedings of the IEEE/CVF International Conference on Computer Vision, Seoul, Republic of Korea, 27–28 October 2019; pp. 5007–5016.
14. Park, W.; Kim, D.; Lu, Y.; Cho, M. Relational knowledge distillation. In Proceedings of the IEEE Conference on Computer Vision and Pattern Recognition, Long Beach, CA, USA, 15–20 June 2019; pp. 3967–3976.
15. Heo, B.; Kim, J.; Yun, S.; Park, H.; Kwak, N.; Choi, J.Y. A comprehensive overhaul of feature distillation. In Proceedings of the IEEE/CVF International Conference on Computer Vision, Seoul, Republic of Korea, 27–28 October 2019; pp. 1921–1930.
16. Adriana, R.; Nicolas, B.; Samira, E.; Antoine, C.; Carlo, G.; Yoshua, B. Fitnets: Hints for Thin Deep Nets. In Proceedings of the International Conference on Learning Representations, San Diego, CA, USA, 7–9 May 2015.
17. Zhao, B.; Cui, Q.; Song, R.; Qiu, Y.; Liang, J. Decoupled knowledge distillation. In Proceedings of the IEEE/CVF Conference on Computer Vision and Pattern Recognition, New Orleans, LA, USA, 18–24 June 2022; pp. 11953–11962.
18. Hao, Z.; Guo, J.; Han, K.; Hu, H.; Xu, C.; Wang, Y. VanillaKD: Revisit the Power of Vanilla Knowledge Distillation from Small Scale to Large Scale. *arXiv* **2023**, arXiv:2305.15781.
19. Zheng, Z.; Ye, R.; Hou, Q.; Ren, D.; Wang, P.; Zuo, W.; Cheng, M.M. Localization distillation for object detection. *IEEE Trans. Pattern Anal. Mach. Intell.* **2023**, *45*, 10070–10083. [CrossRef]
20. Zhao, B.; Cui, Q.; Song, R.; Liang, J. DOT: A Distillation-Oriented Trainer. In Proceedings of the IEEE/CVF International Conference on Computer Vision, Vancouver, BC, Canada, 18–22 June 2023; pp. 6189–6198.
21. Scott, D.W. *Multivariate Density Estimation: Theory, Practice, and Visualization*; John Wiley & Sons: Hoboken, NJ, USA, 2015.
22. Van der Maaten, L.; Hinton, G. Visualizing data using t-SNE. *J. Mach. Learn. Res.* **2008**, *9*, 2579–2605.

23. Wang, D.; Lu, H.; Bo, C. Visual tracking via weighted local cosine similarity. *IEEE Trans. Cybern.* **2014**, *45*, 1838–1850. [CrossRef]
24. Krizhevsky, A.; Hinton, G. *Learning Multiple Layers of Features from Tiny Images;* University of Toronto: Toronto, ON, Canada, 2009.
25. Le, Y.; Yang, X. Tiny imagenet visual recognition challenge. *CS 231N* **2015**, *7*, 3.
26. Ahn, S.; Hu, S.X.; Damianou, A.; Lawrence, N.D.; Dai, Z. Variational information distillation for knowledge transfer. In Proceedings of the IEEE/CVF Conference on Computer Vision and Pattern Recognition, Long Beach, CA, USA, 16–20 June 2019; pp. 9163–9171.
27. Keskar, N.S.; Mudigere, D.; Nocedal, J.; Smelyanskiy, M.; Tang, P.T.P. On large-batch training for deep learning: Generalization gap and sharp minima. *arXiv* **2016**, arXiv:1609.04836.
28. Dinh, L.; Pascanu, R.; Bengio, S.; Bengio, Y. Sharp minima can generalize for deep nets. In Proceedings of the International Conference on Machine Learning, PMLR, Sydney, Australia, 6–11 August 2017; pp. 1019–1028.
29. Izmailov, P.; Podoprikhin, D.; Garipov, T.; Vetrov, D.; Wilson, A.G. Averaging weights leads to wider optima and better generalization. *arXiv* **2018**, arXiv:1803.05407.
30. Cho, J.H.; Hariharan, B. On the efficacy of knowledge distillation. In Proceedings of the IEEE/CVF International Conference on Computer Vision, Seoul, Republic of Korea, 27–28 October 2019; pp. 4794–4802.
31. Li, H.; Xu, Z.; Taylor, G.; Studer, C.; Goldstein, T. Visualizing the loss landscape of neural nets. *Adv. Neural Inf. Process. Syst.* **2018**, *31*, 6391–6401. [CrossRef]

electronics

Article

Multitasking Feature Selection Using a Clonal Selection Algorithm for High-Dimensional Microarray Data

Yi Wang [1], Dan Luo [2,*] and Jian Yao [1]

[1] School of Information Engineering, Hubei University of Economics, Wuhan 430205, China; yiwang@hbue.edu.cn (Y.W.); yaojian@hbue.edu.cn (J.Y.)
[2] Business School, Putian University, Putian 351100, China
* Correspondence: annlo@ptu.edu.cn

Abstract: Effective gene feature selection is critical for enhancing the interpretability and accuracy of genetic data analysis, particularly in the realm of disease prediction and precision medicine. Most evolutionary feature selection algorithms tend to become stuck in local optima and incur high computational costs, particularly when dealing with the complex and high-dimensional nature of genetic data. To address these issues, this study proposes a multitasking feature selection method based on clone selection for high-dimensional microarray data, which identifies optimal features by transferring useful knowledge across two related tasks derived from the same microarray dataset. First, a dual-task generation strategy is designed, where one task selects features based on the Relief-F method, and the other task is generated from the original features. Second, a new mutation operator is introduced to share useful information between the multiple tasks. Finally, an improved clonal selection algorithm is proposed to strengthen the global and local search abilities. The experimental results on six high-dimensional microarray datasets demonstrate that our method significantly outperforms four state-of-the-art feature selection methods, highlighting its effectiveness and efficiency in tackling complex feature selection problems.

Keywords: gene feature selection; evolutionary multitasking; clonal selection algorithm; immune algorithm; evolutionary algorithm

1. Introduction

In the fields of medicine and biology, gene feature selection (FS) plays a crucial role in disease diagnosis [1], enhances the accuracy of genetic association studies [2], and advances personalized medicine [3]. This process involves identifying the most relevant genetic features from the original microarray datasets, which helps mitigate the challenges associated with the 'curse of dimensionality', thereby typically enhancing classification accuracy and decreasing computational expenses [4].

Feature selection methods are commonly classified into four categories: filter, wrapper, embedded, and hybrid [5]. Filter methods [6] evaluate features based on their inherent characteristics, employing statistical metrics to determine their relevance to the target variable. Wrapper methods [7] select feature subsets by directly evaluating the performance of a particular learning algorithm. Embedded methods [8] integrate feature selection into the model training process itself. They automatically select relevant features while building the model. In general, filter methods are independent of any specific algorithm and offer high computational efficiency, while wrapper methods achieve better accuracy by considering feature interactions; however, they are computationally expensive. In contrast, embedded methods balance efficiency and accuracy by considering feature interactions during training, although they can be complex to implement and are dependent on the chosen model. Hybrid methods [9] combine the strengths of different feature selection techniques, enhancing both accuracy and efficiency.

Clonal selection algorithms (CSAs) [10], based on the natural immune response of the human body to foreign antigens, have been widely used in the field of feature selection [11]. These algorithms have several advantages for feature selection, such as the ability to find optima due to the diversity introduced by the cloning and mutation processes. Moreover, they are easy to implement for feature selection. For example, a two-stage hybrid FS method was proposed in [12], in which Fisher scoring is used to reduce the dimensionality of the search space in the first stage, and then an improved CSA method is employed to select a feature subset. Chai et al. [13] proposed a decomposition multi-objective CSA method for FS, which initializes the population based on symmetric uncertainty and uses a population update strategy to improve the evolutionary process. However, most CSAs are limited by premature convergence and significant computational costs, particularly in the context of high-dimensional data.

Evolutionary multitasking (EMT) [14,15] is an innovative approach for tackling optimization problems, allowing for the simultaneous resolution of multiple related tasks by sharing information across different tasks. Consequently, these approaches provide benefits such as robust search capabilities and rapid convergence rates. Chen et al. [16] proposed a novel high-dimensional feature selection method based on particle swarm optimization, in which evolutionary multitasking is used to enhance feature selection performance and decrease computational costs. It generates two tasks from the same dataset: one task involves selecting features from the whole dataset, while the other focuses on choosing promising features based on Relief-F. Li et al. [17] introduced three filtering methods to improve a multitask generation strategy and employed a competitive swarm optimizer to tackle the four associated tasks by facilitating the transfer of useful knowledge. Lin et al. [18] integrated an innovative searching technique and a transformation method into the evolutionary multitasking framework, significantly boosting the efficacy of the multi-objective feature selection algorithm.

Based on the aforementioned analysis, we propose a multitasking feature selection method based on clone selection for high-dimensional microarray data, called CSA-EMT, which aims to improve the quality of feature subsets and reduce computational costs by introducing evolutionary multitasking. To the best of our knowledge, little attention has been given to combining a clonal selection algorithm with multitasking to improve the performance of high-dimensional feature selection algorithms. The key contributions of this study are summarized as follows:

(1) An effective multitasking feature selection method is proposed, which improves the performance of FS by transferring useful knowledge across two related tasks;
(2) A dual-task generation strategy is adopted, in which one task is constructed using the Relief-F method, while the other is derived from the original features;
(3) A clonal selection algorithm is improved to enhance search capabilities and accelerate the rate of evolution by introducing a new mutation operator that shares useful information between multiple tasks.

The structure of the rest of this paper is as follows. Section 2 reviews the related works on evolutionary multitasking, clonal selection algorithms, and feature selection. Section 3 introduces the proposed CSA-EMT method in detail. Section 4 presents the experimental setup and results. Finally, Section 5 concludes this paper with a discussion of the findings and future directions.

2. Related Works

2.1. Evolutionary Multitasking

Evolutionary multitasking is an emerging research field in optimization that aims to solve multiple optimization tasks simultaneously. Instead of focusing on a single problem, EMT leverages the synergies between different tasks, enabling knowledge transfer across tasks during the evolutionary process. EMT methods are usually classified into two categories: multifactorial-based methods and multi-population methods [19]. Multifactorial-based methods are a type of evolutionary multitasking that use a single population to solve multiple optimization tasks simultaneously. In these methods, each individual in the population is evaluated on multiple tasks, and the knowledge transfer between tasks happens implicitly as the population evolves. Gupta et al. [20] proposed a famous multifactorial evolutionary algorithm (MFEA) that optimizes multiple tasks simultaneously by evolving a single population within a shared search space. The method begins by initializing a population where each individual is associated with a task based on its skill factor. Crossover operations are then performed between individuals with high skill factors from different tasks, enabling cross-domain knowledge transfer. Since then, a large number of variant algorithms have been proposed. For example, Bali et al. [21] proposed an enhanced MFEA, in which an online transfer parameter estimation mechanism is used to allow effective multitasking across multiple tasks, even with varying intertask relationships. Xing et al. [22] developed an adaptive multifactorial evolutionary algorithm for constrained optimization problems, which incorporates an archiving strategy, an adaptive mutation probability, and a mutation strategy. Additionally, empirical research has explored multifactorial differential evolution [23] and multifactorial particle swarm optimization [24].

Multi-population EMT methods are another class of multitasking algorithms, where each task is assigned to a separate population, which evolves independently. The populations are designed to solve specific tasks, but controlled interactions between populations allow for knowledge transfer (such as migration or crossover), enabling the sharing of useful information between tasks. For example, Feng et al. [25] employed explicit genetic transfer using autoencoders to transfer useful information between different tasks, helping improve overall performance across tasks. Lin et al. [26] used an effective positive transfer strategy to improve the convergence of the target task, wherein solutions are transferred from the neighbors of those that achieved successful knowledge transfer. Zhang et al. [27] introduced adaptive dual knowledge transfer into differential evolution, which integrates unified search space-based transfer with domain adaptation-based transfer to enhance the performance of EMT. Li et al. [28] employed dual information transfer alongside a mating strategy to minimize the negative effects of migration. Compared with multifactorial-based methods, multi-population methods allow for task-specific evolution, enabling each population to focus on solving its own task without interference from others. They also carefully control the interactions between populations, allowing for more flexible and targeted knowledge sharing between tasks. Therefore, our algorithm adopts a multi-population EMT pattern.

2.2. Clonal Selection Algorithm

The clonal selection algorithm is an important technique derived from the immune system's adaptive mechanisms, particularly focusing on the clonal selection theory [29]. In this theory, immune cells recognize antigens and undergo proliferation and mutation to better adapt to detected foreign entities. This biological process is emulated in computational applications by cloning candidate solutions, introducing controlled variations, and then selecting the best-adapted clones. Through iterative selection, clonal expansion, and mutation, the algorithm can search the solution space effectively, avoiding local optima while enhancing global search capabilities.

Initially introduced by de Castro [30], the CSA has been widely used in various optimization tasks due to its ability to maintain diversity while ensuring convergence. In recent years, a large number of variant algorithms have been proposed. Yan et al. [31] used a non-uniform mutation along with an arithmetic crossover to improve the performance of the CSA. In [32], a CSA was combined with a negative selection algorithm to accelerate searches, and network suppression was employed to reduce premature convergence. Wang et al. [33] employed multiple mutation strategies based on differential evolution and an adaptive parameter mechanism derived from [34] to mitigate the semi-blindness caused by hypermutations. To enhance population diversity, Li et al. [35] adopted vertical distances instead of crowding distances to determine the number of clones for each antibody. The effectiveness of CSAs in the field of optimization has been proven, especially when applied to high-dimensional datasets. Therefore, this study utilizes a CSA for feature selection, aiming to identify the most relevant features while maintaining diversity within the population and improving overall search efficiency.

2.3. Feature Selection for Microarray Data

Feature selection is a critical step in the analysis of microarray data, which typically involves a high-dimensional dataset with a large number of gene expressions and a relatively small sample size. The primary goal of feature selection in microarray data is to identify the most relevant genes that contribute significantly to classification or prediction tasks, thereby improving model performance and interpretability while reducing computational costs.

Various methods have been proposed to address the challenge of feature selection in microarray data. These methods can be broadly classified into four categories: filter, wrapper, embedded, and hybrid methods. Filter methods are typically based on statistical techniques that evaluate the relevance of features independently of the learning algorithm. Ouaderhman et al. [36] proposed the Psitop filter FS method for mixed-type DNA microarray data, which ranks features based on Psitop scores derived from two nonparametric association coefficients: Psicor and partial Psicor. Lee et al. [37] proposed a Markov blanket-based multivariate feature ranking method, which considers both feature relevance and redundancy to improve gene selection and microarray data classification accuracy. A least-loss feature selection method was proposed in [38], which reduces data dimensionality by removing weakly correlated variables while maintaining classifier performance through probability-based similarity scoring. Filter methods are computationally efficient and easy to implement, but they evaluate features independently, often ignoring feature interactions, which can result in suboptimal subsets for complex tasks.

Wrapper methods incorporate a learning algorithm to evaluate subsets of features by directly optimizing the performance of a classifier. Techniques such as particle swarm optimization [39], CSAs [40], and gray wolf optimization [41] have been extensively used for wrapper-based feature selection in microarray data. They provide high accuracy by evaluating feature subsets using a learning algorithm but are computationally expensive, especially with high-dimensional data.

Embedded methods perform feature selection during the learning process of a model, and examples include decision trees and regularization techniques. For example, in [42], four embedded FS methods were compared, and the most effective one was selected for the diagnosis of Alzheimer's disease. Fu et al. [8] proposed an embedded FS method for GMM, which accounts for feature interdependencies and offers feature relevance ranking as a byproduct. These FS methods strike a balance between computational efficiency and effectiveness, as they take into account interactions between features while being integrated with the learning algorithm.

Hybrid methods integrate multiple types of feature selection algorithms, combining the strengths of both filter and wrapper approaches to enhance overall performance. These methods usually first use filter techniques to quickly reduce the number of irrelevant features or improve solution quality. Then, a wrapper method is applied to the reduced feature subset to further refine and select the optimal set by evaluating the performance of a learning algorithm on the selected features. For example, Vommi et al. [43] proposed a filter-wrapper FS method for COVID-19 case classification, which uses Relief-F and fuzzy entropy to remove unimportant features, followed by an improved equilibrium optimizer to further refine the feature subset. Ke et al. [44] proposed a two-stage FS method, which improves the quality of the initial population in the genetic algorithm or ant colony optimization by utilizing the feature ranking information from the first stage.

In summary, compared to related FS approaches, the proposed method offers several key contributions. While most multitasking feature selection methods rely on particle swarm optimization, genetic algorithms, or competitive swarm optimizers, integrating a clonal selection algorithm with multitasking remains relatively unexplored. This integration presents a promising alternative for optimizing high-dimensional feature selection, thanks to its robust search capabilities and ease of implementation. Additionally, we introduce an enhanced clonal selection algorithm that enables efficient knowledge transfer across tasks, population initialization based on feature weights, and an adaptive parameter control mechanism, all of which support robust global and local search performance.

3. The Proposed CSA-EMT Method

This section introduces the CSA-EMT method, covering its general framework, dual-task generation strategy, an improved clonal selection algorithm for enhanced performance, and a runtime complexity analysis, offering a comprehensive feature selection approach for high-dimensional data.

3.1. The General Framework of CSA-EMT

The proposed method integrates an immune algorithm with evolutionary multitasking to optimize gene feature selection. The flowchart of CSA-EMT is shown in Figure 1. It primarily encompasses two critical steps: a dual-task generation strategy and an improved clonal selection algorithm tailored for gene selection. The dual-task generation strategy is initially employed to create two related tasks, as explained in detail in Section 3.2. This approach allows the algorithm to effectively explore diverse search spaces. Next, an improved clonal selection algorithm is applied to optimize feature selection by facilitating knowledge transfer between the two tasks, thereby enhancing the search process and preventing the algorithm from becoming trapped in local optima, as discussed in Section 3.3. In the final step, the best-performing antibodies from both tasks are selected and output as the final solution, ensuring robust and efficient feature selection. The pseudocode for the CSA-EMT framework is shown in Algorithm 1.

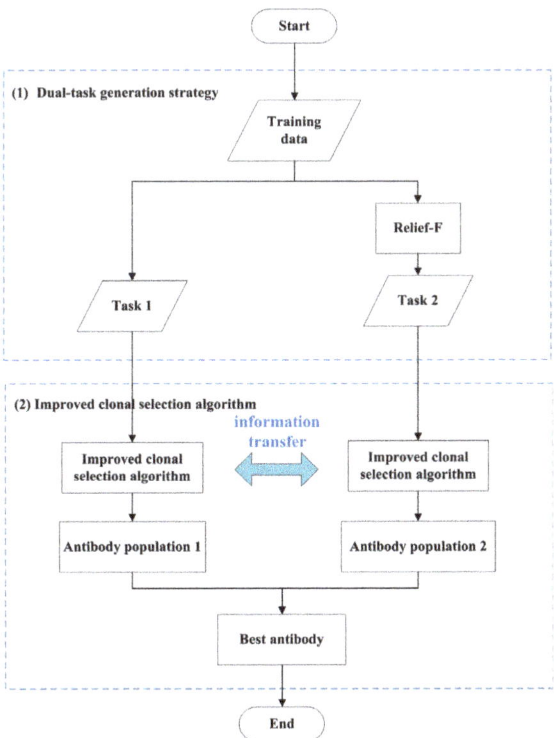

Figure 1. The general framework of CSA-EMT.

Algorithm 1 Framework of CSA-EMT

Input: training data *Data*,
maximum number of iterations G_{max}.
Output: best antibody ab_b.

```
G = 1;
task1,task2 = GenerateTasks(Data);
InitializePopulation(task1);
InitializePopulation(task2);
while G <= G_max do
    ExecICSA(task1);
    ExecICSA(task1);
    G = G + 1;
end while
ab_b = GetBestAntibody(task1,task2);
return ab_b
```

3.2. Dual-Task Generation Strategy

In this study, Task 1 retains all features from the original dataset. Task 2 contains important features identified by the Relief-F and knee point methods. In Task 2, features are ranked according to their weight values, which are computed using the Relief-F algorithm. Then, the knee point method, based on these weights, is used to automatically determine the important features. Features are included in Task 2 if their weight values exceed the threshold defined by the knee point method.

3.3. An Improved Clonal Selection Algorithm

The CSA-EMT method uses a modified clonal selection algorithm to simultaneously address two relevant tasks. The flowchart is shown in Figure 2. It primarily includes population initialization, affinity evaluation, selection, cloning, mutation, and memory cell formation. Specifically, the process begins by generating an initial population of antibodies for Task 1, selected randomly, and for Task 2, based on feature weights. This initialization provides a diverse starting set for optimization. In each iteration, antibodies are evaluated for their affinities, and those with higher affinity values are selected for cloning. Following cloning, each clone undergoes a mutation process. This step introduces diversity by making small alterations and facilitates knowledge transfer between the two tasks, enabling the algorithm to explore a broader range of potential solutions and avoid local optima. Finally, the best clones are selected to form the updated population, replacing the weakest antibodies from the previous generation. This iterative process ensures that the population's overall quality improves with each generation and continues until a termination condition is met. Here, we focus on introducing the improvement steps (population initialization, an affinity function, and a mutation strategy), which are described as follows:

(1) Population initialization

Real numbers are used to characterize the feature masks of antibodies, which allow for smoother mutation operations in continuous space. When the value is greater than 0.5, the corresponding feature is selected; otherwise, it is not selected. For Task 1, each component of the antibody is randomly generated from a uniform distribution in the [0, 1] range. For Task 2, each component corresponds to a normalized weight value determined by the Relief-F method.

(2) Affinity function

CSA-EMT uses Equation (1) as the affinity function, which aims to minimize the error rate and the number of selected features:

$$Affinity = \gamma \times Err_b + (1-\gamma) \times \frac{|F|}{|D|} \tag{1}$$

$$Err_b = 1 - \left(\frac{1}{C} \sum_{i=1}^{C} Acc_i \right) \tag{2}$$

where Err_b represents the balanced error rate, which offers particular benefits in handling imbalanced datasets. It calculates the average error rate for each class and ensures that all classes contribute equally to the final error rate, regardless of their frequency in the dataset. C is the number of classes, and Acc_i is the accuracy for class i. The right-hand side of the equation represents the ratio of the number of selected features ($|F|$) to the total number of features ($|D|$). The value of γ is set to 0.999999.

(3) Mutation strategy

Knowledge is transferred between Task 1 and Task 2 through the mutation strategy applied to each antibody, which can improve the quality of antibodies and lead to faster convergence. During the mutation process, a transfer probability, P_t, is predefined to determine whether to perform information exchange between the two tasks. Then, a random number is generated between 0 and 1. If its value is greater than P_t, the knowledge transfer will occur using Equation (3); otherwise, antibodies will undergo mutation without knowledge transfer, using Equation (4).

$$v_i = x_i + F_i \cdot (x_{gbest} - x_i) + F_i \cdot (x_{r1} - \tilde{x}_{r2}) \tag{3}$$

$$v_i = x_i + F_i \cdot (x_{cbest} - x_i) + F_i \cdot (x_{r1} - \tilde{x}_{r2}) \tag{4}$$

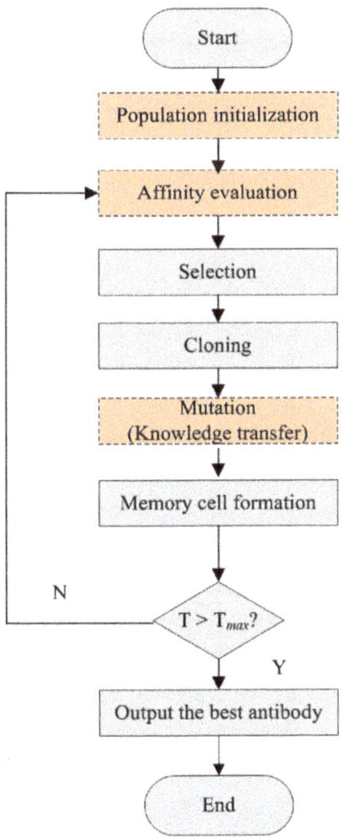

Figure 2. The flowchart of the improved clonal selection algorithm.

These mutation operators are DE-based mutation strategies, which use superior and inferior antibodies to guide the search directions. Two integers, $r1$ and $r2$, are randomly selected from the range of 1 to the population size. They are distinct from each other and neither equals i. The antibodies x_{cbest} and x_{gbest} are randomly selected from the best-performing antibodies of the current task and from all tasks, respectively. The antibody

$\tilde{x}_{r2}$ is randomly selected from a set that combines an external archive of inferior solutions with the current population. F_i is a scaling factor for the ith antibody within the range [0, 1]. After mutation, the mutant antibodies will undergo crossover:

$$u_i^j = \begin{cases} v_i^j & if\ rand \leq CR_i\ or\ j == j_{rand} \\ u_i^j & otherwise \end{cases} \tag{5}$$

where j denotes the jth feature of the ith antibody. The parameter CR_i refers to the crossover probability of the ith antibody, with a value that ranges between 0 and 1. The term j_{rand} is randomly selected between 1 and the number of features.

The parameter update process for F_i and CR_i in SHADE 1.1 [45] is retained, with the modification that the last elements in the memory pools start with a value of 0.9. In particular, it initializes with two memory pools that store the historically successful values of F_i and CR_i. Each element, except for the last one, is initialized with a value of 0.5, while the last element is set to 0.9. In each generation, the control parameters F_i and CR_i are computed based on the following equations:

$$F_i = randc(MP_{r_k}^F, 0.1) \tag{6}$$

$$CR_i = \begin{cases} 0 & MP_{r_k}^{CR} = \perp \\ randn(MP_{r_k}^{CR}, 0.1) & otherwise \end{cases} \tag{7}$$

F_i is sampled from a Cauchy distribution with a location parameter MP_k^F and a scale parameter of 0.1. If the sampled value exceeds 1, it is clipped to 1. If the sampled value is less than 0, it is resampled from the Cauchy distribution until it falls within the valid range (0, 1]. The index k is randomly selected from 1 to the memory pool size. CR_i is sampled from a normal distribution, with a mean of MP_k^{CR} and a standard deviation of 0.1, and the clipped value stays within [0, 1].

After each generation, our method collects information about F and CR from the successful individuals and updates the memory pools using Algorithm 2.

Algorithm 2 Memory update process

Input: array of F values from successful individuals S^F,
array of CR values from successful individuals S^{CR}.
Output: Memory Pools MP^F and MP^{CR}.

```
if S^F ≠ ∅ and S^CR ≠ ∅ then
    if MP_k^CR ≠ ⊥ and MP_max^CR ≠ 0 then
        MP_k^CR = mean_L(S^CR);
    else
        MP_k^CR = ⊥;
    end if
    MP_k^F = mean_L(S^F);
    k = k + 1;
    if k > PoolSize then
        k = 1;
    end if
end if
return MP^F and MP^CR
```

The function $meanL()$ computes the weighted Lehmer mean of the successful F and CR values, as follows:

$$mean_L(S) = \frac{\sum_{k=1}^{|S|} w_k \cdot (S_k)^2}{\sum_{k=1}^{|S|} w_k \cdot S_k} \tag{8}$$

$$w_k = \frac{|(f(v_k) - f(x_k))|}{\sum_{i=1}^{|S|} |(f(v_i) - f(x_i))|} \tag{9}$$

$|.|$ is the improvement in fitness between the parent and the offspring.

3.4. Runtime Complexity Analysis

The analysis of the time complexity of CSA-EMT is as follows:

Step 1: Generate dual tasks by separately applying Relief-F and using the original training data with m samples and d features. The time complexity follows $O(mds)$, where s represents the number of times the algorithm randomly samples instances from the dataset.

Step 2.1: Initialize the population with N antibodies and evaluate the affinity values. The time complexity follows $O(Nd + EN)$, where E represents the time taken for affinity evaluation.

Step 2.2: Select the N_s best antibodies for cloning, which has a time complexity of $O(N_s)$.

Step 2.3: Each selected antibody is cloned N_c times, which has a time complexity of $O(N_s N_c d)$.

Step 2.4: Each clone undergoes mutation and has its affinity value evaluated. The time complexity follows $O(N_s N_c d + E N_s N_c)$.

Step 2.5: Update the population, which has a time complexity of $O((N_s N_c + N) log(N_s N_c + N))$.

Step 2.6: The evolutionary process runs for G generations.

The total time complexity is as follows:

$O(mds + G(Nd + EN + N_s + N_s N_c d + N_s N_c d + E N_s N_c + (N_s N_c + N) log(N_s N_c + N))$

$= O(mds + G(Nd + EN + N_s N_c d + E N_s N_c + (N_s N_c + N) log(N_s N_c + N))$

From this, it is clear that the population size N, the number of selected antibodies N_s, the number of clones N_c, and the number of evolutionary iterations G are all key factors that impact the algorithm's time complexity. As our algorithm can achieve faster convergence with a smaller population size N, it can reduce the number of evolutionary iterations and effectively decrease the training time.

4. Experimental Results and Discussion

This section presents three experiments to evaluate the performance of CSA-EMT. First, we compare CSA-EMT with the 1NN classifier using the full feature set. Second, we benchmark CSA-EMT against other well-established feature selection methods. Finally, we examine the impact of different generation strategies on the performance of CSA-EMT.

4.1. Experimental Setup

For this study, we utilized six microarray datasets to evaluate the performance of the proposed CSA-EMT method. The details are provided in Table 1 and are available at https://github.com/lyceia/FS-DB (accessed on 20 October 2024). The training and test sets were generated using 10-fold cross-validation, which is widely used in feature selection due to its ability to effectively balance bias and variance [17,46]. In this method, nine folds are designated for training, and the remaining fold is used for testing. Furthermore, we employed stratified sampling to ensure that the class distribution remained consistent during the splitting of the datasets, which helps mitigate the impact of class imbalance during cross-validation.

The experiments were conducted on a system with an Intel Core i9 processor and 32 GB of RAM in a Windows 11 environment. The CSA-EMT algorithm was implemented using the JAVA WekaClassalgos development package, which can be accessed at http://wekaclassalgos.sourceforge.net (accessed on 20 October 2024). The main parameters were as follows: the population size for each task was set to 5; the top 20% of antibodies were selected for cloning, with each selected antibody producing one clone; the historical memory pool size for each task was set to 5; the maximum number of evolutions was set to 50; and the 1NN classifier was used to evaluate the performance of the methods. Each method was run 20 times on each dataset to reduce bias.

Table 1. The details of the benchmark datasets.

Dataset	Features	Instances	Classes	Imbalance Ratio
SRBCT	2308	83	4	2.64
Leukemia1	5327	72	3	4.22
DLBCL	5469	77	2	3.05
Brain Tumor1	5920	90	5	15.00
Brain Tumor2	10,367	50	4	2.14
Leukemia2	11,225	72	3	1.40

4.2. Performance Evaluation

We evaluated the performance of CSA-EMT based on accuracy and the number of selected features. Figures 3 and 4 illustrate the comparative results between CSA-EMT and the 1NN classifier using all features.

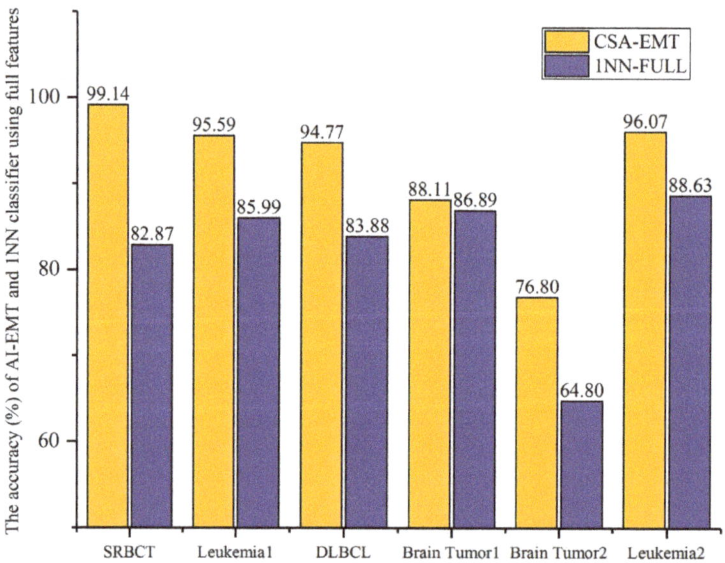

Figure 3. The accuracy (%) of CSA-EMT vs. that of the 1NN classifier using all features.

In Figure 3, the accuracy (%) of the proposed CSA-EMT method is compared with that of the 1NN classifier using all feature sets across six datasets. The x-axis represents the datasets, while the y-axis indicates the classification accuracy as a percentage. As shown, CSA-EMT consistently outperformed the 1NN classifier across all datasets, demonstrating its effectiveness in selecting high-quality feature subsets, which improved classification accuracy. Compared to using all features, the classification accuracy increased by at least 7.44% on five datasets, with SRBCT showing the largest improvement, achieving a 16.27% increase.

In Figure 4, the percentage of the average number of selected features relative to the total number of features is presented, with the x-axis representing each dataset and the y-axis indicating the proportion of selected features. The results show that CSA-EMT significantly reduced the feature subset by at least 95.86%, selecting a smaller subset while retaining relevant information. Leukemia1 exhibited the most significant reduction, decreasing by 99.01%.

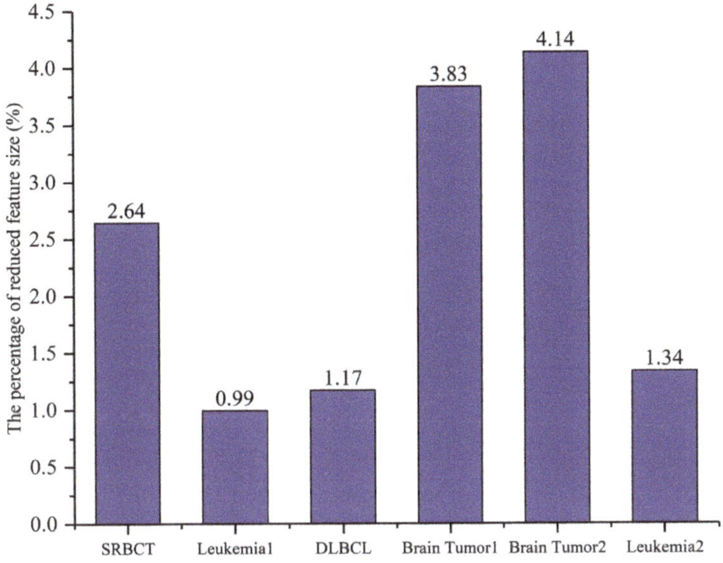

Figure 4. The percentage of selected features relative to the total number of features (%).

In summary, these results highlight the robust feature selection capability of CSA-EMT, which significantly reduces dimensionality while enhancing the predictive power of the classifier.

4.3. Comparison with Feature Selection Methods

To demonstrate the effectiveness and efficiency of CSA-EMT, we compared it with four state-of-the-art, well-known feature selection algorithms, including MF-CSO [17], VLPSO-LS [47], the GA (genetic algorithm), and the CSA (clonal selection algorithm). MF-CSO is an evolutionary multitasking-based feature selection method that employs a competitive swarm optimizer to tackle the four tasks generated using three filtering methods. VLPSO-LS is a one-stage feature selection method that employs a variable-length representation to accelerate the search speed. The GA and CSA are well-known evolutionary algorithms with powerful global search abilities.

Table 2 presents the comparison results with other state-of-the-art feature selection methods, where $|S|$ represents the number of selected features, $|Avg|$ represents the average accuracy, and $|T|$ represents the running time. The symbols "−", "+", and "≈" denote whether the compared methods outperformed, underperformed, or performed similarly to CSA-EMT.

The results indicate that CSA-EMT outperformed the comparative methods in both accuracy and running time on five out of six datasets. Compared with the traditional GA and CSA-based feature selection methods, CSA-EMT not only achieved the highest accuracy but also required fewer features across all datasets. The average accuracy improved by at least 8.07%, except for Brain Tumor1. Compared with VLPSO-LS, although CSA-EMT selected more features on four datasets, it enhanced the performance across all datasets except for SRBCT, surpassing VLPSO-LS in overall effectiveness. This is because CSA-EMT adopts the evolutionary multitasking technique to share information across different tasks. Compared with MF-CSO using EMT, CSA-EMT showed obvious advantages in average accuracy across all datasets. The most notable enhancement was observed in Brain Tumor1, where the accuracy increased by at least 13.18%. Regarding the average running time, CSA-EMT was the top performer, followed by GA, VLPSO-LS, CSA, and MF-CSO.

Table 2. Comparison of CSA-EMT with four feature selection methods.

Dataset	Eval. Meas.	MF-CSO	VLPSO-LS	GA	CSA	CSA-EMT
SRBCT	$\|S\|$	**57**	78	950	1152	61
	Avg	95.13 ± 6.81	**99.83 ± 0.40**	84.53 ± 2.90	84.63 ± 2.64	99.14 ± 0.95
	$\|T\|$	105.88	**9.74**	23.71	46.88	10.71
Leukemia1	$\|S\|$	95	59	1957	2661	**53**
	Avg	89.75 ± 14.45	92.90 ± 1.95	85.95 ± 2.11	85.86 ± 1.72	**95.59 ± 1.37**
	$\|T\|$	113.31	42.01	40.70	60.76	**20.95**
DLBCL	$\|S\|$	**35**	60	2151	2743	64
	Avg	93.85 ± 9.92	93.17 ± 3.46	84.64 ± 2.31	82.79 ± 1.31	**94.77 ± 2.09**
	$\|T\|$	108.85	60.37	46.79	87.92	**23.53**
Brain Tumor1	$\|S\|$	127	**98**	2190	2957	227
	Avg	74.93 ± 17.24	78.38 ± 3.44	87.89 ± 0.92	87.11 ± 1.33	**88.11 ± 1.93**
	$\|T\|$	130.99	57.83	60.56	70.64	**29.87**
Brain Tumor2	$\|S\|$	133	**65**	3746	5187	429
	Avg	71.65 ± 21.43	73.54 ± 4.35	65.40 ± 3.23	66.40 ± 2.80	**76.80 ± 4.07**
	$\|T\|$	140.68	82.22	40.68	227.82	**50.22**
Leukemia2	$\|S\|$	101	**66**	3495	5609	150
	Avg	91.94 ± 10.98	94.83 ± 1.14	86.77 ± 2.29	88.00 ± 2.21	**96.07 ± 2.20**
	$\|T\|$	146.84	128.49	75.53	250.37	**46.53**
	$\|S\|$	91	71	2415	3385	164
	AVG	86.21	88.78	82.53	82.46	91.75
	$\|T\|$	124.42	63.44	48.00	124.06	30.30
	$-/+/\approx$	6/0/0	5/1/0	6/0/0	6/0/0	

4.4. Impact of Different Generation Strategies

In this section, we analyze the effect of three generation strategies on the performance of CSA-EMT. We implemented three generation strategies: information gain, mRMR, and Relief-F. Each strategy was tested using the same initial parameters to ensure a fair comparison. Table 3 shows the comparison results of CSA-EMT using different generation strategies. CSA-EMT-IG employs information gain and the knee point method to generate features in Task 2. CSA-EMT-mRMR utilizes the top 10% of the important features generated by mRMR to produce Task 2.

The results indicate that CSA-EMT and CSA-EMT-mRMR achieved similar accuracies; however, CSA-EMT selected fewer features and had a shorter running time. CSA-EMT-IG, on the other hand, performed worse overall. These findings suggest that while the Relief-F and knee point methods are effective, other methods, such as mRMR, are also viable for feature selection. The choice of method can impact both the efficiency and accuracy of the results. Therefore, it is essential to explore the use of various filter-based feature selection methods to generate multiple tasks to improve overall performance. Here, we have used only the Relief-F and knee point methods, but we are not limited to these.

Table 3. Comparison of CSA-EMT performance using different generation strategies.

Dataset	Eval. Meas.	CSA-EMT-IG	CSA-EMT-mRMR	CSA-EMT
SRBCT	$\|S\|$	**56**	76	61
	Avg	98.50 ± 1.07	98.07 ± 1.79	**99.14 ± 0.95**
	$\|T\|$	10.63	**10.58**	10.71
Leukemia1	$\|S\|$	55	163	**53**
	Avg	94.68 ± 1.38	**96.02 ± 0.78**	95.59 ± 1.37
	$\|T\|$	25.95	23.11	**20.95**

Table 3. *Cont.*

Dataset	Eval. Meas.	CSA-EMT-IG	CSA-EMT-mRMR	CSA-EMT
DLBCL	$\|S\|$	92	179	**64**
	Avg	93.29 ± 3.42	93.77 ± 1.13	**94.77 ± 2.09**
	$\|T\|$	28.30	26.89	**23.53**
Brain Tumor1	$\|S\|$	240	**203**	227
	Avg	86.00 ± 1.74	**88.89 ± 1.41**	88.11 ± 1.93
	$\|T\|$	37.77	**27.45**	29.87
Brain Tumor2	$\|S\|$	563	**333**	429
	Avg	77.60 ± 3.07	**79.00 ± 2.57**	76.80 ± 4.07
	$\|T\|$	70.90	**45.05**	50.22
Leukemia2	$\|S\|$	**134**	336	150
	Avg	95.45 ± 1.38	95.00 ± 1.91	**96.07 ± 2.20**
	$\|T\|$	57.70	49.21	**46.53**
	$\|S\|$	190	215	164
	AVG	90.92	91.79	91.75
	$\|T\|$	38.54	30.38	30.30
	$-/+/\approx$	5/1/0	3/3/0	

5. Conclusions

In this study, we proposed an evolutionary multitasking feature selection approach based on an immune algorithm to address the challenges of high-dimensional microarray data analysis. Multitask learning is introduced to leverage the clonal selection algorithm to solve multiple feature selection tasks simultaneously. By sharing information across tasks, the method enhances convergence and reduces computational costs, resulting in more robust feature selection. The dual-task generation strategy and the improved clonal selection algorithm are the key components of our proposed algorithm. The dual-task generation strategy uses the Relief-F method and the original features to generate two tasks. Meanwhile, the improved clonal selection algorithm enhances the exploration and exploitation capabilities of the CSA. Through experiments on six high-dimensional microarray datasets, the CSA-EMT method demonstrated a better trade-off between the number of selected features, classification accuracy, and computational time when compared to other feature selection methods across most datasets. However, it presented some limitations. Notably, it tended to select slightly more features, as observed in the Brain Tumor1 and Brain Tumor2 datasets. For future research, we plan to enhance the search capabilities of the clone selection process to address this limitation, potentially by incorporating local search techniques or developing a more effective knowledge transfer strategy.

Author Contributions: Conceptualization, Y.W.; Methodology, Y.W.; Validation, Y.W., D.L., and J.Y.; Resources, J.Y.; Writing—original draft, Y.W. and D.L.; Supervision, D.L.; Funding acquisition, Y.W. All authors have read and agreed to the published version of the manuscript.

Funding: This research was funded by the National Natural Science Foundation of China (Grant No. 62102146).

Data Availability Statement: The original contributions presented in the study are included in the article. Further inquiries can be directed to the corresponding author.

Conflicts of Interest: The authors declare no conflicts of interest.

References

1. Umirzakova, S.; Ahmad, S.; Mardieva, S.; Muksimova, S.; Whangbo, T.K. Deep learning-driven diagnosis: A multi-task approach for segmenting stroke and Bell's palsy. *Pattern Recognit.* **2023**, *144*, 109866. [CrossRef]
2. Sun, S.; Dong, B.; Zou, Q. Revisiting genome-wide association studies from statistical modelling to machine learning. *Briefings Bioinform.* **2021**, *22*, bbaa263. [CrossRef] [PubMed]

3. Masciocchi, C.; Gottardelli, B.; Savino, M.; Boldrini, L.; Martino, A.; Mazzarella, C.; Massaccesi, M.; Valentini, V.; Damiani, A. Federated cox proportional hazards model with multicentric privacy-preserving LASSO feature selection for survival analysis from the perspective of personalized medicine. In Proceedings of the 2022 IEEE 35th International Symposium on Computer-Based Medical Systems (CBMS), Shenzhen, China, 21–23 July 2022; IEEE: Piscataway, NJ, USA, 2022; pp. 25–31.
4. Osama, S.; Shaban, H.; Ali, A.A. Gene reduction and machine learning algorithms for cancer classification based on microarray gene expression data: A comprehensive review. *Expert Syst. Appl.* **2023**, *213*, 118946. [CrossRef]
5. Firdaus, F.F.; Nugroho, H.A.; Soesanti, I. A review of feature selection and classification approaches for heart disease prediction. *IJITEE (Int. J. Inf. Technol. Electr. Eng.)* **2021**, *4*, 75–82. [CrossRef]
6. Bommert, A.; Welchowski, T.; Schmid, M.; Rahnenführer, J. Benchmark of filter methods for feature selection in high-dimensional gene expression survival data. *Briefings Bioinform.* **2022**, *23*, bbab354. [CrossRef] [PubMed]
7. Maldonado, J.; Riff, M.C.; Neveu, B. A review of recent approaches on wrapper feature selection for intrusion detection. *Expert Syst. Appl.* **2022**, *198*, 116822. [CrossRef]
8. Fu, Y.; Liu, X.; Sarkar, S.; Wu, T. Gaussian mixture model with feature selection: An embedded approach. *Comput. Ind. Eng.* **2021**, *152*, 107000. [CrossRef]
9. Pramanik, R.; Pramanik, P.; Sarkar, R. Breast cancer detection in thermograms using a hybrid of GA and GWO based deep feature selection method. *Expert Syst. Appl.* **2023**, *219*, 119643. [CrossRef]
10. Haktanirlar Ulutas, B.; Kulturel-Konak, S. A review of clonal selection algorithm and its applications. *Artif. Intell. Rev.* **2011**, *36*, 117–138. [CrossRef]
11. Wang, Y.; Tian, H.; Li, T.; Liu, X. A two-stage clonal selection algorithm for local feature selection on high-dimensional data. *Inf. Sci.* **2024**, *677*, 120867. [CrossRef]
12. Zhu, Y.; Li, W.; Li, T. A hybrid artificial immune optimization for high-dimensional feature selection. *Knowl.-Based Syst.* **2023**, *260*, 110111. [CrossRef]
13. Chai, Z.; Li, W.; Li, Y. Symmetric uncertainty based decomposition multi-objective immune algorithm for feature selection. *Swarm Evol. Comput.* **2023**, *78*, 101286. [CrossRef]
14. Wei, T.; Wang, S.; Zhong, J.; Liu, D.; Zhang, J. A review on evolutionary multitask optimization: Trends and challenges. *IEEE Trans. Evol. Comput.* **2021**, *26*, 941–960. [CrossRef]
15. Wu, X.; Wang, W.; Zhang, T.; Han, H.; Qiao, J. Improved evolutionary multitasking optimization algorithm with similarity evaluation of search behavior. *IEEE Trans. Evol. Comput.* **2024**. [CrossRef]
16. Chen, K.; Xue, B.; Zhang, M.; Zhou, F. An evolutionary multitasking-based feature selection method for high-dimensional classification. *IEEE Trans. Cybern.* **2022**, *52*, 7172–7186. [CrossRef]
17. Li, L.; Xuan, M.; Lin, Q.; Jiang, M.; Ming, Z.; Tan, K.C. An evolutionary multitasking algorithm with multiple filtering for high-dimensional feature selection. *IEEE Trans. Evol. Comput.* **2023**, *27*, 802–816. [CrossRef]
18. Lin, J.; Chen, Q.; Xue, B.; Zhang, M. Evolutionary multitasking for multi-objective feature selection in classification. *IEEE Trans. Evol. Comput.* **2023**, 1. [CrossRef]
19. Li, J.Y.; Zhan, Z.H.; Tan, K.C.; Zhang, J. A meta-knowledge transfer-based differential evolution for multitask optimization. *IEEE Trans. Evol. Comput.* **2021**, *26*, 719–734. [CrossRef]
20. Gupta, A.; Ong, Y.S.; Feng, L. Multifactorial evolution: Toward evolutionary multitasking. *IEEE Trans. Evol. Comput.* **2015**, *20*, 343–357. [CrossRef]
21. Bali, K.K.; Ong, Y.S.; Gupta, A.; Tan, P.S. Multifactorial evolutionary algorithm with online transfer parameter estimation: MFEA-II. *IEEE Trans. Evol. Comput.* **2019**, *24*, 69–83. [CrossRef]
22. Xing, C.; Gong, W.; Li, S. Adaptive archive-based multifactorial evolutionary algorithm for constrained multitasking optimization. *Appl. Soft Comput.* **2023**, *143*, 110385. [CrossRef]
23. Yu, Y.; Zhu, A.; Zhu, Z.; Lin, Q.; Yin, J.; Ma, X. Multifactorial differential evolution with opposition-based learning for multi-tasking optimization. In Proceedings of the 2019 IEEE Congress on Evolutionary Computation (CEC), Wellington, New Zealand, 10–13 June 2019; IEEE: Piscataway, NJ, USA, 2019; pp. 1898–1905.
24. Tang, Z.; Gong, M.; Xie, Y.; Li, H.; Qin, A.K. Multi-task particle swarm optimization with dynamic neighbor and level-based inter-task learning. *IEEE Trans. Emerg. Top. Comput. Intell.* **2021**, *6*, 300–314. [CrossRef]
25. Feng, L.; Zhou, L.; Zhong, J.; Gupta, A.; Ong, Y.S.; Tan, K.C.; Qin, A.K. Evolutionary multitasking via explicit autoencoding. *IEEE Trans. Cybern.* **2018**, *49*, 3457–3470. [CrossRef] [PubMed]
26. Lin, J.; Liu, H.L.; Tan, K.C.; Gu, F. An effective knowledge transfer approach for multiobjective multitasking optimization. *IEEE Trans. Cybern.* **2020**, *51*, 3238–3248. [CrossRef] [PubMed]
27. Zhang, T.; Gong, W.; Li, Y. Multitask differential evolution with adaptive dual knowledge transfer. *Appl. Soft Comput.* **2024**, *165*, 112040. [CrossRef]
28. Li, X.; Wang, L.; Jiang, Q. Multipopulation-based multi-tasking evolutionary algorithm. *Appl. Intell.* **2023**, *53*, 4624–4647. [CrossRef]
29. Tauber, A.I.; Podolsky, S.H. *The Generation of Diversity: Clonal Selection Theory and the Rise of Molecular Immunology*; Harvard University Press: Cambridge, MA, USA, 2000.
30. De Castro, L.N.; Von Zuben, F.J. Learning and optimization using the clonal selection principle. *IEEE Trans. Evol. Comput.* **2002**, *6*, 239–251. [CrossRef]

31. Yan, X.; Li, P.; Tang, K.; Gao, L.; Wang, L. Clonal selection based intelligent parameter inversion algorithm for prestack seismic data. *Inf. Sci.* **2020**, *517*, 86–99. [CrossRef]
32. Etaati, B.; Ghorrati, Z.; Ebadzadeh, M.M. A full-featured cooperative coevolutionary memory-based artificial immune system for dynamic optimization. *Appl. Soft Comput.* **2022**, *117*, 108389. [CrossRef]
33. Wang, Y.; Li, T.; Liu, X.; Yao, J. An adaptive clonal selection algorithm with multiple differential evolution strategies. *Inf. Sci.* **2022**, *604*, 142–169. [CrossRef]
34. Awad, N.H.; Ali, M.Z.; Suganthan, P.N.; Reynolds, R.G. An ensemble sinusoidal parameter adaptation incorporated with L-SHADE for solving CEC2014 benchmark problems. In Proceedings of the 2016 IEEE Congress on Evolutionary Computation (CEC), Vancouver, BC, Canada, 24–29 July 2016; IEEE: Piscataway, NJ, USA, 2016; pp. 2958–2965.
35. Li, L.; Lin, Q.; Li, K.; Ming, Z. Vertical distance-based clonal selection mechanism for the multiobjective immune algorithm. *Swarm Evol. Comput.* **2021**, *63*, 100886. [CrossRef]
36. Ouaderhman, T.; Chamlal, H.; Janane, F.Z. A new filter-based gene selection approach in the DNA microarray domain. *Expert Syst. Appl.* **2024**, *240*, 122504. [CrossRef]
37. Lee, J.; Choi, I.Y.; Jun, C.H. An efficient multivariate feature ranking method for gene selection in high-dimensional microarray data. *Expert Syst. Appl.* **2021**, *166*, 113971. [CrossRef]
38. Thabtah, F.; Kamalov, F.; Hammoud, S.; Shahamiri, S.R. Least Loss: A simplified filter method for feature selection. *Inf. Sci.* **2020**, *534*, 1–15. [CrossRef]
39. Alrefai, N.; Ibrahim, O. Optimized feature selection method using particle swarm intelligence with ensemble learning for cancer classification based on microarray datasets. *Neural Comput. Appl.* **2022**, *34*, 13513–13528. [CrossRef]
40. Zhu, Y.; Li, T.; Lan, X. Feature selection optimized by the artificial immune algorithm based on genome shuffling and conditional lethal mutation. *Appl. Intell.* **2023**, *53*, 13972–13992. [CrossRef]
41. Mafarja, M.; Thaher, T.; Too, J.; Chantar, H.; Turabieh, H.; Houssein, E.H.; Emam, M.M. An efficient high-dimensional feature selection approach driven by enhanced multi-strategy grey wolf optimizer for biological data classification. *Neural Comput. Appl.* **2023**, *35*, 1749–1775. [CrossRef]
42. Mahendran, N.; PM, D.R.V. A deep learning framework with an embedded-based feature selection approach for the early detection of the Alzheimer's disease. *Comput. Biol. Med.* **2022**, *141*, 105056. [CrossRef]
43. Vommi, A.M.; Battula, T.K. A hybrid filter-wrapper feature selection using Fuzzy KNN based on Bonferroni mean for medical datasets classification: A COVID-19 case study. *Expert Syst. Appl.* **2023**, *218*, 119612. [CrossRef]
44. Ke, L.; Li, M.; Wang, L.; Deng, S.; Ye, J.; Yu, X. Improved swarm-optimization-based filter-wrapper gene selection from microarray data for gene expression tumor classification. *Pattern Anal. Appl.* **2023**, *26*, 455–472. [CrossRef]
45. Tanabe, R.; Fukunaga, A. Success-history based parameter adaptation for differential evolution. In Proceedings of the 2013 IEEE Congress on Evolutionary Computation, Cancun, Mexico, 20–23 June 2013; IEEE: Piscataway, NJ, USA, 2013; pp. 71–78.
46. Braik, M.; Hammouri, A.; Alzoubi, H.; Sheta, A. Feature selection based nature inspired capuchin search algorithm for solving classification problems. *Expert Syst. Appl.* **2024**, *235*, 121128. [CrossRef]
47. Tran, B.; Xue, B.; Zhang, M. Variable-length particle swarm optimization for feature selection on high-dimensional classification. *IEEE Trans. Evol. Comput.* **2019**, *23*, 473–487. [CrossRef]

electronics

MDPI

Article

Optimization of SM2 Algorithm Based on Polynomial Segmentation and Parallel Computing

Hongyu Zhu [1,2], Ding Li [3,4,*], Yizhen Sun [1,2], Qian Chen [5], Zheng Tian [1,2] and Yubo Song [3,4]

[1] State Grid Hunan Electric Power Company Limited Information and Communication Company, Changsha 410004, China; zhuhy17@hn.sgcc.com.cn (H.Z.); sunyz2@hn.sgcc.com.cn (Y.S.); tianz5@hn.sgcc.com.cn (Z.T.)
[2] Hunan Key Laboratory for Internet of Things in Electricity, Changsha 410004, China
[3] School of Cyber Science and Engineering, Southeast University, Nanjing 211189, China; songyubo@seu.edu.cn
[4] Purple Mountain Laboratories, Nanjing 211111, China
[5] State Grid Hunan Electric Power Co., Ltd., Changsha 410007, China; chenq31@hn.sgcc.com.cn
* Correspondence: ld1ng@seu.edu.cn

Abstract: The SM2 public key cryptographic algorithm is widely utilized for secure communication and data protection due to its strong security and compact key size. However, the intensive large integer operations it requires pose significant computational challenges, which can limit the performance of Internet of Things (IoT) terminal devices. This paper introduces an optimized implementation of the SM2 algorithm specifically designed for IoT contexts. By segmenting large integers as polynomials within a modified Montgomery modular multiplication algorithm, the proposed method enables parallel modular multiplication and reduction, thus addressing storage constraints and reducing computational redundancy. For scalar multiplication, a Co-Z Montgomery ladder algorithm is employed alongside Single Instruction Multiple Data (SIMD) instructions to enhance parallelism, significantly improving efficiency. Experimental results demonstrate that the proposed scheme reduces the computation time for the SM2 algorithm's digital signature by approximately 20% and enhances data encryption and decryption efficiency by about 15% over existing methods, marking a substantial performance gain for IoT applications.

Keywords: Montgomery modular multiplication; SIMD; Montgomery ladder; parallel processing; elliptic curve cryptography; modular arithmetic optimization; efficiency improvement

1. Introduction

Elliptic curve cryptography (ECC), compared with the RSA cryptographic algorithm, offers better computational efficiency and requires less key storage space. Consequently, ECC has become a crucial alternative to RSA. Major countries worldwide have established ECC standards and are promoting their use to safeguard information security.

ECC is applied in various scenarios. For instance, the U.S. government uses ECC as a fundamental cryptographic component to ensure data security in the Tor project [1]. In the foundational technology of Bitcoin [2] blockchain, Nakamoto employs ECC as the authentication mechanism. However, international ECC standards are not completely secure. Internal memos leaked by former NSA employee Edward Joseph Snowden [3] reveal that the NSA left a backdoor in the NIST's ECC technical standards, where the pseudo-random number generator Dual_EC_DRBG [4] can have its output predicted under certain conditions. Therefore, it is crucial to adopt cryptographic algorithms independently developed by our country for critical information systems.

In 2010, the National Cryptography Administration of China introduced the SM2 public key cryptography algorithm based on ECC, aimed at replacing the RSA algorithm. As a national cryptographic algorithm, SM2 has been applied in various commercial cryptographic products, such as electronic certification systems and key management systems. Additionally, due to its high security and short key length, the SM2 algorithm is widely used for key agreement and data encryption transmission among IoT devices. IoT devices have brought significant convenience to our production and daily life, from simple smart home controls to complex industrial automation equipment. However, these devices face numerous limitations in computational capacity and storage space, placing higher demands on the performance of the SM2 algorithm. Specifically, because it relies on operations over elliptic curve groups, the computational load is high, its structure is complex, and it suffers from low operational efficiency and high resource consumption on resource-limited IoT terminals.

Recently, researchers have proposed various solutions for the SM2 algorithm tailored to different application scenarios, primarily focusing on applications [5–9], with less emphasis on optimization implementation. Since the SM2 algorithm has not been available for long, it does not adapt well to some existing ECC computational algorithms, hindering its broader adoption. Discussing the integration of these algorithms with the SM2 computational algorithm is crucial for enhancing the computational efficiency of the SM2 algorithm.

The main contributions of this paper are as follows:

1. Efficient elliptic curve group computation: we utilize an improved Montgomery algorithm based on polynomial expansion, where large integers are expanded into polynomials to interleave modular multiplication and modular reduction operations. This approach achieves efficient and stable modular multiplication. Additionally, the Montgomery ladder algorithm based on Co-Z operations reduces redundant calculations in elliptic curve scalar multiplication, further enhancing the efficiency of point addition and doubling.
2. Effective use of parallel computing: we introduce SIMD instruction set optimization to enable parallel processing of multiple data. In particular, the combination of SIMD technology with Montgomery point multiplication significantly improves performance.
3. Comprehensive implementation of the SM2 national cryptographic algorithm: we fully implement the SM2 public key encryption algorithm and digital signature algorithm, ensuring wide applicability in practical applications. Our design is compared with other public algorithms such as the SM2 signature algorithm based on OpenSSL 1.1.1, the SM2 encryption and decryption algorithm, ECDSA (secp256k1), and ECIES (secp256k1). Metrics such as runtime and throughput are used as evaluation criteria.

2. Related Work

Numerous scholars worldwide have extensively researched the ECC algorithm. The optimization of field operations primarily targets computationally intensive modular multiplication. In 1985, mathematician Montgomery proposed Montgomery multiplication [10], significantly speeding up large integer modular multiplication. Building on this, Koc et al. [11] integrated the steps of the Montgomery reduction algorithm, proposing five optimized versions that further improved efficiency. In 1987, Montgomery introduced a point multiplication algorithm over binary extension fields [12], which only requires processing the X coordinate during point multiplication, thus reducing space requirements. In 1999, literature [13] extended the Montgomery point multiplication algorithm to LD coordinate representation, reducing the need for inversion operations in binary fields. In 2010, Ref. [14] used a bottom-up approach to optimize the ECC point multiplication algorithm, employing Jacobi coordinates, extended Twisted Edwards coordinates, and the Galbraith–LinScott (GLS) method, achieving about a 30% improvement in computational speed.

Since Intel introduced the SIMD instruction set in 1996, many researchers have used this instruction set to optimize various symmetric cryptographic algorithms. Parallel implementation schemes for the SM4 algorithm [15] and the ZUC algorithm [16] have subsequently been proposed. The key steps of elliptic curve-based public key cryptographic algorithms are large integer operations and elliptic curve operations. Hisil et al. [4], based on the Montgomery ladder point multiplication algorithm [12], designed a four-way vectorized Montgomery point multiplication algorithm for Montgomery form elliptic curves, utilizing AVX2 and AVX512 instruction sets. Nath et al. [17] further proposed optimized algorithms for variable base point and fixed-base point scalar multiplication, reducing the number of multiplications in point operations. They implemented a four-way vectorized Montgomery point multiplication algorithm for Curve25519 and Curve448 curves using assembly language and the AVX2 instruction set, significantly reducing the runtime. Cheng et al. [18] further improved the throughput of scalar multiplication on the Curve25519 curve based on the AVX2 instruction set. Huang et al. [19] extended this approach to the SM2 elliptic curve, implementing a two-way parallel large integer operation and scalar multiplication algorithm using the AVX2 instruction set, which reduced the latency of constant-time scalar multiplication on SM2. Gueron et al. [20] developed a highly optimized cryptographic library for the NIST P-256 curve on the x86_64 platform, optimizing the fixed-base scalar multiplication computation process using SIMD instructions, which can be directly extended to OpenSSL. Bernstein et al. [21] proposed techniques for accelerating fixed-base scalar multiplication on the Ed25519 curve, increasing the running speed of the EdDSA scheme. Faz-Hernández et al. [22] designed a precomputation table for the Ed25519 curve using SIMD instructions, further optimizing the performance of fixed-base scalar multiplication.

Additionally, various other optimization efforts have been made. F. Chen et al. [23] proposed a low-cost, high-speed parallel modular multiplication implementation for SM2, executing the two steps of multiplication and reduction in parallel. They improved the classic Karatsuba algorithm, executing it in eight parts, combined with subsequent parallel reduction computations. Wang et al. [24] proposed a modular squaring unit using a fast partial Montgomery reduction algorithm, significantly reducing area. Modular squaring operations can be completed in only four clock cycles, and modular multiplication and squaring can be computed in parallel for high speed. Xingran Li et al. [25] proposed a new parallel efficient algorithm to accelerate scalar multiplication, introducing a new regular halving and addition method, effective with projective coordinates. They compared various algorithms for double addition and halving addition, finally combining the best methods to obtain a new faster parallel algorithm. Mai et al. [26] developed a new SM2 algorithm implementation called Yog-SM2, leveraging the parallel computing capabilities of modern processors, such as the AVX2 instruction set, significantly enhancing execution speed while maintaining security. Hu et al. [27] proposed a high-performance ECC architecture based on a half-word multiplier, where PM operations consist of point addition (PA) and point doubling (PD) operations. They introduced a novel schedule for PA and PD to reduce MM operations and enhance the parallelism of multiplication and fast reduction operations.

3. Preliminaries

3.1. SM2 Public Key Cryptographic Algorithm

The SM2 algorithm is a type of ECC algorithm. It provides higher security strength than 2048-bit RSA and operates faster than RSA. The National Cryptography Administration of China has decided to use the SM2 algorithm to replace RSA after thorough research. The SM2 elliptic curve public key cryptography algorithm was developed and formulated by China, incorporating existing research from both domestic and international sources, and it possesses independent intellectual property rights.

An elliptic curve system over a prime field typically consists of the following parameters:

(1) The field size p, where p is a prime number greater than 3;
(2) The elliptic curve equation $y^2 = x^3 + ax + b$, with coefficients a and b;
(3) The base point $G(G_x, G_y)$ on the elliptic curve;
(4) The order n of the base point;
(5) The cofactor h of the base point.

SM2 digital signature algorithm: the SM2 elliptic curve cryptography algorithm includes digital signature generation and verification, as well as encryption and decryption. Given a message, M, to be signed, the signature, (r, s), the public key, P, and the private key,

d, the elliptic curve equation over the finite prime field, p, is defined as $y^2 = x^3 + ax + b$ with the base point G. The signing process is as follows. Let Z_A be the hash value of the user A, M be the message to be signed, and d_A be the private key of user A:

(1) Concatenate Z_A and M, denoted as M', i.e., $M' = Z_A \parallel M$;
(2) Compute the hash value of M', denoted as e, i.e., $e = H_v(M')$;
(3) Generate a random number $k \in [1, n-1]$;
(4) Compute the elliptic curve point $(x_1, y_1) = [k]G$;
(5) Compute $r = (e + x_1) \mod n$. If $r = 0$ or $r + k = n$, return to step 3;
(6) Compute $s = [(1 + d_A)^{-1} \cdot (k - r \cdot d_A)] \mod n$. If $s = 0$, return to step 3;
(7) Output the digital signature (r, s) for the message M.

SM2 encryption algorithm: given the message M to be sent as a bit string of length $klen$, the SM2 encryption algorithm operates as follows:

(1) Generate a random number $k \in [1, n-1]$;
(2) Compute the elliptic curve point $C_1 = (x_1, y_1) = [k]G$;
(3) Compute the elliptic curve point $S = [h]P_B$. If $S = O$, report an error and exit;
(4) Compute the elliptic curve point $(x_2, y_2) = [k]P_B$;
(5) Compute $t = KDF(x_2 \parallel y_2, klen)$. If t is an all-zero bit string, return to step 1;
(6) Compute $C_2 = M \oplus t$;
(7) Compute $C_3 = H_v(x_2 \parallel M \parallel y_2)$;
(8) Output the ciphertext $C = C_1 \parallel C_2 \parallel C_3$.

3.2. Montgomery Modular Multiplication

The classic Montgomery modular multiplication algorithm leverages the properties of residue systems to transform standard modular operations into shift and addition operations. The algorithm computes $S = A \times B \times R^{-1} \mod M$. Select large integers A and B such that $0 \leq A, B < M$ and $\mathrm{GCD}(M, R) = 1$, and choose a base, R, where $R > M$. Parameters R^{-1} and M' are selected to satisfy $0 < R^{-1} < M$, $0 < M' < R$, and $R \times R^{-1} - M' \times M = 1$, ensuring the following conditions hold:

$$
\begin{aligned}
R \times R^{-1} &\equiv 1 \pmod{M} \\
M' &\equiv -M^{-1} \pmod{R}
\end{aligned}
\tag{1}
$$

The classic Montgomery algorithm consists of four main steps:

1. Multiply the large integers A and B to obtain the product T: $T = A \times B$;
2. Take the lower n bits of T, multiply by M', and again take the lower n bits to obtain the quotient q: $q = (T \mod R) \times M' \mod R$;
3. Multiply q by the modulus M, add T, and take the higher n bits to obtain S: $S = \frac{T + q \times M}{R}$;
4. If $S > M$, return $S - M$; otherwise, return S.

By analyzing the classic Montgomery algorithm and combining it with Equation (1), we obtain:

$$
q \times M \equiv -T \pmod{R} \tag{2}
$$

and

$$
S \times R \equiv T \pmod{R}, \text{ which implies } S \equiv T \times R^{-1} \pmod{M} \tag{3}
$$

Since $0 \leq T + q \times M < 2 \times M \times R$, an additional step, as shown in step 4, is necessary to obtain the final result. The classic Montgomery algorithm involves two n-bit large integer multiplications and two $2n$-bit large integer additions, making the logic operations more complex and time-consuming with wider bit-widths.

3.3. Montgomery Ladder Algorithm

The Montgomery ladder algorithm is designed for computing non-fixed-point scalar multiplication on Montgomery curves. This algorithm focuses only on the X coordinate, eliminating many Y coordinate operations. In the main loop, each iteration performs a point addition and a point doubling operation, with a time complexity of only $5M + 4S$, making it significantly more efficient than other elliptic curve algorithms. The algorithm's implementation involves conditional swaps to resist side-channel attacks, making it highly suitable for ECDH protocols requiring efficient non-fixed-point scalar multiplication.

As shown in Algorithm 1, the Montgomery point multiplication algorithm is presented. It starts by computing the initial values $R_0 = G$ and $R_1 = 2G$ based on the base point G. It then performs point addition and doubling operations on R_0 and R_1 according to the binary encoding of the integer k. The loop computes the final point multiplication result based on the binary digits of k.

Algorithm 1 Montgomery Point Multiplication

Input: $k = (k_{n-1}, \ldots, k_0)$, point G
Output: $Q = kG$
Initialize $R_0 = G, R_1 = 2G, i = n-2$
while $i \geq 0$ **do**
  if $k_i == 0$ **then**
    $R_1 = R_0 + R_1$, $R_0 = 2R_0$
  else
    $R_0 = R_0 + R_1$, $R_1 = 2R_1$
  end if
  $i = i - 1$
end while
$Q = R_0$

4. Methods

4.1. Polynomial Expansion Cross Montgomery Modular Multiplication Algorithm

This paper presents an improved version of the classical Montgomery modular multiplication algorithm, resulting in a polynomial expansion cross Montgomery modular multiplication algorithm. This algorithm consists of two main loops, referred to as Loop 1 and Loop 2. Loop 1 calculates the intermediate parameter, q_i, used in modular reduction, and Loop 2 performs multiple iterations to complete both the modular multiplication and reduction operations, with Loop 3 embedded within it to handle individual iterations of these operations.

In this algorithm, the input parameters—the modulus, multiplicand, and multiplier—are represented as polynomials:

$$M = \sum_{j=0}^{k_2-1} m_j \times (r_A)^j, \quad A = \sum_{j=0}^{k_2-1} m_j \times (d_A)^j, \quad y = r_A = 2^y, \quad k_2 = \frac{n}{y} \tag{4}$$

$$A = \sum_{j=0}^{k_2-1} a_j \times (r_A)^j = \sum_{j=0}^{k_2-1} a_j \times (d_A)^j, \quad y = r_A = 2^y, \quad 0 \leq A \leq 2M, \quad k_2 = \frac{n}{y} \tag{5}$$

$$B = \sum_{i=0}^{k_1-1} b_i \times (r_B)^j = \sum_{i=0}^{k_1-1} b_i \times (d_B)^j, \quad x = r_B = 2^x, \quad 0 \leq B \leq 2M, \quad 4M < 2^{k_1 x} \tag{6}$$

The input parameter is M_0', which represents the lower x bits of the modular multiplicative inverse of M (denoted M'), $S_0 = 0$. The output parameter is S.

The algorithm proceeds as follows:

Step 1: Sequentially take the low x bits of B (denoted b_i) and multiply by the low x bits of A (denoted $A[0]$). Add the low x bits of the intermediate result S_i (denoted $S_i[0]$). After the multiply–accumulate operation, retain the low x bits and multiply by M_0'. Finally, take the low x bits to obtain the parameter q_i. As shown in Algorithm 2, the iterative calculation of the intermediate parameter q_i is performed to ensure computational accuracy and efficiency.

Algorithm 2 Iterative Calculation of Intermediate Parameter q_i

for $i = 0$ to $k_1 - 1$ **do** ▷ Loop 1
  if $i == 0$ **then** ▷ Initialize
    $S_i = 0$
    $q_i = (((S_i[0] + A[0] \times b_i) \mod x) \times M_0') \mod x$
  end if
end for

Step 2: Utilize a nested loop structure, consisting of Loop 2 and Loop 3. In each iteration of the inner loop (Loop 3), sequentially take the y bits of A (denoted a_j) and multiply them by the x bits of B (denoted b_i, where i ranges from 0 to 30). Accumulate the result with the y bits of the previous iteration S_i (denoted $S_{i,j}$) and the carry $C\_AB_{i+1,j}$. This yields the modular multiplication result. Subsequently, multiply q_i by the y bits of the modulus M (denoted m_j) and add the carry $C\_qm_{i+1,j}$ and the accumulated result $S\_AB_{i+1,j+1}$ to complete the modular reduction operation, as shown in Algorithm 3.

Algorithm 3 Nested Modular Multiplication and Reduction Algorithm

for $i = 0$ to $k_1 - 1$ **do** ▷ Loop 2
  if $i == 0$ **then** ▷ Initialize
    $S_i = 0$
  end if
  for $j = 0$ to $k_2 - 1$ **do** ▷ Loop 3
    if $j == 0$ **then** ▷ Initialize
      $C\_AB_{i+1,j} = 0$
    end if
    $(C\_AB_{i+1,j+1}, S\_AB_{i+1,j+1}) = b_i \times a_j + S_{i,j} + C\_AB_{i+1,j}$
    $(C\_qm_{i+1,j+1}, S\_qm_{i+1,j+1}) = q_i \times m_j + S\_AB_{i+1,j+1} + C\_qm_{i+1,j}$
  end for
  $S_{i+1} = \frac{S\_qm_{i+1}}{x}$
end for

Step 3: The algorithm expands the range of input data, thereby eliminating the need for the subtraction operation used in the classical Montgomery modular multiplication algorithm. The computation concludes with the output result S.

4.1.1. Polynomial Expansion

Assuming the n-bit large integer B is represented with base r_B, $B = (b_{k_1-1}, b_{k_1-2}, \ldots, b_1, b_0)r_B$, with $r_B = 2^x$. Each part is represented by b_i, where b_i ranges from 0 to x, and is calculated according to Equation (4). Here, i ranges from 0 to $k_1 - 1$, and the integers x and k_1 satisfy $4M < 2^{(k_1 x)}$, resulting in the k_1-bit large integer B (Equation (5)):

$$b_i = (B \gg (x \times i)) \mod r_B \tag{7}$$

$$B = \sum_{i=0}^{k_1-1} b_i \times (r_B)^i \tag{8}$$

Additionally, the k_1-bit large integer B can also be expanded as a polynomial of degree $k_1 - 1$, as shown in Equation (6), where $d_B = r_B$:

$$B(d_B) = \sum_{i=0}^{k_1-1} b_i \times (d_B)^i \tag{9}$$

Similarly, assuming the n-bit large integer A is represented with base r_A, $A = (a_{k_2-1}, a_{k_2-2}, \ldots, a_1, a_0)r_A$, with $r_A = 2^y$. Each part is represented by a_j, where a_j ranges from 0 to y, and is calculated according to Equation (7). Here, j ranges from 0 to $k_2 - 1$, and $k_2 = \left\lceil \frac{n}{y} \right\rceil$, resulting in A:

$$a_j = (A \gg (d_A \times j)) \mod r_A \tag{10}$$

$$A = \sum_{j=0}^{k_2-1} a_j \times (r_A)^j \tag{11}$$

Moreover, the k_2-bit large integer A can also be expanded as a polynomial of degree $k_2 - 1$, as shown in Equation (9), where $d_A = r_A$:

$$A(d_A) = \sum_{j=0}^{k_2-1} a_j \times (d_A)^j \tag{12}$$

$$T = A \times B = A(d_A) \times B(d_B) = \sum_{i=0}^{k_1-1} \left\{ b_i \times (d_B)^i \times \left(\sum_{j=0}^{k_2-1} (a_j \times (d_A)^j) \right) \right\} \tag{13}$$

If the input data are the n-bit multiplicand A and the multiplier B, the computation process will produce an intermediate result of up to $2n$ bits. By expanding the input data as polynomials and performing multi-precision calculations, each operation only involves parts of A and B (i.e., a_j and b_i), reducing the intermediate result to $(x + y)$ bits. In hardware implementation, this multiplier can be reused, and its size will affect the circuit's area, making this operation beneficial for saving area costs.

4.1.2. Cross Execution of Modular Multiplication and Modular Reduction

This paper illustrates the use of the polynomial expansion modular multiplication algorithm, which involves multiplication and modular reduction operations, by combining it with Step 2 of the polynomial expansion cross Montgomery modular multiplication algorithm. Step 2 primarily consists of Loop 2 and Loop 3, with Loop 3 nested within Loop 2. Loop 3 executes the operations described in Equations (11) and (12), achieving modular multiplication and modular reduction, respectively. The computation within Loop 2 is as shown in Equation (13):

$$S\_AB_{i+1} = b_i \times \left(\sum_{j=0}^{k_2-1} a_j \times (d_A)^j \right) = b_i \times A \tag{14}$$

$$S\_qm_{i+1} = q_i \times \left(\sum_{j=0}^{k_2-1} m_j \times (d_B)^j \right) + S\_AB_{i+1} = q_i \times M + S\_AB_{i+1} \tag{15}$$

$$S\_qm = \left(\sum_{i=0}^{k_1-1} q_i \times (d_A)^i \right) \times M + \left(\sum_{i=0}^{k_1-1} b_i \times (d_A)^i \right) \times A = q \times M + B \times A \tag{16}$$

This paper introduces a method for the cross execution of modular multiplication and modular reduction operations using polynomial expansion. Unlike the classical Montgomery modular multiplication algorithm, the proposed algorithm performs modular multiplication with a smaller bit-width before initiating the modular reduction operation, thereby reducing the start time for modular reduction. These enhancements make the modular multiplication algorithm more suitable for hardware implementation involving large integer modular multiplication. By alternating the execution of modular multiplication and modular reduction using smaller bit-widths, computational efficiency is increased. The new algorithm conserves hardware resources by minimizing the multiplier area, resulting in efficient modular multiplication with low resource consumption.

4.2. Parallel Montgomery Ladder Algorithm Based on Co-Z Operations

The Montgomery ladder algorithm based on Co-Z operations improves the efficiency of scalar multiplication by eliminating the need for Z coordinate calculations in the main loop. In the Montgomery point multiplication algorithm, irrespective of the value of k_i, each iteration of the loop involves computing both point addition and point doubling, which are independent operations that can be executed in parallel. To optimize these operations, Co-Z operations are introduced. When the Z coordinates of two different points are equal in Jacobian projective coordinates, the addition operation can omit certain calculations involving the Z coordinate, thus enhancing the efficiency of the addition operation. The ladder step in the main loop of the traditional Montgomery ladder algorithm is replaced with the following.

First, perform one Co-Z conjugate addition operation, then perform one Co-Z addition operation. The algorithm proceeds as follows:

1. $a = (k_i + k_{i+1}) \mod 2$
2. $XYCZ\_addC(R_{1-a}, R_a)$;
3. $XYCZ\_add(R_a, R_{1-a})$;

This method restores the Z coordinate at the final stage of the Montgomery ladder algorithm with minimal additional cost. The optimized point multiplication operation reduces the time complexity by the equivalent of 6 modular multiplications.

To fully leverage the parallelism of the SIMD instruction set, we carefully analyzed the execution flow of Co-Z Jacobian operations. We found that most prime field operations lack data dependencies and can be executed in parallel. Algorithms 4 and 5 provide parallel optimized implementations of Co-Z addition and Co-Z conjugate addition, respectively, involving only the (X, Y) coordinates. These algorithms implement elliptic curve point operations using parallel prime field operations with AVX2. In these algorithms, each line represents the simultaneous execution of the same operation on two sets of data. However, during the parallelization of Co-Z operations, some operations in Algorithm 4 cannot be paired; these are relatively simple addition and subtraction operations. Conversely, Algorithm 5 ensures that all operations can be paired by precomputing A' and T'.

Algorithm 4 PCZ-ADD: Parallel Co-Z Addition Operation

Input: $P = (X_P, Y_P), Q = (X_Q, Y_Q)$
Output: $(R, R') = (P + Q, P')$

#	Operation		Comment
1	$T_1 = X_P - X_Q$	$T_2 = Y_Q - Y_P$	{mod sub}
2	$A = T_1^2$	$D = T_2^2$	{mod square}
3	$B = X_P A$	$C = X_Q A$	{mod mul}
4	$T_1 = B + C$		{mod add}
5	$X_R = D - T_1$	$T_3 = C - B$	{mod sub}
6	$T_1 = B - X_R$		{mod sub}
7	$T_1 = T_1 T_2$	$E = Y_P T_3$	{mod mul}
8	$Y_R = T_1 - E$		{mod sub}
9	**return** $((X_R, Y_R), (B, E))$		

Compared with the sequential implementation of Co-Z addition, the time complexity of parallel Co-Z addition is nearly halved, reducing from $4M + 2S + 7A$ to $2\ddot{M} + 1\ddot{S} + 5\ddot{A}$, where $\ddot{M}$, $\ddot{S}$, and $\ddot{A}$ represent bidirectional parallel modular multiplication, modular squaring, and modular addition/subtraction operations, respectively. The counts of modular multiplication and modular squaring are thus reduced by 50%. Additionally, the bidirectional parallel scheduling of the Co-Z conjugate addition lowers the time complexity from $5M + 3S + 11A$ to $3\ddot{M} + 1\ddot{S} + 6\ddot{A}$.

Algorithm 5 PCZ-ADDC: Parallel Co-Z Conjugate Addition Operation

Input: $P = (X_P, Y_P), Q = (X_Q, Y_Q), A' = (X_Q - X_P)^2, T' = (X_Q - X_P)A' = C' - B'$
Output: $(R, R') = (P + Q, P - Q)$

Operation		Comment
$C = X_Q A'$	$E = Y_P T'$	{mod mul}
$B = C - T'$	$T_1 = Y_Q - Y_P$	{mod sub}
$T_2 = B + C$	$T_3 = Y_P + Y_Q$	{mod add}
$D = T_1^2$	$F = T_3^2$	{mod square}
$X_R = D - T_2$	$X'_R = F - T_2$	{mod sub}
$T_2 = B - X_R$	$T_4 = X'_R - B$	{mod sub}
$T_2 = T_2 T_1$	$T_3 = T_3 T_4$	{mod mul}
$Y_R = T_2 - E$	$Y'_R = T_3 - E$	{mod sub}
return $((X_R, Y_R), (X'_R, Y'_R))$		

Analyzing the computational processes in Co-Z addition and Co-Z conjugate addition reveals a total time complexity of $9M + 5S + 18A$. Rivain [28] proposed an optimization scheme that replaces one multiplication with one squaring and four additions, reducing the Co-Z ladder algorithm's time complexity to $8M + 6S + 22A$. Since these operations are even-numbered in prime fields, theoretically, the lowest time complexity for a bidirectional parallel Co-Z ladder algorithm is $4\ddot{M} + 3\ddot{S} + 11\ddot{A}$. However, the total time complexity for sequential execution of Algorithms 4 and 5 is $5\ddot{M} + 2\ddot{S} + 11\ddot{A}$, which does not reach the theoretical minimum. Therefore, we merged Co-Z conjugate addition and Co-Z addition to achieve the lowest theoretical time complexity. Before entering the main loop, we precompute two large integers, $A' = (X_Q - X_P)^2$ and $T' = (X_Q - X_P)A'$, and repeatedly update them during the main loop. This significantly reorders the operations in the Co-Z ladder algorithm to reduce the parallelized algorithm's time complexity to $4\ddot{M} + 3\ddot{S} + 13\ddot{A}$, very close to the theoretical minimum, requiring only two additional modular addition operations. Detailed steps are in Algorithm 6. Except for the last two operations, all can be processed in parallel, making Algorithm 6 highly suitable for bidirectional parallel implementation. Compared with the sequential combined implementation of Co-Z conjugate addition and Co-Z addition with a time complexity of $5\ddot{M} + 2\ddot{S} + 11\ddot{A}$, our optimization reduces the Co-Z ladder algorithm's time complexity to the minimum. Our scheme replaces $1\ddot{M}$ with $1\ddot{S} + 2\ddot{A}$. By comparing the clock cycles of bidirectional parallel modular multiplication and squaring operations, our scheme effectively enhances the efficiency of the Co-Z ladder algorithm. The overall time complexity optimization effect of the improved algorithm is compared, as shown in Table 1.

Table 1. Improved time complexity of the parallel Co-Z algorithm.

Algorithm	Sequential Execution	Parallel Execution
Co-Z Addition	4M + 2S + 7A	$2\ddot{M} + 1\ddot{S} + 5\ddot{A}$
Co-Z Combined Addition	5M + 3S + 11A	$3\ddot{M} + 1\ddot{S} + 6\ddot{A}$
Sequential Execution	9M + 5S + 18A	$5\ddot{M} + 2\ddot{S} + 11\ddot{A}$
Precomputation A', T'	8M + 6S + 22A	$4\ddot{M} + 3\ddot{S} + 13\ddot{A}$

Algorithm 7 demonstrates the complete process of the Montgomery ladder algorithm based on parallel Co-Z operations. This algorithm initializes two elliptic curve points $(R_1, R_0) = (2P, P)$ using the INIT algorithm, making their Z coordinates equal, allowing them to use Co-Z operations.

Algorithm 6 PCZ-LADDER: Parallel Co-Z Ladder Algorithm

Input: $P = (X_P, Y_P) = R_a$, $Q = (X_Q, Y_Q) = R_{1-a}$, $A' = (X_Q - X_P)^2$, $T' = (X_Q - X_P)A' = C' - B'$, $a \in \{0, 1\}$, R_a, R_{1-a} are two Co-Z coordinates points updated in the Montgomery ladder algorithm.
Output: $(R_a, R_{1-a}) = (2R_a, R_a + R_{1-a})$ with updated $A' = (X_{R_a} - X_{R_{1-a}})^2$ and $T' = (X_{R_{1-a}} - X_{R_a})A'$

Operation		Comment
$C' = X_Q A'$	$E' = Y_P T'$	{mod mul}
$B' = C' - T'$	$T_1 = Y_Q - Y_P$	{mod sub}
$T_2 = B' + C'$	$T_3 = Y_P + Y_Q$	{mod add}
$D' = T_2^2$	$F' = T_3^2$	{mod square}
$X_R = D' - T_2$	$X'_R = F' - T_2$	{mod sub}
$T_2 = B' - X_R$	$T_4 = X'_R - B'$	{mod sub}
$T_2 = T_2 T_1$	$T_4 = T_3 T_4$	{mod mul}
$Y_R = T_2 - E'$	$Y'_R = T_4 - E'$	{mod sub}
$T_1 = X'_R - X_R$	$T_2 = Y'_R - Y_R$	{mod sub}
$A = T_1^2$	$D = T_2^2$	{mod square}
$X_P = B = X_R A$	$C = X'_R A$	{mod mul}
$T_3 = T_2 + B$	$T_4 = B + C$	{mod add}
$X_Q = D - T_4$	$T_1 = C - B$	{mod sub}
$T_4 = X_Q - X_P$	$T_3 = T_3 - X_Q$	{mod sub}
$A' = T_4^2$	$T_3 = T_3^2$	{mod square}
$T' = T_4 A'$	$X_P = E = Y_R T_1$	{mod mul}
$T_1 = D + A'$	$T_2 = E + E$	{mod add}
$T_3 = T_3 - T_1$		{mod sub}
$Y_Q = \frac{1}{2}(T_3 - T_2)$		{mod sub}
return $((X_Q, Y_Q), (X_P, Y_P))$		

Algorithm 7 Montgomery Ladder Algorithm Based on Co-Z Operation

Input: Elliptic curve point $P \neq \infty$, a scalar $k \in \mathbb{F}_p$, and $k_{n-1} = 1$.
Output: The result of the scalar multiplication $k \cdot P$.

$(R_1, R_0) = INIT(P)$
$A' = (X_0 - X_1)^2$, $T' = (X_0 - X_1)A'$
for i from $n - 2$ by 1 down to 0 **do**
    $a = (k_i + k_{i+1}) \mod 2$
    $(R_a, R_{1-a}, A', T') = PCZ - LADDER(R_a, R_{1-a}, A', T')$
end for
$a = (k_0 + k_1) \mod 2$
$(R_a, R_{1-a}) = PCZ - ADDC(R_a, R_{1-a}, A', T')$
$\frac{\lambda}{Z}$ = Final_Inv_Z(R_{1-a}, R_a, P, a)
$(R_0, R_1) = PCZ - ADD(R_0, R_1)$
return $((\frac{\lambda}{Z})^2 X_0, (\frac{\lambda}{Z})^3 Y_0)$

After initializing the elliptic curve points R_1 and R_0, we precompute the items $A' = (X_Q - X_P)^2$ and $T' = (X_Q - X_P)A'$ mentioned in the Co-Z ladder algorithm to adjust the calculation order in the main loop and reduce the time complexity. Entering the main loop of the Montgomery ladder algorithm, we replace the traditional trapezoidal algorithm $P_1 = 2P_1; P_2 = P_1 + P_2$ with the following equations:

$$(R_{1-a}, R_a) = (R_a + R_{1-a}, R_a - R_{1-a})$$
$$R_a = R_{1-a} + R_a$$

where $a = (\lceil k_i + k_{i+1} \rceil \mod 2)$. As shown in Algorithm 7, the Montgomery ladder algorithm based on parallel Co-Z operations executes one parallel Co-Z ladder algorithm per iteration, thus having a regular execution flow and fixed execution time. The precomputed items A' and T' are updated once in each iteration of the Co-Z ladder algorithm. After the main loop ends, we need to convert the elliptic curve points from Co-Z Jacobian projective coordinates back to affine coordinates. This process is achieved through the Final_Inv_Z algorithm, which computes $Z = X_P Y_{R_a}(X_{R_0} - X_{R_1})$ and $\lambda = y_P X_{R_a}$, and outputs $\frac{\lambda}{Z}$. The algorithm's time complexity is $1I + 3M + 1A$, requiring one inversion operation in the prime field.

5. Evaluation

This section presents performance data of our optimized implementation of the SM2 cryptographic algorithm. We evaluate execution time and throughput as key performance metrics, and compare our approach with other available schemes (e.g., the SM2 signature algorithm and ECDSA (secp256k1) based on OpenSSL 1.1.1). We selected OpenSSL 1.1.1 (LTS) as it is a widely used version that supports server security in many industrial applications, making our evaluation more representative. The test environment is shown below, as presented in Table 2.

Table 2. Comparison of experimental hardware configurations.

Processor	Frequency	Memory	Operating System	SIMD Support
quad-core ARM Cortex-A7	900 MHz	1 GB	Raspbian OS	NEON
4th gen Intel Core i5-4402EC	2.5 GHz	8 GB	Ubuntu 18.04 LTS	AVX2

We conducted tests on both processors using the standard SM2 algorithm, the optimized SM2 algorithm, and ECDSA for encryption, decryption, signing, and verification operations. Each operation was performed 3000 times, and the average time was recorded. The time statistics do not include hashing time, and the data length for encrypted messages was set to 1 KB. The experimental results are shown in Table 3.

Table 3. Performance comparison between SM2 and our SM2 on different processors.

Operation	Processor	SM2 (ms)	Our SM2 (ms)	Improvement (%)
Signing	ARM Cortex-A7	2045.8	1634.3	20.1%
	Intel Core i5	1010.3	701.2	30.6%
Verification	ARM Cortex-A7	2189.2	1780.6	18.7%
	Intel Core i5	1078.3	850.1	21.2%
Encryption	ARM Cortex-A7	4285.3	3352.4	21.8%
	Intel Core i5	1997.5	1348.1	32.5%
Decryption	ARM Cortex-A7	2324.7	1867.2	19.7%
	Intel Core i5	1140.8	854.2	25.1%

As shown in the data, the optimization scheme brings significant performance improvements on both Intel Core i5 and low-power ARM Cortex-A7 processors. The improvement is especially notable on the Intel Core i5 processor, which supports more advanced SIMD instruction sets (AVX2). On the ARM processor, despite limited SIMD support, the optimization still achieves approximately 20% performance gains in resource-constrained environments.

For the comparison with other schemes, we primarily used the Intel Core i5 processor for testing. This choice is based on the following considerations:

- Intel Core i5 processor supports a wider range of SIMD instructions, which better demonstrate the performance advantage of the optimization scheme.
- The computational capability of this processor is commonly found in edge devices for IoT, providing a certain level of representativeness.

Therefore, in the following comparative analysis, we mainly base our discussion on the test results of the Intel processor.

Utilizing precomputation techniques is an effective way to enhance the performance of SM2 algorithm implementation. Precomputation significantly improves program efficiency. Many protocols in the SM2 public key cryptosystem require repeated point multiplications of the base point "G". In our implementation, we precompute these multiples of the base point G and store them in the code, allowing for quick lookup and retrieval during runtime, as summarized in Table 4.

Table 4. SM2 base point calculation table.

i	j	**Storage Point**	i	j	**Storage Point**
0	1	$1G$	2	1	$2^{16}G$
0	2	$2G$	2	2	$2^{16} \times 2G$
...	...	...	...	...	...
0	255	$255G$	2	255	$2^{16} \times 255G$
1	1	2^8G	...	...	...
1	2	$2^8 \times 2G$	31	1	$2^{31}G$
...	...	...	...	...	...
1	255	$2^8 \times 255G$	31	255	$2^{31} \times 255G$

In the SM2 signature algorithm, it is necessary to calculate $s = \left((1 + d_A)^{-1} \cdot (k - r \cdot d_A)\right)$ mod n, where $(1 + d_A)^{-1}$ requires a modular inverse operation. To enhance efficiency when signing large numbers of data with a given key, the value of $(1 + d_A)^{-1}$ can be precomputed and subsequently utilized in each signing process.

Table 5 compares the number of operations required for point addition and point doubling in various coordinate systems. Here, I, M, and S denote modular inversion, modular multiplication, and modular squaring, respectively. It is evident that Jacobian coordinates offer superior performance compared with other methods. For point addition, the computation requires 12 modular multiplications and four modular squarings; similarly, for point doubling, the computation also requires 12 modular multiplications and four modular squarings.

Table 5. Comparison of point addition and doubling operations in different coordinate systems.

	Affine Coordinates	**Standard Projective Coordinates**	**Jacobian Coordinates**
Point Addition	$I + 2M + S$	$13M + 2S$	$12M + 4S$
Doubling	$I + 2M + 2S$	$8M + 5S$	$4M + 6S$

I: Modular inversion. Computationally expensive operation, especially in large field arithmetic.

M: Modular multiplication. Requires significant computational resources but fewer than modular inversion.

S: Modular squaring. Special case of modular multiplication, generally faster but still computationally significant.

Compared with the commonly used affine coordinates and standard projective coordinates, Jacobian coordinates eliminate the need for modular inversion operations. In affine coordinates, point addition requires one modular inversion, which is typically computationally intensive. However, Jacobian coordinates enable point addition and point doubling without any inversion operations, significantly improving computational efficiency. Moreover, Jacobian coordinates exhibit higher efficiency in point doubling operations due to fewer required multiplications and squarings. While standard projective coordinates also avoid modular inversion and allow for simpler mathematical representation, they generally incur higher arithmetic overhead. Additionally, Jacobian coordinates are highly compatible with Montgomery point multiplication, further enhancing computational efficiency.

5.1. Montgomery Modular Multiplication

For Montgomery modular multiplication, we optimized the classical Montgomery modular multiplication algorithm to better suit hardware implementations for large integer modular multiplication. This improved algorithm alternates between modular multiplication and modular reduction with a small bit-width, thereby enhancing computational efficiency. By reducing the multiplier's size, the new algorithm minimizes hardware resource usage, achieving efficient modular multiplication with low resource consumption. We performed comparative evaluations between the fast modular multiplication scheme based on the improved Montgomery algorithm and several other public algorithms. Given that modular multiplication accounts for approximately 70% of the computational overhead in the entire SM2 algorithm, we tested the runtime of the entire SM2 protocol using randomly generated public–private key pairs. The results are presented in Table 6.

Table 6. Performance test results of SM2 algorithm under different modular multiplication algorithms.

Modular Multiplication Algorithm	SM2 Signature Time (s)	SM2 Verification Time (s)	SM2 Encryption Time (s)	SM2 Decryption Time (s)
Montgomery Mult [10]	0.6528	1.2938	1.2763	0.6490
SOS [11]	0.2581	0.4988	0.5039	0.2182
FIOS [11]	0.3696	0.7224	0.7221	0.3671
Literature [29]	0.4129	0.8105	0.8070	0.4103
Literature [30]	0.2199	0.4220	0.4292	0.2182
This Work	0.2065	0.3951	0.4024	0.2045

5.2. Parallel Montgomery Ladder Algorithm

Table 7 presents the execution times for the sequential and parallel implementations of Co-Z addition, Co-Z conjugate addition, Co-Z ladder algorithm, and the Montgomery ladder algorithm based on Co-Z operations. Our parallel implementations significantly outperform the corresponding sequential implementations, with speedup ratios ranging from 1.26 to 1.60. Specifically, the bidirectional parallel implementation of the Montgomery ladder algorithm based on Co-Z operations achieves an execution time of 274,908 clock cycles, making it 1.31 times faster than its sequential counterpart.

Table 7. Comparison of clock cycles for sequential and parallel implementation of Co-Z operations and Montgomery ladder based on Co-Z operations.

Implementation Method	Co-Z Addition	Co-Z Diagonal Addition	Co-Z Ladder Algorithm	Montgomery Ladder Algorithm
Sequential Implementation	555	786	1,334	359,868
Parallel Implementation	439	489	1,001	274,908
Speedup Ratio	1.26	1.60	1.33	1.31

Table 8 compares the time complexity and clock cycles of the Montgomery ladder algorithm based on Co-Z operations on the SM2, Curve25519, and NIST P-256 curves. Since SM2 and Curve25519 utilize Co-Z coordinates, modular inversion is not required in scalar multiplication, significantly reducing computational complexity. Curve25519, as an efficient Montgomery curve, further optimizes performance by supporting operations with only the X coordinate. Additionally, the mathematical properties and precomputation requirements of each curve influence performance. SM2, based on the short Weierstrass form, requires additional coefficient calculations and affine transformations, while Curve25519, adopting the Montgomery form, simplifies computational complexity. Overall, Curve25519 demonstrates the best performance, while SM2 on this processor also performs within the expected range; in contrast, NIST P-256, without Co-Z optimization, shows higher clock cycle requirements. (In this context, "C" represents a single multiplication by a curve constant, which is typically much faster than a standard modular multiplication.)

Table 8. Comparison of time complexity and clock cycles for AVX2 implementation of Montgomery ladder based on Co-Z operations and other fixed-point multiplication algorithms.

Implementation Method	Time Complexity per Bit	Additional Time Complexity	Clock Cycles
SM2 (This Work)	$4\ddot{M} + 3\ddot{S} + 13\ddot{A}$	$I + 8M + 7S + 12A$	274,908 (CL)
Curve25519	$3\ddot{M} + 2\ddot{S} + 1\ddot{C} + 4\ddot{A}$	$I + 1M$	156,500 (H)
NIST P-256	n/a	n/a	312,000 (H)

5.3. Performance of Digital Signature Algorithm Implementations

In this section, we conduct comparative testing on the SM2 signature algorithm based on OpenSSL 1.1.1, ECDSA (secp256k1), work [30], work [31], and our implemented SM2 signature algorithm to evaluate the overall performance of the optimized SM2 cryptographic algorithm designed in this study. The time consumed by the hashing process in these signature algorithms is excluded from the time statistics. To minimize statistical errors, we performed 10 rounds of tests for each algorithm, with each round comprising 3000 signatures and verifications. In the final statistics, the maximum and minimum values from each round were discarded, and the average was calculated to obtain the final test results for 3000 signatures and verifications, as shown in Table 9.

In signature and verification operations, the time consumed by the hashing algorithm increases as the data size grows. As the number of data to be tested increases, the proportion of time spent on the hashing process in the overall signature and verification operations also gradually increases. Consequently, in cases with large data sizes, the total time for signature and verification is dominated by the hashing time. To eliminate the impact of SM3 and SHA256 on the test duration, we excluded the hashing process in this section's tests. The essence of a digital signature is to use a public-key cryptographic scheme to encrypt the hash value to obtain a data digest. Therefore, by excluding the hashing process, the tests effectively measure the encryption of the data digest directly. Furthermore, since both SM3 and SHA256 produce a fixed output length of 256 bits, the length of the data digest remains constant, indicating that the test results in this section are independent of the length of the data to be signed.

Table 9. Time consumption for 3000 signatures without hashing.

Time Consumption (ms)	SM2	Our SM2	ECDSA	Work [30]	Work [31]
Signature	1012.0	705.7	1087.2	802.5	827.9
Verification	1079.2	870.4	1207.3	902.3	944.8

The data from Table 9 allow us to derive a performance comparison chart for signature and verification, depicted in Figure 1. The horizontal axis indicates the time consumed for 3000 signatures or verifications by each algorithm, measured in milliseconds.

The data in Table 9 and Figure 1 show that our optimized SM2 implementation demonstrates superior performance in both signing and verification operations compared with other algorithms and implementations. For 3000 signature operations, our SM2 implementation requires 705.7 milliseconds, significantly less than the 1012.0 milliseconds for the standard SM2 and 1087.2 milliseconds for ECDSA, highlighting its higher signing efficiency. Similarly, for verification, our SM2 implementation achieves a time of 870.4 milliseconds, which is faster than both the standard SM2 at 1079.2 milliseconds and ECDSA at 1207.3 milliseconds. Compared with other works (work [30] and work [31]), our implementation consistently shows lower time consumption for both signing and verification. This improvement is particularly noticeable because the SM2 signing algorithm involves more point doubling operations on the base point "G" than the verification algorithm. By precomputing the base point "G", we achieve a more significant speedup in this aspect, resulting in a noticeable difference in the time required for signing and verification.

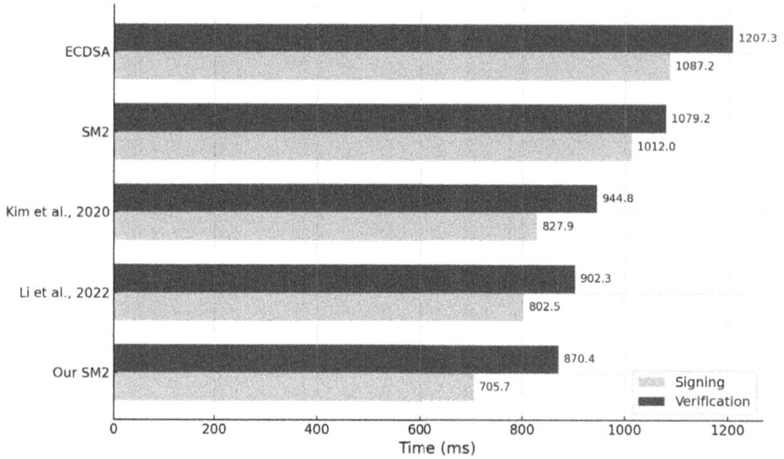

Figure 1. Performance comparison of SM2 digital signature implementations.

5.4. *Performance of SM2 Data Encryption Algorithm Implementation*

This section presents performance overhead tests for our implemented SM2 data encryption algorithm. We tested encryption on data sizes of 32 B, 64 B, 128 B, 256 B, 512 B, 1 KB, 2 KB, 4 KB, 8 KB, 16 KB, 32 KB, 64 KB, 128 KB, and 256 KB. For each data size, randomly generated data were used to eliminate potential biases.

The performance testing followed these steps: (1) randomly generate the test data; (2) encrypt and decrypt each group of test data 300 times, repeating this process 10 times; and (3) exclude the maximum and minimum values from each group's results and calculate the average to obtain the final test result for that data size.

For comparative purposes, we selected ECIES (secp256k1) as a reference algorithm in addition to our implemented SM2 data encryption algorithm. The SM3 algorithm was used as the hash function within the SM2 algorithm. The organized test results are presented in Tables 10 and 11.

Table 10. The duration of 300 encryption processes.

Time/ms	SM2 use SM3	Our SM2 Use SM3	ECIES secp256k1
32 B	181.0	104.3	249.1
64 B	181.6	104.5	254.4
128 B	183.6	103.9	260.0
256 B	187.3	109.1	267.4
512 B	194.8	116.7	278.6
1 KB	210.3	131.5	295.1
2 KB	239.5	166.8	324.2
4 KB	298.1	207.6	378.6
8 KB	415.4	320.1	483.4
16 KB	647.4	549.2	693.4
32 KB	1113.4	1021.2	1116.2
64 KB	2054.0	1912.6	1976.9
128 KB	3969.7	3847.3	3938.0
256 KB	7784.4	7654.8	7644.2

Table 11. The duration of 300 decryption processes.

Time/ms	SM2 Use SM3	Our SM2 Use SM3	ECIES secp256k1
32 B	97.4	73.2	116.2
64 B	98.3	73.9	124.3
128 B	99.5	74.8	130.8
256 B	100.7	75.7	138.7
512 B	104.9	78.8	145.2
1 KB	113.5	85.3	159.3
2 KB	129.2	97.1	185.2
4 KB	159.8	120.0	206.6
8 KB	222.9	167.3	308.5
16 KB	347.4	260.7	387.2
32 KB	556.6	447.6	541.0
64 KB	994.4	821.0	849.5
128 KB	1704.3	1578.4	1528.0
256 KB	3546.9	3165.3	3061.6

From Figures 2 and 3, it is clear that our implemented SM2 data encryption algorithm improves encryption and decryption speeds compared with the original implementation. The time overhead for the signing and verification process is reduced by approximately 20% compared with the existing OpenSSL implementation, while the time overhead for data encryption and decryption is reduced by about 25% for smaller data sizes. The proportion of overhead from the hash function in the data encryption algorithm increases with the size of the data to be encrypted, and the time consumption of the encryption algorithms using the same hash function tends to converge as data size increases.

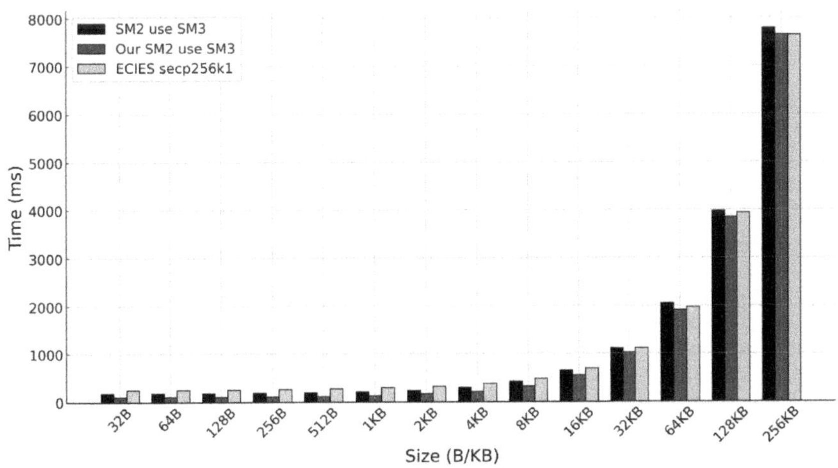

Figure 2. The duration of 300 encryption processes.

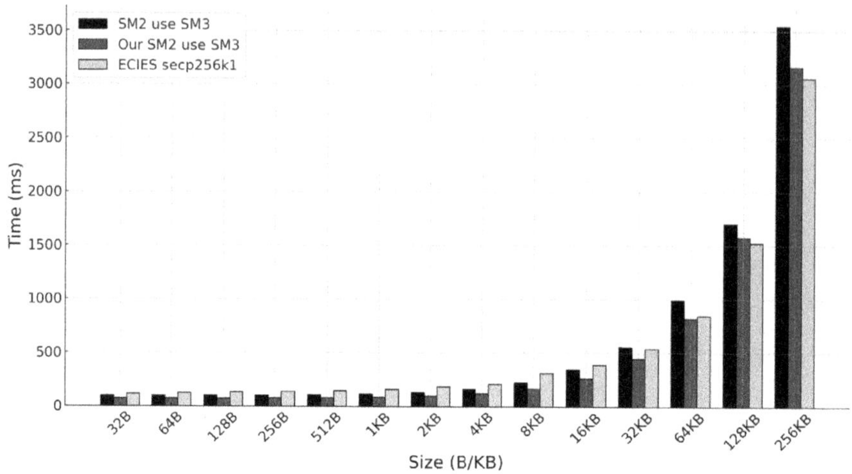

Figure 3. The duration of 300 decryption processes.

6. Discussion

Although our work has achieved significant improvements in the computational efficiency of the SM2 algorithm, several limitations remain.

First, while the proposed optimizations effectively reduce execution time, additional factors, such as power consumption and memory requirements, also influence the adoption of the algorithm in real-world IoT devices. Experimental results show that memory usage remains largely unchanged, as the reduction in computational redundancy is counterbalanced by the increased demand from SIMD parallel instruction sets. However, the parallelism achieved through SIMD instructions may lead to higher power consumption during cryptographic operations, which is a critical concern for resource-constrained IoT environments. Balancing execution speed, power consumption, and memory usage will be a focus of future research. For example, exploring low-power architectures and optimizing instruction-level parallelism could mitigate the increased energy demands, while adaptive strategies that adjust computational methods dynamically based on device contexts may further enhance practical applicability.

Second, although resilience to side-channel attacks is a critical consideration for cryptographic algorithms, especially in IoT devices, this study primarily focuses on optimizing computational efficiency through software-level improvements. Techniques such as constant-time algorithms, scalar randomization, and secure memory access are commonly used to address side-channel vulnerabilities [31–34]. However, integrating such countermeasures typically involves trade-offs between security and performance, which were beyond the scope of this work. Future studies will explore software-based strategies to enhance side-channel attack resistance, such as algorithmic masking and timing attack mitigations, aiming to improve the security of the optimized SM2 algorithm without significantly compromising its performance gains.

In the future, we aim to investigate solutions that simultaneously address the above limitations. By integrating power-efficient optimizations and side-channel countermeasures, the proposed algorithm can be further refined to meet the stringent requirements of IoT applications, ensuring both high performance and robust security.

7. Conclusions

With the ongoing increase in computational power, traditional ECC algorithms are encountering performance bottlenecks. To address these issues, we optimized elliptic curve group computation by introducing a cross Montgomery modular multiplication algorithm based on polynomial expansion and leveraging SIMD technology to accelerate the Montgomery ladder algorithm using Co-Z operations. This approach enhances ECC performance and bolsters information security. By segmenting large integer operations into polynomials, we perform modular multiplication and reduction simultaneously, reducing storage demands and streamlining the Montgomery multiplication process. The incorporation of SIMD technology enables parallel processing, significantly boosting computational efficiency through optimized instruction scheduling and loop unrolling, which minimizes control overhead and enhances micro-level execution. Our results show that the optimized SM2 digital signature algorithm reduces computation time by approximately 20%, while the SM2 data encryption algorithm achieves a 25% performance improvement in encryption and decryption times for smaller data sizes. These optimizations advance ECC performance and provide strong support for information security.

Author Contributions: Conceptualization, H.Z. and Y.S. (Yubo Song); methodology, H.Z. and Y.S. (Yubo Song); software, H.Z. and D.L.; validation, H.Z. and Y.S. (Yizhen Sun); investigation, Y.S. (Yizhen Sun); formal analysis, H.Z.; data curation, Y.S. (Yizhen Sun); resources, H.Z.; writing—original draft, H.Z. and D.L.; writing—review and editing, Q.C.; visualization, D.L. and Q.C.; supervision, H.Z. and Q.C.; project administration, H.Z. and Z.T.; funding acquisition, Z.T. All authors have read and agreed to the published version of the manuscript.

Funding: This work is supported by State Grid Electric Power Co., Ltd. research project No. 5700-202323607A-3-2-ZN and Hunan Key Laboratory for Internet of Things in Electricity, P.R.China No. 2019TP1016.

Data Availability Statement: The data used in this study were randomly generated fixed-size text files, which were used solely for testing the performance of the optimized SM2 algorithm. As these datasets do not have intrinsic research value, they have not been publicly archived.

Conflicts of Interest: Authors Hongyu Zhu, Yizhen Sun, and Zheng Tian were employed by the State Grid Hunan Electric Power Company Limited Information and Communication Company, Qian Chen was employed by State Grid Hunan Electric Power Co., Ltd. The remaining authors declare that the research was conducted in the absence.

References

1. Rivest, R.L.; Shamir, A.; Adleman, L. A method for obtaining digital signatures and public-key cryptosystems. *Commun. ACM* **1978**, *21*, 120–126. [CrossRef]
2. Fagoyinbo, J.B. *The Armed Forces: Instrument of Peace, Strength, Development and Prosperity*; Author House: Bloomington, IN, USA, 2013.
3. Nakamoto, S. Bitcoin: A Peer-to-Peer Electronic Cash System. *Satoshi Nakamoto* 2008. Available online: https://static.upbitcare.com/931b8bfc-f0e0-4588-be6e-b98a27991df1.pdf (accessed on 18 November 2024).
4. Hisil, H.; Egrice, B.; Yassi, M. Fast 4 Way Vectorized Ladder for the Complete Set of Montgomery Curves. *IACR Cryptology ePrint Archive* **2020**, 2020/388. Available online: https://eprint.iacr.org/2020/388.pdf (accessed on 11 June 2024).
5. Perlroth, N. Government announces steps to restore confidence on encryption standards. *The New York Times*, 11 September 2013.
6. Barker, E.B.; Kelsey, J.M. *Recommendation for Random Number Generation Using Deterministic Random Bit Generators (Revised)*; US Department of Commerce, Technology Administration, National Institute of Standards and Technology, Computer Security Division, Information Technology Laboratory: Washington, DC, USA, 2007.
7. Li, M.; Li, N.; Liu, H.; Cheng, S.; Hu, X.; Li, J. Implementation of a Safe and Efficient Point Multiplication for SM2 Algorithm. In Proceedings of the 2023 IEEE 6th Information Technology, Networking, Electronic and Automation Control Conference (ITNEC), Chongqing, China, 24–26 February 2023; pp. 137–141. [CrossRef]
8. Liu, D.; Yuan, Y.; Xue, T.; Chen, L. An Efficient Batch Verification Scheme for SM2 Signatures. In Proceedings of the 2021 8th International Conference on Dependable Systems and Their Applications (DSA), Yinchuan, China, 5–6 August 2021; pp. 208–212. [CrossRef]
9. Chinbat, M.; Wu, L.; Batsukh, A.; Khuchit, U.; Zhang, X.; Mongolyn, B.; Xu, K.; Yang, W. Performance Comparison of Finite Field Multipliers for SM2 Algorithm based on FPGA Implementation. In Proceedings of the 2020 IEEE 14th International Conference on Anti-counterfeiting, Security, and Identification (ASID), Xiamen, China, 30 October–1 November 2020; pp. 69–72. [CrossRef]
10. Montgomery, P.L. Modular multiplication without trial division. *Math. Comput.* **1985**, *44*, 519–521. [CrossRef]
11. Koc, C.; Acar, T.; Bailey, R., Jr. Analyzing and comparing Montgomery multiplication algorithms. *IEEE Micro* **1996**, *16*, 26–33. [CrossRef]
12. Montgomery, P.L. Speeding the Pollard and elliptic curve methods of factorization. *Math. Comput.* **1987**, *48*, 243–264. [CrossRef]

13. López, J.; Dahab, R. Fast multiplication on elliptic curves over GF(2m) without precomputation. In Proceedings of the International Workshop on Cryptographic Hardware and Embedded Systems, Berlin, Germany, 12–15 August 1999; Springer: Berlin/Heidelberg, Germany, 1999; pp. 316–327.
14. Longa, P.; Gebotys, C. Efficient techniques for high-speed elliptic curve cryptography. In Proceedings of the International Workshop on Cryptographic Hardware and Embedded Systems, Berlin, Germany, 17–20 August 2010; Springer: Berlin/Heidelberg, Germany, 2010; pp. 80–94.
15. Zhang, X.C.; Guo, H.; Zhang, X.Y.; Wang, C.; Liu, J. Fast Software Implementation of SM4. *J. Cryptologic Res.* **2020**, *7*, 799–811. [CrossRef]
16. Zhang, Y.P.; Gao, Y.; Yan, Y.; Liu, X. Fast Software Implementation of ZUC Algorithm. *J. Cryptologic Res.* **2021**, *8*, 388–401. .
17. Nath, K.; Sarkar, P. Efficient 4-way vectorizations of the Montgomery ladder. *IEEE Trans. Comput.* **2022**, *71*, 712–723. [CrossRef]
18. Cheng, H.; Großschädl, J.; Tian, J.Q.; Rønne, P.B.; Ryan, P.Y. High-Throughput Elliptic Curve Cryptography Using AVX2 Vector Instructions. In *Selected Areas in Cryptography—SAC 2020*; Springer: Cham, Switzerland, 2021; pp. 698–719._27. [CrossRef]
19. Huang, J.H.; Liu, Z.; Hu, Z.; Großschädl, J. Parallel Implementation of SM2 Elliptic Curve Cryptography on Intel Processors with AVX2. In *Australasian Conference on Information Security and Privacy*; Springer: Cham, Switzerland, 2020; pp. 204–224._11. [CrossRef]
20. Gueron, S.; Krasnov, V. Fast Prime Field Elliptic-Curve Cryptography with 256-Bit Primes. *J. Cryptogr. Eng.* **2015**, *5*, 141–151. [CrossRef]
21. Bernstein, D.J.; Duif, N.; Lange, T.; Schwabe, P.; Yang, B.Y. High-Speed High-Security Signatures. *J. Cryptogr. Eng.* **2012**, *2*, 77–89. [CrossRef]
22. Faz-Hernández, A.; López, J.; Dahab, R. High-Performance Implementation of Elliptic Curve Cryptography Using Vector Instructions. *ACM Trans. Math. Softw.* **2019**, *45*, 1–35. [CrossRef]
23. Chen, F.; Liu, Y.; Zhang, T.; Xu, Y.; Huang, Z. SM2-based low-cost and efficient parallel modular multiplication. *Microprocess Microsyst.* **2022**, *94*, 104650. [CrossRef]
24. Wang, D.; Lin, Y.; Hu, J.; Li, J.; Wang, Z. FPGA Implementation for Elliptic Curve Cryptography Algorithm and Circuit with High Efficiency and Low Delay for IoT Applications. *Micromachines* **2023**, *14*, 1037. [CrossRef] [PubMed]
25. Li, X.; Yu, W.; Li, B. Parallel and Regular Algorithm of Elliptic Curve Scalar Multiplication over Binary Fields. *Secur. Commun. Netw.* **2020**, *2020*, 4087873 . [CrossRef]
26. Mai, L.; Yan, Y.; Jia, S.; Liao, X.; Liu, X. Accelerating SM2 digital signature algorithm using modern processor features. In Proceedings of the International Conference on Information and Communications Security, Cham, Switzerland, 19–22 November 2019; Springer: Cham, Switzerland, 2019; pp. 430–446.
27. Hu, X.; Zheng, X.; Zhang, S.; Chen, S.; Shi, Y. A high-performance elliptic curve cryptographic processor of SM2 over GF(p). *Electronics* **2019**, *8*, 431. [CrossRef]
28. Rivain, M. Fast and Regular Algorithms for Scalar Multiplication over Elliptic Curves. *IACR Cryptol. ePrint Arch.* **2011**, 2011/338. Available online: https://eprint.iacr.org/2011/338 (accessed on 11 June 2024).
29. Yan, M. Fast implementation and optimization of SM2 digital signature and verification algorithm based on GPU. Ph.D. Thesis, Shanghai Jiaotong University, Shanghai, China, 2020.
30. Li, B.; Zhou, Q.L.; Chen, X.J.; Wu, L.; Zhang, Y. Optimization of reconfigurable SM2 algorithm over prime field. *J. Commun.* **2022**, *43*, 30–41.
31. Kim, K.H.; Choe, J.; Kim, S.Y.; Kim, N.; Hong, S. Speeding up regular elliptic curve scalar multiplication without precomputation. *Adv. Math. Commun.* **2020**, *14*, 703 [CrossRef]
32. Das, D.; Nath, M.; Chatterjee, B.; Ghosh, S.; Sen, S. STELLAR: A generic EM side-channel attack protection through ground-up root-cause analysis. In Proceedings of the 2019 IEEE International Symposium on Hardware Oriented Security and Trust (HOST), McLean, VA, USA, 5–10 May 2019; pp. 11–20.
33. Das, D.; Danial, J.; Golder, A.; Ghosh, S.; Sen, S. EM and power SCA-resilient AES-256 through> 350× current-domain signature attenuation and local lower metal routing. *IEEE J. Solid-State Circuits* **2020**, *56*, 136–150. [CrossRef]
34. Das, D.; Maity, S.; Nasir, S.B.; Ghosh, S.; Raychowdhury, A.; Sen, S. High efficiency power side-channel attack immunity using noise injection in attenuated signature domain. In Proceedings of the 2017 IEEE International Symposium on Hardware Oriented Security and Trust (HOST), Mclean, VA, USA, 1–5 May 2017; pp. 62–67.

electronics

MDPI

Article

Distributed Semi-Supervised Partial Multi-Label Learning over Networks

Zhen Xu [1,2,†] **and Weibin Chen** [2,3,*,†]

1 College of Computer Science and Artificial Intelligence, Wenzhou University, Wenzhou 325006, China; 20200588@wzu.edu.cn
2 The Metaverse and Artificial Intelligence Institute of Wenzhou University, Wenzhou University, Wenzhou 325006, China
3 Center for Applied Mathematics of Jiangsu Province, Nanjing University of Information Science and Technology, Nanjing 210044, China
* Correspondence: sun@wzu.edu.cn
† These authors contributed equally to this work.

Abstract: Inthis paper, a distributed semi-supervised partial multi-label learning (dS^{2}PML) algorithm is proposed, which can be used to address the problem of distributed classification of partially multi-labeled data and unlabeled data. In this algorithm, we utilize the multi-kernel function together with the label correlation term to construct the discriminant function. In addition, to obtain a decentralized implementation, we design a reconstructed error on the labeling confidence based on globally common basic data that are selected by a distributed strategy. By exploiting the similarity structure among feature and label spaces under the sparsity constraint, the labeling confidences of partially multi-labeled and unlabeled data are estimated in a decentralized manner. Meanwhile, by using the sparse random feature map to approximate the kernel feature map, the multi-label classifier can be trained under the supervision of the estimated labeling confidence. Experiments on multiple real datasets are conducted to evaluate the learning performance of the proposed approach. According to the experimental results, the average ranks of all the comparison algorithms evaluated on five evaluation metrics are computed. The ranking results show that the average ranks of our algorithm in terms of hamming loss, one error, average precision, ranking loss, and coverage are 3.16, 2.27, 2.15, 2.38, and 2.18, respectively. The average ranks of the dS^{2}PML are second only to the corresponding centralized S^{2}PML (cS^{2}PML) algorithms and higher than other existing comparison algorithms in five evaluation metrics. The average rank differences in terms of Hamming loss, one error, average precision, ranking loss, and coverage between our proposed algorithm and the closest comparison algorithm are 0.28, 1.67, 1.80, 1.15, and 1.62, respectively. Additionally, owing to the distributed storage and decentralized processing of training data, our proposed dS^{2}PML algorithm reduces CPU time by more than 65% and memory consumption by more than 6% compared to the centralized comparison algorithms. The experimental results indicate that our proposed algorithm outperforms the other state-of-the-art algorithms in classification accuracy, CPU time, and memory consumption.

Keywords: distributed processing; semi-supervised partial multi-label learning; multi-kernel function; label correlation

1. Introduction

Multi-label learning (MLL) is a crucial learning paradigm. It can be used to handle the scenario where each training data sample is simultaneously associated with multiple valid labels. In recent years, many MLL algorithms have been developed [1–9] and successfully utilized in the areas of text categorization [1,6], image annotation [2], and computer vision [3]. For these previous multi-label learning studies, a fundamental assumption is that each training data sample is precisely annotated with all of its relevant labels [1–3].

However, in many real-world applications, collecting a large number of precisely annotated training data is a time-consuming and costly process. Instead, it is more common that only data samples with ambiguity-supervised information can be obtained, where each training data sample is allocated with a set of candidate labels, of which only a portion are correct.

To handle such a learning scenario, a novel learning framework, called partial multi-label learning (PML), has been formulated, and a series of PML methods have been presented [10–17]. Among them, an easy and straightforward solution for handling the partially multi-labeled data is to completely ignore the detrimental impact brought by noisy labels, and directly exploit the current MLL algorithms (ML-*k*NN and Binary Relevance) to induce the predictor model [12,14]. However, the hidden noisy labels cannot be properly treated, which may result in unsatisfactory performance. Another major strategy proposes to use iterative approaches to estimate the confidence of each candidate label [13,15,16] and then train the predictor by exploiting the supervised information from the labels with high confidences. In [11], an approach, namely PARVLS, has been developed to elicit credible labels from the candidate label set via label propagation and induce the predictive model under the supervision of credible labels. Extensive experiments in [11,13,15,16] have shown that the accuracy of classification can be improved to some extent by eliminating the effect of the labels with low confidence during the training of the predictive model.

Nevertheless, there are two potential limitations to most of the previous works on PML. Firstly, typical PML methods suppose that the candidate labels are accessible for the whole training data [11,13,15,16]. But, in many real-world situations, this assumption hardly holds due to the high cost and difficulty in collecting a large-size partially labeled dataset. Instead, obtaining a lot of unlabeled data without any supervised information is relatively easy and/or cheap [18,19]. When it is difficult to learn effective models based only on a limited number of labeled data, it becomes crucial to extract valuable information from both partially labeled and unlabeled data. So, the first limitation of the above PML methods is that they fail to utilize vast amounts of unlabeled data.

Secondly, it is easy to notice that these PML methods only concentrate on centralized learning, which requires all the training data must be centrally stored and processed at a single fusion center. However, in many real applications, as shown in Figure 1, a large amount of training data are usually collected/stored across multiple nodes [20–24]. In such a scenario, due to the privacy protection of training data, the load of the communication infrastructure, and the restricted compute capability of one node, it is infeasible to transmit all the data samples into the fusion center for centralized processing. So, developing a distributed S^{2}PML (dS^{2}PML), which induces the global-like multi-label classifier at each individual node by transmitting only a few parameters among neighbors, is preferred.

In this paper, jointly taking distributed learning, semi-supervised learning and PML into account, we develop a dS^{2}PML algorithm. For clarity, a brief flowchart of the dS^{2}PML algorithm is illustrated in Figure 1.

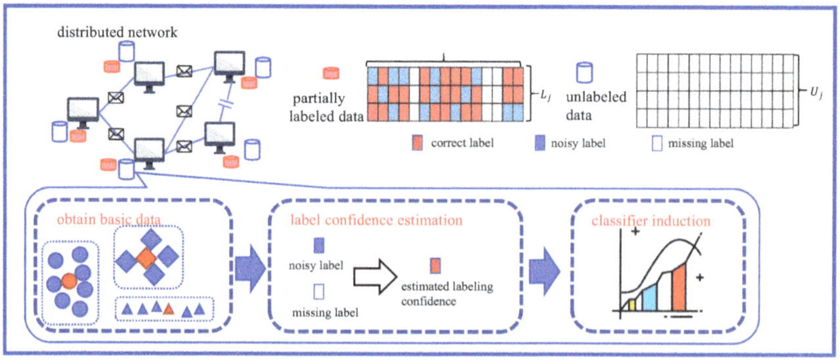

Figure 1. An example of the distributed network and flowchart of the proposed dS^{2}PML algorithm.

The main contributions of this paper are summarized as follows:

1. We use the multi-kernel function and the label correlation term to construct the discriminant function in order to achieve non-linear classification and effectively exploit the label correlation.
2. We design a reconstructed error on the labeling confidence based on globally common basic data that are selected using a distributed strategy. Based on the proposed reconstructed error term, we achieve the decentralization of the global objective function. Then, by exploiting the similarity structure among feature and label spaces, the labeling confidence of partially labeled data and unlabeled can be distributively learned. Meanwhile, the l_0-norm constraint is integrated into the objective function to ensure the sparsity of the labeling confidence vector, so that the negative effect of incredible labels with low confidence can be effectively eliminated.
3. The dS^{2}PML algorithm is proposed, which is used for solving the distributed semi-supervised PML problem. In this algorithm, the kernel feature map of the multi-kernel function is approximated by the sparse random feature map, so that the multi-label classifier can be adaptively learned under the supervision of the estimated labeling confidence.
4. The complexity of the proposed algorithm is analyzed in theory.

2. Related Work

There exist four related machine learning paradigms related to dS^{2}PML, that is, MLL [1–6], semi-supervised learning [7–9], distributed processing [21,25,26], and partial label learning [27–29].

MLL is a crucial learning paradigm designed to handle scenarios in which each training data sample is simultaneously associated with multiple valid labels without any ambiguity. There are three main types of strategies for handling label correlation. The first-order methods [4] treat each class label independently, and completely disregard the label correlation among labels. The second-order approaches exploit the correlation of a pair of labels to boost the learning performance [6]. High-order approaches take the label correlations among some or all of the class labels into account [5].

Semi-supervised learning develops the predictive model using a training dataset that includes a limited quantity of labeled data and a substantial number of unlabeled data [7–9]. Based on the commonly used smoothness assumption in semi-supervised learning methods [18], plenty of unlabeled data can be used to exactly characterize the distribution of the whole dataset, which is helpful to improve the learning performance. Lately, some attempts have been made to address the problem of semi-supervised MLL. In the literature [7], a semi-supervised MLL approach has been presented to handle semi-supervised multi-label learning issues by utilizing the similarity of instances on labeled and unlabeled data using weighted graphs. In [8], the authors propose to incorporate the principles of co-training and manifold learning to exploit label correlation among multiple labels. In [9], a new methodology is provided that takes label and instance correlations into account to recover missing labels and makes use of a huge quantity of unlabeled data to boost classification performance.

Distributed learning aims to induce the predictor model based on the supervision information provided by their own local data and exchanged from one-hop neighbors. Owing to its commendable learning efficacy and flexibility to node and/or link failures, distributed learning has been extensively utilized across various domains, including fault diagnosis [20], Internet of Things [30], environmental supervision [31], and machine learning [21,23] etc. Recently, there have been a few attempts made to extend the MLL into a distributed environment. In [21], two distributed information-theoretic semi-supervised multi-label learning algorithms are proposed, which employ a distributed matrix completion algorithm to distributively exploit the label correlation among label spaces. In [25], a distributed MLL is proposed to leverage federated learning principles to address MLL problem. In [26], a distributed ensemble MLL method is proposed to utilize a heterogeneous ensemble model for handling large-scale datasets. Nevertheless, neither semi-supervised MLL nor distributed MLL can directly solve the problem concerned in this study, since they assume that the labeled training data are only associated with the ground truth labels.

Partial label learning is used to deal with the problem that the training data is annotated with a group of candidate labels, but only one is correct. Among the existing partial single-label learning methods, the key is to disambiguate the candidate labels via average-based strategies [24,28,29] or identification-based strategies [27]. The former ones treat all the candidate labels equally initially, and determine the candidate labels with the highest confidence as the unique ground-truth label. The latter ones treat the unique ground-truth label as a hidden variable, and then optimize the objective function by aggregating the model outputs. Among these above disambiguation strategies, an implicit assumption is that there is only one ground-truth label among the candidate labels. But, for PML, more than one label within candidate labels is the ground-truth label, and thus, the disambiguation strategy cannot be directly applied to labeling confidence estimation.

Consequently, some solutions have been specially developed to address the problem of PML recently. In [13], authors consider all the candidate labels to be the correct ones, and then utilize some off-the-shelf methods to alternatively estimate the labeling confidence for classifier induction. In [14], a PML approach has been proposed to simultaneously identify the noisy labels and learn a multi-label classifier based on the observed label matrix. In [11], a two-stage PML approach is suggested to determine credible labels based on the estimated labeling confidence of the candidate label. Subsequently, a multi-label predictor is induced based on credible labels. In [17], the error-correcting output code is employed to convert the PML learning problem into multiple binary learning problems for further processing, thereby avoiding the process of estimating labeling confidence for each candidate label. In [16], a granular ball-based PML method is developed to jointly seek feature selection and classifier induction. Despite the advances made by these approaches, one possible limitation is that they are not considered to learn from unlabeled data, which is inapplicable to the problem concerned in this study.

To simultaneously handle partially multi-labeled and unlabeled data, lately, a novel S^2PML algorithm has been proposed in [18]. This algorithm estimates the labeling confidence by leveraging the similarity structure in a low-dimensional embedding space, and then guides the induction of a multi-label predictor using the estimated labels propagated from labeled data. Lately, a novel SSPML [19] has been proposed to link the spaces of features and labels for co-training, and construct an embedded subspace to estimate the label variables of partially labeled data and unlabeled data. Nevertheless, there are two potential limitations to the previous studies on S^2PML. Firstly, the classification efficacy of the aforementioned methods heavily depends upon the accuracy of the label propagation. When data distribution is imbalanced, label propagation becomes inefficient, potentially impairing classification performance. Secondly, these S^2PML approaches necessitate extensive high-dimensional matrix multiplication and inversion calculations during the training process, making them unsuitable for large-scale data sets.

3. Distributed S^2PML Algorithm

The issue of the distributed classification of partially multi-labeled and unlabeled data over a network is formulated, and then, a dS^2PML algorithm is proposed in this section. The diagram of the procedure for the proposed dS^2PML algorithm is schematically illustrated in Figure 2.

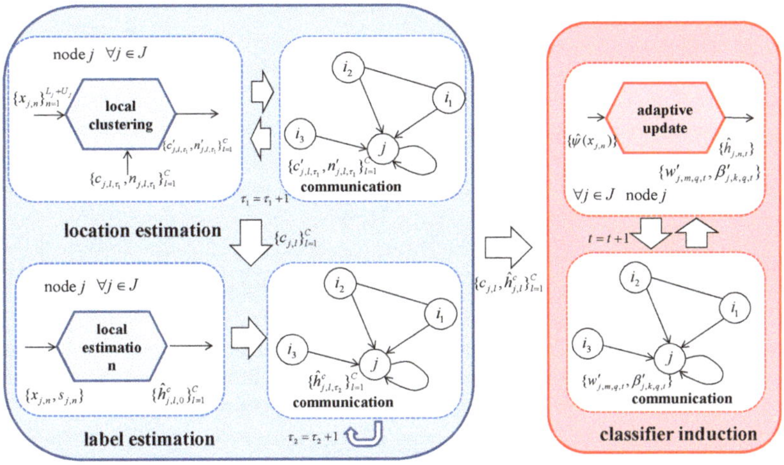

Figure 2. Diagram of the procedure of proposed dS^{2}PML algorithm.

3.1. Problem Formulation

In this paper, we focus on a connected network consisting of J nodes distributed across a geographical region. Without sacrificing any generality, we present this network as a connected graph $\mathcal{G} = (\mathcal{J}, \mathcal{E})$, which includes the set of nodes $\mathcal{J}$ and the set of edges $\mathcal{E}$. To carry out the following diffusion cooperative strategy, we let $\mathcal{B}_j$ denote the set of neighbors of node j, including itself. At each node j, the local training data consists of $L_j + U_j$ data, including L_j partially multi-labeled data $\mathcal{X}^l = \{\boldsymbol{x}_{j,n}, \boldsymbol{s}_{j,n}\}_{n=1}^{L_j}$ and U_j unlabeled data $\mathcal{X}^u = \{\boldsymbol{x}_{j,n}\}_{n=L_j+1}^{L_j+U_j}$. For the whole network, there exist a total L partially multi-labeled data $(L = \sum_{j=1}^{J} L_j)$ and U unlabeled data $(U = \sum_{j=1}^{J} U_j)$. Here, $\boldsymbol{x}_{j,n} \in \mathcal{X}^d$ denotes the input vector, and $\boldsymbol{s}_{j,n} = [s_{j,n,1}, \ldots, s_{j,n,Q}]^T \in \{0,1\}^Q$ denotes the candidate label vector composed of Q class labels. In this setting, $s_{j,n,q} = 1$ if the q-th label is the candidate label of the n-th sample at node j, and 0 otherwise. Only some of the candidate labels in $\boldsymbol{s}_{j,n}$ are the ground-truth ones, while the others are irrelevant for $\boldsymbol{x}_{j,n}$. The objective of each node j is to seek the Q optimal discriminant functions for all the class labels based on the information exploited by the local data and exchanged from one-hop neighbors $\mathcal{B}_j$.

3.2. Design of Global Objective Function

Assuming that the considered PML problem is non-linear, without loss of generality, the discriminant function should be formulated as the linear combination of a series of kernel functions associated with the whole dataset. However, the traditional kernel function relies on a properly preselected kernel width, which requires a lot of background knowledge. In order to overcome this constraint, the multi-kernel function [32,33], which can select multiple kernels with different kernel widths from the prescribed dictionary, is used to construct the discriminant function $f_q(\boldsymbol{x}_n)$ with respect to (w.r.t.) the q-th label as follows:

$$f_q(\boldsymbol{x}_n) = \left\{ \sum_{v} \sum_{m=1}^{P} \eta_{m,v,q} k_m(\boldsymbol{x}_v, \boldsymbol{x}_n) \right\}, \tag{1}$$

where $k_m(\cdot,\cdot)$ denotes a basis kernel function determined by the inner product of two data vectors. Here, a series of kernel functions with different kernel widths are chosen in advance, and then adaptively combined with the weight coefficient $\eta_{m,v,q}$. Let $\phi_m(\cdot)$

be the m-th non-linear kernel feature map, we have $k_m(x_v, x_n) = < \phi_m(x_v), \phi_m(x_n) >$. Furthermore, the discriminant function $f_q(x_n)$ becomes

$$f_q(x_n) = \left\{ \sum_{m=1}^{P} w_{m,q}^T \cdot \phi_m(x_n) \right\}, \tag{2}$$

where the weight vector is a linear combination of the weight coefficient $\eta_{m,v,q}$ and the kernel feature map $\phi_m(x_v)$, i.e., $w_{m,q} = \sum_v \eta_{m,v,q}\phi_m(x_v)$.

However, the weight vector is comprised of a series of infinite-dimensional kernel feature maps, which can not be explicitly expressed. Additionally, the computation of the kernel matrix quadratically grows as the number of data increases, which brings a heavy burden to the computation system.

To explicitly express the model parameter and reduce the computation burden, the finite-dimensional random feature map $\hat{\phi}(\cdot)$ is adopted to replace the original kernel feature map $\phi(\cdot)$, so that the m-th basis kernel function can be approximated by [33–35]

$$k_m(x_v, x_n) \approx < \hat{\phi}_m(x_v), \hat{\phi}_m(x_n) > . \tag{3}$$

In this paper, a well-known kernel, namely, the Gaussian kernel with multiple kernel bandwidths, is focused on. Correspondingly, the z-th dimension of the approximated random feature map of the m-th basis kernel function can be defined as [33–35]

$$[\hat{\phi}_m(x_n)]_z = \begin{cases} \frac{1}{\sqrt{D}} \cos(\omega_{m,\frac{z+1}{2}}^T \cdot x_n), & 0 < z < D, \quad \text{odd}, \\ \frac{1}{\sqrt{D}} \sin(\omega_{m,\frac{z}{2}}^T \cdot x_n), & 0 < z < D, \quad \text{even}, \end{cases} \tag{4}$$

where $\omega_{m,z}$ is obtained by randomly sampling the probability distribution $\mathbf{p}(\omega_m) = (2\pi)^{(D/2)} \exp(-||\omega_m||_2^2/2)$.

To achieve good learning performance, a large-dimensional random feature map (a large D) can be expected, which implies high computational complexity. To address this issue, the sparse random projection [36] is utilized to make a balance between the learning performance and the complexity of communication. Let s be the dimension reduction ratio; the sparse random projection matrix $R \in \mathbb{R}^{\lfloor D/s \rfloor \times D}$ can be obtained with its nl-th element

$$R_{nl} = \sqrt{s} \begin{cases} +1, & \text{with probability } \frac{1}{2s}, \\ 0, & \text{with probability } 1 - \frac{1}{s}, \\ -1, & \text{with probability } \frac{1}{2s}, \end{cases}$$

where $\lfloor \cdot \rfloor$ denotes that the operation rounds an element to the nearest integer less than or equal to that element.

By substituting the kernel feature map with a sparse random feature map, we have

$$\hat{\psi}_m(x_n) = \sqrt{\frac{1}{\lfloor D/s \rfloor}} R\hat{\phi}_m(x_n). \tag{5}$$

The weight vector can be explicitly expressed as a $\lfloor D/s \rfloor$-dimensional vector (i.e., $w_{m,q} = \sum_v \eta_{m,v,q}\hat{\psi}_m(x_v)$), which can be adaptively estimated using the diffusion cooperative strategy without sharing the original data across nodes. Additionally, the computation of the multi-kernel function only linearly grows as the data size increases, which controls the computation complexity to an acceptable level.

Furthermore, to efficiently exploit the label correlation among multiple labels, the label correlation is integrated into the discriminant function for directly correcting the outputs of non-linear regression. Benefited by the interplay between the label correlation and the weight vector, the classification performance can be boosted. Therefore, the novel discriminant function for the q-th label can be re-modeled by

$$f_q(\boldsymbol{x}_n) = \left\{ \sum_{m=1}^{P} \boldsymbol{w}_{m,q}^T \cdot \hat{\psi}_m(\boldsymbol{x}_n) + \sum_{q \neq k} \beta_{q,k} y_{n,k} \right\}, \tag{6}$$

where $y_{n,k}$ denotes the k-th ground-truth label of the n-th data vector, and $\beta_{q,k}$ measures the degree of correlation between the q-th and k-th labels.

However, according to the basic settings of the S^{2}PML, the collected labels are ambiguous or missing, and thus, the ground-truth labels cannot be directly obtained. To tackle this problem, we use the estimate of the labeling confidence $\hat{h}_{n,k}$ to replace the ground-truth label $y_{n,k}$, and rewrite the novel discriminant function as follows:

$$f_q(\boldsymbol{x}_n) = \left\{ \sum_{m=1}^{P} \boldsymbol{w}_{m,q}^T \cdot \hat{\psi}_m(\boldsymbol{x}_n) + \sum_{q \neq k} \beta_{q,k} \hat{h}_{n,k} \right\}, \tag{7}$$

where $\hat{\boldsymbol{h}}_n = [\hat{h}_{n,1}, \ldots, \hat{h}_{n,Q}]^T \in [0,1]^Q$ is used to denote the estimate of the labeling confidence of data vector $\boldsymbol{x}_n$, with $\hat{h}_{n,k}$ being the estimate of k-th label.

Given a series of training data, we develop the global objective function by incorporating the novel discriminant function into the loss function, which is given by

$$\begin{aligned}
\min_{\hat{h}_{n,q}, \boldsymbol{w}_{m,q}, \beta_{q,k}} \quad \mathcal{L} = & \frac{\gamma_A}{2L} \sum_{n=1}^{L} \sum_{q=1}^{Q} (s_{n,q} - \hat{h}_{n,q})^2 + \frac{\gamma_B}{2(L+U)} \sum_{n=1}^{L+U} \sum_{q=1}^{Q} \left(\hat{h}_{n,q} - \sum_{l=1}^{L+U} \Omega_{n,l} \hat{h}_{l,q} \right)^2 \\
& + \left(\frac{C_L}{2L} \sum_{n=1}^{L} \sum_{q=1}^{Q} (\hat{h}_{n,q} - f_q(\boldsymbol{x}_n))^2 + \frac{C_U}{2U} \sum_{n=L+1}^{L+U} \sum_{q=1}^{Q} (\hat{h}_{n,q} - f_q(\boldsymbol{x}_n))^2 \right) \\
& + \left(\frac{\gamma_C}{2} \sum_{q=1}^{Q} \sum_{m=1}^{P} ||\boldsymbol{w}_{m,q}||_2^2 + \frac{\gamma_D}{2} \sum_{q \neq k} |\beta_{q,k}|^2 \right) + \sum_{n=1}^{L+U} \gamma_E ||\hat{\boldsymbol{h}}_n||_0.
\end{aligned} \tag{8}$$

The objective function is composed of five parts.

(1) Estimated Error of Labeling Confidence: The first part is the estimated error between the originally candidate labels and the estimated labeling confidence w.r.t. all the partially multi-labeled data with the weight parameter γ_A. Incorporating this term into the objective function can exploit information from the candidate labels for guiding the labeling confidence estimation.

(2) Reconstructed Error of Labeling Confidence: The second part is the reconstructed error on the labeling confidence among all the training data with the weight parameter γ_B. As the ground-truth labels are devoid of noise, it is reasonable to anticipate that the similarity structure in the feature space can maintain in the ground-truth label space. So, we can estimate the labeling confidence of the candidate label by minimizing the reconstructed error. Here, $\Omega_{n,l}$ denotes the similarity between $\boldsymbol{x}_n$ and $\boldsymbol{x}_l$, which satisfies $\sum_l \Omega_{n,l} = 1$.

(3) Loss Function: The third part consists of loss functions of the partially multi-labeled and unlabeled data with their weight coefficients C_L and C_U.

(4) Regularization: The fourth part is the regularization term w.r.t. the model parameters $\boldsymbol{w}_{m,q}$ and $\beta_{q,k}$, which can be used to control the complexity of model parameters. Their weight coefficients $\gamma_C, \gamma_D > 0$ can be used to regulate the degree of the complexity penalty.

(5) Sparse Constraint: The last part is the sparse constraint term with weight parameter γ_E that ensures the sparsity of the labeling confidence vector $\hat{\boldsymbol{h}}_n$. As training data are assigned with only a small number of ground-truth labels, this implies that the majority of entities in $\hat{\boldsymbol{h}}_n$ should be equivalent to 0. To avoid the bad effect of incredible

labels with small confidence on the performance of the classifier, we incorporate this term into the objective function for enforcing the labeling confidence of incredible labels to be zeros.

However, considering that the l_0-norm $||\hat{\boldsymbol{h}}_n||_0$ is non-convex, and that its minimization is non-polynomial hard, we use a continuous function to approximate the l_0-norm [37,38],

$$||\hat{\boldsymbol{h}}_n||_0 \approx \sum_{q=1}^{Q}(1 - e^{-\delta|\hat{h}_{n,q}|}), \tag{9}$$

where Q is the dimension of $\hat{\boldsymbol{h}}_{j,n}$, and δ is a positive constant. Here, the two sides in (9) are strictly equal when $\delta \rightarrow +\infty$. According to the basic settings, the labeling confidence of each class label $\hat{h}_{n,q}$ is greater than 0, and thus, the approximation of the l_0-norm can be simplified as follows:

$$||\hat{\boldsymbol{h}}_n||_0 \approx \sum_{q=1}^{Q}(1 - e^{-\delta\hat{h}_{n,q}}). \tag{10}$$

Based on the above approximation, we have the q-th element in the derivative of the l_0-norm as follows:

$$\xi(\hat{h}_{j,n,q}) = \begin{cases} -(\delta^2\hat{h}_{j,n,q} - \delta), & \text{if } 0 < \hat{h}_{j,n,q} \leq \frac{1}{\delta}, \\ 0, & \text{elsewise}, \end{cases} \quad q = 1, \ldots, Q. \tag{11}$$

3.3. Decentralization of Global Objective Function

To obtain the global optimal solution in a fully decentralized manner, the global objective function should be decentralized.

However, from (8), we can find that computing the second term requires the entire dataset. Due to the dispersed storage of data samples across multiple nodes, it is challenging to directly update the labeling confidence without gathering all the training data into a fusion center for centralized processing. To solve this problem, several globally common basic data $\{\boldsymbol{c}_l\}_{l=1}^{M}$ are exploited in prior as the representatives of the whole dataset for labeling confidence estimation [21,23,39]. According to the smoothness assumption commonly used in semi-supervised [21,23], in the high-density region, the samples that are in close proximity should also have similar outputs (labels). So, if the number of selected basic data is sufficient to cover the high-density regions, then basic data can give a good characterization for the global data distribution. The labeling confidence estimated based on the global basic data is close to the corresponding estimates obtained based on the whole dataset. Based on this consideration, we construct the reconstructed error based on these globally basic data instead of the whole dataset, and reformulate the global objective function as

$$\begin{aligned} \min_{\hat{h}_{n,q}, \boldsymbol{w}_{m,q}, \beta_{q,k}} \mathcal{L} = & \frac{\gamma_A}{2L}\sum_{n=1}^{L}\sum_{q=1}^{Q}(s_{n,q} - \hat{h}_{n,q})^2 + \frac{\gamma_B}{2(L+U)}\sum_{n=1}^{L+U}\sum_{q=1}^{Q}\left(\hat{h}_{n,q} - \sum_{l=1}^{M}\Omega_{n,l}^{c}\hat{h}_{l,q}^{c}\right)^2 \\ & + \left(\frac{C_L}{2L}\sum_{n=1}^{L}\sum_{q=1}^{Q}(\hat{h}_{n,q} - f_q(\boldsymbol{x}_n))^2 + \frac{C_U}{2U}\sum_{n=L+1}^{L+U}\sum_{q=1}^{Q}(\hat{h}_{n,q} - f_q(\boldsymbol{x}_n))^2\right) \\ & + \left(\frac{\gamma_C}{2}\sum_{q=1}^{Q}\sum_{m=1}^{P}||\boldsymbol{w}_{m,q}||_2^2 + \frac{\gamma_D}{2}\sum_{q\neq k}|\beta_{q,k}|^2\right) + \gamma_E\sum_{n=1}^{L+U}\sum_{q=1}^{Q}(1 - e^{-\delta\hat{h}_{n,q}}), \end{aligned} \tag{12}$$

where $\hat{h}_{l,q}^{c}$ in the second term denotes the confidence of the q-th label for the l-th basic data, and the scalar $\Omega_{n,l}^{c}$ is used to quantify the degree of similarity between the n-th training data and the l-th basic data, which satisfies $\sum_l \Omega_{n,l}^{c} = 1$. Additionally, M represents the total number of basic data.

Therefore, the key for decentralization is to select suitable basic data from dispersed distributed training data. An efficient strategy is to employ data clustering, which selects more basic data (data centers) from the high-density region and less from the low-density region based on data distribution. To achieve this, a decentralized algorithm can be developed, which includes two main steps: location and label prediction.

3.3.1. Location Estimation of Basic Data

In this part, a decentralized version of the clustering algorithm is developed to obtain several global consensus cluster centers, which can be utilized as globally common basic data. To achieve this, a loop indexed by τ_1 is set. At the initial state of the loop, we set $\tau_1 = 0$, and initialize the locations of M cluster centers with random values. The main procedures at each iteration τ_1 are summarized as follows:

(1) Partition Calculation: At each iteration τ_1, for each node j, the squared Euclidean distance between the cluster center and the training data $\mathcal{D}(\boldsymbol{x}_{j,n}, \boldsymbol{c}_{j,l})$ is computed. Then, the training data $\boldsymbol{x}_{j,n}$ can be clustered to the nearest partition $P_{j,l}$ according to the rule $\boldsymbol{x}_{j,n} \in P_{j,l}$, if $\mathcal{D}(\boldsymbol{x}_{j,n}, \boldsymbol{c}_{j,l}) \leq \mathcal{D}(\boldsymbol{x}_{j,n}, \boldsymbol{c}_{j,r}), \forall r$.

(2) Local Estimation: According to the partition results, the partition counts $n'_{j,l}(\tau_1)$ can be determined, and the cluster centers can be updated by

$$\boldsymbol{c}'_{j,l}(\tau_1) = \frac{\sum_{n \in P_{j,l}} \boldsymbol{x}_{j,n}}{n'_{j,l}(\tau_1)}. \tag{13}$$

(3) Information Exchange and Fusion: Each node j transmits the local cluster results to its one-hop neighbors. The local estimation of the cluster center can be updated by

$$\boldsymbol{c}_{j,l}(\tau_1) = \frac{\boldsymbol{c}'_{j,l}(\tau_1) n'_{j,l}(\tau_1) + \exp(-\tau_1/J) \sum_{i \in \mathcal{B}_j} \boldsymbol{c}'_{i,l}(\tau_1) n'_{i,l}(\tau_1)}{n'_{j,l}(\tau_1) + \exp(-\tau_1/J) \sum_{i \in \mathcal{B}_j} n'_{i,l}(\tau_1)}, \tag{14}$$

where $\exp(-\tau_1/J)$ is the time-varying coefficient, which gradually reduces the influence of neighbors' results as the cluster results update continuously until convergence.

(4) Termination Condition Judgment: If the difference between cluster results at iteration τ_1 and $\tau_1 - 1$ is smaller than the threshold ϵ, i.e., $\max_l ||\boldsymbol{c}_{j,l}(\tau_1) - \boldsymbol{c}_{j,l}(\tau_1 - 1)||_2 < \epsilon, \forall j \in \mathcal{J}$, the loop terminates. Otherwise, the loop continues to the next iteration, i.e., $\tau_1 = \tau_1 + 1$.

Algorithm 1 provides a summary of the key steps of location estimation of basic data for clarity.

Algorithm 1 Location estimation of basic data

Require: Input training data $\{\boldsymbol{x}_{j,n}\}_{n=1}^{L_j+U_j}$, and initialize cluster centers $\{\boldsymbol{c}_{j,l,0}\}_{l=1}^{M}$.

repeat
  for $j = 1, \ldots, J$ **do**
    Cluster the training data $\boldsymbol{x}_{j,n}$ to the nearest partition.
    Determine the partition counts $n'_{j,l}(\tau_1)$ and update cluster centers via (13).
    Transmit $\{\boldsymbol{c}'_{n,l}(\tau_1), n'_{j,l}(\tau_1)\}_{l=1}^{M}$ to its one-hop neighbors.
  end for
  for $j = 1, \ldots, J$ **do**
    Update the cluster center via (14).
  end for
until convergence
Obtain the final estimation of the cluster centers as basic data $\{\boldsymbol{c}_{j,l}\}_{l=1}^{M}$.

3.3.2. Label Prediction of Basic Data

To estimate the predicted labels of basic data $\hat{\boldsymbol{h}}_l^c = [\hat{h}_{l,1}^c, ..., \hat{h}_{l,Q}^c]^T \in [0,1]^Q$ over a network, we construct another loop indexed by τ_2. The main procedures in the loop are summarized as follows.

(1) Local Estimation: At the beginning of the loop ($\tau_2 = 0$), the locally predicted labels of the basic data $\hat{\boldsymbol{h}}_{j,l,0}^c$ can be initially calculated based on the local partially multi-labeled data:

$$\hat{\boldsymbol{h}}_{j,l,0}^c = \sum_{n=1}^{L_j} \Omega_{j,n,l}^c \boldsymbol{s}_{j,n}, \quad l = 1, \ldots, M. \tag{15}$$

(2) Information Exchange and Fusion: At each iteration τ_2 of the loop, each node j exchanges its intermediate estimations with its one-hop neighbors $i \in \mathcal{B}_j$. Then, the predicted labels of basic data can be updated by combining the intermediate estimates exchanged from neighbors within $\mathcal{B}_j$, i.e.,

$$\hat{\boldsymbol{h}}_{j,l,\tau_2+1}^c = \sum_{i \in \mathcal{B}_j} v_{ji} \hat{\boldsymbol{h}}_{i,l,\tau_2}^c, \quad l = 1, \ldots, M, \quad \tau_2 = 0, ..., T_2 - 1, \tag{16}$$

where the cooperative coefficient v_{ji} is designed according to the Metropolis rule [22].

(3) Global Consensus Estimation: The maximum number of loops is set to T_2. The global consensus estimations of the predicted labels of basic data $\hat{\boldsymbol{h}}_l^c = [\hat{h}_{l,1}^c, ..., \hat{h}_{l,Q}^c]^T \in [0,1]^Q$ can be obtained after T_2 iterations, i.e., $\hat{\boldsymbol{h}}_l^c = \hat{\boldsymbol{h}}_{1,l,T_2}^c = ... = \hat{\boldsymbol{h}}_{J,l,T_2}^c$.

For clarity, the main steps of labeling confidence estimation of basic data are summarized in Algorithm 2.

Algorithm 2 Label prediction of basic data

Require: Input basic data $\{\boldsymbol{c}_l\}_{l=1}^M$ and training data $\{\boldsymbol{x}_{j,n}, \boldsymbol{s}_{j,n}\}_{n=1}^{L_j}$.

```
for j = 1, ..., J do
    Initialize the predicted labels of the basic data {ĥ^c_{j,l,0}}_{l=1}^M via (15).
end for
for τ2 = 0, ..., T2 − 1 do
    for j = 1, ..., J do
        Transmit {ĥ^c_{j,l,τ2}}_{l=1}^M to its one-hop neighbors.
    end for
    for j = 1, ..., J do
        Update the intermediate estimates {ĥ^c_{j,l,τ2+1}}_{l=1}^M via (16).
    end for
end for
Obtain the final global consensus estimates {ĥ^c_{j,l,T2}}_{l=1}^M.
```

3.3.3. Decentralized Implementation

Given the global consensus estimations of the labeling confidence of basic data, by using the local parameters $\{\boldsymbol{w}_{j,m,q}, \beta_{j,q,k}\}_{j=1}^J$ to replace the global ones and adding the consensus equality constraints on the model parameters, we can decentralize the global objective function (12) as

$$
\begin{aligned}
\min_{\hat{h}_{j,n,q}, w_{j,m,q}, \beta_{j,q,k}} \quad \mathcal{L} = & \sum_{j=1}^{J} \Bigg\{ \frac{\gamma_A}{2L} \sum_{n=1}^{L_j} \sum_{q=1}^{Q} (s_{j,n,q} - \hat{h}_{j,n,q})^2 + \frac{\gamma_B}{2(L+U)} \sum_{n=1}^{L_j+U_j} \sum_{q=1}^{Q} \left(\hat{h}_{j,n,q} - \sum_{l=1}^{M} \Omega^c_{j,n,l} \hat{h}^c_{l,q} \right)^2 \\
& + \left(\frac{C_L}{2L} \sum_{n=1}^{L_j} \sum_{q=1}^{Q} (\hat{h}_{j,n,q} - f_q(x_{j,n}))^2 + \frac{C_U}{2U} \sum_{n=L_j+1}^{L_j+U_j} \sum_{q=1}^{Q} (\hat{h}_{j,n,q} - f_q(x_{j,n}))^2 \right) \\
& + \left(\frac{\gamma_C}{2J} \sum_{q=1}^{Q} \sum_{m=1}^{P} ||w_{j,m,q}||_2^2 + \frac{\gamma_D}{2J} \sum_{q \neq k} |\beta_{j,q,k}|^2 \right) + \gamma_E \sum_{n=1}^{L_j+U_j} \sum_{q=1}^{Q} (1 - e^{-\delta \hat{h}_{j,n,q}}) \Bigg\} \\
= & \sum_{j=1}^{J} \mathcal{L}_j, \\
\text{s.t.} \quad & w_{j,m,q} = w_{i,m,q}, \quad \beta_{j,q,k} = \beta_{i,q,k}, \quad j \in \mathcal{J}, \quad i \in \mathcal{B}_j.
\end{aligned}
\tag{17}
$$

Lemma 1. *If the network is connected, supposing that* $(w_{j,m,q}, \beta_{j,q,k})_{j=1}^{J}$ *is a feasible solution of (17), then* $w_{j,m,q} = w_{m,q}$ *and* $\beta_{j,q,k} = \beta_{q,k}, \forall j \in \mathcal{J}$*, where* $(w_{m,q}, \beta_{q,k})$ *represents a feasible solution of (12).*

The proof of Lemma 1 can refer to Appendix A of [23]. Lemma 1 implies that as long as the network is connected, the decentralization of the objective function has no impact on the feasible solution.

3.4. Classifier Induction

An alternating minimization method [21,22] is used to estimate the labeling confidences and jointly seek the optimal model parameters of the classifier $\{w^*_{j,m,q}, \beta^*_{j,q,k}\}$. At each iteration t, two sub-optimization problems can be iteratively solved until convergence.

(1) Updating $\{\hat{h}_{j,n,q}\}$: With $w_{j,m,q}$ and $\beta_{j,q,k}$ fixed, we can update the labeling confidence of the training data $\{\hat{h}_{j,n,q}\}$ by optimizing the following problem:

$$
\{\hat{h}_{j,n,q,t+1}\} = \arg\min_{\hat{h}_{j,n,q}} \mathcal{L}_j(\hat{h}_{j,n,q}, w_{j,m,q,t}, \beta_{j,q,k,t}). \tag{18}
$$

Based on (18), we would like to use the gradient descent (GD) method to update the labeling confidence $\hat{h}_{j,n,q}$, i.e.,

$$
\hat{h}_{j,n,q,t+1} = \hat{h}_{j,n,q,t} - \mu_{1,t+1} \nabla_{\hat{h}_{j,n,q}} \mathcal{L}_j(\hat{h}_{j,n,q}, w_{j,m,q,t}, \beta_{j,q,k,t}), \tag{19}
$$

where $\mu_{1,t+1}$ denotes the learning rates satisfying the diminishing conditions, and $\nabla_{\hat{h}_{j,n,q}} \mathcal{L}_j$ denotes the gradient of $\mathcal{L}_j$ w.r.t. $\hat{h}_{j,n,q}$.

(2) Updating $\{w_{j,m,q}, \beta_{j,q,k}\}$: With $\hat{h}_{j,n,q}$ fixed, the weight vector and the label correlation coefficient $\{w_{j,m,q}, \beta_{j,q,k}\}$ are optimized by

$$
\begin{aligned}
\{w_{j,m,q,t+1}, \beta_{j,q,k,t+1}\} &= \arg \min_{w_{j,m,q}, \beta_{j,q,k}} \mathcal{L}_j(\hat{h}_{j,n,q,t+1}, w_{j,m,q}, \beta_{j,q,k}), \\
\text{s.t.} \quad w_{j,m,q} &= w_{i,m,q}, \quad \beta_{j,q,k} = \beta_{i,q,k}, \quad j \in \mathcal{J}, \quad i \in \mathcal{B}_j.
\end{aligned}
\tag{20}
$$

To seek the globally optimal classifier in the distributed network, we redesign the global-like objective function as the combination of the local objective function and the distance on the model parameters obtained at a pair of neighboring nodes j and i, that is,

$$\begin{aligned}\{\boldsymbol{w}_{j,m,q,t+1}, \beta_{j,q,k,t+1}\} = &\arg \min_{\boldsymbol{w}_{j,m,q}, \beta_{j,q,k}} \mathcal{L}_j(\hat{h}_{j,n,q,t+1}, \boldsymbol{w}_{j,m,q}, \beta_{j,q,k}) \\ &+ \sum_{i \in \mathcal{B}_j \backslash j} \sum_{q=1}^{Q} \sum_{m=1}^{P} a_{ji} ||\boldsymbol{w}_{j,m,q} - \boldsymbol{w}'_{i,m,q}||_2^2 + \sum_{i \in \mathcal{B}_j \backslash j} \sum_{q \neq k} a_{ji} (\beta_{j,q,k} - \beta'_{i,q,k})^2,\end{aligned} \tag{21}$$

where $\boldsymbol{w}'_{i,m,q}$ and $\beta'_{i,q,k}$ stand for the immediate local estimates at node i, and the non-negative coefficient a_{ji} satisfies $\sum_{i \in \mathcal{B}_j} a_{ji} = 1$ and $a_{ji} = 0$ if $i \notin \mathcal{B}_j$.

Taking the gradient of (21) w.r.t. $\boldsymbol{w}_{j,m,q,t}$, we have the recursive equations as follows:

$$\boldsymbol{w}_{j,m,q,t+1} = \boldsymbol{w}_{j,m,q,t} - \mu_{2,t+1} \nabla_{\boldsymbol{w}_{j,m,q}} \mathcal{L}_j(\hat{h}_{j,n,q,t+1}, \boldsymbol{w}_{j,m,q}, \beta_{j,q,k,t}) - \rho \sum_{i \in \mathcal{B}_j \backslash j} a_{ji} (\boldsymbol{w}_{j,m,q,t} - \boldsymbol{w}'_{i,m,q,t}), \tag{22}$$

where $\mu_{2,t+1}$ denotes the time-varying step size, and ρ denotes a positive invariant constant. Additionally, $\nabla_{\boldsymbol{w}_{j,m,q}} \mathcal{L}_j$ denotes the gradients of $\mathcal{L}_j$ w.r.t. $\boldsymbol{w}_{j,m,q}$.

To efficiently carry out the diffusion cooperation strategy, referring to [21,22], the new immediate estimates of $\boldsymbol{w}'_{j,m,q,t+1}$ are introduced, such that the update equation in (22) can be respectively accomplished in two steps, that is,

$$\boldsymbol{w}'_{j,m,q,t+1} = \boldsymbol{w}_{j,m,q,t} - \mu_{2,t+1} \nabla_{\boldsymbol{w}_{j,m,q}} \mathcal{L}_j(\hat{h}_{j,n,q,t+1}, \boldsymbol{w}_{j,m,q}, \beta_{j,q,k,t}), \tag{23a}$$

$$\boldsymbol{w}_{j,m,q,t+1} = \boldsymbol{w}'_{j,m,q,t+1} - \rho \sum_{i \in \mathcal{B}_j \backslash j} a_{ji} (\boldsymbol{w}_{j,m,q,t} - \boldsymbol{w}'_{i,m,q,t}). \tag{23b}$$

Utilizing the current estimates $\boldsymbol{w}'_{j,m,q,t+1}$ ($\boldsymbol{w}'_{i,m,q,t+1}$) to replace the $\boldsymbol{w}_{j,m,q,t}$ ($\boldsymbol{w}'_{i,m,q,t}$) in (23b), we have

$$\begin{aligned}\boldsymbol{w}_{j,m,q,t+1} &= \boldsymbol{w}'_{j,m,q,t+1} - \rho \sum_{i \in \mathcal{B}_j \backslash j} a_{ji} (\boldsymbol{w}'_{j,m,q,t+1} - \boldsymbol{w}'_{i,m,q,t+1}) \\ &= (1 - \rho \sum_{i \in \mathcal{B}_j \backslash j} a_{ji}) \boldsymbol{w}'_{j,m,q,t+1} + \rho \sum_{i \in \mathcal{B}_j \backslash j} a_{ji} \boldsymbol{w}'_{i,m,q,t+1} \\ &= \sum_{i \in \mathcal{B}_j} v_{ji} \boldsymbol{w}'_{i,m,q,t+1},\end{aligned} \tag{24}$$

where the cooperative coefficient $v_{ji} = \rho a_{ji}$, $v_{jj} = 1 - \rho \sum_{i \in \mathcal{B}_j \backslash j} a_{ji}$.

Similarly, the label correlation coefficient $\beta_{j,q,k}$ can be updated via adaption and combination steps, i.e.,

$$\beta'_{j,q,k,t+1} = \beta_{j,q,k,t} - \mu_{3,t+1} \nabla_{\beta_{j,q,k}} \mathcal{L}_j(\hat{h}_{j,n,q,t+1}, \boldsymbol{w}_{j,m,q,t}, \beta_{j,q,k}), \tag{25a}$$

$$\beta_{j,q,k,t+1} = \sum_{i \in \mathcal{B}_j} v_{ji} \beta'_{i,q,k,t+1}, \tag{25b}$$

where $\mu_{3,t+1}$ denotes the time-varying step size, and $\nabla_{\beta_{j,q,k}} \mathcal{L}_j$ denotes the gradients of $\mathcal{L}_j$ w.r.t. $\beta_{j,q,k}$.

Algorithm 3 summarizes the pseudo-code of the proposed dS^{2}PML algorithm.

Algorithm 3 dS^{2}PML algorithm

Require: Input training data $\{\boldsymbol{x}_{j,n}, s_{j,n}\}_{n=1}^{L_j}$ and $\{\boldsymbol{x}_{j,n}\}_{n=L_j+1}^{L_j+U_j}$. Initialize $\boldsymbol{w}_{j,m,q,0} = \boldsymbol{0}_{\lfloor D/s \rfloor}$ and $\beta_{j,q,k,0} = 0$.

```
Obtain basic data {c_l, ĥ_l^c}_{l=1}^M via Algorithm 1 and Algorithm 2.
Map data x_{j,n} into sparse feature space via (4) and (5).
for t = 0, 1, ... do
    for j = 1, ..., J do
        Calculate {ĥ_{j,n,q,t+1}} according to (19).
    end for
    for j = 1, ..., J do
        Calculate {w'_{j,m,q,t+1}, β'_{j,q,k,t+1}} according to (23a) and (25a).
        Transmit {w'_{j,m,q,t+1}, β'_{j,q,k,t+1}} to one-hop neighbors.
    end for
    for j = 1, ..., J do
        Calculate {w_{j,m,q,t+1}, β_{j,q,k,t+1}} according to (24) and (25b).
    end for
end for
```

3.5. Performance Analysis

The performance analysis of the proposed dS^{2}PML algorithm in terms of complexity and convergence is presented in this subsection.

3.5.1. Convergence Analysis

To conduct the subsequent convergence analysis, we initially present some assumptions frequently employed in the context of distributed learning.

Assumption 1. *For a connected network $\mathcal{G}$, the cooperative coefficient matrix V with its entity $V_{ji} = v_{ji}$ satisfies the condition of doubly stochasticity, i.e, $V\mathbf{1}_J = \mathbf{1}_J$, $\mathbf{1}_J^T V = \mathbf{1}_J^T$, and the spectral norm of the matrix $V - \frac{1}{J}\mathbf{1}_J\mathbf{1}_J^T$ satisfies the condition of not being greater than 1.*

Theorem 1. *If Assumption 1 holds, for all $j \in \mathcal{J}$, the local estimates of labeling confidence $\hat{\boldsymbol{h}}_{j,n,t}$, the model parameter $\boldsymbol{w}_{j,m,q,t}$ and the label correlation coefficient $\beta_{j,q,k,t}$ converge to their respective optimal values $\boldsymbol{h}_{j,n}^*$, $\boldsymbol{w}_{m,q}^*$ and $\beta_{q,k}^*$ when t approaches infinity.*

Theorem 1 may be proven using the proof presented in [21,22]. Theorem 1 proves that each node in the distributed network can obtain the global optimal classifier as good as the centralized algorithm by exchanging and combining the model parameters with its neighbors.

3.5.2. Complexity Analysis

The computation complexity and communication cost of the proposed dS^{2}PML algorithm are analyzed. The complexity of computation is assessed by the number of addition operations (AO) and multiplication operations (MO). Table 1 summarizes the computation cost at each step for each node j of the proposed dS^{2}PML algorithm during the process of obtaining basic data, labeling confidence estimation of basic data, and model induction. From the above analysis, we can notice that the computation complexity depends on the number of basic data M, the number of kernel functions P, the number of one-hop neighbors $|\mathcal{B}_j|$, and the dimension of the sparse random feature map $\lfloor D/s \rfloor$, except for the characteristics of training datasets. As the one-hop neighbors of nodes are usually not very large in practical networks, the computation complexity is acceptable, provided that the values of M, P and $\lfloor D/s \rfloor$ can be controlled into suitable regions.

Table 1. Computation complexity in terms of number of MOs and AOs per iteration per node j.

$\{c_{j,l}\}_{l=1}^{M}$	MO	$Md(1+2\vert\mathcal{B}_j\vert)$
	AO	$Cd(\vert\mathcal{P}_{j,l}\vert+2\vert\mathcal{B}_j\vert)$
$\{\hat{h}_{j,l}^{c}\}_{l=1}^{M}$	MO	$MQ(L_j+\vert\mathcal{B}_j\vert)$
	AO	$CQ(L_j+\vert\mathcal{B}_j\vert)$
$\{\hat{h}_{j,n}\}_{n=1}^{L_j+U_j}$	MO	$L_jQ(3+M+Q)+U_jQ(2+M+Q)$
	AO	$L_jQ(3+M+Q)+U_jQ(2+M+Q)$
$\{w_{j,m,q}\}_{m,q}$	MO	$QP\lfloor D/s\rfloor(1+L_j+U_j+\vert\mathcal{B}_j\vert)$
	AO	$QP\lfloor D/s\rfloor(1+2L_j+2U_j+\vert\mathcal{B}_j\vert)$
$\{\beta_j\}_{q,k}$	MO	$\frac{1}{2}Q^2(3+L_j+U_j+\vert\mathcal{B}_j\vert)$
	AO	$\frac{1}{2}Q^2(3+L_j+U_j+\vert\mathcal{B}_j\vert)$

In addition, during the process of obtaining basic data, at each step τ_1, Md scalar transmission is required at node j. During the process of predicting the labeling confidence of basic data, each node j requires to transmit MQ scalars to its neighbors at each iteration τ_2. During the process of model induction, at each iteration t, for each node j, the number of scalars transmitted among neighboring nodes becomes $QP\lfloor D/s\rfloor + \frac{1}{2}Q^2$. As the one-hop neighbors of nodes are usually moderate in actual networks in practical networks, the communication cost is deemed to be acceptable.

4. Experiment

In this section, to test the learning performance of the proposed algorithm, we carry out a series of simulations on a wide variety of datasets.

In the following experiments, to generate a synthetic partially multi-labeled dataset, referring to [11], we randomly add some extra irrelevant labels into the candidate label sets, such that the average number of candidate labels (avg. CLs) is equivalent to a special value. Here, avg. CLs and the corresponding average number of ground-truth labels (avg. GLs) are considered to be controlled parameters. Table 2 summarizes the characteristics of these datasets, including the number of training data (♯Training Data), the number of testing data (♯Testing Data), the dimension of data samples (♯Dimension), the number of class labels (♯Label), Avg. CLs and Avg. GLs. To show the classification performances of different algorithms with a certain proportion of partially multi-labeled and unlabeled data, a new measure, namely, the Percentage of Partially Multi-labeled data in the whole dataset (PPM) is defined. Moreover, to assess the classification effectiveness of different comparison algorithms from a variety of perspectives, five evaluation metrics, namely, the hamming loss, one error, average precision, ranking loss, and coverage, are used. Small values of hamming loss, one error, ranking loss and coverage, and a large value of average precision are expected for a good classifier. For their detailed definitions, please refer to [11].

Additionally, to carry out the following simulations, a randomly generated network with $J = 10$ nodes and $|\mathcal{E}| = 23$ links is considered, and then all the training data are allocated to these nodes. At each trail of simulation, the parameters are set as $C_L = 1$, $C_U = 0.1$, $\gamma_A = 1$, $\gamma_B = 0.5$, $\gamma_C = 0.1$, $\gamma_D = 0.01$, $\gamma_E = 0.05$, and $\delta = 10$, and the dimension of $\hat{\psi}(\cdot)$ is set as 200 (i.e., $D = 600, s = 3$). In addition, the multi-kernel function combined with three different single kernel functions using kernel widths 0.2, 1, and 5 is employed to construct the discriminant function. Additionally, we set the step size $\mu_{1,t} = 0.3/t^{0.5}, \mu_{2,t} = \mu_{3,t} = 0.1/t^{0.5}$, the maximum number of loops $T_2 = 10$, and the threshold $\epsilon = 0.1$.

Table 2. Summary of characteristics of used datasets.

Dataset	♯ Training Data	♯ Testing Data	♯ Dimension	♯ Label	Avg. CLs	Avg. GLs
genbase 1	1580	406	1185	27	7.25	1.25
genbase 2	1580	406	1185	27	11.25	1.25
medical 1	2060	520	1449	45	9.24	1.24
medical 2	2060	520	1449	45	13.24	1.24
CHD49 1	2660	670	49	6	3.58	2.58
CHD49 2	2660	670	49	6	4.08	2.58
flag 1	1550	390	19	7	4.39	3.39
flag 2	1550	390	19	7	4.89	3.39
TMC2007 1	17200	4319	500	22	8.23	2.23
TMC2007 2	17200	4319	500	22	10.23	2.23
emotion	5460	1373	98	11	5.30	2.42

By taking the hamming loss as an example metric for illustration, we set the value of PPM = 0.3, and depict the learning curves of the proposed dS^{2}PML algorithm and the centralized S^{2}PML (cS^{2}PML) algorithm on the "genbase 1", "medical 1" and "TMC2007 1" datasets in Figure 3. In addition, to testify the robustness of the dS^{2}PML algorithm against network settings, we perform the simulations on multiple networks with different configuration parameters, where the configuration parameters of the network are characterized by the number of nodes J and the number of links $|\mathcal{E}|$. All the learning curves are depicted in Figure 3.

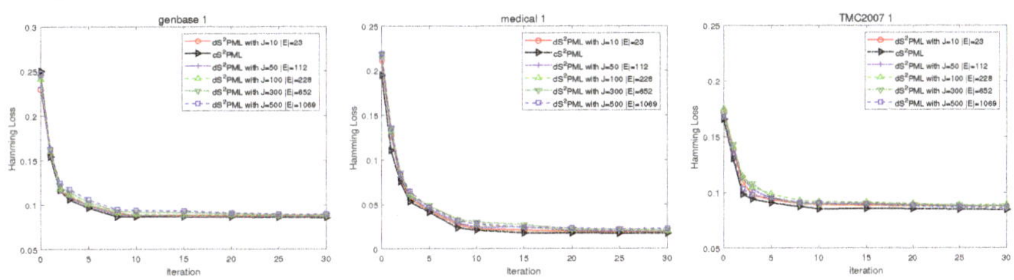

Figure 3. Learning curves of dS^{2}PML with different network topologies and cS^{2}PML on "genbase 1", "medical 1" and "TMC2007 1" datasets.

Three sub-figures of Figure 3 show similar trends. All the learning curves rapidly converge at initial iterations. After about 20 iterations, the values of the learning curves remain nearly invariant. The learning performances of our proposed dS^{2}PML method with different network topologies are similar, indicating that the proposed algorithms are insensitive to the network topologies. Additionally, the learning performances of dS^{2}PML using different network topologies are very close to that of the corresponding cS^{2}PML method on the three used datasets, which verifies the effectiveness of the distributed learning.

We investigate the influences of seven parameters, C_L, C_U, γ_A, γ_B, γ_C, γ_D, and γ_E, on the classification performance on the "genbase 1", "medical 1", and "TMC2007 1" datasets. The simulation results are presented in Figures 4–6. According to the results in Figures 4–6, we can notice that provided that the parameters can be set within appropriate regions, the classification performance of our proposed algorithm is not sensitive to the parameters. So, we can draw the conclusion that appropriate parameter values should be set as $C_L \in (10^0, 10^1)$, $C_U \in (10^{-1}, 10^0)$, $\gamma_A \in (10^0, 10^1)$, $\gamma_B \in (10^{-1}, 10^0)$, $\gamma_C \in (10^{-1}, 10^0)$, $\gamma_D \in (10^{-2}, 10^{-1})$ and $\gamma_E \in (10^{-2}, 10^{-1})$, respectively.

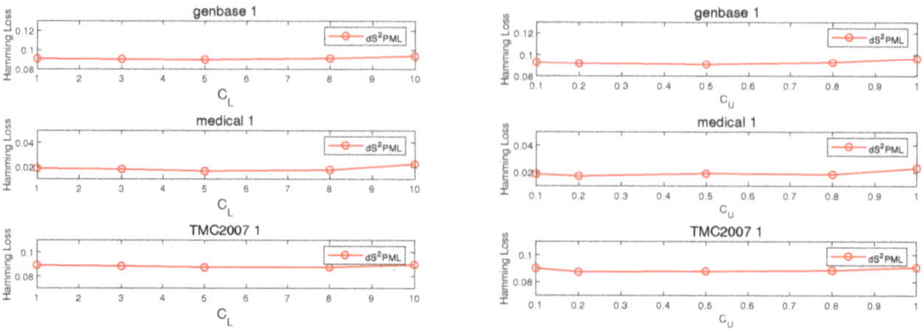

Figure 4. Hamming loss of dS²PML versus the values of parameters C_L and C_U on "genbase 1", "medical 1", and "TMC2007 1" datasets.

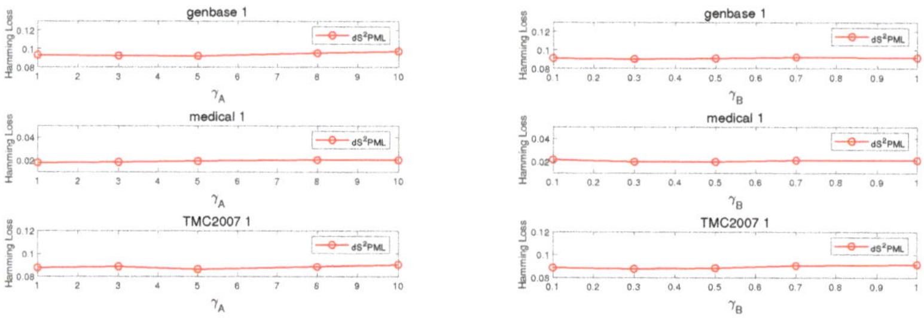

Figure 5. Hamming loss of dS²PML versus the values of parameters γ_A and γ_B on "genbase 1", "medical 1", and "TMC2007 1" datasets.

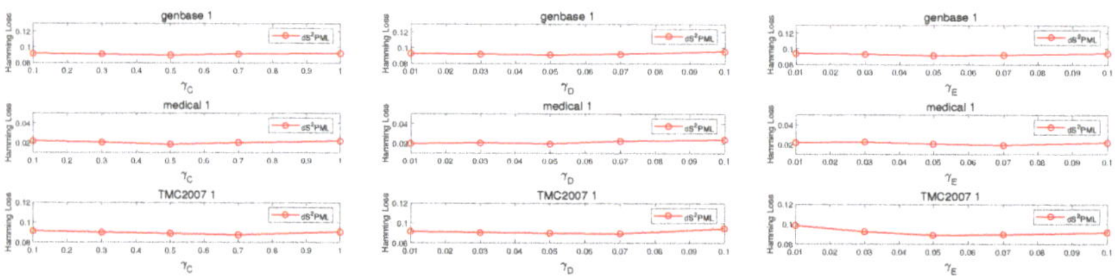

Figure 6. Hamming loss of dS²PML versus the values of parameters γ_C, γ_D and γ_E on "genbase 1", "medical 1", and "TMC2007 1" datasets.

In addition, we also investigate the influences of the number of kernel functions and the values of kernel widths on the learning performance of the proposed algorithm. The changing curves of the hamming loss of the proposed dS²PML using one single kernel function with varying kernel widths are depicted in Figure 7 with a blue line. It can be observed that as long as the kernel width is selected within [0.1,5], good learning performance can be achieved. Additionally, we also compare the hamming loss of the proposed dS²PML with different numbers of kernel functions. Here, we conduct the experiments of the multi-kernel function by varying the number of kernel functions while keeping the kernel width unchanged. The specific values of kernel widths are listed in the caption of Figure 7. The experiment results in Figure 7 verify the effectiveness of the multi-kernel function. The performance of the proposed algorithm improves with the increasing number of kernel functions. Even for the dS²PML using two kernel functions, its hamming loss is still smaller than dS²PML using a single kernel function with the optimal kernel width. As the number of kernel functions further increases, the magnitude of performance improvement gradually decreases. Therefore, it is suitable to combine three kernel functions with kernel widths of 0.2, 1, and 5 to construct the discriminant function.

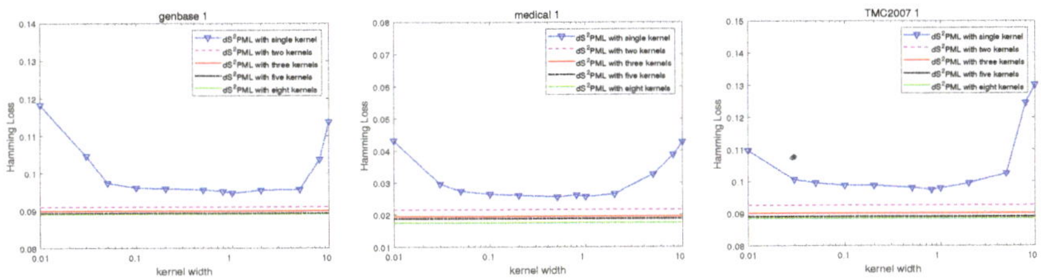

Figure 7. Hamming loss of dS^{2}PML versus the number of kernel functions and the value of kernel widths on "genbase 1", "medical 1", and "TMC2007 1" datasets. It is noted that dS^{2}PML using two kernels with kernel widths $\sigma = 0.8, 1$, dS^{2}PML using three kernels with kernel widths $\sigma = 0.2, 1, 5$, dS^{2}PML using five kernels with kernel widths $\sigma = 0.2, 0.5, 1, 2, 5$, and dS^{2}PML using eight kernels with kernel widths $\sigma = 0.2, 0.4, 0, 8, 1, 2, 3, 4, 5$.

The impact of the number of basic data M on the accuracy of classification of the proposed dS^{2}PML algorithm is also studied. The left sub-figure of Figure 8 depicts the steady-state hamming loss of dS^{2}PML versus the number of basic data M. The hamming loss of the cS^{2}PML algorithm is also presented, serving as a benchmark. It can be observed that as the number of basic data increases, the hamming losses decrease gradually. When the value of M is more than 20, the number of basic data is sufficient to cover all high-density areas, and is capable of characterizing the global data distribution. So, a high-precision labeling confidence can be estimated for each candidate label, so that dS^{2}PML can achieve almost as good classification performances as the corresponding cS^{2}PML algorithm. Considering that the increasing of basic data can increase the computational complexity, a suitable choice of M should lie within (20, 30).

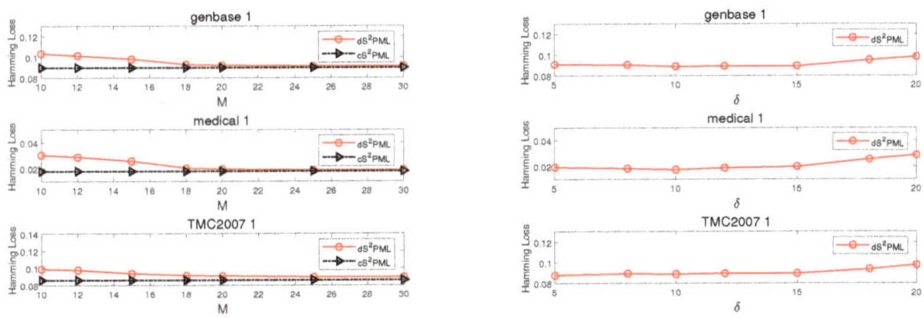

Figure 8. Hamming loss of dS^{2}PML versus the number of basic data M and the value of parameter δ on "genbase 1", "medical 1", and "TMC2007 1" datasets.

We also investigate the hamming loss of the proposed algorithm with varying values of δ in the right sub-figure of Figure 8. The simulation results suggest that the proper value of δ should be set within $(5, 15)$. By employing the sparse constraint term w.r.t. $\hat{\boldsymbol{h}}_{j,n}$ with a proper δ, we can reduce the label confidence whose value is less than the threshold to a value close to zero, which can eliminate the negative effect of these noisy labels efficiently.

To further prove this, by fixing the value of δ to 10, we depict the changing curves of the average number of noisy labels with confidence close to 0 (denoted by N^0) of the dS^{2}PML and cS^{2}PML algorithms in Figure 9. Note that in the "genbase 1", "medical 1", and "TMC2007 1" datasets, we artificially add 6, 8, and 6 noisy labels to each training data, respectively. By observing Figure 9, we can notice that the changing curves of dS^{2}PML and cS^{2}PML algorithms are similar. The initial values of all the change curves are 0. Through a few iterations, the values of N^0 of two algorithms rapidly increase, and the values of N^0 of cS^{2}PML are slightly higher than that of dS^{2}PML. After about 20 iterations, the changing curves gradually converge, and the steady-state values of N^0 of dS^{2}PML are very close to that of cS^{2}PML. The experimental results indicate that we successfully reduce the labeling confidences of more than five noisy labels to very low values after 30 iterations. This proves that employing sparse constraints with a proper threshold is helpful to reduce the negative effect of noisy labels, and the distributed storage of data can not affect the update of label confidence.

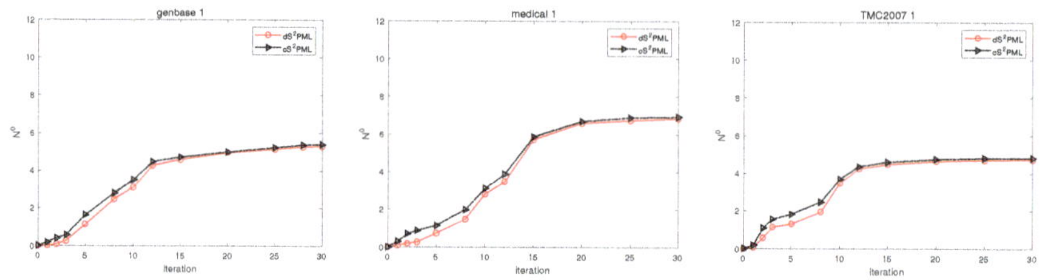

Figure 9. Changing curves of the average number of noisy labels with confidence close to 0 of dS^{2}PML and cS^{2}PML on "genbase 1", "medical 1", and "TMC2007 1" datasets. Here, the labeling confidence whose values are less than 0.03 can be regarded as close to 0.

In Figure 10, we test the impact of the dimension of the random feature map D and the value of s on the hamming loss of the proposed dS^{2}PML algorithm on the "genbase 1", "medical 1", and "TMC2007 1" datasets. We carry out the experiments by varying the value of s while setting different fixed values for D. Figure 10 demonstrates that the changing trends of the hamming losses in three sub-figures are similar to each other. When the value of D is larger than 600 and the value of s is selected within (2,5), the learning performance of the proposed algorithm is insensitive to both D and s. So, in practice, $D \in (600, 1000)$ and $s \in (2, 5)$ are recommended in the simulations.

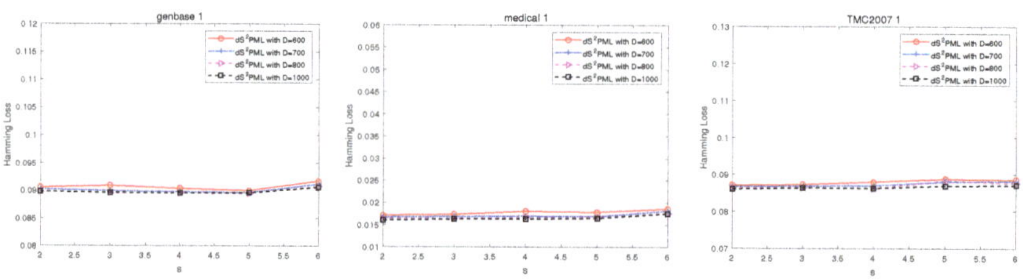

Figure 10. Hamming loss of dS^{2}PML versus different values of D and s on "genbase 1", "medical 1", and "TMC2007 1" datasets.

To further demonstrate the advantages of the proposed algorithm, its classification performance is also tested on more datasets, including genbase 2 [40], medical 2 [40], CHD49 1 [40], CHD49 2 [40], TMC2007 2 [40], flag 1 [40], flag 2 [40], and emotion [11]. The detailed characteristics of all the used datasets are summarized in Table 2. Additionally, the performance of some typical state-of-the-art algorithms is also investigated for comparison. However, so far as we know, there has been no prior work addressing the issue of the distributed S^{2}PML. Instead, we simulate the performance of one distributed semi-supervised MLL (dITS^{2}MLL [21]), one distributed supervised multi-label learning (FMLL) [25], one centralized PML using credible label elicitation (PARVLS [11]), one centralized PML using noisy label identification (PMLNI [15]), two centralized semi-supervised PML based on embedding subspace (SSPML-SL [18] and CS2PML-SL [19]) and one distributed semi-supervised partial single-label learning (dS^{2}PLL [24]). To provide further evidence for the effectiveness of distributed learning, the performance of the cS^{2}PML is also assessed. To highlight the advantages of semi-supervised learning, the classification performance of the corresponding distributed supervised PML (denoted by dPML) is also given, serving as a benchmark. The comprehensive experimental results of all the comparison algorithms in terms of five metrics are shown in Tables 3–7. The average ranks of all the comparison algorithms are depicted in Figure 11.

Table 3. Hamming loss of different algorithms versus PPM on 11 used datasets, where the best performances are shown in bold face.

Hamming Loss						
Dataset	**Genbase 1**	**Genbase 2**	**Medical 1**	**Medical 2**	**CHD49 1**	**CHD49 2**
PPM	**0.5**	**0.5**	**0.5**	**0.5**	**0.5**	**0.5**
dS²PML	0.058	0.120	0.020	0.023	0.242	0.270
cS²PML	0.057	0.108	**0.019**	**0.021**	**0.238**	**0.263**
dPML	0.060	0.123	0.025	0.029	0.265	0.298
dITS²MLL	**0.026**	**0.042**	0.035	0.034	0.332	0.339
PARVLS	0.062	0.127	0.024	0.028	0.268	0.302
PMLNI	0.062	0.085	0.022	0.027	0.261	0.280
SSPML-SL	0.027	0.047	0.024	0.028	0.266	0.279
dS²PLL	0.035	0.076	0.033	0.035	0.324	0.328
CS2PML-SL	0.029	0.051	0.028	0.033	0.270	0.282
FMLL	0.061	0.124	0.043	0.057	0.337	0.355

Hamming Loss					
Dataset	**TMC2007 1**	**TMC2007 2**	**Flag 1**	**Flag 2**	**Emotion**
PPM	**0.5**	**0.5**	**0.5**	**0.5**	**0.5**
dS²PML	0.088	0.107	0.066	0.081	0.322
cS²PML	**0.084**	0.104	**0.060**	**0.075**	**0.316**
dPML	0.092	0.110	0.093	0.117	0.332
dITS²MLL	0.093	0.113	0.101	0.125	0.325
PARVLS	0.087	0.182	0.143	0.181	0.326
PMLNI	0.086	0.106	0.131	0.160	0.322
SSPML-SL	0.090	**0.098**	0.092	0.105	0.323
dS²PLL	0.093	0.113	0.079	0.114	0.327
CS2PML-SL	0.091	0.101	0.095	0.108	0.324
FMLL	0.096	0.129	0.126	0.172	0.338

Table 4. One error of different algorithms versus PPM on 11 used datasets, where the best performances are shown in bold face.

One Error						
Dataset	**Genbase 1**	**Genbase 2**	**Medical 1**	**Medical 2**	**CHD49 1**	**CHD49 2**
PPM	**0.5**	**0.5**	**0.5**	**0.5**	**0.5**	**0.5**
dS²PML	0.147	0.234	0.310	0.343	0.112	0.154
cS²PML	**0.133**	0.222	**0.299**	**0.328**	**0.108**	**0.143**
dPML	0.159	0.255	0.361	0.425	0.155	0.189
dITS²MLL	0.142	0.316	0.621	0.687	0.249	0.287
PARVLS	0.172	0.280	0.381	0.406	0.198	0.205
PMLNI	0.145	**0.221**	0.369	0.392	0.142	0.180
SSPML-SL	0.185	0.272	0.341	0.354	0.145	0.149
dS²PLL	0.163	0.351	0.642	0.653	0.230	0.253
CS2PML-SL	0.159	0.246	0.347	0.364	0.150	0.160
FMLL	0.173	0.314	0.665	0.674	0.239	0.295

One Error					
Dataset	**TMC2007 1**	**TMC2007 2**	**Flag 1**	**Flag 2**	**Emotion**
PPM	**0.5**	**0.5**	**0.5**	**0.5**	**0.5**
dS²PML	0.379	0.380	0.019	0.021	0.479
cS²PML	**0.367**	**0.372**	**0.017**	**0.017**	**0.460**
dPML	0.397	0.426	0.030	0.035	0.509
dITS²MLL	0.470	0.470	0.057	0.065	0.535
PARVLS	0.452	0.453	0.031	0.043	0.522
PMLNI	0.433	0.436	0.020	0.023	0.514
SSPML-SL	0.389	0.394	0.025	0.049	0.492
dS²PLL	0.470	0.470	0.079	0.114	0.540
CS2PML-SL	0.391	0.405	0.025	0.029	0.497
FMLL	0.470	0.470	0.076	0.091	0.558

Table 5. Average precision of different algorithms versus PPM on 11 used datasets, where the best performances are shown in bold face.

			Average Precision			
Dataset	**Genbase 1**	**Genbase 2**	**Medical 1**	**Medical 2**	**CHD49 1**	**CHD49 2**
PPM	**0.5**	**0.5**	**0.5**	**0.5**	**0.5**	**0.5**
dS^{2}PML	0.893	0.812	0.763	0.745	0.910	0.886
cS^{2}PML	**0.898**	0.818	**0.765**	**0.752**	**0.917**	**0.895**
dPML	0.873	0.776	0.739	0.712	0.878	0.859
dITS^{2}MLL	0.885	0.745	0.566	0.558	0.811	0.770
PARVLS	0.865	0.736	0.705	0.700	0.881	0.854
PMLNI	0.883	**0.823**	0.714	0.710	0.885	0.867
SSPML-SL	0.864	0.769	0.745	0.735	0.887	0.860
dS^{2}PLL	0.865	0.717	0.568	0.561	0.825	0.781
CS2PML-SL	0.869	0.764	0.739	0.728	0.879	0.856
FMLL	0.871	0.713	0.556	0.547	0.819	0.765
			Average Precision			
Dataset	**TMC2007 1**	**TMC2007 2**	**Flag 1**	**Flag 2**	**Emotion**	
PPM	**0.5**	**0.5**	**0.5**	**0.5**	**0.5**	
dS^{2}PML	0.684	0.679	**0.975**	0.972	0.603	
cS^{2}PML	**0.686**	**0.683**	0.973	**0.974**	**0.608**	
dSPML	0.663	0.641	0.960	0.964	0.585	
dITS^{2}MLL	0.601	0.597	0.941	0.939	0.568	
PARVLS	0.643	0.637	0.951	0.947	0.563	
PMLNI	0.657	0.649	0.962	0.958	0.577	
SSPML-SL	0.669	0.657	0.961	0.960	0.591	
dS^{2}PLL	0.603	0.595	0.973	0.970	0.569	
CS2PML-SL	0.661	0.650	0.957	0.952	0.578	
FMLL	0.597	0.582	0.942	0.938	0.559	

Table 6. Ranking loss of different algorithms versus PPM on 11 used datasets, where the best performances are shown in bold face.

			Ranking Loss			
Dataset	**Genbase 1**	**Genbase 2**	**Medical 1**	**Medical 2**	**CHD49 1**	**CHD49 2**
PPM	**0.5**	**0.5**	**0.5**	**0.5**	**0.5**	**0.5**
dS^{2}PML	0.033	0.057	0.038	0.040	0.101	0.139
cS^{2}PML	**0.030**	0.051	**0.036**	**0.038**	**0.099**	**0.135**
dSPML	0.040	0.067	0.051	0.067	0.128	0.156
dITS^{2}MLL	0.039	0.095	0.078	0.081	0.211	0.255
PARVLS	0.043	0.064	0.046	0.050	0.132	0.172
PMLNI	0.039	**0.050**	0.040	0.044	0.124	0.159
SSPML-SL	0.042	0.066	0.041	0.043	0.120	0.146
dS^{2}PLL	0.047	0.094	0.072	0.086	0.192	0.241
CS2PML-SL	0.041	0.073	0.043	0.048	0.126	0.154
FMLL	0.043	0.098	0.081	0.087	0.209	0.258
			Ranking Loss			
Dataset	**TMC2007 1**	**TMC2007 2**	**Flag 1**	**Flag 2**	**Emotion**	
PPM	**0.5**	**0.5**	**0.5**	**0.5**	**0.5**	
dS^{2}PML	0.089	0.091	0.033	0.046	0.258	
cS^{2}PML	**0.087**	**0.090**	**0.029**	**0.042**	**0.252**	
dSPML	0.098	0.102	0.042	0.058	0.264	
dITS^{2}MLL	0.124	0.125	0.063	0.074	0.286	
PARVLS	0.106	0.107	0.057	0.066	0.284	
PMLNI	0.095	0.097	0.047	0.051	0.263	
SSPML-SL	0.099	0.102	0.049	0.056	0.262	
dS^{2}PLL	0.116	0.117	0.031	0.049	0.287	
CS2PML-SL	0.101	0.104	0.058	0.069	0.268	
FMLL	0.127	0.131	0.102	0.108	0.296	

Table 7. Coverage of different algorithms versus PPM on 11 used datasets, where the best performances are shown in bold face.

Coverage						
Dataset	**Genbase 1**	**Genbase 2**	**Medical 1**	**Medical 2**	**CHD49 1**	**CHD49 2**
PPM	**0.5**	**0.5**	**0.5**	**0.5**	**0.5**	**0.5**
dS^2PML	0.052	0.082	0.050	0.052	0.356	0.384
cS^2PML	**0.049**	0.079	**0.045**	**0.048**	**0.352**	**0.378**
dPML	0.063	0.095	0.059	0.064	0.373	0.398
dITS^{2}MLL	0.061	0.129	0.085	0.098	0.447	0.463
PARVLS	0.066	0.090	0.055	0.065	0.379	0.408
PMLNI	0.061	**0.078**	0.052	0.058	0.370	0.397
SSPML-SL	0.064	0.092	0.058	0.061	0.380	0.396
dS^2PLL	0.078	0.128	0.083	0.102	0.432	0.449
CS2PML-SL	0.068	0.097	0.055	0.064	0.384	0.403
FMLL	0.082	0.138	0.087	0.096	0.466	0.497

Coverage					
Dataset	**TMC2007 1**	**TMC2007 2**	**Flag 1**	**Flag 2**	**Emotion**
PPM	**0.5**	**0.5**	**0.5**	**0.5**	**0.5**
dS^2PML	0.189	0.190	0.359	0.362	0.428
cS^2PML	**0.188**	**0.189**	**0.356**	**0.358**	**0.424**
dPML	0.196	0.215	0.371	0.385	0.457
dITS^{2}MLL	0.236	0.266	0.399	0.402	0.454
PARVLS	0.208	0.211	0.387	0.389	0.452
PMLNI	0.190	0.193	0.377	0.382	0.456
SSPML-SL	0.203	0.210	0.375	0.378	0.430
dS^2PLL	0.227	0.236	0.365	0.367	0.453
CS2PML-SL	0.208	0.224	0.378	0.383	0.445
FMLL	0.273	0.301	0.402	0.408	0.473

From Tables 3–7 and Figure 11, we can notice that our proposed dS^2PML and the corresponding cS^2PML rank the top two among all the comparison algorithms, indicating that our proposed algorithm is capable of handling the tasks of reliable labeling confidence estimation, label correlation exploitation, and classification induction in an effective manner. For clarity, we can summarize the observed experimental results into three points:

(1) It can be observed that the classification performance of our proposed dS^2PML is close to that of the corresponding cS^2PML algorithm, and significantly superior to that of the corresponding dPML method in all the evaluation metrics. Such a simulation result demonstrates the effectiveness of distributed learning. Additionally, by comparing the learning performances of dS^2PML and dPML, we can find that utilizing the information from unlabeled data can enhance classification performance.

(2) It can be observed that FMLL, dITS^{2}MLL, and dS^2PLL perform relatively poorly in these comparison algorithms. The possible reason is that as a distributed supervised learning method, FMLL learns the classifier based on the dispersed distributed labeled data. So, it is not only unable to handle the negative effect of noisy labels on the learned model, but it also fails to exploit the information from unlabeled data. Different from FMLL, dITS^{2}MLL utilizes the logistic loss and information entropy to take the information from both labeled and unlabeled data into account. So, dITS^{2}MLL performs better than FMLL, but it is still inferior to the other PML comparison methods affected by the noisy labels concealed in candidate labels. Additionally, dS^2PLL belongs to semi-supervised single partial label learning methods, which disambiguate the candidate labels based on the learned labeling confidence. So, the learning performance of dS^2PLL is better than that of FMLL. But, due to the ignoring of potential correlation among multiple labels, its performance is still poorer than that of the other PML algorithm.

(3) It can be observed that four PML/S^2PML algorithms, including CS2PML-SL, PARVLS, PMLNI, and SSPML-SL, perform better than the FMLL, dITS^{2}MLL, and dS^2PLL methods, but their performances are still inferior to that of our proposed method. The possible reasons are explained as follows. These PML/S^2PML algorithms utilize a series of strategies to eliminate the negative effect of noisy labels on the learning

performance and exploit the label correlation in depth. So, they outperform the other comparison algorithms. However, PARVLS and PMLNI, which are supervised learning methods, do not consider the information from unlabeled data during the training process, which may have a negative effect on their learning performance. Additionally, the performances of PARVLS, SSPML-SL, and CS2PML-SL heavily depend on the accuracy of label propagation. When data distribution is imbalanced, label propagation becomes inefficient, potentially impairing classification performance.

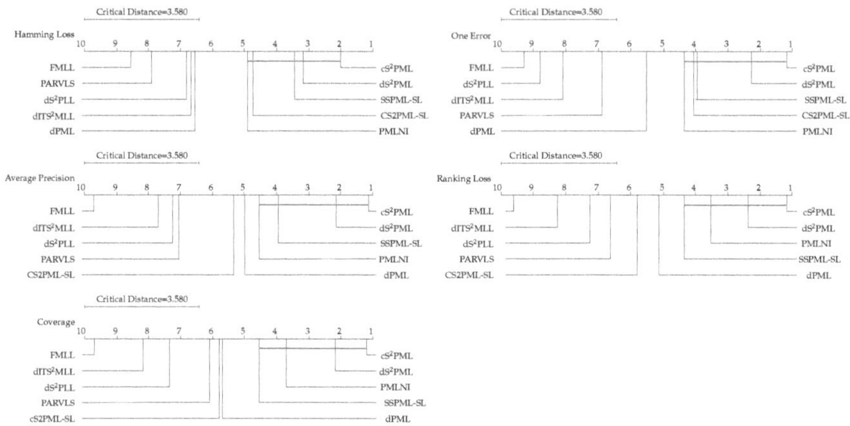

Figure 11. Comparison of dS^{2}PML and cS^{2}PML (the control algorithm) in contrast to other comparing algorithms using the Bonferroni–Dunn test.

Additionally, we employ the Friedman test to determine whether there exists a significant performance difference among comparison algorithms. Let $k_A = 10$ represent the number of comparison algorithms, and set $N_D = 11$ denote the number of used datasets. We calculate the value of the Friedman statistics, denoted by F_F, as well as the critical values corresponding to all the used metrics. As shown in Table 8, for each evaluation metric, the null hypothesis that the performances of these comparison algorithms are indistinguishable from each other is rejected when the significance level is set at 0.05.

Table 8. Summary of the Friedman statistics F_F and the critical value in teams of each evaluation metric.

Metric	F_F	Critical Value ($\alpha = 0.05$)
Hamming loss	11.34	
One Error	29.52	
Average Precision	17.33	1.986
Ranking Loss	18.46	
Coverage	21.50	

The relative performance difference between the control algorithm and another comparison algorithm is assessed using the Bonferroni–Dunn test. Figure 11 exhibits the critical difference (CD) diagrams on each metric by using the cS^{2}PML algorithm as the control method, where the average ranks of all the used algorithms are depicted with black lines. In each subfigure, a red line depicts the link between a comparison algorithm and the control algorithm if the difference between their average ranks is less than one CD at the significance level 0.05. Otherwise, no link is depicted. In each subfigure, it can be found that among all the comparison algorithms, the proposed cS^{2}PML shows superior learning performance, with an average rank distinctly different from that of dPML, PARVLS, dS^{2}PLL, dITS^{2}MLL, and FMLL in all the evaluation metrics. Additionally, the proposed dS^{2}PML and cS^{2}PML algorithms are the two highest-ranked among the comparison algorithms in each metric. This observation demonstrates that our proposed dS^{2}PML algorithm is efficient for solving the distributed S^2PML problem. Its performance is fairly close to that of the centralized method and noticeably superior to that of the other comparison algorithms.

Finally, to highlight the computation efficiency of our proposed algorithm, we have compared the CPU times and memory consumption of the proposed dS^2PML and the other comparison algorithms on different datasets. The results are presented in Tables 9 and 10, respectively. It is noted that the semi-supervised learning methods induce predictive models based on both labeled and unlabeled data, but supervised learning methods only take the information of labeled data into account during the training process. So, directly comparing the CPU time and memory consumption of comparison algorithms on the originally training dataset is unfair for semi-supervised learning methods. In this experiment, for the sake of fairness, all the training data are set as labeled to ensure that the amount of training dataset for all the comparison algorithms, whether supervised learning algorithms or semi-supervised learning algorithms, is the same. Considering that the proposed dS^2PML is completely equivalent to the corresponding dPML algorithm in this experiment, the CPU time and memory consumption of the dPML algorithm are not given here. Additionally, the size of datasets and the number of class labels are the same for pairs of datasets: genbase 1/2, medical 1/2, CHD49 1/2, TMC2007 1/2, and flag 1/2. For simplicity, the simulation results for these pairs of datasets are combined into one column.

Table 9. CPU time (s) of different algorithms on used datasets, where the minimum values are shown in bold face.

	CPU Time (s)					
Dataset	**Genbase 1/2**	**Medical 1/2**	**CHD49 1/2**	**TMC2007 1/2**	**Flag 1/2**	**Emotion**
dS^2PML	**31.45**	**64.31**	16.79	**294.40**	**10.36**	**39.24**
cS^2PML	276.72	578.77	147.89	2.56×10^3	89.90	355.15
dITS^2MLL	52.62	106.28	27.87	534.97	17.54	71.04
PARVLS	165.05	427.05	146.78	5.62×10^3	85.17	463.74
PMLNI	84.06	163.08	50.42	993.30	33.60	133.06
SSPML-SL	161.74	419.69	143.75	5.79×10^3	74.43	434.77
dS^2PLL	31.58	65.41	**16.35**	317.42	10.86	42.56
CS2PML-SL	164.98	436.44	137.49	5.43×10^3	76.42	461.64
FMLL	87.05	170.61	39.28	772.18	26.19	110.03

Table 10. Memory consumption (MB) of different algorithms on used datasets, where the minimum values are shown in bold face.

	Memory Consumption (MB)					
Dataset	**Genbase 1/2**	**Medical 1/2**	**CHD49 1/2**	**TMC2007 1/2**	**Flag 1/2**	**Emotion**
dS^2PML	**1013**	1020	1028	**1074**	**1016**	**1032**
cS^2PML	1076	1083	1095	1305	1074	1128
dITS^2MLL	1048	1051	1057	1145	1046	1080
PARVLS	1342	1563	1904	7356	1318	3556
PMLNI	1131	1142	1155	1293	1117	1165
SSPML-SL	1320	1535	1874	7227	1307	3527
dS^2PLL	1015	**1017**	**1026**	1078	1019	1049
CS2PML-SL	1296	1508	1853	6875	1278	3462
FMLL	1113	1135	1147	1259	1126	1153

From the results given in Tables 9 and 10, we can notice that, different from the centralized learning algorithms, all the training data are dispersedly stored at J individual nodes and then processed in parallel in distributed learning algorithms. Owing to the dispersed storage and parallel processing of training data, the CPU time and the memory consumption of the distributed learning algorithm are smaller than those of the other centralized comparison algorithms. Additionally, comparing the results of these distributed comparison algorithms, we can find that the CPU times and the memory consumption of the proposed dS^2PML and dS^2PLL are close to each other, and both of them are significantly smaller than those of dITS^2MLL and FMLL. The possible reasons for this phenomenon are that dS^2PML and dS^2PLL only need to compute and store a few model parameters at each iteration. However, the dITS^{2}MLL necessitates a substantial number of high-dimensional matrix multiplication operations and inversion computations during the initial stages of the training process. For FMLL, the process of building decision trees also requires a large amount of computation and memory.

Referring to the simulation results, jointly considering the classification performance, running time, and memory consumption, we conclude that our proposed algorithm outperforms the other existing comparison algorithms in both accuracy and efficiency.

5. Conclusions

In this paper, we have developed a dS^{2}PML algorithm. In the proposed algorithm, the multi-kernel function together with the label correlation has been used to construct the discriminant function. Based on several globally common basic data, the decentralized implementation of the global objective function has been achieved. By utilizing an alternating minimization method, the labeling confidence can be estimated, and then, a multi-label classifier has been collaboratively trained with transmitting only a few parameters among neighbors. Experiments have been conducted on a series of datasets, and the experimental results have confirmed that the proposed algorithm outperforms the other existing comparison algorithms in both accuracy and efficiency.

In addition, considering that in some real applications, the data distributions can vary across different nodes due to systematic factors or the sensitivity of detection sensors, we would like to develop some distributed personalized algorithms to deal with heterogeneous data distributions in the future. Additionally, our proposed algorithm ignores the requirement of data privacy protection in the distributed network. But, in many real applications, the private information of original data is sensitive, and the direct transmission of local estimations may result in privacy breaches. So, we would also like to develop some privacy-preserving dS^{2}PML algorithms in the future. Furthermore, developing a dynamic information cooperation strategy to adapt to dynamic networks is also one of the possible research directions in the future.

Author Contributions: Conceptualization, W.C.; Methodology, Z.X.; Software, Z.X.; Validation, W.C.; Formal analysis, Z.X.; Investigation, W.C.; Resources, W.C.; Data curation, W.C.; Writing—original draft, Z.X.; Writing—review & editing, W.C.; Supervision, W.C.; Project administration, W.C.; Funding acquisition, W.C. All authors have read and agreed to the published version of the manuscript.

Funding: This work was partly supported by the National Natural Science Foundation of China (Grant Nos. 62201398) and supported by the Open Project of Center for Applied Mathematics of Jiangsu Province (Nanjing University of Information Science and Technology).

Data Availability Statement: All data generated or analyzed during this study are included in this published article.

Conflicts of Interest: The authors declare no conflicts of interest.

References

1. Lin, J.; Su, Q.; Yang, P.; Ma, S.; Sun, X. Semantic unit-based dilated convolution for multi-label text classification. In Proceedings of the 2018 Conference on Empirical Methods in Natural Language Processing, Brussels, Belgium, 31 October–4 November 2018; pp. 4554–4564.
2. Chen, Z.M.; Wei, X.S.; Wang, P.; Guo, Y. Multi-label image recognition with graph convolutional networks. In Proceedings of the 2019 IEEE Conference on Computer Vision and Pattern Recognition, Long Beach, CA, USA, 15–20 June 2019; pp. 5177–5186.
3. Deng, J.; Ding, N.; Jia, Y.; Frome, A.; Murphy, K.; Bengio, S.; Li, Y.; Neven, H.; Adam, H. Large-scale object classification using label relation graphs. In Proceedings of the European Conference on Computer Vision, Zurich, Switzerland, 6–12 September 2014; pp. 48–64.
4. Zhang, M.L.; Li, Y.K.; Liu, Y.Y.; Geng, X. Binary relevance for multi-label learning: An overview. *Front. Comput. Sci.* **2018**, *12*, 191–202. [CrossRef]
5. Tsoumakas, G.; Katakis, I.; Vlahavas, I. Random *k*-labelsets for multi-label classification. *IEEE Trans. Knowl. Data Eng.* **2011**, *23*, 1079–1089. [CrossRef]
6. Zhang, M.L.; Wu, L. Lift: Multi-label learning with label-specific features. *IEEE Trans. Pattern. Anal. Mach. Intell.* **2015**, *37*, 107–120. [CrossRef] [PubMed]

7. Du, G.D.; Zhang, J.; Zhang, N.; Wu, H.R.; Wu, P.L.; Li, S.Z. Semi-supervised imbalanced multi-label classification with label propagation. *Pattern Recogn.* **2024**, *150*, 110358. [CrossRef]
8. Li, J.X.; Zhu, X.Y.; Wang, H.R.; Zhang, Y.; Wang, J.Y. Stacked co-training for semi-supervised multi-label learning. *Inf. Sci.* **2024**, *677*, 120906. [CrossRef]
9. Xie, Z.X.; Li, P.P.; Jiang, J.L.; Wu, X.D. Semi-supervised multi-Label learning with missing labels via correlation information. In Proceedings of the 2023 International Joint Conference on Neural Networks (IJCNN), Gold Coast, Australia, 18–23 June 2023; pp. 1–8.
10. Chen, Z.S.; Wu, X.; Chen, Q.C.; Hu, Y.; Zhang, M.L. Multi-view partial multi-label learning with graph-based disambiguation. In Proceedings of the 34th AAAI Conference on Artificial Intelligence, New York, NY, USA, 7–12 February 2020; pp. 3553–3560.
11. Fang, J.P.; Zhang, M.L. Partial multi-label learning via reliable label elicitation. In Proceedings of the 33rd AAAI Conference on Artificial Intelligence, Honolulu, HI, USA, 27 January–1 February 2019; pp. 3518–3525.
12. Wang, H.; Liu, W.; Zhang, Y.; Hu, T.; Chen, G. Discriminative and correlative partial multi-label learning. In Proceedings of the 28th International Joint Conference on Artificial Intelligence, Macao, China, 10–16 August 2019; pp. 3691–3697.
13. Sun, L.; Feng, S.; Wang, T.; Lang, C.; Jin, Y. Partial multi-label learning by low-rank and sparse decomposition. In Proceedings of the 33rd AAAI Conference on Artificial Intelligence, Honolulu, HI, USA, 27 January–1 February 2019; pp. 5016–5023.
14. Xie, M.K.; Huang, S.J. Partial multi-label learning. In Proceedings of the 32nd AAAI Conference on Artificial Intelligence, New Orleans, LA, USA, 2–7 February 2018; pp. 4302–4309.
15. Xie, M.K.; Huang, S.J. Partial multi-label learning with noisy label identification. *IEEE Trans. Pattern Anal. Mach. Intell.* **2022**, *44*, 3676–3687.
16. Qian, W.B.; Tu, Y.Q.; Huang, J.T.; Ding, W.P. Partial multi-label learning via robust feature selection and relevance fusion optimization. *Knowl.-Based Syst.* **2024**, *286*, 111365. [CrossRef]
17. Liu, B.Q.; Jia, B.B.; Zhang, M.L. Towards enabling binary decomposition for partial multi-label learning. *IEEE Trans. Pattern Anal. Mach. Intell.* **2023**, *45*, 13203–13217. [CrossRef]
18. Xie, M.K.; Huang, S. Semi-supervised partial multi-Label learning. In Proceedings of the IEEE International Conference on Data Mining (ICDM), Sorrento, Italy, 17–20 November 2020; pp. 691–700.
19. Tan, A.; Wu, W.Z. Partial multi-label learning via semi-supervised subspace collaboration. *Knowl.-Based Syst.* **2024**, *287*, 111444. [CrossRef]
20. Miao, X.D.; Liu, Y.; Zhao, H.Q.; Li, C.G. Distributed online one-class support vector machine for anomaly detection over networks. *IEEE Trans. Cybern.* **2019**, *49*, 1475–1488. [CrossRef]
21. Xu, Z.; Liu, Y.; Li, C. Distributed information theoretic semi-supervised learning for multi-label classification. *IEEE Trans. Cybern.* **2022**, *52*, 821–835. [CrossRef]
22. Xu, Z.; Liu, Y.; Li, C. Distributed semi-supervised learning with missing data. *IEEE Trans. Cybern.* **2021**, *51*, 6165–6178. [CrossRef] [PubMed]
23. Liu, Y.; Xu, Z.; Li, C. Distributed online semi-supervised support vector machine. *Inf. Sci.* **2018**, *466*, 236–257. [CrossRef]
24. Liu, Y.; Xu, Z.; Zhang, C. Distributed semi-supervised partial label learning over networks *IEEE Trans. Artif. Intell.* **2022**, *3*, 414–425.
25. Ghasemkhani, B.; Varliklar, O.; Dogan, Y.; Utku, S.; Birant, K.; Birant, D. Federated Multi-Label Learning (FMLL): Innovative Method for Classification Tasks in Animal Science. *Animals* **2024**, *14*, 2021. [CrossRef] [PubMed]
26. Guehria, S.; Belleili, H.; Azizi, N. Distributed Approach for Large-Scale Ensemble Multi-Label Classification. In Proceedings of the 2nd International Conference on Scientific and Innovative Studies, Konya, Turkey, 11–12 September 2024; pp. 834–840.
27. Zhou, Y.; He, J.; Gu, H. Partial label learning via Gaussian processes. *IEEE Trans. Cybern.* **2017**, *47*, 4430–4450. [CrossRef] [PubMed]
28. Yu, F.; Zhang, M.L. Maximum margin partial label learning. *Mach. Learn.* **2017**, *106*, 573–593. [CrossRef]
29. Tang, C.; Zhang, M.L. Confidence-rated discriminative partial label learning. In Proceedings of the 31st AAAI Conference on Artificial Intelligence, San Francisco, CA, USA, 4–9 February 2017; pp. 2611–2617.
30. Liu, M.Q.; Yang, K.; Zhao, N.; Chen, Y.F.; Song, H.; Gong, F.K. Intelligent signal classification in industrial distributed wireless sensor networks based industrial internet of things. *IEEE Trans. Ind. Inf.* **2020**, *17*, 4946–4956. [CrossRef]
31. Carminati, M.; Kanoun, O.; Ullo, S.L.; Marcuccio, S. Prospects of distributed wireless sensor networks for urban environmental monitoring. *IEEE Aerosp. Electron. Syst. Mag.* **2019**, *34*, 44–52. [CrossRef]
32. Liu, X.; Wang, L.; Zhu, X.; Li, M.; Yin, J. Absent multiple kernel learning algorithms. *IEEE Trans. Pattern. Anal. Mach. Intell.* **2020**, *42*, 1303–1316. [CrossRef]
33. Shen, Y.; Chen, T.; Giannakis, G.B. Online multi-kernel learning with orthogonal random features. In Proceedings of the 2018 IEEE International Conference on Acoustics, Speech and Signal Processing (ICASSP), Calgary, AL, Canada, 15–20 April 2018; pp. 6289–6293.
34. Rahimi, A.; Recht, B. Random features for large-scale kernel machines. In Proceedings of the 21th International Conference on Neural Information Processing System, Vancouver, BC, Canada, 3–6 December 2007; pp. 1177–1184.
35. Sreekanth, V.; Vedaldi, A.; Zisserman, A.; Jawahar, C. Generalized RBF feature maps for efficient detection. In Proceedings of the 21st British Machine Vision Conference, Aberystwyth, UK, 31 August–3 September 2010; pp. 1–11.

36. Yuan, X.; Wang, Z.; Deng, J.; Liu, Q. Efficient χ^2 kernel linearization via random feature maps. *IEEE Trans. Neural Netw. Learn. Syst.* **2016**, *27*, 2448–2453. [CrossRef] [PubMed]
37. Liu, Y.; Li, C.; Zhang, Z. Diffusion sparse least-mean squares over networks. *IEEE Trans. Signal. Process* **2012**, *60*, 4480–4485. [CrossRef]
38. Gu, Y.; Jin, J.; Mei, S. l_0-norm constraint LMS algorithm for sparse system identification. *IEEE Signal. Process. Lett.* **2009**, *16*, 774–777.
39. Pu, X.K.; Li, C.G. Online Semisupervised Broad Learning System for Industrial Fault Diagnosis. *IEEE Trans. Ind. Inf.* **2021**, *17*, 6644–6654. [CrossRef]
40. Tsoumakas, K.G.; Vlahavas, I. Mulan Repository of Multi-Label Machine Learning Databases. Available online: http://mulan.sourceforge.net/index.html (accessed on 1 May 2024).

electronics

MDPI

Article

Knowledge Extraction from LLMs for Scalable Historical Data Annotation

Fabio Celli *and Dmitry Mingazov

Maggioli Research, Via Bornaccino 101, 47822 Santarcangelo di Romagna, Italy
* Correspondence: fabio.celli@maggioli.it

Abstract: This paper introduces a novel approach to extract knowledge from large language models and generate structured historical datasets. We investigate the feasibility and limitations of this technique by comparing the generated data against two human-annotated historical datasets spanning from 10,000 BC to 2000 CE. Our findings demonstrate that generative AI can successfully produce historical annotations for a wide range of variables, including political, economic, and social factors. However, the model's performance varies across different regions, influenced by factors such as data granularity, historical complexity, and model limitations. We highlight the importance of high-quality instructions and effective prompt engineering to mitigate issues like hallucinations and improve the accuracy of generated annotations. The successful application of this technique can significantly accelerate the development of reliable structured historical datasets, with a potentially high impact on comparative and computational history.

Keywords: large language models; knowledge extraction; cliodynamics

1. Introduction

Structured or semi-structured historical datasets, such as Seshat [1] and Chronos [2], are valuable tools for extracting models of societal evolution, cultural change [3], response to social crises [4] and geo-political patterns [5]. For example, data and models demonstrate that the evolution of warfare techniques alone can account for more than half of the increase in the hierarchical complexity of past societies. Additionally, improvements in governance specialization explain one-third of the increase in agricultural productivity [6].

Unfortunately, the development of trusted historical datasets is costly, time-consuming, not scalable and prone to errors and limitations. There are three open challenges in particular:

- Data integrity is a primary challenge in developing datasets of this nature, as certain phenomena, such as immaterial historical records, are difficult to quantify [7]. Specifically, historical data are inherently biased due to missing records [8], a problem that becomes more pronounced as we examine increasingly distant past periods.
- Subjectivity poses another significant challenge. Reaching consensus on historical data annotation is difficult due to the subjective nature of historical interpretation.
- A third challenge is knowledge representation, particularly how to compress historical information into a structured format. The Seshat dataset contains data about polities from 35 different natural geographic areas (NGAs) and provides many dimensions that report the presence or absence of a cultural trait in a polity at a specific point in time, for example, the presence/absence of copper, fortifications, firearms, written literature, coins and many others. These cultural dimensions can be computationally represented using one-hot encoding (OHE), a common technique for converting categorical features into numerical ones. OHE represents each category as a binary vector, where a '1' indicates presence and a '0' indicates absence. However, OHE often leads to high information sparsity in the transformed data, meaning that many values are zero. This sparsity can hinder the extraction of models using statistical or machine learning techniques [9].

Time-series interpolation techniques are employed to address data integrity issues and crowdsourcing to address subjectivity. While they have a positive effect [10], crowdsourcing is ineffective in mitigating subjectivity, as human judgment is often influenced by cultural biases [11]. This work mainly addresses the challenge of knowledge representation and contributes to the improvement of AI-generated historical data with the application of a new compression technique.

1.1. Related Work

To solve the knowledge representation problem, one-hot encoded features are usually transformed into coarse-grained variables with compression techniques like principal component analysis (PCA) or autoencoders [12]; however, once compressed, the data lose their transparency, making it very difficult to interpret the models from a human perspective. However, techniques like time-resolved variables (TRVs) can compress historical data into meaningful scales [13]. In essence, TRVs transform categorical variables into interpretable numerical scales. Each level of the scale represents a developmental stage of a specific dimension, ordered chronologically by its first known historical appearance. For instance, a scale of military technologies might place stone at the first level, copper at the second, bronze at the third, iron at the fourth, and so on.

The hypothesis that motivates this work is that knowledge extraction from large language models (LLMs) can be exploited to annotate structured historical datasets in a scalable and cheaper way. The field of knowledge extraction from LLMs is quite novel, but there are successful applications. For example, prompts to perform knowledge extraction in structured data are used for testing the risk of LLMs to leak sensitive information [14]. Another successful application is tabular data augmentation (TDA), which enhances an existing dataset in a tabular format with additional structured data, with the aim of improving machine learning models [15]. However, the most popular use of LLMs for generating structured data might be synthetic data generation: systems like DiffLM, based on autoencoders and diffusion models [16], can generate tabular data similar to an original table, with the same data distribution but without privacy issues. A previous attempt to benchmark LLMs in historical data generation showed that LLMs can generate correct outputs, but there is considerable room for improvement in this task [17]. Crucially, recent advancements in LLMs have substantially mitigated their tendency to hallucinate, enabling the first real-world applications of LLM-based tabular data generation. In this domain, context-rich prompts have proven to significantly enhance both data generation quality and training efficiency [18].

This work is the first attempt to exploit knowledge extraction from LLMs for producing structured historical datasets in a scalable manner. To do so, we review evaluation methods in a previous study on the generation of structured data with LLMs (Section 1.2); then, we define our method (Section 2), provide description of the data Section 2.1, describe the experiments and the results of our evaluation (Section 3) and then draw our conclusion and outline potential future directions (Section 4).

1.2. Evaluation of Generative Models

It is not easy to evaluate the validity of AI-generated, synthetic structured data. The literature suggests five main metrics for this kind of evaluation [19]:

- The Pearson correlation coefficient is a general purpose measure that quantifies the linear relationship between two variables. It ranges from -1 to 1, with larger absolute values indicating a stronger linear correlation. This metric can quantitatively assess the similarity between generated and real data. When dealing with time series, like in historical data, the correlation coefficient can also evaluate how much the trend of generated and real data is similar [20].
- F1-score, the harmonic mean of precision and recall, is a metric to assess the accuracy of classification models. It measures how well a model's predicted discrete values

align with the ground truth values. This metric is often used in zero-shot or few-shot classification tasks [21].
- The Kolmogorov–Smirnov test, a statistical method used to determine if two datasets originate from the same underlying distribution, compares the cumulative distribution functions of two datasets and it is used in synthetic numerical data generation [22].
- Kullback–Leibler divergence is a metric that measures the difference between two probability distributions. A lower score signifies greater similarity between the two distributions. Unlike the Kolmogorov–Smirnov test, which uses statistics to express this difference, Kullback–Leibler divergence quantifies the information difference between one distribution and another [23].
- Edit distance, often referred to as Levenshtein distance, is a metric used to quantify the difference between two sequences and takes values from 0 to infinity. Applied on text, it measures the minimum number of single-character edits (insertions, deletions, or substitutions) required to transform one string into another. It is used in the evaluation of code similarity [24].

We select average edit distance and correlation coefficient as metrics to evaluate structured historical data. Average edit distance is an error metric (lower scores mean greater similarity), while correlation coefficient should be close to 1 to indicate a good performance. Previous work in structured data generation obtained a minimum correlation of $\rho = 0.693$ on census income data [25] and a maximum $\rho = 0.983$ on air carrier statistics data [26], We refer to these results as baseline, as no previous evaluation is available for generated historical data.

2. Materials and Methods

Figure 1 illustrates our method for generating and evaluating structured historical data. We begin with Seshat and Chronos, two human-annotated historical datasets detailed in Section 2.1. First, we interpret the feature values for each of the two datasets in order to design specific instructions on how to categorize, extract and structure data. Then, we incorporate these instructions into the corresponding prompts (see Section 2.2).

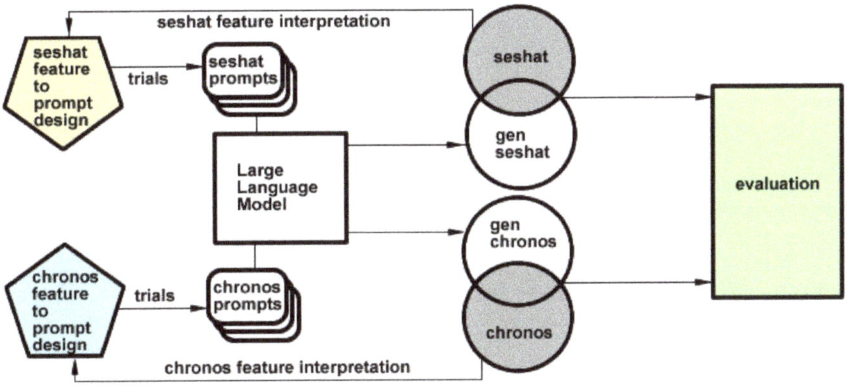

Figure 1. Schema of the method adopted.

In order to cover a wide spectrum of cases, we perform three different trials with Gemini 1.5 flash, Llama 3.1 and GPT-4o, testing parameters such as temperature and grounding, without any fine-tuning (see Section 3). We perform three runs with the same prompts, one per dataset, changing the NGAs: Turkey (which had a early development), Japan (intermediate development) and Ecuador (late development). The input to the LLM includes the prompt and an example of the desired output taken from the original data. The prompts contain instructions to estimate the desired categories, and there is the possibility to generate null values. Then, we align the generated data with the original dataset via timestamping.

Finally, we evaluate the correlation and edit the distance and coverage for each trial, run and dataset to obtain a comparison of the synthetic and original data.

2.1. Data

We use two publicly available datasets annotated with historical records: Seshat and Chronos. Seshat released many replication sets and we selected the social complexity dataset [27] which contains PCA-compressed variables about polities, such as population, territory, type of texts, type of government, currency, infrastructure, social scale and others, sampled from 30 NGAs with a timestep of 100 years. The weak point of Seshat is that the PCA-compressed variables are difficult to interpret and explain through instructions for the language model to replicate them. The strong point is that the timestep of 100 years is good for the alignment; hence, we expect high coverage. Polity identifiers in Seshat were not encoded following strict rules. Thus, we expect a poor edit distance in their replication.

Chronos is more detailed than Seshat, providing numerous variables for polities in 18 NGAs. These variables include quantitative data like population and territory size, as well as information expressed using TRVs. The use of TRVs simplifies interpretation, and this is a valuable feature of the Chronos dataset. Additionally, the consistent encoding of polity identifiers suggests potential for accurate alignment and low edit distances. However, Chronos's 10-year timestep might hinder alignment with generated datasets, possibly leading to lower coverage.

Gemini 1.5 flash, Llama 3.1 and GPT-4o have a knowledge cutoff between October and December 2023. Seshat has been published for the first time in 2017, so it is possible that LLMs contain it in a raw format. Chronos, instead, has been published in December 2024 and was not available at the time we ran the experiments; hence, it is impossible that LLMs contain it or access it with grounding.

2.2. Prompts

We create two specific prompts, one for Seshat and one for Chronos, which contain explanation for data annotation based on feature interpretation. We select a subset of comparable features from both datasets. For Seshat, the selected features are the following: **polity population** (PolPop) is the log-transformed polity population and **polity territory** (PolTerr) is the log-transformed territory size;

type of money (economy) is the OHE-PCA summarizing the presence/absence of precious metals, tokens, articles, paper currency, indigenous and foreign coins;

type of texts (infomedia) is the OHE-PCA of calendars, lists, sacred text, practical literature, scientific literature, fiction, and philosophy;

infrastructure (infrastructure) is the OHE-PCA of bridges, markets, mines and quarries, canals, roads, drinking water supply, ports, irrigation or production systems, food storage sites;

Social scale (scale) is the OHE-PCA of polity population, polity territory and the population of the largest settlement and **Specialization of governance** (government): the OHE-PCA of presence or absence of full-time bureaucrats, professional officers, priests, soldiers, examination systems, specialized buildings for government, full-time judges, formal legal code, courts, lawyers, merit promotion.

As part of the feature interpretation phase, all variables in Seshat were normalized to a 0–1 scale. This operation allowed us to manually check the descriptions of three polities at each scale level (0.1, 0.2, 0.3 and so on) to interpret these values and create textual instructions for the prompt. For instance, a population value of 0.1 roughly corresponded to a polity with 100–1000 people. All instructions are detailed in Figure 2. This method is inherently error-prone, and we expect a high edit distance. We also ask the LLM to generate a description of the historical period in order to perform a qualitative assessment of the output.

```
Generate a table in json format with information about the polities that exist in the [NGA] between 10000 BC and 2010 CE.
The structure of the table must be a century per row and the following columns:
NGA: location of the society or site;
polID: the polity ID, as the concat of two characters for civilization (where the population come from, use the two char state
abbreviation), three characters for culture (use abbreviation of population name, ruling dynasty or type site), one char for the
social type (c=community, n=nomad community, k=kingdom, e=empire, r=republic) and one character for the civilization stage (i=incipient,
f=formative, e=early, m=middle, l=late, t=terminal, *=any);
time: (values below 0 represent years BC, timestep of 100 years, for example, -1000, -900, -800 and so on);
‘‘PolPop’’: polity population: 0=around 100 people, 0.1=between 100 and 1000 people, 0.2=between 1000 and 5000 people, 0.3=between 5 and
10 thousand people, 0.4=between 10 and 50 thousand people, 0.5=between 50 and 100 thousand people, 0.6=between 100 thousand and 1 million
people, 0.7=between 1 and 100 million people, 0.8=between 100 and 500 million people, 0.9=between 500 million and 1 billion people,
1.0=population above 1 billion;
‘‘PolTerr’’: polity territory class: 0.1=less than 100 km2, 0.2=between 100 and 500 km2, 0.3=between 500 and 1000 km2, 0.4=between 1
and 10 thousand km2, 0.5=between 10 and 50 thousand km2, 0.6=between 50 and 100 thousand km2, 0.7=between 100 and 500 thousand km2,
0.8=between 500 thousand and 1 million km2, 0.9=between 1 and 10 million km2, 1.0=more than 10 million km2;
government: 0=no institutions, 0.1=government by a chief, 0.2=government of a chief over other rulers, 0.3=government with ruler
and aristocrats, 0.4=government with an assembly, 0.5=government with assembly and religious institutions, 0.6=rule of more than
one religious institutions, 0.7=rule of one religious/ideological institution, 0.8=imperial rule of religion or ideology over other
governments, 0.9=imperial religious/ideological rule with bureaucracy, 1.0=government with religion/ideology bureaucracy and legal
institutions;
infrastructure: level of infrastructures: 0=no infrastructures, 0.1=routes, 0.2=quarries, 0.3=monuments or special buildings,
0.4=production and irrigation systems, 0.5=urban markets, 0.6=canals dikes or aqueducts, 0.7=ports, 0.8=supply transport systems,
0.9=small portual systems, 1.0=large portual systems;
infomedia: level of mediated information: 0=inferred oral tradition, 0.1=calendars, 0.4=symbols, 0.5=written laws, 0.7=presence of
religious/philosophical texts, 0.8=presence of written literature, 0.9=presence of written fiction, 1.0=presence of all kind of written
texts;
economy: level of economy: 0=subsistence, 0.1=subsistence and barter, 0.2=barter, 0.3=use of tokens and barter, 0.5=use of tokens
and precious metals, 0.6=use of precious metals and foreign coins, 0.7=use of coins, 0.8=credit system, 0.9=banks, 1.0=paper currency,
1.1=stock market
scale: level of social scale complexity as 0=hunter-gatherer groups, 0.1=nomad hunters and sparse villages, 0.2=sparse villages,
0.3=large villages, 0.4=simple domains, 0.5=complex domains, 0.6=kingdoms, 0.7=archaic state, 0.8=state, 0.9=state-empire, 1.0=empire,
1.1=state-nation
description: text notes with a summary of maximum 400 characters about historical events happened in the century. Focus on the
following types of events: wars or battles; reforms; rulers; population; elites; disasters or epidemics; alliances or treaties;
socio-conomic context; famines or financial stress; protests or movements; changes of elite; main type site; religions and philosophies.
When possible, report the scientific references about the information in the text notes.
When values are unknown, set ‘‘null’’ to a value.
Below is an example of the desired output.

‘‘NGA’’: ‘‘Konya Plain’’, ‘‘PolID’’: ‘‘TrBrzER’’, ‘‘Time’’: ‘‘-2300’’, ‘‘PolPop’’: ‘‘1.0’’, ‘‘PolTerr’’: ‘‘1.0’’, ‘‘government’’: ‘‘0.2’’, ‘‘infrastr’’: ‘‘0.4’’,
‘‘infomedia’’: ‘‘0.0’’, ‘‘economy’’: ‘‘0.5’’, ‘‘scale’’: ‘‘0.3’’, ‘‘description’’: ‘‘This period begins with controversy, because the transition from
Late Chalcolithic to Early Bronze Age is not clear. Some scholars argue that beginning of the Early Bronze Age should be dated to around
3000 BCE.’’
```

Figure 2. Prompt for Seshat social complexity dataset generation.

In the Chronos dataset, all variables except population and territory were encoded as TRVs. This allowed for straightforward interpretation because, as reported in Section 1, the meaning of scales expressed as TRVs is known in advance.

The features selected from the Chronos dataset in order to be comparable to the ones in Seshat are the following: **polity population** (PolPop) is the estimated population in the polity at the time as an integer and **polity territory** (PolTerr) is the estimated size of polity territory in km^2.

Economic scale (economy) encodes the progression of economic evolution, with subsistence and exogamy [28] at the base level, bartering with precious goods at the first level [29], metals and weights at the second [30], coinage at the third, paper money as the fourth and stock market the fifth level [31].

Information management (infomedia) encodes the level of information and amount of contents that a culture can elaborate. The basic stage of this scale is oral tradition with its earliest evidence dating to 38,000 BC [32]. The first level in the scale is symbolism, which appeared around 9000 BC in Göbekli Tepe, Turkey [33], and around 6000 BC in Jiahu, China [34]. The second level is administration with written text, such as lists, laws or calendars [35]; at the third stage, there are religious/philosophical/scientific texts [36], followed by fiction at the fourth level [37] and news and opinions at the fifth level [38].

Infrastructure scale (infrastructure) encodes the level of control over infrastructures. The first stage includes routes and quarries [39]; at the second level, there are special buildings like circular towers in Tell Qaramel that are dated around 10,000 BC [40]. At the third stage, there are irrigation and production systems [41]: irrigation for the polities relied on massive agriculture and production systems for those polities who relied mainly on animal husbandry [42]. At the fourth step, there are urbanization and markets [43], followed by portual systems for goods' supply, evolved through the bronze, iron and early modern ages [44]. At the sixth stage, there are railways and telecommunications, while the seventh, space systems, started in 1998 with the launch of the International Space Station.

Social scale (scale): encodes the evolutive steps of societies growing in population and territory [45]. At the base level, there are small groups of hunter–gatherers, dominant up to the Neolithic Period [46]; at the first level, there are sparse villages, started after the agricultural revolution [47]. At the second level, there are simple domains with a capital and connected villages, a dominant pattern in the chalcolithic [48]. At the third step, there are complex domains or archaic empires, started with Sargon of Akkad around 2500 BC [49]. At the fourth step, there are archaic states up to one million people [50]. At the fifth level, there are states and empires up to several million people; at the sixth step of the scale, there are state-nations, up to hundred million people; finally, at the seventh step, there are large nations, up to one billion people and more.

Political system (government) encodes the development of the power limits imposed to the rulers. At the base level, there is a sole ruler or chiefdom; hence, there is no limit to their power at all. At the first level, there are collective assemblies, possibly appeared in large agricultural villages [51]. At the second level, we have representatives of the population, which started in the republican Rome with the Tribunes of the Plebs [52]. The third stage involves legal impeachment, which empowers an institution like the parliament to nullify the ruler's authority without resorting to physical harm. The instructions included in the Chronos prompt (Figure 3) are derived from these descriptions of TRVs.

```
Generate a table in json format with information about the polities existed in the [NGA] between 10000 BC and 2010 CE.
The structure of the table must be a century per row and the following columns:
NGA: location of the society or site;
PolID: the polity ID, as the concat of two characters for civilization (where the population come from, use the two char state
abbreviation), three characters for culture (use abbreviation of population name, ruling dynasty or type site), one char for the
social type (c=community, n=nomad community, k=kingdom, e=empire, r=republic) and one character for the civilization stage (i=incipient,
f=formative, e=early, m=middle, l=late, t=terminal, *=any) ;
Time:  (values below 0 represent years BC, timestep of 100 years, for example -1000, -900, -800 and so on);
PolPop:  estimated population in the polity at the time;
PolTerr:  estimated size of polity territory in km2;
government:  scale of government/politic system; 0.0=no limits to ruler (monarchy), 0.1=assembly (aristocracy), 0.2=population
representatives (democracy), 0.3=rule of law with ruler check (legal impeachment)
infrastructure:  level of infrastructures:  0.1=routes/quarries, 0.2=common/special buildings, 0.3=production systems/irrigation,
0.4=urbanization/markets, 0.5=portual good supply systems, 0.6=railways/telecommunications, 0.7=space supply system
infomedia:  level of mediated information:  0.0=presence of oral tradition/gossip, 0.1=presence of written symbols, 0.2=presence of
laws/calendars, 0.3=presence of religious/philosophical texts, presence of 0.4=literature/fiction, presence of 0.5=newspapers/press,
economy:  level of economy:  0.0=subsistence/exogamy, 0.1=barter with goods/livestock, 0.2=precious metals by weight, 0.3=coins,
0.4=paper currency, 0.5=stock market
scale:  0.0=hunter-gatherers groups, 0.1=sparse villages, 0.2=simple domain, 0.3=complex domain or archaic empire, 0.4=archaic state or
kingdom, 0.5=modern state or empire, 0.6=state-nation, 0.7=modern nation
description:  text notes with a summary of maximum 400 characters about historical events happened in the century.  Focus on the
following types of events:  wars or battles; reforms; rulers; population; elites; disasters or epidemics; alliances or treaties;
socio-conomic context; famines or financial stress; protests or movements; changes of elite; main type site; religions and philosophies.
When possible, report the scientific references about the information in the text notes.
When values are unknown put null as value.
Below is an example of the desired output.

''NGA'': ''Adana'', ''PolId'':  ''TrOttem'', ''time'':  ''1600'', ''PolPop'':  ''27014772'', ''PolTerr'':  ''4930769'', ''government'':  ''0.2'', ''infrastr'':
''0.5'', ''infomedia'':  ''0.4'', ''economy'':  ''0.3'', ''scale'':  ''0.5'', ''description'':  ''Sultans Suleiman II and Ahmed II. Great Turkish War
in the 1690s:  the armies of the Holy League pushed the Ottomans back to the Balkans.  End of expansionist policies in Europe, series
of grand viziers from the Köprülü family.  Conquest of Cyprus in 1571 led to the naval defeat against the Holy League in the Battle of
Lepanto'',
```

Figure 3. Prompt for Chronos data generation.

3. Experiments and Results

We performed the experiments as zero-shot tasks, without any fine-tuning of LLMs. Experiments include three different trials per dataset, with three different settings, and three different runs on the selected NGAs: Turkey, Japan and Ecuador. We compare three different LLMs: Gemini-1.5-flash002, Llama 3.1 and GPT-4o. The experimental settings aim to test also temperature and grounding. The temperature parameter controls randomization in token selection and may affect the generation of correct labels and polity identifiers. A higher temperature can lead to more freedom in token selection. We tested the default value (1) and a more strict setting with a temperature of 0.5. The grounding parameter links the model output to verifiable sources of information through a Google search.

This technology connects Gemini with world knowledge and up-to-date information on the Internet. A dynamic retrieval configuration evaluates whether a prompt requires knowledge about real world or recent events and activates grounding accordingly. For example, a prompt like "Who won the latest F1 grand prix?" activates grounding search that helps the LLM generate correct answers. This feature is only available for the Gemini model and is useful in situations where accuracy and reliability are important. We test the importance of this option against the other LLMs that do not provide this feature.

Results, reported in Table 1, show several interesting things:

- Gemini yields the best coverage and has competitive correlation coefficients; Llama has the best edit distance and GPT the best correlation. The result of GPT is consistent with the results reported in multiple-choice question answering about historical data [17].
- Grounding has a positive impact on coverage: repeating the experiments using Gemini without the grounding option yields lower coverage (0.250 on Seshat and 0.492 on Chronos). The results of Gemini without grounding are in line with the other LLMs.
- Larger timesteps do not yield higher coverage: we expected higher coverage with Seshat, which has a timestep of 100 years, but this is true only with Gemini, not with the other LLMs.
- Temperature has no clear impact on the task: in particular, we expected better results in terms of edit distance on Chronos, where polity identifiers are more strict than in Seshat, but there is no evidence of this.
- The highest correlation coefficients are in general obtained with the Chronos dataset: this suggests a stronger relationship between the generated narratives and the ground truth data. This might be due to the higher granularity of the Chronos dataset and the transparency of TRVs, which allowed us to create better instructions in the prompt.

Table 1. Results on the different experimental settings: t1 = temperature 1, t0.5 = temperature 0.5. The best results are marked in bold.

Dataset	Settings	Avg Coverage	Avg Edit Distance	Avg Correlation
seshat	gemini1.5f-t1-grounding	**0.690**	1.737	0.804
seshat	gemini1.5f-t0.5-grounding	0.660	1.758	0.765
chronos	gemini1.5f-t1-grounding	0.667	1.583	0.847
chronos	gemini1.5f-t0.5-grounding	0.602	1.675	0.871
seshat	llama3.1-t1	0.248	1.589	0.505
seshat	llama3.1-t0.5	0.284	**1.524**	0.558
chronos	llama3.1-t1	0.484	1.951	0.705
chronos	llama3.1-t0.5	0.475	1.851	0.491
seshat	gpt4o-t1	0.242	1.533	0.806
seshat	gpt4o-t0.5	0.327	1.583	0.868
chronos	gpt4o-t1	0.366	1.785	0.884
chronos	gpt4o-t0.5	0.345	1.637	**0.902**

Overall, the best performing LLM is Gemini with grounding because it has the highest coverage. Tt the same time, it is competitive in terms of correlation coefficients and edit distance. We also report per-variable details of the best runs.

3.1. Detailed Variable Analysis

Detailed results of the trials with the best results are reported in Table 2. Coverage is consistent within a single run because it is referred to the NGA. These details reveal that Turkey has generally the lowest coverage, suggesting challenges in annotating historical data for a region with a long history. In particular, the LLM tends to annotate the polities in the far past with a timestep of 1000 years in order to keep informative content when information is scarce. Ecuador, on the other hand, has the highest coverage because the ground-truth data contained only few centuries, starting from 1500 CE. In fact, the impossibility to compute some correlation coefficients for this region is due to the poor availability of annotated data. Nevertheless, all LLMs produced data since 10,000 BC for this region. Gemini produced annotations starting from 9000 BC, reporting that there is a lack of evidence for that period; Llama reported data from neighboring cultures starting from 9800 BC, and GPT started from 5000 BC generally referring to "early hunter–gatherer groups". We could evaluate only the validity of the labels after 1500 CE, as the gold standard contains data only for that period of time. The edit distance shows that the models struggle with the "polity" variable, suggesting difficulties in accurately annotating polity identifiers, as expected. Crucially, correlation coefficients are high, especially for infomedia and infrastructure. This is surprising, especially in Seshat, given that the instructions extracted from the OHE-PCA variables are error-prone.

Table 2. Details of the trials with the best results.

Dataset/Run	Variable	Coverage	Edit Distance	Correlation
gemini1.5f-t1-seshat-turkey	polity	0.254	4.321	
gemini1.5f-t1-seshat-turkey	economy	0.254	0.892	0.817
gemini1.5f-t1-seshat-turkey	infomedia	0.254	2.285	0.901
gemini1.5f-t1-seshat-turkey	polpop	0.254	0.821	0.772
gemini1.5f-t1-seshat-turkey	polterr	0.254	0.964	0.527
gemini1.5f-t1-seshat-turkey	infrastr	0.254	1.464	0.857
gemini1.5f-t1-seshat-turkey	gov	0.254	1.142	0.927
gemini1.5f-t1-seshat-turkey	scale	0.254	0.964	0.884
gemini1.5f-t1-seshat-japan	polity	0.818	6.055	
gemini1.5f-t1-seshat-japan	economy	0.818	0.999	0.547
gemini1.5f-t1-seshat-japan	infomedia	0.818	2.388	0.899
gemini1.5f-t1-seshat-japan	polpop	0.818	0.833	0.848
gemini1.5f-t1-seshat-japan	polterr	0.818	0.833	0.712
gemini1.5f-t1-seshat-japan	infrastr	0.818	1.0	0.903
gemini1.5f-t1-seshat-japan	gov	0.818	0.944	0.489
gemini1.5f-t1-seshat-japan	scale	0.818	0.777	0.791
gemini1.5f-t1-seshat-ecuador	polity	1.000	6.000	
gemini1.5f-t1-seshat-ecuador	economy	1.000	1.000	1.000
gemini1.5f-t1-seshat-ecuador	infomedia	1.000	2.000	
gemini1.5f-t1-seshat-ecuador	polpop	1.000	1.000	
gemini1.5f-t1-seshat-ecuador	polterr	1.000	1.000	
gemini1.5f-t1-seshat-ecuador	infrastr	1.000	1.000	
gemini1.5f-t1-seshat-ecuador	gov	1.000	2.000	
gemini1.5f-t1-seshat-ecuador	scale	1.000	1.000	1.000
llama3.1-t0.5-seshat-turkey	polity	0.036	3.750	
llama3.1-t0.5-seshat-turkey	economy	0.036	1.000	0.992
llama3.1-t0.5-seshat-turkey	infomedia	0.036	1.750	0.970
llama3.1-t0.5-seshat-turkey	polpop	0.036	0.750	0.973
llama3.1-t0.5-seshat-turkey	polterr	0.036	1.500	0.812
llama3.1-t0.5-seshat-turkey	infrastr	0.036	1.000	0.926
llama3.1-t0.5-seshat-turkey	gov	0.036	1.750	0.846
llama3.1-t0.5-seshat-turkey	scale	0.036	0.500	0.990
llama3.1-t0.5-seshat-japan	polity	0.318	4.000	
llama3.1-t0.5-seshat-japan	economy	0.318	1.143	0.573
llama3.1-t0.5-seshat-japan	infomedia	0.318	1.429	0.933
llama3.1-t0.5-seshat-japan	polpop	0.318	1.286	0.918
llama3.1-t0.5-seshat-japan	polterr	0.318	1.571	0.874
llama3.1-t0.5-seshat-japan	infrastr	0.318	0.857	0.944
llama3.1-t0.5-seshat-japan	gov	0.318	1.000	0.811
llama3.1-t0.5-seshat-japan	scale	0.318	1.286	0.928
llama3.1-t0.5-seshat-ecuador	polity	0.500	4.000	
llama3.1-t0.5-seshat-ecuador	economy	0.500	2.000	−1.000
llama3.1-t0.5-seshat-ecuador	infomedia	0.500	0.500	
llama3.1-t0.5-seshat-ecuador	polpop	0.500	1.000	

Table 2. *Cont.*

Dataset/Run	Variable	Coverage	Edit Distance	Correlation
llama3.1-t0.5-seshat-ecuador	polterr	0.500	1.000	−1.000
llama3.1-t0.5-seshat-ecuador	infrastr	0.500	1.000	
llama3.1-t0.5-seshat-ecuador	gov	0.500	1.500	
llama3.1-t0.5-seshat-ecuador	scale	0.500	1.000	−1.000
gpt4o-t0.5-chronos-turkey	polity	0.070	4.750	
gpt4o-t0.5-chronos-turkey	economy	0.070	0.000	1.000
gpt4o-t0.5-chronos-turkey	infomedia	0.070	0.500	0.949
gpt4o-t0.5-chronos-turkey	polpop	0.070	3.500	0.956
gpt4o-t0.5-chronos-turkey	polterr	0.070	3.750	0.989
gpt4o-t0.5-chronos-turkey	infrastr	0.070	0.500	0.949
gpt4o-t0.5-chronos-turkey	gov	0.070	1.000	0.187
gpt4o-t0.5-chronos-turkey	scale	0.070	0.750	0.944
gpt4o-t0.5-chronos-japan	polity	0.217	4.800	
gpt4o-t0.5-chronos-japan	economy	0.217	0.600	0.866
gpt4o-t0.5-chronos-japan	infomedia	0.217	0.600	0.986
gpt4o-t0.5-chronos-japan	polpop	0.217		
gpt4o-t0.5-chronos-japan	polterr	0.217		
gpt4o-t0.5-chronos-japan	infrastr	0.217	0.600	0.938
gpt4o-t0.5-chronos-japan	gov	0.217	0.800	0.963
gpt4o-t0.5-chronos-japan	scale	0.217	0.600	0.973
gpt4o-t0.5-chronos-ecuador	polity	0.750	5.667	
gpt4o-t0.5-chronos-ecuador	economy	0.750	0.667	1.000
gpt4o-t0.5-chronos-ecuador	infomedia	0.750	1.333	0.945
gpt4o-t0.5-chronos-ecuador	polpop	0.750		
gpt4o-t0.5-chronos-ecuador	polterr	0.750		
gpt4o-t0.5-chronos-ecuador	infrastr	0.750	0.667	0.945
gpt4o-t0.5-chronos-ecuador	gov	0.750	1.000	0.756
gpt4o-t0.5-chronos-ecuador	scale	0.750	0.667	0.990

3.2. Limitations

LLMs differ in the generation of data about polity population and polity territory expressed as integer numbers. Gemini does not generate annotations for these variables, while Llama always tries to generate estimates, and GPT can generate population and territory estimates only for recent polities, although no command for estimating values was given in the prompt. This means that bins and ranges are required in the instructions, and precise data cannot be generated. From this perspective, TRVs have a positive impact on prompt design. A manual qualitative analysis revealed a hallucination of Gemini, which placed the Edo period both in 1700 and in 1900, annotating the wrong type of government in 1900. This means that hallucinations are possible even with grounding.

While this study demonstrates the feasibility of generating structured historical samples using LLMs, it is critical to emphasize that these samples cannot be directly integrated into Seshat or Chronos without rigorous verification by domain experts.

4. Discussion and Conclusions

This paper presented the first attempt to automatically generate an annotation of historical data by means of LLMs. Trusted historical datasets are valuable tools for extracting models of societal evolution, geo-political patterns and response to social crises. The manual annotation of trusted historical data are costly and unscalable; hence, generative AI can help to produce scalable annotations, reducing costs. We compared the performance of an LLM generating annotations on two historical datasets–Seshat and Chronos–starting from 10,000 BC to 2000 CE with a timestep of 100 years. This study revealed that historical annotation generation is possible and promising; however, there are challenges. The quality and quantity of the training data for each region could influence the model's performance. A lack of high-quality historical data for certain regions, like Ecuador, might contribute to lower accuracy and difficulty in the evaluation. Nevertheless, we demonstrate that it is possible to instruct an LLM to recognize broad categories of history, such as economy and social scale, even if the complexity of historical events and political structures in different regions can pose challenges for the model. Finally, despite the possibility to ground the LLM with search engines, hallucinations might happen. We suggest that our evaluation technique can help to spot these cases. However, further research is needed in prompt engineering in order to keep this problem under control.

We believe that there is still room for improvement for future research in this topic. Exploring advanced language models and training techniques, such as fine-tuning on specific historical datasets, can enhance accuracy. Moreover, incorporating more contextual information and examples in prompts, such as geographical, cultural, and political factors, can improve the model's ability to generate accurate and nuanced historical labels. By addressing these factors, future research can aim to improve the accuracy and coverage of automatic historical annotation, particularly for complex regions like Turkey and Ecuador.

Author Contributions: Conceptualization, methodology and data curation: F.C.; software and experiments: D.M. All authors have read and agreed to the published version of the manuscript.

Funding: This research was supported by the European Commission, grant 101120657: European Lighthouse to Manifest Trustworthy and Green AI—ENFIELD.

Data Availability Statement: The Chronos dataset is available online as a Google sheet (https://docs.google.com/spreadsheets/d/1OW6CtmUudN3WTJ1VvWRZYZdTWVEjDJGns6Q8_I6EBwk/edit?usp=sharing, accessed on 18 November 2024) for collaborative open science. The Seshat project provides replication datasets available online at https://seshat-db.com/downloads_page/ (accessed on 18 November 2024).

Acknowledgments: This research employed data from the Seshat Databank (seshatdatabank.info, accessed on 18 November 2024) under Creative Commons Attribution Non-Commercial (CC By-NC SA) licensing.

Conflicts of Interest: The authors declare no conflicts of interest.

Abbreviations

The following abbreviations are used in this manuscript:

LLMs	Large language models
TRVs	Time-resolved variables
OHE	One-hot encoding
PCA	Principal component analysis
NGA	Natural geographic area
TDA	Tabular data augmentation

References

1. Turchin, P.; Whitehouse, H.; François, P.; Hoyer, D.; Alves, A.; Baines, J.; Baker, D.; Bartokiak, M.; Bates, J.; Bennet, J.; et al. An introduction to Seshat: Global history databank. *J. Cogn. Hist.* **2020**, *5*, 115–123. [CrossRef]
2. Celli, F.; Basile, V. History Repeats: Historical Phase Recognition from Short Texts. In Proceedings of the CLIC-it 2024, Pisa, Italy, 4–6 December 2024.
3. Richerson, P.J. A Dynamic Analysis of American Socio-Political History. A Review of Ages of Discord: A Structural Demographic Analysis of American History by Peter Turchin (Beresta Books, 2016). *Cliodynamics* **2017**, *8*, 229–239. [CrossRef]
4. Turchin, P. Multipath forecasting: The aftermath of the 2020 American crisis. In *How Worlds Collapse*; Routledge: Oxfordshire, UK, 2023; pp. 397–416.
5. Collins, R. A dynamic theory of battle victory and defeat. *Cliodynamics* **2010**, *1*, 3–25. [CrossRef]
6. Turchin, P.; Whitehouse, H.; Gavrilets, S.; Hoyer, D.; François, P.; Bennett, J.S.; Feeney, K.C.; Peregrine, P.; Feinman, G.; Korotayev, A.; et al. Disentangling the evolutionary drivers of social complexity: A comprehensive test of hypotheses. *Sci. Adv.* **2022**, *8*, eabn3517. [CrossRef]
7. Horsley, N. What can a knowledge complexity approach reveal about big data and archival practice? In Proceedings of the 2017 IEEE International Conference on Big Data (Big Data), Boston, MA, USA, 11–14 December 2017; IEEE: Piscataway, NJ, USA, 2017; pp. 2246–2250.

8. Demartini, G.; Roitero, K.; Mizzaro, S. Data bias management. *Commun. ACM* **2023**, *67*, 28–32. [CrossRef]
9. Ul Haq, I.; Gondal, I.; Vamplew, P.; Brown, S. Categorical features transformation with compact one-hot encoder for fraud detection in distributed environment. In *Data Mining: 16th Australasian Conference, AusDM 2018, Bahrurst, NSW, Australia, 28–30 November 2018*; Revised Selected Papers 16; Springer: Berlin/Heidelberg, Germany, 2019; pp. 69–80.
10. Oh, C.; Han, S.; Jeong, J. Time-series data augmentation based on interpolation. *Procedia Comput. Sci.* **2020**, *175*, 64–71. [CrossRef]
11. Barbera, D.L.; Maddalena, E.; Soprano, M.; Roitero, K.; Demartini, G.; Ceolin, D.; Spina, D.; Mizzaro, S. Crowdsourced Fact-checking: Does It Actually Work? *Inf. Process. Manag.* **2024**, *61*, 103792. [CrossRef]
12. Chiarot, G.; Silvestri, C. Time series compression survey. *ACM Comput. Surv.* **2023**, *55*, 1–32. [CrossRef]
13. Celli, F.; Lepri, B. Feature Engineering for Quantitative Analysis of Cultural Evolution. *SocArXiv* **2023**. [CrossRef]
14. Yan, B.; Li, K.; Xu, M.; Dong, Y.; Zhang, Y.; Ren, Z.; Cheng, X. On protecting the data privacy of large language models (llms): A survey. *arXiv* **2024**, arXiv:2403.05156.
15. Cui, L.; Li, H.; Chen, K.; Shou, L.; Chen, G. Tabular data augmentation for machine learning: Progress and prospects of embracing generative ai. *arXiv* **2024**, arXiv:2407.21523.
16. Zhou, Y.; Wang, X.; Niu, Y.; Shen, Y.; Tang, L.; Chen, F.; He, B.; Sun, L.; Wen, L. DiffLM: Controllable Synthetic Data Generation via Diffusion Language Models. *arXiv* **2024**, arXiv:2411.03250.
17. Hauser, J.; Kondor, D.; Reddish, J.; Benam, M.; Cioni, E.; Villa, F.; Bennett, J.S.; Hoyer, D.; Francois, P.; Turchin, P.; et al. Large Language Models' Expert-level Global History Knowledge Benchmark (HiST-LLM). In Proceedings of the Thirty-Eight Conference on Neural Information Processing Systems Datasets and Benchmarks Track, Vancouver, BC, Canada, 10–15 December 2024.
18. Banday, B.; Thopalli, K.; Islam, T.Z.; Thiagarajan, J.J. On The Role of Prompt Construction In Enhancing Efficacy and Efficiency of LLM-Based Tabular Data Generation. *arXiv* **2024**, arXiv:2409.03946.
19. Kim, D.K.; Ryu, D.; Lee, Y.; Choi, D.H. Generative models for tabular data: A review. *J. Mech. Sci. Technol.* **2024**, *38*, 4989–5005. [CrossRef]
20. Lin, Y.T.; Chen, Y.N. Llm-eval: Unified multi-dimensional automatic evaluation for open-domain conversations with large language models. *arXiv* **2023**, arXiv:2305.13711.
21. Abburi, H.; Suesserman, M.; Pudota, N.; Veeramani, B.; Bowen, E.; Bhattacharya, S. Generative ai text classification using ensemble llm approaches. *arXiv* **2023**, arXiv:2309.07755.
22. Siska, C.; Marazopoulou, K.; Ailem, M.; Bono, J. Examining the robustness of LLM evaluation to the distributional assumptions of benchmarks. In Proceedings of the 62nd Annual Meeting of the Association for Computational Linguistics (Volume 1: Long Papers), Bangkok, Thailand, 11–16 August 2024; pp. 10406–10421.
23. Wu, T.; Tao, C.; Wang, J.; Yang, R.; Zhao, Z.; Wong, N. Rethinking kullback-leibler divergence in knowledge distillation for large language models. *arXiv* **2024**, arXiv:2404.02657.
24. Song, Y.; Lothritz, C.; Tang, D.; Bissyandé, T.F.; Klein, J. Revisiting Code Similarity Evaluation with Abstract Syntax Tree Edit Distance. *arXiv* **2024**, arXiv:2404.08817.
25. Xia, J.; Zhang, S.; Cai, G.; Li, L.; Pan, Q.; Yan, J.; Ning, G. Adjusted weight voting algorithm for random forests in handling missing values. *Pattern Recognit.* **2017**, *69*, 52–60. [CrossRef]
26. Valdiviezo, H.C.; Van Aelst, S. Tree-based prediction on incomplete data using imputation or surrogate decisions. *Inf. Sci.* **2015**, *311*, 163–181. [CrossRef]
27. Turchin, P.; Brennan, R.; Currie, T.; Feeney, K.; Francois, P.; Hoyer, D.; Manning, J.; Marciniak, A.; Mullins, D.; Palmisano, A.; et al. Seshat: The global history databank. *Cliodynamics* **2015**, *6*, 77–107. [CrossRef]
28. Dow, G.K.; Reed, C.G.; Woodcock, S. The Economics of Exogamous Marriage in Small-scale Societies. *Econ. Inq.* **2016**, *54*, 1805–1823. [CrossRef]
29. Khalaily, H.; Valla, F.R. Obsidian in Natufian context: The case of Eynan (Ain Mallaha), Israel. In *The Natufian Foragers in the Levant. Terminal Pleistocene Social Changes in Western Asia*; Berghahn Books: Oxford, UK, 2013; pp. 193–202.
30. Ialongo, N.; Hermann, R.; Rahmstorf, L. Bronze Age weight systems as a measure of market integration in Western Eurasia. *Proc. Natl. Acad. Sci. USA* **2021**, *118*, e2105873118. [CrossRef] [PubMed]
31. Hafer, R.W.; Hein, S.E. *The Stock Market*; Bloomsbury Publishing USA: New York, NY, USA, 2006.
32. Matchan, E.L.; Phillips, D.; Jourdan, F.; Oostingh, K. Early human occupation of southeastern Australia: New insights from 40Ar/39Ar dating of young volcanoes. *Geology* **2020**, *48*, 390–394. [CrossRef]
33. Ayaz, O. Self-Revelation: An Origin Myth Interpretation of the Göbekli Tepe Culture (An Alternative Perspective on Anthropomorphic Themes). *Yüzüncü Yıl Üniv. Sos. Bilim. Enstitüsü Derg.* **2023**, *60*, 191–208. [CrossRef]
34. Li, X.; Harbottle, G.; Zhang, J.; Wang, C. The earliest writing? Sign use in the seventh millennium BC at Jiahu, Henan Province, China. *Antiquity* **2003**, *77*, 31–44. [CrossRef]
35. Woods, C. The earliest Mesopotamian writing. In *Visible Language: Inventions of Writing in the Ancient Middle East and Beyond*; Institute for the Study of Ancient Cultures Museum: Chicago, IL, USA, 2010; pp. 33–50.
36. Willard, R.H. Weights and Measures in Egypt. In *Encyclopaedia of the History of Science, Technology, and Medicine in Non-Western Cultures*; Springer: Dordrecht, The Netherlands, 2008; pp. 2244–2251. [CrossRef]
37. Tigay, J.H. *The Evolution of the Gilgamesh Epic*; Bolchazy-Carducci Publishers: Wauconda, IL, USA, 2002.
38. Barker, H. *Newspapers and English Society 1695–1855*; Routledge: Oxfordshire, UK, 2014.

39. Aurenche, O.; Galet, P.; Régagnon-Caroline, E.; Évin, J. Proto-Neolithic and Neolithic cultures in the Middle East—The birth of agriculture, livestock raising, and ceramics: A calibrated 14C chronology 12,500–5500 cal BC. *Radiocarbon* **2001**, *43*, 1191–1202. [CrossRef]
40. Mazurowski, R.F.; Michczyńska, D.J.; Pazdur, A.; Piotrowska, N. Chronology of the early Pre-Pottery Neolithic settlement Tell Qaramel, northern Syria, in the light of radiocarbon dating. *Radiocarbon* **2009**, *51*, 771–781. [CrossRef]
41. Kurt, A. *Ancient near East V1*; Routledge: Oxfordshire, UK, 1996.
42. Makarewicz, C.A.; Arbuckle, B.S.; Öztan, A. Vertical transhumance of sheep and goats identified by intra-tooth sequential carbon (δ13C) and oxygen (δ18O) isotopic analyses: Evidence from Chalcolithic Köşk Höyük, central Turkey. *J. Archaeol. Sci.* **2017**, *86*, 68–80. [CrossRef]
43. Altenmüller, H. Old Kingdom: Fifth Dynasty. *Oxf. Encycl. Anc. Egypt* **2001**, *2*, 601.
44. Knapp, A.B. Thalassocracies in Bronze Age eastern Mediterranean trade: Making and breaking a myth. *World Archaeol.* **1993**, *24*, 332–347. [CrossRef]
45. Turchin, P. *Ultrasociety: How 10,000 Years of War Made Humans the Greatest Cooperators on Earth*; Beresta Books: Chaplin, CT, USA, 2016.
46. Marlowe, F.W. Hunter-gatherers and human evolution. *Evol. Anthropol. Issues News Rev.* **2005**, *14*, 54–67. [CrossRef]
47. Barker, G. *The Agricultural Revolution in Prehistory: Why Did Foragers Become Farmers?* Oxford University Press: Oxford, UK, 2006.
48. Heyd, V. Growth and expansion: Social, economic and ideological structures in the European Chalcolithic. In *Is There a British Chalcolithic*; Oxbow Books: Oxford, UK, 2012; pp. 96–112.
49. Steinkeller, P. The Sargonic and Ur III Empires. In *The Oxford World History of Empire: Volume Two: The History of Empires*; Oxford University Press: Oxford, UK, 2020; Volume 43, pp. 43–72.
50. Adams, R.M. Complexity in archaic states. *J. Anthropol. Archaeol.* **2001**, *20*, 345–360. [CrossRef]
51. Hodder, I. Staying egalitarian and the origins of agriculture in the Middle East. *Camb. Archaeol. J.* **2022**, *32*, 619–642. [CrossRef]
52. Smith, C. The Origins of the Tribunate of the Plebs. *Antichthon* **2012**, *46*, 101–125. [CrossRef]

electronics

MDPI

Article

Efficient Statistical Computation for K-Player Basketball Lineups Using Semilattice Structures

Michalis Mountantonakis [1,2]

[1] Institute of Computer Science, FORTH-ICS, 700 13 Heraklion, Greece; mountant@ics.forth.gr
[2] Computer Science Department, University of Crete, 700 13 Heraklion, Greece

Abstract: Basketball games are characterized by the large number of lineups that can be used by the coach during a game, e.g., with 12 players there are 792 possible lineups. This has led to the development of several statistics for the combinations of players on the court since team performance depends on synergy among players. It is of primary importance for a basketball team to understand the team performance and aid the coaching staff in making the proper decisions. In this work, we apply data mining and knowledge extraction techniques to basketball analytics. In particular, we propose an algorithm for answering questions (including filtering and maximization) about the team performance when any K-Player lineup is on the court ($1 \leq K \leq 5$). The algorithm uses a semilattice representation and a depth-first search traversal that incrementally computes the statistics by exploiting set theory properties. As a case study, we provide experiments by using lineups mainly from the EuroLeague Basketball but also from the National Basketball Association (NBA). Regarding the results, the proposed method is more than 30× faster than the baseline for the EuroLeague and 200× faster for the NBA. Indicatively, we can compute the key traditional cumulative and average statistics for all K-Player combinations of players of the EuroLeague of a single season in less than 1 s. Finally, we introduce indicative statistics using the computations mentioned.

Keywords: semilattice; K-Player lineups; EuroLeague; Hasse diagram; NBA; power set

1. Introduction

Sports analytics is an emerging topic for all the popular sports (see such surveys in [1,2]), including basketball, which, according to the International Basketball Federation (FIBA), is the second most popular sport globally behind football, with more than 3.3 billion fans (http://bit.ly/3QK136X, accessed on 15 May 2025). Basketball is a dynamic, fast-paced sport, where the team performance depends not only on a single player, but also on the synergy among players on the court. For this reason, a basketball game is characterized by the large number of lineups that can be used by the coach during a game, e.g., 12 players result in 792 possible 5-Player lineups. Moreover, it has been mentioned that a basketball game can be similar to a chess game, according to the chess master Magnus Carlsen (https://www.gq.com/story/nba-chess-club, accessed on 15 May 2025). Traditional statistical analysis often focuses on individual player metrics or full 5-player lineup efficiencies. On the other hand, a deeper understanding of team dynamics, team chemistry, player synergy, and tactical effectiveness, requires evaluating the impact of any K-Player basketball lineup, i.e., ($1 \leq K \leq 5$).

As mentioned in [3], it is of primary importance for a sports team to be able to understand the performance of the team/player, to make the correct decisions. Moreover, as stated in [4], "It is widely accepted that some groups of players work better together than others, creating synergistic lineups that transcend the sum of their individual parts". For example, some combinations may enhance offensive efficiency, while others may strengthen defensive stability. Generally, there have been approaches that provide statistics over combinations of lineups, such as [4], the official website of the National Basketball Association, i.e., NBA (https://www.nba.com/stats/lineups/traditional, accessed on 15 May 2025), and the website Hack-a-Stat (https://hackastat.eu/en/EuroLeague-stats/, accessed on 15 May 2025), a repository of statistics from major European basketball tournaments, including EuroLeague. On the other hand, our focus is on how to provide a method for enabling the fast computation of statistics for any given question that requires computation over K-Player Lineups. The objective is to allow for the fast evaluation of the impact of different K-Player lineups, which can be of primary importance to allow the decision-making of the coaching and technical staff, e.g., see [5].

From a mathematical perspective, analyzing all possible K-Player combinations requires computing the restricted power set of combinations of up to 5 players. Such a combinatorial approach can enable us to systematically evaluate the performance of every possible K-Player group on the court, allowing for a more granular analysis of team dynamics. The research questions are as follows:

- *RQ1*: How can set theory properties be exploited to reuse computations from previous lineups (i.e., lineups for which the statistics have already been computed)?
- *RQ2*: How can fast statistics be computed for any combination of K-Player lineups for maximization/minimization and filtering problems?

In our running example in Figure 1, suppose that the user desires to find the K-Player lineup of Panathinaikos (2023–2024), for $1 \leq K \leq 3$, with the highest value team points/minute (i.e., how many points the team has scored per minute when the given combination of players was together on the court). Thereby, it is a maximization problem. Figure 1 presents a part of the semilattice, and each node represents a K-Player lineup. Due to reasons of space, it shows the best lineup of each K and some other K-Player combinations. In particular, in the bottom part, we can see the single players, in the middle part, pairs of players, and in the upper part, triads of players. For example, the node on the lower left side (with the label "Sloukas") provides the following information: Panathinaikos has scored 1922 points in the 893.1 min that "Sloukas" was on the court, i.e., 2.152 points per minute.

Furthermore, we can see that for cumulative statistics, such as the number of team points, their value decreases as we visit the supersets, e.g., see the number of minutes of "Sloukas" and "Sloukas, Nunn" nodes in Figure 1. In this way, filtering conditions are easy to execute, i.e., if the condition was the combination of players to have played at least 280 min, then there was no need to compute statistics about any 2,3,4,5-player lineups, including "Papapetrou" (since he has played 273 min in total). On the other hand, it does not hold for the average statistics, e.g., the value of the team points per minute when "Nunn" is on the court is lower than when "Nunn" and "Papapetrou" are on the court.

Regarding our contribution, this paper provides (a) a semilattice-based incremental algorithm that is based on set theory properties for computing the statistics of the restricted power set of the players of a team, (b) comparative results by using a baseline approach and the incremental algorithm, and (c) indicative statistics over the past three EuroLeague seasons and an NBA regular season. Concerning novelty, to the best of our knowledge, this is the first work that tries to compute fast K-Player lineup statistics by using a semilattice approach based on set theory properties.

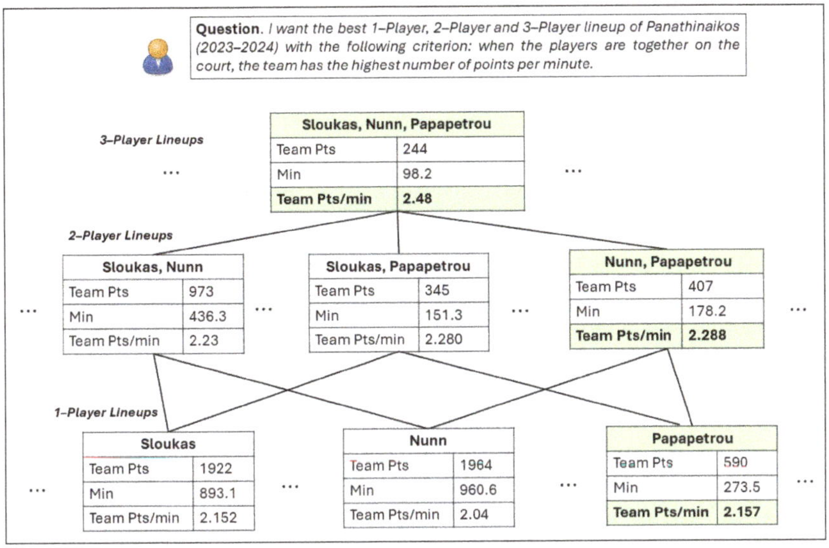

Figure 1. Running Example—visualization of a semilattice for a question for K-Player lineups.

The rest of this paper is organized as follows: Section 2 discusses the related work, Section 3 introduces the problem statement and the competency questions, and Section 4 describes the steps of the approach and the incremental algorithm. Moreover, Section 5 provides an experimental evaluation, and finally Section 6 concludes the paper and provides directions for future work.

2. Related Work

This section presents related approaches for basketball analytics, then discusses approaches using lattice-based techniques for power set computations, and finally mentions the differences with the related work and the novelty of this paper.

2.1. Basketball Analytics

First, data mining and knowledge discovery techniques have been used for decades for basketball, e.g., see a data mining application for the NBA that was proposed in 1997 [6]. Concerning lineup prediction, the authors in [7] studied the problem of how to choose the best lineup against an opponent team, and they provided graph theory techniques. In [8], a statistical Markov chain model was developed to compare the evolution and performance of players' positions, to aid the coach in making optimal decisions regarding the player's rotation line-ups. Moreover, the authors in [9], analyzed and compared statistical data of the NBA and EuroLeague Basketball, and they concluded that EuroLeague "is becoming quantitatively and qualitatively more similar to the NBA".

In the study of [10], the authors provided a benchmark with existing performance analytics used in the literature for evaluating teams and players, whereas in [11], a framework was introduced for simulating games by calculating different synergies of NBA teams, by comparing their 5-player lineups in several categories. Furthermore, in [12], the authors used a generalized version of Shapley value for evaluating the importance of each player in a given lineup. Also, in [13], a statistical analysis was performed on the historical evolution of the EuroLeague. In addition, the author in [14] exploited dynamic programming techniques, for finding optimal substitution strategies. In addition, there is a benchmark available, called SportQA [15], which contains 70 thousand questions for several sports (including basketball) and can be used for complex analysis.

There are also several works that exploit machine learning techniques for providing basketball analytics. For instance, in [16], the authors exploited machine learning algorithms to predict the winner of European basketball matches, by using over 5000 boxscores, whereas [17] introduced a machine learning framework for predicting the results of NBA games. In addition, ref. [18] surveyed approaches using machine learning algorithms to classify and extract patterns from the movement data of the players. Concerning other data mining techniques in the context of basketball analytics, the authors in [19] exploited association rule mining techniques for uncovering recovery and economic impacts in NBA basketball. Moreover, in [20], such techniques were applied to identify patterns concerning the performance of NBA players quarter-by-quarter.

Furthermore, the authors in [21] used the Shapley additive explanations (SHAP) method for predicting the outcome of an NBA game. SHAP was also exploited in [22] for predicting the next game lineup in collegiate basketball. In particular, SHAP values suggested the important factors for each prediction to aid coaches in making the proper decisions. In addition, ref. [23] proposes a classifier that relies on individual player order statistics for predicting the performance of a five-person basketball lineup. Moreover, ref. [24] introduced counterfactual predictions for evaluating the decision-making skills of players in basketball games.

Regarding the computations of statistics involving combinations of lineups, the official website of the NBA (https://www.nba.com/stats/lineups/traditional, accessed on 15 May 2025) provides statistics over any K-Player combination in tables for the NBA league. Moreover, the website Hack-a-Stat (https://hackastat.eu/en/EuroLeague-stats/, accessed on 15 May 2025) provides Excel files with such statistics for 5-Player lineups for several European Leagues, including EuroLeague. However, there are no details of how they are computed.

2.2. Lattice-Based Measurements over Power Sets

In the past, we have used lattice-based structures for computing content-based measurements in the field of Linked Open Data, i.e., [25]. The objective was to perform several set operations over hundreds of Knowledge Graphs (or datasets), such as to find (i) the intersection of common elements among any combination of datasets in [26], and (ii) the union and complement between the datasets in [27]. Similarly to this paper, we exploited a bottom-up lattice-based approach, which was the fastest one and enabled the computations of millions of combinations in a few seconds.

2.3. Comparison and Novelty

In comparison with the related work, this paper mainly focuses on how to answer fast maximization/minimization questions over any combination of K-Player lineups, instead of trying to predict either the best lineups (e.g., [7]) or the scores of basketball games (e.g., [16,17]). Also, compared to [26,27], we apply lattice-based algorithms to another domain that has different properties. As regards data mining techniques (such as association rules mining [19,20]), we decided to use semilattice structures, since the target is to enable the computation of statistics for any combination of players and not to discover statistically significant patterns in the data that frequently co-occur. On the other hand, these two techniques could be combined, i.e., apply association rule mining to evaluate and prioritize the results of the proposed algorithm based on statistical significance.

Moreover, compared to the website of the NBA, which contains such statistics for any K-Player lineup for the NBA, and the Hack-a-stat website, which provides 5-player lineups statistics for EuroLeague, we focus on the fast computation of the statistics even for maximization and filtering problems. Finally, regarding the novelty, to the best of our knowledge, this is the first work to compute such fast K-Player combination statistics by using a semilattice approach based on set theory properties.

3. Problem Statement and Competency Questions

This section introduces the problem statement and a list of competency questions.

3.1. Problem Statement

The key notations can be seen in Table 1 and are described below.

Table 1. The key notations of the problem statement and their definitions.

Notation	Definition
T	Set of Teams
$Pl(T_i)$	Players of a Team
$P(Pl(T_i))$	Power set of any combinations of players of a team
$P_{\leq 5}(Pl(T_i))$	Restricted power set of combinations up to 5 players of a team
$L_5(Pl(T_i))$	Lineups of 5 players of a team having played together at least 1 s
B	A subset of players
$L(B)$	All the lineups including the subset of players B
St	A given statistic
$CNum(St, B)$	The cumulative number for a statistic and a subset of players
$Avg(St, B)$	The average value of a given statistic and a subset of players
$CNumBest(St)$	The best subset of players maximizing a cumulative statistic
$AvgBest(St)$	The best subset of players maximizing a statistic with average values
$CNum_f(St, B, F)$	The cumulative statistic for a subset of players B using a filter F
$Avg_f(St, B, F)$	The average statistic for a subset of players B using a filter F

Teams and Players. First of all, we define T as the set of teams $T = \{T_1, \ldots, T_n\}$, and $Pl(T_i)$ as all players of a team, i.e., $Pl(T_i) = \{P_1, \ldots, P_n\}$, where $T_i \in T$.

Power Set of Players of a Team. We define $P(Pl(T_i))$ as the power set of any combination of players in a team, i.e., $P(Pl(T_i)) = \{L \mid L \subseteq Pl(T_i)\}$. This power set contains any combination of players, e.g., pairs, triads, quads, quintets, hexads, and so forth.

Restricted Power Set of Players of a Team. The goal is to calculate the statistics for any K-Player combinations of players when they are together on the court. However, since there cannot be more than five players on the court, we restrict the power set to only those subsets that represent legal lineups (e.g., we exclude hexads and so on). Therefore, below, we define the restricted power set of $Pl(T_i)$ up to combinations of five.

$$P_{\leq 5}(Pl(T_i)) = \{L \subset Pl(T_i), 1 \leq |L| \leq 5\} \quad (1)$$

Meet-semilattice. It is a partially ordered set $(P, \leq)$ in which every pair of elements $a, b \in P$ has a greatest lower bound (also called the *meet*, denoted $a \wedge b$), which is also in P. The set $P_{\leq 5}(\mathrm{Pl}(T_i))$, together with the subset relation $\subseteq$, forms a *meet-semilattice*. The meet of any two elements A_1 and A_2 is given by their intersection, i.e., $A_1 \wedge A_2 = A_1 \cap A_2$.

Hasse Diagram. A semilattice can be visualized as a Hasse diagram, which is a graphical representation of a finite partially ordered set $(P, \leq)$. Specifically, each element of P is represented by a node, an edge is drawn between two elements a and b if $a < b$ and there is no $c \in P$ such that $a < c < b$ (i.e., b *covers* a), and the diagram is drawn so that if $a < b$, then b appears higher than a in the layout, and edges are directed implicitly upward (edges are not labeled with arrows). An example is given in Figure 1.

Number of Maximum K-Player Combinations. The total number of subsets in $P_{\leq 5}(Pl(T_i))$ is given by summing the binomial coefficients:

$$\sum_{n=1}^{5} C(|Pl(T_i)|, n),\ where\ C(|Pl(T_i)|, n) = \frac{|Pl(T_i)|!}{n!(|Pl(T_i)| - n)!} \tag{2}$$

For instance, if there are 15 players in a team roster, it results in 3003 5-player combinations, 1365 4-player combinations, 455 3-player combinations, 105 2-player combinations, and 15 1-player combinations, i.e., a total of 4943 combinations.

The 5-player Lineups. Since any time there are lineups of five on the court, we start by defining the lineups having played together for at least 1 s as follows:

$$L_5(Pl(T_i)) = \{L \in P_{\leq 5}(Pl(T_i)) \mid |L| = 5\ and\ Minutes(L) > 0\} \tag{3}$$

All the lineups including a K-Player combination. For a given combination of players, say $B \in P_{\leq 5}(Pl(T_i))$, we need to find all the 5-player lineups in which they have participated as follows:

$$L(B) = \{L \in L_5(Pl(T_i)) \mid B \subseteq L, 1 \leq |B| \leq 5\} \tag{4}$$

How to measure the statistics. We want to compute the team statistics when the combination B is on the court. First, we define as $CNum(St, B)$ the cumulative number for a given statistic St (points, assists, three points made, minutes, etc.) and a combination $B \in P_{\leq 5}(Pl(T_i))$. The $CNum(St, B)$ is computed for the desired statistic St by taking the sum for St for each 5-player lineup that includes all the players of B. For example, for finding all the points of the lineups, including both "Grant" and "Nunn", we need to take the sum of the points of all the 5-Player lineups, including these two players. Apart from statistics concerning cumulative numbers, there can be statistics, including average values, i.e., $Avg(St, B)$. In such cases, we need to combine cumulative statistics to find the average, e.g., for finding the points per minute we need to divide the number of points by the number of minutes $CNum('Points', B)/CNum('Minutes', B)$.

Set theory Properties. By the given two combinations of players $B, B' \in P_{\leq 5}(Pl(T_i))$, where it holds that $B \subset B'$, we know from the set theory that $L(B) \supseteq L(B')$ (i.e., see [28]). For instance, if $B = \{Grant, Nunn\}$ and $B' = \{Grant, Nunn, Sloukas\}$, we know that the lineups that include "Grant and Nunn" is a superset of the lineups, including "Grant, Nunn, and Sloukas". Also, if we know that "Lessort and Yurtseven" have never played together, it means that any 3–4 and 5-player combination, including these two players, have never played together in any game. Finally, for the cumulative stats, we know that if $B \subset B'$, then $CNum(St, B) \geq CNum(St, B')$.

Objective. The objective is to compute any of the statistics of each K-Player combination in an incremental way for exploiting the mentioned set theory properties.

Maximization Questions. One target is to provide an answer to the maximization questions, i.e., give me the combination of players B that maximize the following criteria:

$$CNumBest(St) = arg_B max\ CNum(St, B) \tag{5}$$

$$AvgBest(St) = arg_B max\ Avg(St, B) \tag{6}$$

For the first one, an example can be to find which combination of players has the highest plus/minus (when they are on the court); for the second case, it can find which combination of players the team has the highest three-point percentage. Correspondingly, it can be used for minimization problems, e.g., for statistics, such as the number of turnovers, i.e., "give me the K-Player lineups that minimize the number of turnovers".

Filtering Questions. Another case is to compute filtering questions for a given value F such as $CNum_f(St, B, F) = CNum(St, B) \geq F$, e.g., find all the combinations having played at least 40 min and $Avg_f(St, B, F) = Avg(St, B) \geq F$, e.g., find all the combinations of players that, when they are on the court, the team has over 2 points per minute. In any case, one question can include one or more filtering conditions and one or more maximization/minimization conditions.

3.2. Competency Questions

We provide different types of questions based on their computation, i.e., a set of questions is given below:

[Q1. General Question]: For each K-Player combination of players, give me all the team statistics, when they are on the court.

[Q2. Maximization Question]: With which 3-player combination does the team have the highest number of points per minute?

[Q3. Filtering and Maximization Question]: Give me the best K-Player combination of Panathinaikos, including Kendrick Nunn, that maximizes the value of the 3-Point percentage (extra filtering condition: at least 50 min on the court)?

[Q4. Comparative and Filtering Question]: Compare the best K-Player combinations for all the statistics for the Panathinaikos team for the 2023–2024 and 2024–2025 seasons (that have played together at least 80 min on the court)?

[Q5. Minimization Question]: Give me the top-5 3-player lineups in EuroLeague for the 2023–2024 season that, when they are on the court, the team has the lowest number of opponent points per minute.

[Q6. Distribution Question]: Give me the minutes of each K-Player lineup (for a given K) to check their distribution (e.g., power-law distribution).

4. The Steps and Semilattice Incremental Computations

This section provides the steps for computing the desired metrics, the traversal that is used by the algorithms, a baseline method, the proposed incremental algorithm, and how it can be adjusted for questions requiring some maximization and/or filtering conditions.

4.1. The Steps and the Focus of This Paper

We present the steps and the focus of this paper, which are also depicted in Figure 2.

Data Collection. The first step includes the analysis of the play-by-play for the desired games (left part of Figure 2). The target is to collect all the statistics for all 5-player lineups (i.e., $L_5(Pl(T_i))$) that have played together (at least one second) for each team. As a result, we have all the statistics for all the 5-player lineups of each team. Certainly, in that step, one can exclude specific lineups/games, e.g., to collect only the home or away games, the games that the team won or lost, the lineups in the last quarter, etc. Since more and more games are played as time passes in a single season, the 5-player lineups should be updated. In the example of Figure 2, we can see such 5-player lineups for a given team and some indicative statistics (minutes, points).

User Interface and Data Computation. The user, e.g., a data analyst, a coach, can express a question (see the upper right part of Figure 2) to conduct an analysis for a single team and/or several teams. The main notion is that the algorithm finds the desired 5-player lineups (and statistics) based on the given question and uses them as input for the computations. For instance, if the question is about all the teams, e.g., "Give me the K-Player lineup of each team that maximizes the number of assists per 40 min", then the algorithm will perform separately the computation for each team and will produce the results, which are finally returned to the user.

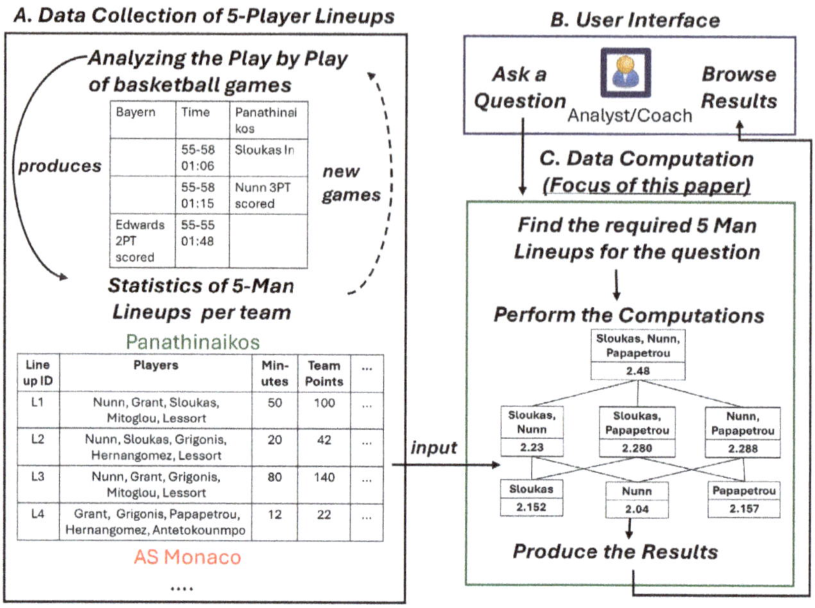

Figure 2. The steps and the focus of this paper.

Focus of this paper. The focus of this paper is the computation phase, i.e., the effective computation of the measurements of any K-Player combination based on precomputed 5-player lineup statistics. For this reason, we use existing precomputed statistics for all 5-player lineups of all teams that are available in the Hack-a-stat and NBA websites. We have stored them in TSV (Tab-Separated Values) format, and we update them periodically. On the other hand, the ultimate target is to extend this work by analyzing the play-by-play from existing APIs and updating the statistics (even in real time), e.g., for EuroLeague, this can be completed through the EuroLeague API (https://live.euroleague.net/api/PlaybyPlay?gamecode=333&seasoncode=E2023, accessed on 15 May 2025). In this way, we expect to have such an analysis even during a given game, e.g., at half-time, since for the time being, we do not handle dynamic updates. Finally, we plan to provide an interactive user interface to analysts/coaches for expressing their questions by enabling the selection of specific teams, players, etc.

4.2. The Depth-First Search Traversal

For the algorithms (including the baseline), we follow a Depth-First Search (DFS) traversal. An example with all the combinations of four players is depicted in Figure 3. The figure shows the visiting order (with red color). We always go upwards, and we never visit a combination of players twice. We can clearly see that we first compute all the combinations, including "Nunn", then all the combinations, including "Grant" (but without "Nunn", since they have been computed previously), and so forth. Due to this traversal, we can visit and compute the metrics for any K-Player combination at run time. This means that we do not pre-construct a data structure for the lattice. Finally, it allows us to stop the computation at any K.

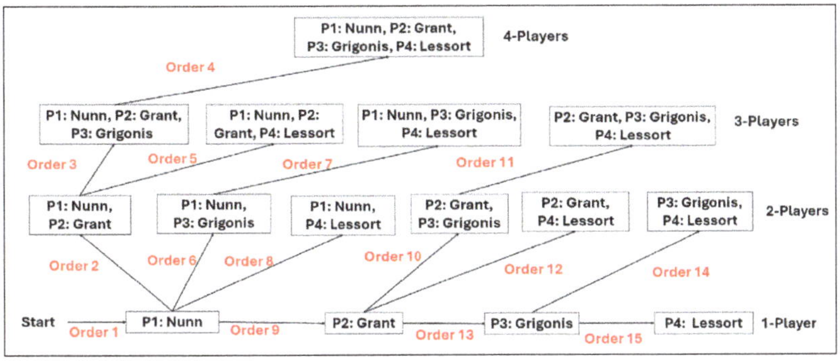

Figure 3. The (Depth-First Search) DFS traversal for 4 players.

4.3. Baseline Method

For the baseline, we follow the mentioned DFS traversal for a given team. In particular, we start from the bottom, and for each subset $B \in P_{\leq 5}(Pl(T_i))$, we iterate over each $L' \in L_5(Pl(T_i))$. For each iteration, we check if $B \subseteq L'$ and only if it holds, we take the sum of the desired cumulative statistic(s), and in the end, we can compute the average statistics.

Example of the Baseline. Suppose that we perform the traversal of Figure 3 for computing all the metrics by using as input the collected 5-player Lineups that are depicted on the left lower side of Figure 2. Thereby, we will start from "Nunn", and we will check for each of the four 5-player lineups (of Figure 2) if they contain "Nunn". Afterwards, we will visit the pair "Nunn, Grant", and we will check again for each of the four 5-player lineups if they contain both "Nunn" and "Grant". Generally, we perform the same process for each K-Player lineup of the given team.

Time and Space Complexity. In this way, we need each K-Player combination to check each 5-player lineup of the team, i.e., we need $|P_{\leq 5}(Pl(T_i))| * |L_5(Pl(T_i))|$ iterations, and the time complexity is $\mathcal{O}(|P_{\leq 5}(Pl(T_i))| * |L_5(Pl(T_i))|)$. Although it can be expensive to compute the statistics for all the K-Player lineups, this method is suitable for answering questions for a single $K-$Player combination, e.g., give me all the statistics when the players {Nunn, Hernangomez, Lessort} are on the court. The space complexity is $\mathcal{O}(|L_5(Pl(T_i))|)$.

4.4. Semilattice-Based Incremental Algorithm

The problems with the baseline model are that (a) we need to iterate over all the $L_5(Pl(T_i))$ for each K-Player combination, (b) we can even perform computations for combinations that have never played together, and (c) we do not reuse statistics, which is important for some queries, e.g., for the cumulative statistics, we know that if $B \subset B'$, then $L(B) \supseteq L(B')$ and also $CNum(St, B) \geq CNum(St, B')$.

Input. The algorithm (see Algorithm 1) uses as input post-match static data. Specifically, it receives as parameters the players of a team, a number i to know the order of the players, the current combination of players B, and the 5-player lineups, including all the players of B, i.e., $L(B)$.

Initial Call. First, we call the function (see line 14) with the following parameters: $Pl(T_x)$, i.e., all the players of the desired team, $i = 0$, i.e., to start from the first player, the emptyset ({}), since we start from the bottom. We also give all the 5-player lineups of the team that have played together at least 1 s.

Procedure. We start from the bottom, iterate over the players of the team, add in our current K-Player combination B' the player P_j, and initialize some variables (lines 3–6). Afterwards, we iterate over all the lineups $L(B)$, and we check if the players of our current lineup exist in each 5-player lineup. If it is true, we add the 5-player lineup L' to the lineups of B', and we increase the value of the cumulative statistics (lines 7–10). For instance, if the first player is "Nunn", then we keep each 5-player lineup, including "Nunn". After having computed the cumulative statistics, we can also compute the average statistics (if we desire), i.e., line 11.

Algorithm 1: Semilattice incremental computation of statistics for all K-Player lineups ($1 \leq K \leq 5$)

Input: $Pl(T_x)$: Set of players for team T_x
$L_5(Pl(T_x))$: Set of all 5-player lineups from $Pl(T_x)$ having played together
Output: Statistics for all K-Player combinations (where $1 \leq K \leq 5$)

1 **Procedure** SemilatticeStats(*$Pl(T_x)$, order i, subset B, lineups $L(B)$*)
2   **foreach** $P_j \in Pl(T_x)$, *where* $j \geq i$ **do** `// Iterate over players starting from index` i
3     $B' \leftarrow B \cup \{P_j\}$ `// Extend the current subset with player` P_j
4     $L(B') \leftarrow \emptyset$ `// Initialize lineups containing` B'
5     $CNum(St, B') \leftarrow 0$ `// Initialize cumulative statistics`
6     $Avg(St, B') \leftarrow 0$ `// Initialize average statistics`
7   **foreach** $L' \in L(B)$ **do** `// For each lineup in` $L(B)$
8   **if** $P_j \in L'$ **then** `// If the new player` P_j `in lineup` L'
9         $L(B') \leftarrow L(B') \cup \{L'\}$ `// Add 5-player lineup to` B'`'s lineup`
10         $CNum(St, B') \leftarrow CNum(St, B') + CNum(St, L')$ `// Update cumulative stats`
11   Compute $Avg(St, B')$ `// Finalize average statistics for` B'
12   **if** $|B'| < 5$ ***and*** $|L(B')| > 0$ **then** `// Recurse if size` < 5 `and there is at least one 5-player lineup in` $L(B')$
13   SemilatticeStats($Pl(T_x), i+1, B', L(B')$)

14 **Initial Call:** SemilatticeStats($Pl(T_x), 0, \emptyset, L_5(Pl(T_x))$)

Recursion. The next step is to continue upwards in a recursive way (lines 11–13). We increase the value of i, we "transfer" the lineups of the current combination B' since we know from the set theory that if $B \subset B'$, then $L(B) \supseteq L(B')$. Therefore, in the next recursion, a new player will be added to the combination, and we will perform the same computations by reusing the $L(B)$ from the previous lineup. If our combination of players reaches 5, there is no need to continue upwards and compute any statistics (there cannot be more than 5 players on the court); thereby, we return to the previous level (recursively). Moreover, if we do not find any lineups $L(B')$, including the combination B', there is also no need to continue upwards.

Example of the Incremental Algorithm. In Figure 4, we perform the computations for any combination of four players of a given team. The task is to compute the total team points when any K-Player lineup (of these players) is on the court. As an input, we use the statistics from the 5-player lineups (see the bottom part of Figure 4). We start from "Nunn", we find in which 5-player lineups $L(B)$ he has participated in, and we compute the statistics. Indeed, "Nunn" was part of the lineups with IDs L_1, L_2, L_3, and the sum of the team points in these lineups was 282 points.

The next step is to continue upwards, by transferring $L(B)$ and by adding a new player, e.g., "Grant" (line 3 of Algorithm 1). We iterate only over the lineups, including "Nunn", and if they also include "Grant", we keep them (see $L(B)$ for that pair of players) and we use them to compute the statistics (lines 7–10 of Algorithm 1). Therefore, the difference in our example with the baseline algorithm is that for the baseline, we needed to iterate over all four lineups to check if "Nunn" and "Grant" were part of each 5-player lineup. On the contrary, here, we iterate over the three lineups, including "Nunn" (with IDs L_1, L_2, L_3), and we check if Grant is part of each of these lineups (i.e., he is part of lineups with IDs L_1, L_3). In this way, as we go upwards, the size of $L(B)$ decreases, e.g., when we reach the top node, we perform a check only for one 5-player lineup (i.e., L_3). In the end, the final result is that we have computed the total team points for each combination.

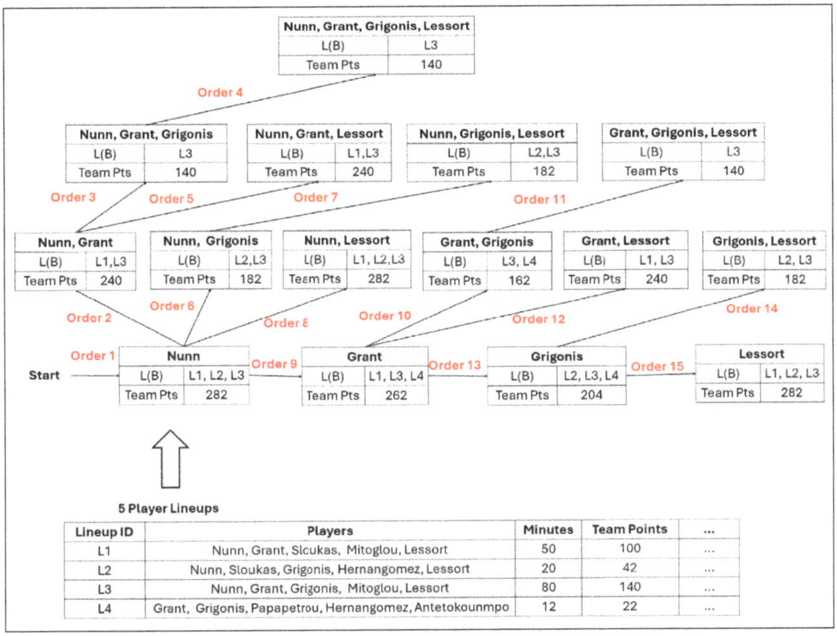

Figure 4. The semilattice depth-first search traversal for a subset of players—the task is to find the number of team points when the players are on the court.

Time and Space Complexity. Since we follow a DFS, in the worst case (where any combination of players have played together for at least one second), we visit each node (combination of players) once, and we create one edge per K-Player combination, i.e., $|P_{\leq 5}(Pl(T_i))| + |P_{\leq 5}(Pl(T_i))|$. For each combination of players B', we iterate over $L(B)$ entries for finding the $L(B')$. Therefore, the time complexity here is $\mathcal{O}(|P_{\leq 5}(Pl(T_i))| * avg(L(B)))$, where $avg(L(B))$ denotes the average number of $L(B)$ that we need to iterate for finding the 5-player lineups for each K-Player combination. Concerning space complexity, it is $O(|B'| * avg(L(B)))$, where $B' = \{B_i, \ldots, B_n\}$ are the subsets that occur in the maximum depth d of the lattice (maximum is 5 in our case).

4.5. Filtering, Maximization, and Order of Players

Here, we discuss how the algorithm can be adjusted for filtering, maximization/minimization, and we discuss the visiting order of players.

Filtering and Maximization/Minimization. In Algorithm 1, in line 11, we can add code to keep the maximum or minimum values, e.g., to find the $CNumBest(St)$, the $AvgBest(St)$, etc. Regarding filtering, we can perform more checks in line 12. For example, we can stop at any K (e.g., triads of players), and we can keep the maximum/minimum or the top-X values (e.g., top-10). Also, we can stop if a cumulative statistic is higher/lower than a given value, e.g., $CNum_f(Minutes, B, 40)$, to compute the statistics only for K-Player lineups that have played at least 40 min together, and so forth. In this way, fewer nodes

(K-Player combinations) will be visited. As an example, in Figure 4, in case we desire K-Player combinations with at least 200 team points, there is no need to visit the quad of players since we already know that when "Nunn, Grant, Grigonis" were on the court, the team scored less than 200 points.

Is the order of players important? Since we transfer $L(B)$ of a given B to B', the order of players can be of primary importance. As an example in Figure 5, we can see the computations of the AS Monaco players. In the lower part, we observe that "James" occurs in five 5-player lineups, "Theis" in three, and "Jaiteh" in one. In the upper left side, we use a descending order regarding the number of 5-player lineups per player. Thus, we start with "James", and then by visiting "James, Theis", we transfer five 5-player lineups and we keep only the three 5-player lineups, including both players. Then, we visit the triad of players, and we transfer the three 5-player lineups; however, since this triad of players have never played together, the $L(B)$ is empty. Generally, with that order, we visit all the nodes, and we transferred, in total, 16 5-player lineups. Therefore, more iterations are needed in line 7 of Algorithm 1. On the upper right side, for the same players, we follow an ascending order. We start from "Jaiteh", and since he has participated only in one 5-player lineup, we transferred that lineup to the pair "Jaiteh, Theis". However, since these two players have never played together (they are both Centers), and $L(B)$ is empty, we do not need to visit the triad of players. By using this order, we visited fewer nodes and performed fewer iterations.

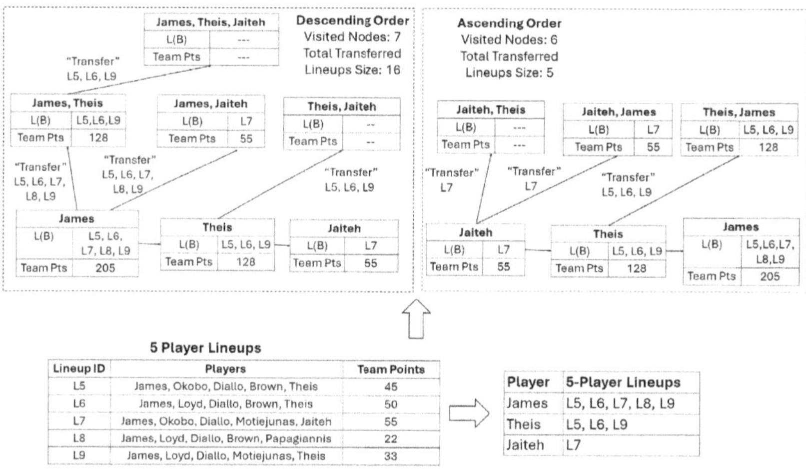

Figure 5. An example for the ascending versus descending order with respect to the number of 5-player lineups per player for the semilattice incremental algorithm.

In the experiments, we evaluate different orders of players, i.e., an ascending order (e.g., right part of Figure 5), a descending order (e.g., left part of Figure 5), and a random order. For each order, we provide results about a) the number of visited nodes (K-Player combinations) and b) the number of the total and average iterations, i.e., to find $L(B)$.

5. Experimental Evaluation

We first provide some details for the datasets and the experimental setup, then we discuss comparative results on the algorithms, and we present some indicative statistics on the lineups. Finally, we provide a discussion and specific research directions.

5.1. Datasets

Since we focus on EuroLeague, we use the 5-player lineups from EuroLeague 2022–2023, 2023–2024, and 2024–2025 (until the regular season since it is an ongoing season) from Hack-a-Stat (https://hackastat.eu/en/EuroLeague-stats/, accessed on 15 May 2025). Moreover, we manually collected all the 5-player Lineup statistics for the NBA regular season 2023–2024 from the NBA website (https://www.nba.com/stats/lineups/traditional, accessed on 15 May 2025) since we wanted to also perform the measurements in a larger dataset, i.e., NBA contains 30 teams and they play over 1200 games per season, while the EuroLeague includes 18 teams, and the number of games is approximately 330.

The initial datasets are in .tsv format (tab separated values), and an overview is provided in Table 2. The initial datasets contain only the statistics of the 5-player lineups. Also, in that table, for each $K \in [1, 4]$, we see the number of combinations that have played together for each season for all the teams (computed using the algorithms presented in this paper). In the NBA, there are approximately 2.6× more K-Player lineups than in the EuroLeague.

Table 2. Datasets used in the experiments and the distinct number of K-Player lineups. For $1 \leq K \leq 4$, the statistics were derived after the computations using the proposed algorithm.

Dataset	5-Player Lineups (Initial Dataset)	4-Player Lineups	3-Player Lineups	2-Player Lineups	1-Player Lineups	Total K-Player Lineups
EuroLeague 2022–2023	5709	10,976	6835	1994	297	25,811
EuroLeague 2023–2024	5804	11,497	7151	2037	295	26,784
EuroLeague 2024–2025 (regular season)	5840	11,523	7225	2101	303	26,992
NBA regular season 2023–2024	15,902	29,853	19,111	5330	662	70,858

5.2. GitHub Page, Software, and Hardware

The GitHub page (https://github.com/mountanton/Basketball_K-Player_Lineups, accessed on 15 May 2025) contains the input files and the output files with all the statistics for all the K-Player combinations of EuroLeague for the 2022–2023, 2023–2024, and 2024–2025 seasons.

Software. The GitHub page also provides the code which has been written in JAVA programming language. The current version of the code enables the user to run the experiments for the datasets of Table 2. The users can test all the methods for computing the statistics for all the K-Player combinations. Also, it has an example for a maximization and filtering query to compute the best K-Player lineup having the most points per minute.

Hardware. For all the experiments, we use a single machine having an i5 core, 16 GB main memory, and 500 GB disk space.

5.3. Experimental Setup

First, for the efficiency measurements, we provide the execution time for the general competency question Q1. In particular, we compute a set of 38 key cumulative and average statistics for all the combinations of players of all the datasets by using (a) the baseline model (described in Section 4.3) and (b) the semilattice incremental method (described in Section 4.4). For the semilattice method, we provide results with a different order of players: (b1) semilattice (asc), i.e., an ascending order according to the number of lineups that the players of a team have participated in (e.g., if a player P_1 has participated in the fewer lineups, we will start from player X), (b2) semilattice (desc), i.e., the opposite of the previous one, and (b3) semilattice (rand), i.e., a random order of players.

We have performed 10 independent runs for each method to account for variability in execution time and ensure statistical robustness. We provide the following results for each dataset: (i) average execution time per method, (ii) p-value (statistical significance) between each pair of methods, and (iii) number of visited nodes and iterations per method. Finally, we provide an example for the competency questions Q2 to Q6.

5.4. Efficiency Results

Execution Time per Method. We can see the average execution time per method (average for the 10 runs) for each EuroLeague season in Figure 6. The semilattice methods are much faster than the baseline one for all the EuroLeague seasons. Indeed, we managed to compute all the statistics for all the K-Player combinations of players ($1 \leq K \leq 5$) very fast, e.g., on average, 0.67 s for the 2023–2024 season, whereas for the baseline method, we needed 19.35 s, i.e., 28.61× faster. Concerning the other seasons, for 2022–2023, the semilattice (asc) method was 23.18× faster, and for 2024–2025, it was 36.29× faster. As regards NBA, Figure 7 shows that the difference is much higher, i.e., we computed the statistics, on average, in 2.11 s, whereas for the baseline, we needed 488 s, i.e., 230× faster. Moreover, Figures 8 and 9 show the execution time per run, for the Euroleague 2023–2024 and for NBA regular season 2023–2024. Generally, the execution time for the semilattice methods is more stable, whereas the baseline shows a higher variance in execution time.

Statistical significance (p-values). Table 3 shows the statistical significance between the method pairs. Specifically, the paired t-tests conducted on execution times across the three EuroLeague seasons, as well as the NBA dataset, show that all method pairs exhibit statistically significant differences in performance ($p < 0.05$ in every comparison). Specifically, we observe highly significant performance differences between the baseline and the semilattice methods.

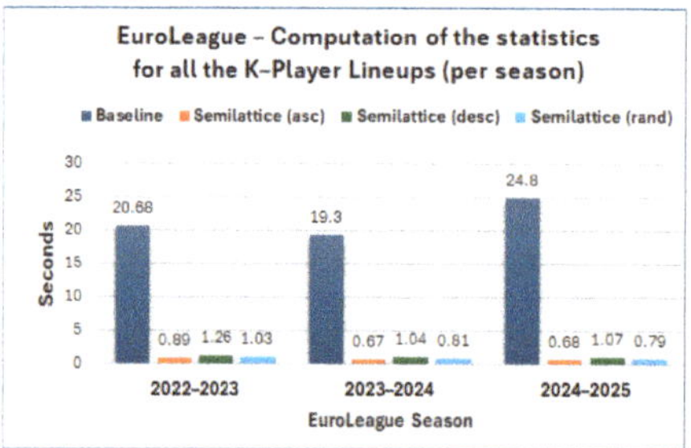

Figure 6. Average execution time (10 runs) for all the K-Player combinations of players (EuroLeague).

Visited nodes and iterations per method. This time difference is important for real-time queries and can be explained by checking Tables 4 and 5 for the EuroLeague and NBA, respectively (for 2023–2024 season). The main reason is that for the baseline method, we need to check all the possible K-Player combinations (since it does not exploit set theory properties), and we need to iterate each time over all the 5-player lineups of a team for each K-Player combination. More specifically, for the baseline, we needed EuroLeague (2023–2024) to check 153 thousand K-Player combinations and perform over 5 million iterations to find the $L(B)$. In contrast, by using the semilattice (asc) method, we managed to compute the statistics by visiting 48 thousand K-Player combinations by performing only 57 thousand iterations (i.e., 7.8 per K-Player combination). Regarding the regular 2023–2024 NBA season, where more teams and lineups are included, the difference is much higher, and it is worth mentioning that for the baseline method, we needed to visit over 1.5 million K-Player combinations and perform over 1 billion iterations.

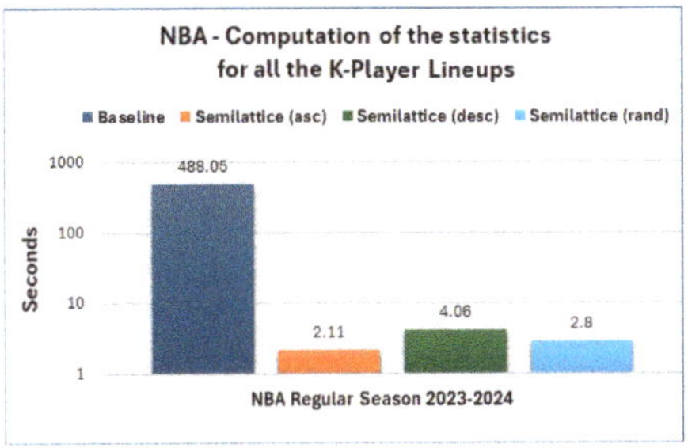

Figure 7. Average execution time (10 runs) for all the K-Player combinations of players—NBA regular season 2023–2024.

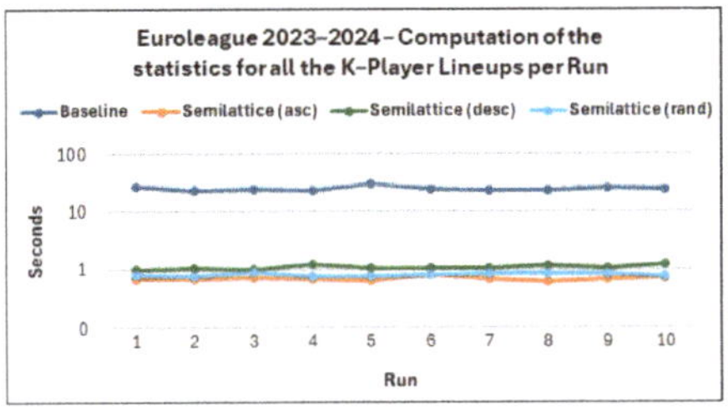

Figure 8. Execution time per run for each method for Euroleague 2023–2024 (log-linear plot).

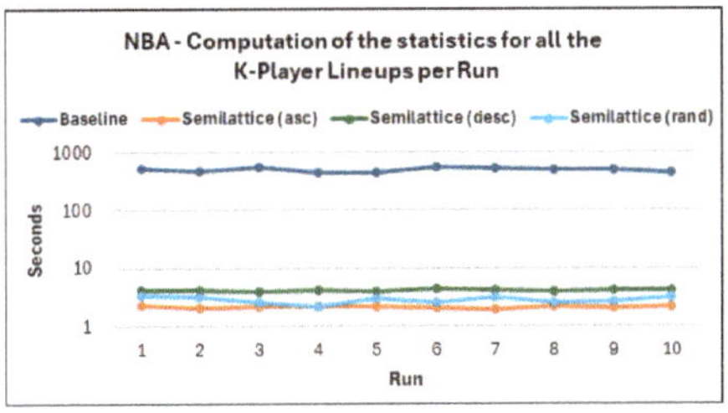

Figure 9. Execution time per run for each method for NBA 2023–2024 (log-linear plot).

Table 3. Paired t-test p-values comparing execution times between baseline (BS) and semilattice methods across EuroLeague (EL) seasons and the NBA dataset.

Paired T-Test	EL 2022–2023	EL 2023–2024	EL 2024–2025	NBA 2023–2024
BS vs. Semilattice (asc)	1.23×10^{-15}	1.26×10^{-16}	2.16×10^{-10}	2.88×10^{-10}
BS vs. Semilattice (desc)	2.21×10^{-15}	2.45×10^{-16}	2.65×10^{-10}	2.94×10^{-10}
BS vs. Semilattice (rand)	8.46×10^{-16}	1.25×10^{-16}	2.27×10^{-10}	2.86×10^{-10}
Semilattice (asc vs. desc)	5.67×10^{-8}	4.67×10^{-7}	7.85×10^{-7}	4.59×10^{-11}
Semilattice (asc vs. rand)	5.95×10^{-5}	3.30×10^{-3}	3.89×10^{-4}	4.06×10^{-4}
Semilattice (desc vs. rand)	2.05×10^{-5}	1.48×10^{-5}	2.78×10^{-5}	3.74×10^{-6}

Table 4. Comparative results for computing the statistics for all K-Player combinations of all EuroLeague Teams—2023–2024 season. Bold text indicates the lowest numbers.

Method	Visited K-Player Nodes	Total Iterations	Avg Iterations per K-Player Node
Baseline	153,884	5,233,4384	340.08
Semilattice (asc)	**48,458**	**570,849**	**11.78**
Semilattice (desc)	100,650	1,365,731	13.56
Semilattice (rand)	66,143	878,219	13.27

Table 5. Comparative results for computing the statistics for all the K-Player combinations of all NBA teams—2023–2024 regular season. Bold text indicates the lowest numbers.

Method	Visited K-Player Nodes	Total Iterations	Avg Iterations per K-Player Node
Baseline	1,579,077	1,030,346,843	652.49
Semilattice (asc)	**161,001**	**1,882,607**	**11.69**
Semilattice (desc)	464,762	6,068,807	13.05
Semilattice (rand)	248,351	3,343,350	13.46

Comparison of semilattice methods. The ascending order of players (e.g., starting from the player with the fewest number of minutes on the court) was the most effective one, i.e., on average, 1.56× faster than the descending order and 1.2× faster than a random order. For all the semilattice orders, we needed, on average, fewer iterations per combination; however, for the random and descending one, we visited much more lattice nodes (i.e., K-Player combinations), i.e., see Tables 4 and 5.

5.5. *Indicative Statistics for Competency Questions—EuroLeague*

Here, we provide some indicative statistics for the remaining competency questions as follows: (Q2) the best 3-player combination of players in each team with the highest number of points per minute (season 2023–2024) for K-Player combinations having played at least 80 min on the court, (Q3) the best K-Player combination including "K. Nunn" that maximizes the 3-point percentage, (Q4) the best K-Player combination of Panathinaikos for a set of 10 statistics for the 2023–2024 and 2024–2025 seasons (regular season), (Q5) the top-5 3-player lineups with the lowest number of opponent points per minute (at least 50 min on the court) for the 2023-2024 season, and (Q6) checking for power-law distribution for the minutes of K-Player lineups (EuroLeague 2023–2024 season).

Question Q2. Table 6 shows the results for Q2, for all the EuroLeague teams, and the highest number of points per minute achieved by the triad of players {Campazzo, Causeur, Deck} of Real Madrid with 2.54 points per minute.

Question Q3. From the measurements, we found that the best K-Players for the given question (2023–2024 season) was {Nunn, Sloukas, Papapetrou, Mitoglou} with a 3-point percentage 53.1%, i.e., when these four players were on the court, the team had 17 out of 32 that made three-points shots. Regarding the 2024–2025 season, the best K-Player group was {Nunn, Grant, Sloukas, Mitoglou} with a 3-point percentage of 49.2% (32 out of the 65).

Question Q4. From Table 7, we can observe that for the 2023–2024 season, J. Grant was a key player of Panathinaikos for most of the categories, both on offense and defense, whereas for the 2024–2025 season (ongoing, regular season), when "J. Grant, J. Hernangomez, and P. Kalaitzakis" are on the court, the team seems to be effective in many categories, such as the number of rebounds per minute and the performance index rating.

Table 6. The best 3-player combination of each team giving the team the highest number of points per minute (EuroLeague 2023–2024). Bold text indicates the best combination.

Team	3-Player Combination	Points per Minute
AS Monaco	James, Loyd, Okobo	2.33
Asvel Villeurbanne	De Colo, Lauvergne, Scott	2.35
Baskonia	Howard, Kotsar, Moneke	2.49
Bayern	Ibaka, Edwards, Francisco	2.20
Alba Berlin	Delow, Koumadje, Thiemann	2.30

Table 6. *Cont.*

Team	3-Player Combination	Points per Minute
Red Star Belgrade	Giedraitis, Hanga, Teodosic	2.50
Efes Pilsen	Beaubois, Larking, Oturu	2.36
Barcelona	Abrines, Laprovittola, Satoransky	2.39
Fenerbahce	Biberovic, Wilbekin, Motley	2.51
Milano	Lo, Mirotic, Voigtmann	2.24
Maccabi Tel Aviv	Blatt, Dibartolomeo, Webb	2.50
Olympiacos	Papanikolaou, Walkup, Williams Goss	2.39
Panathinaikos	Nunn, Papapetrou, Sloukas	2.48
Partizan Belgrade	Dozier, Kaminsky, Nunnally	2.45
Real Madrid	**Campazzo, Causeur, Deck**	**2.54**
Valencia	Davies, Inglis, Jovic	2.35
Virtus Bologna	Belinelli, Lundberg, Hackett	2.32
Zalgiris	Birutis, Evans, Manek	2.41

Table 7. The best K-Player combination, where Panathinaikos achieves the best values when the players are on the court at least 80 min.

ID	Team Statistic	K-Player, Season 2023–2024	Value	K-Player, Season 2024–2025 (Regular Season)	Value
1	Highest Plus/Minus	Sloukas, Lessort	213.0	Hernangomez, Nunn	131.0
2	Points per min	Grant, Grigonis, Lessort, Mitoglou, Sloukas	2.52	Gabriel, Mitoglou	2.59
3	Less Opp points per minute	Grant, Grigonis, Hernangomez, Lessort	1.54	Grant, Hernangomez, Kalaitzakis	1.62
4	Highest Ast/To ratio	Grant, Grigonis Lessort, Mitoglou, Sloukas	2.46	Brown, Hernangomez, Yurtseven	2.65
5	Total Rebs per minute	Grant, Kalaitzakis	1.08	Grant, Hernangomez, Kalaitzakis	1.09
6	Steals Per Minute	Grant, Hernangomez, Nunn	0.28	Grant, Gabriel, Hernangomez	0.27
7	PIR per minute	Grant, Grigonis, Lessort, Mitoglou, Sloukas	3.46	Grant, Hernangomez, Kalaitzakis	3.29
8	Highest FG%	Grant, Grigonis, Lessort, Mitoglou, Sloukas	57.0%	Gabriel, Mitoglou	59.0%
9	Highest 2PT%	Grant, Grigonis, Lessort, Mitoglou, Sloukas	67.1%	Grant, Lessort, Nunn	67.3%
10	Highest 3PT%	Grant, Papapetrou, Lessort	53.8%	Grant, Mitoglou, Nunn, Sloukas	49.2%

Question Q5. Table 8 provides the top-5 3-player lineups (2023–2024 season), with the lowest opponent points per minute, and as we can see, the top triad of players allowed only 1.32 points per minute for the opponents.

Question Q6. In Figure 10, we can clearly observe a power-law distribution for the minutes played of the K-Player lineups in EuroLeague, for every K in the range $[2, 5]$. It is worth mentioning that half of the 5-player lineups played together less than 2 min in the whole season.

Table 8. The top-5 best 3-player combinations in the 2023–2024 season with less opponent points per minute.

Ranking	Team	3-Player Combination	Opponent Points per Minute
1	Barcelona	Jokubaitis, Laprovitola, Vesely	1.32
2	Valencia	Jovic, Reuvers, Toure	1.36
3	Panathinaikos	Nunn, Hernangomez, Antetokounmpo	1.38
4	Real Madrid	Abalde, Llull, Poirier	1.42
5	Olympiacos	Larentzakis, Papanikolaou, Fall	1.44

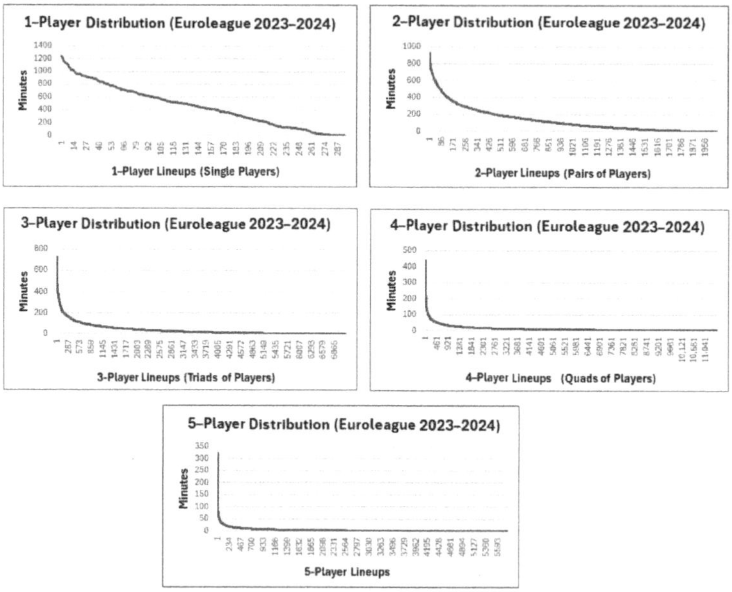

Figure 10. K-Player distributions in EuroLeague 2023–2024 (having played together at least 1 s).

5.6. Discussion, Limitations, and Future Directions

By using the semilattice approach, we managed to answer the research questions *RQ1* and *RQ2*, i.e., for *RQ1*, we exploited set theory properties through the semilattice methods for reusing previous measurements, whereas for *RQ2*, we managed to compute the statistics very fast, i.e., in 2.1 s for the NBA and less than 1 s in the EuroLeague, which is of primary importance for real-time questions. Moreover, the difference was high compared to a baseline approach, i.e., it was even more than 200× faster. Certainly, for many questions, there is no need to compute all the statistics and visit all the nodes, e.g., for the competency question Q3, we need to compute the metrics only for Panathinaikos and only for the lineups including "Nunn".

Regarding limitations which are targets of future work, at the time being, we use existing post-match 5-player lineups statistics, and we do not collect them in real time. Moreover, although the code is provided and offers some basic scenarios, there is no available interactive web interface. Thereby, the target is to automate the whole process by collecting statistics automatically by creating a crawler and offer an interactive web application that provides real-time answers, by providing the opportunity to the user to ask different types of questions (e.g., like the Competency Questions). One other direction is to use and/or create a Knowledge Graph for enabling the expression of more advanced questions, e.g., "Give me the statistics of lineups including at least three players with height over 2.05" since we can retrieve the height of each player from a KG (and any desired information, like age, college, position, NBA draft number, etc.). Another interesting direction could be to provide measurements for analyzing the performance of a specific player in a given K-Player lineup, e.g., "In which 3-player lineup, did Kendrick Nunn maximize his 3-point percentage?". Such a question requires each 5-player Lineup to keep the exact statistics for each of the players in the lineup, which can also be done in the case of creating our own crawler.

6. Concluding Remarks

In this paper, we presented a semilattice algorithm for computing the team statistics of a basketball team, when any K-Player combination of players is on the court ($1 \leq K \leq 5$). The algorithm exploits set theory properties and follows a depth-first search traversal, for reusing computations of lineups, and is essential for maximization/minimization and filtering problems, e.g., for finding which K-Player lineup maximizes a given statistic. Regarding the experiments, we used real datasets from EuroLeague and NBA, and indicatively we managed to compute in 0.67 s a key set of statistics for all the K-Player combinations that have played together in EuroLeague (2023–2024) and in 2.1 s for the NBA regular season (2023–2024). Compared to a baseline method, the proposed algorithm was more than 200× faster for the computations for the NBA and over 30× faster for the EuroLeague. Finally, we presented indicative statistics for the EuroLeague.

As future work, we plan to (a) use a crawler to analyze the play-by-play of each game, e.g., for including/excluding specific games and for providing more advanced statistics (even in real time), (b) create a user-friendly web application for enabling the fast answering of any maximization/minimization or/and filtering questions by using the proposed algorithms, (c) create an ontology and a knowledge graph for enabling the execution of more complex queries regarding the statistics, boxscores, and play-by-play of basketball games, and (d) use the same incremental algorithm in other sports.

Funding: This research received no external funding.

Institutional Review Board Statement: Not applicable.

Informed Consent Statement: Not applicable.

Data Availability Statement: All the datasets of this study, experimental results, and code for running the experiments are available in https://github.com/mountanton/Basketball_K-Player_Lineups, accessed on 15 May 2025.

Conflicts of Interest: The authors declare no conflicts of interest.

References

1. Singh, N. Sport analytics: A review. *Learning* **2020**, *9*, 64–69. [CrossRef]
2. Ghosh, I.; Ramasamy Ramamurthy, S.; Chakma, A.; Roy, N. Sports analytics review: Artificial intelligence applications, emerging technologies, and algorithmic perspective. *Wiley Interdiscip. Rev. Data Min. Knowl. Discov.* **2023**, *13*, e1496. [CrossRef]
3. Piette, J.; Pham, L.; Anand, S. Evaluating basketball player performance via statistical network modeling. In Proceedings of the 5th MIT Sloan Sports Analytics Conference, Boston, MA, USA, 4–5 March 2011; pp. 4–5.
4. Devlin, S.; Uminsky, D. Identifying group contributions in NBA lineups with spectral analysis. *J. Sport. Anal.* **2020**, *6*, 215–234. [CrossRef]
5. Vinué, G.; Epifanio, I. Archetypoid analysis for sports analytics. *Data Min. Knowl. Discov.* **2017**, *31*, 1643–1677. [CrossRef]
6. Bhandari, I.; Colet, E.; Parker, J.; Pines, Z.; Pratap, R.; Ramanujam, K. Advanced scout: Data mining and knowledge discovery in NBA data. *Data Min. Knowl. Discov.* **1997**, *1*, 121–125. [CrossRef]
7. Ahmadalinezhad, M.; Makrehchi, M.; Seward, N. Basketball lineup performance prediction using network analysis. In Proceedings of the IEEE/ACM International Conference on Advances in Social Networks Analysis and Mining, Vancouver, BC, Canada, 27–30 August 2019; pp. 519–524. [CrossRef]

8. Kolias, P.; Stavropoulos, N.; Papadopoulou, A.; Kostakidis, T. Evaluating basketball player's rotation line-ups performance via statistical markov chain modelling. *Int. J. Sport. Sci. Coach.* **2022**, *17*, 178–188. [CrossRef]
9. Mandić, R.; Jakovljević, S.; Erčulj, F.; Štrumbelj, E. Trends in NBA and Euroleague basketball: Analysis and comparison of statistical data from 2000 to 2017. *PLoS ONE* **2019**, *14*, e0223524. [CrossRef]
10. Sarlis, V.; Tjortjis, C. Sports analytics—Evaluation of basketball players and team performance. *Inf. Syst.* **2020**, *93*, 101562. [CrossRef]
11. Maymin, A.; Maymin, P.; Shen, E. NBA chemistry: Positive and negative synergies in basketball. *Int. J. Comput. Sci. Sport* **2013**, *12*, 4–23. [CrossRef]
12. Metulini, R.; Gnecco, G. Measuring players' importance in basketball using the generalized Shapley value. *Ann. Oper. Res.* **2023**, *325*, 441–465. [CrossRef]
13. Katris, C. Exploring Euroleague History using Basic Statistics. *arXiv* **2023**, arXiv:2301.02443.
14. Hughes, D.W. An Approximate Dynamic Programming Approach to Determine the Optimal Substitution Strategy for Basketball. Ph.D. Thesis, George Mason University, Fairfax, VA, USA, 2017.
15. Xia, H.; Yang, Z.; Wang, Y.; Tracy, R.; Zhao, Y.; Huang, D.; Chen, Z.; Zhu, Y.; Wang, Y.; Shen, W. Sportqa: A benchmark for sports understanding in large language models. *arXiv* **2024**, arXiv:2402.15862.
16. Lampis, T.; Ioannis, N.; Vasilios, V.; Stavrianna, D. Predictions of European basketball match results with machine learning algorithms. *J. Sport. Anal.* **2023**, *9*, 171–190. [CrossRef]
17. Thabtah, F.; Zhang, L.; Abdelhamid, N. NBA game result prediction using feature analysis and machine learning. *Ann. Data Sci.* **2019**, *6*, 103–116. [CrossRef]
18. Stephanos, D.K.; Husari, G.; Bennett, B.T.; Stephanos, E. Machine learning predictive analytics for player movement prediction in NBA: Applications, opportunities, and challenges. In Proceedings of the ACM Southeast Conference, Virtual, 15–17 April 2021; pp. 2–8. [CrossRef]
19. Sarlis, V.; Papageorgiou, G.; Tjortjis, C. Leveraging Sports Analytics and Association Rule Mining to Uncover Recovery and Economic Impacts in NBA Basketball. *Data* **2024**, *9*, 83. [CrossRef]
20. Iatropoulos, D.; Sarlis, V.; Tjortjis, C. A Data Mining Approach to Identify NBA Player Quarter-by-Quarter Performance Patterns. *Big Data Cogn. Comput.* **2025**, *9*, 74. [CrossRef]
21. Ouyang, Y.; Li, X.; Zhou, W.; Hong, W.; Zheng, W.; Qi, F.; Peng, L. Integration of machine learning XGBoost and SHAP models for NBA game outcome prediction and quantitative analysis methodology. *PLoS ONE* **2024**, *19*, e0307478. [CrossRef]
22. Sharma, S.; Divakaran, S.; Kaya, T.; Raval, M. Athletic signature: Predicting the next game lineup in collegiate basketball. *Neural Comput. Appl.* **2024**, *36*, 21761–21780. [CrossRef]
23. Martonosi, S.E.; Gonzalez, M.; Oshiro, N. Predicting elite NBA lineups using individual player order statistics. *J. Quant. Anal. Sport.* **2023**, *19*, 51–71. [CrossRef]
24. Fujii, K.; Takeuchi, K.; Kuribayashi, A.; Takeishi, N.; Kawahara, Y.; Takeda, K. Estimating counterfactual treatment outcomes over time in complex multiagent scenarios. *arXiv* **2024**, arXiv:2206.01900v4. [CrossRef]
25. Mountantonakis, M. *Services for Connecting and Integrating Big Numbers of Linked Datasets*; IOS Press: Amsterdam, The Netherlands, 2021; Volume 50. [CrossRef]
26. Mountantonakis, M.; Tzitzikas, Y. On measuring the lattice of commonalities among several linked datasets. *Proc. VLDB* **2016**, *9*, 1101–1112. [CrossRef]
27. Mountantonakis, M.; Tzitzikas, Y. Content-based union and complement metrics for dataset search over RDF knowledge graphs. *J. Data Inf. Qual. (JDIQ)* **2020**, *12*, 1–31. [CrossRef]
28. Hrbacek, K.; Jech, T. *Introduction to Set Theory, Revised and Expanded*; CRC Press: Boca Raton, FL, USA, 2017. [CrossRef]

electronics

Article

A Multi-Source Embedding-Based Named Entity Recognition Model for Knowledge Graph and Its Application to On-Site Operation Violations in Power Grid Systems

Lingwen Meng [1], Yulin Wang [2], Guobang Ban [1], Yuanjun Huang [3], Xinshan Zhu [2] and Shumei Zhang [2,*]

[1] Electric Power Research Institute of Guizhou Power Grid Co., Ltd., Guiyang 550002, China; menglw000@163.com (L.M.); banforks@163.com (G.B.)
[2] School of Electrical Automation and Information Engineering, Tianjin University, Tianjin 300072, China; yulin_2000@tju.edu.cn (Y.W.); xszhu@tju.edu.cn (X.Z.)
[3] Southern Power Grid Digital Grid Group Co., Ltd., Guizhou Branch, Guiyang 550002, China; 18198350949@139.com
* Correspondence: shumeizhang@tju.edu.cn

Abstract: With the increasing complexity of power grid field operations, frequent operational violations have emerged as a major concern in the domain of power grid field operation safety. To support dispatchers in accurately identifying and addressing violation risks, this paper introduces a profiling approach for power grid field operation violations based on knowledge graph techniques. The method enables deep modeling and structured representation of violation behaviors. In the structured data processing phase, statistical analysis is conducted based on predefined rules, and mutual information is employed to quantify the contribution of various operational factors to violations. At the municipal bureau level, statistical modeling of violation characteristics is performed to support regional risk assessment. For unstructured textual data, a multi-source embedding-based named entity recognition (NER) model is developed, incorporating domain-specific power lexicon information to enhance the extraction of key entities. High-weight domain terms related to violations are further identified using the TF-IDF algorithm to characterize typical violation behaviors. Based on the extracted entities and relationships, a knowledge graph of field operation violations is constructed, providing a computable and inferable semantic representation of operational scenarios. Finally, visualization techniques are applied to present the structural patterns and distributional features of violations, offering graph-based support for violation risk analysis and dispatch decision-making. Experimental results demonstrate that the proposed method effectively identifies critical features of violation behaviors and provides a structured foundation for intelligent decision support in power grid operation management.

Keywords: knowledge graph construction; on-site power grid operations; named entity recognition (NER); violation behaviors

1. Introduction

As a fundamental pillar of national energy infrastructure, the electric power industry plays a critical role in industrial, economic, and societal domains, holding strategic importance for the realization of national revitalization objectives [1]. Field operations in power grids involve high-voltage electrical equipment and complex power systems, where accidents or faults can easily lead to severe consequences such as casualties, equipment damage, and large-scale power outages. Therefore, ensuring the safety of field operations in power grids is essential for protecting human life, maintaining the integrity of equipment, and safeguarding socioeconomic interests [2]. At present, safety supervision of field operations primarily relies on on-site inspections by professionals or remote video monitoring. For instance, Peng et al. [3] developed an object detection approach called CORY-Net, which combines contrastive self-supervised learning with the YOLOv5 framework and applied it to intelligent safety surveillance in power grid construction environments. As artificial intelligence continues to evolve, the State Grid Corporation of China is actively promoting the digitalization and intelligent upgrading of the power industry, prioritizing the enhancement of risk prevention and control capabilities and positioning safety assurance as a core development objective [4]. A large volume of multimodal data has become available in power grid operations, providing a rich resource for analysis and application. However, traditional data analysis techniques are increasingly inadequate in addressing the exponential growth of data volume. There is an urgent need to introduce more intelligent and systematic analytical approaches to achieve a deeper understanding and more effective prevention of violation behaviors.

With the rapid advancement of machine learning and deep learning technologies, it has become feasible to conduct efficient mining and intelligent analysis of the massive data generated by smart grids. Zhou et al. [5], based on historical data from power companies, conducted an in-depth investigation into the relationship between field operation behaviors and violation incidents, providing data-driven support and theoretical foundations for enhancing safety management in power operation sites. Wang [6] proposed the Multi-DeT model, which adopts a single-encoder, multi-decoder architecture under a multi-task learning framework. The model effectively captures the coupling relationships among various energy loads to achieve joint prediction tasks, demonstrating strong performance in both prediction accuracy and generalization capability. This provides essential technical support for the coordination and management of integrated energy systems. Tan [7] developed a deep multi-task learning approach with practical application value, integrating multimodal feature extraction and a soft parameter-sharing structure. This approach mitigates the limitations in feature extraction and error accumulation commonly encountered in multi-node load forecasting, thereby improving the overall prediction performance. Zhang [8] developed a quantitative characterization model for power equipment fault diagnosis, incorporating the number of alarms and their temporal distribution during the fault process as classification features. These features were integrated into a diagnostic framework to enable joint identification of fault types and faulty equipment. The method was validated using both simulation systems and real fault cases, demonstrating high applicability and diagnostic precision. Cao [9] designed an integrated intelligent early warning system for power grids based on multi-source data fusion. By integrating heterogeneous data sources such as EMS, fault recording systems, OMS, and meteorological monitoring, and applying intelligent algorithms, the system enables real-time monitoring of equipment operating status and efficient warning of defect risks. Sun [10] addressed safety risks in the power construction process by proposing a safety early warning model based on particle swarm optimization and support vector machines (PSO-SVM). The model improves generalization capability and warning performance through parameter optimization, and experimental results indicate superior performance over traditional SVM models. Ke [11] introduced a substation intelligent safety perception and early warning approach that integrates multi-dimensional information. By combining key technologies such as sensor-based perception, cloud-edge collaboration, transfer learning, and semantic segmentation, the method achieves intelligent identification and real-time warning of unsafe operation distances, violation behaviors, misoperation, and hazardous gases, thereby enhancing the safety and intelligent management of substation field operations.

Power grid systems encompass not only large volumes of structured data but also extensive unstructured textual information, such as operation records and inspection logs. Efficiently extracting valuable information from such heterogeneous data sources and presenting it in a logically coherent and well-structured manner has become a key challenge in addressing the rapid expansion of domain knowledge within the power sector. As a semantic-level knowledge organization framework, knowledge graphs can represent and analyze real-world concepts and their interactions in a structured format by capturing entities and the semantic relationships among them. This facilitates complex querying and logical reasoning [12]. Due to their strong capabilities in knowledge representation and management, knowledge graphs have been widely applied in fields such as search engine technologies, financial risk control, and biomedical research [13], and are increasingly demonstrating substantial potential in power systems—particularly in critical tasks such as intelligent questioning [14], fault diagnosis [15], and decision support [16].

Tang et al. [17] constructed a knowledge graph for power equipment and proposed an information retrieval method based on graph search strategies, which effectively improved the level of intelligence in the lifecycle management of power assets. Liu et al. [18] designed a Chinese entity recognition model based on BERT–BiLSTM–CRF, integrating BERT's contextual semantic representation capability, BiLSTM's sequential modeling strength, and CRF's label dependency constraints. This model achieved accurate extraction of fault-related entities and their semantic relations in power equipment and further supported automated fault diagnosis and intelligent question answering by constructing a Neo4j-based knowledge graph system. The approach significantly enhanced the precision of entity recognition in Chinese power-related literature. Addressing the rapidly growing demand for ultra-high-voltage (UHV) infrastructure in power grid development, Hu [19] proposed a knowledge graph construction method that integrates multi-view graph convolutional networks (GCN) with a Haar convolution pooling mechanism. By jointly aggregating node attribute information and subgraph structural features, the method enabled accurate classification of UHV projects, achieving superior accuracy and generalization performance on both the UHV and NCI-1 datasets. In addition, Y et al. [20] focused on centralized monitoring and intelligent alerting in smart grid control systems, constructing an accident knowledge graph based on monitoring data. By incorporating grid topology and historical alarm rules into the modeling of entities and relationships, the method enhanced the identification of correlations among alarm events and improved both the efficiency of accident analysis and the reliability of control systems.

Research on on-site construction operation scenarios in the electric power sector remains relatively limited, with existing studies commonly exhibiting limitations such as a narrow range of data types, weak inter-information associations, and insufficient visualization capabilities. To tackle these challenges, this study introduces a knowledge graph-driven approach for modeling and profiling violations in power grid field operations, aiming to enable comprehensive modeling and precise representation of non-compliant behaviors, thereby providing data-driven support for scheduling and planning decisions. For structured data, violation behaviors are statistically analyzed using rule-based methods, and a mutual information algorithm is employed to identify correlations between violations and seven key operational factors: operation entity, task source, operation type, professional category, voltage level, risk level, and working mode. Additionally, stage-wise statistical modeling is conducted at the municipal level to inform regional violation risk assessments. For unstructured textual data, a multi-source embedding-based named entity recognition (NER) model is developed, incorporating domain-specific power lexicon information to enhance the extraction of key entities. High-weight domain terms related to violations are further identified using the TF-IDF algorithm to characterize typical violation behaviors. Based on the extracted entities and relationships, a knowledge graph of field operation violations is constructed, providing a computable and inferable semantic representation of operational scenarios. Finally, visualization techniques are applied to present the structural patterns and distributional features of violations, offering graph-based support for violation risk analysis and dispatch decision-making. Experimental results demonstrate that the proposed method effectively identifies critical features of violation behaviors and provides a structured foundation for intelligent decision support in power grid operation management. The main contributions and innovations of this study are outlined as follows:

(1) A knowledge graph is specifically constructed for the field of on-site operation violations in power systems, which focuses on a unique and underexplored domain that involves highly unstructured and safety-critical textual data.
(2) A curated power operation vocabulary is used as prior semantic knowledge to enhance the named entity recognition (NER) process, which significantly improves the recognition of key entities (e.g., person, object).
(3) It enables power grid personnel to analyze violations, assess potential risks, and derive targeted safety insights, which supports the decision-making in real-world settings and improves the effectiveness of safety management.

2. Construction of a Knowledge Graph for Violations in Power Grid Field Operations

2.1. Framework for Constructing a Knowledge Graph of Violations in Power Grid Field Operations

As a natural language processing technique, knowledge graphs fundamentally aim to model real-world concepts and their interrelations in the form of "entity–relation–entity" triples, thereby constructing a structured semantic network [21]. This study employs a top-down design strategy to construct a domain-specific knowledge graph specifically for modeling violation scenarios in power grid field operations. The complete framework is depicted in Figure 1. This knowledge graph focuses on the in-depth modeling and analysis of on-site violation data associated with power grid personnel and encompasses the entire process from semantic modeling to practical graph-based applications.

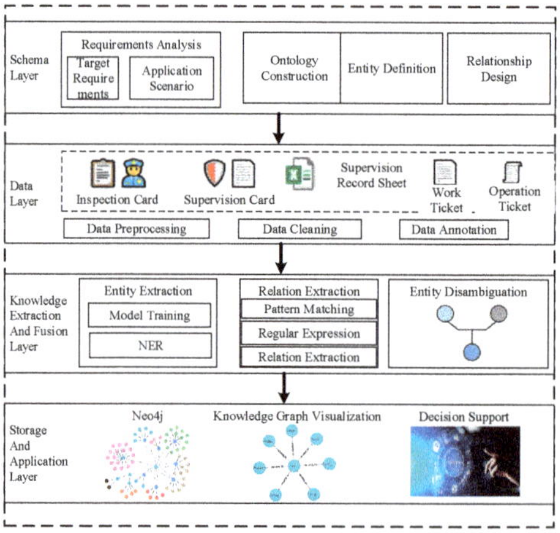

Figure 1. Framework for constructing a KG of violations in power grid field operations.

Specifically, the schema layer provides a semantically explicit and structurally complete conceptual framework for the knowledge graph through requirement analysis, entity definition, relationship design, and ontology construction. This layer serves as the logical foundation for knowledge graph construction and inference. The data layer primarily relies on historical structured documents related to power grid field operations (e.g., work permits and operation tickets) and violation records (e.g., inspection cards and supervision records), supplemented by general dictionaries and domain-specific power-related lexicons. It supports data cleaning, annotation, and normalization of raw inputs. The knowledge extraction and fusion layer combines rule-based approaches and deep learning techniques to extract key information related to violation behaviors from structured and semi-structured data. Named Entity Recognition (NER) is employed to identify key operational entities in textual data, and semantic relationships between entities are obtained through rule-based extraction or pattern matching methods. These are further integrated and transformed into standardized triples. Finally, the storage and application layers store the extracted triples into a Neo4j graph database, following predefined construction rules and aligning with operational requirements of power grid field scenarios. This enables efficient knowledge visualization and supports decision-making in dispatching-related applications.

Figure 2 illustrates the overall workflow of the proposed method for constructing a power grid operation knowledge graph. It begins with ontology modeling to define entities and relationships. Then, it processes structured data related to operational factors and unstructured text describing violations. The structured data undergoes preprocessing and statistical analysis to extract the probability distribution of key operational factors. Meanwhile, the violation text data is annotated with BMES tagging, followed by a named entity recognition model that integrates multi-source embeddings to extract power-specific terminology. Subsequently, in knowledge fusion, the TF_IDF algorithm is used to extract key power-specific terms. These results are then used, based on predefined relationships and entities, to extract triples for building a knowledge graph. The knowledge graph for on-site power grid operation violations is constructed in neo4j. The resulting knowledge graph supports downstream applications such as visualization and key information queries, providing a structured and interpretable representation of historical violation patterns for risk analysis and decision support.

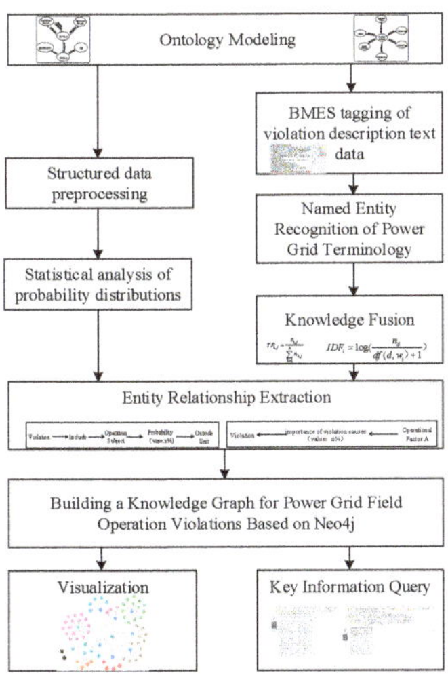

Figure 2. Overview workflow diagram.

2.2. Ontology Modeling

Ontology is a semantic model that formally describes concepts, entities, their attributes, and interrelations in the real world. It is widely utilized in knowledge graph construction and information retrieval [22]. Within a knowledge graph system, ontology serves as a fundamental component, providing a standardized foundation for unified knowledge modeling and semantic reasoning. The construction of a knowledge ontology involves defining key concepts, specifying relationship types, formulating attribute constraints, and modeling semantic structures such as "entity—relationship—entity" and "entity—relationship—attribute" in a consistent manner.

To address the multi-source and heterogeneous nature of historical data from power grid field operations, as well as its application requirements in violation control, this study designs and develops a domain knowledge ontology model for violation profiling in grid field operations, both at the overall level and at the level of local municipal bureaus. The model is constructed based on the seven-step methodology for ontology development and incorporates the stage-wise distribution characteristics of violation data along with the division of management dimensions. It systematically models grid operation behaviors, with the objective of providing structured semantic support for violation profiling and auxiliary decision-making.

At the overall level, a power grid field operation plan is typically associated with multiple key operational factors, including the operation entity, task source, operation type, specialty type, voltage level, risk level, and working mode. Based on historical violation data, the knowledge ontology is required to support correlation analysis and contribution assessment between each operational factor and violation occurrence. Additionally, it should enable statistical modeling of the probability distribution of violations across factor values, the distribution of violation incidents across local municipal bureaus, and the behavioral characteristics of violators. This facilitates the provision of a quantifiable and interpretable foundation for violation profiling to support dispatch management. As illustrated in Figure 3, the semantic structure among relevant concepts is explicitly defined and represented through ontology modeling.

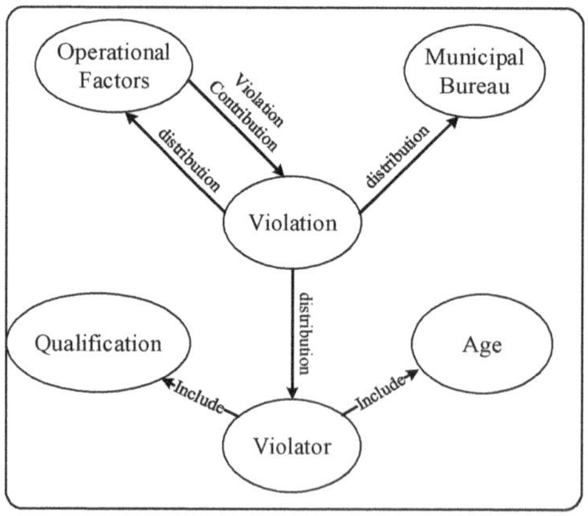

Figure 3. Ontology representation at the overall level.

At the level of the local municipal bureau, ontology modeling focuses on capturing the statistical characteristics and behavioral profiles of regional historical violation data. First, the probability distributions of key operational factors—including operation entity, task source, operation category, specialty type, voltage level, risk level, and work mode—are analyzed based on violation samples to reveal the structural features of regional operational risk. Second, the distributions of problem types, violation categories, and violation severity levels (A, B, C, D) are modeled to characterize violation patterns in terms of frequency and severity. Based on this analysis, the five most frequently occurring violation codes in the historical records are identified and labeled as representative non-compliant behaviors.

Finally, drawing on the historical behavioral records of personnel involved in violations, individuals are categorized as either occasional or habitual violators. This classification is based on the frequency of violation occurrences associated with each individual in the dataset. A predefined threshold is applied: if the number of violations attributed to a person exceeds a certain value, the individual is labeled as a habitual violator; otherwise, the person is considered occasional. The corresponding results, as shown in Figure 4, provide structured and visualized knowledge support for regional violation management and risk mitigation.

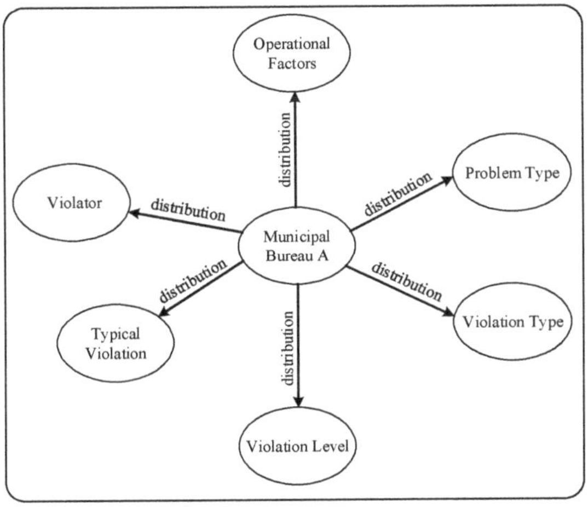

Figure 4. Ontological representation at the local municipal bureau level.

2.3. Data Preprocessing

Structured knowledge refers to a form of knowledge representation characterized by clear semantic definitions and standardized data formats, which can be effectively organized and expressed through data structures or models. In the context of violations in power grid field operations, the structured construction of knowledge is based on original field records such as picket cards, inspection cards, inspection record sheets, work tickets, and operation tickets. For these heterogeneous data sources, systematic data cleaning and preprocessing are first conducted, including steps such as completion of missing fields, unification of data formats, elimination of invalid values, and derivation of key features. This processing stage significantly enhances the structural integrity and semantic consistency of the raw data, thereby providing a high-quality and standardized foundation for subsequent knowledge graph construction, statistical modeling, and decision support system development.

Unstructured knowledge refers to information that lacks a clear structure and standardized representation format, making it difficult to organize, classify, or manage directly. Compared with structured knowledge, unstructured knowledge exhibits greater complexity and variability, and its processing and utilization typically require advanced techniques such as artificial intelligence, natural language processing (NLP), and image recognition [23]. In the domain of power grid field operation violations, unstructured knowledge primarily originates from textual descriptions of violations found in operation records. These texts are semantically rich and expressed in diverse forms, rendering them unsuitable for direct transformation into structured "entity—relationship—entity" triples through conventional approaches. Instead, they must undergo a series of language normalization and information extraction procedures to be converted into computable knowledge representations.

To address this, the following text preprocessing workflow is designed for handling violation-related texts in power grid field operations:

1. Text Cleaning and Normalization: This step involves the removal of invalid characters and special symbols, as well as the semantic restoration and standardization of non-standard abbreviations, shorthand notations, and semantically ambiguous expressions, in order to improve the uniformity and readability of the text.
2. Domain Dictionary Construction: To address the challenge of highly specialized terminology in power grid operation scenarios, a domain-specific terminology dictionary for violation behaviors is developed in collaboration with industry experts. This dictionary serves as a corpus resource to support subsequent entity annotation tasks. Specifically, historical violation description texts were collected and processed using jieba word segmentation, followed by term frequency statistics. The top 1500 high-frequency candidate terms were extracted and reviewed in conjunction with domain experts. Based on both their frequency and relevance to power grid operations, a subset of these terms was selected as domain-specific entities, forming the final version of the power domain dictionary.
3. Named entity recognition (NER) is conducted using the BMES annotation scheme to identify and classify key entities within the text. In this study, five entity types are defined: Person, Object, File, Action, and Surrounding. The specific annotation guidelines for each entity type are detailed in Table 1.

Table 1. Table of entity types.

Entity Type	Entity Beginning Tag	Entity Inside Tag	Entity Ending Tag
Action	B-Action	M-Action	E-Action
Object	B-Object	M-Object	E-Object
File	B-File	M-File	E-File
Person	B-Person	M- Person	E-Person
Surrounding	B-Surrounding	M-Surrounding	E-Surrounding

To guarantee the accuracy and reliability of the annotated dataset during the BMES tagging process, all annotation tasks were carried out by two independent annotators with domain knowledge. After the initial annotation round, the results were compared to identify and review any inconsistencies. Disagreements were resolved through a two-step procedure: the annotators first discussed the disputed cases to reach a consensus, and if no agreement could be reached, the final decision was made by a senior expert in the power grid domain. This process ensured the consistency and accuracy of the final annotated corpus.

The preprocessing system provides a critical foundation for the standardized representation and triple-based extraction of unstructured knowledge, thereby significantly enhancing the usability and structural quality of unstructured textual information in power grid field operation scenarios.

As an illustrative example, Table 2 presents the labeling results for the phrase "未佩戴安全帽 (Not Wearing a Safety Helmet)".

Table 2. Examples of entity type labeling.

Text Sequence	English Translation	NER Tag
未	Not	O
佩	Wearing	B-Action
戴		E-Action
安		B-Object
全	Safety Helmet	M-Object
帽		E-Object

2.4. *Knowledge Extraction from Violation Description Texts in Grid Field Operations*

Entity extraction refers to the identification of entities with explicit semantic types from natural language text. Based on pre-labeled data in the BMES format, entities such as Person, Object, File, Action, and Surrounding are extracted from the text. In power grid field operation violation texts, entity expressions are highly variable and strongly context-dependent, making it difficult for traditional rule-based or shallow learning methods to effectively capture complex semantic relationships and contextual features, which often results in limited extraction accuracy.

To address this challenge, this paper presents a Chinese named entity recognition (NER) model specifically designed for extracting power-related entities from field operation violation texts in the power grid domain, leveraging multi-source embeddings to improve the identification of entity boundaries. The model architecture, depicted in Figure 5, consists of three functional components:

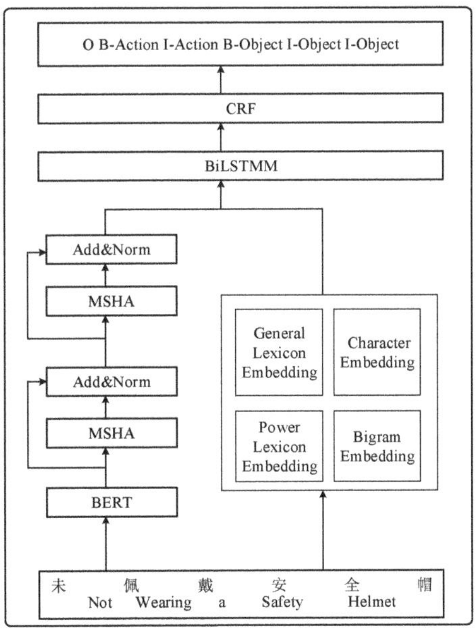

Figure 5. Named entity recognition model with multi-source embedding fusion.

1. Multi-source Embedding Fusion Layer: This layer integrates multi-source embedding vectors, including the pre-trained BERT embeddings, character-level, word-level, and domain-specific power lexicon information. It effectively enhances the semantic representation capability of the input and enhances the model's ability to recognize domain-specific terminology.

2. Feature Encoding Layer: A deep neural network based on BiLSTM is employed as a context-aware encoder to capture deep semantic features and contextual dependencies within the input sequence.
3. Label Decoding Layer: A Conditional Random Field (CRF) is used for label sequence modeling, enabling global optimization of entity boundary and type predictions, thereby significantly improving recognition accuracy.

By combining multidimensional semantic representations with context-aware modeling and incorporating structured prior knowledge, the proposed model offers a robust and accurate method for identifying electric power entities in field operation violation descriptions of power grids.

2.4.1. Word-Character Fusion Feature Embedding Layer

Multi-source embedding includes BERT embeddings, single-character embeddings, bi-character embeddings, generic dictionary embeddings, and power domain dictionary embeddings. The dictionary integration approach follows the method proposed by Ma et al. [24], in which external lexical information is incorporated to enhance the performance of named entity recognition. Besides, this strategy is extended by introducing a power operation domain-specific lexicon that provides specialized semantic cues for the identification of technical terms in violation descriptions. Importantly, this domain lexicon is designed to be flexible and extensible, allowing for incremental updates as new terminology, regional variations, or internal jargon emerge over time or across different power grid units. This adaptability ensures the sustained effectiveness of the NER model in diverse and evolving operational contexts.

BERT Embedding: The BERT pre-trained model can generate dynamic character-level vector representations for input text sequences. An example input sequence, "未佩戴安全帽 (Not Wearing a Safety Helmet)" is illustrated in Figure 6. Unlike the original BERT architecture, the proposed model feeds the output of BERT into an additional Multi-Head Self-Attention Residual Module to enhance context modeling and extract higher-level semantic features.

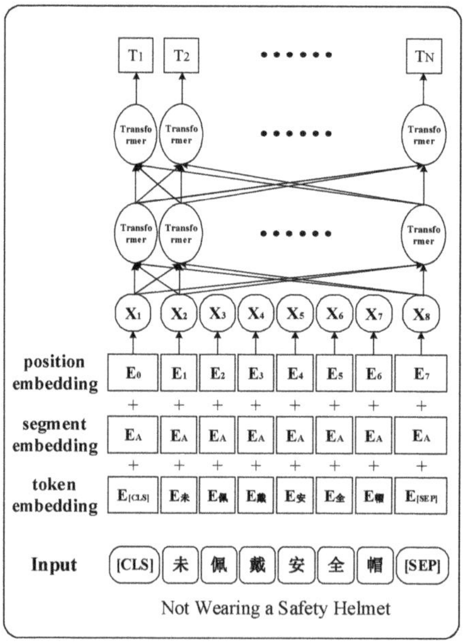

Figure 6. BERT input representation diagram.

Single-character, Bi-character, and Generic Lexicon Embeddings: To capture lexical information at different granularities, this study adopts the same external lexicon used in Lattice-LSTM [25] to obtain embedding representations at the single-character, bi-character, and word levels. These embeddings complement BERT by incorporating fine-grained lexical cues into the model.

Power Domain Dictionary Embedding: In the data preprocessing stage, a power domain-specific dictionary is constructed using violation description texts from grid field operation records as the training corpus. The Skip-gram algorithm within the Word2Vec framework is employed to train word vectors, resulting in specialized embeddings tailored to the power grid domain. These embeddings enhance the model's capability to represent domain-specific terminology and improve recognition accuracy in specialized contexts.

Word2Vec [26], created by Google in 2013, is an efficient word embedding model widely used in various NLP tasks. It consists of two main architectures: Continuous Bag of Words (CBOW) and Skip-Gram. CBOW predicts the target word from surrounding context, while Skip-Gram does the reverse by predicting context words from a center word.

Figure 7 illustrates the architecture of the Word2Vec model, which comprises an input layer, a projection layer, and an output layer. Trained on large-scale corpora, Word2Vec maps words into a low-dimensional continuous vector space, allowing semantically related words to cluster together. This structure effectively captures the semantic relationships between words.

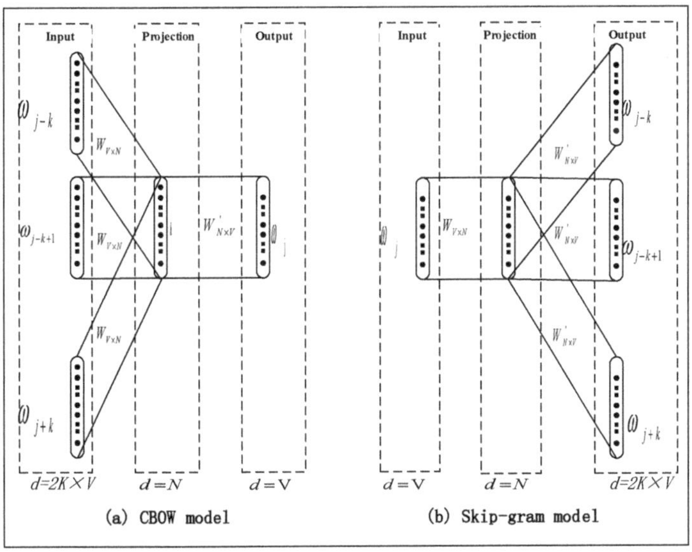

Figure 7. Architecture diagram of Word2Vec model.

The Skip-Gram model typically generates more accurate semantic representations than the CBOW model and demonstrates superior performance, especially in handling low-frequency words within small-scale corpora. Therefore, this study adopts Skip-Gram architecture for training word vectors on violation description texts from power grid field operations.

The core objective of the Skip-Gram model is to maximize the conditional probability of context words given a center word. Its optimization objective function is:

$$L = \sum_{\omega_j \in V} \lg P(\omega_{j-k}, \omega_{j-k+1}, \cdots, \omega_{j+k} | \omega_j) \tag{1}$$

Here, V represents the set of all words in the corpus, k denotes the size of the context window, and ω_j is the center word. The fundamental idea of the Skip-Gram model is to predict the probability of the k surrounding context words based on the given center word ω_j. This probability is modeled using the softmax function as follows:

$$P(\omega_{j-k}, \omega_{j-k+1}, \cdots, \omega_{j+k} | \omega_j) = \frac{\exp(u_j^T h)}{\sum_i \exp(u_i^T h)} \quad (2)$$

where h is the input vector of the center word (i.e., the column vector from the input matrix), u_j is the output vector of a context word (i.e., the row vector from the output matrix), and V denotes the vocabulary size. The model parameters are optimized using stochastic gradient descent (SGD).

The four embeddings, namely single-character embedding, bi-character embedding, generic dictionary embedding, and power domain dictionary embedding, are all trained with a dimensionality of 50. The BERT embedding, after processing, yields a 256-dimensional representation. These multi-source embeddings are concatenated and fed into the feature encoding layer as the final input.

2.4.2. Feature Encoding Layer

To encode contextual information from input embeddings, this study employs a bidirectional LSTM (BiLSTM) in the feature encoding layer. As a variant of the traditional RNN, LSTM is designed to handle long-range dependencies by regulating information flow through a gating mechanism, thereby alleviating the issues of gradient vanishing and explosion. The unit structure includes three gates: input, forget, and output, as shown in Figure 8.

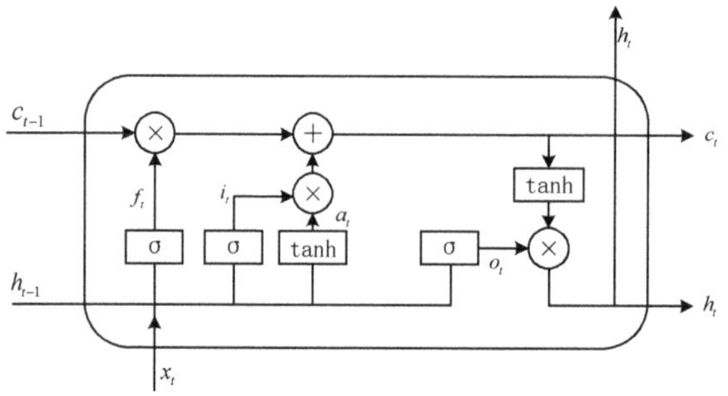

Figure 8. Architecture of the LSTM model.

The input gate i_t controls the extent to which new information from the current input is integrated into the cell state. The forget gate f_t is responsible for filtering out unnecessary components of the previous cell state c_{t-1}. Meanwhile, the output gate o_t regulates how much of the updated cell state c_t contributes to the hidden state h_t. The updated equations for these three gates are provided in Equations (3)–(7).

$$i_t = \sigma(W_i \cdot [h_{t-1}, x_t] + b_i) \quad (3)$$

$$f_t = \sigma(W_f \cdot [h_{t-1}, x_t] + b_f) \quad (4)$$

$$o_t = \sigma(W_o \cdot [h_{t-1}, x_t] + b_o) \quad (5)$$

$$c_t = f_t \times c_{t-1} + i_t \times \tanh(W_s \cdot [h_{t-1}, x_t] + b_s) \quad (6)$$

$$h_t = o_t \times \tanh(c_t) \quad (7)$$

Here, σ, W, b, x_t represent the activation function, weight matrix, bias term, and the input to the current unit, respectively.

A single-layer LSTM model can only capture unidirectional features of the target word and fails to fully account for contextual information. Therefore, a bidirectional LSTM (BiLSTM) network is adopted in this study. Figure 9 illustrates the model architecture of BiLSTM.

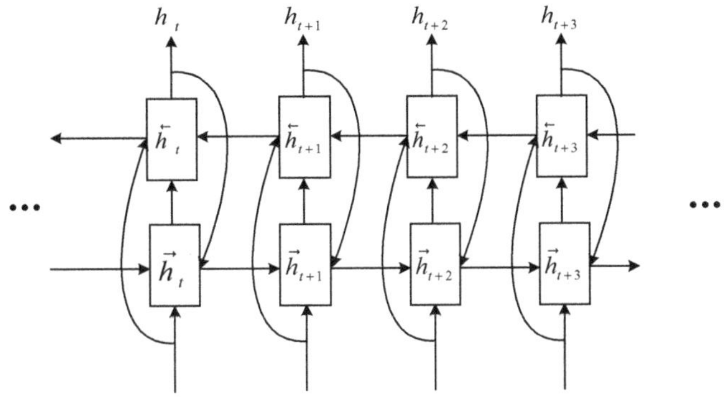

Figure 9. Architecture of the BiLSTM model.

The BiLSTM layer receives the multi-source embedding outputs and utilizes both forward and backward LSTM networks to compute the forward representation $\overrightarrow{h}_t$ and the backward representation $\overleftarrow{h}_t$ of each input character at time step t. Subsequently, the model concatenates the hidden states from both directions to produce the final BiLSTM output h_t, as defined in Equation (8).

$$h_t = [\overrightarrow{h}_t; \overleftarrow{h}_t] \tag{8}$$

2.4.3. Label Decode Layer

Although the BiLSTM model is capable of generating token-level label predictions, it does not effectively account for the dependencies between adjacent labels in sequence labeling tasks. For instance, under the BMES tagging scheme, a label such as "B-Object" should logically be followed by "M-Object" or "E-Object", but not by unrelated tags like "S-File" or "O". Similarly, the initial character in a sequence is typically labeled as "B-" (beginning) or "S-" (single), rather than "M-" (middle) or "E-" (end). These label transition rules imply that BiLSTM outputs alone may violate structural constraints, resulting in invalid sequences. To resolve this limitation, a Conditional Random Field (CRF) [27] layer is applied on top of the BiLSTM. The CRF models the dependencies between adjacent labels through a learnable transition matrix, which assigns scores to permissible label transitions. By considering the entire label sequence during decoding, the CRF ensures that the final output adheres to the syntactic structure imposed by the BMES scheme, thereby yielding globally optimal and consistent predictions.

To obtain a valid label sequence, the BiLSTM layer generates a score matrix $S \in R^{n \times m}$, where each element s_{ij} represents the emission score for assigning the jth label to the ith character x_i in the input sequence. The scoring function used to evaluate a predicted label sequence for a given input is formulated as:

$$score(X,Y) = \sum_{i=0}^{n} A_{y_i,y_{i+1}} + \sum_{i=1}^{n} S_{i,y_i} \tag{9}$$

In this formulation, $A \in R^{(m+2)\times(m+2)}$ represents the transition score matrix, where $A_{yi,yi+1}$ encodes the transition likelihood from label y_i to label y_{i+1}. The emission component $S_{i,yi}$ captures the confidence score of assigning label y_i to the character at position i in the input.

The probability of the output label sequence Y is computed using the softmax normalization function, as defined below:

$$P(Y|X) = \frac{e^{score(X,Y)}}{\sum_{\widetilde{Y} \in Y_X} e^{score(X,\widetilde{Y})}} \tag{10}$$

Here, Y_X denotes the complete set of candidate label sequences, and $\widetilde{Y}$ represents the ground-truth annotation.

To identify the most probable label sequence for a given input X, the Viterbi algorithm is employed to search for the sequence Y^* that maximizes the overall score. Specifically, Y^* corresponds to the label configuration with the highest output probability, and is computed as:

$$Y^* = \underset{Y \in Y_X}{\mathrm{argmax}}\, score(X, \widetilde{Y}) \tag{11}$$

2.5. Knowledge Fusion

After processing unstructured violation description texts from power grid field operations using Named Entity Recognition (NER) techniques, a large number of entity terms are typically extracted. These often exhibit semantic ambiguity, redundancy, or inconsistent formatting [28]. Among such entities, many synonymous or semantically similar expressions may exist—for example, "梯子 (ladder)" and "扶梯 (step ladder)", or "围栏 (fence)" and "遮栏 (barrier)". Without further processing, these terms can result in a proliferation of redundant entities in the knowledge graph, thereby compromising structural accuracy and significantly reducing the efficiency of query and reasoning operations. Therefore, it is necessary to perform knowledge fusion on the extracted entities.

The core objective of knowledge fusion is to unify and standardize different expressions of the same concept. This is achieved through techniques such as entity alignment and synonym merging, ensuring that each normalized entity is assigned a unique identifier, and thus maintaining the consistency and completeness of the knowledge graph structure. Specifically, when the semantic similarity between two extracted entities exceeds a predefined threshold, they are merged and normalized to the entity that has the larger frequency count in the corpus, which improves graph compactness while preserving dominant terminology usage.

In addition, considering the variations in on-site working environments, management practices, and safety cultures across different municipal bureaus, this study further incorporates TF-IDF algorithms to compute the importance weights of entities extracted by the NER model from violation descriptions. High-frequency domain-specific terms that characterize violation behaviors in each region are identified, enabling the construction of representative violation profiles for different municipal bureaus and providing support for subsequent risk analysis and behavior profiling. TF-IDF is computed as follows:

$$TF_{i,j} = \frac{n_{i,j}}{\sum_{k=1}^{k} n_{k.j}} \tag{12}$$

where $n_{i,j}$ denotes the frequency of term ω_i in document d_j, and the denominator represents the total number of term occurrences in the document, calculated as the sum of frequencies of all terms. Here, k denotes the number of unique terms contained in the document.

IDF formula:

$$IDF_{\mathrm{i}} = \log(\frac{n_d}{df(d,w_i)+1}) \quad (13)$$

where n_d refers to the overall size of the document collection and $df(d, w_i)$ indicates the count of documents in which the term w_i appears. To prevent division by zero, the denominator is adjusted by adding 1.

2.6. Entity Relationship Extraction

After completing the named entity recognition of unstructured text data and the statistical analysis of probability distributions in structured data, the semantic associations between entities are further clarified based on the predefined entity-relationship rules defined in the schema layer. Subsequently, a knowledge graph for grid operation violations is constructed. This graph represents various entities and their associated attributes within the grid operation scenario in a structured manner, thereby enhancing the organization and semantic interpretability of the data.

As an illustrative example, the construction result of the knowledge graph corresponding to the probability distribution of "outside unit" under the dimension of "operation subject" at the overall level is presented in Figure 10. This figure demonstrates the entity's relational structure and associated weight information within the context of actual operational data.

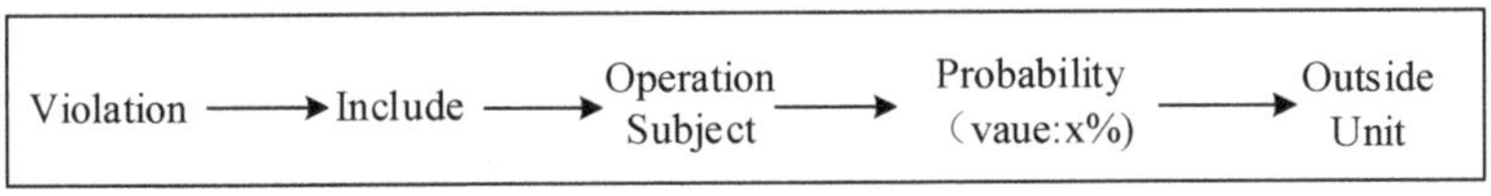

Figure 10. Example of probability distribution relationship construction at the overall level.

In addition, this study also considers the contribution of operational factors to violation analysis at the overall level. A mutual information–based method [29] is employed to assess the degree of association between operational factors and violations. The data used for this analysis are derived from the historical on-site operation violation records, specifically from the columns corresponding to operational factors—namely operation entity, task source, operation category, specialty type, voltage level, risk level, and working mode—and the violation label column. All variables involved are discreet.

To quantify the correlation between each operational factor and the occurrence of violations, mutual information is computed. The strength of the association between an operational factor and violation behavior increases with the mutual information value. Mutual information is computed as follows:

$$I(X;Y) = \sum_{x\in X}\sum_{y\in Y} p(x,y)\log(\frac{p(x,y)}{p(x)p(y)}) \quad (14)$$

$$\text{contribution}_{\mathrm{i}} = \frac{I(X_i;Y)}{\sum_{j=1}^{d} I(X_i;Y)} \quad (15)$$

Here, X represents the operational factor (e.g., operation entity) and Y denotes the violation status. $p(x,y)$ represents the joint probability distribution over X and Y; $p(x)$ and $p(y)$ correspond to the marginal probability distributions of X and Y; and $I(X;Y)$ denotes the mutual information of X and Y.

In practical computation, the joint probability distribution $p(x,y)$ and the marginal probabilities $p(x)$ and $p(y)$ are estimated by counting the co-occurrence frequencies of each operational factor and the violation category in the historical dataset. For example, considering the operational factor "operation entity", which takes values such as internal unit and external unit, the co-occurrence frequencies between each value and violation status are calculated. Based on these statistics, the mutual information is computed to quantify the contribution of this operational factor to violations. An illustrative example is shown in Figure 11.

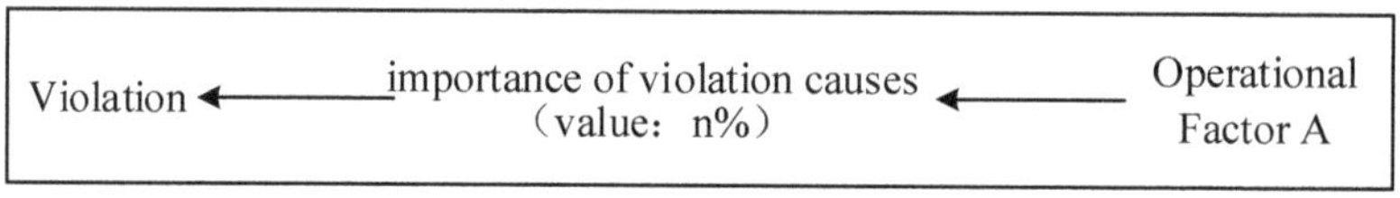

Figure 11. Example of relationship construction for violation contribution of operational factors.

3. Experimental Evaluation and Result Analysis

3.1. Data Introduction and Preprocessing

A complete set of power grid field violation inspection records from the year 2023 was obtained from a power grid company. These records include various types of information, such as operational factors, violation details, municipal bureaus, and violators. Both the textual descriptions of field operation violations and the structured tabular data were processed through a series of preprocessing steps. As a result, a total of 47,980 meaningful violation inspection records were retained.

For the violation description texts, five entity categories were defined based on expert knowledge in the power domain: Action, Object, File, Person, and Surrounding. Entity annotation was then performed accordingly. The YEDDA annotation tool was adopted due to its efficiency in sequence labeling tasks, and the BMES tagging scheme was used for annotating the violation descriptions.

In this tagging scheme, B denotes the beginning of an entity, M and E represent the middle and end of an entity, respectively, while S indicates a single-character entity. The final annotation was independently conducted by two annotators with domain expertise. Any discrepancies were resolved through discussion and re-annotation to ensure consistency and quality of the labeled data.

A total of 32,380 entities were annotated in the electric grid violation dataset. Among them, Action, Object, File, Person, and Surrounding entities account for approximately 32.7%, 30.1%, 12.7%, 10.0%, and 14.5%, respectively. In the experimental validation process, we partitioned the annotated dataset of textual descriptions for field operation violations into training, validation, and test sets, using a 7:2:1 ratio.

3.2. Evaluation Metrics for Chinese NER Model

Named Entity Recognition (NER) is typically evaluated using three key metrics: *Precision, Recall,* and *F1*-Score. The *F1*-Score, calculated as the harmonic means of precision and recall, provides a balanced evaluation of the model's overall effectiveness. The formulas for these evaluation metrics are given in Equations (16)–(18):

$$Precision = \frac{TP}{(TP + FP)} \tag{16}$$

$$Recall = \frac{TP}{(TP + FN)} \tag{17}$$

$$F1 = \frac{2 \times (Precision \times \mathrm{Re}call)}{(Precision + \mathrm{Re}call)} \tag{18}$$

Here, TP (True Positive) is the count of correctly identified positive samples, FP (False Positive) is the count of negative samples wrongly labeled as positive, and FN (False Negative) is the count of positive samples incorrectly labeled as negative.

Precision, *Recall*, and *F1*-Score range from 0 to 1, with values closer to 1 indicating superior model performance.

3.3. Experimental Results of Chinese NER Model

To evaluate the effectiveness of the proposed model, five commonly used named entity recognition models are selected for comparison, i.e., BiLSTM-CRF [30], LR-CNN [31], Lattice-LSTM [25], BERT-CRF [32], and BERT-BiLSTM-CRF [33], using BERT-BiLSTM-CRF as the baseline model. To ensure experimental rigor, we set the batch size to 32, aligning with the typical length of violation description texts in the historical power grid field operation records.

To further ensure a fair comparison, all models, including the proposed one, adopt the Adam optimizer with an identical learning rate setting of 0.0001, and the number of training epochs is set to 128. The detailed comparison results are presented in Table 3.

Table 3. Evaluation of model performance on the power grid violation description dataset.

Model	P	R	F1
BiLSTM-CRF [30]	82.73%	76.14%	79.30%
LR-CNN [31]	79.19%	54.88%	65.84%
Lattice-LSTM [25]	84.55%	88.33%	86.40%
BERT-CRF [32]	90.01%	89.23%	89.62%
BERT-BiLSTM-CRF [33]	92.67%	93.85%	93.26%
Our Model	**95.73%**	**94.87%**	**95.30%**

The proposed model demonstrates superior performance across all three key metrics (Precision, Recall, and F1-score) compared to comparative methods, as shown in Table 3, highlighting its enhanced accuracy in recognizing entities within power grid violation descriptions. The comparative results between the proposed model and both BiLSTM-CRF and BERT-CRF clearly demonstrate the advantage of utilizing BERT, which excels at capturing deep semantic information from textual data. Furthermore, the comparison between the proposed model and BERT-BiLSTM-CRF indicates that the multi-source embedding layer introduced in this study provides richer semantic representations than using BERT embeddings alone. By incorporating additional lexical and contextual cues, the proposed model is able to extract more informative features and achieve enhanced entity recognition performance. Moreover, the comparison with classical Chinese lexical fusion models such as Lattice-LSTM and LR-CNN further validates the effectiveness of the proposed lexical fusion mechanism and the introduced Multi-Head Self-Attention Residual Module, which jointly contribute to more robust and accurate entity recognition.

To further evaluate the real-world effectiveness of the proposed method, a robust analysis was conducted using raw violation description texts from power grid operation records, without any preprocessing. These texts commonly contain various types of noise, including:

1. Omissions, such as using incomplete terms like "试验标签 (test label)" instead of the correct "试验合格标签 (qualified test label)", or "安全技术交底 (safety technical disclosure)" instead of "安全技术交底单 (safety technical disclosure form)";
2. Typographical errors, such as "师机 (machine master, incorrect)" for "司机 (driver)", "安全遮拦 (safety barricade, incorrect)" for "安全遮栏 (safety fence)", and "实验 (experiment, incorrect)" mistakenly used for "试验 (test)";

3. Abbreviations, such as "安措 (abbrev. for safety measures)" for "安全措施 (safety measures)" and "接地 (grounding, abbreviated)" for "接地线 (grounding wire)".

Such inconsistencies frequently occur in field documentation and can affect the performance of named entity recognition. Therefore, a comparative evaluation between the proposed model and the baseline model is designed to assess their ability to handle noisy inputs.

As shown in Table 4, the performance of both models declines when evaluated on noisy data, which simulates common real-world issues such as omissions, typographical errors, and abbreviations. The BERT-BiLSTM-CRF model exhibits a notable F1 drop of 5.54%, highlighting its limited robustness in handling such irregularities. In contrast, the proposed model shows a much smaller degradation of only 1.71%, demonstrating superior resilience to input noise.

Table 4. Comparison of F1 performance on clean vs. noisy data.

Model	Clean Data (%)	Noisy Data (%)	F1 Degradation (%)
BERT-BiLSTM-CRF	93.26	87.72	5.54
Our Model	95.30	93.59	1.71

The robustness can be attributed to the integration of a multi-source lexical embedding mechanism, particularly the inclusion of domain-specific gazetteers. Many noise-affected terms—such as omissions, typographical errors, abbreviations—are explicitly covered in the curated dictionaries. As a result, the proposed model can still identify entity boundaries accurately even when the input text contains inconsistencies or non-standard terminology. This underscores the practical applicability of the method in real-world power grid operation scenarios where data quality cannot always be guaranteed.

To assess cross-domain performance, we extended our evaluation to the general-domain Weibo dataset. The results, presented in Table 5, show that the model achieves an average improvement of approximately 1% across all three metrics on this dataset. The evaluation results in general domains validate the robustness of the proposed model.

Table 5. Comparison of model performance on the general Weibo dataset.

Model	P	R	F1
BERT-BiLSTM-CRF	95.75%	95.28%	95.51%
Our Model	96.55%	96.26%	96.41%

To offer a more comprehensive evaluation of the performance advantages of the proposed model, a statistical significance test was conducted using paired two-tailed t-tests on the F1-scores obtained across multiple runs. The results are summarized in Table 6.

Table 6. *t*-test results for F1-score differences between models.

Dataset	Compared Models	Mean F1 Gap	*p*-Value	Significance
Power Grid Violation Dataset	Our Model vs. BERT-BiLSTM-CRF	+2.04%	0.008	Significant
General Weibo Dataset		+0.90%	0.032	Significant

For the Power Grid Violation Description Dataset (Table 3), the F1-score improvements of the proposed model over the strongest baselines (e.g., BERT-BiLSTM-CRF) were found to be statistically significant ($p < 0.01$). Similarly, for the general Weibo dataset (Table 6), the improvement in F1-score also reached statistical significance with $p < 0.05$.

These results indicate that the observed performance gains are unlikely to be due to random variation.

3.4. *Knowledge Graph Construction Results*

3.4.1. Knowledge Graph Construction Results at the Overall Level

The overall knowledge graph comprises 73 entity nodes and 79 relational edges. Entities are organized according to their semantic functions, with the "violation" node serving as the central risk entity. Surrounding it are seven operational factor nodes: operation entity, task source, operation category, specialty type, voltage level, risk level, and work mode. These factors are linked to 39 corresponding value nodes with explicit labels (e.g., "external unit", "internal unit").

To reflect the regional hierarchy, the graph includes one overall-level municipal bureau node and 16 subordinate municipal bureau nodes (e.g., A and B Power Supply Bureau). Additionally, a violator node is introduced and further refined based on qualification ("three types of personnel") and age range, resulting in a total of eight feature nodes, details can be found in Table 7.

Table 7. Structural table of knowledge graph violators at the overall level.

Entity	Relation	Entity		
violator	include (2)	Qualification (three types of personnel)	distribution (2)	Y; N.
		age	distribution (4)	Under 30; 30–40; 40–50; above 50

The graph structure contains 8 "include" relationships (violation → factors), 61 "probability distribution" relationships (factors → values), and 7 "violation cause importance" relationships (factors → violation), with importance scores calculated using mutual information.

The entire knowledge graph has been deployed and stored in the Neo4j graph database. Figure 12 provides a detailed illustration of relationship attributes, where all probability and contribution values are embedded as edge attributes. Table 8 lists the structure of the overall-level knowledge graph, and the complete visualization is shown in Figure 13.

Figure 12. Entity-relationship attribute diagram.

Table 8. Table of structural overview of the overall-level knowledge graph.

Entity	Relation	Entity	Relation	Entity
violation	include (7) importance of violation causes (7)	operation entity	distribution (2)	internal unit; external unit
		task source	distribution (4)	infrastructure; production; marketing; dispatch
		operation category	distribution (5)	infrastructure; technical improvements and repairs; overhaul test and fixed inspection maintenance category; marketing; operation
		specialty type	distribution (7)	distribution; substation; marketing; transmission; secondary system; generation; civil engineering
		voltage level	distribution (13)	10 kV; 0.4 kV; 0.22 kV; 110 kV; 35 kV; 500 kV; 220 kV; 6.3 kV; 0.62 kV; low voltage; 20 kV; 350 kV; 11 kV
		risk level	distribution (5)	low; medium; high; acceptable; none
		working mode	distribution (3)	power-off; live-line; live work
	include (2)	municipal bureau	distribution (16)	power supply bureau A-P
		violator	include (2)	qualification (three types of personnel); age

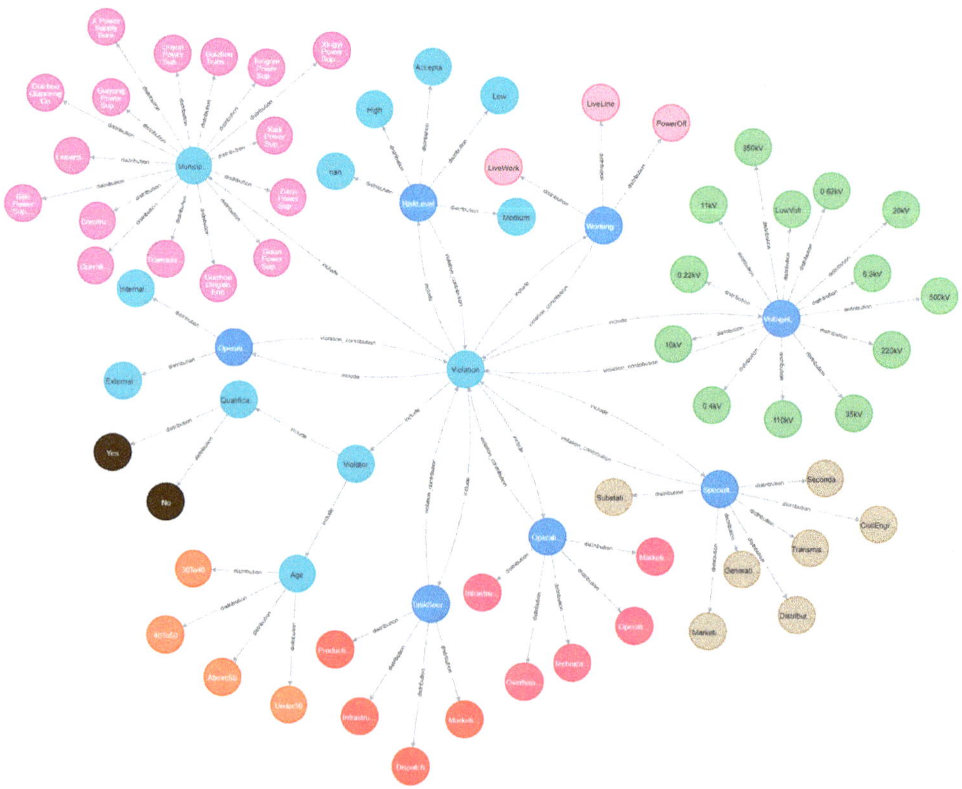

Figure 13. Visualization results of the knowledge graph at the overall level.

3.4.2. Named Entity Recognition for X Power Supply Bureau

From a preprocessed dataset comprising 15,183 historical records from a power grid company, 1328 records corresponding to X Power Supply Bureau were extracted. The unstructured text data describing on-site operational violations from these records were analyzed using the pre-trained multi-source hybrid embedding named entity recognition (NER) model, as detailed in Section 3.3. The model was applied to identify five categories of power-related entities—Person, Action, Object, File, and Surrounding—within the violation description texts. To validate the effectiveness of the proposed model, a specific violation description from the X Power Supply Bureau—"工作班人员没有戴安全帽 (The staff on duty did not wear safety helmets)"—is selected as a case study.

As shown in Figure 14, the named entity recognition process of the proposed model is demonstrated using the violation description "工作班人员没有戴安全帽 (The staff on duty did not wear safety helmets)". The Gazetteer-Matching module aligns each character in the input sequence with matched lexical entries from multiple resources. For example, the character "工" matches entries such as "工", "工作", and "工作班"; "安" matches "安", "安全", and "安全帽"; and "帽" is matched as part of "安全帽". The complete gazetteer match list for this input includes entries from single-character, bi-character, general lexicon, and power-domain lexicon sources.

Input	工作班人员没有戴安全帽(The staff on duty did not wear safety helmets).	The NER recognition process
Gazetteer-Matching	[['工', '工作', '工作班'], ['作'], ['班'], ['人', '人员'], ['员'], ['没', '没有'], ['有'], ['戴'], ['安', '安全', '安全帽'], ['全'], ['帽']]	
Predicted Labels	['B-Person', 'M-Person', 'M-Person', 'M-Person', 'E-Person', 'O', 'O', 'S-Action', 'B-Object', 'M-Object', 'E-Object']	
Recognized Entities	Entity(type="Person", text="工作班人员",span=0-5)	
	Entity (type="Action", text="戴",span=7-8)	
	Entity(type="Object", text="安全帽",span=8-11)	
Status	Extraction successful; 3 entities identified.	
Input	Violation Description Text	Figure Legend
Gazetteer-Matching	Matched Terms from Lexicons (e.g., single-character, bi-character, general, and power-domain gazetteers)	
Predicted Labels	Sequence of Predicted Entity Tags (BMES format)	
Recognized Entities	NER Output with Entity Type and Span	
Status	Extraction Result Summary	

Figure 14. Example of entity extraction process using the proposed model.

Compared with the baseline BERT-BiLSTM-CRF model, which relies solely on contextual embeddings from general-domain corpora, the proposed model integrates multi-source hybrid embeddings, including character-level, bi-character, general lexicon, and power-domain-specific lexicon embeddings. This rich lexical information enables the model to accurately distinguish entity boundaries and identify domain-specific terms. For instance, in this case, the model successfully extracts three entities: "工作班人员" (Person), "戴" (Action), and "安全帽" (Object). This result demonstrates that the combination of domain-specific lexical knowledge with general and fine-grained lexical cues significantly improves recognition performance in technical violation texts.

A comparative analysis with baseline models is presented in Table 9. Specifically, the baseline model BERT-BiLSTM-CRF identified only ["工作班人员 (the staff on duty)", "戴 (wear)"] and failed to recognize the critical domain-specific entity "安全帽 (safety helmet)". In contrast, the proposed model correctly extracted the complete entity sequence, including "工作班人员", "戴", and "安全帽", demonstrating superior capability in handling power grid terminology in real-world violation texts. The baseline model relies solely on BERT, which is pre-trained on general-domain Chinese corpora and captures contextual semantics at a broad level. However, it lacks the capacity to fully recognize specialized terminology specific to the power grid domain, especially in domain-specific contexts. In contrast, the proposed model integrates multi-source hybrid embeddings, including character-level, bi-character, general lexicon, and power-domain lexicon embeddings. The inclusion of power-specific lexical information enhances the model's ability to accurately identify entity boundaries, even when the context is ambiguous. This contributes to improved named entity recognition performance for specialized texts in the power grid domain.

Table 9. Comparative NER results on a sample violation description.

Input Text	Ground Truth Entities	Prediction Results of Baseline Model	Prediction Results of the Proposed Model
工作班人员没有戴安全帽 [The staff on duty did not wear safety helmets]	工作班人员 (Person), 戴 (Action), 安全帽 (Object)	工作班人员 (Person), 戴 (Action)	工作班人员 (Person), 戴(Action), 安全帽 (Object)

As shown in Table 10, the inference time of the proposed model is comparable to that of the baseline model, with only a slight increase in average processing time per sample (0.0729 s vs. 0.0676 s). Despite this minimal overhead, the proposed model achieves significantly better performance in accurately identifying entity boundaries, particularly for domain-specific terminology in power grid violation texts. It demonstrates that the model maintains practical feasibility for deployment in operational monitoring environments while delivering enhanced recognition accuracy.

Table 10. Comparison of inference time between the proposed model and baseline model.

Model	Run 1	Run 2	Run 3	Run 4	Run 5	Run 6	Run 7	Run 8	Run 9	Run 10	Average Time (s)
Baseline Model	0.0780	0.0740	0.0740	0.0590	0.0668	0.0670	0.0597	0.0670	0.0580	0.0720	0.0676
Proposed Model	0.0730	0.0710	0.0790	0.0620	0.0700	0.0690	0.0700	0.0830	0.0800	0.0720	0.0729

After completing named entity recognition on all field operation violation description texts associated with X Power Supply Bureau, this study further applies the TF-IDF algorithm to extract the top five high-weight power-related terms that best represent the characteristics of the bureau—namely, "接地线 (grounding wire)", "填写 (filling in)", "安全交代 (safety briefing)", "施工作业票 (work operation permit)", and "围栏 (barrier)". These selected terms effectively capture the typical violation patterns in the region and serve as foundational data for subsequent modeling of representative violations in X Power Supply Bureau.

3.4.3. Knowledge Graph Construction Results at the Municipal-Level

Table 11 illustrates the structure of the municipal-level knowledge graph, taking the X Power Supply Bureau as a representative example. A visualization of the field operation violation knowledge graph is provided in Figure 15, comprising 86 entity nodes and 86 relational edges, and is modeled across three dimensions.

Table 11. Structural overview of the municipal-level knowledge graph.

Entity	Relation	Entity	Relation	Entity
X Power Supply Bureau	include (11)	operation entity	distribution (2)	internal unit; external unit
		task source	distribution (3)	infrastructure; production; marketing
		operation category	distribution (5)	infrastructure; technical improvements and repairs; overhaul test and fixed inspection maintenance category; marketing; operation
		specialty type	distribution (4)	distribution; substation; marketing; transmission
		voltage level	distribution (7)	10 kV;0.4 kV;0.22 kV;110 kV;35 kV; 500 kV;220 kV
		risk level	distribution (4)	low; medium; high; acceptable
		working mode	distribution (3)	power-off; live-line; live work
		violation level	distribution (4)	A, B, C, D
		typical violation	distribution (5)	"接地线 (grounding wire)", "填写 (filling in)", "安全交代 (safety briefing)", "施工作业票 (work operation permit)", "围栏 (barrier)".
		problem type	distribution (3)	management; behavioral (operational); equipment
		violation type	distribution (5)	two-ticket file; personnel behavior; tool protection; message transmission; operating environment
		violator	include (2)	occasional; habitual

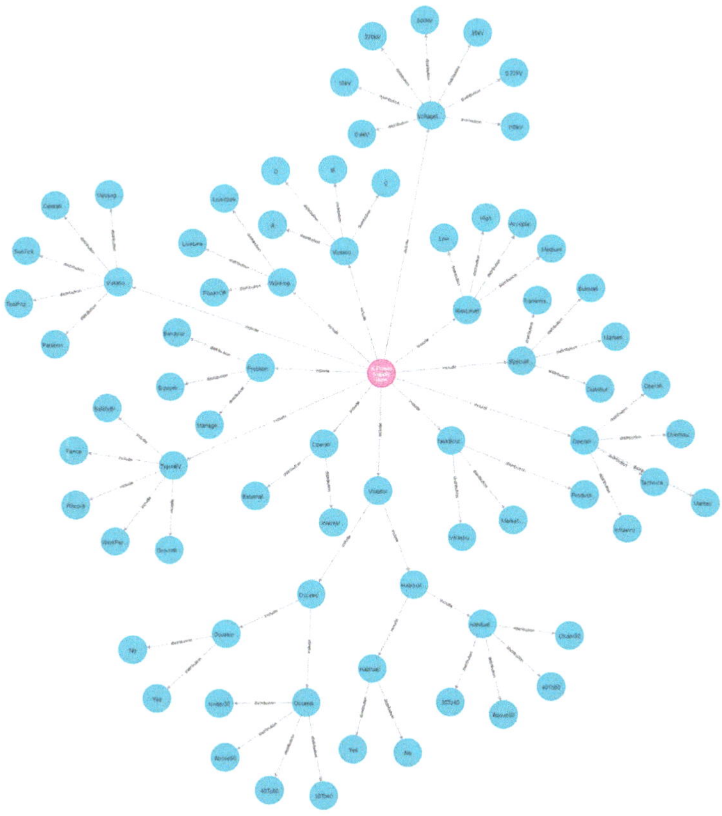

Figure 15. Knowledge graph visualization of X municipal Power Supply Bureau.

In the operational factors dimension, seven first-level factor nodes (e.g., distributions of operation entities and task sources) and their corresponding value nodes are constructed, totaling 46 nodes. These are connected through 7 including relationships and 39 probability distribution relationships.

In the violation situation dimension, the graph includes four violation factor nodes—problem type, violation type, violation level, and typical violations—linked to 17 value nodes. This includes 4 included relationships and 17 additional connections (12 probability distribution and 5 included relationships) to represent typical behavioral patterns. All probability values are stored as edge attributes, consistent with the overall-level model.

In the violator dimension, the graph refines violator characterization by distinguishing between habitual violators and occasional violators. The municipal-level knowledge graph contains 19 nodes and 19 edges in this dimension; details can be seen in Table 12.

Table 12. Structural table of knowledge graph violators at the local municipal level.

Entity	Relation	Entity	Relation	Entity	Relation	Entity
violator	include (2)	occasional	include	qualification (three types of personnel)	distribution (2)	Y; N.
				age	distribution (4)	Under 30; 30–40; 40–50; above 50
		habitual	include	qualification (three types of personnel)	distribution (2)	Y; N.
				age	distribution (4)	Under 30; 30–40; 40–50; above 50

3.4.4. Key Information Query Under the Support of the Knowledge Graph

Beyond the visualization of on-site power grid operation knowledge graphs at both the overall and city levels, the constructed knowledge graph also enables the querying of critical information. The knowledge graph for on-site power grid operations presented in this invention is constructed based on data collected over a specific period. It transforms textual and structured tabular data into visualized graph data, thereby reflecting the on-site power grid during that period.

At the overall level, it is possible to query the violation contribution or distribution of operational factors during this period—including Operation Entity, Task Source, Operation Category, Specialty Type, Voltage Level, Risk Level, and Working Mode—as well as the age and qualification status of violators. As shown in Figure 16, the following Cypher query retrieves the violation contributions of operational factors, sorted in descending order: (

MATCH (f)-[r:violation_contribution]->(v:Violation)
RETURN f.name AS Factor, r.value AS Contribution
ORDER BY toFloat(r.value) DESC

)

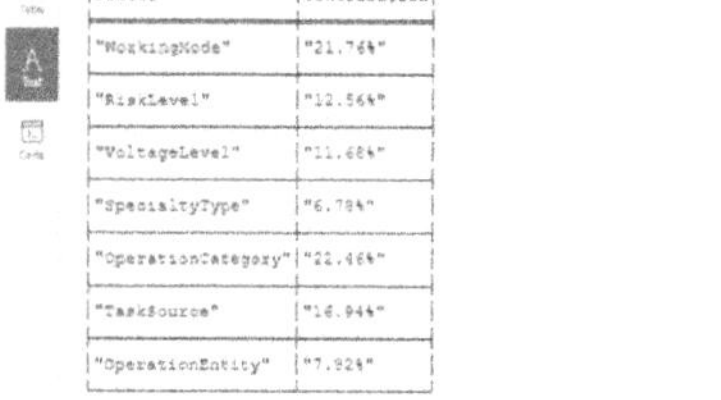

Figure 16. Example chart for querying violation contribution at the overall level.

At the municipal bureau level, it is also possible to query the distribution of operational factors during a given period, including Operation Entity, Task Source, Operation Category, Specialty Type, Voltage Level, Risk Level, and Working Mode. In addition, for a specific municipal bureau, the age and qualification distributions of violators under habitual and occasional violations can be retrieved. For instance, the following Cypher query retrieves the age distribution of violators under habitual violations within the X Power Supply Bureau: (

```
MATCH (b: MunicipalBureau {name: 'X Power Supply Bureau'})-[:include]->
(v_root:X_Violator_Distribution)
MATCH (v_root)-[:include]->(h:X_HabitualViolator)
MATCH (h)-[:include]->(age:X_HabitualAge_Distribution)
MATCH (age)-[r:distribution]->(val:X_HabitualAge_Value)
RETURN val.name AS AgeGroup, r.value AS Proportion
ORDER BY toFloat(r.value) DESC
)
```

Figure 17 displays the query result corresponding to the presented example.

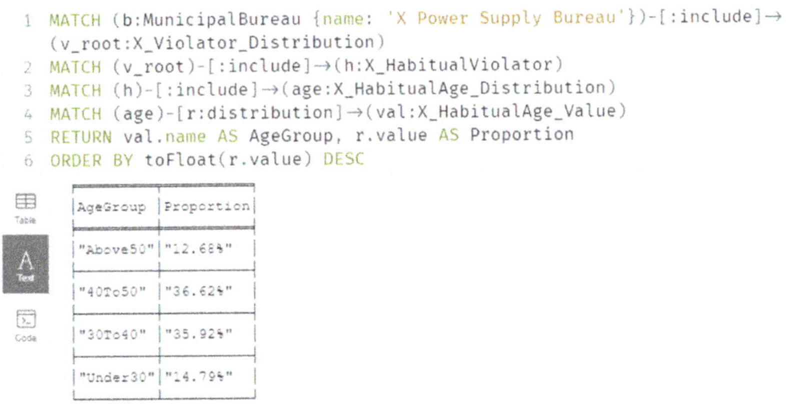

Figure 17. Example chart for querying voltage level distribution at the municipal bureau level.

4. Conclusions

The focus of this work is analyzing the data traits associated with field operation violations in the power grid domain and designing a knowledge ontology by integrating the experience and requirements of power grid professionals. This ontology is used to guide the extraction and knowledge mapping of historical data related to grid field operation violations. A multi-source embedded Chinese NER model is proposed to address the limitations of classical NER models in handling grid-related textual data. By deeply integrating multiple feature representations, the model innovatively incorporates a domain-specific dictionary constructed from grid field operation text data, which markedly enhances the accuracy of identifying power-related entities in the text of power grid field violations. The Neo4j graph database is utilized to store the knowledge related to grid field operation violations, and a visual knowledge graph is constructed to support grid operation planners and provide safeguards for violation prevention in the power sector. The data types and modalities in the field of power grid operations are rich and diverse. In the future, the integration of large language models will be considered to explore new approaches for handling multimodal data, thereby further enhancing the intelligent and visual representation of domain knowledge.

The proposed method is designed to construct a knowledge graph of on-site power grid operations based on historical violation records. Since such records require a period of accumulation, the current approach focuses on converting existing textual and structured tabular data into visualized graph data, enabling retrospective analysis and key information querying. Therefore, the knowledge graph reflects historical violations over a defined time span and is not intended for real-time processing. It is more suitable for periodic updates, which can be performed at regular intervals to incorporate new violations and reflect evolving patterns.

In terms of scalability, the current system relies on predefined dictionaries and graph query interfaces. Future work will explore the integration of large language models (LLMs) to improve scalability and user interaction. In particular, natural language interfaces will be introduced to enable key information retrieval using plain language queries, removing the need for users to write Cypher or other graph query languages when interacting with the knowledge graph.

Author Contributions: Methodology, Y.W. and S.Z.; Validation, L.M. and Y.W.; Conceptualization, L.M. and S.Z.; Software, G.B.; Investigation, G.B.; Formal analysis, Y.H.; Visualization, Y.H.; Resources, G.B.; Data curation, X.Z.; Project administration, X.Z.; Writing—original draft preparation, L.M. and Y.W.; Writing—review and editing, S.Z.; Supervision, S.Z.; Funding acquisition, L.M. All authors have read and agreed to the published version of the manuscript.

Funding: This research was funded by Guizhou Power Grid Co. Ltd., grant number GZKJXM20222320.

Data Availability Statement: Data is available upon request from the corresponding authors or works cited in the article.

Conflicts of Interest: Author Lingwen Meng was employed by the Electric Power Scientific Research Institute of Guizhou Power Grid Guizhou. The authors declare that this study received funding from the authors' affiliated institution (Guizhou Power Grid Co. Ltd., grant number GZKJXM20222320.). The funder had involvement in study design, data collection and analysis, decision to publish, and preparation of the manuscript.

References

1. Qiu, W.; Liu, X.; Ban, G.B.; Fu, L.; Zhou, J.C. Recognition of Complex Operator Operation Features Based on Neural Network. *Power Syst. Big Data* **2024**, *27*, 81–90.
2. Chen, J.; Wu, G.; Qin, L.; Peng, Z.; Zhang, X. Power Grid Field Operation Intelligent Safety Supervision System. In Proceedings of the 2024 Boao New Power System International Forum-Power System and New Energy Technology Innovation Forum (NPSIF), Boao, China, 8–10 December 2024; IEEE: Piscataway, NJ, USA, 2024; pp. 617–621.
3. Peng, G.; Lei, Y.; Li, H.; Wu, D.; Wang, J.; Liu, F. CORY-Net: Contrastive res-YOLOv5 network for intelligent safety monitoring on power grid construction sites. *IEEE Access* **2021**, *9*, 160461–160470. [CrossRef]
4. AlHaddad, U.; Basuhail, A.; Khemakhem, M.; Eassa, F.E.; Jambi, K. Towards sustainable energy grids: A machine learn-ing-based ensemble methods approach for outages estimation in extreme weather events. *Sustainability* **2023**, *15*, 12622. [CrossRef]
5. Zhou, F.; Lu, H.; Jiang, C. Violation with concerns of safety: A study on non-compliant behavior and the antecedent and consequent effects in power grid construction. *Saf. Sci.* **2024**, *170*, 106353. [CrossRef]
6. Wang, C.; Wang, Y.; Ding, Z.; Zheng, T.; Hu, J.; Zhang, K. A transformer-based method of multienergy load forecasting in integrated energy system. *IEEE Trans. Smart Grid* **2022**, *13*, 2703–2714. [CrossRef]
7. Tan, M.; Hu, C.; Chen, J.; Wang, L.; Li, Z. Multi-node load forecasting based on multi-task learning with modal feature ex-traction. *Eng. Appl. Artif. Intell.* **2022**, *112*, 104856. [CrossRef]
8. Zhang, X.; Du, M.; Wang, Y.; Zhang, H.; Guo, Y. Research on power grid fault diagnosis based on a quantitative representation of alarm information. *IEEE Trans. Ind. Electron.* **2022**, *70*, 9582–9592. [CrossRef]
9. Cao, Z.; Sun, J.; Du, X.; Zhang, J. Research on power grid comprehensive intelligent warning system based on multi-source data fusion. In Proceedings of the Fourth International Conference on Sensors and Information Technology (ICSI 2024), Xiamen, China, 5–7 January 2024; SPIE: Bellingham, CA, USA, 2024; Volume 13107, pp. 136–141.
10. Sun, Y.; Zhu, J.; Yu, X.; Ye, C.; Fan, G. Research on early warning of power grid construction safety based on PSO-SVM model. *J. Phys. Conf. Ser.* **2020**, *1449*, 012037. [CrossRef]

11. Ke, Y.; Chen, H.; Liu, Z.; Yang, Z. Perception and early warning technology of power substation safety construction operation based on multi-dimensional information fusion. *Int. J. Wirel. Mob. Comput.* **2024**, *26*, 408–415. [CrossRef]
12. Peng, C.; Xia, F.; Naseriparsa, M.; Osborne, F. Knowledge graphs: Opportunities and challenges. *Artif. Intell. Rev.* **2023**, *56*, 13071–13102. [CrossRef]
13. Wu, L.; Lin, H.; Gao, Z.; Zhao, G.; Li, S.Z. A teacher-free graph knowledge distillation framework with dual self-distillation. *IEEE Trans. Knowl. Data Eng.* **2024**, *39*, 4375–4385. [CrossRef]
14. Ma, Z.; Yan, K.; Wang, H. BERT-based question answering using knowledge graph embeddings in nuclear power domain. In Proceedings of the 2023 26th International Conference on Computer Supported Cooperative Work in Design (CSCWD), Rio de Janeiro, Brazil, 24–26 May 2023; IEEE: Piscataway, NJ, USA, 2023; pp. 267–272.
15. Zhou, Y.; Lin, Z.; Tu, L.; Song, Y.; Wu, Z. Big Data and Knowledge Graph Based Fault Diagnosis for Electric Power Systems. *EAI Endorsed Trans. Ind. Netw. Intell. Syst.* **2022**, *9*, 1. [CrossRef]
16. Li, C.; Wang, B. A knowledge graph method towards power system fault diagnosis and classification. *Electronics* **2023**, *12*, 4808. [CrossRef]
17. Tang, Y.; Liu, T.; Liu, G.; Li, J.; Dai, R.; Yuan, C. Enhancement of power equipment management using knowledge graph. In Proceedings of the 2019 IEEE Innovative Smart Grid Technologies-Asia (ISGT Asia), Sichuan, China, 21–24 May 2019; IEEE: Piscataway, NJ, USA, 2019; pp. 905–910.
18. Liu, P.; Tian, B.; Liu, X.; Gu, S.; Yan, L.; Bullock, L.; Ma, C.; Liu, Y.; Zhang, W. Construction of power fault knowledge graph based on deep learning. *Appl. Sci.* **2022**, *12*, 6993. [CrossRef]
19. Hu, J.; Xu, G.; Qi, L.; Qie, X. Knowledge reasoning in power grid infrastructure projects based on deep multi-view graph convolutional network. *Front. Energy Res.* **2024**, *11*, 1339416. [CrossRef]
20. Liu, Y.; Huang, X.; Li, S.; Gao, S.; Ji, K.; Li, H.; Xu, H. A construction method of power grid monitoring knowledge graph. *J. Phys. Conf. Ser.* **2022**, *2166*, 012010. [CrossRef]
21. Chen, X.; Jia, S.; Xiang, Y. A review: Knowledge reasoning over knowledge graph. *Expert Syst. Appl.* **2020**, *141*, 112948. [CrossRef]
22. Guizzardi, G.; Halpin, T.; Guizzardi, G.; Halpin, T. Ontological foundations for conceptual modelling. *Appl. Ontol.* **2008**, *3*, 1–12. [CrossRef]
23. Su, L.; Wang, Z.; Ji, Y.; Guo, X. A survey based on knowledge graph in fault diagnosis, analysis and prediction: Key technologies and challenges. In Proceedings of the 2020 International Conference on Artificial Intelligence and Computer Engineering (ICAICE), Beijing, China, 23–25 October 2020; IEEE: Piscataway, NJ, USA, 2020; pp. 458–462.
24. Ma, R.; Peng, M.; Zhang, Q.; Huang, X. Simplify the usage of lexicon in Chinese NER. *arXiv* **2019**, arXiv:1908.05969.
25. Zhang, Y.; Yang, J. Chinese NER using lattice LSTM. *arXiv* **2018**, arXiv:1805.02023.
26. Mikolov, T.; Chen, K.; Corrado, G.; Dean, J. Efficient estimation of word representations in vector space. *arXiv* **2013**, arXiv:1301.3781.
27. Lafferty, J.; McCallum, A.; Pereira, F. Conditional random fields: Probabilistic models for segmenting and labeling sequence data. In Proceedings of the International Conference on Machine Learning, Williamstown, MA, USA, 28 June–1 July 2001; Volume 1, p. 3.
28. Melluso, N.; Grangel-González, I.; Fantoni, G. Enhancing industry 4.0 standards interoperability via knowledge graphs with natural language processing. *Comput. Ind.* **2022**, *140*, 103676. [CrossRef]
29. Huang, L.; Zhou, X.; Shi, L.; Gong, L. Time Series Feature Selection Method Based on Mutual Information. *Appl. Sci.* **2024**, *14*, 1960. [CrossRef]
30. Huang, Z.; Xu, W.; Yu, K. Bidirectional LSTM-CRF models for sequence tagging. *arXiv* **2015**, arXiv:1508.01991.
31. Gui, T.; Ma, R.; Zhang, Q.; Zhao, L.; Jiang, Y.G.; Huang, X. CNN-Based Chinese NER with Lexicon Rethinking. In Proceedings of the International Joint Conference on Artificial Intelligence, Macao, China, 10–16 August 2019.
32. Souza, F.; Nogueira, R.; Lotufo, R. Portuguese named entity recognition using BERT-CRF. *arXiv* **2019**, arXiv:1909.10649.
33. Liu, Y.; Wei, S.; Huang, H.; Lai, Q.; Li, M.; Guan, L. Naming entity recognition of citrus pests and diseases based on the BERT-BiLSTM-CRF model. *Expert Syst. Appl.* **2023**, *234*, 121103. [CrossRef]

electronics

MDPI

Article

Resilient Event-Triggered $\mathcal{H}_\infty$ Control for a Class of LFC Systems Subject to Deception Attacks

Yunfan Wang [1,2], Zesheng Xi [1,2], Bo Zhang [1,2], Tao Zhang [1,2,*] and Chuan He [1,2]

[1] China Electric Power Research Institute, Nanjing 210003, China; wangyunfan@epri.sgcc.com.cn (Y.W.); xizesheng@epri.sgcc.com.cn (Z.X.); zhangbo6@epri.sgcc.com.cn (B.Z.); hechuan@epri.sgcc.com.cn (C.H.)

[2] State Grid Laboratory of Power Cyber-Security Protection and Monitoring Technology, Nanjing 210003, China

* Correspondence: zhangtao3@epri.sgcc.com.cn

Abstract: This paper explores an event-triggered load frequency control (LFC) strategy for smart grids incorporating electric vehicles (EVs) under the influence of random deception attacks. The aggressive attack signals are launched over the channels between the sensor and controller, compromising the integrity of transmitted data and disrupting LFC commands. For the purpose of addressing bandwidth constraints, an event-triggered transmission scheme (ETTS) is developed to minimize communication frequency. Additionally, to mitigate the impact of random deception attacks in public environment, an integrated networked power grid model is proposed, where the joint impact of ETTS and deceptive interference is captured within a unified analytical structure. Based on this framework, a sufficient condition for stabilization is established, enabling the concurrent design of the $\mathcal{H}_\infty$ controller gain and the triggering condition. Finally, two case studies are offered to illustrate the effectiveness of the employed scheme.

Keywords: LFC; ETTS; random deception attacks; $\mathcal{H}_\infty$ control

1. Introduction

Modern electric power grids are a typical example of networked control architectures, where generation facilities, sensing equipment, and control units are interconnected via large-scale communication infrastructures [1–4]. Within these systems, load frequency control (LFC) is vital for suppressing frequency deviations induced by variations in power demand [5–8]. In recent developments, electrical vehicles (EVs) [9,10] have emerged as promising technologies due to their potential to curb emissions of greenhouse gases and lessen the dependence on fossil-based energy. EVs can both draw power from and supply power to the grid, presenting new opportunities for integration with power systems. This bidirectional interaction enables EVs to provide auxiliary services, such as frequency and voltage regulation, thereby enhancing grid stability and efficiency.

LFC is a critical component of smart grids, responsible for maintaining optimal system frequency and managing power exchanges between areas [11]. In modern smart grids, the LFC system heavily relies on advanced communication technologies, which also introduce various security vulnerabilities. Typically, data acquisition systems forego high-level encryption for authentication due to the stringent real-time demands of LFC data, rendering them highly susceptible to cyberthreats such as deception attacks [12,13] and denial-of-service (DoS) attacks [14,15]. DoS attacks interfere with the communication between the phasor measurement unit (PMU) and the LFC system, while deception attacks undermine data integrity, thereby impairing the control center's ability to make informed decisions. In some extreme cases, such attacks may cause significant frequency deviations, potentially resulting in power system failure [16]. Consequently, it is imperative to explore robust control techniques that can withstand deceptions in power systems, which ensure both system stability and smart grid network security.

The integration of Smart Microgrids (SMGs) into LFC has been extensively studied in the literature [17–20]. For instance, by designing an appropriate feedback controller and leveraging SMGs participation, LFC can effectively regulate frequency deviations and enhance overall power system stability. However, power systems operating within wired/wireless communication networks face unavoidable issues including communication delays, packet dropouts, and cyberattacks. In recent years, these issues have attracted significant attention from researchers [21–23]. For example, in [17], an adaptive multi-objective fuzzy proportional-integral-derivative controller is proposed for the LFC of islanded SMGs. Hu et al. [21] have proposed multi-power systems subject to unknown load disturbances and intermittent denial-of-service (DoS) attacks, and a resilient load frequency controller has been devised. Peng et al. have discussed an adaptive event-triggering $\mathcal{H}_\infty$ LFC scheme, where the event-triggering threshold can be dynamically adjusted to save more resources, while maintaining the expected control performance. In [24], a robust cooperative LFC strategy for multi-area power systems via a hierarchical control approach has been devised. Despite these advancements, the influence of EVs on frequency domains for power systems warrants a deeper exploration.

Notably, most existing investigations adopt a time-triggered scheme, where sensors sample system outputs at fixed intervals and immediately transmit the data to the controller. In this building, the sampling period is chosen conservatively to ensure the system performance even under worst-case conditions, To maintain system effectiveness under adverse conditions, such as severe disturbances, prolonged delays, or undesired noises, the sampling period is deliberately set with a conservative margin. Nevertheless, since such scenarios occur infrequently, this conservative strategy results in redundant sampling, yielding unnecessary bandwidth consumption and increased computational burden on the controller. As a result, developing an efficient yet resource-conscious scheduling algorithm named event-triggered communication scheme has been recognized as reliable control approach [25–29]. Under this scheme, sampled measurements are transmitted only when specific conditions are met, effectively reducing communication overhead in the network. However, combining event-triggered schemes with LFC to construct a unified model poses significant challenges, which encourages us to study deeply.

It should be highlighted that in a networked power system, both control and communication signals are often delivered via open-access networks, which exposes them to significant cyberattack risks [30,31]. For instance, as reported in [32], cyberattacks can lead to severe consequences, including information leakage, destruction of critical infrastructure, and other devastating impacts. Consequently, ensuring the security of power systems is an issue of paramount importance. A wealth of research has been conducted in this area (see [12,33,34]). Among various cyberthreats, deception attacks stand out as one of the most critical, as they compromise data integrity by altering its content. There has been an increasing focus on investigating deception attacks (see [30,34,35]). For example, the optimal linear deception attacks targeting remote state estimation has been explored in [32], and the metric of K-L divergence has been adopted for measuring the statistical distribution of transmission sequence. As a typical deception attacks, a class of zero trace stealthy attacks has been researched for distributed secondary control in DC microgrids (DCmGs) [36], which can degrade the control objective while keep stealthy to implemented detectors. Furthermore, a recursive filter design problem was considered in [35] for a type of time-varying discrete sequential systems under deception attacks. As typical networked systems, power systems for LFC are particularly vulnerable to malicious adversaries [23].

However, despite the critical nature of this issue, cyberattack resilience in the LFC of power systems remains less examined. Addressing this gap serves as the second key motivation of this research.

In this work, an event-triggered $\mathcal{H}_\infty$ controller has been developed within the context of power systems. It is evident that the research into LFC controller design is still in its infancy and the challenges underlying this study stem from the following aspects: (1) How can we formulate a comprehensive model that incorporates the LFC dynamics, random deception attacks, and the event-triggered mechanism? (2) How can we design the suitable communication protocol for reducing computational overhead? (3) How can we deploy a resilient $\mathcal{H}_\infty$ controller to effectively mitigate the adverse impacts of cyberattacks?

Based on the previous analysis, this study investigates $\mathcal{H}_\infty$ load frequency control in power systems subject to limited bandwidth and exposed communication channels. For optimizing communication resources while enhancing control performance, an event-triggered transmission scheme (ETTS) is put forward, which enables more efficient data transmission and reduces unnecessary communication. In order to capture real-world complexities, the concerned system model also accounts for randomly occurring deception attacks; an event-triggered feedback controller is designed to ensure the asymptotically mean-square stability (AMSS) of power systems, with rigorously derived sufficient conditions. Furthermore, the controller gain and event-triggered parameter are jointly optimized by solving linear matrix inequalities, thereby achieving both security and efficiency. The main contributions of this work are outlined below:

- An integrated model of a networked power system is established, which simultaneously accounts for communication delays, stochastic deception attacks, and ETTS.
- An ETTS is proposed to minimize redundant transmission while enhancing control performance. Different from the traditional time-triggered scheme, ETTS effectively utilizes sampled data selectively, reducing the computation burden fairly.
- An event-triggered $\mathcal{H}_\infty$ LFC design method is carefully developed to jointly optimize the output-feedback controller gain along with the communication parameters. Unlike conventional time-triggered controllers, the proposed $\mathcal{H}_\infty$ LFC controller enhances control performance by effectively utilizing available information, even in the presence of deception attacks, achieving superior resilience compared to standard approaches.

Organizations: The remainder of this paper is organized as follows. Section 1 introduces the system description and fundamental concepts, covering the system model and the relevant ETTS used in the following analysis. Section 3 presents the stability criterion for the power systems under investigation. In Section 4, two cases are given to validate the usefulness of the developed method. Lastly, Section 5 summarizes this work.

Notations: The notation used in this paper follows standard conventions unless otherwise specified. The set of natural numbers is denoted by $\mathbb{N}$. The symbols $\mathbb{R}$, $\mathbb{R}^n$, and $\mathbb{R}^{n\times m}$ represent the set of real numbers, the space of n-dimensional real numbers, and the space of $n \times m$ real matrices, respectively. The transpose of a matrix A is denoted by A^T. The notation $[A_{ij}]_{n\times n}$ indicates an $n \times n$ block matrix, where the block at the ith row and jth column is A_{ij}. The identity matrix of appropriate dimensions is represented by I. The function diag$\{\cdot\}$ constructs a diagonal matrix. The notation $||\cdot||$ denotes the Euclidean norm for vectors and the induced 2-norm for matrices. Lastly, $\mathbb{E}\{\cdot\}$ represents the expectation of a given stochastic variable.

2. Problem Setup

This part presents the dynamic modeling of load frequency control (LFC) systems integrated into electric vehicles (EVs), taking into account load disturbances to better reflect the actual behavior of power systems, as discussed in [37]. The proposed system architecture is depicted in Figure 1; based on the information flow and transfer functions illustrated, the entire control loop involves the following modules, including EVs, governors, turbines, and generators. The controller generates output signals that regulate the power frequency deviation of the generator through two control subloops. In the first path, the controller output is distributed to the governor via a regulation gain. The signal then passes through the governor dynamics and the governor droop characteristics to produce a speed control signal, which is further processed by the turbine dynamics to generate the turbine output power. In another subloop, the controller output is allocated to the EVs module, leading to the incremental change in the EVs' output power. Taking external disturbance into account, the total generation power can be calculated from the turbine and the EVs unit. The relevant physical variables are summarized in Table 1. Moreover, two definitions are added.

Definition 1 (State-space method). *The state-space method is a modeling method describing system dynamics with a set of differential or difference equations, which are especially suitable for analyzing multi-input multi-output (MIMO) systems.*

Definition 2 (Asymptotically mean-square stability (AMSS)). *Mathematically, a stochastic system is said to be AMSS if*

$$\lim_{k\to\infty} \mathbb{E}\left\{||x_k||^2\right\} = 0,$$

where x_k denotes the system state at instant k.

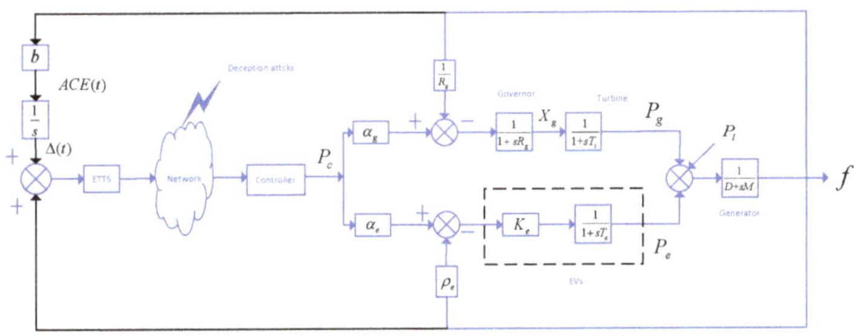

Figure 1. Block of the LFC system model.

Table 1. Notations.

Parameters	Meaning
f	frequency deviation
X_g	governor valve position
P_g	turbine output power
P_e	incremental changes in EVs
P_l	load disturbance
P_c	control input
α_g	thermal turbine
α_e	participation factor
D	load damping coefficient
M	inertia constant

Table 1. *Cont.*

Parameters	Meaning
R_g	governor
ρ_e	droop characteristic
T_g	speed governor
T_t	turbine time constant
K_e	gain constant
T_e	time constant
b	frequency bias constant

On the basis of the flow chart included in Figure 1, one has

$$\begin{cases} f(s) = \dfrac{1}{D+sM}(P_g(s) + P_e(s) - P_l(s)), \\ X_g(s) = \dfrac{1}{1+sT_g}(\alpha_g P_c(s) - \dfrac{1}{R_g} f(s)), \\ P_g(s) = \dfrac{1}{1+sT_t} X_g(s), \\ P_e(s) = \dfrac{K_e}{1+sT_e}(\alpha_e P_c(s) - \rho_e f(s)), \\ \Delta(s) = \dfrac{1}{s} ACE(s) = \dfrac{1}{s} b f(s). \end{cases} \tag{1}$$

By applying the inverse Laplace Transform for (1), one has

$$\begin{cases} \dot{f}(t) = \dfrac{1}{M}(P_g(t) + P_e(t) - P_l(t) - Df(t)), \\ \dot{X}_g(t) = \dfrac{1}{T_g}(\alpha_g P_c(t) - \dfrac{1}{R_g} f(t) - X_g(t)), \\ \dot{P}_g(t) = \dfrac{1}{T_t}(X_g(t) - P_g(t)), \\ \dot{P}_e(t) = \dfrac{K_e}{T_e}(\alpha_e P_c(t) - \rho_e f(t)) - \dfrac{1}{T_e} P_e(t), \\ \dot{\Delta}(t) = b f(t). \end{cases} \tag{2}$$

Define

$$\begin{aligned} x(t) &= [f(t), \quad X_g(t), \quad P_g(t), \quad P_e(t), \quad \Delta(t)]^T, \\ y(t) &= [f(t), \quad \Delta(t)]^T, \\ u(t) &= P_c(t), \\ \varpi(t) &= P_l(t). \end{aligned}$$

According to the state-space method in Definition 1, the LFC system has the following expression.

$$\begin{cases} \dot{x}(t) = Ax(t) + Bu(t) + D\varpi(t), \\ y(t) = Cx(t), \end{cases} \tag{3}$$

where A, B, C, and D indicate system matrices, $x(t)$, $u(t)$, and $\varpi(t)$ represent the state vector, the control input, and external disturbance, respectively, and

$$A=\begin{bmatrix} -\frac{D}{M} & 0 & \frac{1}{M} & \frac{1}{M} & 0 \\ -\frac{1}{R_g T_g} & -\frac{1}{T_g} & 0 & 0 & 0 \\ 0 & \frac{1}{T_t} & -\frac{1}{T_t} & 0 & 0 \\ -\frac{\rho_e K_e}{T_e} & 0 & 0 & -\frac{1}{T_e} & 0 \\ b & 0 & 0 & 0 & 0 \end{bmatrix},$$
$$B=\begin{bmatrix} 0 & \frac{\alpha_g}{T_g} & 0 & \frac{\alpha_e K_e}{T_e} & 0 \end{bmatrix}^T,$$
$$C=\begin{bmatrix} 1 & 0 & 0 & 0 & 0 \\ 0 & 0 & 0 & 0 & 1 \end{bmatrix},$$
$$D=\begin{bmatrix} -\frac{1}{M} & 0 & 0 & 0 & 0 \end{bmatrix}^T.$$

2.1. ETTS

This subsection introduces an event-based communication protocol to optimize the utilization of communication bandwidth while maintaining optimal system performance. Defining h as the sampling period of the concerned LFC systems. The most recent triggering instant and the next triggering instant are indicated by $t_k h$ and $t_{k+1}h$, respectively, and the next triggering instant can be determined by:

$$\begin{aligned} &t_{k+1}h \triangleq t_k h + \min_{i\in\mathbb{N}}\left\{ih | e^T(t)\Psi e(t) > \sigma x^T(t_k h)\Psi x(t_k h)\right\}, \\ &e(t) \triangleq x(t_k h + ih) - x(t_k h), \end{aligned} \tag{4}$$

where Ψ denotes the triggering threshold matrix and $0 < \sigma \leq 1$ represents the threshold value.

Remark 1. *In practical systems, transmitted signals are susceptible to various anomalies, including malicious attacks, network-induced delays, data packet losses, and so forth. Though irregularities may occur with low probability from a statistical standpoint, they can still pose significant threats to the system performance. It is worth noting that the employed ETTS plays a crucial role in mitigating the impact of abnormal signals and relieving computation burden. As expressed in (3), the adopted ETTS reduces to the general time-triggered manner when $\sigma = 0$.*

It is well-known that time delay is a common yet unavoidable network-induced phenomenon in LFC systems, which must be carefully considered in network communication. In this article, as shown in Figure 2, the interval between $t_1 h$ and $t_2 h$ can be divided into five subintervals according to the designed principle. Consequently, by means of the virtual partition method proposed in [25], for any given time period between two consecutive triggering instants $t_k h$ and $t_{k+1}h$, after considering the respective time delays at the triggering instant from the sensor to the controller, it can be expressed by the following subperiods:

$$\begin{aligned} &[t_k h + \mu_{t_k}, t_{k+1}h + \mu_{t_{k+1}}) = \bigcup_{i=0}^{f_M} \mathcal{I}_i, \\ &\begin{cases} \mathcal{I}_0 = [t_k h + \mu_{t_k}, (t_k+1)h + \bar{\mu}), \\ \mathcal{I}_i = [(t_k+i)h + \bar{\mu}, (t_k+i+1)h + \bar{\mu}), i = 1, \ldots, f_M - 1, \\ \mathcal{I}_{f_M} = [(t_k+f_M)h + \bar{\mu}, t_{k+1}h + \mu_{t_{k+1}}), \end{cases} \end{aligned} \tag{5}$$

where $\bar{\mu}$ indicates the upper bound of μ_{t_k}.

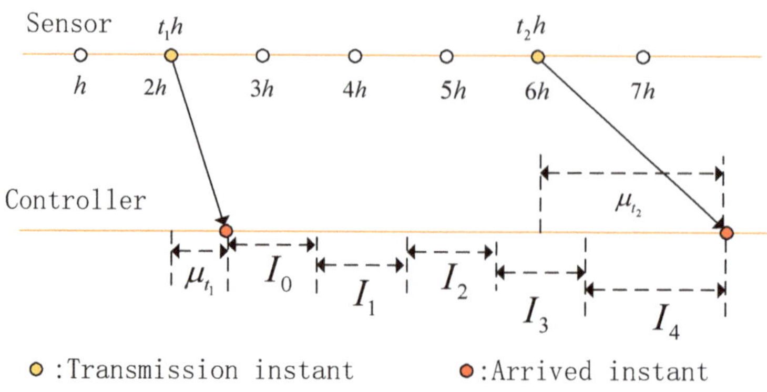

Figure 2. The sketch of event-triggered transmission scheme.

We now consider the following two cases:
Case 1: If $t_{k+1}h + \mu_{t_{k+1}} \leq t_k h + h + \bar{\mu}$, define a function $\mu(t)$ as

$$\mu(t) = t - t_k h, \quad t \in [t_k h + \mu_{t_k}, t_{k+1}h + \mu_{t_{k+1}}). \tag{6}$$

Obviously, $\mu_{t_k} \leq \mu(t) \leq (t_{k+1} - t_k)h + \mu_{t_{k+1}} \leq h + \bar{\mu}$.
Case 2: If $t_k h + h + \bar{\mu} < t_{k+1}h + \mu_{t_{k+1}}$, one has

$$\mu(t) = \begin{cases} t - t_k h, & t \in \mathcal{I}_0, \\ t - t_k h - ih, & t \in \mathcal{I}_i, i = 1, \ldots, f_M - 1, \\ t - t_k h - f_M h, & t \in \mathcal{I}_{f_M}. \end{cases} \tag{7}$$

Therefore, we have

$$\begin{cases} \mu_{t_k} \leq \mu(t) \leq h + \bar{\mu}, & t \in \mathcal{I}_0, \\ \mu_{t_k} \leq \bar{\mu} \leq \mu(t) \leq h + \bar{\mu}, & t \in \mathcal{I}_i, i = 1, \ldots, f_M - 1, \\ \mu_{t_k} \leq \bar{\mu} \leq \mu(t) \leq h + \bar{\mu}, & t \in \mathcal{I}_{f_M}, \end{cases} \tag{8}$$

and $0 \leq \mu_{t_k} \leq \mu(t) \leq h + \bar{\mu} \triangleq \mu_M$. From (4), one has

$$e(t) = \begin{cases} 0, & t \in \mathcal{I}_0, \\ x(t_k + ih) - x(t_k h), & t \in \mathcal{I}_i, i = 1, \ldots, f_M - 1, \\ x(t_k + f_M h) - x(t_k h), & t \in \mathcal{I}_{f_M}. \end{cases} \tag{9}$$

Therefore

$$e(t) = x(t - \mu(t)) - x(t_k h), \quad t \in \mathcal{I}_i. \tag{10}$$

2.2. Random Deception Attacks

In this article, it is assumed that the measurement signals are subject to random deception attacks governed by malicious adversaries. On the basis of the above analysis, an indicator variable $\lambda(t)$ is introduced to formulate this scene, and the actual measurement signal is as follows:

$$\bar{y}(t) = (1 - \lambda(t))y(t) + \lambda(t)\psi(y(t)), \tag{11}$$

where $\psi(y(t))$ denotes the injected data during the process of deception attack, and satisfies the following:

$$||\psi(y(t))||_2 \leq ||Gy(t)||_2, \tag{12}$$

with G being a known matrix of appropriate dimensions. Specifically, the random variable $\lambda(t)$ follows a Bernoulli distribution with the following expression:

$$\begin{aligned}\Pr\{\lambda(t)=1\}&=\bar{\lambda},\\ \Pr\{\lambda(t)=0\}&=1-\bar{\lambda},\end{aligned} \tag{13}$$

where $\bar{\lambda}\in[0,1]$.

Remark 2. *According to (7), (8) and (9), it can be observed that the matrix G represents the upper bound of the nonlinearity of $\psi(y(t))$. On the other hand, $\lambda(t)$ regulates the randomness of the deception attacks. Particularly, when $\lambda(t)=1$, this indicates that the system is under attack. Conversely, when $\lambda(t)=0$, the system runs normally. From the stand of defender, the randomness of the attacks stems from the fact that their success heavily depends on the fluctuating detection capabilities of protective equipment or software. Moreover, the modified measurement signal $\psi(y(t))$ is supposed to be bounded, as deception attacks with large amplitudes are more likely to be detected by attackers, making subtle attacks preferable.*

To mitigate the adverse impacts caused by randomly occurring deception attacks, the output feedback controller can be designed as follows:

$$\begin{aligned}u(t)=&-Ky(t_kh)\\ =&-(1-\lambda(t))KC(x(t-\mu(t))-e(t))-\lambda(t)K\psi(y(t_kh)),\end{aligned} \tag{14}$$

thereby, one has

$$\dot{x}(t)=Ax(t)-(1-\lambda(t))BKC(x(t-\mu(t))-e(t))-\lambda(t)BK\psi(y(t_kh))+D\varpi(t). \tag{15}$$

This paper aims to develop the event-based controller (10) to ensure that the system (3), running under the ETTS (4) and subject to randomly occurring deception attacks (7), achieves AMSS while meeting the $\mathcal{H}_\infty$ performance index. Correspondingly, the following requirements should be satisfied:

- The LFC system (3), in the absence of external disturbances $\varpi(t)$, should be AMSS;
- Under zero initial conditions, the system satisfies the performance requirement $\mathbb{E}\{||y(t)||^2\}\leq\mathbb{E}\{\gamma^2||\varpi(t)||^2\}$ for any nonnegative noises $\varpi(t)\in L_2[0,\infty)$, where $\gamma>0$ represents a prescribed performance bound.

3. Main Results

For paving the way of subsequent analysis, the following lemma is employed in the proof of the main results.

Lemma 1 ([38]). *Give the symmetric matrix S with the following expression:*

$$S=\begin{bmatrix}S_{11} & S_{12}\\ S_{12}^T & S_{22}\end{bmatrix},$$

then the following statements are equivalent:

- $S<0$;
- $S_{11}<0, S_{22}-S_{12}^TS_{11}^{-1}S_{12}<0$;
- $S_{22}<0, S_{11}-S_{12}S_{22}^{-1}S_{12}^T<0$.

This section formulates two theorems to tackle key challenges concerning the AMSS of the closed-loop LFC system, its disturbance suppression capability, and the gain computation for the event-based $\mathcal{H}_\infty$ controller.

Theorem 1. *Given fixed values of σ, κ, μ_M, and γ and a specified feedback gain K, the LFC system (3) is AMSS with an $\mathcal{H}_\infty$ performance bound γ, provided that there exist positive definite matrices $P > 0$, $Q > 0$, $\Psi > 0$, and $R > 0$, Z meeting*

$$\begin{bmatrix} \Gamma_{11} & * \\ \Gamma_{21} & \Gamma_{22} \end{bmatrix} < 0, \tag{16}$$

$$\begin{bmatrix} R & Z^T \\ Z & R \end{bmatrix} > 0, \tag{17}$$

where $\Gamma_{11} = [\Theta]_{2\times 2}$ and $\kappa = \sqrt{\lambda(1-\lambda)}$, and

$$\begin{aligned}
&\Theta_{11}^{11} = A^T P + PA + Q - R, \\
&\Theta_{11}^{21} = (1-\bar{\lambda})C^T K^T B^T P + R - Z, \\
&\Theta_{11}^{22} = \sigma\Psi - 2R + Z + Z^T, \\
&\Theta_{21}^{11} = Z, \Theta_{21}^{12} = R - Z, \\
&\Theta_{21}^{21} = -(1-\bar{\lambda})C^T K^T B^T P, \\
&\Theta_{21}^{22} = -\sigma\Psi, \Theta_{21}^{31} = \bar{\lambda} C^T K^T B^T P, \Theta_{21}^{41} = D^T P, \\
&\Theta_{22} = diag\left\{-Q - R, \sigma\Psi - \Psi, -\bar{\lambda}P, -\gamma^2 I\right\}, \\
&\Gamma_{21} = col\{\mu_M R\Lambda_1, \mu_M R\Lambda_2, \Upsilon_1, \Upsilon_2\}, \\
&\Gamma_{22} = diag\{-R, -R, -P, -I\}, \\
&\Lambda_1 = [A, -(1-\bar{\lambda})BKC, 0, (1-\bar{\lambda})BKC, -\bar{\lambda}BKC, D], \\
&\Lambda_2 = [0, \kappa BKC, 0, -\kappa BKC, -\kappa BKC, 0], \\
&\Upsilon_1 = [0, \sqrt{\bar{\lambda}}PGC, 0, -\sqrt{\bar{\lambda}}PGC, 0, 0], \\
&\Upsilon_2 = [C, 0, 0, 0, 0, 0].
\end{aligned}$$

Proof. Construct the Lyapunov functional as follows:

$$V(t) = x^T(t)Px(t) + \int_{t-\mu_M}^{t} x^T(\zeta)Qx(\zeta)d\zeta + \mu_M \int_{t-\mu_M}^{t}\int_{\zeta}^{t} \dot{x}^T(s)R\dot{x}(s)dsd\zeta. \tag{18}$$

For $t \in \mathcal{I}_i$, applying the infinitesimal operator [39] on $V(t)$, one has

$$\begin{aligned}
\mathbb{E}\{\mathcal{L}(V(t))\} =& x^T(t)Qx(t) + 2\dot{x}^T(t)Px(t) - x^T(t-\mu_M)Qx(t-\mu_M) \\
&+ \mu_M^2 \dot{x}^T(t)R\dot{x}(t) - \mu_M \int_{t-\mu_M}^{t} \dot{x}^T(\zeta)R\dot{x}(\zeta)d\zeta - e^T(t)\Psi e(t) \\
&+ e^T(t)\Psi e(t) - y^T(t)y(t) + \gamma^2\varpi^T(t)\varpi(t) + y^T(t)y(t) \\
&- \bar{\lambda}\psi^T(y(t_k h))P\psi(y(t_k h)) + \bar{\lambda}\psi^T(y(t_k h))P\psi(y(t_k h)) \\
&- \gamma^2\varpi^T(t)\varpi(t).
\end{aligned} \tag{19}$$

Furthermore, from (4), one has

$$e^T(t)\Psi e(t) \le \sigma(x^T(t-\mu(t)) - e^T(t))\Psi(x(t-\mu(t)) - e(t)). \tag{20}$$

In addition, it can be seen from (8) that there exists a symmetric matrix P satisfying

$$\psi^T(y(t_kh))P\psi(y(t_kh)) \leq (x^T(t-\mu(t)) - e^T(t))C^TG^TPGC(x(t-\mu(t)) - e(t)). \tag{21}$$

On the other hand, the reciprocally convex method in [40] is used to tackle the cross item in (19). Hence, we have

$$-\mu_M \int_{t-\mu_M}^{t} \dot{x}^T(\zeta)R\dot{x}(\zeta)d\zeta \leq \begin{bmatrix} \varsigma_1^T & \varsigma_2^T \end{bmatrix} \begin{bmatrix} R & Z^T \\ Z & R \end{bmatrix} \begin{bmatrix} \varsigma_1 \\ \varsigma_2 \end{bmatrix}, \tag{22}$$

where $\varsigma_1 = x(t) - x(t-\mu(t))$, $\varsigma_2 = x(t-\mu(t)) - x(t-\mu_M)$.

Therefore, one can attain from (18)–(22) that

$$\mathbb{E}\{\mathcal{L}(V(t))\} \leq \vartheta^T(t)(\Gamma_{11} - \Gamma_{21}^T\Gamma_{22}^{-1}\Gamma_{21})\vartheta(t) - y^T(t)y(t) + \gamma^2\varpi^T(t)\varpi(t), \tag{23}$$

where $\vartheta(t) = [x^T(t), x^T(t-\mu(t)), x^T(t-\mu_M), e^T(t), \psi^T(x(t)), \omega^T(t)]^T$.

By utilizing Schur complement Lemma 1 from (16), one has

$$\Gamma_{11} - \Gamma_{21}^T\Gamma_{22}^{-1}\Gamma_{21} \leq 0.$$

In addition, one has

$$\mathbb{E}\{\mathcal{L}(V(t))\} \leq -y^T(t)y(t) + \gamma^2\varpi^T(t)\varpi(t). \tag{24}$$

Integrating both sides of (24) from 0 to ∞, and under zero initial conditions, it is easy to derive that

$$\int_0^\infty y^T(\zeta)y(\zeta)d\zeta \leq \int_0^\infty \gamma^2\varpi^\zeta\varpi(\zeta)d\zeta, \tag{25}$$

i.e., $\mathbb{E}\{||y(t)||^2\} \leq \mathbb{E}\{\gamma^2||\varpi(t)||^2\}$. Hence, the disturbance suppression index is ensured. When $\varpi(t) = 0$, it can be summarized that the system (3) is AMSS. This ends the proof. □

The addressed event-triggered $\mathcal{H}_\infty$ controller has successfully considered both AMSS and $\mathcal{H}_\infty$ performance. Meanwhile, the matrix constraints established in Theorem 1 provide a set of sufficient conditions for the relevant performance indices. However, determining the event-triggered controller gain remains a significant challenge, which serves as the drive for the listed theorem.

Theorem 2. *Given preset parameters σ, κ, μ_M, γ, ϱ, and ε, the LFC system (3) is AMSS with an $\mathcal{H}_\infty$ norm threshold γ, when there exist matrices $H > 0$, $\check{Q} > 0$, $\check{\Psi} > 0$, $\check{R} > 0$, $\check{Z}$, M, and Y meeting*

$$\begin{bmatrix} \Gamma_{11} & * \\ \Gamma_{21} & \Gamma_{22} \end{bmatrix} < 0, \tag{26}$$

$$\begin{bmatrix} \check{R} & \check{Z}^T \\ \check{Z} & \check{R} \end{bmatrix} > 0, \tag{27}$$

$$\begin{bmatrix} -\varepsilon I & * \\ MC - CH & -I \end{bmatrix} < 0, \tag{28}$$

where $\check{\Gamma}_{11} = [\check{\Theta}]_{2\times 2}$, $\kappa = \sqrt{\bar{\lambda}(1-\bar{\lambda})}$, *and*

$$\begin{aligned}
&\check{\Theta}_{11}^{11} = AH + HA^T + \check{Q} - \check{R},\\
&\check{\Theta}_{11}^{21} = (1-\bar{\lambda})C^TY^TB^T + \check{R} - \check{Z},\\
&\check{\Theta}_{11}^{22} = \sigma\check{\Psi} - 2\check{R} + \check{Z} + \check{Z}^T,\\
&\check{\Theta}_{21}^{11} = \check{Z}, \check{\Theta}_{21}^{12} = \check{R} - \check{Z},\\
&\check{\Theta}_{21}^{21} = -(1-\bar{\lambda})C^TY^TB^T,\\
&\check{\Theta}_{21}^{22} = -\sigma\check{\Psi}, \check{\Theta}_{21}^{31} = \bar{\lambda}C^TY^TB^T, \check{\Theta}_{21}^{41} = D^T,\\
&\check{\Theta}_{22} = diag\left\{-\check{Q} - \check{R}, \sigma\check{\Psi} - \check{\Psi}, -\bar{\lambda}H, -\gamma^2 I\right\},\\
&\check{\Gamma}_{21} = col\{\mu_M\check{\Lambda}_1, \mu_M\check{\Lambda}_2, \check{Y}_1, \check{Y}_2\},\\
&\check{\Gamma}_{22} = diag\left\{\varrho^2\check{R} - 2\varrho H, \varrho^2\check{R} - 2\varrho H, -H, -I\right\},\\
&\check{\Lambda}_1 = [AH, -(1-\bar{\lambda})BYC, 0, (1-\bar{\lambda})BYC, -\bar{\lambda}BYC, D],\\
&\check{\Lambda}_2 = [0, \kappa BYC, 0, -\kappa BYC, -\kappa BYC, 0],\\
&\check{Y}_1 = [0, \sqrt{\bar{\lambda}}GCH, 0, -\sqrt{\bar{\lambda}}GCH, 0, 0],\\
&\check{Y}_2 = [CH, 0, 0, 0, 0, 0].
\end{aligned}$$

Then, the event-triggered $\mathcal{H}_\infty$ controller gain can be derived as $K = YM^{-1}$.

Proof. For brevity, define

$$\begin{aligned}
&H = P^{-1}, \check{Q} = HQH, \check{R} = HRH,\\
&\check{Z} = HZH, \check{\Psi} = H\Psi H,\\
&\Omega_1 \triangleq \mathrm{diag}\{H, H, H, H, H, I\},\\
&\Omega_2 \triangleq \mathrm{diag}\left\{R^{-1}, R^{-1}, H, I\right\}.
\end{aligned}$$

With the aid of the following inequality:

$$-H\check{R}^{-1}H \le \varrho^2\check{R}^{-1} - 2\varrho H,$$

and pre- and postmultiplying both sides of (16) and (17) by $\mathrm{diag}\{\Omega_1, \Omega_2\}$ and $\mathrm{diag}\{H, H\}$, respectively. Naturally, (26) and (27) can be obtained. Then, KCH and CH are substituted with YC and MC, respectively. Following a similar control design technique as in [41], we establish that

$$(MC - CH)^T(MC - CH) = 0.$$

According to Lemma 1, the above equation can be reformulated into an optimization problem with the format of (28). This completes the proof. □

Remark 3. *A key assumption in simulation-based methods, such as those proposed in [21,22], is that the controller gains must be known a priori. If these gains are not prefixed, the aforementioned methods become inapplicable. Nevertheless, as illustrated in this study, the controller gains can be designed using Theorem 2, which highlights a key advantage of the proposed scheme.*

According to Theorems 1 and 2, the state stability, $\mathcal{H}_\infty$ performance, and synthesis of the expected event-triggered controller are designed through the application of matrix techniques, stochastic methods, Lyapunov stability theory, and other advanced approaches. Since this article considers complex factors such as the event-based communication scheme and stochastic deception attacks, the derived sufficient criteria inherently incorporate these elements. Moreover, the matrix constraints included in two theorems have been gained using Matlab R2018b simulation technology.

To illustrate the implementation of Theorem 2 and derive the gain for the designed event-triggered $\mathcal{H}_\infty$ controller, the following Algorithm 1 is given in this section.

Algorithm 1 Event-based $\mathcal{H}_\infty$ controller design algorithm.

Step 1.	Initialize values of $x(0)$, γ, δ, κ, μ_M, G, $\psi(y(t))$, $\varpi(t)$;
Step 2.	Formulate kinetic model (3) of the LFC system;
Step 3.	Design the employed event-based $\mathcal{H}_\infty$ controller (10) that satisfies AMSS and the $\mathcal{H}_\infty$ performance index;
Step 4.	Solve the LMIs in Theorem 2 and derive the controller gain K.

4. Case Studies

This section focuses on evaluating the effectiveness of the proposed control strategy by analyzing a power system with LFC subject to stochastic deception attacks. Certain electrical parameters are expressed in Table 2.

Table 2. System parameters of the LFC scheme.

D	M	R_g	T_g	T_t	ρ_e	K_e	T_e	b	α_g	α_e
0.0083	0.1667	2.4	0.08	0.3	0.42	1	1	0.425	0.8	0.2

Set $x(0) = [0.2; 0.5; 0.5; 0.2; 0.3]$, with other parameters given as $\gamma = 10$, $\delta = 0.5$, $\bar{\lambda} = 0.5$, $\mu_M = 0.1s$, $G = \text{diag}\{0.2, 0.1\}$ and $\psi(y(t)) = [-\tanh(0.2y_1(t)), \tanh(0.1y_2(t))]$. $\varpi(t)$ follows:

$$\varpi(t) = \begin{cases} 0.01, & 0 < t \leq 40, \\ 0, & t > 40. \end{cases}$$

An event-triggered $\mathcal{H}_\infty$ controller is employed to regulate the nominal frequency of the power system (e.g., near-zero frequency difference). Define the controller without considering network attacks as Controller 1, and the controller with considering network attacks as Controller 2. To verify the effectiveness of the proposed control method against deception attacks, two cases are examined.

- Case 1: This case demonstrates that, in the absence of deception attacks, both Controller 1 and Controller 2 successfully stabilize the power system;
- Case 2: In this case, random deception attacks are introduced. Simulation results show that, compared to Controller 1, Controller 2 provides a significantly smoother and improved system response.

Figure 3 illustrates that the system (3) achieves the AMSS by Controller 1 and 2 in the absence of deception attacks; Figure 4 reflects that when deception attacks occur, Controller 2 still preserves good system performance more effectively while Controller 1 fails. The negative impacts brought from deception attacks are counteracted to a great extent. Therefore, it is apparent to see that the designed $\mathcal{H}_\infty$ controller (Controller 2) in this study can realize stronger control performance under cyberattacks.

On the other side, Figures 5 and 6 show the triggering instants and the triggering intervals in this article, respectively. Compared to the conventional time-triggered scheme, the proposed ETTS demonstrates significantly greater ability to optimize network bandwidth utilization. In Figure 7, the red asterisk and the green dot represent the attack instant and trigger sequences, respectively, where the developed event-triggered mechanism regulates the number of triggered data packets according to the frequency of deception attacks.

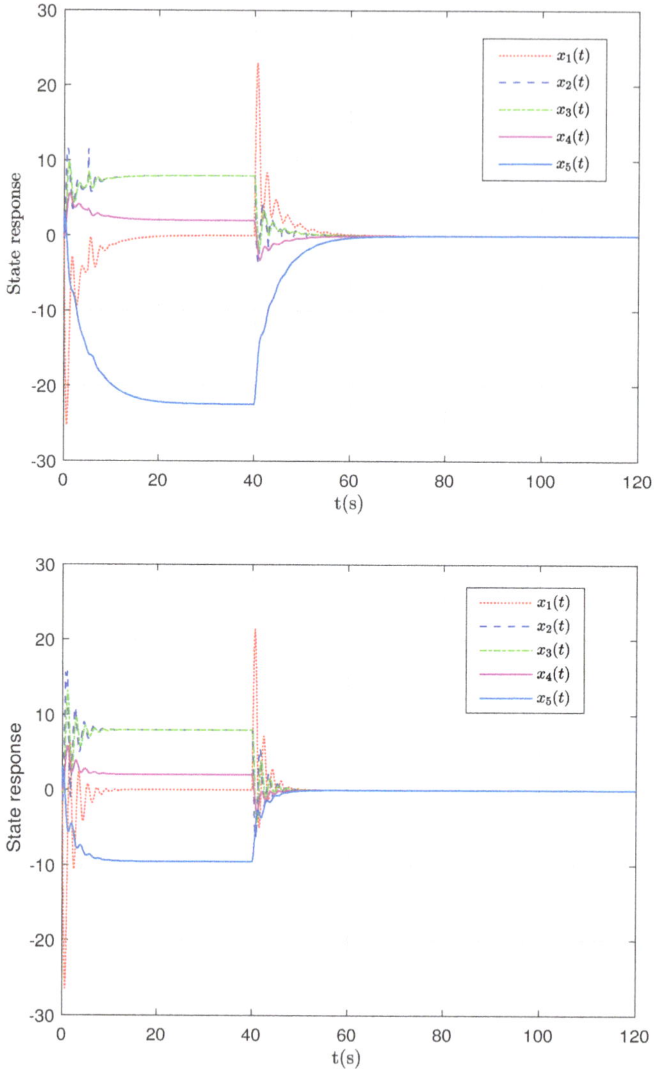

Figure 3. Simulation results in Case 1. Top: State trajectories of $x(t)$ with Controller 2; Bottom: State trajectories of $x(t)$ with Controller 1.

Specially, as depicted in Figures 5 and 6, the number of triggering events decreases in the presence of attacks. The reason behind this is that the proposed triggered fashion strategically reduces data packet transmissions when cyberattacks or other anomalies happen, hence minimizing the risk of packet corruption. In other words, under such communication protocols, the system demonstrates strong resilience to deception attacks and effectively mitigates false triggers caused by cyberattacks.

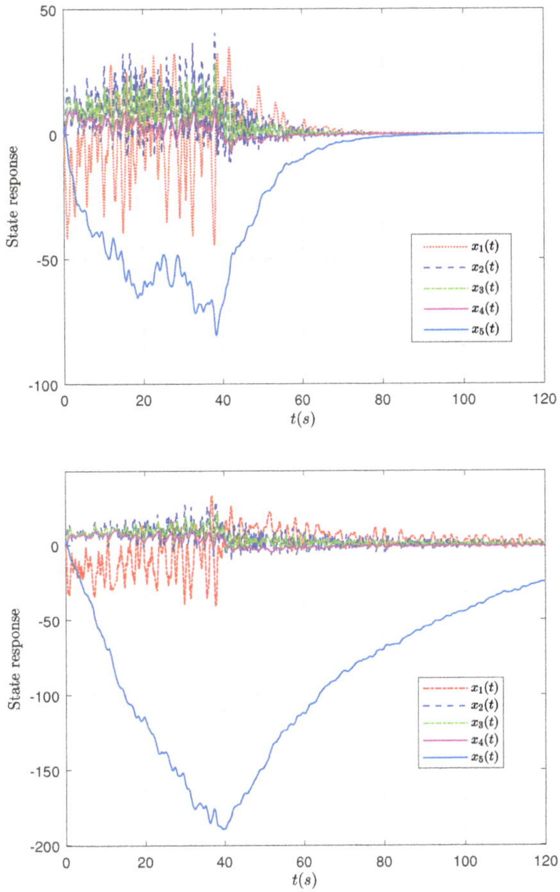

Figure 4. Simulation results in Case 2. Top: State trajectories of $x(t)$ with Controller 2; Bottom: State trajectories of $x(t)$ with Controller 1.

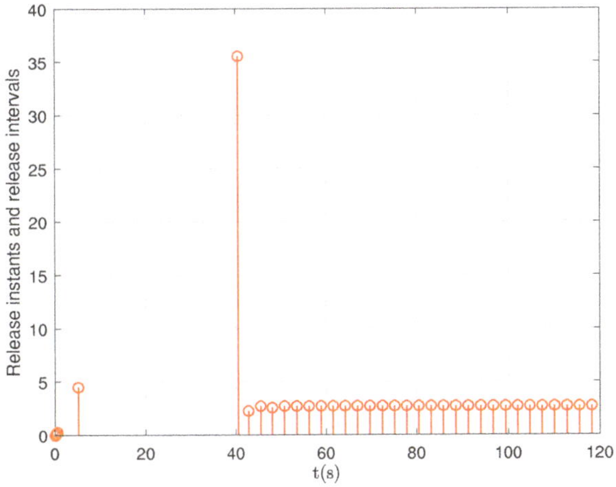

Figure 5. Release intervals without deception attacks.

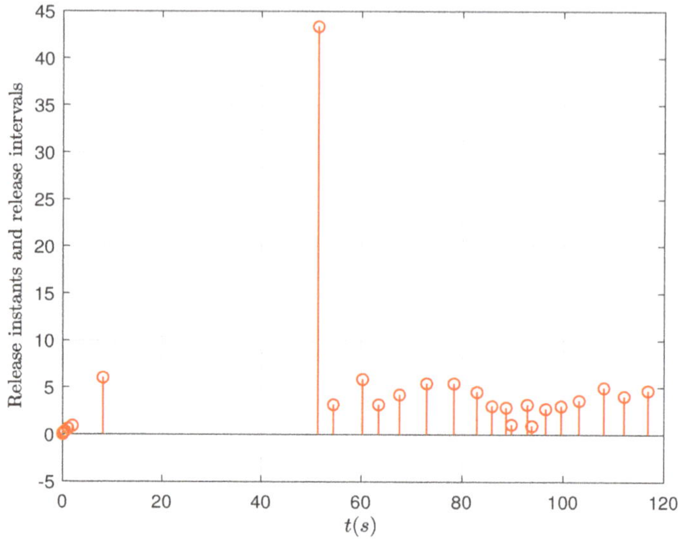

Figure 6. Release intervals with deception attacks.

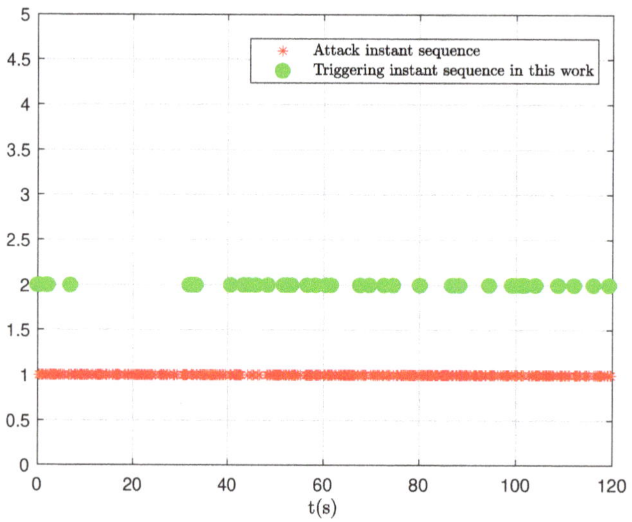

Figure 7. The deception attack and triggering instant sequences.

5. Conclusions

This study presents an event-triggered $\mathcal{H}_\infty$ load frequency control (LFC) strategy for power systems, particularly incorporating electric vehicles (EVs). By employing an event-based communication scheme, the data transmission and the network burden can be reduced and alleviated, while maintaining satisfactory control performance in contrast to conventional time-triggered approaches. Specially, it compensates for the detrimental effects of random deception attacks through the resilient controller. Sufficient conditions for the AMSS of the closed-loop system has been obtained by utilizing the Lyapunov theory in terms of LMIs. The simulation results illustrate the feasibility and availability of the proposed method for power systems under limited bandwidth and cyberthreats. Future work involves exploring distributed and full decentralized event-triggered LFC schemes, as well as data-driven and model-free control methods for resilient controller design in large-scale power networks [42].

Author Contributions: Methodology, Y.W. and B.Z.; Software, Z.X.; Formal analysis, C.H.; Investigation, B.Z.; Resources, Y.W.; Data curation, Z.X.; Writing—original draft, C.H.; Writing—review & editing, Y.W.; Supervision, T.Z.; Project administration, T.Z. All authors have read and agreed to the published version of the manuscript.

Funding: This research was funded by the National Key Research and Development Program of China, grant number 2022YFB3104300.

Data Availability Statement: The data presented in this study are available on request from the corresponding author.

Conflicts of Interest: The authors declare no conflicts of interest.

References

1. Yilmaz, M.; Krein, P.T. Review of the impact of vehicle-to-grid technologies on distribution systems and utility interfaces. *IEEE Trans. Power Electron.* **2013**, *28*, 5673–5689. [CrossRef]
2. Prabhakar, K.; Jain S.K.; Padhy P.K. Inertia estimation in modern power system: A comprehensive review. *Electr. Power Syst. Res.* **2022**, *211*, 10822. [CrossRef]
3. Liu, D.; Zhang, X.; Tse, C.K. Effects of high level of penetration of renewable energy sources on cascading failure of modern power systems. *IEEE J. Emerg. Sel. Top. Circuits Syst.* **2022**, *12*, 98–106. [CrossRef]
4. Liu, M.; Teng, F.; Zhang, Z.; Ge, P.; Sun, M.; Deng, R. Enhancing cyber-resiliency of DER-based smart grid: A survey. *IEEE Trans. Smart Grid* **2024**, *15*, 4998–5030. [CrossRef]
5. Shangguan, X.C.; He, Y.; Zhang, C.K.; Jin, L.; Yao, W.; Jiang, L.; Wu, M. Control performance standards-oriented event-triggered load frequency control for power systems under limited communication bandwidth. *IEEE Trans. Control Syst. Technol.* **2022**, *30*, 860–868. [CrossRef]
6. Zhang, Z.; Deng, R.; Yau D.K.Y. Vulnerability of the load frequency control against the network parameter attack. *IEEE Trans. Smart Grid* **2024**, *15*, 921–933. [CrossRef]
7. Bu, X.; Yu, W.; Cui, L.; Hou, Z.; Chen, Z. Event-triggered data-driven load frequency control for multiarea power systems. *IEEE Trans. Ind. Inf.* **2022**, *18*, 5982–5991. [CrossRef]
8. Zhong, Q.; Yang, J.; Shi, K.; Zhong, S.; Li, Z.; Sotelo, M.A. Event-triggered $\mathcal{H}_\infty$ load frequency control for multi-area nonlinear power systems based on non-fragile proportional integral control strategy. *IEEE Trans. Intell. Transp. Syst.* **2022**, *23*, 12191–12201. [CrossRef]
9. Wang, H.; Chen, S.; Li, M.; Zhu, C.; Wang, Z. Demand-driven charging strategy-based distributed routing optimization under traffic restrictions in internet of electric vehicles. *IEEE Internet Things J.* **2024**, *11*, 35917–35927. [CrossRef]
10. Islam, S.; Iqbal, A.; Marzband, M.; Khan, I.; Al-Wahedi, A.M. State-of-the-art vehicle-to-everything mode of operation of electric vehicles and its future perspectives. *Renew. Sustain. Energy Rev.* **2022**, *166*, 112574. [CrossRef]
11. Liu, S.; Luo, W.; Wu, L. Co-design of distributed model-based control and event-triggering scheme for load frequency regulation in smart grids. *IEEE Trans. Syst. Man Cybern. B Cybern.* **2018**, *50*, 3311–3319. [CrossRef]
12. Yang, S.; Lao, K.-W.; Hui, H.; Chen, Y. Secure distributed control for demand response in power systems against deception cyber-attacks with arbitrary patterns. *IEEE Trans. Power Syst.* **2024**, *39*, 7277–7290. [CrossRef]
13. Liu, X.; Yang, G.-H. Optimal intermittent deception attacks with energy constraints for cyber-physical systems. *IEEE Trans. Man Cybern. B Cybern.* **2024**, *54*, 5889–5900. [CrossRef]
14. Lu, K.D.; Wu, Z.-G. Resilient event-triggered load frequency control for cyber-physical power systems under DoS attacks. *IEEE Trans. Power Syst.* **2023**, *38*, 5302–5313. [CrossRef]
15. Zhou, S.; Deng, C.; Fan, S.; Wang, B.; Che, W.-W. Resilient distributed Nash equilibrium control for nonlinear MASs under DoS attacks. *IEEE Trans. Cybern.* **2025**, *55*, 2316–2326. [CrossRef]
16. Zhang, G.; Li, J.; Bamisile, O.; Xing, W.; Cai, D.; Huang, Q. An $\mathcal{H}_\infty$ load frequency control scheme for multi-area power system under cyber-attacks and time-varying delays. *IEEE Trans. Power Syst.* **2023**, *38*, 1336–1349. [CrossRef]
17. Khooban, M.H.; Niknam, T.; Shasadeghi, M.; Dragicevic, T.; Blaabjerg, F. Load frequency control in microgrids based on a stochastic noninteger controller. *IEEE Trans. Sustain. Energy* **2018**, *9*, 853–861. [CrossRef]
18. Hu, S.; Ge, X.; Chen, X.; Yue, D. Resilient load frequency control of islanded AC microgrids under concurrent false data injection and denial-of-service attacks. *IEEE Trans. Smart Grid* **2023**, *14*, 690–700. [CrossRef]

19. Zhao, N.; Yue, D.; Dou, C.; Shi, T. Distributed dynamic event-triggered cooperative control of multiple TCLs and HESS for improving frequency regulation. *IEEE Trans. Ind. Inf.* **2024**, *20*, 1539–1549. [CrossRef]
20. Hossain, M.M.; Peng, C.; Wang, Y.-L.; Du, X. Handshake logic-based event-triggered load frequency control for smart grids under DoS attacks. *IEEE Trans. Ind. Inf.* **2022**, *18*, 3863–3872. [CrossRef]
21. Hu, S.; Ge, X.; Zhang, W.; Yue, D. DoS-resilient load frequency control of multi-area power systems: An attack-parameter-dependent approach. *IEEE Trans. Inf. Forensics Secur.* **2024**, *19*, 3423–3434. [CrossRef]
22. Peng, C.; Zhang, J.; Yan, H. Adaptive event-triggering $\mathcal{H}_\infty$ load frequency control for network-based power systems. *IEEE Trans. Ind. Electron.* **2018**, *65*, 1685–1694. [CrossRef]
23. Peng, C.; Li, J.; Fei, M. Resilient event-triggering $\mathcal{H}_\infty$ load frequency control for multi-area power systems with energy-limited DoS attacks. *IEEE Trans. Power Syst.* **2016**, *32*, 4110–4118. [CrossRef]
24. Hu, Z.; Zhang, K.; Su, R.; Wang, R.; Li, Y. Robust cooperative load frequency control for enhancing wind energy integration in multi-area power systems. *IEEE Trans. Autom. Sci. Eng.* **2024**, *22*, 1508–1518. [CrossRef]
25. Yue, D.; Tian, E.; Han, Q.-L. A delay system method for designing event-triggered controllers of networked control systems. *IEEE Trans. Autom. Control* **2013**, *58*, 475–481. [CrossRef]
26. Hossain, M.M.; Peng, C.; Su, H.-T.; Xie, S. Bandwidth allocation-based distributed event-triggered LFC for smart grids under hybrid attacks. *IEEE Trans. Smart Grid* **2022**, *13*, 820–830. [CrossRef]
27. Zhai, J. Event-triggered control for p-normal uncertain nonlinear systems. *Nonlinear Dyn.* **2024**, *112*, 3661–3677. [CrossRef]
28. Ren, H.; Cheng, Z.; Qin, J.; Lu, R. Deception attacks on event-triggered distributed consensus estimation for nonlinear systems. *Automatica* **2023**, *154*, 111100. [CrossRef]
29. Zhang, L.; Zhao, Z.; Ma, Z.; Zhao, N. Prescribed performance adaptive neural event-triggered control for switched nonlinear cyber–physical systems under deception attacks. *Neural Netw.* **2024**, *179*, 106586. [CrossRef]
30. Guo, Z.; Shi, D.; Johansson, K.-H.; Shi, L. Optimal linear cyber-attack on remote state estimation. *IEEE Trans. Control Netw. Syst.* **2017**, *4*, 4–13. [CrossRef]
31. Li, T.; Wang, Z.; Zou, L.; Chen, B.; Yu, L. A dynamic encryption–decryption scheme for replay attack detection in cyber–physical systems. *Automatica* **2023**, *151*, 110926. [CrossRef]
32. Guo, Z.; Shi, D.; Johansson, K.-H.; Shi, L. Worst-case stealthy innovation-based linear attack on remote state estimation. *Automatica* **2018**, *89*, 117–124. [CrossRef]
33. Liang, G.; Zhao, J.; Luo, F.; Weller, S.R.; Dong, Z.Y. A review of false data injection attacks against modern power systems. *IEEE Trans. Smart Grid* **2017**, *8*, 1630–1638. [CrossRef]
34. Chen, P.; Zhang, D.; Yu, L.; Yan, H. Dynamic event-triggered output feedback control for load frequency control in power systems with multiple cyber attacks. *IEEE Trans. Syst. Man Cybern. B Cybern.* **2022**, *52*, 6246–6258. [CrossRef]
35. Li, X.; Wei, G.; Ding, D.; Liu, S. Recursive filtering for time-varying discrete sequential systems subject to deception attacks: Weighted try-once-discard protocol. *IEEE Trans. Syst. Man Cybern. B Cybern.* **2021**, *52*, 3704–3713. [CrossRef]
36. Liu, Q.; Zhao, C.; Liu, M.; Deng, R.; Cheng, P. Submodularity-based false data injection attack strategy in DC microgrids. *IEEE Trans. Inf. Forensics Secur.* **2025**, *20*, 2342–2352. [CrossRef]
37. Pham, T.N.; Nahavandi, S.; Trinh, H.; Wong, K.P. Static output feedback frequency stabilization of time-delay power systems with coordinated electric vehicles state of charge control. *IEEE Trans. Power Syst.* **2017**, *32*, 3862–3874. [CrossRef]
38. Zhang, X.-M.; Han, Q.-L.; Yu, X. Survey on Recent Advances in Networked Control Systems. *IEEE Trans. Ind. Inf.* **2016**, *12*, 1740–1752. [CrossRef]
39. Zhang, X.M.; Han, Q.-L.; Ge, X. A novel approach to $\mathcal{H}_\infty$ performance analysis of discrete-time networked systems subject to network-induced delays and malicious packet dropouts. *Automatica* **2022**, *136*, 110010. [CrossRef]
40. Park, P.; Ko, J.-W.; Jeong, C. Reciprocally convex approach to stability of systems with time-varying delays. *Automatica* **2011**, *47*, 235–238. [CrossRef]
41. Crusius, C.A.; Trofino, A. Sufficient LMI conditions for output feedback control problems. *IEEE Trans. Autom. Control* **1999**, *44*, 235–238. [CrossRef]
42. Xiao, Z.; Jiang, Y.; Yao, Z.; He, Z.; Jiang, Y.; Li, Y. A hybrid data-driven power loss minimization method of dual-active bridge converters. *IEEE Trans. Power Electron.* **2024**, *39*, 5820–5832. [CrossRef]

electronics

MDPI

Article

Assessing Cross-Domain Threats in Cloud–Edge-Integrated Industrial Control Systems

Lei Zhang, Yi Wang, Cheng Chang and Xingqiu Shen *

Institute of Big Data, Fudan University, Shanghai 200437, China; ibd_zhanglei@fudan.edu.cn (L.Z.); yiwang_@fdu.edu.cn (Y.W.); changcheng@fudan.edu.cn (C.C.)
* Correspondence: shenxingqiu@fudan.edu.cn

Abstract: As Industrial Control Systems (ICSs) increasingly adopt cloud–edge collaborative architectures, they face escalating risks from complex cross-domain cyber threats. To address this challenge, we propose a novel threat assessment framework specifically designed for cloud–edge-integrated ICSs. Our approach systematically identifies and evaluates security risks across cyber and physical boundaries by building a structured dataset of ICS assets, attack entry points, techniques, and impacts. We introduce a unique set of evaluation indicators spanning four key dimensions—system modules, attack paths, attack methods, and potential impacts—providing a holistic view of cyber threats. Through simulation experiments on a representative ICS scenario inspired by real-world attacks, we demonstrate the framework's effectiveness in detecting vulnerabilities and quantifying security posture improvements. Our results underscore the framework's practical utility in guiding targeted defense strategies and its potential to advance research on cloud–edge ICS security. This work not only fills gaps in the existing methodologies but also provides new insights and tools applicable to sectors such as smart grids, intelligent manufacturing, and critical infrastructure protection.

Keywords: industrial control systems (ICSs); cloud–edge integration; cross-domain attacks; risk assessment; cyber–physical security

1. Introduction

Industrial Control Systems (ICSs) have evolved dramatically since their inception in the 1960s, when highly automated production processes first saw widespread industrial use [1]. With the advent of initiatives like smart manufacturing and Industry 4.0, modern ICSs have transformed into complex cyber–physical systems (CPSs) that tightly couple physical processes with digital control, greatly improving efficiency and responsiveness [2,3]. In parallel, advances in computing have fostered new architectures for ICSs. Cloud–edge collaboration has emerged as a promising paradigm that combines the powerful data processing capabilities of cloud computing with the low-latency responsiveness of edge computing [4,5]. This integration provides higher operational efficiency and real-time data processing and has begun to gain attention in domains such as manufacturing ICSs [6], smart power grids [7], and intelligent transportation systems [8]. An ICS is no longer just a collection of automated devices but an intelligent network that can monitor and analyze data across an entire product lifecycle in real time.

However, the adoption of cloud–edge-integrated architectures also introduces new security challenges. In cloud–edge collaborative environments, ICSs face *cross-domain attacks* that span cyber and physical domains and often involve multiple layers of the system. Notably, several high-profile cyber–physical attacks have illustrated the complexity and multi-dimensional nature of such threats. For example, the Stuxnet worm of 2010 leveraged both cyber exploits and physical sabotage to infiltrate an air-gapped ICS network, illustrating one of the first globally recognized cross-domain ICS attacks [9]. Another case is the 2015 Ukraine power grid cyberattack, where attackers remotely compromised control systems and caused a widespread blackout [10]. Similarly, the 2017 *NotPetya* malware spread from IT networks to disrupt industrial operations worldwide, resulting in significant physical and economic damage (citelika2018notpetya). These incidents highlight the vulnerability of ICS to Advanced Persistent Threats (APTs) that traverse multiple domains (IT networks, control networks, and physical equipment), combining cyber techniques, physical disruption, and even social engineering.

Traditional cybersecurity assessment methods struggle to fully address such multi-faceted, cross-domain threats. Extensive research has been conducted on ICS security evaluation using tools like attack graphs (formal models that map potential sequences of exploits across system components), attack trees (hierarchical diagrams that decompose attacker goals into subgoals), and Bayesian networks (probabilistic graphical models capturing dependencies and uncertainties in attack scenarios) [11–13]. These approaches provide valuable insights into network vulnerabilities and attack probabilities. However, relatively few studies focus specifically on *cross-domain* attacks in cloud–edge scenarios, where the dynamic, distributed architecture and real-time requirements of cloud–edge ICS render many existing methods insufficient. Early work did not deeply explore the risks arising from interactions across different layers and domains in a cloud–edge-integrated ICS. For instance, conventional models lack the ability to evaluate dynamic cross-layer attack paths or the cascading effects of attacks that move between cyber (information) domain and physical domain.

In this context, this paper proposes a comprehensive framework and methodology to fill the research gap and provide a systematic solution for enhancing ICS security in cloud–edge collaborative scenarios. The main contributions are as follows:

1. **Systematic Framework Construction**: We systematically construct a cross-domain attack evaluation framework for cloud–edge collaborative ICS by detailed collection and classification of system assets, cross-domain attack entry points, attack methods, and attack impacts. This includes identifying various types of ICS assets, categorizing potential attack entry points, surveying attack techniques/tools, and classifying attack impacts. These preparatory steps establish the necessary data foundation and basic structure for subsequent attack evaluation.
2. **Cross-Domain Attack Indicator System**: We develop a novel cross-domain attack evaluation indicator system tailored to cloud–edge ICS scenarios. This indicator system accounts for the unique characteristics of cross-domain attacks in ICS and covers four key dimensions: system modules, attack paths, attack methods, and their potential impacts. It provides a standardized theoretical basis and methodology for identifying, evaluating, and defending against cross-domain attacks.
3. **Simulation-Based Validation**: We conduct simulation experiments under a representative ICS topology to test the practical effectiveness of the proposed evaluation method. The experiments verify the validity and feasibility of the approach in identifying weak points of the system and improving overall security.

2. Related Work

To address the escalating security threats in Industrial Control Systems (ICSs), especially in the context of cloud–edge collaboration, various attack assessment approaches have been proposed. A summary of representative works and their comparative characteristics is provided in Table 1. We categorize the existing research into four classes: static structural modeling, dynamic probabilistic analysis, cross-domain propagation modeling, and cloud–edge-tailored evaluation frameworks.

(1) Static Structural Assessment. Early studies primarily relied on fixed-attack structures such as attack trees and graphs to identify vulnerabilities. Wang et al. [12] employed attack–defense trees to quantify risk in ICS environments, capturing attacker and defender behavior in a static hierarchy. Zhou et al. [11] further extended attack-graph-based methods by introducing correlation among vulnerabilities to dynamically generate exploit paths. Zhu et al. [14] proposed a risk evaluation model for distribution cyber–physical systems by simulating static attack paths combined with system fault analysis. While insightful, these models lack adaptability to dynamic topology or temporal propagation, limiting their application in evolving ICS environments.

(2) Dynamic Risk Inference and Bayesian Modeling. To better capture uncertainty in ICS security, probabilistic approaches have been developed. Zhang et al. [15] constructed a Bayesian network to estimate the probability of sensor and actuator compromise, enabling physical-level risk prediction. Fu et al. [16] integrated fuzzy logic with Bayesian networks to assess cross-domain risk propagation in distribution systems. Huang et al. [17] proposed an association analysis method based on system state variables and security events, revealing probabilistic correlations among risk factors. Jin et al. [18] explored cloud–fog architectures for autonomous industrial CPS, emphasizing dynamic 3C (communication–computation–control) coupling and security-aware automation strategies. These works provide valuable insights but generally assume fixed data sources and are limited in modeling multi-layer interactions.

(3) Cross-Domain Attack Propagation Models. To address attack transitions between IT and OT domains, several studies have proposed integrated propagation frameworks. Liu et al. [19] combined colored Petri nets with Bayesian game theory to evaluate cyber–physical risk in power grid control systems, modeling both attacker strategies and system responses. Tan and Li [20] used attack graph models augmented by reinforcement learning to simulate attack progression across domains. Cao et al. [21] presented a deep-learning-based spatiotemporal detection framework (FedDynST) for ICS DDoS detection in cloud–edge settings, which inherently models cross-domain behavior via federated temporal features.

(4) Cloud–Edge Collaborative Evaluation. Despite the above progress, only limited work explicitly addresses the structural dynamics introduced by cloud–edge collaboration in the ICS. Liu et al. [22] analyzed cyber contingencies in active distribution networks using a co-simulation approach but did not focus on the cloud–edge architecture. Li et al. [23] proposed an optimization-based framework to assess worst-case attack strategies under resource constraints. Zheng et al. [24] surveyed cybersecurity solutions for edge-integrated IIoT and ICS networks, identifying specific risks in edge-cloud communication and recommending layered mitigation techniques. Wu et al. [25] proposed a federated-learning-based real-time threat scoring model for edge-enabled ICS, improving detection latency and decentralization robustness. However, none of these frameworks fully model the cloud–edge-specific deployment layers or account for real-time adaptive changes in such hybrid architectures. Our proposed method fills this gap by integrating multi-source indicators—entry points, propagation paths, method complexity, and impact types—into a unified scoring system suitable for cloud–edge ICS risk assessment.

Table 1. Summary of ICS threat assessment literature.

Category	Method	Key Contribution	Model	Simulator	Dataset	Strength	Limitation
Static	Wang et al. [12]	ICS risk via attack–defense trees	Attack–defense tree	N/A	Synthetic configs	Formal attacker logic	No dynamics
	Zhou et al. [11]	Correlated attack graph	Correlation-based graph	N/A	Case study	Better exploit prediction	Still static
	Zhu et al. [14]	Fault-aware static risk evaluation	Fault + attack path	System simulator	CPS substation	Considers fault impact	No timing model
Dynamic	Zhang et al. [15]	Bayesian ICS inference	Bayesian network	ICS emulator	Synthetic logs	Sensor-actuator linkage	Fixed priors
	Fu et al. [16]	Cross-domain via fuzzy-Bayes	Fuzzy Bayes net	Grid emulator	SCADA flows	Models fuzzy transitions	Limited scale realism
	Huang et al. [17]	Event-state association mining	Association analysis	Event logger	ICS logs	Data-driven risk links	No causality
	Jin et al. [18]	Fog-Cloud 3C coupling	Cloud–fog architecture	Digital twin	Co-simulated ICPS	Dynamic ICPS modeling	Deployment cost
Cross-Domain	Liu et al. [19]	Petri-game cyber–physical modeling	Petri Net + Bayes game	Power emulator	Grid logs	Game-theoretic attacker	Hard-coded rules
	Tan et al. [20]	RL-trained attack propagation	Graph + RL	MDP simulator	Hybrid ICS	Learns adaptive tactics	High training cost
	Cao et al. [21]	FedDynST for DDoS detection	Fed-GCN + T-CNN	Edge testbed	ICS-DDoS traces	Federated DDoS learning	Specific to DDoS
Cloud–Edge	Liu et al. [22]	Co-simulation of contingencies in distribution networks	Co-simulation	Distribution network simulator	Synthetic grid	Fault propagation modeling	No cloud–edge focus
	Li et al. [23]	Optimizing worst-case attacker strategies	Optimization framework	Simulated ICS environment	Synthetic configs	Resource-aware attacker modeling	Lacks distribution
	Zheng et al. [24]	Survey on edge-IIoT threats	Threat taxonomy	N/A	N/A	Comprehensive taxonomy	No empirical eval
	Wu et al. [25]	FL-based edge threat scoring	Anomaly detection	ICS edge testbed	Labeled logs	Real-time scoring	Needs labeled data

3. Methodology

3.1. Framework Overview

Figure 1 presents our end-to-end framework for evaluating cross-domain attacks in a cloud–edge–field ICS. Unlike traditional cloud-only security assessments—which typically treat edge and field devices as passive data sources, assume unlimited compute and persistent connectivity, and apply homogeneous controls—our design explicitly captures the heterogeneity, resource constraints, intermittent connectivity, and physical accessibility of edge nodes, as well as the strict timing and safety requirements of field controllers. By integrating telemetry and configuration data across all three tiers (cloud, edge, and field), we can model multi-layer attack paths that span different domains and dynamically adjust risk estimates as conditions evolve.

- Cloud Layer: centralized analytics, long-term data storage, containerized services.
- Edge Layer: distributed compute nodes deployed near physical processes, often with constrained resources and minimal hardening.
- Field Layer: programmable logic controllers (PLCs), sensors, actuators, and associated industrial protocols.

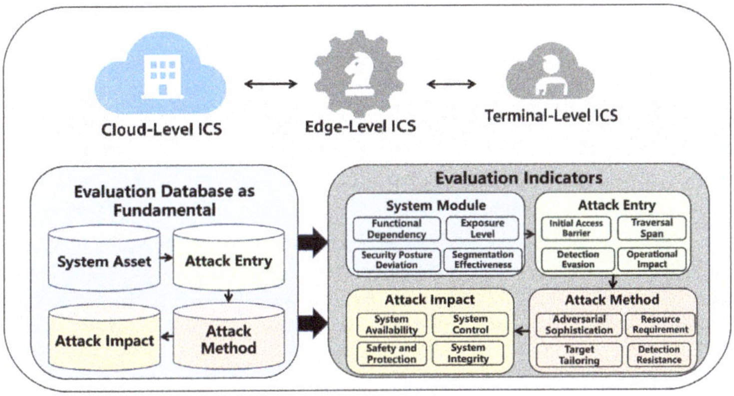

Figure 1. Our proposed framework for cross-domain attack evaluation in a cloud–edge collaborative ICS.

By integrating telemetry and configuration data from all three layers, we achieve a unified cross-domain view of attacker capabilities and system vulnerabilities. This multi-phase framework comprises the following:

1. Data Collection and Threat Modeling: inventory of assets and mapping of known ICS techniques.
2. Indicator Quantification: computation of 16 tailored metrics across four risk dimensions.
3. Score Aggregation and Analysis: synthesis into a composite risk score for benchmarking and "what-if" exploration.

In Phase 1, we focus on assembling a detailed dataset and threat model for an Industrial Control System (ICS) within a cloud–edge architecture. The process begins with the systematic inventory of the ICS assets, which is derived from our private dataset. This dataset provides comprehensive details about the hardware, software, and network assets across the environment, forming the foundation for the entire evaluation. These assets are meticulously catalogued to identify key components and their attributes, such as entry points, attack methods, and potential impacts. One crucial aspect of this phase is identifying and categorizing cross-domain attack entry points. These are potential vulnerabilities where an attacker could breach the network to affect OT devices or vice versa. By following the MITRE ATT&CK for the ICS framework (see Figure A1), we map out known attack methods, tools, and the corresponding impacts on system operations and safety. This provides us with a thorough understanding of how an attacker might exploit various components in the cloud–edge architecture. This comprehensive dataset and attack model, which merges detailed asset information with structured threat data, form the cornerstone for the subsequent development of attack indicators and risk evaluation.

In Phase 2, we develop and compute a set of evaluation *indicators* across four dimensions: (a) system module metrics, (b) attack path metrics, (c) attack method metrics, and (d) attack impact metrics. These indicators quantitatively characterize different aspects of cross-domain threats. The details of each indicator and their calculation methods are provided in Section 3.2. In developing our indicator set, we deliberately selected 16 metrics to ensure both theoretical rigor and practical relevance across the cloud–edge–field architecture. First, we drew on an extensive literature review of risk-quantification techniques in industrial contexts—dependency metrics that capture cascading failures in multi-component systems [26], exposure-surface scoring methods for networked services [27], and probabilistic models of detection avoidance [28]—to inform our measures of module importance, interface exposure, and stealth potential. However, conventional frameworks invariably assume either cloud-only or on-premises deployments and thus overlook the distinct threats introduced by edge computing. In particular, edge nodes often operate with minimal security hardening in physically accessible locations, rendering them susceptible to tampering, intermittent connectivity, and rapid reconfiguration. To address these gaps, we devised novel indicators—such as Security Posture Deviation and Segmentation Effectiveness—that explicitly account for the resource constraints and physical coupling of edge devices. Finally, we ensured that each metric produces a normalized, interpretable score so that operators overseeing hundreds of distributed assets can rapidly compare and prioritize security investments. By combining well-established dependency and exposure measures with edge-specific risk factors and by structuring all sixteen indicators into four coherent dimensions, our framework advances beyond traditional ICS assessments to deliver a unified, actionable portrait of cross-domain vulnerability.

In the final phase, the various indicator values are aggregated to produce overall scores, which facilitate analysis of the system's security posture. Specifically, we derive a composite score for each dimension (System Module Score, Attack Path Score, Attack Method Score, and Attack Impact Score), which are then combined into a single *overall attack evaluation score* for the ICS. This overall score provides a high-level quantitative measure of the cross-domain attack risk facing the system. By examining the contributions of each dimension, system defenders can pinpoint critical weaknesses (e.g., a particular module with high risk, or an attack path that is especially vulnerable and stealthy) and prioritize mitigation strategies. Figure 1 presents our end-to-end framework for evaluating cross-domain attacks in a cloud–edge–field ICS. Unlike traditional cloud-only security assessments—which typically treat edge and field devices as passive data sources, assume unlimited compute and persistent connectivity, and apply homogeneous controls—our design explicitly captures the heterogeneity, resource constraints, intermittent connectivity, and physical accessibility of edge nodes, as well as the strict timing and safety requirements of field controllers. By integrating telemetry and configuration data across all three tiers (cloud, edge, and field), we can model multi-layer attack paths that span IT and OT domains and dynamically adjust risk estimates as conditions evolve.

3.2. Indicator Definition and Calculation

In this section, we define the evaluation indicators for each of the four dimensions and present their calculation formulas. The indicator definitions take into account the unique features of cloud–edge-integrated ICS and cross-domain attack behavior.

3.2.1. System Module Indicators

This dimension evaluates the scope and significance of system components affected by the attack. We define four indicators for system modules:

1. Functional Dependency Score (FDS): This indicator FDS_i measures the degree to which other modules in the system depend on module i for correct operation. Instead of subjective importance, FDS_i is computed by analyzing the system's functional dependency graph. A module that supports many downstream components or processes has a higher FDS_i, indicating that its compromise could cause cascading failures. Let d_i be the number of modules directly dependent on module i and $\max(d)$ the maximum such value across all modules:

$$FDS_i = \frac{d_i}{\max(d)}\,. \tag{1}$$

2. Exposure Level (EL): EL_i reflects the number and type of interfaces through which module i communicates with other internal or external components, representing its potential attack surface. Interfaces may include APIs, network ports, or wireless connections. A module with many exposed endpoints or Internet-facing services has a higher risk of being targeted. Let e_i be the number of such interfaces, normalized by the maximum observed value:

$$EL_i = \frac{e_i}{\max(e)}\,. \tag{2}$$

3. Security Posture Deviation (SPD): SPD_i quantifies how much module i diverges from the recommended security configuration baseline. This includes outdated patches, misconfigurations, or policy violations. It is derived from audit data or security scans. A higher SPD_i means the module has more security gaps. Let s_i represent a normalized deviation score based on violations and $\max(s)$ be the worst-case deviation:

$$SPD_i = \frac{s_i}{\max(s)}\,. \tag{3}$$

4. Segmentation Effectiveness (SE): SE_i evaluates how well module i is isolated from the rest of the system, based on logical or physical segmentation. Modules within high-trust or tightly segmented zones will have higher SE_i values, limiting lateral movement. This score is obtained via architectural analysis (e.g., network design and VLAN separation). Let z_i be the assigned isolation score:

$$SE_i = \frac{z_i}{\max(z)}\,. \tag{4}$$

These indicators provide a balanced view of each module's role and security posture: FDS_i captures operational dependency, EL_i the exposure to threats, SPD_i the internal configuration state, and SE_i the isolation strength. A module with high dependency, high exposure, poor configuration, and weak segmentation represents a critical vulnerability.

We define the overall *System Module Score (SMS)* to summarize these risks across all n modules by integrating the indicators into a weighted risk expression:

$$\text{SMS} = \frac{1}{n}\sum_{i=1}^{n} \frac{FDS_i \times EL_i \times SPD_i}{SE_i}, \tag{5}$$

where a higher SMS indicates greater systemic vulnerability in the module layer.

3.2.2. Attack Path Indicators

For the attack paths dimension, we consider metrics that characterize the nature of each possible attack path an adversary might take through the system (as represented in the attack graph). We define four indicators for an attack path j:

1. Initial Access Barrier (IAB): IAB_j represents the difficulty an attacker faces in gaining the initial foothold required to begin traversing path j. This includes required credentials, network reachability, and exploit availability. A higher IAB_j means that starting the path requires more effort or privilege. Let b_j be a normalized score reflecting access barriers:
$$IAB_j = b_j\,. \tag{6}$$
2. Traversal Span (TS): TS_j measures how broadly path j stretches across different zones, layers, or security domains. It captures lateral movement capability and the scope of compromise. Let z_j be the number of unique zones traversed, normalized by Z, the maximum across all paths:
$$TS_j = \frac{z_j}{Z}\,. \tag{7}$$
3. Detection Evasion Potential (DEP): DEP_j indicates how likely it is that attacks along path j will evade detection. We assess the residual undetected risk r_i at each node i based on sensor coverage, logging, and response latency. Averaging across n_j nodes yields the following:
$$DEP_j = \frac{1}{n_j}\sum_{i=1}^{n_j} r_i\,. \tag{8}$$
4. Operational Impact Potential (OIP): OIP_j estimates the damage to operations if path j is successfully exploited. This considers whether the path leads to critical process disruption, safety risks, or data loss. Let o_j be a normalized score derived from threat impact analysis:
$$OIP_j = o_j\,. \tag{9}$$

Together, these indicators provide insight into path feasibility (IAB_j), scope (TS_j), stealth (DEP_j), and impact (OIP_j). A low-barrier, wide-spanning, undetectable path with high impact represents the highest threat.

The overall Attack Path Score (APS) summarizes the severity of all M attack paths:

$$\text{APS} = \frac{1}{M}\sum_{j=1}^{M} \frac{DEP_j + OIP_j}{IAB_j + TS_j}, \tag{10}$$

which captures the ratio between attack benefits and required effort across paths.

3.2.3. Attack Method Indicators

For the attack methods dimension, we evaluate the techniques that an adversary employs at various stages of the attack. We define four indicators to characterize each attack method k used in cross-domain scenarios:

1. Adversarial Sophistication (AS): AS_k assesses the novelty and advancement of method k based on whether it is typically associated with advanced persistent threats (APTs), novel exploits, or automation. Higher AS_k implies the use of modern, often less detectable techniques.
2. Resource Requirement (RR): RR_k measures the effort, tools, and expertise needed to execute method k. This includes programming knowledge, availability of exploit kits, or hardware requirements. A higher score means fewer attackers are capable of using it.
3. Target Tailoring (TT): TT_k evaluates how specifically the method is designed for the victim system. Custom-built payloads or exploits tailored to particular ICS platforms yield high TT_k scores, signaling targeted intent and reconnaissance.
4. Detection Resistance (DR): DR_k reflects the inherent stealthiness of method k, considering whether it uses encrypted channels, fileless execution, or blending with legitimate processes. Higher DR_k indicates higher evasion capability.

These indicators ensure a comprehensive evaluation of the attacker's means from multiple perspectives: adversarial sophistication (how novel and advanced the method is), resource demand (the level of skill and tooling required), target tailoring (the degree of customization to the victim system), and detection resistance (the stealthiness of the method). By analyzing attack methods through these metrics, defenders can better understand the threat landscape and prioritize their responses accordingly—for instance, by improving detection mechanisms for stealthy, tailored attacks or focusing mitigation efforts on techniques requiring minimal attacker resources.

Suppose the total number of distinct attack methods considered is K. We can compute average values for each of the four metrics across all methods:

$$AS = \frac{1}{K}\sum_{k=1}^{K} AS_k\,, \qquad RR = \frac{1}{K}\sum_{k=1}^{K} RR_k\,, \tag{11}$$

$$TT = \frac{1}{K}\sum_{k=1}^{K} TT_k\,, \qquad DR = \frac{1}{K}\sum_{k=1}^{K} DR_k\,. \tag{12}$$

Finally, we define an overall *Attack Method Score (AMS)* by combining these four aspects. One simple approach is to take the arithmetic mean:

$$\text{AMS} = \frac{AS + RR + TT + DR}{4}\,, \tag{13}$$

resulting in a normalized 0–1 score that represents the cumulative threat posed by the attack techniques. Higher values of AMS correspond to more advanced, targeted, and stealthy methods that may require prioritized attention in system defenses.

3.2.4. Attack Impact Indicators

Finally, for the attack impact dimension, we categorize and quantify the potential consequences that cross-domain attacks could inflict on the industrial system. Drawing inspiration from the impact taxonomy in frameworks like MITRE ATT&CK [29], we classify attack impacts into the following categories:

- Loss of Availability (LA)—reduction in or loss of system availability, causing downtime.
- Loss of Productivity and Revenue (LPR)—direct impact on production output and financial losses due to disruption.
- Loss and Denial of Control (LDC)—attacker gains or denies control of the system, e.g., via disabling control commands or performing unauthorized control actions (akin to Denial-of-Service or command hijacking).

- Manipulation of Control (MC)—attacker issues malicious or altered control commands, causing the system to operate unsafely or incorrectly.
- Loss of Safety (LS)—compromised safety mechanisms, potentially endangering human operators or equipment (e.g., disabling alarms or safety interlocks).
- Loss of Protection (LP)—disabling or bypassing security protections, such as encryption, authentication, or physical security measures.
- Damage to Property (DP)—physical destruction or damage to equipment, facilities, or products as a result of the attack.
- Theft of Operational Information (TOI)—exfiltration of sensitive operational data, such as proprietary process recipes, engineering drawings, or system configurations.

For clarity, Table 2 shows how these specific impacts are grouped into broader impact categories affecting different aspects of the system. Each category addresses a dimension of potential damage: availability, control, safety/protection, and integrity of physical or informational assets.

Table 2. Impact categories, specific indicators, and calculation methods.

Impact Category	Specific Indicators	Explanation and Calculation
System Availability	LA, LPR	$\text{LA} = \frac{\text{downtime}_{\text{hrs}}}{\max(\text{downtime}_{\text{hrs}})}$; LPR = production-loss (USD) linearly scaled from [USD 0–USD 1M] into [0,1].
System Control	LDC, MC	$\text{LDC} = \frac{\text{\#denied commands}}{\text{\#total commands}}$; $\text{MC} = \frac{\text{\#malicious commands executed}}{\text{\#total commands}}$.
Safety and Protection	LS, LP	$\text{LS} = \frac{\text{safety-interlock failures}}{\max(\text{failures})}$; $\text{LP} = \frac{\text{auth/crypto bypass events}}{\max(\text{bypass events})}$.
Integrity and Information	DP, TOI	DP = cost (USD) mapped to [0,1] via thresholds (e.g., 0–USD $10^4 = 0$, USD 10^4–USD $10^5 = 0.25$, …, ≥USD $10^7 = 1$); $\text{TOI} = \frac{\text{exfiltrated data (GB)}}{\max(\text{data (GB)})}$.

Each of the eight specific impacts (LA, LPR, LDC, MC, LS, LP, DP, and TOI) can be viewed as an indicator on its own. We assess each impact type in terms of severity for the given scenario. To quantify the impact severity, we adopt a qualitative scoring approach: each impact is assigned a severity level from 0 to 4 (five levels), which is then mapped to a numerical score from 0 to 1 in equal increments. For example, an impact assessed as negligible would be level 0 (score 0), minor impact level 1 (score 0.25), moderate impact level 2 (score 0.5), serious impact level 3 (score 0.75), and catastrophic impact level 4 (score 1). The scoring criteria can be customized for each impact type. As an illustration, consider the Damage to Property (DP) impact: one could define the levels in terms of estimated financial loss in dollars. For instance,

$$\text{DP score} = \begin{cases} 0 & \text{if loss} < USD10^4; \\ 0.25 & USD10^4 \leq \text{loss} < USD10^5; \\ 0.5 & USD10^5 \leq \text{loss} < USD10^6; \\ 0.75 & USD10^6 \leq \text{loss} < USD10^7; \\ 1 & \text{if loss} \geq USD10^7. \end{cases} \quad (14)$$

where the thresholds (USD 10^4, USD 10^5, etc.) are chosen as example ranges for property damage costs. Similar piecewise definitions can be established for other impacts (e.g., downtime duration for LA, safety incident severity for LS, etc.).

By covering impacts from the cyber layer (information theft) to the physical layer (equipment damage), the evaluation system achieves a comprehensive view of potential damages. Our impact categorization is informed by the MITRE ATT&CK impact metrics [29], ensuring that the evaluation method is grounded in a well-vetted taxonomy and remains systematic and scientific. The outcome of this impact assessment is a clear quantitative analysis of attack consequences that can aid system managers in understanding worst-case scenarios.

Once each of the eight impact indicators is assigned a score (between 0 and 1), we compute the overall *Attack Impact Score (AIS)* as the average of these values:

$$\mathrm{AIS} = \frac{\mathrm{LA} + \mathrm{LPR} + \mathrm{LDC} + \mathrm{MC} + \mathrm{LS} + \mathrm{LP} + \mathrm{DP} + \mathrm{TOI}}{8}, \tag{15}$$

where each term is the score for that impact type. This yields a single figure representing the overall severity of impacts an attacker could cause, on average, given the scenario.

3.3. Overall Evaluation Score

Based on the computed scores for each dimension (modules, paths, methods, and impacts), we derive a final aggregated metric, the Attack Evaluation Score (or simply Score), for the system. We define it as

$$\mathrm{Score} = \mathrm{SMS} + \mathrm{APS} + \mathrm{AMS} + \mathrm{AIS}, \tag{16}$$

summing the System Module Score, Attack Path Score, Attack Method Score, and Attack Impact Score. This overall score encapsulates the comprehensive risk level of cross-domain attacks on the cloud–edge-integrated ICS. Higher values indicate a more insecure system (greater combined risk across all dimensions). In practice, this score can be used as a benchmark to compare different system configurations or to track security improvements over time (for instance, after implementing mitigations, one would expect the score to decrease).

It is worth noting that while we use an unweighted sum here for simplicity, the framework could be extended by applying weighting factors to each component of the score if certain dimensions are considered more critical in a given context. For this study, we treat them equally to emphasize a balanced consideration of all aspects.

4. Experiments and Results

After constructing the cross-domain attack evaluation method, we validated its effectiveness and practicality through a repeatable digital-twin testbed. All scenarios and attacks described below are, therefore, fully deployable by third parties who reproduce the released testbed images and scripts.

4.1. Experimental Scenario Design

To thoroughly exercise the evaluation framework, we designed a test scenario inspired by real-world security incidents. In particular, we base our simulation on the 2015 Ukraine power grid cyberattack, which exemplified a coordinated multi-stage, cross-domain attack. This scenario was chosen because it fully reflects the complexity and multi-dimensional nature of cross-domain attacks, involving network intrusions, operational technology manipulations, and physical consequences.

The simulated ICS environment (shown in Figure 2) is a representative cloud–edge collaborative architecture. It includes a *cloud layer* for high-level data analytics and decision support, an *edge layer* comprising edge controllers and gateways that interface with field equipment, and a *terminal device layer* containing the on-site controllers (PLCs and RTUs), sensors, and actuators on the factory floor or power grid substation. This architecture captures the typical multi-layer structure of modern ICS deployments that leverage cloud and edge computing. We carefully designed the network topology and communication patterns to reflect realistic configurations (for instance, how edge devices communicate with both cloud services and local controllers and how corporate IT networks connect to control networks under certain constraints). The attack graph for this scenario includes multiple entry points (e.g., phishing entry via corporate network, direct malware on an HMI workstation, etc.) and multiple known vulnerabilities that an attacker could exploit at various stages.

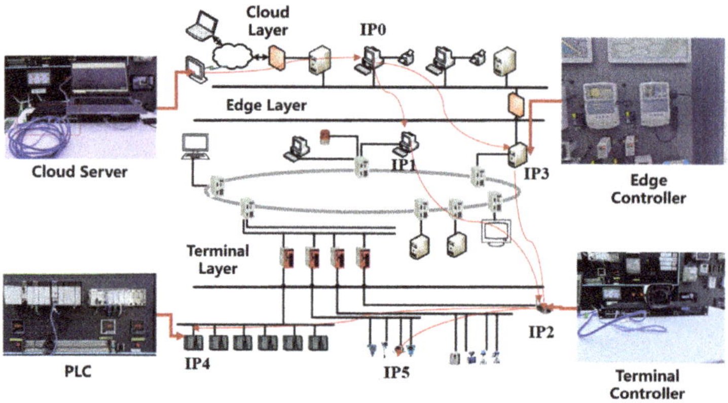

Figure 2. Topology of our simulated ICS environment.

The details of our simulated ICS environment setting are as follows (Figure 2):

- Cloud layer—a three-node Kubernetes1.30 cluster (each node: 4vCPU@2.4GHz, 16 GB RAM, 100 GB SSD) running analytic micro-services and a TimescaleDB historian.
- Edge layer—two ARM-based gateways (RaspberryPi4B, 4 GB RAM) equipped with Modbus and OPCUA protocol adapters and an Nvidia JetsonNano (128-CUDA core, 4 GB RAM) for on-prem inference.
- Field/terminal layer—three OpenPLCv3 virtual controllers (compiled for x86), emulating Siemens S7-1200-class PLCs, each interfaced with a MiniCPS physics model of a power-distribution feeder; sensors/actuators exchange data via Modbus/TCP at 100 ms scan cycles.

We ran multiple iterative trials of the simulation to ensure stability, reliability, and reproducibility of the results. Each experimental scenario was executed 30 times under independent random seeds, influencing factors such as traffic timing and attacker decision branches. By repeating the experiment several times and averaging the results, we reduce the impact of random factors or simulation noise on the evaluation metrics and obtain statistically rigorous estimates. We report the mean and 95% confidence intervals using bootstrapping with 2000 resamples.

During the simulation, data on system state, attack progression, and detection events were collected dynamically, feeding into the calculation of the evaluation indicators in real time. This emulates how, in a real deployment, security monitoring and data acquisition would continuously provide input to our evaluation algorithm. Across all repetitions, the maximum confidence interval half-width observed for the overall score is 0.04, indicating high stability and reliability of the results. Furthermore, to ensure reproducibility and avoid environment-induced variability, we fixed the software versions and dependencies used in our experiments, preventing version skew and ensuring that identical experiments yield consistent results over time.

4.2. Results and Analysis

To systematically quantify the security gains and trade-offs offered by distinct defense mechanisms in our cloud–edge ICS deployment, we defined four experimental scenarios to evaluate the impact of targeted mitigations on overall risk posture:

- Scenario A—Baseline: The system operates with default settings (PLC firmware v3.4.5, flat network topology, no VLAN/ACL rules), representing the unprotected risk posture.
- Scenario B—Targeted Patch at IP1: Deploy vendor hotfix on the PLC at IP1 (firmware upgraded to v3.4.6 via our CI/CD pipeline), closing the known exploit while retaining original network segmentation.
- Scenario C—Micro-Segmentation of IP2: Enforce strict isolation on the edge controller at IP2 by migrating its interface into a dedicated VLAN 42 and applying ACLs that block all IT-subnet ingress, plus a stateful firewall on Modbus TCP port 502 (deny-by-default), effectively severing lateral attack pathways.
- Scenario D—Combined Defenses: Apply both the IP1 firmware patch (v3.4.6) and IP2 micro-segmentation together, removing the easy entry vector and reinforcing the critical pivot to demonstrate compounded security improvements.

Using the designed scenario, we applied our evaluation framework to compute the security scores for the system under the simulated attack. The inputs to the evaluation included the system topology and the constructed cross-domain attack graph (as illustrated in Figures 2 and 3). Figure 3 presents a layered view of the attack, showing the attacker's utilized entry points, the specific vulnerabilities exploited, and the resultant attack paths through the system under different scenarios. The layered visualization makes clear how the attacker moves through the cloud–edge collaborative environment, highlighting cross-domain transitions between the IT network, cloud services, edge layer, and physical control layer.

Based on the indicators and formulas defined in Section 3.2, we calculated the score contributions for each dimension. Table 3 summarizes the security evaluation results for each scenario across the four dimensions (System Module, Attack Path, Attack Method, and Attack Impact) and the overall cross-domain attack score. The scores reflect the system's risk exposure in each scenario, with lower values indicating a more secure posture.

As expected, Scenario A (Baseline) exhibits the highest risk across all dimensions, yielding an overall score of 3.04. With no safeguards in place, the System Module Score is relatively high (0.41) due to unpatched vulnerabilities and lack of isolation, the Attack Path Score is 1.00 (indicating an accessible multi-step attack chain), the Attack Method Score is 0.90 (common exploits are readily applicable), and the Attack Impact Score is 0.73 (significant potential damage if the attack succeeds). This baseline highlights the system's weak points—notably, the vulnerability at IP1 and the pivotal role of IP2 in the attack chain—which contribute to an elevated cross-domain attack risk.

Table 3. Comparison of security evaluation scores under different scenarios.

Scenario	System Module Score	Attack Path Score	Attack Method Score	Attack Impact Score	Overall Score
A (Baseline)	0.41 ± 0.02	1.00	0.90 ± 0.03	0.73	3.04 ± 0.05
B (Patch IP1)	0.30 ± 0.01	1.00	0.60	0.73	2.63 ± 0.01
C (Isolate IP2)	0.30 ± 0.01	0.60	0.80	0.60	2.30 ± 0.01
D (Both Mitigations)	0.21 ± 0.02	0.50	0.40	0.40	1.51 ± 0.02

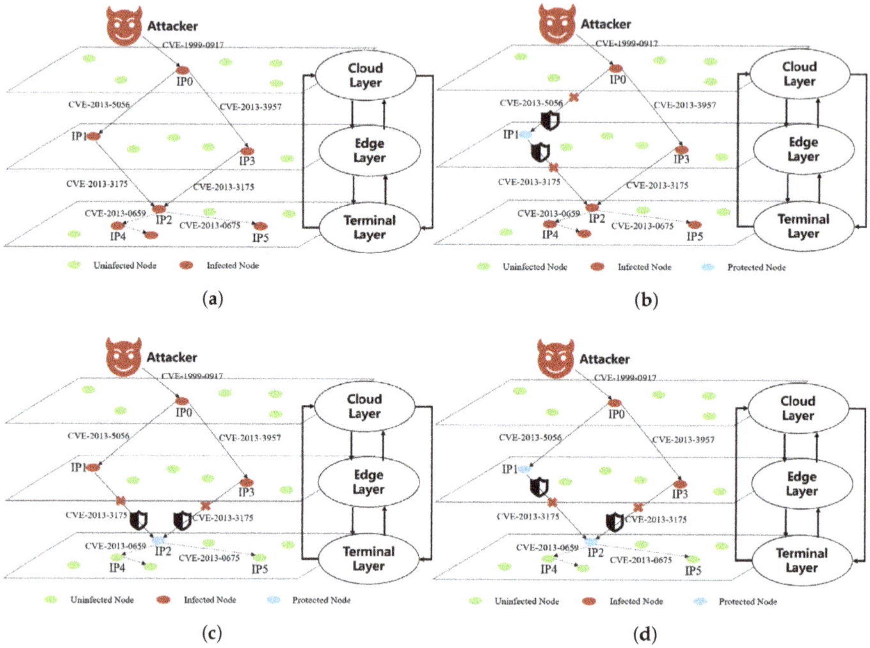

Figure 3. Attack graphs under different scenarios in the simulated ICS environment. Subfigures illustrate the attack surfaces under four configurations: (**a**) Scenario A—Baseline. (**b**) Scenario B—Mitigation at IP1. (**c**) Scenario C—Mitigation at IP2. (**d**) Scenario D—Both Mitigations.

In Scenario B (Patch IP1), the act of patching the known vulnerability at node IP1 strengthens that node's security, reflected by a lower System Module Score (0.30) compared to the baseline 0.41. Eliminating the easy exploit also forces the attacker to consider more complex or less direct attack methods, which reduces the Attack Method Score from 0.90 to 0.60. These changes result in a moderate improvement in the overall score (down to 2.63). However, because the network topology and IP2's status are unchanged in this scenario, the Attack Path Score remains at 1.00, and the Attack Impact Score stays high (0.73)—an attacker who somehow gains a foothold at IP1 (e.g., via an alternative method or credential theft) could still traverse to IP2 and inflict similar impact as in the baseline. Thus, patching IP1 alone addresses the specific vulnerability and improves the security posture to a degree, but significant risk remains via the critical IP2 pathway.

In Scenario C (Isolate IP2), only the isolation measure is applied at node IP2, while IP1's vulnerability is left unpatched. Here, we observe a substantial reduction in the Attack Path Score (from 1.00 down to 0.60) because isolating IP2 erects a barrier in the attack chain—the attacker's path is curtailed, and crossing into the protected segment becomes significantly more difficult. The isolation also limits the potential spread and consequences of an attack, lowering the Attack Impact Score to 0.60 (versus 0.73 baseline) since a breach is less likely to reach critical assets beyond IP2. The System Module Score (0.30) is slightly improved relative to baseline, thanks to the increased isolation degree of that important module (even though IP1 remains vulnerable). Notably, the Attack Method Score (0.80) in Scenario C is still relatively high because the initial exploit on IP1 is still available to the adversary—the attacker does not need a more sophisticated method to compromise IP1. Overall, Scenario C achieves an improved overall score of 2.30, which is a greater risk reduction than Scenario B. This underscores the effectiveness of isolating the key node (IP2) in disrupting cross-domain attack paths and containing potential damage, even though one vulnerability (IP1) remains open.

Scenario D (Both Mitigations) yields the best security outcomes by combining the two defenses. In this scenario, the System Module Score drops to 0.21, the lowest of all cases, indicating that the system's inherent resilience is greatly improved when IP1's vulnerability is patched and IP2 is isolated. The Attack Path Score is reduced to 0.50—the attack graph is effectively broken; the path to the target is highly restricted by the IP2 isolation (requiring elevated privileges or extraordinary steps to bypass) and the initial entry is no longer trivial. Likewise, the Attack Method Score declines to 0.40 because the attacker must now resort to significantly more complex and less certain exploits at every stage (the previously available exploit at IP1 is gone, and additional specialized techniques would be needed to penetrate the isolated IP2). The Attack Impact Score also falls to 0.40, reflecting the fact that with the attack unable to reach its final target layer, the worst-case impact is substantially mitigated. Consequently, the overall cross-domain attack score in Scenario D improves to 1.51, which is roughly a 50% reduction in risk compared to the baseline scenario. This dramatic improvement confirms that addressing both identified weaknesses in tandem provides a compounded security benefit: the patch at IP1 removes an easy entry point, and the isolation of IP2 protects the critical pivot in the attack chain. Together, these measures reinforce each other and provide the strongest security posture, drastically reducing the system's vulnerability to cross-domain attacks.

In summary, the comparative evaluation across the four scenarios clearly demonstrates the value of targeted defenses in a cloud–edge ICS. Scenario B (patching IP1) reduced the System Module and Attack Method Scores but left the Attack Path and Impact largely unchanged, yielding a moderate overall improvement. Scenario C (isolating IP2) proved more effective at severing attacker pathways and containing damage, producing a greater drop in overall risk than patching alone. The combined mitigations in Scenario D achieved the most substantial reduction—over 50% lower overall score relative to baseline—by simultaneously eliminating the easy exploit at IP1 and fortifying the critical pivot IP2. These results validate our framework's ability to quantify security gains from specific countermeasures and to guide defenders toward the most impactful interventions.

5. Conclusions and Future Work

In this paper, we presented a comprehensive framework for assessing cross-domain threats in cloud–edge-integrated Industrial Control Systems. The framework systematically combines data collection, multi-dimensional indicator analysis, and scoring to evaluate the risk posed by attacks that span cyber and physical domains. By introducing a novel set of 16 evaluation indicators across system modules, attack paths, attack methods, and impacts, our approach addresses the limitations of traditional methods in dynamic, distributed cloud–edge environments.

Through a simulated case study based on a real-world attack scenario, we demonstrated that the framework can effectively identify critical vulnerabilities and attack pathways in an ICS. The evaluation results provided both a quantitative security score and qualitative insights into the system's weak points, thereby enabling targeted defensive measures. After applying mitigations, the framework could validate an increase in overall security, highlighting its utility not just in assessment but also in iterative improvement of ICS defenses.

This work offers theoretical and practical guidance for the secure deployment of cloud–edge technologies in industrial settings. For practitioners, the indicator system and scoring method can be used as a tool to continuously monitor and assess an ICS as it evolves, ensuring that emerging cross-domain risks are recognized promptly. For researchers, our framework fills a gap by blending cyber and physical security analysis in a unified model and suggests several avenues for future work. One direction is to further refine the weighting and aggregation techniques for the indicators, potentially incorporating machine learning to adapt weights based on historical incident data. Another is to expand the framework to consider proactive defense measures (e.g., how quickly an attack could be quarantined once detected). Moreover, while our simulation was illustrative, testing the framework on more extensive real or emulated environments (such as digital twins of industrial facilities) would provide deeper validation.

Looking ahead, quantum computing introduces novel threat vectors and defensive opportunities for ICS security. Future investigations may explore quantum-enabled attack scenarios—such as accelerated key search and quantum-enhanced cryptanalysis—and evaluate quantum-resistant cryptographic primitives, including lattice-based and hash-based schemes tailored for resource-constrained edge devices. Moreover, the design of hybrid classical–quantum key management architectures could be examined to balance performance and long-term confidentiality in cloud–edge communications.

Advances in machine learning and automated defense mechanisms offer pathways to enhance the framework's adaptability and responsiveness. Subsequent work might apply supervised and reinforcement learning to historical incident archives and live telemetry data, enabling dynamic indicator weighting and threshold tuning. The incorporation of explainable AI techniques could facilitate transparent risk assessments, while research into real-time mitigation strategies—such as automated micro-segmentation, adaptive traffic control, and rapid quarantine triggers—could inform best practices for maintaining operational continuity under attack.

To ensure practical applicability at scale, the framework could be validated through deployment on large-scale digital twins and pilot studies with industry partners. Such efforts would assess performance under high-throughput conditions, characterize scoring latency, and identify integration challenges. Additionally, further exploration of privacy-preserving data sharing methods—such as secure multi-party computation and homomorphic encryption—and blockchain-based provenance tracking for firmware updates may strengthen supply chain and data integrity. Finally, extending safety and resilience metrics to incorporate human factors and recovery objectives could yield a more holistic understanding of system robustness and post-incident restoration capabilities.

Author Contributions: Conceptualization, L.Z. and X.S.; methodology, L.Z.; software, L.Z.; validation, L.Z. and X.S.; formal analysis, L.Z. and Y.W.; investigation, L.Z., Y.W. and C.C.; resources, X.S.; data curation, Y.W.; writing—original draft preparation, L.Z. and Y.W.; writing—review and editing, L.Z., Y.W., C.C. and X.S.; visualization, L.Z. and Y.W.; supervision, X.S.; project administration, X.S.; funding acquisition, X.S. All authors have read and agreed to the published version of the manuscript.

Funding: This research was funded by National Key R&D Program of China (2022YFB3104300).

Data Availability Statement: Data available on request from the authors.

Conflicts of Interest: The authors declare no conflicts of interest.

Appendix A

Figure A1 (available at https://attack.mitre.org/matrices/ics/ (accessed on 10 July 2025)) shows the MITRE ATT&CK ICS Matrix, which categorizes adversarial tactics and techniques specific to industrial control systems.

Figure A1. MITRE ATT&CK ICS Matrix.

References

1. Stouffer, K.; Falco, J.; Scarfone, K. Guide to industrial control systems (ICS) security. *NIST Spec. Publ.* **2011**, *800*, 16.
2. Lee, E.A. Cyber physical systems: Design challenges. In Proceedings of the 2008 11th IEEE International Symposium on Object and Component-Oriented Real-Time Distributed Computing (ISORC), Orlando, FL, USA, 5–7 May 2008; pp. 363–369.
3. Rajkumar, R.; Lee, I.; Sha, L.; Stankovic, J. Cyber-physical systems: The next computing revolution. In Proceedings of the 47th Design Automation Conference, Anaheim, CA, USA, 13–18 June 2010; pp. 731–736.
4. Shi, W.; Cao, J.; Zhang, Q.; Li, Y.; Xu, L. Edge computing: Vision and challenges. *IEEE Internet Things J.* **2016**, *3*, 637–646. [CrossRef]
5. Bonomi, F.; Milito, R.; Zhu, J.; Addepalli, S. Fog computing and its role in the internet of things. In Proceedings of the First Edition of the MCC Workshop on Mobile Cloud Computing, Helsinki, Finland, 17 August 2012; pp. 13–16.
6. Wang, K.; Wang, Y.; Sun, Y.; Guo, S.; Wu, J. Green industrial Internet of Things architecture: An energy-efficient perspective. *IEEE Commun. Mag.* **2016**, *54*, 48–54. [CrossRef]
7. Samie, F.; Bauer, L.; Henkel, J. Edge computing for smart grid: An overview on architectures and solutions. In *IoT for Smart Grids: Design Challenges and Paradigms*; Springer: Cham, Switzerland, 2018; pp. 21–42.
8. Arthurs, P.; Gillam, L.; Krause, P.; Wang, N.; Halder, K.; Mouzakitis, A. A taxonomy and survey of edge cloud computing for intelligent transportation systems and connected vehicles. *IEEE Trans. Intell. Transp. Syst.* **2021**, *23*, 6206–6221. [CrossRef]
9. Langner, R. Stuxnet: Dissecting a cyberwarfare weapon. *IEEE Secur. Priv.* **2011**, *9*, 49–51. [CrossRef]
10. Case, D.U. Analysis of the cyber attack on the Ukrainian power grid. *Electr. Inf. Shar. Anal. Cent. (E-ISAC)* **2016**, *388*, 3.
11. Zhou, Y.; Zhang, Z.; Zhao, K.; Zhang, Z. A Novel Dynamic Vulnerability Assessment Method for Industrial Control System Based on Vulnerability Correlation Attack Graph. *Comput. Electr. Eng.* **2024**, *119*, 109482. [CrossRef]
12. Wang, S.; Ding, L.; Sui, H.; Gu, Z. Cybersecurity Risk Assessment Method of ICS Based on Attack-Defense Tree Model. *J. Intell. Fuzzy Syst.* **2021**, *40*, 10475–10488. [CrossRef]
13. Zhang, Q.; Zhou, C.; Tian, Y.C.; Xiong, N.; Qin, Y.; Hu, B. A fuzzy probability Bayesian network approach for dynamic cybersecurity risk assessment in industrial control systems. *IEEE Trans. Ind. Inform.* **2017**, *14*, 2497–2506. [CrossRef]
14. Zhu, M.; Li, Y.; Xu, W. A Quantitative Risk Assessment Model for Distribution Cyber-Physical System under Cyber Attack. *IEEE Trans. Smart Grid* **2022**, *13*, 545–555.
15. Huang, K.; Zhou, C.; Tian, Y.-C.; Yang, S.; Qin, Y. Assessing the Physical Impact of Cyberattacks on Industrial Cyber-Physical Systems. *IEEE Trans. Ind. Electron.* **2018**, *65*, 8153–8162. [CrossRef]
16. Fu, Y.; Wang, X.; Liu, J.; Zhang, R. Cross-Space Risk Assessment of Cyber-Physical Distribution System under Integrated Attack Based on Fuzzy Bayesian Networks. *IEEE Trans. Ind. Inform.* **2021**, *17*, 6423–6433.
17. Huang, L.; Zhang, X.; Luo, C. Association Analysis-Based Cybersecurity Risk Assessment for Industrial Control Systems. *IEEE Access* **2020**, *8*, 131479–131490.
18. Jin, J.; Pang, Z.; Kua, J.; Zhu, Q.; Johansson, K.H.; Marchenko, N.; Cavalcanti, D. Cloud–Fog Automation: The New Paradigm towards Autonomous Industrial Cyber–Physical Systems. *arXiv* **2025**, arXiv:2504.04908. [CrossRef]
19. Liu, Y.; Zhang, J.; Huang, Z.; Zhang, P. Cyber-Physical Risk Assessment of Power Grid Control Systems Based on Colored Petri Nets and Bayesian Games. *J. Electr. Comput. Eng.* **2024**, *2024*, 1–15.

20. Tan, R.; Li, M. Analyzing the Impact of Cross-Domain Attacks on Industrial Control Systems Using Attack Graph Models. SSRN Preprint, Posted 15 December 2024, 18p. Available online: https://ssrn.com/abstract=5056771 (accessed on 12 July 2025).
21. Cao, Z.; Liu, B.; Gao, D.; Zhou, D.; Han, X.; Cao, J. A Dynamic Spatiotemporal Deep Learning Solution for Cloud–Edge Collaborative Industrial Control System Distributed Denial of Service Attack Detection. *Electronics* **2025**, *14*, 1843. [CrossRef]
22. Liu, Y.; Chen, T.; Zhang, P. Operational Risk Evaluation of Active Distribution Networks Considering Cyber Contingencies. *IEEE Trans. Smart Grid* **2019**, *10*, 5003–5013.
23. Li, H.; Zhao, J.; Wu, C.; Sun, Y. An Integrated Cyber-Physical Risk Assessment Framework for Worst-Case Attacks in Industrial Control Systems. *arXiv* **2023**, arXiv:2304.07363.
24. Zheng, T.; Kumar, I.; Inam, R.; Naz, N.; Elmirghani, J.M. Cybersecurity Solutions for Industrial Internet of Things–Edge A Comprehensive Survey. *Sensors* **2025**, *25*, 213. [CrossRef]
25. Wu, Y.; Song, T.; Zhou, M.; Fang, J. Federated Real-Time Threat Scoring in Cloud–Edge Collaborative ICS: A Lightweight Anomaly Detection Approach. *Electronics* **2025**, *14*, 2050. [CrossRef]
26. Baybulatov, A.; Promyslov, V. Industrial Control System Availability Assessment with a Metric Based on Delay and Dependency *IFAC-PapersOnLine* **2021**, *54*, 472–476. [CrossRef]
27. Ross, R.S. Guide for Conducting Risk Assessments 2012. Special Publication (NIST SP) 800-30 Rev 1, National Institute of Standards and Technology, Gaithersburg, MD, USA, September 2012 (Updated January 2020). Available online: https://nvlpubs.nist.gov/nistpubs/Legacy/SP/nistspecialpublication800-30r1.pdf (accessed on 8 July 2025).
28. Wang, S.; Ko, R.K.; Bai, G.; Dong, N.; Choi, T.; Zhang, Y. Evasion attack and defense on machine learning models in cyber-physical systems: A survey. *IEEE Commun. Surv. Tutorials* **2023**, *26*, 930–966. [CrossRef]
29. Strom, B.E.; Applebaum, A.; Miller, D.P.; Nickels, K.C.; Pennington, A.G.; Thomas, C.B. Mitre att&ck: Design and philosophy. In *Technical Report*; The MITRE Corporation: Bedford, MA, USA, 2018.

MDPI AG
Grosspeteranlage 5
4052 Basel
Switzerland
Tel.: +41 61 683 77 34

Electronics Editorial Office
E-mail: electronics@mdpi.com
www.mdpi.com/journal/electronics

www.ingramcontent.com/pod-product-compliance
Lightning Source LLC
Chambersburg PA
CBHW061508220926
51850CB00004B/204
9783725852130